LAND ECONOMICS

LAND ECONOMICS
PRINCIPLES, PROBLEMS, AND POLICIES
IN UTILIZING LAND RESOURCES

REVISED EDITION

By **ROLAND R. RENNE**

President, Montana State College

Harper & Brothers   Publishers   New York

LAND ECONOMICS, REVISED EDITION

HD
111
R4
1958

CONTENTS

v

PART IV. PROPERTY IN LAND

PART V. DISTINCTIVE FEATURES OF MAJOR LAND USES

PART VI. IMPROVEMENT OF LAND USE

FIGURES

TABLES

PREFACE TO THE FIRST EDITION

LAND HAS certain unique characteristics which distinguish it from the other major factors of production and which cause its users to respond in special ways to the stimulation of price shifts or institutional changes. Methods of using land and its share in the national income are therefore determined according to principles whose applications are sufficiently different from those of other production factors to justify separate study. Hence, the social science of land economics, the purpose of which is the formulation of a systematic body of knowledge concerning the characteristics and utilization of land that society may employ in determining allocations and uses that will best serve to achieve desired ends.

The content and arrangement of the subject matter of this book are the outgrowth of nearly two decades of experience in teaching. Part I presents certain definitions and relationships to give the student the essential background and perspectives for a proper understanding and appreciation of the field of land economics. Part II analyzes the fundamental principles of the economic and social processes of land utilization, operating within the system of property rights as construed by the prevailing economic philosophy. These principles are designed to shape the tools by which the problems of land use may be attacked and resulting policies and programs understood. Part III describes the spatial requirements and most important characteristics peculiar to the seven major land uses. These chapters provide the factual basis for a comprehensive understanding of the land utilization pattern and the competition of land uses in producing economic goods and services.

Part IV analyzes the major land use problems of tenure and tenancy, valuation and credit, taxation and conservation, and the policies and programs that have been established or which would be most effective in solving them. These problems have been analyzed in Part IV rather than in the seven chapters of Part III describing major land uses, in order to focus attention and thinking on the *economic and social problems* associated with land utilization. For example, tenure and tenancy problems in utilizing agricultural land are discussed in Chapter XIV, "Land Tenure and Tenancy," along with tenure and tenancy problems of the other major types of use, rather than in Chapter VII, "Agricultural Land." Some contend that land credit and land taxation problems are land tenure problems arising from aspects of human behavior in which property rights in land are the dominant directing factor, just as are tenancy problems. Land credit and taxation problems are so large and significant, however, and courses of study, research, and administration have already been established in these fields, that it seems best to devote separate chapters to these problems.

The last section of the book (Part V) is devoted to an analysis of planning and control of land use in the interests of improving the quality of human living. Far-reaching economic and social changes have recently shaken the very foundations of society, and present new and interesting problems for solution. The content of land economics must be geared to and determined by the efforts of the nation and the world to improve human living, including full employment and higher nutritional levels. Over large parts of the world the mass of the people can improve their lot chiefly by improving their ways of using the soil and other natural resources.

The author wishes to acknowledge the encouragement and assistance of many colleagues, friends, and students in the preparation of this volume. G. H. Craig was particularly helpful in the preparation of the first six chapters. Virgil Hurlburt's critical reading and constructive criticism of Parts III and V improved these chapters. Oswald Brownlee gave valuable assistance in reading and criticizing Chapters V and VII; Victor Sullam, Chapter IV; Rainer Schickele, Chapter XIV; M. Slade Kendrick, Chapter XVI, and Arthur C. Bunce, Chapter XVII. John J. Haggerty and the late Leonard A. Salter, Jr., made general suggestions concerning the organization and presentation of the material, and Miss Erdine Maxwell assisted in preparing the charts. The author is particularly indebted to John Ise for his careful editing of the entire manuscript and his many helpful suggestions throughout. Finally, I am grateful to Miss Margaret Austin, who prior to her death in May, 1944, assisted in the preparation of the entire first draft, and to her sister, Miss Nancy Austin, for her efficient help in the preparation of the final copy and the mechanics of publication.

June, 1946

ROLAND R. RENNE

PREFACE TO THE REVISED EDITION

THE RECEPTION accorded the first edition by teachers and students has been gratifying. This revision is designed to bring the pertinent data and interpretations up to date and to make the volume more readable and teachable by careful editing and rearrangement of the materials based on more than a decade of classroom use in many institutions. Some descriptive materials have been omitted and some new materials added, including the entire final chapter on land reform.

In the preparation of this revised edition the author is indebted to the many teachers throughout the country who have sent in their suggestions for improvements based on their experiences in using the volume in their classes over a period of several years. Experiment station workers and staff members of various state and federal agencies involved in land resources development and utilization programs, especially in the United States Department of Agriculture, have made numerous helpful suggestions that have improved the volume throughout. Dr. Layton Thompson and Dr. Roy E. Huffman, staff associates, have been especially helpful in making valuable suggestions on the reorganization of the subject matter and rearrangement of the chapters. Comments and suggestions of students in Dr. Thompson's classes in Land Economics have been very useful in preparing the revision.

The author is deeply grateful to Miss Jeannie Dixon for her tireless and skilled efforts in editing the entire manuscript, assisting in checking reference and source materials, and helping in the preparation of the final copy and with the mechanics of publication.

January 1, 1958

ROLAND R. RENNE

part **1**

THE FIELD OF
LAND ECONOMICS

LAND ECONOMICS AS A SOCIAL SCIENCE
LAND PROBLEMS, POLICIES, AND PROGRAMS

chapter 1

LAND ECONOMICS AS A SOCIAL SCIENCE

LAND AND LIFE

Strategic Role of Land Resources—Influence of Land on Culture—Influence of Culture on Land

THE SUBJECT MATTER OF LAND ECONOMICS

Definition and Scope of Land Economics—Land Economics as an Applied Field of Economics—Recent Interest in Land Economics

LAND ECONOMICS concerns itself with economic problems associated with man's use of land to produce economic goods and services. It attempts to formulate a systematic body of knowledge covering basic principles and policies that individuals and society may employ to determine land allocations and uses that will most effectively achieve desired goals.

LAND AND LIFE

Climate, land forms, and natural resources (soils, water, minerals, natural vegetation, and native animal life) combine to make up the physical environment within which man exists. The basic earth resources are transformed by labor into economic goods and services that satisfy human wants. The great importance of land in determining man's economic and cultural progress is attributable largely to the diversification, relative scarcity, and localization of its resources. Arable farm land and the most useful minerals, especially, are not distributed evenly over the earth's surface but are highly localized.

STRATEGIC ROLE OF LAND RESOURCES

The struggle for political control of raw materials indicates the highly localized nature of land resources. Discoveries of new land bodies and new

3

natural resources have been milestones along the path of economic progress and cultural development. The discovery and extraction of minerals are almost always among the principal objectives in exploration and colonization, because nations controlling the most important minerals can forge ahead and may be better able to wage successful defensive or offensive warfare. Since mineral supplies are fixed and limited, international rivalry grows more intense as their consumption increases. Even if an equitable redistribution of mineral resources were politically possible, it would be physically impossible, because some deposits are unique and others too limited to be divided among the numerous would-be users.

Access to useful minerals and diverse types of arable lands enables industrial and agricultural technology to advance. The encouragement of inventive genius frequently associated with harnessing the forces of nature is a significant example of land's influence on human progress. Nations with relatively favorable natural environments have usually developed greater industrial plants and more complex technology than have nations comparatively poor in accessible natural resources. For example, Great Britain's rapid development into a world power was caused largely by the industrial and commercial lead it secured while the Continent was engaged in the Napoleonic Wars. This early leadership was made possible by Britain's readily available water-power sites; deposits of coal used in steam engines; limestone and iron ore necessary for making steel; and ready access to the sea, the major transportation medium of the time. The United States, because of her rich, arable lands and large, accessible deposits of the more useful minerals, has made great material progress and is one of the leading powers of the twentieth-century world.

INFLUENCE OF LAND ON CULTURE

Although physical environment does not specifically predetermine man's way of living, it does set certain limits to the development of his activities and institutions. Soils, climate, and mineral resources are highly localized; the amount of arable land suited to the growth of important foodstuffs and fibers varies widely among nations. Such natural conditions as topography and the amount, nature, and timing of precipitation influence not only technical practices but the people themselves and their entire economic and social organization. If it is to survive over a long period of time, human culture must be in harmony with physical environment.

Physical environment is a major determinant of the pattern of man's economic and social organization in a relatively primitive society, but in highly industrialized societies, physical environment is considerably less influential. This "geographic determinism" does not mean that cultures become exactly alike under similar physical conditions. Rather, it implies that the effect of climate, topography, fertility, and other physical factors upon all cultures will be relatively predictable.

A somewhat barren controversy has developed between advocates of "geographic determinism" [1] and "cultural determinism." [2] Both schools tend to oversimplify the relationship between nature, culture, and the economic and social organization of society. In reality the functioning societal structure is produced by a mutual adaptation of the physical and cultural environment.

The necessity of harmonizing human culture with physical environment may be illustrated by the American experience with Western land settlement. The 160 acres allotted to each settler under early homestead policies proved satisfactory in the comparatively humid Middle West, but this acreage was insufficient to support a family in the more arid Great Plains.[3] Allotments were doubled in 1909, and in 1916 a full section was allotted if the land was to be used for ranching.

Unfortunately, much of the land had already been subdivided into small, uneconomic parcels. This subdivision and the resulting land system were important causes of overgrazing, soil blowing, and farm abandonment. These became so acute that in the thirties the federal government inaugurated a submarginal land purchase and development program in parts of the Great Plains, to repair some of the damage caused by earlier land policies and to bring about tenure and utilization practices more suited to the natural environment. Exploitative cutting and abandonment occurred in the case of forest lands. Thus, American experience in land settlement is evidence that climate and land forms are strategic in forcing cultural adaptation.

INFLUENCE OF CULTURE ON LAND

Land is not simply an active agent causing cultural adaptation, but is itself subject to rather significant changes. Its rough forest profiles may be transformed into smooth airplane runways or terraced rice paddies. Many man-made land structures become permanent and thereafter subject to the same economic treatment as the structures laid down by nature.

During the last two centuries rapid strides have been made in the use of earth strata unutilized before the development of modern machinery

[1] See particularly Ellsworth Huntington, *Civilization and Climate*, Yale University Press, 1924, and his other writings; Ellen C. Semple, *Influences of Geographic Environment*, Holt, 1911; R. H. Whitbeck and O. J. Thomas, *The Geographic Factor: Its Role in Life and Civilization*, Appleton-Century, 1932.

[2] See especially Wilson D. Wallis, *Culture and Progress*, McGraw-Hill, 1930. Advocates of cultural determinism emphasize the influence of culture on determining the economic and social organization of society.

[3] The Great Plains area is, roughly speaking, that section of the United States lying between the 98th meridian and the eastern edge of the Rocky Mountains.

and technology. The subsurface has been made to yield its fossil fuels (oil, gas, and coal) and its metals to make machines that use these fuels. Railroads, automobiles, and trucks have been responsible for many changes in the earth's profile; and water also has come to be used more intensively for various purposes such as irrigation. Development of aircraft, the radio, television, and the modern skyscraper has permitted greater use of the supersurface (air) for transportation, communication, and other purposes.

Since the use of land is no longer confined to the earth's surface, area and acreage have become less dependable measures of the total economic supply of land. These changes, with the development of technology, have increased the economic supply of land far beyond earlier potentialities in most lines of production. Improved transportation and production methods accompanying the application of science and machine technique to mining, manufacturing, and agriculture have made available land that was formerly useless because of its inaccessibility or inferior quality. Land now responds much more readily to increases in demand for its products with increases in the amount of land available.

Agricultural land use in modern technological, commercial economies is much more complex than that in a simple hand-labor, animal-energy economy. Nonagricultural uses are even more numerous and complex, competing for land not only with agriculture but also among themselves, though they are closely interrelated. Modern society is characterized by the expanded, accelerated use of natural resources to satisfy human wants. Study of the principles governing the economic utilization of land is, therefore, increasingly important.

THE SUBJECT MATTER OF LAND ECONOMICS

Man's attempt to appropriate land for his use and possession is the subject matter of land economics. Only when land becomes scarce do economic problems arise. So long as land is relatively abundant, as it is under primitive conditions where population is small and soil use unspecialized, serious difficulties will probably not occur.

The early nomad did not bother to appropriate any part of the lands grazed by his flocks as long as he was sure that in his wanderings he could always find the needed pasture. But as the land was tilled and used more intensively to satisfy the wants of a growing population, the right to use certain lands became more valuable and more fiercely contested. Legal rights of property or ownership of land resulted from scarcity of land with desirable location or productiveness, and from use of human labor and accumulated capital goods to produce food and fiber from the tilled acres.

Land economics focuses attention on situations and problems in which the use of land is the *strategic, limiting,* or *decisive* factor. Since land could not be a limiting factor if it were superabundant, and since property in land would not exist under such conditions, the problems with which land economics is concerned are those associated with the institution of property in land. Property governs men's relations to one another in utilizing land.

Study of economic problems in land use is not an end in itself but a means to determine principles and methods by which human welfare may be improved. This betterment of the conditions of living is the standard by which all policies and programs of land utilization, public or private, should be measured.

DEFINITION AND SCOPE OF LAND ECONOMICS

Land economics deals with the problems of cost, price, value, income, and control in using land to produce economic goods and services. It has been said that all human creation is basically re-creation and all production reproduction. Producers of economic wealth do not make anything completely new, but perform a process of "extraction" and "conversion" reworking the basic element, land, into useful things ("wealth"). Land, the basic natural earth resource, is transformed into usable, desirable goods through the efforts of agriculture, industry, and commerce.

Land economics deals with economic problems involved in utilizing soils, forests, minerals, water, topography, and climate for production of food, fuel, fiber, lumber, metals, recreation, irrigation and drainage, location sites (dwelling, business, and industrial sites), and transportation. Most land economists have been trained in the field of agricultural economics, and have, therefore, devoted most of their energies to determining principles and solving problems applicable to farm and ranch lands. *Agricultural land economics,* like farm management or agricultural marketing, may be considered a subdivision of agricultural economics; but the full scope of land economics is a distinct, applied field of the parent discipline—economics.

Land economics, even when limited to consideration of agricultural land utilization, is clearly distinguishable from farm management, although the two fields are not mutually exclusive. In farm management, the strategic or limiting factor is management, while in land economics it is *land,* either because of its natural qualities of location and fertility, or because of the institutions or behavior patterns established to govern its use. Farm management focuses attention on the management problems of an individual firm and the choice of enterprises for a farm or ranch, or group of farms and ranches. Land economics considers especially how the individual firm affects land use and how it affects groups using or interested in the land.

The problems with which the farm management economist is concerned are the individual farm operator's decisions with respect to alternative enterprises—such as grain or livestock production. The land economist is interested in community, state, or national problems, such as tenancy, land taxation, foreclosure, and soil depletion. The institution of property in land is the focus of attention in land economics since it determines the major relations of man to land, and since most of the problems of land economics are intimately connected with the exercise of property rights as construed by the prevailing economic philosophy.

LAND ECONOMICS AS AN APPLIED FIELD OF ECONOMICS

Land economics can be conceived in its proper relationship to other fields of study only as a distinct, applied field of the parent discipline—economics. Economics defined in a very general way is "the social science which treats of the phenomena arising from the wealth-getting and wealth-using activities of man." [4] Or economics may be defined as "the science which treats of those 'social phenomena' which are due to the activities of man in producing, acquiring, and using material goods and services." [5] Land economics as a field within the broader parent social science of economics is limited to those social phenomena arising from *man's activities in using land* to produce, acquire, and utilize material goods and services.

There are three major purposes to which the social sciences should be oriented, and land economics as a branch of economics is subject to the same orientation. The first purpose is to provide an adequate explanation of a broad area of social phenomena. The second is to develop an adequate system of "welfare" guidance in the formulation or evaluation of social policy. The third is to formulate effective solutions for specific problems of particular economies or societies.

One writer holds that in satisfying these three purposes economics becomes a social philosophy in the first case, a moral philosophy in the second, and a practical technology in the third.[6] These three purposes are equally applicable to the branch field of land economics.

The term "social philosophy" is in many respects a more appropriate designation for economics or land economics than "social science," although the latter term is generally used. The economist and the land economist, like the physical scientist, seek rigor and precision in their

[4] Richard T. Ely and Ralph H. Hess, *Outlines of Economics,* Macmillan, 6th ed., 1937, p. 4.

[5] Edwin F. Dummeier and Richard B. Hefflebower, *Economics with Applications to Agriculture,* McGraw-Hill, 1940, p. 5.

[6] Robert A. Solo, "Economics as Social Philosophy, Moral Philosophy, and Technology," in Robert A. Solo (ed.), *Economics and the Public Interest,* Rutgers University Press, 1955, p. 5.

explanations of economic phenomena, but because of differences in the available data, economic systems are not equivalent to systems of natural science. There are no identical relationships in the social universe as there are in the physical sciences. No two wars, or two depressions, or two corporations are identical. Moreover, the irreducible unit of all sociological study, the individual, is in many ways similar to but in no sense identical with his fellow men.

Finally, because the individual is free, neither his actions nor his social responses are predictable in accordance with natural laws established from observation of individual actions or of social responses to past known stimuli. Consequently, the economist cannot reduce social phenomena into their underlying uniformities like the natural scientist, because the uniformities are nonexistent. Instead, he selects a set of social relationships, institutions, and psychological drives and responses which he postulates as "normal" or "typical," and from them derives a "usual" or "typical" explanation of economic phenomena.

The importance of recognizing the limitations of exact science and its methods in dealing with characteristic economic and social problems has been pointed out by many [7] but is summed up appropriately by Solo: "If the premises at the base of the deductive systems of economics are not considered as *philosophic essences,* but rather are asserted as scientific principles (as they have been) —beyond subjective evaluation, beyond the challenges of individual judgment, frozen into convention, shielded from doubt—then between partisans there can be no fruitful meeting of the minds, and the social philosophies may not be of help to us in finding our way through the swift, hard, shifting currents of history, but may instead lead us into monumental error." [8]

The economist is concerned not only with explaining economic phenomena or "what is," but also with "what ought to be." This, of course, involves subjective evaluation and requires criteria of a moral or ethical order. Economics should not only describe or explain economic phenomena but offer a general guide to the formulation of social policy or to social goals. In the last analysis, social policy and social goals should emphasize those phases of human welfare that improve living conditions and the well-being of the great majority if not all members of a given community or economy.

In fulfilling the third purpose of economics—suggesting effective solutions for particular problems of a given community—the economist should try to discover ways of achieving agreement on a common purpose

[7] Leonard A. Salter, Jr., *A Critical Review of Research in Land Economics,* University of Minnesota Press, 1948, pp. 39–51.

[8] Solo, *op. cit.,* p. 9.

or assist in its fulfillment. This agreement must be sound enough to secure common action in dealing with the particular problem or a particular group of problems.

Such a welfare technology or action-oriented approach will lead to formulation of more adequate public policies and programs. In the case of land economics, this approach should be instrumental in helping to solve some of the more pressing problems associated with land utilization, including tenure, credit, taxation, and conservation.

RECENT INTEREST IN LAND ECONOMICS

The subject of land economics is a comparatively new one in American college and university curriculums, and in the thinking of agricultural and business leaders.[9] A Division of Land Economics in the United States Bureau of Agricultural Economics was established in 1918, but not until the thirties were soil conservation, resettlement and rehabilitation, agricultural adjustment, subsistence homesteads, county agricultural planning, farm tenancy reform, control of floods and water facilities, and related legislation made a part of our national program. Each of these is primarily concerned with working out better economic relationships between man and land to make possible a more permanent and satisfactory American agriculture, industry, and level of living.

This increased interest in land economics is the result of forces operative during a considerable period of our history—forces which have brought about land-use problems so acute and spectacular that serious public concern has been aroused. The American policy of quickly transferring the public domain to private ownership resulted in rapid settlement, speculation, and widespread resource exploitation. The increase of absentee ownership and tenancy associated with speculation and finance capitalism increased the tendency to wasteful, planless exploitation of natural resources. Feverish business activity and high prices in the World War I period postponed the conservation movement begun in Theodore Roosevelt's administration after the disappearance of the free land and the devastation of much of our wildlife and forest land; and the industrial and technological expansion and investment speculation of the postwar twenties, in spite of widespread agricultural depression, further postponed it.

However, dust storms in the West, floods in the East, serious longtime disparities between farm and nonfarm prices, loss of foreign markets,

[9] In a survey, made by the author in 1940, of 44 state agricultural colleges and state universities, 37 were offering at least one course in land economics. The distribution of these 37, by periods in which their first land economics course was offered, is: Prior to 1930, 11; 1930–1934 inclusive, 12; 1935–1940, 14. Thus 26 (nearly three-fourths of those offering land economics courses) offered a course for the first time during the thirties.

heavy mortgages, high interest rates, and excessive taxes have made us more conscious of the harmful effects of soil erosion and rapid resource exploitation. The business depression of the thirties and the efforts to reduce unemployment further encouraged public activity in the improvement of land-use practices and in the development of sound conservation methods. The progress made along these lines just prior to World War II, which began in Europe in September, 1939, was an important factor in preventing a duplication of the rape of our natural resources, particularly agricultural lands, that occurred during World War I.

These causative forces and events will be considered more fully in the chapters that follow. The general approach of the science of land economics to the solution of the problems growing out of these forces and events is briefly sketched in the following chapter.

REFERENCES FOR FURTHER READING

Geiger, G. R., *The Theory of the Land Question*, The Macmillan Company, New York, 1936, Chap. I.

Huntington, Ellsworth, *Civilization and Climate*, Yale University Press, New Haven, 3d ed., 1933.

Salter, Leonard A., Jr., *A Critical Review of Research in Land Economics*, University of Minnesota Press, Minneapolis, 1948, Chap. III.

Semple, Ellen C., *Influences of Geographic Environment*, Henry Holt and Company, Inc., New York, 1911.

Solo, Robert A. (ed.), *Economics and the Public Interest*, Rutgers University Press, New Brunswick, N.J., 1955, Chap. I.

Wallis, Wilson D., *Culture and Progress*, McGraw-Hill Book Company, Inc., New York, 1930.

Whitbeck, R. H., and Thomas, O. J., *The Geographic Factor: Its Role in Life and Civilization*, D. Appleton-Century Company, Inc., New York, 1932.

Whittlesey, Derwent, *The Earth and the State*, Henry Holt and Company, Inc., New York, 2d ed., 1944, Chap. III.

Zimmermann, Erich, *World Resources and Industries*, Harper & Brothers, New York, rev. ed., 1951, Chaps. VII, VIII, and IX.

chapter

2

LAND PROBLEMS, POLICIES, AND PROGRAMS

LAND ECONOMIC PROBLEMS

Basic Economic Problems—Principal Problem Areas

LAND POLICIES

Objectives of Land Policy—United States Land Policy

LAND PROGRAMS

Early Land Programs in the United States—Recent United States Programs: RESOURCE CONSERVATION, RE-ACQUISITION AND MANAGEMENT OF PUBLIC LANDS, CLASSIFICATION AND RESOURCE EVALUATION, ZONING AND LAND-USE CONTROL, LAND CREDIT, PRODUCTION CONTROL

THE LIMITS of a field of study or a scientific discipline are not fixed, but change as new methods, new approaches, new problems and solutions emerge. Furthermore, a field of study cannot be satisfactorily described by reference to its subject matter only. It is more adequately identified by reference to its methodology, its analytical tools and techniques, the kinds of problems confronted, and the types of projects and studies engaged in by those trained for and working in the field. The major determinant of the vigor and influence of a field of study is the responsiveness of its workers to current and emerging problems within its scope.

Land economics is a comparatively young field of study, but it has been since its beginnings a field close to existing social problems. The point of emphasis has varied according to conditions. Major concern and investigations began in land economics as a result of the growth in farm tenancy. The ideal of "best land use" came to hold a strong position in the profession, and land economists have become interested in problems of credit, mortgage foreclosures, land taxation and tax delinquency, soil conversation, land-use adjustments, zoning, and family-farm policy. Land economists have consistently been interested in social problems and public policy.

LAND ECONOMIC PROBLEMS

Land economics is concerned with the economic problems arising out of the institutions that man has created to guide and control the use of land. Problems arise within the gap or spread that occurs between existing land-use conditions and those desired. These problems reflect conflicts, confusions, and uncertainties regarding future courses of action in the use of land. Changes within man-to-man and man-to-land relationships that arise in land utilization and tenure arrangements are necessary if conflicts of interests are to be resolved or problems solved. Generally, land economics deals with problems that involve policy decisions and frequently require some type of action, public or private.

BASIC ECONOMIC PROBLEMS

The use of land, like the use of other economic goods, is subject to economic forces such as those of supply and demand. Land has certain unique characteristics that distinguish it from other major factors of production and cause it to respond in special ways to the stimulation of price shifts or institutional changes. Two such characteristics not common to the human element or to capital in production are *permanence of land and its fixity in space.* The method of using land and its share in the national income are therefore determined according to principles whose applications are sufficiently different from other production factors to justify separate study.

These differences in the response to price or institutional changes give rise to serious problems. Should income from land be taxed differently from other income? Does land ownership give the owner peculiar monopolistic control because of land's nonreproducible nature, the scarcity of certain kinds of land, and the lack of substitutability among individual parcels? Answers to these questions involve careful study of the characteristics of landed property and the particular economic system within which it operates.

American public and private land-use policies have developed in a commercialized price economy where the principle of specialization and division of labor is generally accepted and applied. Land resources are used to produce want-satisfying goods and services in an economic environment dominated by private enterprise and production for sale and profit.

The price system gives rise to many land utilization problems that would not occur in a more primitive, self-sufficing economy. Land economists are concerned with prices because land use is determined largely by the market price of products of land and the costs of producing them.

Price fluctuations create many land utilization problems. For example, if prices of farm products decline rapidly, the farmer must adjust his costs of production, among other things, in order to survive. Two major means of adjustment for the farmer are tightening his belt or mining the soil. He may reduce his level of living, as a means of reducing costs of production, but frequently this is not enough. Some other approach must then be made to the problem of living within his reduced income.

Too often the adjustment takes the form of "mining" or exploiting the soil. For example, a farmer may apply insufficient fertilizer or till inadequately, allowing undue decline in fertility, spread of weeds, expedited erosion, and soil blowing. Price changes are therefore extremely significant in land economics, since price disparities between things bought and sold often cause those who utilize land resources directly to mine them through ill-adapted, short-sighted practices.

Property rights ill adapted to the general welfare are often responsible for exploitation of land resources. A notorious case is that of allowing separate drilling of oil wells by different owners into a common pool. The race to obtain the most oil first drains supplies much more quickly than the relative needs of present and future would make desirable.

PRINCIPAL PROBLEM AREAS

Two major problem areas have been the principal focal points of land economics since the turn of the century. These are: (1) problems in the conversion of land from one major use to another general use, arising out of social changes or social processes; (2) problems in the attainment of land-tenure objectives, whether or not they are associated with land-use changes. This second group of problems also arises from social changes.[1]

One of the most challenging problems for land economics is determining those resource changes for land, labor, and capital that are necessary to achieve efficient resource use and uniformly high income returns. Another important task is the naming and testing of public programs conceived to bring about these changes.[2] Changes in land use, in size of farm or operating firm, in employment of capital and labor that are necessary to increase the productivity of the human agent to the level in the more advanced areas of economic development are needed, and programs must be suggested to bring about these changes.

A grouping of land economic problem areas into a few major categories would include, among others, the following: [3]

[1] Leonard A. Salter, Jr., *A Critical Review of Research in Land Economics*, University of Minnesota Press, 1948, p. 38.

[2] Harold G. Halcrow (ed.), *Contemporary Readings in Agricultural Economics*, Prentice-Hall, 1955, p. 299.

[3] Cf. V. Webster Johnson and Raleigh Barlowe, *Land Problems and Policies*, McGraw-Hill, 1954, pp. 4–5, and Salter, *op. cit.*, pp. 232–235.

1. Problems associated with changing land uses in which an area undergoes a transformation in the sense that space devoted to enterprises with certain land requirements are put to uses with different requirements. For example, in transforming a farm unit into residential units, a shift in the entire pattern of economic space units is involved. Problems result from changes in the holding and evaluating of property rights.

2. Problems growing out of land use at the use margins, i.e., where relatively small changes in conditions cause comparatively wide changes in uses, as on the farm-grazing fringe or the farm-urban fringe.

3. Problems involved in land development, land settlement, and land retirement programs.

4. Problems connected with landlord-tenant relations, including lease terms, sharing of returns from the land, effects on land deterioration and erosion, extent of management supervision supplied by the owner, and problem situations in regard to acquiring, maintaining, and transferring land ownership.

5. Problems associated with the changing nature of the locational qualities of land and the locational characteristics of space units. The influence of roads on farm land and land use is one type of problem in this category. Another is that of freight rates and trade barriers, with their associated marketing and pricing problems.

6. Problems in the use and control of water as an economic resource: irrigation, drainage, flood control, and administrative and organizational procedures and policies in the use and development of water resources.

7. Problems arising from land resource conservation programs and policies and the changing character and quality of tangible resources. These problems must be analyzed in relation to food and fiber needs and inducements for achieving conservation and wise use of land resources.

8. Problems of land valuation, capitalization of benefit payments into land values, appraisal and credit problems, imperfections in the land market, and similar problems.

9. Problems of land taxation, equalization of tax burdens among various land users, tax policies and assessment procedures, and local governmental organization and operation as conditioners of land use and occupancy.

10. Problems of determining and effecting the most profitable or socially desirable combination of the factors of land, labor, capital, and management in the production of goods and services under varying product price and cost conditions, varying efficiency and capacity of lands for use, and presence of scarce or limiting supplies of certain productive factors.

Land economists try to discover and explain why and how these problems develop, and how they can be solved or their adverse effects reduced to a minimum. Their purpose is that by so doing individuals and agencies will be assisted in formulating policies and programs that will bring about better use of land resources and a higher level of general welfare.

LAND POLICIES

A *policy* is a specific plan or settled course adopted and followed by a government, a group, an institution, or an individual to achieve desired ends.[4] Land policies may be considered as major lines of public action aimed to improve the use of land resources and the conditions of property rights under which people work and live on the land.[5] The major problems with which land policy is concerned, therefore, occur in the fields of (1) land use, conservation, and development; and (2) land tenure.

Land policies, public or private, but especially public, form the field of operations within which individuals plan land use; and one of the functions of land economics is to analyze these policies and the principles upon which they are based, to determine whether they are the most consistent or the most feasible means of achieving the goals of maximum welfare.

The land policy of a nation is "an evolutionary growth in which politics, ambitions, fear, prejudices, traditions, beliefs true or untrue, and myths each and all have an influence." [6] Physical factors such as soil characteristics, topography, and humidity; technological inventions and developments; biological factors such as improved varieties of plants and better types and breeds of animals; economic and political factors such as taxes, import duties, export subsidies, tariffs, nationalism, and self-sufficiency—all assert their influence on a nation's land-use policy, some working together, some against each other. The resulting policy is formed by an intricate mosaic of factors.

OBJECTIVES OF LAND POLICY

The objectives of land policy are governed by what people want or think they should have, and what the functions of government are conceived to be in bringing about better land use and tenure. Changes in land use and tenure are desired only when people are dissatisfied with existing conditions or when people conceive of better land-use and tenure practices and procedures. These conceptions or notions as to how things ought to be, may be called *value judgments* or *goals*.

[4] The term "policy" in its most comprehensive meaning has been defined as implying "a more or less carefully considered and fundamental course of action followed consistently for a period of years." (See John D. Black, "The Problem of Determining an Economic Policy for American Agriculture," in E. A. Duddy [ed.], *Economic Policy for American Agriculture,* University of Chicago Press, 1932, p. 1.)

[5] Cf. John F. Timmons and William G. Murray (eds.), *Land Problems and Policies,* Iowa State College Press, 1950, p. 277.

[6] A. G. Black, "Agricultural Policy and the Economist," *Journal of Farm Economics,* Vol. XVIII, No. 2, May, 1936, p. 311.

Land-policy goals must be geared to and subservient to the major goals toward which the economy as a whole is pointed and which society is striving to attain. Land policy is but one segment of the broader goals of economic policy. The two master goals of American economic policy are: (1) to increase to the maximum the social product over time, and (2) to achieve optimum distribution of income among people. The first is concerned with problems of misuse of human and physical resources in the production process, and the second with problems of inequities in the distribution of real income among families.[7]

In more precise terms, land-use policy goals, as distinguished from land-tenure policy goals, strive for that degree of use intensity and that system of use practices which will result in a more efficient allocation of resources and consequently bring about a larger social net product. This standard is particularly appropriate for land-use, conservation, and development policies.

Land-tenure policy goals strive for optimum distribution of income. It is true that tenure arrangements influence land use, conservation, and the productive process in general, but they are primarily important because they determine how land income is distributed among various holders of property rights. The best income distribution is one that equalizes opportunity among all individuals of society, and at the same time gives each individual the liberty to develop according to his peculiar skills, talents, and aspirations, which of necessity makes for unequal real incomes.[8] Maldistribution of income is more likely to be strongly resented than malallocation of resources, and public policy is much more often and directly concerned with improving income distribution than with increasing the social product. Progressive taxation and minimum wage and similar legislation have as their goals not product maximization, but income redistribution in a direction and to a degree that more adequately meets some distributive standard, vague though its conception may be.

Although the greatest possible increase of product and the most favorable distribution of income generally constitute the prime objectives of land policy, other objectives may become paramount under certain conditions. The exigencies of war often force nations to utilize natural resources at rates and in ways inconsistent with these master objectives and soil conservation. Military considerations have also caused some nations to pursue population policies inconsistent with goals emphasizing individual well-being. Similarly, the avoidance of dangerous dependence on foreign sources of food supplies and raw materials has resulted in agri-

[7] Rainier Schickele, "Objectives of Land Policy," in Timmons and Murray, *op. cit.,* p. 6.
[8] *Ibid.,* p. 9.

cultural and land-use policies that would be hard to defend except on grounds of military security.

The United States has been more fortunate than most nations in meeting its military needs without drastically modifying its peacetime utilization pattern of natural resources. The great diversity of American output and the tremendous productive capacity of United States technology, both industrial and agricultural, have reduced dependence on foreign sources of supply. Nevertheless, the great drain upon certain resources during wartime and in recent years has reduced United States reserves and is a matter of increasing concern to Americans.

The other objectives or goals, under certain conditions may be of major significance in determining the utilization of land resources. The first of these is *political stability*. Experience has demonstrated that farm owners are basically conservative, and political considerations have resulted in major redistributions of land in some countries. After World War I in Europe, significant distributions of land occurred, and after World II more sweeping redistributions occurred in central and eastern Europe. The land reform movement in the newly created nations of Asia has emphasized improved tenure systems and recognizes the significance of widespread land ownership to economic growth and political stability. The breaking up of large estates or holdings into numerous small, owner-operated family farm units has characterized land reform programs throughout the world.

The other objective tending to exert a major influence on land utilization in some countries is *conservation*. Too often conservation is considered merely as a matter of postponing resource utilization. But conservation is more than simply depriving ourselves in the present in order to pass on natural resources to future generations. A considerable part of the most serious destruction of resources is sheer waste that benefits none or only a few, without corresponding benefits, and often to the serious detriment of the community and the country as a whole. Conservation of natural resources, particularly in fields such as soil conservation, has developed very gradually in the United States and has become an important part of our public land policy only in very recent years.

UNITED STATES LAND POLICY

The land policy of the United States up to the turn of the century, if indeed we had a genuine land policy,[9] was primarily one of transferring

[9] The eminent land policies historian, Dr. B. H. Hibbard, more than a quarter century ago, in commenting on our land policies, said, "Thus far there has been no genuine land policy in and for the United States. True enough, there have been temporizing plans, some of them good for a time, and for certain sections. But a plan involving and comprehending the welfare of the whole nation, varied to fit the different parts of the country, we have not had." Benjamin H. Hibbard, *A History of the Public Land Policies*, Macmillan, 1924, p. 562.

the public domain to private ownership as quickly as possible and leaving desirable adjustments to be worked out by the forces of competition. Little consideration was given to the uses for which land was best adapted or to the effective demand for products of the land.

This policy, together with fundamental economic and social changes in the nation that became apparent after World War I, necessitated corrective action, either on the part of the government or through more unified private initiative. Congressional legislation passed "to do something for agriculture" or "to place agriculture on a basis of economic equality with other industries" has involved a reconsideration of our use of land, particularly agricultural land. Soil erosion, dust storms, and the simultaneous decline of foreign markets and increase in domestic agricultural output have strengthened the land-resource conservation movement.

The land-use policy of the United States has gradually become one of improving methods of utilizing land resources so as to maintain and improve soil fertility and productive capacity. It is now felt that an adequate land policy must provide not only for the preservation of soil fertility but also for the directed adjustment of production to demand, the economic utilization of marginal lands, and the maintenance of a balance among the various segments of the economy.

United States land policy should be developed and continuously appraised with due consideration for the land and population problems of the rest of the world. Our production and land-utilization policies and practices will be deeply influenced by the needs of other nations for agricultural and industrial products and the overall development of their economies. The more we are aware of the oneness of the modern world, the broader in scope and more truly beneficial our land policy will become.

The land policies of individual nations, if they are to be fully effective in meeting general welfare objectives, should be formulated as a part of a coördinated, world-wide framework to meet global needs. However, since there is no world government, the formulation of world land policies can be no more than nations voluntarily helping other nations to analyze their land problems and to arrive at sound land policies that will weld a peaceful society of nations and contribute to higher levels of living for people in all parts of the world. Through the United Nations and United States technical assistance, much can be done to achieve these highly desirable objectives. The basic principles and objectives are, in general, amenable to world-wide application, but the specific objectives and the various ways by which they can and should be implemented must be closely adapted to the institutions and economic and social conditions of each nation.

LAND PROGRAMS

Current phases of a land policy are referred to as *programs*. Reference to *programs* is ordinarily to immediate events, plans, or institutions, which are the contemporary manifestations of the longer-time, more fundamental policy.[10] Land-use programs, in other words, represent current efforts to achieve the objectives implicit in the prevailing land policy. They are the means by which the policy is translated into action. They include efforts of private and public agencies to set up rules and administrative procedures for achieving immediate goals.

The great number of federal, state, and local agencies engaged in land-use and land-adjustment programs have created a large body of rules, interpretations, and administrative procedures, often conflicting and contradictory, which make it somewhat difficult to determine at any time the fundamental land-use plan or policy of the nation. It is important that the student distinguish clearly between the terms "policy" and "program" in land economics. Unless otherwise indicated, the term "land policy" will be used in this text to designate the more permanent, long-time guiding principles governing land utilization practices. "Land programs" will mean current procedures used to implement and attain the land policy.

EARLY LAND PROGRAMS IN THE UNITED STATES

During the first 125 years of our history as a nation, the disposal of the public domain was the chief concern in public land policy, and land programs during this period were designed to carry out this major policy objective. Principal programs included public acquisition of title to lands on the frontier, the sale of these lands to private buyers or settlers, and various settlement acts enabling settlers to earn title to land by living on it and developing it rather than by purchasing it.

Land-sales programs underwent numerous changes during the more than a century that lands were offered for sale at public auctions to the highest bidders. Concessions were made to settlers by reducing the minimum size of units purchasable, by lowering the minimum purchase price, by use of an ill-starred credit system, and by recognition of squatters' rights through adoption of the preëmption principle.

Military bounties were granted to soldiers and veterans and were eventually modified to permit their ready transfer, which encouraged speculation. Swampland, education, and other grants were made to the states, to be disposed of by them as they determined, and large grants were made to railroads.[11]

---

[10] A. G. Black, *op. cit.*, p. 312.
[11] Johnson and Barlowe, *op. cit.*, pp. 64–65.

Settlement acts included the Homestead Act of 1862 and later modifications of its 160-acre gift provisions through passage of the Kinkaid Act, the Enlarged Homestead Act, the Stock-raising Homestead Act, the Desert Land Act, and the Timber Culture Act. There was much violation of the spirit and purpose of these acts by land speculators and timber barons during the last half of the nineteenth century.

RECENT UNITED STATES LAND PROGRAMS

A growing public awareness, in the last three decades of the nineteenth century, that the land disposal and settlement programs were not compatible with the public interest resulted in enactment of the Land Reform Act of 1891. This law repealed the Timber Culture Act and the preëmption laws, amended the homestead laws and the Desert Land Act, stopped the program of land sales at public auctions, and authorized setting aside timber areas for national parks by the President.[12]

Since the turn of the century, various land programs have been adopted affecting the use, conservation, and development of the land resources of the nation. In general, these have been designed to achieve better land-use practices and to improve the economic well-being of those who own, occupy, or use the land. Some of the more important land-use aspects emphasized include resource conservation, reacquisition and management of public lands, land classification and resource evaluation, retirement of submarginal lands, reclamation and land development, zoning and land-use control, land credit, low-cost housing, and production control.[13]

Resource Conservation. Early beginnings of the conservation movement started around the turn of the century. National concern prevailed over a feared shortage of production resources, and the problem was attacked on three fronts—increased agricultural research to make two blades of grass grow where one had grown previously; establishment of a National Forest Products Laboratory to find more economical forest-product use; and creation of the Bureau of Reclamation to construct irrigation works and reclaim public lands. More public lands were reserved for forest, park, mineral, and water-power-site purposes, but not until the advent of the New Deal in 1933 did resource conservation really come into its own. The Soil Conservation Service was established in the United States Department of Agriculture to deal with problems involved in conserving and building up the soil resources of the nation. By mid-century more than 2300 soil conservation districts covering about three-fourths of the farm land had been organized in the various states.

In addition to the Soil Conservation Program, after 1938 the Agricultural Adjustment Administration and its successors, the War Food

[12] Roy M. Robbins, *Our Landed Heritage*, Peter Smith, 1950, pp. 296–297.
[13] Johnson and Barlowe, *op. cit.*, p. 66.

Administration and the Production and Marketing Administration, carried on agricultural conservation programs in which farmers adopted soil-building and range-building practices. Some of these are list-terracing, use of green manure and cover crops, crop-residue management, field strip cropping, contour farming, pasture seeding, farm drainage, sodding of waterways, tree planting, and construction of dams for providing stock water and for erosion control.[14]

Reacquisition and Management of Public Lands.   Another important program of the New Deal was the retiring of millions of acres of submarginal lands from their current uses. The Taylor Grazing Act of 1934, amended in 1936, authorized withdrawal of 142 million acres of vacant, unappropriated, and unreserved public lands for inclusion in grazing districts. In 1935 President Franklin Roosevelt withdrew the remaining public domain from private appropriation. Additional millions of acres were purchased by the federal government for national forests, parks, and recreational areas, for reclamation, flood control, rural resettlement, wildlife, military uses, and other purposes. In addition, many states and counties acquired considerable acreages of private lands through chronic tax delinquency in the thirties.

Classification and Resource Evaluation.   The first general classification of the nation's resources was completed during the early years of the New Deal. This classification contributed a great deal to the development of sound conservation and public management programs. Under the Land Use Planning Program of the United States Department of Agriculture, between 1938 and 1941, in coöperation with the states, nearly all the counties in the nation were expected to inventory and classify their land resources, analyze their problems, and develop programs to improve local situations. A great variation in results occurred among the counties, some doing a thorough and competent job and developing successful action programs, others doing a superficial job with net results little more than preparation of a land-use map.

Zoning and Land-Use Control.   The twentieth century has experienced increasing emphasis on programs involving greater social control over individual land-use practices. Among the more important land-use direction and control programs that have developed are those involved in the zoning of land uses, prescribing of building restrictions, and establishing of special districts to deal with soil and grazing land management and conservation. Practically all cities of any size now have zoning regulations, and most of the states have authorized various types of rural zoning. Timber-cutting regulations, grazing-permit regulations, and mining regulations covering health and safety standards represent other means of

[14] *Ibid.,* p. 68.

exercising the power of the government in directing and controlling types of land use.

Land Credit. One of the most significant and successful programs contributing to sound land-use practices in the United States in recent years is provision of adequate credit facilities for American farmers. Long-term credit facilities have been provided by the federal land bank system established in 1917. In 1933 the Farm Credit Administration was established, and in addition to supervising the land banks, it serves local production credit associations through the federal intermediate credit banks. It also provides emergency feed and crop loans to farmers who cannot secure credit from other sources, and makes loans to farmer coöperative associations. The Farmers Home Administration, established in 1946, and preceded by the Farm Security Administration and the Resettlement Administration, has helped many farm families that ordinarily would not have had adequate or any sources of real-estate and production credit available for their use.

Federal government activity in the real-estate credit field has not been limited to agricultural credit. Home mortgage defaults and foreclosures in the thirties led to enactment of mortgage-moratorium statutes. These restricted foreclosure rights, lengthened redemption periods, and limited deficiency judgments. The chartering of federal savings and loan associations was encouraged, and a Federal Savings and Loan Insurance Corporation was established in 1934 to insure deposits of shareholders in savings and loan associations. The Federal Housing Administration, established in 1934, insures approved risks taken by private lenders and thus provides a more certain mortgage market and stimulates a freer flow of credit for construction and property improvement.

Production Control. In 1933 the Agricultural Adjustment Administration embarked on a national program of production controls in an attempt to reduce depressing farm surpluses and bolster agricultural prices. Acreage allotments were established for basic crops. The allotment system was soon supplemented by use of marketing quotas. In more recent years, production adjustment has been tied to conservation with lands shifted from so-called *soil-depleting* to *soil-conserving* crops. Payments are made to farmers for following certain recommended land-use practices. In 1956 the Soil Bank Act was passed, and farmers are paid to "deposit" certain of their lands in the bank by withdrawing them from production of commercial crops.

Some of the effects of the production-control programs on land use, as they have been administered in the last two decades, include: intensification of land use; shifting of the margins of crop transference for several crops as lands that appear submarginal for higher uses are shifted into competition with lands normally adapted for lower uses; placing a natural premium on ownership or control of properties that have the proper historical base for a sizable allotment or quota; significant impacts on the size of operating units, increasing them under certain conditions and decreasing them under others; adding to the attractiveness of farm investments, both for farm and nonfarm investors; and adding greatly to the security of farm ownership.[15]

The chapters immediately following analyze the principles of the economic and social processes of land utilization. These principles are designed to shape the tools by which the problems of land use may be attacked and resulting policies and programs understood.

REFERENCES FOR FURTHER READING

Ely, R. T., and Morehouse, E. W., *Elements of Land Economics,* The Macmillan Company, New York, 1924, Chaps. I and IV.

Halcrow, Harold G. (ed.), *Contemporary Readings in Agricultural Economics,* Prentice-Hall, Inc., Englewood Cliffs, N.J., 1955, pp. 298–305.

Hibbard, Benjamin H., *A History of the Public Land Policies,* The Macmillan Company, New York, 1924, Chap. XXVIII.

Johnson, V. Webster, and Barlowe, Raleigh, *Land Problems and Policies,* McGraw-Hill Book Company, Inc., New York, 1954, Chaps. I and IV.

Robbins, Roy M., *Our Landed Heritage,* Peter Smith, New York, 1950, Chaps. XVIII, XIX, XX, and XXIV.

Salter, Leonard A., Jr., *A Critical Review of Research in Land Economics,* University of Minnesota Press, Minneapolis, 1948, Chap. VIII.

Timmons, John F., and Murray, William G. (eds.), *Land Problems and Policies,* Iowa State College Press, Ames, 1950, Chaps. II, XV, and XVI.

[15] For a more complete analysis of these and other effects, see Johnson and Barlowe, *op. cit.,* pp. 66–93.

part II

PRINCIPLES OF
LAND UTILIZATION

THE SUPPLY OF LAND
LAND SUPPLIES FOR SPECIFIC USES
THE DEMAND FOR LAND
LAND REQUIREMENTS FOR SPECIFIC USES
THE PROCESS OF RESOURCE ALLOCATION
ECONOMIC RESPONSES IN LAND USE
LAND CONSERVATION

chapter 3

THE SUPPLY OF LAND

SUPPLY ASPECTS OF LAND IN PRODUCTION

Physical and Economic Supply of Land—Elasticity of Supply of Land—Economic Response of Land to Production

INCREASING THE ECONOMIC SUPPLY OF LAND

Extension of Land Area Used—More Intensive Utilization of Land Resources Now in Use—Removal of Obstacles to Most Efficient Land Utilization—Adjusting Consumption to Products Most Easily Produced—Military Conquest of Additional Lands—Control of Foreign Trade—Physical Conditions and Economic Response of Land

CLASSIFICATION OF LAND RESOURCES

Objectives of Land Classification: CLASSIFICATION AND WISE LAND SETTLEMENT, CLASSIFICATION AS AN AID IN PUBLIC LAND PURCHASE AND DEVELOPMENT, CLASSIFICATION AS AN AID IN PLANNING THE ORGANIZATION AND DISTRIBUTION OF LOCAL GOVERNMENTAL SERVICES, CLASSIFICATION AS AN AID IN DISTRIBUTING PUBLIC FUNDS TO LOCAL AREAS, CLASSIFICATION AND EXTENSION OF LAND CREDIT, CLASSIFICATION AND TAX ASSESSMENT, CLASSIFICATION AS A GUIDE IN DEVELOPING AND ADMINISTERING PROGRAMS FOR IMPROVED LAND UTILIZATION PRACTICES, CLASSIFICATION AS AN AID IN DETERMINING TYPE AND SIZE OF OPERATING UNITS— *Requirements of a Suitable Classification—Types of Land Classification—Physical Classification of Land—Use Classification of Land—Development of Land Classification in the United States—Weaknesses of Land Classification in the United States—The Future of Land Classification*

THE UTILIZATION of land as well as that of other goods is subject in a general way to economic forces such as those of interplay of supply and demand. However, the conditions of supply and demand are not exactly the same for each of the factors of production, nor do they operate in precisely the same manner to determine land income or rent as they do to determine labor income (wages), capital returns (interest), or management income (profits).

In order to develop mature judgment concerning the response that land and land users will make to the stimuli of cultural forces and of price, property, or administrative rulings, students must acquire a knowledge of the physical supply of land and, more important, an understanding of the characteristic economic responses of land and land suppliers.

SUPPLY ASPECTS OF LAND IN PRODUCTION

PHYSICAL AND ECONOMIC SUPPLY OF LAND

The supply of land considered in a strict physical sense consists of the whole earth—its land surface and subsurface, water areas, and atmosphere. The total physical supply of land on the earth, therefore, may be considered fixed and limited. Another aspect of land supply is of greater economic and social significance than absolute physical supply. This is the economic supply of land that may be defined as the schedule of land units which will enter particular uses in response to price at a given time and at given places. For certain purposes a supply function will be used to denote the response of land to factors other than price, such as government rules and regulations, subsidies, or other forms of stimulating the use of land.

The potential economic supply of land—all land that might possibly or ultimately be used for any purpose—differs from total physical supply because the entire physical supply of land may not be economically available or usable for certain purposes, either now or at any time in the future. The present economic supply of land—that which is now being used for all economic production—reflects current utilization practices and takes into account current economic availability and adaptability for specific uses. It represents the economic response to demand for land under existing cultural and technological conditions.

A complete inventory of the world's physical supply of land resources cannot be presented. Many mineral deposits of great value to man no doubt have not yet been discovered. In many parts of the world, moreover, land resources have not been carefully surveyed to make possible any adequate inventory or classification of existing physical resources. To make a complete inventory of present economic supply, it would be necessary to outline the areas now used by man for various purposes. Although data showing physical resources, together with present land utilization patterns, are helpful in giving the student of land economics some understanding of existing relationships between man and land, it is more important for him to have a clear understanding of the man-land relationships that determine present economic supply for each of the uses to which land is put. The term "supply of land," therefore, will mean the present economic supply for each use—that is, the economic supply currently available for agriculture, forestry, recreation, mining, transportation, and urban uses. This meaning of supply of land takes into account the influence of both physical and human factors upon the availability of land when used for these various purposes.

ELASTICITY OF SUPPLY OF LAND

In the present largely capitalistic world, owners and users of land decide the type and intensity of use according to the price the land will bring in the market. If the demand for grazing land is such that a high price can be paid for its use, many acres will enter production, which otherwise would be too far up the mountain or too poorly covered with vegetation to be used profitably.

The elasticity of supply of land for any particular use or combination of uses is determined in large part by *scarcity, fertility,* and *accessibility.* Since the supply of land, from the economic standpoint, reflects the relationship between the amount of land available and its price, landowners respond by making their land available, both in the aggregate and for alternative uses according to various reservation prices.

Land may be considered to have no supply price to the extent that it is a permanent good. Land in the sense of surface is fixed, whereas in the sense of the totality of natural contribution it is not fixed but highly dynamic. Land changes constantly in response to the impact of changing human attitudes and actions and of ever-changing culture.

For short periods, scarcity and reservation prices of owners are the only determining factors. When possible alternative uses of the land exist, they influence the supply prices that will be established. For example, in depleting or conserving crops, shifts in supply will occur only when either: (1) some change occurs in landowners' ideas with respect to future prices or profits, or (2) when new knowledge or technological developments occur that affect the supply of the land itself.

The demand for land rises from the various direct and indirect uses to which it can be put. Direct uses include those in which land itself is a consumption good, such as utilization for recreation purposes or homesites. Indirect uses include those in which land is used as a means of producing goods and services to be used in industry or for final consumption. In the latter case, the demand for land is a *derived demand,* which springs from the demand for the goods and services produced, including food and fiber.

The demand for land is the schedule of the amounts of land that users will take at varying prices. Shifts will occur with any change in the basic demand for the goods and services derived from land utilization or when any changes occur in prices of these goods and services. Shifts in the demand for land may also occur when any change comes in the market for the other factors of production—capital, labor, or entrepreneurship, either through price changes or through innovations. Innovations are largely ones that cause a change in substitutability among the factors.

Improved methods of transportation, farming, factory and home construction, and trade and exchange make available for profitable production and use land formerly unprofitable and therefore unused because of inaccessibility or inferior quality, or make land already available more accessible or more productive.

With primitive techniques of production, transportation, and trade, physical conditions are highly important in determining land use. In a modern nation, such as the United States with its mineral-using industries, well-developed transportation system, and widespread application of machine technique, land economically available for use is far in excess of current human requirements for many of its products. The same physical resources from which the native Indians produced so little now produce tremendous quantities of food and fiber products, as well as huge quantities of minerals and mineral products. Irrigation has made land productive that was formerly unfit for crop production. Development of hybrid corn has increased the yield of corn; the effect is the same as increasing the supply of cornland. The supply of land has been further increased through reclamation, drainage, leveling, regrassing, and other means.

Man has so modified the effects of climate or the physical conditions controlling land utilization that areas once relatively uninhabitable or unproductive except for very limited use have been made fruitful and pleasant, and the supply of land has again been increased.[1] When mining was on a small-scale, selective basis, richness of ore deposits was an all-important factor; but nowadays the exploitation of relatively lean or poor-grade mineral deposits is possible because of the opportunity of applying greater doses of capital under modern technology. Leaner or poorer deposits may produce a larger profit than the richer deposits that do not permit an equal degree of intensive capitalistic development. Oil refining is a good example. Thus, availability and applicability of capital

---

[1] Frost or storm warnings broadcast over the radio to help farmers protect their crops or livestock serve as an example of modern techniques which help to overcome climatic hazards.

are of paramount importance in modern times, and land is not as serious a limiting factor as it once was.[2] Land supply has been made more elastic. When no alternatives are available the supply curve is inelastic.

ECONOMIC RESPONSE OF LAND TO PRODUCTION

While the influence of natural characteristics in determining the land supply available has declined, temperature, moisture, topography, and soils, often referred to as "the four physical frontiers of agriculture," still determine the absolute limits of cultivability or physical productivity for agricultural land. However, these physical factors now operate less directly, since their influence has been overcome, within limits, or so taken into account that only ultimately do they determine production. These physical frontiers indicate the limits of agricultural potentiality, but the extent to which agriculture is actually practiced depends on the state of societal and technical arts, population pressure, standards of living, and related economic, social, and cultural factors.[3] For example, while 1 acre in 10 of the world's surface acreage is physically suitable for wheat production, this tenth greatly exceeds present human requirements, and less than 1 acre in 10 of this physically adapted supply is now being used for wheat. Moreover, since other crops such as corn, oats, hay, and vegetables must also be grown on land suitable for wheat, "it appears unlikely that over 3 percent of the world's land surface will ever be devoted to wheat production." [4]

Technological development of a nation is an important determinant of the extent to which physically adapted supply will be utilized for economic production. In China, for example, less than a third of the acreage physically suitable for crops is cultivated, in spite of a large population, but some 40 percent is so used in the United States. On a per capita basis, from five to six times as much land is cultivated in the United States as in China, or between 2½ and 3 acres per capita in the United States compared with about a half acre in China.[5]

In China, only the very best lands can be worked, because poorer lands will not yield enough to sustain life under hand-labor methods. Where

[2] Erich W. Zimmermann, *World Resources and Industries,* Harper, rev. ed., 1951, pp. 83–84.

[3] According to Zimmermann, "It is safe to assume that in the calculable future the world's food supply will depend primarily on the development of the arts, especially on increased knowledge of agronomy, better techniques of plant and animal breeding, revolutionary discoveries in the field of biology, the increasing availability and efficiency of capital equipment, and, above all, on the fuller use of inanimate energy. But it will also depend on improved knowledge of diatetics and the prevailing attitude toward food consumption. For the calculable future, therefore, the question of the physical limits of cultivability will remain a purely academic one." (*Ibid.,* p. 86.)

[4] O. E. Baker, "The Potential Supply of Wheat," *Economic Geography,* Vol. I, No. 1, March, 1925, p. 31.

[5] Cf. Zimmermann, *op. cit.,* p. 88.

animals are used as a source of energy, they use as feed a considerable portion of what they help to produce. Use of modern machinery reduces the amount of land required for food and feed production, so that a profit may be made even where less productive lands are utilized, while under hand-labor conditions there might not be a sufficient margin of yield over and above that required to support the hand laborer's family.[6]

Use of machine energy leads to agricultural surpluses, and consequently to trade and to cash crops or salable animal products; that is, exchange economies develop an agriculture resting on a more commercialized, profit-seeking basis than that in hand-labor, locally self-sufficing economies. Cultivation of the soil in commercialized economies tends to be more impersonal and exploitative than that in a hand-labor, self-sufficing economy, and this tendency may have serious consequences for the soil itself. The elasticity in the amount of land that will be used, or respond to production, will vary more in a commercialized economy where business activity, purchasing power, and related economic conditions vary considerably in different periods. These variations cause significant variations in the amount of land actually utilized for production (the economic response) and in the physical supply suitable for such utilization.

Thus, while the physical properties of land are directly related to the economic supply of land, the relationship is not fixed but is constantly in flux. Increases in population ordinarily tend to increase demand, while improvements in the technique or art of obtaining products or services from land usually tend to increase the supply. If chemists should ever discover an economically feasible process for the manufacture of food in test tubes and laboratory, the economic supply of agricultural land might conceivably become unlimited.

INCREASING THE ECONOMIC SUPPLY OF LAND

The limits of the economic supply of land in a price economy at any given time are set by the ratio between the price of the product and the cost of overcoming certain physical obstacles in production. Thus, the decline in value of agricultural land in the United States, beginning in

[6] In the United States, increased use of the tractor and automobile and substitution of gasoline and tractor fuel for horsepower since 1918 have released 78 million acres of cropland and 55 million acres of pastureland, formerly needed to produce feed for horses and mules, for production of food for human consumption. (U.S. Department of Agriculture, *Agricultural Land Resources in the United States,* Agricultural Information Bulletin No. 140, Government Printing Office, June, 1955, p. 80.)

Some 87 percent of the total energy used in the United States is now derived from the fossil fuels (coal, oil, and natural gas) and 7 percent from water power, leaving only 6 percent of work to be done by men and animals. It is estimated that by 1960 human beings will contribute only 2.5 percent of the total energy output of the nation. (Zimmermann, *op. cit.,* p. 58.)

1920, reflected the increasing economic supply of land resulting largely from increased efficiency of agricultural production and decreasing price of agricultural products.

The economic supply of land may be increased in six important ways.[7] (1) New areas previously unused can be brought into production, constituting an extension of the land used. (2) Areas in use can be utilized more intensively—that is, more labor and capital can be applied in a given area to increase yields and production. (3) Certain drawbacks or hindrances to the complete or fullest possible use of the area already utilized may be removed, thus permitting greater output. This is "economizing land utilization," or using the land more economically. (4) Consumption of products of the land may be controlled so that people will desire what the earth can produce most readily. (5) Military conquest of additional lands may take place. (6) Foreign trade may be controlled so as to reduce exports of agricultural and industrial products to other nations or increase imports of such products from abroad, thus increasing the economic supply of land within a given nation. Obviously, this method would be ineffective for the world as a whole, but it does cause significant shifts in land utilization and in the economic supplies available for various uses in specific parts of the world.

EXTENSION OF LAND AREA USED

The principal areas of great natural resources as yet undeveloped are: (1) the tropics, (2) the temperate zone outside the range of present intensive development, (3) the arctic, and (4) the sea. The tropics, which may be defined as the areas of the earth approximately within the boundaries of the isotherms of mean annual temperature of 25° C. or 77° F.,[8] contain half the arable land of the earth and are rich in undeveloped natural resources but, for the most part, are not now suited to permanent occupation by the white race. Though colored races are able to live in the tropics, they have been backward in developing the natural resources. Nevertheless, the fact that Java and Madura, Puerto Rico, and some other tropical areas now support a population relatively large in comparison with their land area is evidence that other parts of the tropics may eventually be made to support comparatively large populations. Java and Madura, which have a total area only slightly smaller than Montana, have a population of more than 42 million compared with about a half million in Montana; and Puerto Rico has a population density of 520 per square mile.

[7] Ely and Morehouse mention the first four of these methods. (See R. T. Ely and E. W. Morehouse, *Elements of Land Economics,* Macmillan, 1924, pp. 63–67.)

[8] Isaiah Bowman (ed.), *Limits of Land Settlement,* Council on Foreign Relations, 1937, p. 381.

Perhaps the best example of an area awaiting development within the temperate zones is northwestern Canada, which contains large areas of excellent soil, comparatively rich deposits of valuable minerals, and abundant water-power resources. However, better prices for minerals and food and improved transportation facilities are the two main requirements for increased utilization of these land resources. Many undeveloped lands in this area require drainage, irrigation, or clearing before they can be used effectively for agriculture; and the distance from railroads is so great as to make any intensive form of agriculture impracticable. To use another example, the Trans-Siberian Railway has made possible the use of a strip some 50 to 100 miles wide across Asia for agricultural purposes, but the surrounding land is commercially nonexistent, though much of it is physically suitable for agricultural use and contains relatively rich deposits of certain minerals. Until mineral and food prices reach a level high enough to repay the cost of constructing additional transportation facilities and related production costs, these areas will remain undeveloped.

Expeditions to the relatively unexplored polar regions have recently indicated great potential food and mineral resources in the arctic and antarctic. The sea is a potential source of food; and in addition to fish and other sea foods, certain minerals and products such as iodine, salt, or even gold may be recaptured from oceans or other bodies of water. Bowman, in *The Pioneer Fringe*, defines the remaining areas considered as "pioneer" areas as "regions of potential settlement in which man may have a reasonably safe and prosperous life, but regions in most of which he is required to make certain special adaptations." [9]

These adaptations are many and varied. In some cases, adaptations to very cold or very hot climates must be made through plant and animal breeding. In arid regions, drought-resistant varieties must be established or irrigation must be developed. In other areas, insect pests must be controlled to the point where they are not too destructive, or swampy lowland strips must be reclaimed through drainage, or a too porous soil may be a factor that man must contend with before he can efficiently utilize the area. In any case, remaining areas of undeveloped natural resources do not constitute a broad, unbroken belt, but rather "a series of scattered patches and strips loosely disposed in belt-like form beyond the fringe of present settlement," [10] each continent having its share (see Figure 1).

On the continent of North America, pioneer belts include a strip of land lying roughly along the 100th meridian in the United States, and a

[9] Isaiah Bowman, *The Pioneer Fringe*, American Geographical Society, Special Publication 13, 1931, p. 51.
[10] *Ibid*.

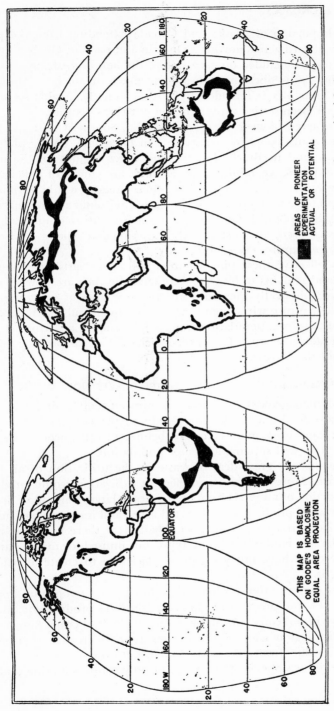

Figure 1. Pioneer Belts of the World. (Adapted from Isaiah Bowman, *The Pioneer Fringe*, American Geographical Society, Special Publication 13, 1931.)

considerable portion of Alaska and Canada extending from the prairie provinces eastward across northern Ontario and parts of Quebec. In Asia, much territory is included on each side of the belt of settlement that has followed the Trans-Siberian Railway, and much of northern Manchuria and Inner Mongolia is included (refer to Figure 1). Arable sections in this area have been settled rapidly in the last three decades.

There are large pioneer areas in Australia, Southern Africa, and the continent of South America, particularly in Patagonia, on the plateau of Mato Grosso, and in Brazil, Bolivia, and other regions on the eastern slope of the Andes. Remaining pioneer lands are chiefly of deficient and less reliable rainfall. Scientific study of such climates would permit man to make land-use adaptations to fit the basic environment most efficiently. Much study is required if land is to be most fully utilized and its highest possibilities realized; and certainly the experimental type of land on the pioneer fringe requires even more study.

Just how effective these pioneer areas will be in satisfying man's demand for land remains to be seen. Economically they are now relatively unimportant; physically they constitute a large area of great potentialities, and their future will depend largely upon demand for the products of land resulting from population trends and standard of living achieved, and on the advancement of science, which will make possible efficient utilization of these areas.

MORE INTENSIVE UTILIZATION OF LAND RESOURCES NOW IN USE

Improved management and large applications of capital and labor result in more food and fiber being produced per acre, and fewer acres will do the same work more acres did before. In other words, the same number of acres will support a greater population.

There has been a great deal of waste in the utilization of all major land resources. More intensive and efficient utilization would produce a larger proportion of minerals from ore bodies, a larger amount of finished lumber and wood products from forested acres, and increased agricultural output per acre from farm lands. In urban areas there is, in the aggregate, considerable land plotted for city use but unused for urban purposes because the cities have not yet grown sufficiently to create an effective demand for it.

Systematic crop rotations, using soil-building crops (crops that improve tilth), legumes, and grasses to retain soil and food productivity, are not only effective in soil conservation but increase yields of crops. Substituting higher-quality legumes for other hays results in increased tonnage and higher feed value from the same tonnage. Contour tillage (farming around the hill or slope, on the level) not only controls erosion and conserves moisture but increases yields.[11] Applications of lime and phosphate to pastures increase the livestock-carrying capacity of pastures, especially in the eastern and southern United States.

Use of certain soil amendments in the form of chemicals and soil elements vital to plant growth has increased yields per acre considerably. Many plant diseases have been traced to deficiency of certain soil elements. Lack of magnesium may cause sand-drown of tobacco or chlorosis of tomatoes, while adding zinc to the soil and using it in orchard sprays remedies pecan rosette, peach little leaf, and similar diseases. Recent studies show that crackstem of celery, internal cork of apples, and several other diseases can be controlled or prevented by adding small amounts of boron to the soil.[12] Application of such soil amendments results in greatly increased yields as well as improved quality.

More intensive farm woodlot utilization and the shift in the South to pulpwood production for the paper industry have greatly increased the annual forest product yield per acre. Extensive forest fire and insect pest control by the U.S. Forest Service has increased the growth of high-quality, valuable timber on public forest lands. Yields of forest lands in such countries as Germany, where intense utilization has been developed, indicate the potential increase in output possible under such conditions.

Use of more efficient machinery in extracting minerals is another example of increased output made possible by intensification. In certain United States gold-producing areas placered many years ago and abandoned, large modern dredges have extracted gold from the same land previously panned by hand.

One of the boldest of twentieth-century technical plans to intensify utilization of previously used land by the application of great doses of capital, labor, and management is the plan referred to as "Antleuropa," evolved by a Munich architect. This plan would convert the Mediterranean into an inland lake in order to utilize part of its water power for productive purposes and reclaim much land along its European and African shore lines for agricultural and urban use.[13]

Although the preceding examples indicate ways in which more intensive land resource utilization can result in increased production, this

[11] In a short test in one area, contour farming boosted corn yields from 5 to 23 bushels per acre, and it was estimated that probably about 15 million acres of corn grown annually on sloping land in the western corn belt in the United States could be farmed on the contour. It is estimated that a concentrated program of contouring in the western corn belt could provide an increase in corn production of about 50 million bushels. (See U.S. Department of Agriculture, *Technology on the Farm*, Government Printing Office, August, 1940, p. 29.)

[12] *Ibid.*, p. 31.

[13] "Plugging up the Mediterranean Projected in Giant German Plan," *Christian Science Monitor*, September 30, 1933.

intensified utilization—whether applied to agricultural, forest, mineral, recreational, or urban land, or land used for transportation—will probably not occur unless prices of land products rise sufficiently to justify the additional expense, or unless the intensified methods result in lower costs of production so that greater profits can be secured at current prices.

REMOVAL OF OBSTACLES TO MOST EFFICIENT LAND UTILIZATION

Inadequate transportation is an important hindrance to most efficient or complete utilization of land resources in many areas. There is an economic limit to which a farmer, a lumberman, or a miner can go to transport his commodity, depending upon the scale of productive operations, state of the roads, means of transport, cost of labor, and market value of the product.[14] Railroad construction has been of tremendous importance to American agriculture. Railroads opened the interior to commercial farming, but lack of satisfactory side roads running into the back country on both sides of the right-of-way and dependence upon horses as the source of transport power prevented extension of commercial crop farming beyond these relatively narrow strips. Ranching was developed more extensively back from the main railroad lines, since cattle and sheep could be driven relatively long distances to market.

Webb tells of the efforts of Texans at the close of the Civil War to connect the 4-dollar Texas cow with the 40-dollar Northern market. Their immediate objectives in driving cattle northward were railheads from which the cattle could be shipped east. By 1866, several railroads—among these the Missouri Pacific, which had reached Sedalia, Missouri—had nosed their way across the Mississippi, following population to the edge of the Great Plains.[15] Cattle trails gradually reached from the Texas ranges to Wyoming, Montana, the Dakotas, and even Canada; and in the space of 15 years the range cattle industry had spread over the entire Great Plains area.[16] Recent great expansion of highway construction accompanying the development of the modern automobile and truck has extended the areas of crop production and widened the areas of buying and selling agricultural produce. Increased use of air transportation, given impetus during World War II, will exert a similar influence. Future technological advances will tend to make for more adequate transportation and thus contribute to increasing the economic supply of land, particularly agricultural land.

The recent rapid growth of rural electrification in the United States has been another important factor reducing obstacles in the way of most

---

[14] Bowman, *The Pioneer Fringe*, p. 64.

[15] The distance from the range areas in Texas to Sedalia, Missouri, averaged between 500 and 850 miles.

[16] W. P. Webb, *The Great Plains*, Ginn, 1931, Chap. VI.

efficient land utilization, especially agricultural land utilization. Modern electrical appliances and equipment make possible greatly increased output of product per worker.

One of the most important recent developments in removal of obstacles to efficient utilization of land is quick-freeze processing of vegetables, which makes out-of-season green vegetables and small fruits available to city consumers. Preserving these vegetables expands the market through increased consumption, provided costs can be kept relatively low.

Continual improvement in farm machinery, in methods of controlling animal and plant diseases, and in disseminating up-to-date agricultural information through agencies established by the federal government and the state agricultural colleges in the United States are good examples of utilizing agricultural land through improvement of agricultural technique. Loss of foreign markets for agricultural products during the twenties and thirties has been another factor contributing to the need for additional agricultural information and improved practices to reduce American agricultural costs of production. Federal and state programs, especially those developed during the thirties, to improve production methods and conserve agricultural lands have been important in meeting this need, with the result that farmers generally are a much more enlightened and progressive group than in earlier years. All of this has contributed to making the utilization of agricultural land more efficient in the United States.

In strict economic terms, *production,* or the *creation of utility,* necessarily includes all the steps in transferring the products from land to final consumers. Consequently, the effect of any circumstances or conditions that delay, waste, reduce the quality of, or destroy the product in its path to the final consumer is the same as a reduction in amount of land used for producing the goods. Lack of market information on the part of producers, lack of quality standards, inefficient purchasing methods of consumers, and similar causes of inefficient distribution of food or other products of the land, such as lumber and mineral products, are all factors effecting a decrease in the economic supply of land.

ADJUSTING CONSUMPTION TO PRODUCTS MOST EASILY PRODUCED

The economic supply of land can be increased by adjusting human consumption to what the earth can produce most efficiently. For example, in the case of agricultural land, the same acres could feed many more people if certain changes in human diet were made. It has been estimated that if the United States reduced its per capita consumption of meat by one-third and compensated for this decrease by a proportionate increase in the use of dairy products and vegetables, the nation could double its population without diminishing its real welfare, and much more than double it if crop production per acre continues to increase as it has since World War II.[17]

Shifts from less productive to more productive crops per acre—especially from grain and hay to fruit and vegetables—resulted in increasing United States crop production by the equivalent of about 14 million acres of crop land between 1919 and 1929. Shifts from less productive to more productive animals per unit of feed consumed—particularly from beef cattle to dairy cattle, hogs, and poultry—resulted in increasing production by the equivalent of about nine million acres of crop land. Consequently, these two shifts accompanying changes in dietary habits increased agricultural production by the equivalent of some 23 million acres during the twenties.

Human diet can be influenced to a large extent by proper education and adequate information. Nutritional research coupled with taxation and government control of certain food products, particularly during war periods or similar emergencies, can do much to control and direct consumption of products most easily produced. The net result of such efforts is to increase the efficiency of the land, which has the same effect as increasing the economic supply. Conversely, shifts in diet in the opposite direction have the effect of reducing the economic supply of land.

Similar conclusions can be applied to urban, forest, mineral, or recreational land, and land used for transportation purposes. If people demand more of those products or services that can be furnished most readily or with the least cost, the economic effect is to increase the supply of land; whereas if they desire from the land more of those goods or services that are most difficult to produce or for which only a limited land supply is available, the net result will be a decrease in the economic supply of land.

While changes in dietary habits affect the economic supply of land for specific uses, the effect of these changes should be distinguished from the effect of changes in population numbers. A declining population, or one in which the rate of increase is declining, will reduce demand for land

[17] The annual consumption of meat per capita in the United States averages over 150 pounds and is much higher than that in some other leading nations. If the annual per capita consumption of meat in the United States were cut to 50 pounds and compensated by a proportionate increase in the consumption of dairy products and vegetables, our diet would be fully as nutritious as before, and would enable the nation to double its population. This is made possible by the fact that a total of less than 4 acres (2.35 acres of crop land and 1.6 acres of pasture land) is required to produce 1,400,000 calories of dairy products, while to produce the same amount with beef requires almost 14 acres (11.3 of crop and 2.5 of pasture). (See O. E. Baker, "Land Utilization in the United States: Geographical Aspects of the Problem," *American Geographical Review*, Vol. XIII, No. 1, January, 1923, pp. 14–15; L. C. Gray and O. E. Baker, *Land Utilization and the Farm Problem*, U.S. Department of Agriculture, Miscellaneous Publication 97, 1930, p. 33; and *Agricultural Land Resources in the United States*, p. 81.)

and consequently have the same effect as an expansion in the economic supply of land. On the contrary, a population expanding rapidly because of a rising birth rate and declining death rate will have the effect of enlarging demand for land and making the current supply of available land resources increasingly inadequate.

MILITARY CONQUEST OF ADDITIONAL LANDS

History is replete with military conquests as a means of extending dominion and control over desired lands. The rise of many nations to world power and improved standards of living has been associated with conquests and colonization of conquered areas. World War II was precipitated principally by the expansionist policies of the Axis Powers involving Germany's drive for *Lebensraum* or "living space," and the insistence of Japan and Italy on "a spot in the sun."

Military conquest obviously does not add to the total economic supply of land except as the conquerors may be more efficient utilizers of the land than the conquered. Lands acquired or lost by military conquest can enrich or impoverish the individual nations concerned by increasing or reducing their economic supply of land.

CONTROL OF FOREIGN TRADE

Another method of increasing the economic supply of land is to reduce agricultural and industrial exports, or to increase the importation of such products. During the World War I period, agricultural and industrial exports expanded greatly. The slogan "Food Will Win the War" resulted in bringing a large additional acreage of agricultural land into use in the United States to supply armies in Europe. The decline in foreign trade after the war and during the thirties reduced the total demand for and depressed prices of agricultural and industrial products.

The foreign trade policy that a nation adopts will influence the land utilization pattern within the nation. For example, the British Isles for many decades encouraged importation of agricultural produce and raw materials by a free trade policy. In the case of exporting nations such as Canada or Argentina, loss of foreign markets or heavy importation of agricultural and industrial products has the same effect as increasing the economic supply of land available to their citizens. The high tariff barriers erected by many nations after World War I brought about significant shifts in land utilization and in the economic supplies available for various uses in different areas of the world.

For the world as a whole, trade policies of individual nations have little effect upon the economic supply of land, because increased imports in one nation are offset by increased exports in another nation, and vice-versa. However, since there is a lag in the time at which land-use adjustments are effected in other nations in response to measures adopted in a given nation, the trade policies of any nation influence the world economic supply of land for various uses.

PHYSICAL CONDITIONS AND ECONOMIC RESPONSE OF LAND

The enumerated methods of increasing or decreasing the economic supply of land all involve human action or man-made inventions or innovations. Man can control these factors so as to alter significantly the amount, quality, and kind of land needed to satisfy his wants. Some of these methods are much more effective than others in determining the elasicity of land supply.

But man does not control all the factors determining elasticity of the supply of land for various uses, although he plays a significant part. Physical factors condition the economic supply of land for various uses, and are in most cases subject to man's control or modification only in a limited way. These physical conditions differ according to the major use to be made of land. The physical factors limiting the economic supply of land for forests are significantly different from those limiting the economic supply of land for agriculture; and those forces limiting the supply for mining, for urban utilization, or for recreation or transportation are all peculiar to the types of use that may be made of the land resource.

CLASSIFICATION OF LAND RESOURCES

The purpose of land classification is to arrange land resources systematically in various classes or groups on the basis of certain similar characteristics so that man may identify and understand their fundamental characteristics and utilize them most intelligently and effectively in satisfying his wants. Thus, classification is important not only in indicating the physical supply of land available for various uses, but also in influencing the economic supply through more intelligent and effective utilization.

Classifications have been developed on many different bases to serve specific purposes. Land bodies may be classified on their relative suitability for some particular use, such as grain production or grazing; or they may be classified to indicate the enterprises, or sizes and types of operating units, which would be most effective in utilizing them. Again, classification may deal with soil types or other physical characteristics of land, or ownership, or some other basis. In any case, the form of classification to be used will be determined by the objectives that classification is to serve.

OBJECTIVES OF LAND CLASSIFICATION

In order to secure the maximum products and services and at the same time conserve resources for the use of future generations, man must adapt his utilization practices to the basic natural capabilities of the land. However, a more specific objective will ordinarily be needed to justify a classification of land, because classification involves considerable time and expense. A clear specific statement of objectives for which classification is to be made helps to show the type of classification procedure that should be followed.

Classification of land is not an end in itself, but a means of obtaining better land use. Specifically, the objectives of classifying land may be grouped into eight major categories: [18] (1) more enlightened and economically sound land settlement policies both public and private; (2) guidance in public land purchase and development; (3) planning the organization and distribution of local governmental services; (4) guidance in the distribution of public aid, particularly federal and state subventions and public relief to local areas; (5) guidance in determining sound real estate lending and borrowing policies; (6) equalization of land assessments for taxation purposes; (7) guidance in developing and administering programs for improved land utilization practices, soil conservation and erosion control measures, and similar practices; and (8) guidance in developing sound farm management policies and organizing the most effective type and size of operating units.

Classification and Wise Land Settlement. Failure to classify land properly before settlement and development has resulted in the disappointment of many private ventures in land utilization. Most of the lands in the United States, Canada, and other nations have been settled without any systematic body of information setting forth the use capabilities or characteristics of the land at the time of settlement. If lands could be classified properly and zones established, based upon the boundaries of lands with common characteristics and adaptabilities for certain uses, and if individuals and agents selling land were required to place in the hands of prospective purchasers an official report setting forth these characteristics and capabilities, much ill-advised and injudicious settlement and utilization of land could be avoided.

Land classification is also essential in establishing districts or zones in which certain detrimental land uses are to be legally discouraged. Before

---

[18] Barnes lists some 14 specific objectives of land classification, many of which are closely related. The accomplishment of one often results indirectly or incidentally in the attainment of others. These 14 objectives can be grouped into the eight major categories indicated. (See C. P. Barnes, "Land Classification: Objectives and Requirements," U.S. Resettlement Administration, Land Utilization Division, Land-Use Planning Publication 1, February, 1936, mimeographed, pp. 3–12.)

the area can be zoned, the land must be classified according to the uses which may or may not be allowed. *Zoning* is one of the more important means of controlling land use and the supply available for various uses.

Classification as an Aid in Public Land Purchase and Development. Public acquisition of rural lands, in addition to public areas such as national parks, highways, national monuments, state parks, primitive areas, watersheds, wildlife refuges, and similar areas has been largely limited to forest lands. However, the federal government embarked in the early thirties upon a policy of purchasing certain "submarginal" areas, particularly in the Great Plains region, as a means of checking undesirable land-use practices.[19] Sound land classification helps determine whether public acquisition should be used to achieve the desire ends— namely, to prevent continuation of land-use practices harmful to the general welfare, or to prevent further loss of individual well-being and capital.

In many areas where land has reverted to public ownership because owners have found it cheaper to lease than to own, or where individuals have been unable to meet their tax payments and have abandoned their lands, land classification helps to determine which of these lands should be returned to private ownership in the interests of the public good, and which should be retained in public ownership for certain definite public uses.

Classification as an Aid in Planning the Organization and Distribution of Local Governmental Services. The cost of local governmental services and necessary facilities, including roads, schools, electric power and telephone lines, and health services, is an important item in rural and urban operating and living costs in many areas. Land classification based upon detailed problem analyses, including cost of production and income studies, helps to determine the productive capacities of the lands, and consequently the capacity of the local areas to meet the costs of these various services. Where the land classification indicates that the established pattern of local governmental services is probably too expensive for the land resources of the community to support, classification is useful in furnishing the basic data for planning the size and organization of alternative local governmental units, in order to bring cost of local public services within the means of the community.

Problems resulting from the disparity between local public service patterns and productivity of the lands are likely to be more acute in

[19] For a statement of the problems associated with public acquisition of submarginal lands, or the retention of lands that are reverting to public ownership through tax delinquency, see *The Problems of Submarginal Areas and Undesirable Adjustments, with Particular Reference to Public Acquisition of Land,* National Land Use Planning Committee and National Advisory Legislative Committee on Land Use, Publication 6, April, 1933.

sparsely settled areas. There are, of course, sparsely settled areas in which occupancy is justified, but a proper land classification is necessary to determine which areas should be occupied and furnished necessary public services. Such a classification would be of considerable assistance to state and federal agencies endeavoring to determine the amount and distribution of public relief and grants-in-aid.

Classification as an Aid in Distributing Public Funds to Local Areas. If current conditions in the community are temporary or of an emergency nature, state and federal grants-in-aid would be justified to assist in supporting local governmental services like schools, roads, and health facilities; but if human occupancy and local governmental services or the present organization and administration of these local services are on a basis disproportionate to productivity of the local land resources, such state and federal grants-in-aid would not be justified without accompanying adjustments.

Classification and Extension of Land Credit. Land classification is particularly useful to borrowers and lenders in guiding extension of credit. Successful loan experience depends to a large extent upon the relationship of the amount loaned to the productivity of the land. By providing physical and economic information concerning production capabilities of the soil, land classification makes possible more intelligent lending and borrowing practices. Such classification is also basic in providing necessary information for satisfactory investment of capital in lands, both rural and urban. Many distress transfers of farm and city properties in past years could have been avoided had suitable land classification data been available and followed at the time the loans were made.

Classification and Tax Assessment. One of the most important uses of land classification data is as a basis for tax assessments. Assessment of lands according to economic productivity is an important factor in reducing tax delinquency and tax deed foreclosures to a minimum. Land classification data which reveal the use capabilities of the lands are important in computing assessments in accordance with productivity.

Studies of present agricultural land assessments indicate that there is a widespread tendency for poorer lands to be most over-assessed in relation to their comparative ability to produce. A soil survey by a soil scientist is desirable to determine productivity ratings of different grades of soil, and use of such data is helpful in making assessments proportionate to the relative productivities of different grades of land.

Classification as a Guide in Developing and Administering Programs for Improved Land Utilization Practices. Land classification if properly done may furnish basic data showing types and boundaries of soils particularly subject to erosion and soil wastage, and types of farm management practices that best conserve land resources. Such agencies as the

Soil Conservation Service have found land classification data particularly useful in showing extent and type of erosion, and have found cropping practices or erosion control measures suited to different soil types, for reducing erosion and conserving soil fertility. In some areas, measures can be effected to reduce soil waste—proper soil management, crop rotations, strip cropping, terracing, or contour furrowing, for instance—without any change in size or type of farm operating unit; and in such areas classification of land will be designed primarily to show cropping or grazing systems or soil management practices suited to the given body of land.

Classification as an Aid in Determining Type and Size of Operating Units. In many areas adjustments are needed in type or size of farm operating unit to secure the most effective land conservation and adequate family living. In some regions most operating units are too small to furnish adequate family living without using the lands in ways that result in erosion and fertility wastage. Ascertaining types of adjustments necessary to improve family living and to conserve land resources requires land classification that will show the fitness of various lands for different combinations of enterprises and the acreage required for efficiency in operation, maintenance of fertility, reduction of erosion to a minimum, and adequate family living.

REQUIREMENTS OF A SUITABLE CLASSIFICATION

If classification of land resources is to be useful, land classes must be simple and distinct, easily understood and easily recognized, measurable, and economically significant. For example, a classification that indicates merely that two pieces of land are composed of soils formed from entirely different materials would not have much practical value for the average farmer, who is concerned with the methods by which these two pieces of land can be most effectively used, and with their relative economic importance or value for specific agricultural uses.

In the past, farm operators have criticized land classifications, particularly of agricultural land, on the grounds that they were too technical and vague, or not stated in practical terms—such as yields per acre in the case of crop lands, or carrying capacities in the case of range lands, or productivity values in dollars and cents. These types of data are very useful in helping farmers and ranchers to understand how they can most effectively use their lands, how much they can afford to pay or borrow, what the assessed valuations of their lands for real estate tax levies should be, and similar questions important in determining the profitableness of farm operations.

Similarly, the classification of transportation, mineral, recreational, urban, and forest lands must be such that the categories are sufficiently listinct and tangible to form the basis for economic appraisals of their relative importance. No one classification can serve all purposes. No system yet developed or in use meets all these requirements, although a few have served well in certain special problem situations.

TYPES OF LAND CLASSIFICATION

The use to be made of land classification determines the basis of classification. There are two major types of land classification—*physical* and *use*. Physical classification groups soils according to their natural qualities, while use classifications include, in addition to these physical factors, all economic forces that condition the use man makes of the land.

Natural land types may be differentiated by climate and surface configuration, by location, size, and shape of individual bodies, and by soil characteristics. A *soil type* includes land that has a specific set of soil characteristics, while a *land type* is broader and consists not only of soil but of relief, vegetation, and related features. In other words, a soil type is only one example of a natural land type.[20] Classification in which the soils are grouped into various types is particularly important in agricultural land utilization, because growth and production of plants depend largely upon the nature of the soil.

Soil is the combined product of climate, living organisms, physical relief, parent material, and age, different combinations of these elements producing different soils.[21] The growth of plants on the soil is closely related to the characteristics of the *soil profile* (a vertical section of soil, commonly from 4 to 8 feet deep). The soil profile is composed of various layers known as *soil horizons*, which vary in texture, structure, thickness, position, and chemical composition. Because of the close relationship between the growth of plants and the characteristics of the profile, it is possible to rate soils for agricultural productivity with the profile characteristics as a base.

It should be kept in mind that soil is only one of many factors that determine value for any given area of land surfaces, even agricultural or forest land; but it is a very important one, and its natural physical or inherent qualities constitute one of the more stable elements determining land productivity and, consequently, land value and use.

The second major type of classification, "use classification," definitely introduces land utilization—the ways in which man employs land for the satisfaction of his wants. Three principal types of land classification,

[20] Barnes, *op. cit.*, p. 13.
[21] *Soils and Men*, U.S. Department of Agriculture *Yearbook*, 1938, p. 988; and R. Earl Storie, *An Index for Rating the Agricultural Productivity of Land*, University of California, Agricultural Experiment Station Bulletin 556, 1933, p. 3.

in terms of use, may be listed: (1) present use, (2) use capabilities, an
(3) recommended use.[22] Thus, in addition to natural qualities of th
land, economic considerations such as market accessibility; size and typ
of operating unit; size, distribution, and composition of the population
location of roads, schools, power lines, stores, factories, and mines; lo
cation, size, and type of properties; type of ownership; economic outloo
and price prospects; transport facilities; costs of production; and relate
economic items must be taken into consideration in determining ho
land can be used most efficiently. In the use classification of land, grade
must be clear and meaningful enough to show those which are sub
marginal for certain types of utilization and those distinctly above th
margin.

PHYSICAL CLASSIFICATION OF LAND

An example of the technique used to classify lands on the basis o
natural or inherent characteristics is the composite index method devel
oped by Storie [23] for classifying agricultural lands. In this method, thre
factors are used: (A) character of the soil profile, (B) soil texture, an
(C) other modifying factors such as drainage, ease of irrigation, alkal
conditions, and other miscellaneous conditions. Each of these thre
factors is evaluated on the basis of 100 percent for the most favorable o
ideal conditions. The composite rating is determined by multiplying to
gether factors A, B, and C. The source of basic data from which such a
composite index is computed is a soil survey, of one of three principal
types—*detailed, reconnaissance,* or *detailed-reconnaissance.*[24]

Factor A evaluates all characteristics of the soil profile except the tex-

[22] The National Resources Planning Board has grouped land classification projects
into five categories, each representing a distinct type of land classification. These five
types are (1) land classification in terms of inherent characteristics, (2) land classification in terms of present use, (3) land classification in terms of use capabilities, (4)
land classification in terms of recommended use, and (5) land classification in terms
of program effectuation. (See National Resources Planning Board, *Land Classification
in the United States,* Report of the Land Committee, 1941, p. 3.)

[23] Storie, *op. cit.*

[24] In the *detailed* soil survey, the land is traversed at intervals of one-fourth mile,
and in addition to such physical features as lakes and streams, relief and stoniness,
the significant culture features, such as ditches, roads, houses, and public buildings
are accurately plotted. In the case of a *reconnaissance* soil survey, mapping units are
defined with less precision, from traverses made at intervals varying from a half mile
to 6 miles. The less intensive the use to which the land is likely to be devoted, the
more likely are traverses to be made at less frequent intervals. A *detailed-reconnaissance* survey has portions surveyed according to the requirements of a detailed soil
survey, and portions according to the less rigid requirements of a reconnaissance survey.
The county is the usual unit of survey, and frequently contains large areas of land
obviously unsuited to intensive agricultural use which are mapped in reconnaissance
and published with the portion mapped in detail, on the same soil map. (Adapted
from Charles E. Kellogg, *Soil Survey Manual,* U.S. Department of Agriculture, Miscellaneous Publication 274, 1937, pp. 12–13.)

ture of the surface soils. These characteristics are used to separate soils into groups known as *soil series*.[25] The soil series is in turn divided into soil types on the basis of *texture* (factor *B*).[26]

Within given soil types there may be differences in relief, erosion, and stoniness significant in the use of the soil when the land is cultivated. Such differences are recognized and mapped as *phases* of specific soil types.[27]

Factor *C* includes other factors influencing soil productivity such as drainage, alkalinity, acidity, infertility, susceptibility to erosion, or weediness.[28]

The ratings for factors *A*, *B*, and *C* are determined on the basis of 100 percent for the very best characteristics of each of these factors, and the final soil rating or index is then obtained by multiplying $A \times B \times C$.[29]

USE CLASSIFICATION OF LAND

This type of classification takes into consideration characteristics of land other than the strictly physical or inherent ones. Thus, land classification, in terms of *present use*, concerns (1) kind of use, (2) characteristics of use, and (3) status of occupancy.[30] In *use-capability* classifications, two types of knowledge are essential—knowledge of the natural qualities of the land, and knowledge of the results of using lands having these natural qualities. In Montana the principal dry-land crop is wheat,

[25] A soil series may be defined as "a group of soils having, in general, the same character of profile—that is, the same range in color, structure, and general sequence of soil and subsoil horizons, the same types of relief and drainage, and a common or similar origin or mode of formation." (C. F. Shaw, *A Glossary of Soil Terms*, American Soil Survey Association Bulletin 9, 1927, pp. 28–58.)

[26] The term "texture" refers to the size of the soil particles, and the term "structure" to their arrangement. (Storie, *op. cit.*, p. 24.)

[27] An example of terms used in designating characteristics of soils is the phrase "Morton silty clay loam, eroded phase." In this phrase, designating a given Montana soil, "Morton" is the series name, "silty clay loam" the type name, and "eroded" the phase (in this case, accelerated loss of surface soil).

[28] For an explanation of the meaning and measurement of some of these factors see Kellogg, *op. cit.*; and U.S. Department of Agriculture, *Soils and Men*, p. 986.

[29] The main reason for multiplying the ratings for the three factors together to determine a composite rating for the soil, rather than adding the score for each of the three factors together as in the case of the score-card method, is that each of the factors considered has a limiting influence upon the total productiveness or value of the soil.

[30] In "kind of use" classification, the land is classified area by area, field by field, to show how it is used. In "characteristics of use" classification, where the objective is agricultural land use, types and yields of crops are mapped; and in the case of mineral lands, types and current production of mines are mapped. "Status of occupancy" classification includes collection of data related to ownership, mortgage indebtedness, tax delinquency and tax-deed foreclosure status, assessed valuation, and related information. It is significant that 53 of the 75 land classification projects studied by the National Resources Planning Board included present use classification. (See National Resources Planning Board, *Land Classification in the United States*, p. 4.)

so that the use classification of such lands is in terms of productivities of this principal crop, and use classification of grazing lands is in terms of carrying capacity for livestock grazing. Quantitatively, bodies of this type of cropland are classified as follows: first grade, 22 bushels or more; second grade, 16 to 21 bushels; third grade, 12 to 15 bushels; and fourth grade, 8 to 11 bushels.[31]

Recommended use classification involves the physical characteristics of each parcel of land, together with its present use and each use to which it might be put. Thus, classification in terms of recommended use is based on the results of each of the preceding three types of land classification, or in any case involves the use of all three of them. Classification in terms of recommended use is based on the constant effort to develop new methods and practices of land utilization that will promote higher economic and social returns. The final purpose of all land classification is some form of action that will put the recommended land uses into effect.

DEVELOPMENT OF LAND CLASSIFICATION IN THE UNITED STATES

The policy of the United States government during the years just after the Revolutionary War was to get large areas of the public domain into private hands with the least possible delay. Although as early as 1796 a law was passed providing that "Every surveyor shall note in his field book the true situation of all mines, salt licks, salt springs, and mill seats which shall come to his knowledge; all watercourses over which the line he runs may pass, and also the quality of the land," [32] the classifications reported by surveyors were very meager. Nearly 100 years later, in 1879, an act was passed providing for classification of public domain land by geological survey directed from the Department of the Interior. However, this classification apparently applied largely to mineral lands and ignored the agricultural quality of the land.[33] In 1889 the Soil Survey Division of the U.S. Department of Agriculture was established to define and map important soil types in the country.[34] Investigations begun by the Soil

[31] For an explanation of the method of arriving at these grades for dry-farm land, as well as that used for arriving at similar grades for grazing land, see L. F. Gieseker, "The Soil Profile and Its Interpretation," Montana Agricultural Experiment Station, 1938, mimeographed; and R. R. Renne and H. H. Lord, *Assessment of Montana Farm Lands,* Montana Agricultural Experiment Station Bulletin 348, October, 1937.

[32] U.S. Department of the Interior, *Manual of Instructions for the Survey of the Public Lands of the United States,* Government Printing Office, 1930, p. 12.

[33] Hibbard divides the history of the classification of the public lands into four periods—from 1785 to 1862, from 1862 to 1879, from 1879 to 1906, and from 1906 to the present. For a concise statement of the types of classifications inaugurated for the public domain during each of these periods, see B. H. Hibbard, *History of the Public Land Policies,* Macmillan, 1924, p. 488; and for the development of land classification in the United States see also National Resources Planning Board, *op. cit.,* Chap. III, pp. 10–22.

[34] U.S. Department of Agriculture, *Soils and Men,* p. 981.

Survey Division have continued, in coöperation with the agricultural experiment stations of the states and territories, up to the present, and much of the country has been covered by reconnaissance or detailed soil surveys. The greater part of the surveyed area has been mapped on a scale of approximately 1 inch to a mile, each map in a majority of cases representing one county.[35] The "rectangular system" of land surveying is shown in Figure 2.

As the science of soil survey has progressed, the classifications have become more scientific and are based more and more upon the natural characteristics of the soil itself. During the late thirties, soil survey work was greatly speeded up in many areas because of the needs of various federal and state action agency programs dealing with agricultural adjustment, particularly the Soil Conservation Service and the agricultural land-use planning activities of the U.S. Department of Agriculture.

Many of the states have undertaken land classification work to meet current land-use problems. The increase in farm tax delinquency and mortage foreclosures in the thirties, and the dust storms and related conditions that developed in some areas increased the need for land classification data. In many states land-use capability classifications have been developed and are being widely used in determining the best land-use adjustment programs for land resources. Considerable variation exists among the states in the techniques used in classifying lands. However, each state should develop land-use capability classifications that fit the situations and land-use problems of its particular area.

WEAKNESSES OF LAND CLASSIFICATION IN THE UNITED STATES

One of the major weaknesses of land classification in the United States, as far as usefulness is concerned, is the technical nature of much of the material that has been mapped and presented covering natural soil characteristics. The terms used have been technical, and not enough effort has been made to translate soil classification data into more practical grades and use-capability classifications that are simple, understandable, and practical.

A second weakness is the tendency to include too much in the land classification process. Land classification has been used to include at one extreme the soil surveys and classification of vegetative cover, and at the other extreme detailed administrative decisions concerning recommended land-use practices by areas. Such a broad concept has caused confusion and misunderstanding. Research and effective planning in resources utiliza-

[35] See Charles Gooze, "Progress in Rural Land Classification in the United States," Land Policy Circular Supplement, Resettlement Administration, Washington, D.C., December, 1935, mimeographed, p. 3; C. E. Kellogg and J. K. Ableiter, *A Method of Rural Land Classification*, U.S. Department of Agriculture, Technical Bulletin 469, 1935.

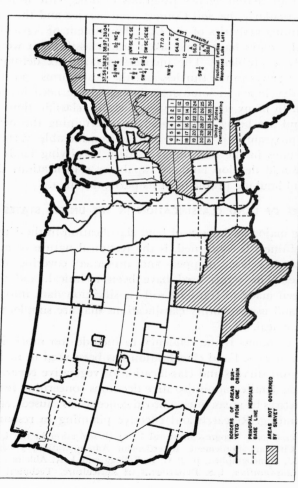

Figure 2. United States Land Survey, Principal Meridians, Base Lines, and Township Numbering. The "rectangular system" of land survey was incorporated in early land laws (1784–1785) after the public domain was acquired. Township lines are run every six miles north and south from the base lines and east and west from the principal meridians. Each township comprises 36 sections of land which are numbered as indicated. Canada reverses the United States order of designating sections. Sections (1 mile square, or 640 acres) are divided into quarter sections, which in turn are divided into 40-acre units. In older parts of the United States and Canada, land is usually described and registered by metes and bounds, natural objects such as trees and rocks designating points connecting surveyors' lines.

tion will be hastened by recognizing the inherent limitation of land classification to "the descriptive art of arranging and sorting land facts cartographically as a tool for the study and planning of resource utilization," [36] not the planning process itself or the final product.

Another weakness is that land classification has been spread over such a long period of time in some states that considerable rechecking is already needed on lands first classified, before all lands of the state have been classified for the first time. Moreover, the time required to make a proper soil survey, which takes into consideration the results of experience and carefully analyzes the physical characteristics and use-capabilities of the soils, handicaps certain efforts at land-use adjustment. The desire of some agencies to push their activities forward rapidly has caused them to make their own soil classifications, with the result that lack of uniformity in the basic soil classification data may occur.

Another important weakness of land classification in the United States is that many lands have been classified for specific purposes in unscientific ways. For example, some states have passed laws requiring land to be classified for tax assessment purposes, but these classifications have not been made by men trained in soil science. The result is that the classifications do not serve the purposes for which the classification was undertaken and are of little use in determining capabilities and best land use.

For example, a western county lists a class of land known as "engine land," including all land that can be farmed with a tractor. In other words, this classification depends largely upon topography and is entirely inadequate for scientific assessment based on productivity. Such classifications tend to undermine the average farmer's confidence in the practical usefulness of land classification work.

These are but a few of the weaknesses of land classification in the United States. Certain types of soil research are badly needed to furnish essential data for improved land classification. Chemical analyses showing composition and available nutrients are lacking for a great many of our important soil types. More precise information is needed about physical and chemical changes that use has produced in arable soils; and research establishing the relationship between nature of the soil and quality of food plants that may be grown on it is highly desirable.[37]

With the emphasis upon improved land use and soil conservation, many of these weaknesses are being overcome and more scientific, improved methods are being developed. A definite need exists for greater coördination of effort among the many agencies interested in land-use

[36] W. F. Musbach and V. Webster Johnson, review of the National Resources Planning Board report, "Land Classification in the United States," in the *Journal of Land and Public Utility Economics*, Vol. XVII, No. 4, November, 1941, pp. 489–493.

[37] For a more complete discussion of soil survey needs, see U.S. Department of Agriculture, *Soils and Men*, pp. 213–215.

adjustment, particularly on agricultural land. The weaknesses indicated above are applicable, in most instances, to classification undertaken for all types of land; but because of the extensive area involved in agricultural land use, weaknesses in classifications of this type of land tend to be especially noticeable.

THE FUTURE OF LAND CLASSIFICATION

Methods of classification have been devised for each of the nation's principal land resources. Some of these are more advanced in technique and coverage than others, but all have produced beneficial results and give promise of accomplishing important results in the future. The trend toward multiple and integrated use of land resources—forest, mineral, water, recreational, and agricultural resources particularly—is likely to increase the general interest in land classification.[38]

The increasing amount of physical and economic data becoming available through current programs indicates that continued improvement in agricultural land classification and the practical applications will become more and more widespread. Similar improvement and increased interest are found in other types of land use, particularly in forest, mineral, and recreational lands. Classification has long been recognized as fundamental to the most effective utilization of urban areas, where the zoning procedure was first used.

REFERENCES FOR FURTHER READING

Bowman, Isaiah, *The Pioneer Fringe*, American Geographical Society, New York, Special Publication 13, 1931.

Ely, R. T., and Morehouse, E. W., *Elements of Land Economics*, The Macmillan Company, New York, 1924, Chap. III.

First National Conference on Land Classification, *Proceedings*, "The Classification of Land," University of Missouri Agricultural Experiment Station Bulletin 421, December, 1940.

Fledderus, Mary L., and Van Kleeck, Mary, *Technology and Livelihood*, Russell Sage Foundation, New York, 1944, Chap. I.

Hibbard, B. H., *A History of the Public Land Policies*, The Macmillan Company, New York, 1924, Chap. XXIV.

[38] The National Resources Planning Board feels that the future will probably win a clearer understanding of the importance of securing adequate coverage in land classification projects within given time intervals, and that piecemeal classification, while it may help to improve methods and techniques, may fail to furnish the materials and understanding required for the development of land-use policies and programs. When this idea of adequate area coverage within a given period of time becomes more general, legislative bodies might allocate funds for land classification work on a long-time basis and thereby increase the utility of classification out of all proportion to the cost. (National Resources Planning Board, *Land Classification in the United States*, p. 21.)

ohnson, V. Webster, and Barlowe, Raleigh, *Land Problems and Policies,* McGraw-Hill Book Company, Inc., New York, 1954, pp. 113–116; 175–179.

Kellogg, C. E., *Soil Survey Manual,* U.S. Department of Agriculture, Washington, D.C., Miscellaneous Publication 274, September, 1937.

Murray, W. G., *Farm Appraisal,* Iowa State College Press, Ames, Iowa, 1940, Part I.

National Resources Planning Board, *Land Classification in the United States,* Report of the Land Committee, Government Printing Office, Washington, D.C., 1941.

Stallings, J. H., *Soil Conservation,* Prentice-Hall, Inc., Englewood Cliffs, N.J., 1957, Chaps. VII and XX.

Timmons, John F., and Murray, William F. (eds.), *Land Problems and Policies,* Iowa State College Press, Ames, Iowa, 1950, pp. 72–81.

U.S. Department of Agriculture, *Technology on the Farm,* Special Report by Interbureau Committee and Bureau of Agricultural Economics, Government Printing Office, Washington, D.C., August, 1940, Chaps. I–IX.

Zimmermann, Erich, *World Resources and Industries,* rev. ed., Harper & Brothers, New York, 1951, Chap. VII.

LAND SUPPLIES FOR SPECIFIC USES

THE SUPPLY OF AGRICULTURAL LAND

Physical Factors Determining Suitability of Land for Agriculture: SOIL CHARACTERISTICS, TOPOGRAPHY, MOISTURE, TEMPERATURE, LOCATION OR SITUATION—*Amount of Land Suitable for Agriculture*

THE SUPPLY OF FOREST LAND

Physical Factors Determining Suitability of Land for Forestry—Amount of Land Suitable for Forestry

THE SUPPLY OF RECREATIONAL LAND

Natural Factors Determining Suitability of Land for Recreation: LAND RELIEF, CLIMATE, WATER RESOURCES, FLORA AND FAUNA—*Amount of Land Suitable for Recreation*

THE SUPPLY OF LAND FOR MINING

Distribution of Major Minerals

THE SUPPLY OF WATER

Availability of Water—A Multiple-Use Resource

SUPPLY OF LAND FOR TRANSPORTATION

Factors Determining Use of Land for Transportation

THE SUPPLY OF URBAN LAND

Factors Determining Suitability of Land for Urban Use —Amount of Land Suitable for Urban Use

THE TOTAL area of the earth is about 197 million square miles, or approximately 126 billion acres, of which the land surface (excluding oceans and similar bodies of water, but including inland streams) is between 57 and 58 million square miles, or approximately 37 billion acres. The water area of the earth (oceans, seas, gulfs, etc.) comprises some 140 million square miles, or about 89 billion acres. Thus, land surface makes up about 30 percent of the earth, and areas covered by water about 70 percent.

Almost a third of the earth's land area is in Asia, nearly a fourth in Africa (55 percent of the total is in these two continents), a little over a sixth in North America, a seventh in South America, and less than a twelfth in Europe and Oceania.

THE SUPPLY OF AGRICULTURAL LAND

Agriculture must compete successfully for the use of land with other major uses. Agricultural land is continually being drawn upon for expanding urban, recreational, industrial, mining, and transportation uses. Less than three-fifths (about 58 percent) of the total arable land of the earth is used either for crops or pasture. Consequently, the economic supply of land for agriculture, viewed from the standpoint of area or acreage, could be almost doubled. Whether this acreage will ever be utilized for agricultural production depends upon the relative profitableness of agriculture compared with other possible uses of the land.

Only about 40 percent of the total land area of the earth outside of the arctic regions, which comprise nearly six million square miles, may be considered arable or cultivable, or about 21 million square miles. Roughly, about a fourth of the earth's land area is in pasture and crops, a third in desert, and two-fifths in forest. Only about 8 percent of the total area is now cultivated. Some 60 percent of the earth's population is directly engaged in cultivating the soil. Consequently, agriculture may be considered the most important of all land uses. However, the importance of agriculture varies greatly among the nations.

PHYSICAL FACTORS DETERMINING SUITABILITY OF LAND FOR AGRICULTURE

Soil characteristics, topography, moisture, temperature, and location determine the areas that are suitable for agriculture and the practices that will be most effective in utilizing them. Within the limits established by these physical factors, human choices determined by economic, cultural, and related forces determine the type and intensity of use.

Soil Characteristics. Although the general soil pattern is determined by nature, the physical make-up of the soil can be changed somewhat by man's land utilization practices.

The soil may be considered a perpetual "storehouse of life," or factory,

which with proper care can be made to produce a large amount of food
and fibers for an indefinite time. With proper care, the soil can be a self
renewable or revolving fund, with a permanent flow of products from i
or from its use. Agriculture, properly operated, is not an extractive
industry, for soil fertility can be improved as well as preserved, generation
after generation.

Topography.   Successful agriculture requires a certain amount of level
ness as well as suitable soil. In some places, man has increased the eco
nomic supply of land for crop production by himself leveling the land
This is frequently done on irrigation projects. Terracing, a form o
leveling, has been practiced for many centuries in parts of Europe and
Asia to bring steep slopes under cultivation and thus make them part o
the economic supply. In general, however, unless man develops certain
adaptation techniques, land that has over 15 feet of fall in a hundred
should not be used for crops.[1]

Not only degree of slope, but direction of slope—that is, whether it i
in a southerly or northerly direction—is frequently important in using
land for certain crops because of associated sunlight and temperature
conditions. For example, a northerly slope where the land is less com
pletely exposed to the direct rays of the sun for a major portion of the
day is considered preferable to a slope in a southerly direction for fruit
trees particularly susceptible to freeze damage. On very sunny slopes
the sap may flow very early in the spring or relatively late in the fall
and increase the possibilities of freeze damage from late spring or early
fall low temperatures.

Man can improve or reduce soil fertility more effectively and on a
larger scale than he can change topography. Only for certain uses re
quiring relatively small land areas can man change topography sufficiently
to adjust the surface formation nearer to his needs. In Figure 3, showing
topographic features of the land area of the United States, the mountainous areas stand out clearly. Note the rough, high character of the West
and the relatively level surface of the Mississippi Valley except for the
Ozark area in the lower central portion.

Moisture.   Plants require water as well as plant nutrients. To man,
therefore, the amount of moisture is a very important feature of the
natural environment. Moisture is made available through the natural
process known as the *hydrologic cycle*. In this cycle, moisture from the
parent seas evaporates and is absorbed into the air in the form of water
vapor. This water vapor is transported over the land by the winds, condensed and precipitated onto the land, and is subsequently returned to
the air through evaporation, or to the seas through streams and rivers
(see Figure 4) .

[1] O. E. Baker, "Land Utilization in the United States: Geographical Aspects of the
Problem," *American Geographical Review*, Vol. XIII, No. 1, January, 1923, p. 17.

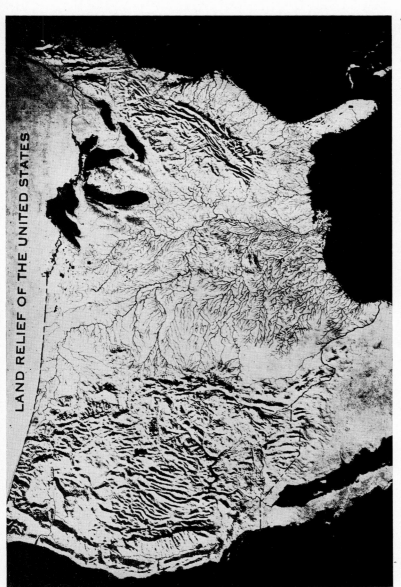

Figure 3. Land Relief, or Topographic Features of the United States. (Source: U.S. Department of Agriculture, Bureau of Agricultural Economics.)

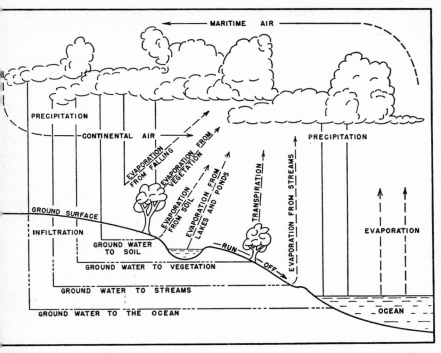

Figure 4. The Hydrologic Cycle. (Adapted from U.S. Department of Agriculture Yearbook, *Climate and Man*, Government Printing Office, Washington, 1941.)

Some areas of the earth have abundant water supplies for all purposes, in which case water is considered a free good. In other areas, water is relatively scarce and various techniques of conserving and utilizing it have been developed. Total precipitation helps to determine type and amount of plant growth; and distribution throughout the year, rate of evaporation, nature of soil and underlying parent material, and form in which the precipitation occurs greatly influence the efficiency of the moisture. For example, rainfall during the growing season is much more effective in determining plant growth in a given season than a similar amount of rainfall in the winter months. A slow steady rain is more effective for plant growth than a short downpour in which runoff is high. If the soil is heavy and the surface crusted and hard, runoff is much greater than where the soil is porous and light with a soft, cultivated surface. Cool cloudy weather following a rain results in much less loss through evaporation than hot, sunny weather and strong winds.

Although the effectiveness of precipitation cannot be measured simply in terms of the total number of inches annually, classification of areas in terms of inches of average annual precipitation does help to indicate their suitability for agriculture. Areas with less than 10 inches of average annual rainfall are ordinarily classed as *arid*, those with 10 to 20 inches as *semiarid*, those with 20 to 30 inches as *subhumid*, and those with more than 30 inches as *humid*.

Areas with less than 10 inches of moisture yearly cannot be used for successful crop production, because of limited grass growth that will support only light grazing. In areas receiving from 10 to 20 inches of rainfall, certain adaptations must be made by man through alternate summer fallow and cropping practices, or development of drought-resistant varieties and special tillage practices to secure successful crops. If the evaporation rate is high, operators must modify their agriculture in areas that have as much as 20 or 30 inches of annual precipitation to insure successful crop production. Such areas will raise grass, and range livestock enterprises will usually be developed on them. More than half the earth's surface is arid, semiarid, or subject to a scarcity of moisture to which its agriculture must be adjusted.

Irrigation is widely practiced in the arid and semiarid regions, in areas of intensive truck and fruit farming, in humid regions where rainfall is irregular, and even, for certain crops, in areas where rainfall is fairly abundant—for example, in the rice fields of India and China. Whenever irrigation water is made available to new land, or whenever the yield is enlarged by applying water to land already used, the economic supply of agricultural land is increased. Possibilities of extending the economic supply of agricultural land through irrigation, however, are limited by the availability of water supplies and by the type of land available. There must be fertile, level land with good drainage and a water supply not only readily accessible but reliable and adequate, if the additional costs of irrigating are to be met and the land is to be an effective part of the economic supply.

Figure 5 shows the average annual precipitation of the United States. Note the arid and semiarid areas in the West, the high rainfall belt along the Pacific Coast, and the generally humid conditions of the eastern half of the nation.

Temperature. Temperature of soil and air largely limits the plants man may grow. The length of time during which a certain average or range of temperature is available is also important if plants are to mature. Temperature conditions of an area are usually measured in terms of average frost-free period and number of heat units during this or a shorter period.[2]

Roughly, mean temperatures of from 50° to 70° are considered tem-

[2] The number of heat units during a day is the average temperature of the day minus a certain constant that is assumed to be the minimum temperature at which general plant growth takes place. This has been tentatively set by some workers at 43° F. (Neil W. Johnson and M. H. Saunderson, *Types of Farming in Montana*, Montana Agricultural Experiment Station Bulletin 328, October, 1936, p. 19.)

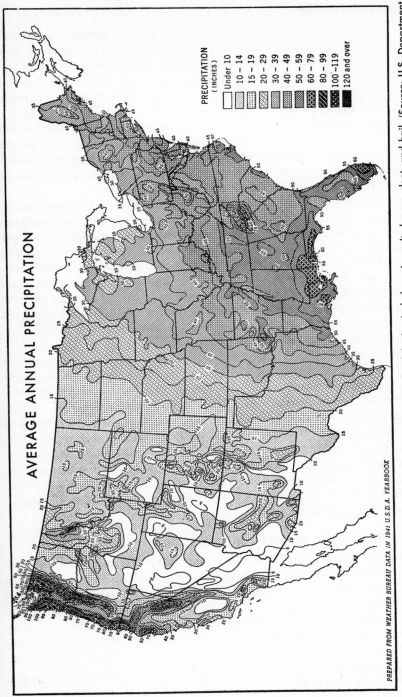

AVERAGE ANNUAL PRECIPITATION

PREPARED FROM WEATHER BUREAU DATA IN 1941 U.S.D.A. YEARBOOK

PRECIPITATION
(INCHES)

Under 10
10 – 14
15 – 19
20 – 29
30 – 39
40 – 49
50 – 59
60 – 79
80 – 99
100 – 119
120 and over

Figure 5. Average Annual Precipitation in the United States. Precipitation includes rain, melted snow, sleet, and hail. (Source: U.S. Department of Agriculture, Bureau of Agricultural Economics.)

perate, and those above 70° or 80°, tropical. A mean temperature of 50°
or below for four or more months strictly limits the variety of crops that
can be grown successfully. Any region having a mean temperature of 50°
or lower for the warmest month is beyond the limit of successful cereal
production, and marks the poleward limit of permanent human occupation, except for a few Eskimos and Lapps.[3]

Figure 6 shows the average length of frost-free season for the United
States. Note the short frost-free season in the high altitude areas of the
West and the most northern sections. Although areas along both coasts
and in the south have comparatively long growing seasons, no portion of
the United States is entirely free from frost.

Although temperature conditions cannot be changed, crops can be
adapted to them, to a limited extent. The breeding of plant varieties
adapted to certain temperature conditions increases the economic supply
of land for some crops. Where the demand is sufficiently great for plants
that will not grow under existing temperature conditions, greenhouses
may be used to supply heat requirements and protect the plant from
outside temperatures. This method is very expensive, however, and the
increase in supply of agricultural land by this method is usually restricted
to the production of flowers, tomatoes, plants for early transplanting,
certain vegetables, and special fruits.

Location or Situation.   Since land is fixed and immobile, no particular
parcel of land is, in a strict physical sense, any more mobile or adaptable
for human use than any other. However the choices of society differentiate locations on the basis of usefulness in want-satisfaction, the location
of agricultural land in relation to concentrations of people is usually of
less importance than the four physical characteristics of soil, topography,
moisture, and temperature, because man, through modern technology,
has greatly reduced the economic significance of physical space and distance. In some special cases, however, because of a combination of circumstances, location may be of major significance in determining the use of
the land for agriculture.

AMOUNT OF LAND SUITABLE FOR AGRICULTURE

Soils, topography, moisture, and temperature determine the absolute
limits of cultivability or physical productivity, and consequently the potential economic supply of land for agriculture. Thus, the total physical
area of the earth suitable for crop production must meet certain requirements under each of these conditions. Areas that are too dry, too cold,
or too mountainous or rough for crops can be quite readily determined,
because there are definite physical limits for each of these three factors,

[3] L. E. Klimm, O. P. Starkey, and N. F. Hall, *Introductory Economic Geography*,
Harcourt, Brace, 1937, p. 72.

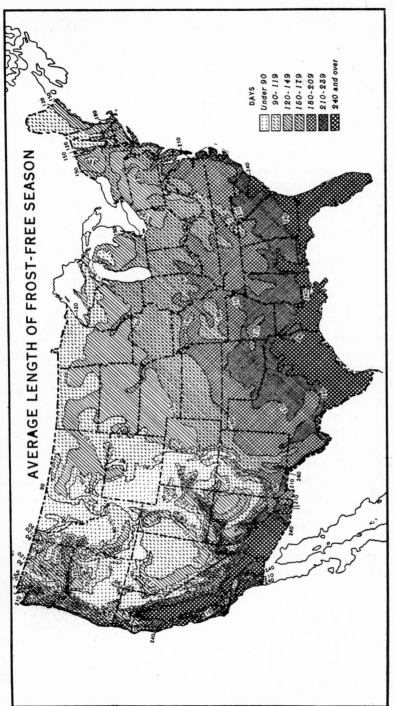

Figure 6. Average Length of Frost-Free Season in the United States. (Source: U.S. Department of Agriculture, Bureau of Agricultural Economics.)

beyond which successful crop production cannot occur. However, in the case of soil conditions, no such definite physical limits can be established. Some soils are too stony, too lacking in plant nutrients, too acid, or too alkaline to permit successful production of certain crops; but almost any soil located in an area that is not too cold, too dry, or too mountainous or rough for successful crop production can grow some crop plants. Whether or not such soils will be utilized depends, of course, upon the profit possibilities.

Of the land area on the earth, about 30 percent is too dry for crops; an additional eighth is too cold; and another twelfth is too rough or mountainous; thus, slightly over half (approximately 50.5 percent) of the total land area of the earth is unsuitable for crops.[4]

Figure 7 shows the distribution of these dry, cold, and mountainous areas unsuitable for crop production among the continents of the world. Note that some areas are too dry, others too cold, others too rough, others too dry and too cold, and still others too dry, too cold, and too rough. Note the relatively large areas too dry for crops without irrigation in the continents of Africa, Asia, and Australia; and note also the comparatively large areas in northern Asia and northern North America that are too cold. The areas in the figure not indicated as too dry, too cold, or too mountainous for crops are not all necessarily arable. Many of these areas are too stony or have soil conditions or geographical formations that make cultivation impossible or so difficult as to be physically impracticable. Many areas indicated in Figure 7 as unsuitable for crops are suitable for pasture and can be used for livestock grazing.

In the United States approximately half (973,000,000 acres) of the land area of 1,905,000,000 acres is physically suited (without irrigation and drainage) for crop production. Of the rest, 468,000,000 acres are arid grazing lands unsuited for any other purpose. Land in forests fit only for forestry with incidental grazing comprises an area of 262,000,000 acres, while some 66,000,000 acres not at present in forest are fit for pasture or forests, but not for crops. Some 67,000,000 acres are wasteland (chiefly desert and rock) unfitted for crops, grazing, or forests. This acreage, with the remainder of about 67,000,000 acres, is used in part for cities, towns, roads, airports, railroads, homesteads, recreation, mining (which ordinarily uses more subsurface than surface areas), and other purposes.

THE SUPPLY OF FOREST LAND

Trees are a crop, and the economic supply of land for forestry is determined by the same physical factors as those that determine the

[4] O. E. Baker, "Land Utilization in the United States," and "The Potential Supply of Wheat," *Economic Geography*, Vol. I, No. 1, March, 1925. Baker lists 52,000,000 square miles as the land surface of the earth, compared with 55,885,000 given in the Rand McNally *Commercial Atlas*, 1931.

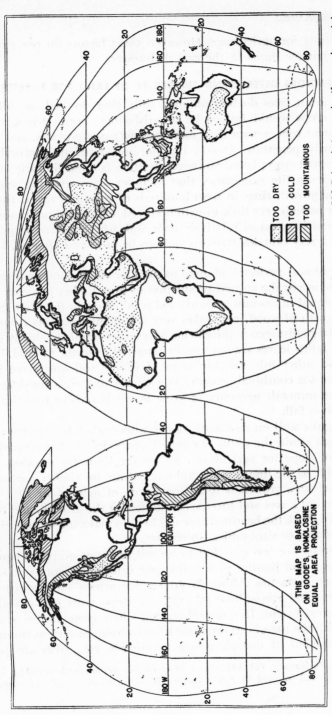

Figure 7. Areas Unsuitable for Tillage, by Continents. Areas considered too cold if no month is as warm as 50° Fahrenheit; too dry if annual precipitation is less than 10 inches. Mountainous areas are adapted from Wellington D. Jones and Derwent S. Whittlesey, *An Introduction to Economic Geography*, University of Chicago Press, 1925. The areas shown on the map are conservative estimates of the limit of cultivation. Present cultivation has by no means reached these limits. (Map prepared by N. Helburn.)

economic supply for agriculture. However, these factors do not operate within such narrow limits in the case of forestry.

PHYSICAL FACTORS DETERMINING SUITABILITY OF LAND FOR FORESTRY

Although forest trees do best on good soils, they do well on soils on which most crops would fail or be unsatisfactory. Forest trees possess more permanent root systems than most crop or pasture plants, and their roots ordinarily penetrate deeper, tapping soil nutrients beyond the reach of the usual crop plants. Moreover, fertility is a less limiting factor, since trees have a life expectancy that includes many growing seasons. Studies of the growth rings in trees hundreds of years old reveal that in some years or periods very little growth occurred, because of poor growing conditions; and in areas of relatively poor soil, where annual growth is rather small, a very valuable tree can perhaps be produced after 50, 75, or 100 years.

Forests are almost perfectly adapted to stony or rough land or to sandy soils in humid areas; the annual production of pine timber in sandy soils is ordinarily equal in amount to hardwood production in the most fertile land. The growth of wood itself takes very few plant nutrients from the soil, and the large nitrogen requirements of trees are obtained chiefly from the air. Since fallen leaves are not usually removed from the ground, lime, magnesia, and other minerals are restored to the soil and serve as a revolving fund for continual growth. As a matter of fact, a considerable portion of the minerals necessary to grow leaves is returned to the soil before the leaves fall.

Trees can grow well on mountain slopes where other forms of vegetation can seldom attain the status of crops. Twenty degrees has been given as the limit of slope for agriculture, 30° as the limit for meadow and pasture, and 40° as the limit for general tree culture for timber purposes.[5] However, much tree growth is found on slopes of more than 40°. The mulch of decaying leaves and litter accumulated on the ground, and leafy branches above check the beating rains and help to make forests peculiarly adaptable to slopes or sites subject to erosion.

Whereas forests are less exacting as to soil and topographic requirements than crop and pasture plants, they are ordinarily more restricted in moisture requirements. Although grasses are grown satisfactorily in the arid regions and are utilized by range livestock, trees will not grow there to any great extent. In semiarid regions where crops can be grown successfully with the use of certain adaptation techniques such as summer-fallow, development of drought-resistant varieties, etc., trees are prac-

---

[5] H. Hausrath, *Forstwesen*, Vol. VII, Part 7, of *Grundriss der Socialokonomik*, J. C. B. Mohr, Tubinger, 1922 (quoted in Zimmermann, *World Resources and Industries*, p. 404).

tically nonexistent. In the far north, however, trees grow with an average annual rainfall of about 18 inches. The conifer trees of this region, with their small, narrow, hard leaves, do not lose much moisture and therefore make efficient use of the limited supply available. Some commercially valuable trees also grow well in swampy land, which is not useful for agriculture without drainage.

Forests are less restricted by low temperatures than many crop and pasture plants. Some forest trees—particularly spruce and fir—are grown successfully at altitudes of 11 or 12 thousand feet, where the mean summer temperature is about 48° F., as for instance in Colorado. An average annual temperature of 68° marks roughly the poleward limits of the palm tree and therefore of tropical plants. Regions with mean temperatures of 50° or below for four months or more are beyond the limits of the oak tree and therefore very largely beyond the limits of the temperate hardwood forest. Some trees will grow where there is frost in every month of the year, and some require comparatively little sunlight.

The distribution of the great commercial forest areas of the world bears no relationship to densities of population (see Figure 8). More than three-fifths of the softwood timber upon which the world depends for construction material is in North America and Europe, which contain only a third of the world's people. China and India, with nearly a billion people, embrace less than 3 percent of the world's forests, while sparsely populated South America contains nearly 30 percent.[6] This disparity in the distribution of forests and populations causes many nations to have less forest area per capita than the minimum needed to provide for cooking and warmth, even at most primitive levels. This minimum is about an acre, but India and the Netherlands have less than this, China less than half an acre, and Syria and Palestine about two-tenths of an acre per person, while at the other extreme Canada has 50 acres per capita.[7]

AMOUNT OF LAND SUITABLE FOR FORESTRY

Forests are a resource that man has been able to destroy very readily. In many instances, forests have been a hindrance or obstacle to be overcome in the development of lands for agricultural use. Consequently, present forest resources of the earth do not often occupy the original forested area, much of which has been cut over. For example, in the United States, forests originally covered more than 822 million acres (see Figure 9), of which some five-sixths has been cut over, only a little more than 138

[6] *Third Report to the Governments of the United Nations by the Interim Commission on Food and Agriculture,* transmitting report of the Technical Committee on Forestry and Primary Forest Products, Charles Lathrop Pack Forestry Foundation, Washington, D.C., 1945, p. 16. See also R. Zon and W. N. Sparhawk, *America and the World's Woodpile,* U.S. Department of Agriculture Circular 21, January, 1928, p. 5.

[7] See *Third Report to the Governments of the United Nations,* p. 16.

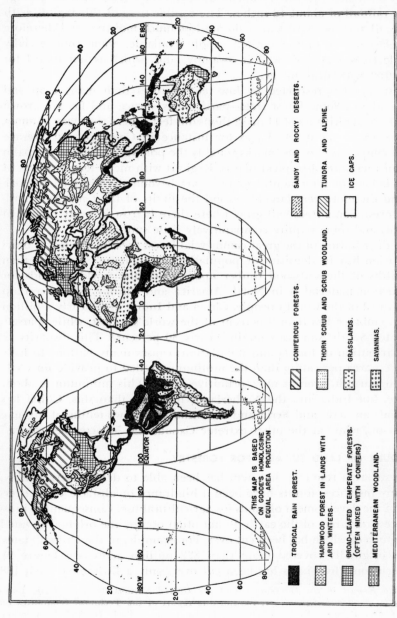

Figure 8. Natural Vegetation of the World. (Adapted from L. E. Klimm, O. P. Starkey, and N. F. Hall, *Introductory Economic Geography*, Harcourt, Brace, 1937.)

NATIVE VEGETATION

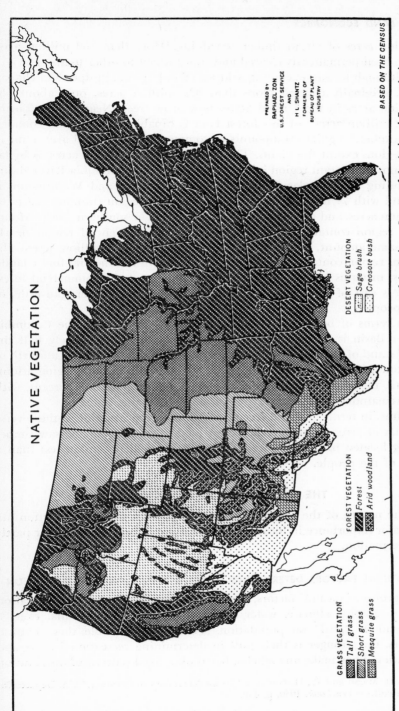

Figure 9. Natural Vegetation of the United States. (Source: U.S. Department of Agriculture, Bureau of Agricultural Economics.)

million acres of virgin timber remaining. More than 350 million acre
have been permanently cleared and transformed to other uses.

Although forests, excluding arid woodland (pinon-juniper and chapar
ral), originally covered more than 822 million acres, only about 63(
million acres in the United States now grow trees. Nearly three-fourth
(462 million acres) of this forest land is capable of producing commer
cial timber.[8] Significant amounts of commercial forest land are found ir
all regions except the Plains. The South, with 203 million acres, is by fa
the most important region in terms of acreage; the Columbia River Basin
including the Douglas fir belt of western Oregon and Washington, i
second with 74 million acres; the northeastern region contains nearly 6(
million acres, and the lake region, 52 million. The southern Rocky Moun
tain region contains about 31 million acres, the central region nearl
the same amount, and the California area about 14 million acres. Th
Plains region contains only 14 thousand acres of commercial forest lands
Thus, in terms of acreage, nearly three-fourths of the commercial fores
land is east of the Plains, in the area that contains over four-fifths o
the people.

In terms of board feet or the amount of saw timber, the Columbi
River Basin is by far the most important with approximately half th
total stand of saw timber of the country. The South has nearly a fourth o
the total, California an eighth, the South Rocky Mountain region a four
teenth, the northeastern about 5 percent, the lake states 3 percent, with
the remainder in the central region and the Plains states.

Thus, in terms of board feet of saw timber, the situation is the reverse
of that of acres of commercial forest land, three-fifths of the saw timber
being located in the area west of the Plains, which contain less than a
fifth of the people.

THE SUPPLY OF RECREATIONAL LAND

The nature of the population and the pattern of its distribution are
of major importance in locating areas that are to be used wholly or partly
for recreation.

NATURAL FACTORS DETERMINING SUITABILITY OF LAND FOR RECREATION

A group of natural factors, principal of which are variety of elevation
or topography, climate, water resources, and flora and fauna, exert a
tremendous "pull" on population. The more favorable these natural
factors, the stronger is their pull in determining recreational areas and
facilities. They make any scheme based on a fixed pattern of distribution

---

[8] R. D. Marsh and W. H. Gibbons, "Forest Resource Conservation," U.S. Department
of Agriculture *Yearbook,* 1940, p. 459.

of recreational areas invalid in serving the needs of a culturally progressive people.

Land Relief. Mountainous or broken terrain with unusual geological formations has distinct advantages in the way of special scenic attractions and peculiar recreational opportunities, like skiing and mountain climbing. The whole of a plain is ordinarily in one life zone, whereas mountain acreages frequently include as many as five life zones giving a variety of flora and fauna.[9] Thus, the flat prairies of Iowa, although excellent for agriculture, do not have great recreational value, while the rugged Rocky Mountain slopes have practically no value for agriculture but have a great deal for scenic and recreational uses. Land relief has been a determining factor in the selection of a majority of the national parks and monuments.

Climate. Favorable precipitation, sunshine, humidity, and temperature, so important for physical comfort, are important factors in determining areas suitable for recreation.

Sections of the country having a high percentage of sunshine in the winter months are especially attractive for recreational use. Any area having 60 percent or more sunshine can be considered as possessing an important natural factor contributing to its desirability for winter recreational use.[10] The Southwest ranks high in this regard. Portions of Arizona and southern California have between 80 and 90 percent of their total possible sunshine for this period. This, combined with warm winter temperatures, makes these areas popular winter recreation spots. Florida is also a popular winter resort for much the same reasons. It is unfortunate that winter sunshine areas are remote from the greatest population centers because most Americans cannot take advantage of them at a time of year when sunshine can contribute so much to good health.

Low humidity (dry atmosphere) areas are much more comfortable than high humidity areas in both summer and winter, summer temperatures being much less depressing and low winter temperatures less chilling and penetrating. The major low humidity areas of the United States are the Southwest and Great Plains regions. They are not available to the great majority of Americans because of their remoteness from heavily populated centers.

Low temperatures in summer and high temperatures in winter are favorable factors for recreational use. Mountain areas are popular in summer and southern areas in winter chiefly because of the low summer temperatures of the former and the relatively high winter temperatures of the latter.

[9] See National Resources Planning Board, "Recreational Use of Land in the United States," *Report on Land Planning*, Government Printing Office, 1938, Part XI, p. 42.
[10] *Ibid.*, p. 45.

Average July and January temperatures of the United States are shown in Figure 10. It is apparent that the areas of densest population, with only limited recreational resources available, have unfavorable summer and winter temperatures. Consequently, those who seek cool summers and warm winters must travel long distances. For summer recreation areas, those having July temperatures averaging between 50° and 60° are greatly desired. These areas occur throughout the Rocky Mountains, the Cascades, and the Sierra Nevadas, located in the far western part of the nation. For winter recreation areas, those having average January temperatures between 50° and 60° are very desirable. All the Gulf states, Southern California, and Arizona contain such areas and are popular winter recreation spots. The southern half of the Florida peninsula has an average January temperature of 60° to 70° and, being convenient to the heavily populated eastern states, it is a great winter recreational ground.

Water Resources. Lakes, bays, oceans, waterfalls, and streams are significant factors in the recreational land-use pattern. These water resources not only contribute beauty to the out-of-doors, but are themselves very useful for active recreation. The recreational value of sea-coasts and beaches is of the highest order. Twenty-one of the 48 states have ocean frontage, and the total length of the seacoast of the continental United States is almost 5000 miles. The total length of tidal shore line, including bodies of tidal waters more than a mile wide that lie close to the main waters, is nearly 12,000 miles. Beaches are one fortunate case of a recreational resource located near centers of greatest human demand. Forty-five percent of the total U.S. population lives within 55 miles of the seacoasts and the Great Lakes.[11]

Flora and Fauna. No area is recreationally complete without the living interest that plant and animal life provide. The importance of plant life is readily recognized in city parks, where a great deal of effort and funds are spent to establish and maintain trees and flowers. Forests and wooded areas greatly enhance recreational values of certain areas. They provide cool, shady retreats in summer, and habitats for birds and game animals. Where tree growth is luxuriant, relatively small areas have a high recreational use value. Fortunately the Atlantic coast and Great Lakes areas are in this category and facilitate the task of providing recreation for the large populations of those regions.

The variety, amount, and distribution of animal life are important factors determining the recreational value of land. The smaller forms of native wildlife, particularly birds, add appreciably to the value of the smallest recreational area such as a city park or residence yard. The larger wildlife species, including big game, require the large areas of their native

[11] *Ibid.*, p. 44.

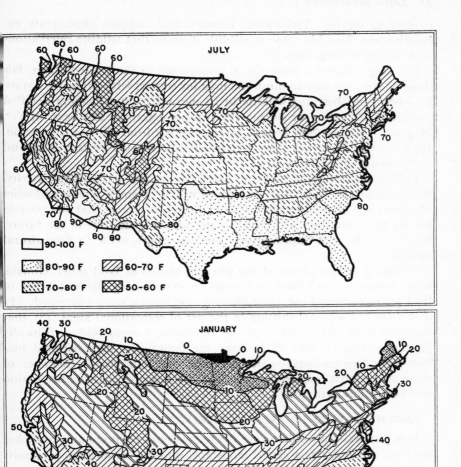

Figure 10. Average July and January Temperatures in the United States. (Source: "Recreational Use of Land in the United States," Report No. 9, National Resources Board, Government Printing Office, 1938.)

habitat to survive. Agriculture, hunters, and trappers persistently encroach upon these big game or wildlife areas so that wildlife reservations with proper management are necessary.

Hunting is of great recreational importance in the United States. For those who do not care to hunt, the urge for contact with primitive nature is satisfied by observing wildlife in its natural habitat, making detailed studies of life habits, or getting close-up photographs. The bears of Yellowstone National Park help to attract tourists from all over the nation. Big game in the United States is most abundant in the western areas and in the South and Lake States.

Fishing is probably the leading American outdoor recreational activity. Although fishing occurs over the entire nation in small and large bodies of water, the best fishing is found in the most remote and inaccessible places. This condition will probably prevail for some time in the future, in spite of the vast improvements that have been made in fish-cultural methods.

Summing up the effects of the physical factors of land relief, climate, water resources, and flora and fauna in determining the suitability of land for recreational use, the following conclusions seem warranted: (1) that there is a seasonal shifting in the use of recreational areas, (2) that the centers of population and the recreational areas seldom coincide, (3) that points (1) and (2) indicate the desirability of a national husbanding of recreational resources, since the "migratory" character of these recreational resources makes them the property of the entire nation and not of local groups.[12]

AMOUNT OF LAND SUITABLE FOR RECREATION

It is physically possible to use for recreational purposes any land that has such attributes as a varied landscape, unusual formations, proximity to bodies of water, particularly enjoyable climate, and interesting flora and fauna. The extent to which such areas will be used for recreation will depend in large part upon their accessibility for large numbers of people.

The physical factors determining suitability of land for recreation are less sharply restrictive than those determining suitability of land for agriculture and forestry. A wide range in climate might be considered "suitable" for recreational purposes, and what might be considered a "varied" landscape or an "unusual" formation would change a great deal with the cultural advancement of the population, amount of leisure time available, income available for recreation, and related economic and social factors. In other words, the limiting factors are more likely to be economic and social than physical. Consequently, it might be said that the

[12] *Ibid.,* p. 48.

total supply of land suitable for recreation could, under certain economic and social conditions, exceed the amount suitable for either forestry or agriculture. In the last analysis, with the exception of a few barren desert spots, almost the whole surface of the earth and some subsurface areas could be considered as conceivably suitable for recreation of one form or another.

In some parts of the United States, the recreation business provides almost the entire income of the community, and in others it provides a major portion. Ordinarily, however, the privately owned land devoted to recreational uses will not make up a large proportion of the total land area of a region.

Some of the more important competitors affecting the supply of attractive recreational areas include water pollution, lumbering, grazing, drainage, and private occupancy of strategic points. Large quantities of oil, refuse from industrial mills, sulphurous water from mines, sewage, and other wastes discharged into rivers, lakes and harbors greatly reduce the attractiveness of these water resources for recreational use, in addition to harming aquatic life. Lumbering, although a necessary land use, does not improve the recreational value of an area. Where overgrazing of an area occurs, erosion is accelerated, reducing the usefulness of the land for wildlife or for any other kind of recreational use. Drainage of swamps and marshes has frequently resulted in serious adverse effects on wildlife. Construction of reservoirs for irrigation and power often destroys scenic, historic, and archeological values. In extremely arid regions, reservoirs often add recreational value, but too often fluctuating water levels leave unsightly, worthless areas. Individual structures in recreational areas, such as private summer homes, dude ranches, and resorts frequently occupy strategic points that control the use of a much larger hinterland.

Recreational use of national resources, therefore, must be correlated with other forms of use, except within areas of primary recreational value. In such primary areas, no competing use should be permitted. Hunting licenses, prevention of stream pollution, preservation of roadside beauty, and similar public activities are essential to continuing recreational use of many areas, because private enterprise, in the search for commerical gain, frequently destroys the characteristics of land resources most valuable for recreation.

THE SUPPLY OF LAND FOR MINING

Physical factors determining the economic supply of land for mining vary with different minerals. For example, ore bodies containing a given percentage of gold or silver might be profitably mined, while the same percentage of copper or zinc in another ore body might be considered very low grade. The location of ores relative to consuming centers is an important factor in the profitableness of many mines, but comparatively insignificant in others. The contiguity of iron ore and coal deposits is very important in determining profitableness of exploitation, while the location of diamond deposits relative to any other metal, or to consuming centers, is relatively unimportant. The quality of the mineral is an important physical factor determining profitableness of utilization, and the type of material found in combination with the mineral in the ore deposit is also a very important physical factor limiting the amount of land used for mining at any given time.[13] Such physical factors as climate, soil characteristics, topography, and the like, which are so important in determining the suitability of land for agriculture, forestry, or recreation are of minor or no influence in determining lands that will be utilized for mineral production.

DISTRIBUTION OF MAJOR MINERALS

The physical supply of the various minerals that may exist in the earth is unknown. In some cases, figures representing the physical supply of certain minerals are given in terms of proved reserves, in which case ore bodies have been rather carefully studied and geologic formations analyzed so that the estimates are relatively accurate. In others, available figures are at best only approximations, estimates, or intelligent guesses. However, the United States is one of the most fortunate nations of the world, from the standpoint of deposits of the major strategic minerals. In spite of certain deficiencies, the United States approaches self-sufficiency in its domestic mineral supply more closely than any other nation.

The United States is noticeably weak in tin and nickel, producing only small amounts of these annually. Other minerals in which the United States is wholly or partly deficient include antimony, asbestos, barite, bauxite, chromite, fluorspar, graphite, magnesite, manganese, mercury, nitrates, pyrites, quartz crystal, talc, and tungsten.[14] Substitutes can be developed for many uses of most of these minerals, and the United States has adequate reserves of some, like barite; but their location relative to consumption centers is disadvantageous, or their grades are unsuited for certain uses. In the case of nitrates, domestic requirements can be met by synthetic production.

---

[13] If the amount of overlying material is small, mining by stripping may be possible; if the deposit is buried more deeply, a shaft must be sunk to or into the deposit, making additional expense. If the beds are very thick, as is frequently the case in coal deposits, it may be difficult to get adequate support for the roofs of necessary horizontal openings or drifts into the deposits. (For a discussion of the effects of position and physical condition of the deposits on mining, see D. H. Davis, *The Earth and Man,* Macmillan, 1942, p. 479.)

[14] National Resources Board, *Report to the President of the United States,* Government Printing Office, December 1, 1934, p. 444; and Army and Navy Munitions Board, "The Strategic and Critical Minerals," Washington, D.C., March, 1940, mimeographed.

Minerals may be divided into three groups: mineral fuel, metallic, and nonmetallic resources. The adequacy of the known supply varies greatly among the different minerals. For some, such as coal, reserves are adequate for centuries ahead; for others, like petroleum, known resources are very small; and for still others, such as tin, the supply of new metal is an immediate problem.

The greatest variety and most adequate reserves are found in the nations bordering on the North Atlantic Ocean—the United States, Canada, and northwestern Europe. With the exception of tin, the United States and Canada have a large supply of the important industrial minerals. Northwestern Europe has a wide variety of metals and coal and lacks only petroleum in large quantities. Although Asia and eastern Europe have metals and fuels in adequate amounts, the deposits are frequently distributed so unevenly and distances between them are so great that their significance is reduced. Excluding Australia, the continents of the Southern Hemisphere have inadequate supplies of coal. In South America, petroleum tends to make up for this deficit, but Africa has practically no oil. Both South America and Africa are rich in metals.

There are between six and seven trillion tons of coal deposits within 6000 feet of the surface of the earth, or enough to last some 6000 years at the present rate of consumption.[15] The distribution of these deposits among the nations is very uneven, however (see Figure 11). The coal reserves of the United States are estimated at 2500 billion short tons, or about 40 percent of the world total.[16]

Although crude petroleum is found in every continent, the major oil fields are restricted largely to North America, northeastern South America, southeastern Europe, southwestern Asia, and the East Indies (see Figure 12). Petroleum has a relatively high value in proportion to its weight and bulk and can be profitably transported long distances from its source to the markets where it is to be used. On the other hand, coal and water power are ordinarily used near their source. Only two important industrial nations, the United States and the U.S.S.R., have adequate petroleum supplies within their boundaries. Thus, petroleum plays a much larger part in world trade than other minerals like coal, frequently traveling thousands of miles to reach its market.

In spite of the fact that the United States has produced and is producing more oil than all the other nations combined, her boundaries contain only about one-sixth of the earth's rock formations favorable for the presence of oil. Fields in the Middle East have about 30 percent of the

---

[15] Klimm, Starkey, and Hall, *op. cit.,* p. 246.
[16] President's Materials Policy Commission, *Outlook for Energy Sources,* Vol. 3 of *Resources for Freedom,* report to the President, Government Printing Office, June, 1952, p. 26.

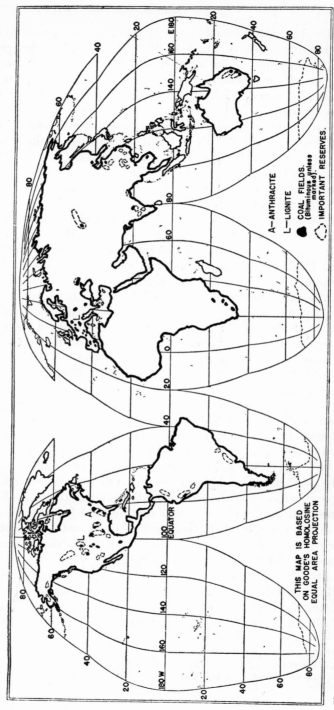

Figure 11. Coal Resources of the World. (Adapted from L. E. Klimm, O. P. Starkey, and N. F. Hall, *Introductory Economic Geography*, Harcourt, Brace, 1937; and D. H. Davis, *The Earth and Man*, Macmillan, 1942.)

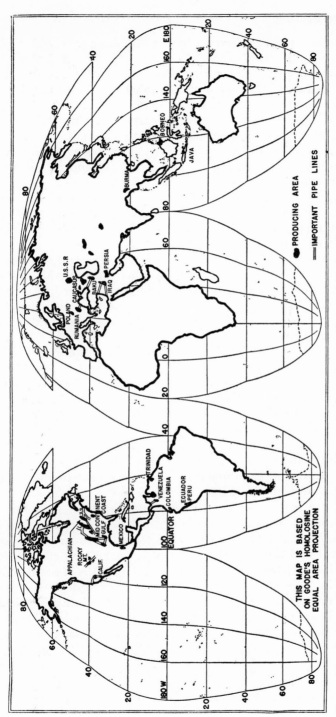

Figure 12. Petroleum Fields of the World. (Adapted from L. E. Klimm, O. P. Starkey, and N. F. Hall, *Introductory Economic Geography*, Harcourt, Brace, 1937.)

probable ultimate world reserves. About a fifth of the probable ultimat world reserves are in Russia, an eighth in the Caribbean Basin, a tentl in the southwest Pacific, and the remaining tenth in the rest of the world

It is estimated that only a tenth of the probable ultimate world reserve of 600 billion barrels can be removed from explored fields by presen methods for sale at present prices. In the case of the United States, ther are between one and one and one-half million square miles in the Unitee States and about six million square miles over the earth as a whole which, from a geological standpoint, favor the presence of oil. On the basis of past experience, about 1 percent of this area, or about 15,00 square miles in the United States, contains oil in commercial quantities All the oil fields developed in the nation to date total only 8000 squar miles. On this basis it would seem that areas at least as large as presen fields remain to be developed.[17]

The third ranking mineral fuel is natural gas. The United States pos sesses greater natural gas reserves than any other country.[18] Much natura gas is wasted in connection with oil production and other inefficient util ization methods. It should always be kept in mind that the mineral fuel —coal, oil, and gas—disappear forever when they are removed from the ground and used.

The major iron ore bodies that meet the conditions essential to make them commercially important today are found in the Lake Superior and southern Appalachian regions in the United States; the Lake Superior region in Canada and in Newfoundland; Cuba; central Chile in South America; Sweden; Great Britain; the U.S.S.R.; Germany; France; and Spain. Less important deposits occur in north China and the Yangtze Valley, and in the Malayan Federation. There are other deposits, some of large amounts of high-grade ores, that are of potential future importance particularly those of eastern Brazil and northeastern India. These deposits are shown in Figure 13.

The iron ore reserves of the United States are both large and wel located. Discontinuous beds of hematite occur in the Appalachians from New York to Alabama. These are mostly low-grade ores, but their associa tion with coal and limestone has resulted in extensive development in the Birmingham, Alabama, area. There are also deposits of possible future significance in the western states. The most important deposits, however are those of the Lake Superior region in the upper peninsula of Michigan, northern Wisconsin, and the Mesabi Range in northeastern Minnesota These Lake Superior ores are not only high grade, but occur so near the

[17] Eugene Holman, "Oil-Product and Pillar of Freedom" (address to New York State Chamber of Commerce, April 6, 1944), Standard Oil Co., New York, 1944. See also L. M. Fanning (ed.), *Our Oil Resources*, McGraw-Hill, 1945, p. 117.

[18] L. F. Terry, "The Future Supply of Natural Gas Will Exceed 500 Trillion Cubic Feet," *Gas Age*, October 26, 1950, p. 58.

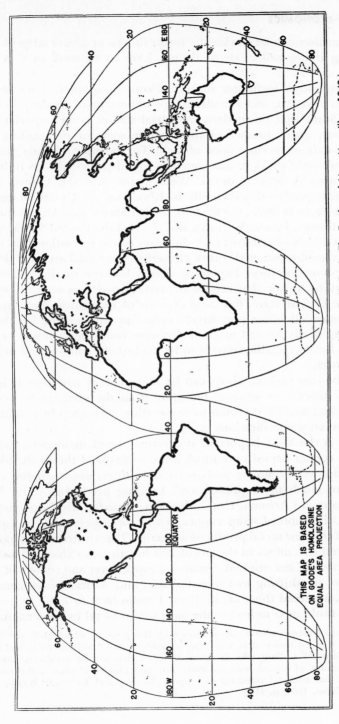

Figure 13. Principal Iron Ore Deposits of the World. (Adapted from D. H. Davis, *The Earth and Man*, Macmillan, 1942.)

THIS MAP IS BASED
ON GOODE'S HOMOLOSINE
EQUAL AREA PROJECTION

surface that they can be worked by steam shovel, or where strip or open pit mining is impossible, shafts do not have to be sunk to very great depths.

The ferroalloys, including nickel, silicon, manganese, molybdenum chromium, tungsten, and vanadium, are important in modern industry It is significant that no modern industrial nation is an important producer of any great number of these, while some of the leading steel producing nations produce none of them. For example, Canada produces most of the world's nickel; manganese is found principally in India, the Caucasus area in Russia, Brazil, West Africa, and the United States Chromium is produced principally in Rhodesia, the United States, and India; vanadium in Peru, the western United States, and Africa; tungsten in China, Burma, Japan, Australia, Bolivia, and the United States. Silicon is the most widely distributed and abundant of the ferroalloys and always occurs in combination with other elements. Some nations have deposits of one or more of these important alloys, but the quality of the or bodies may be so low that economic production is not feasible. For example, the United States has large deposits of manganese and chromite but has depended in the past largely upon imports, because her deposits are geographically located at great distances from the industrial centers or are too low in metallic content to be worked efficiently under ordinary circumstances.

As in the case of iron, alloys can be re-used. It is true that it is comparatively difficult to separate the alloy from the steel scrap, but it is becoming increasingly common to re-use alloy steel scrap in making new steel of the same specifications.

Copper is the most important nonferrous metal in modern industry Workable copper deposits are much more widespread than valuable iron ore deposits, yet economic and social difficulties accompanying copper mining are much more pronounced. Leading producing states in the United States are Arizona, Utah, Montana, Nevada, Michigan, and New Mexico. Utilization of scrap copper or old copper reworked is equal to about half the new metal produced annually. The United States has some of the lowest cost mines in the world, but has already exhausted a considerable portion of her original deposits of copper ore; and centers of world production are shifting to Chile, Canada, and Africa, whose combined reserves now exceed those of the United States by 4 to 1.[19]

Copper ranks next to iron as the most useful metal in modern machine

[19] Reserves of copper should be measured by the price at which they can be produced, and it is estimated that U.S. reserves amount to 21 million tons, and that of foreign nations, 83 million tons in terms of metal that can be produced under past prices. These are, of course, only estimates, but they give some idea of the advancing depletion of our national resources of copper. (See National Resources Board, *Report to the President*, 1934, p. 410.)

ivilization. Technological developments in recent years have made it possible to refine cheap grade ores which a few years ago were considered alueless. Since there are relatively large reserves of comparatively cheap rade ores located in various parts of the earth, the supply of copper is onsidered quite adequate for future needs.

THE SUPPLY OF WATER

The amount of water available for man's use varies considerably among he continents of the earth, as do also the numbers of their inland streams, ivers, and lakes, or their access to large adjacent bodies of water in the orm of oceans, straits, gulfs, or seas. The proportion of the areas of each ontinent receiving a given annual amount of precipitation follows: [20]

	Under 20 Inches	20–40 Inches	Over 40 Inches
Australia	66%	22%	12%
Africa	54	18	28
Asia	67	18	15
North America	52	30	18
Europe	47	49	4
South America	16	8	76

AVAILABILITY OF WATER

There are few areas on the earth where water is not available, or where it cannot be made available with some human effort, to furnish an adequate supply for human consumption, even if it must be used sparingly for other purposes. There is enough fresh water in the world to irrigate all the arid and semiarid lands physically suitable for agriculture; but the juxtaposition of water bodies, or sources of water supplies, and suitable arid and semiarid lands is such that only a very limited percentage of the total area can be economically irrigated.

The most important physical factors limiting the use of water for generating power are volume and rate of stream flow. The amount of water power that can be developed from a given stream during the period when it is at its lowest ebb has been defined as *firm power,* or the amount of horsepower that can be developed on the basis of the flow for the period of two weeks in which the flow of the stream is least. The amount of firm power may be much less than that which can be developed during the high-water months; but if the demand for power is fairly constant during the year, firm power will be the limiting factor determining the horsepower that can be depended upon to satisfy human needs.

Scenic values, fishing possibilities, swimming facilities, winter sports,

[20] Griffith Taylor, "The Frontiers of Settlement in Australia," *Geographical Review,* January, 1926.

boating, and similar opportunities give bodies of water their recreationa value. A greater range of physical qualities can be used effectively to satisfy recreational demands than can be used in the generation of powe or utilization of water for human consumption, or for irrigation. Thus the potential economic supply of water for recreational use is greate than that for the other uses mentioned.

Use of water for navigation and transportation is limited by physica location and depth of the water. Six feet is generally considered the minimum depth for commercial navigation. In many cases, government and private individuals have deepened stream courses to 6 feet or more making year-round navigation possible upon streams formerly navigabl only part of the year, or not at all. The economic supply of water fo transportation, however, is limited largely by depth and by physica location relative to domestic and international markets.

An example of the extreme importance of physical depths of stream can be seen in the effect of fluctuations in the height of water on Grea Lakes shipping. It is claimed that for every inch of decrease in the heigh of water on the Great Lakes in periods of extreme drought, there is ar annual loss to shipping interests of several hundred thousand dollars The big ore boats cannot be loaded to full capacity, and there is a conse quent loss in freight earnings for each inch of reduced displacement During years of low water, increased cost must be incurred to deeper water at the terminals; but this deepening, together with that necessitatec in the channels between the lakes, has had the effect of lowering the gen eral water level.

A MULTIPLE-USE RESOURCE

Water, like forests, is a multiple-use resource, and its uses are no necessarily exclusive. For example, in the case of hydroelectric develop ments for producing water power, the water is still available for trans portation, for irrigation, for navigation, or for recreation. It might even be used for drinking purposes, since its quality is not affected by its use for hydroelectric purposes. In many instances, these various uses supple ment one another and make possible the development of various enter prises that would not be justified by a single use. For example, it may be economically feasible to build an expensive irrigation dam if the water stored behind the dam can be used, at least in part, for the development of electric power (which constitutes an additional source of revenue tc cover part of the construction cost).

These various uses, however, may be antagonistic. To some extent, for example, hydroelectric power and irrigation uses are competitive. Water resources must be carefully studied and their uses adjusted to prevent one desirable undertaking from destroying another use that may be even more important.

SUPPLY OF LAND FOR TRANSPORTATION

Transportation bids high for the services of land, in competition with other uses. Transportation is a higher or more intense land use than agriculture, forestry, or recreation, and it is ordinarily a higher use than urban residence, and frequently than urban industry. Only in the case of very rich ore deposits would a given piece of land be utilized for mining rather than for transportation if the land were situated in the line of transportation development.

FACTORS DETERMINING USE OF LAND FOR TRANSPORTATION

Historically, topography has been one of the major factors determining the location of transportation routes, and most trails, roads, and railroads ran along river valleys, mountain passes, and generally level areas, avoiding mountains and steep hills. In spite of modern technology, the cost of highway construction in mountainous areas, where roadbeds must meet minimum grade requirements for modern sustained speed, is often great enough to compel the use of more level routes.

Aside from topography, natural factors are of minor and usually insignificant importance in determining the transportation route. It is true that some soil characteristics in association with more important factors like strategic location are more desirable than others, but they are not generally so significant as to be the limiting factor. For instance, it may cost more to construct a roadbed in very rocky or clayey soils than in sandy ones, but the difference is a very minor factor in deciding where the road will be built.

Human forces are of major significance in the determination of transportation routes. Land whose principal use is for upholding or supporting strength can hardly be considered as destructible physically through utilization or nonuse, and the value of transportation land is acquired through *situs*. Situs has been defined as the "consensus of human choice and convenience, or the quality aspect of situation." [21] Like all economic utilities, situs is a social product created by man collectively, through preference or choice, and this value may be destroyed by the human choice that created it. Improvements on the land, in the form of roadbed preparation and surfacing, are so large that maintenance of the improvement constitutes the major problem of transportation land use. In this respect, transportation land more nearly resembles urban land than any of the other major types.

[21] H. B. Dorau and A. G. Hinman, *Urban Land Economics*, Macmillan, 1928, p. 167.

THE SUPPLY OF URBAN LAND

Land is fixed and immobile, so that in a strict physical sense no particular parcel of land is any more mobile or adaptable for a given human use than any other. The choices of society, however, differentiate locations on the basis of their usefulness to satisfy wants. The bases of choices of land to be used for urban purposes are very different from those of land for other types of use, especially agricultural and forest use.

FACTORS DETERMINING SUITABILITY OF LAND FOR URBAN USE

The physical characteristics of soil, topography, moisture, and temperature, which are of major importance in determining lands that will be used for agriculture or forestry, are not highly significant, in urban land, but *location,* or *situs,* is of major importance, since a particular site carries with it the trade of a given group for whom it is most convenient. A short distance such as a block, or even less, often makes a great difference in urban land value. In contrast, man will somehow contrive to get at natural wealth wherever it is, so that location does not play such an important role in agricultural, forest, or mining lands.

Cities must, of course, have a water supply from some source. Temperature and sunshine may influence the size and construction of dwellings. Hence, these physical factors affect utilization of land for urban purposes, but not ordinarily in a significant or limiting way. Topography, however, often plays an important role in determining which lands will be used for urban purposes, and the intensity of use. Select residential sites are often on hillsides or ridges, which are highly prized for their picturesque effect and outlook.

AMOUNT OF LAND SUITABLE FOR URBAN USE

No physical factors limit the economic supply of land for urban purposes, aside from the factor of physical space itself, which is a characteristic of all lands; forces other than physical determine the land to be used for cities.

If physical space were the only ultimate limitation to the land available for urban use, urbanization could continue indefinitely, in competition with other uses of land, until the entire surface of the earth had been utilized. In such circumstances, there would be no reason for crowded cities and exorbitant rents on particular sites. However, location within the space occupied by a given city is an extremely important matter.

The "downtown district" of any large city is an example, familiar to almost everyone, of the concentrated use made of such areas and the premium put upon accessibility to the center of the city. Not all parts of the city can be located at or near the center; and different urban land uses are therefore grouped in concentric circles around the center, according to accessibility or ability to pay. Accessibility is a function of the available transportation system or systems, and the circles enlarge as transportation facilities improve.

REFERENCES FOR FURTHER READING

Dana, Samuel T., *Forest and Range Policy,* McGraw-Hill Book Company, Inc., New York, 1956, Chaps. I, II, and III.

Ely, R. T., and Morehouse, E. W., *Elements of Land Economics,* The Macmillan Company, New York, 1924, Chap. V.

Johnson, V. Webster, and Barlowe, Raleigh, *Land Problems and Policies,* McGraw-Hill Book Company, Inc., New York, 1954, pp. 194–208.

Klimm, L. E., Starkey, O. P., and Hall, N. F., *Introductory Economic Geography,* Harcourt, Brace and Company, Inc., New York, 1937, Chaps. VII, VIII, and IX.

President's Materials Policy Commission, *Outlook for Energy Sources,* Vol. III of *Resources for Freedom,* report to the President, 5 vols., Government Printing Office, Washington, D.C., June, 1952, p. 26.

Zimmermann, Erich, *World Resources and Industries,* Harper & Brothers, New York, 1951, Chaps. X, XXIV, and XXV.

THE DEMAND FOR LAND

FACTORS DETERMINING THE CHARACTER OF THE POPULATION

The Land Factor—The Biological Factor—The Cultural Factor

POPULATION AND LAND SETTLEMENT

Total Population—Population Density—The Man-Land Ratio—Population Pressure

POPULATION TRENDS AND THE DEMAND FOR LAND

The Trend of Birth and Death Rates—The Trend of Immigration—World Population Outlook—United States Population Outlook

OPTIMUM POPULATION—THE IDEAL MAN-LAND RATIO

The Concept of Optimum Population—Methods of Attaining Optimum Population—Migration—Population Policies—Future Man-Land Adjustments

THE DEMAND for land arises from the various uses to which it can be put to satisfy man's wants. Man uses land resources directly for homesites, highways, or recreational purposes—or indirectly, in producing goods such as food, feed, fuel, and minerals. Agriculture is by far the most important of the major uses, at least 60 percent of the world's population being engaged directly in cultivating the soil.[1] The proportion of

[1] Ellsworth Huntington, "Agricultural Productivity and Pressure of Population," *Annals of the American Academy of Political and Social Science*, Vol. 198, July, 1938, p. 74. Huntington goes on to say that if merchants, artisans, professional men, and others who serve the agricultural community are included, at least two-thirds of the world's population gets its living quite directly from agriculture, and that if miners,

he population engaged in agriculture varies greatly among the nations, however, and in the United States only about one-tenth of the people ive on farms.

Man selects those land resources, or parts of them, that serve best in the production of economic goods and services to satisfy his wants. In this election, classification of land resources according to inherent physical characteristics and use capabilities, as indicated in Chapter 3, is the first requisite for satisfactory land settlement and most efficient utilization.

The character and amount of land selected for use, as well as the type and method of use, will depend not only on the size and trend of the population but upon its age composition, character, and distribution. The stage of civilization that a people has attained, particularly the stage of science, art, and invention (technology) will also have a very important bearing upon the demand for land.

FACTORS DETERMINING THE CHARACTER
OF THE POPULATION

In more primitive societies, production is largely a matter of combining labor and land; but as civilization develops, capital is created by postponing consumption. A complex pattern of human institutions, customs, and social habits to form what is referred to as culture is built up through time; this culture in turn has an important influence upon the types and methods of utilizing land. We have, therefore, in modern complex society, three very important factors—*available resources,* the *biological factor,* and the *cultural factor*—which are closely interrelated and which determine the character of the population (its size, age composition, distribution, and related characteristics), which in turn determines the character and the amount of land selected for use, as well as the type and method of use.

THE LAND FACTOR

The character of the land resources ultimately determines the limits of population growth and largely conditions the distribution of the population. The physical fact of limited space and limited fertility, or producing ability, sets a limit to the increase of plant and animal life; but space limitations do not operate directly in the case of human beings, because other means of physical limitation become operative before space limitation is the deciding factor. The impossibility of obtaining food

---

lumbermen, factory employees, transportation workers, and others producing and transporting goods consumed by the agricultural population are included, the number of people whose prosperity depends upon that of the farmer probably rises well above 80 percent. All of us are fed, largely clothed, and to some extent sheltered by the direct or indirect products of agriculture.

will operate long before there is "standing room only." In other words the food supply operates to set the upper limits to the world's population

Climate and weather have a very great influence upon the type o crops produced within a given area and the general utilization practice that will be followed, as well as an important influence in determining the density of population and the size and type of buildings and othe improvements that will be made upon the land. Moreover, the climate has a very important effect upon the amount of food required. Basa metabolism seems to be from 5 to 15 percent lower in the tropics than ir the temperate climates, and a person requires a larger supply of food energy in a cold than in a warm climate.[2]

Throughout the greater part of human history, the abundance of game and the fertility of the soil have been the most important factors in determining the amount of population. Wherever the fertility of the soil or the state of the agricultural arts has produced a surplus of food and raw materials beyond the needs of the producers, towns and cities have developed; the proportion of people living in urban areas has always been determined "by the proportion of the agricultural production above that needed to maintain the farm population at or near a subsistence level. Always and everywhere man seems to have developed a town population as large as he could support."[3]

This is typical of a progressive economy because with increased efficiency in production accompanying modern science and technology, including division of labor, a decreased proportion of the total population is required to produce the needed food and fibers. This releases more people to produce nonagricultural goods, and services that are in great demand in a society with modern standards of living. Since man's total wants are practically limitless, as many of the population as are not needed to produce food and fiber pursue other occupations—industrial and professional—that characterize the urban community.

There have been tremendous changes in the amount and distribution of the world's population since the beginning of the Industrial Revolution. Europe and the areas settled by her people, which contained perhaps a sixth of the world's population in 1800, today contain a third or more. The proportion of the rural and urban populations in most of these countries has changed to an even larger degree.

So great have been the effects of industrial development that there is a tendency to disregard the important influences of land in controlling the character of the population. Man, through his inventive genius and

[2] Carl L. Alsberg, "The Food Supply and the Migration Process," in Isaiah Bowman (ed.), *Limits of Land Settlement*, Council on Foreign Relations, 1937, p. 30.

[3] Warren S. Thompson, "The Distribution of Population," *Annals of the American Academy of Political and Social Science*, Vol. 188, November, 1936, p. 250.

cientific advancement, has modified the part which the natural factors, ncluding soil productivity, physical form of the land body, and climate, play in determining the amount and distribution of the population. However, in the marginal areas, or in the near-marginal regions, land plays a very significant role, and even in the more productive and strategic areas, it plays a role of general conditioner too frequently overlooked or underrated.

THE BIOLOGICAL FACTOR

In 1798 Thomas Robert Malthus published an *Essay on the Principles of Population,* in which he argued that the population tends to outrun the food supply.[4] Malthus argued that population tends to increase in a geometric ratio, while food supply or subsistence tends to increase in an arithmetic ratio. His theory implied that in a relatively short time, unless man practiced self-restraint, and other positive checks came into play, pressure of population on food supply would be very great and starvation, pestilence, war, or some similar developments would occur to reduce population to numbers in keeping with the food supply.

Malthus' formulation has been the one around which discussion of population has centered since the publication of his *Essay.* It is a bold, dogmatic statement of the biological concept of population growth; and while it contains an essential truth, it is not tenable as a general theory of population.[5] If one accepts the theory without qualification, the biological inevitability of human population increasing up to the limit of subsistence exonerates the wealthy or more fortunate groups in society from responsibility for existing social ills, poverty, war, disease, and pestilence.[6]

Modern societies demonstrate conclusively that human populations are able to create and maintain powerful checks upon the biological urge to reproduce. The sex appetite is a biological fact, but the reproductive tendency, as shown by the birth rate, is a cultural phenomenon and the development of birth control methods, self-restraint, fear of poverty, desire for a high standard of living, and related factors have enabled man to slow up the rate of increase. In other words, man does not act under biological influences only, and the reduced growth in number of human

---

[4] T. R. Malthus, *Essay on the Principles of Population,* Dent, 1st ed., 1798.

[5] E. B. Reuter, *Population Problems,* Lippincott, rev. ed., 1940, p. 169. Reuter states that "Adequately and sympathetically interpreted, most of Malthus' 'Essay' can be made to appear true, or at least innocuous."

[6] Reuter states that "The privileged classes of England, possessing most of the land and living in luxury among a miserable and starving peasantry, were seduced by a theory, irrelevant as it was to the subject, which seemed to exonerate them from all responsibility for the deplorable social conditions . . . but withal it was highly flattering to the property-owning classes: They were what they were, prosperous and property-owning, because they had the virtues the peasants lacked." (*Ibid.,* p. 167.)

beings in many parts of the world is attributable, at least to a consider able extent, to voluntary control.

About half of the human race, made up largely of the Chinese and the Asiatic Indians, is pushing its population growth to the absolute limit of subsistence.[7] However, within the Western societies, the more advanced groups desire a greater amount of material goods and services for each person, so that they restrict their families even though there is still a greater store of subsistence available to support a much larger population on a lower material level of living.

THE CULTURAL FACTOR

Apparently in some societies the biological factors predominate, while in others they are much more in the background. It would seem apparent, therefore, that amount and distribution of population are determined partly by the physical limitations of the land resources, partly by biolog ical forces, and partly by the cultural pattern, including social usages, institutions, economic organization, technology, and related cultural forces. Ross estimates that the "advanced societies," including perhaps a sixth of the human race, have applied "a brake to their fertility,"[8] and have so modified the influence of the biological factor that numbers are not allowed to increase to the absolute limit of subsistence.

Bryson indicates three distinct stages of cultures: (1) economic strin gency in which both luxuries and necessities (all the elements of sub sistence) are hard to get; (2) relative cheapness of the more necessary things, such as simple food, clothing, and shelter, but great scarcity and expensiveness of secondary elements or luxuries; (3) increasing expen siveness of necessities and relative cheapness of luxuries.[9] The logistic curve of population growth begins in the second stage, for various reasons. Fewer children die of starvation and malnutrition; parents are better fed and can both produce and care for more children; what is more, in the second stage children are economic assets because they are cheap labor. Education is beyond reach; more than simple comfort is impos sible; and forms of vanity are not easily indulged. In the third stage, however, a relatively high standard of living has been established, and its effect is to slow up population growth (or to flatten out the curve) rather than to encourage it.[10]

Obviously, the more culturally mature the society the greater will be the part played by cultural forces, and the less culturally mature the society the greater will be the part played by biological forces. Man, by

[7] Lyman Bryson, "Population and Culture," *Annals of the American Academy of Political and Social Science,* Vol. 162, July, 1932, p. 190.
[8] E. A. Ross, *Standing Room Only?* Century, 1927, p. 5.
[9] Bryson, *op. cit.,* p. 193.
[10] *Ibid.,* p. 195.

his cultural development, has gone beyond the biological phases of the problem and has established adaptive processes through which he has overcome the "inevitable" consequences of population pressing upon the means of subsistence.

POPULATION AND LAND SETTLEMENT

The word "population" ordinarily refers to the number of people inhabiting a given area, or "any group of people bound together with some degree of permanence in time and space, when the emphasis is upon the numbers rather than upon the social organization." [11] The characteristics of the population, including growth, density, age composition, and distribution, as well as total number, are directly and indirectly related to most of the major problems of economic and social life and are of special significance in determining the utilization of land resources.

Growth is one of the principal factors of cultural change. Increase in population numbers and density forces men into new relationships with the land and with their fellow men. The standard of living and the nature of political and social institutions, are conditioned by and in turn condition the character of the population for which land resources are utilized to furnish goods and services.

TOTAL POPULATION

The number of people is not an accurate measure of the importance of the population in determining the amount and character of land used or methods followed in the use of land resources. Numbers combined with cultural development or stage of technological attainment and the trend of population, rather than present population status, are significant. A population growing rapidly influences the wants, arts, and institutions developed by man in a way significantly different from that in which a stagnant, slow-growing, or declining population affects them, and consequently results in different land utilization.

The estimated total population of the earth is in the neighborhood of two and one-half billions. More than half of this number live in Asia, and another fourth in Europe, or more than three-fourths in these two continents (see Figure 14).

POPULATION DENSITY

The distribution of the people of the earth in relation to the land surface varies greatly among the continents (see Figure 15). The density of population also varies greatly among nations within the continents. In North America, the population density varies from over 50 people

[11] Reuter, *op. cit.*, p. 3.

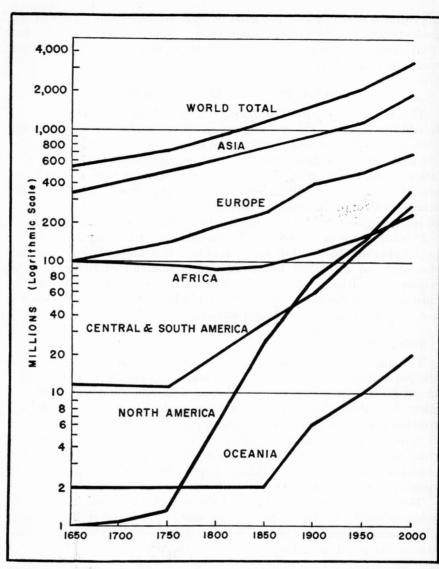

Figure 14. Growth of Population by Continents, 1650–2000. (Data for 1650–1900 from A. M. Carr-Saunders, *World Population*, p. 42; 1900–1950 data based on League of Nations, *World Economic Survey, 1938–1939*, and *Statistical Yearbook, 1938–1939*, and U.S. Department of Commerce, Bureau of the Census, 1950 Census of Population; projected data, 1950–2000 adapted from F. W. Notestein, "Population, the Long View," in T. W. Schultz [ed.], *Food for the World*, University of Chicago Press, 1945, pp. 36–57.)

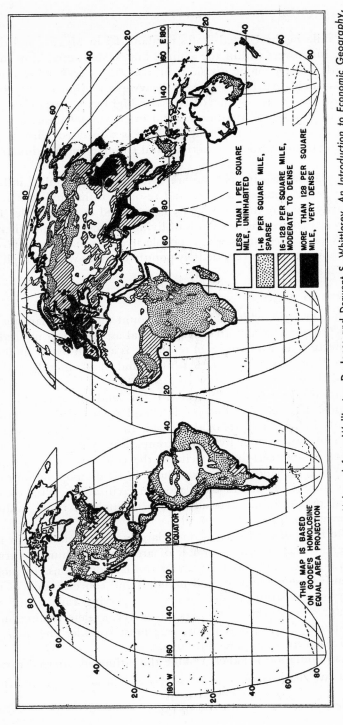

Figure 15. World Population Density. (Adapted from Wellington D. Jones and Derwent S. Whittlesey, *An Introduction to Economic Geography*, University of Chicago Press, 1925, Figure 8.)

per square mile in the United States to about 35 in Mexico and only 4 in Canada. Moreover, within the United States, the population density varies greatly among major divisions or regions, as well as among the states (refer to Figure 15). The very heavy population density of the continent of Europe is associated with the highly industrialized urban areas built upon far-flung commercial and international trade. The comparatively high population density of Asia is associated with the low level of living of the millions of agricultural Chinese and the inhabitants of India.

The population density per square mile has considerable influence upon the type and intensiveness of land resource utilization; but it does not necessarily indicate the levels of living achieved by the people. There are sparsely settled areas where levels of living are very low, and there are also densely populated areas where people live in squalor and poverty. There are, however, other very densely populated areas where a high level of living is maintained.

THE MAN-LAND RATIO

The man-land ratio, which takes into account all the human qualities bearing on productivity and all environmental aspects, both natural and cultural, affecting the availability of resources, is a much better indication of significant relationships between man and land than population density, and the two should not be confused.[12]

The relationship between the capacity of land resources to satisfy human wants, and the size, distribution, and trend of the population differs greatly in various parts of the world. In more primitive societies, where arts and standards of living are comparatively static, the relationship between human carrying capacity of the land (capacity to support human life) and demands made upon the land by the population can be quite easily appraised; but in more modern civilizations, with complex institutional organizations and advancing technology, trade, industry, and commerce, the appraisal is difficult.

When the form of land utilization is largely agricultural, as in more primitive areas, acres or square miles of area indicate human carrying capacity to a large legree, at least under similar conditions. In modern times, extensive use made of subsoil minerals and concentration of these deposits in certain strategic locations make carrying capacity of some areas much greater than that of others. Moreover, in determining human carrying capacity for a given nation, one must consider the area with which the nation trades as part of its area.

Holland's population is almost double the estimated internal carrying

[12] Cf. Erich W. Zimmermann, *World Resources and Industries*, rev. ed., Harper, 1951, p. 92.

capacity of the nation's area; but the human carrying capacity of the Netherlands must include, in addition to the land on the continent of Europe, much of the Dutch East Indies and many other areas of the earth on which, because of her political, commercial, and financial position prior to World War II, she was able to draw for support.[13]

POPULATION PRESSURE

The term "population pressure" is not synonymous with mere numbers or density. Densely populated nations such as India or China have not been, in modern times, driven to aggressive warfare by population pressure. "Pressure of population," in the modern sense, cannot be limited to the direct pressure of the population on the means of subsistence. This direct pressure constitutes the simpler and historic cases, and results in the so-called "hunger" wars where populations are confronted with famine, because of drought or flood or other natural catastrophes.

The three alternatives available to such populations are death by starvation, peaceful migration where available territory makes such migration possible, and invasion of a neighboring territory.[14] In many cases, the last alternative has been chosen, particularly in earlier times when nomadic herdsmen invaded adjacent regions.

Modern "pressure of population" differs greatly from these so-called "hunger" pressures. Nomadic herdsmen fought for new feeding grounds; agricultural peoples fought for new lands; but modern industrial peoples fight for markets, for sources of raw materials, and for opportunities for investment of capital. They fight not to prevent starvation but to safeguard and improve a level of living to which they have become accustomed, or a standard to which they aspire—hence the modern scramble, through aggressive warfare, for "spheres of influence."

A combination of large numbers of people, although the population density may not be abnormally high, and a high standard of living makes population pressure more real than it could possibly be in the case of nations with large numbers and relatively low standards of living. In other words, population pressure becomes economic pressure, and instead of being a matter of mere density or numbers, it takes on certain psychological aspects. It is the *felt* population pressure, rather than the absolute, that causes a nation to resort to aggressive warfare. It reaches its maxi-

[13] Zimmermann refers to such populations as "expansive" compared with "pent up" populations that are unable to draw upon external carrying capacity, either economically or politically, and are led either to birth control, infanticide, or to chronic undernourishment if not starvation, or both. The expansionist populations, not content to live on their own resources, may draw on external carrying capacity through trade, conquest, colonization, commercial or financial penetration, etc. (*Ibid.*, pp. 93–94.)

[14] F. H. Hankins, "Pressure of Population as a Cause of War," *Annals of the American Academy of Political and Social Science,* Vol. 198, July, 1938, p. 103.

mum in a high-standard population with a well-integrated national life when its standard of living is threatened or reduced by the economic policies, real or fancied, of other nations.

POPULATION TRENDS AND THE DEMAND FOR LAND

The rate of increase or decline of a population aside from immigration depends upon the number of births compared with the number of deaths. A high birth rate with high mortality rates may not be as significant in increasing the population as a somewhat lower birth rate and a significantly lower death rate.

THE TREND OF BIRTH AND DEATH RATES

The world's population has increased fourfold since 1650 and has more than doubled since 1800.[15] All sections of the world have participated in this growth (see Figure 14), but it was most pronounced prior to 1900 in Europe and European colonies or areas settled by Europeans. Since 1900 the rate of growth has tended to decline in North America, Europe, and Oceania; but in Africa, Asia, and Central and South America, although accurate data are not available, the rate of growth is apparently still increasing.

This increase in the world's population results largely from a decline in death rates. For example, in the United States the expectation of life at birth has increased from about 34 years in 1879 to more than twice this number of years today. Other nations have made great progress in lowering death rates.

Death rates should continue to decline in nations under the influence of Western civilization. With sanitary and medical advances and the expanding influence of Western civilization growing out of World War II, it is logical to expect appreciable reductions in death rates in those countries where mortality is now highest.

There has been an almost universal reduction in birth rates since the turn of the century. In the United States, birth rates in 1800 were about three and one-half times as large as in 1930 [16] and about two and one-half times as large as in the 1950's. As late as 1880 American women were twice as prolific as today. The rate of material increase of population has diminished in a majority of countries of which statistics are available.

World population is increasing at a rate of approximately 1 percent a year. This could easily lead to a doubling of the population in less than a century. The degree to which this trend will continue depends principally upon fertility and mortality trends over the world.

[15] A. M. Carr-Saunders, *World Population,* Clarendon Press, 1936, p. 42.

[16] National Resources Committee, *The Problems of a Changing Population,* Government Printing Office, 1938, p. 23.

THE TREND OF IMMIGRATION

A third factor affecting the trend of population within a country along with birth and death rates is immigration. In the United States, immigration has been a major factor in the past in determining the size and composition of the nation's population. In some years immigration equaled 1.5 percent of the population and exceeded the million mark annually in several years between 1900 and the outbreak of World War I. In recent years, however, immigration has been greatly reduced by laws and regulations and by unsettled economic and political conditions. It can be assumed that there will continue to be large numbers of persons desirous of taking up residence in this country, and unless immigration is prohibited, its value will vary widely from year to year, depending principally on economic and political conditions here and abroad.

WORLD POPULATION OUTLOOK

Notestein groups the world's population into three demographic types.[17]

I. *Incipient Decline*—Populations in which fertility has fallen below the replacement level or those in which it is near and rapidly approaching that level. Populations of northwestern, southern, and central Europe, North America, Australia, and New Zealand are all in this group. Only immigration or reversal of recent trends in fertility [18] can prevent virtual termination of growth in this group within a generation, but such reversals will be difficult to obtain short of drastic governmental policies.

II. *Transitional Growth*—Populations in which the decline of both fertility and mortality is well established but in which the decline of mortality precedes that of fertility and produces rapid growth. Populations of eastern Europe are nearing the end of this stage, those of Soviet Russia and Japan and certain Latin American countries are in mid-course, while those of Turkey, Palestine, and parts of North America apparently are entering it.

III. *High Growth Potential*—Death and birth rates remain close to pre-modern standards and birth rates have hardly begun to decline. This type includes more than half of the world's population. Egypt, Central Africa, much of the Near East, practically all of Asia excluding Soviet Russia and Japan, the islands of the Pacific and Caribbean, and much of Central and South America fall in this type. If political or economic conditions are bad for prolonged periods in these areas, considerable de-

---

[17] Frank W. Notestein, "Population—The Long View," in T. W. Schultz (ed.), *Food for the World*, University of Chicago Press, 1945, pp. 41–52.

[18] *Fertility* is the number of births per 1000 women of childbearing age, this age being assumed to constitute the period from 15 to 50 years.

population might result, but if a prolonged period of peace and order prevails and production efficiency increases, there would probably be rapid and sustained population growth.

On the basis of this classification of the world's population, it is obvious that populations where fertility has been brought under control enough so that birth rates are in balance with the low death rates permitted by modern conditions are definitely in the minority. Consequently, total world population will continue to increase and may exceed three billions before the year 2000.[19] If by that time fertility is to fall enough to bring about the end of the period of growth, there must be great advances in production and political and social organization. In other words, food output must increase faster than population, and there must be equally rapid advancement in industrial production, education, public health, and government; because it is only when rising levels of living, improved health, and increasing education give new life, value, and dignity to individual life that old customs are discarded and fertility comes under control.

UNITED STATES POPULATION OUTLOOK

United States population for many years grew more and more slowly until 1940, when a marked upturn occurred during the forties and fifties. The decennial rate of increase was above 30 percent for most of the nineteenth century, declined to around 20 percent at the turn of the century, and was only about 7 percent for the intercensal period, 1930 to 1940 (see Table 1).

Whether the upturn in the birthrate that occurred after 1940 (see Figure 16) will continue remains to be seen. In the late nineteen fifties, United States population is increasing at more than three million net per year. At this rate, the nation's population will exceed 180 million by 1960 and about 225 million by 1975. Continued increase at this rate could result in about doubling the national population by the year 2000.

The rate of population increase will probably decline somewhat during the sixties as the women who are now in the child-bearing age group are replaced by the smaller number of women born during the 1930–1940 period when the birthrate was relatively low (see Figure 16). This will likely be only a temporary respite, however, because the large baby crop of the forties and fifties indicates an even larger baby boom in the late sixties and seventies.

The future population of the United States will be determined to a considerable extent by general business conditions, family attitudes, and

[19] Notestein indicates there is considerable chance that the world will reach the three billion level in two generations, with the capacity for growth of its backward populations still unimpaired. (Notestein, *op. cit.*, p. 57.)

Table 1. United States Population, Amount and Percent of Increase by Decades, 1650–1960

Year	Population (Thousands)	Increase (Thousands)	Decennial Percent Increase
1650	52	—	—
1660	85	33	64.0
1670	114	30	35.0
1680	156	41	35.9
1690	214	58	37.2
1700	275	62	28.8
1710	358	82	30.0
1720	474	117	32.7
1730	655	181	38.1
1740	889	234	35.7
1750	1,207	318	35.8
1760	1,610	403	33.4
1770	2,205	595	37.0
1780	2,781	576	26.1
1790	3,929	1,148	41.3
1800	5,308	1,379	35.1
1810	7,240	1,931	36.4
1820	9,638	2,399	33.1
1830	12,866	3,288	33.5
1840	17,069	4,203	32.7
1850	23,260	6,191	36.3
1860	31,502	8,242	35.4
1870	39,904	8,402	26.7
1880	50,262	10,358	26.0
1890	63,056	12,794	25.5
1900	76,129	13,073	20.7
1910	92,267	16,138	21.2
1920	107,190	14,923	16.2
1930	123,091	15,901	14.8
1940	131,669	8,578	7.0
1950	151,132	19,463	14.8
1960 [a]	180,000 est.	29,000 est.	19.2 est.

[a] Estimated.

SOURCE: National Resources Committee, *The Problems of a Changing Population*, Government Printing Office, 1938, pp. 21 and 24; U.S. Department of Commerce, Bureau of the Census, *16th Census of the United States (1940)*, Vol. II, Chap. I, Table 4, and U.S. Department of Agriculture, *Agricultural Statistics, 1954*, U.S. Government Printing Office, Washington, D.C., p. 439.

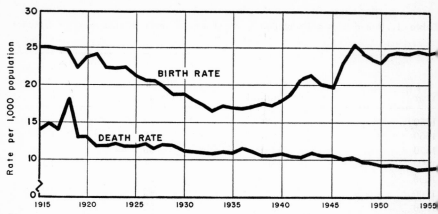

Figure 16.   United States Birth and Death Rates, 1915–1956. (Source: U.S. Department of Commerce, Bureau of the Census.)

prospects for economic security and rising standards of living. If the population reaches a level where any further increase will result in decreasing standards of living for the existing population, Americans will have a very real reason to limit the size of families and to establish and maintain population stability.

OPTIMUM POPULATION—THE IDEAL MAN-LAND RATIO

The population trends that have been noted above will naturally affect resource appraisal. Whether the net result of these population changes and trends will be a better or worse land utilization pattern depends largely on the relationship of population to resources in the various nations. Some countries are more overpopulated than others, but in every case the aim should be the best possible relationship between the supply of and the demand for land, or what might be termed an "ideal man-land ratio."

THE CONCEPT OF OPTIMUM POPULATION

The ideal man-land ratio is often referred to as the "optimum population density," but the word "optimum," or "best," involves subjective appraisal and makes the concept of optimum population a difficult one upon which to secure general agreement and understanding. Since what is best depends upon the basis of appraisal, there are numerous population optima, depending upon the yardstick the appraiser chooses.

The determination of the ideal ratio between the number of people and the area and resources of the land they inhabit is the basic economic problem of land settlement and population. The ideal ratio, expressed in general terms, is that which will give the maximum of human welfare in a certain environment with a given state of development of culture.[20] If we assume that a maximum of creature comforts is worth seeking, the ideal ratio will be attained when " . . . whatever the methods of distribution, per capita production and per capita consumption are at the highest point attainable." [21]

It has also been stated in terms of highest marginal output. If, however, the population of an area is so sparse that additional units will give a larger marginal return, the average output of the group will be raised by population increments beyond the point of highest marginal returns.[22] Some believe that maximization of human happiness is a logical ideal, to be served by all human instrumentalities and activities, although there are many who do not accept this concept.[23] Since welfare and happiness depend upon a great number of considerations other than number of people and quantity or character of economic resources, this concept of maximization of human happiness cannot be used as the criterion of an optimum relation between size of population and available resources.

The concept of maximum economic welfare has similar limitations, for economic welfare includes production, distribution, and consumption of economic goods and services. If this concept were used as the standard to determine the optimum or ideal man-land ratio, the entire field of distribution and consumption, as well as production—in short, every major field of economic theory—would be involved in an adequate explanation of the ideal man-land ratio.

Quantity and quality of resources and the technique of utilizing them are constantly changing in such dynamic economies as characterize modern civilizations. Consequently, in order to determine theoretically what size of population is needed for highest per capita productivity, one must assume a given state of the arts and constant resources of land and raw materials but (theoretically) variable population. The distribution of the product, marketing organization, and monetary system must also be assumed to be such that the output of the productive process at full capacity will be taken off the market for consumption.

If the concept of the maximization of product per unit of cost is accepted as the normative end of economy, economic theorists should be able to work out the concept of the optimum or ideal population in

[20] Cf. Reuter, *op. cit.*, p. 13.

[21] Glenn E. Hoover, "The Quantitative Optimum of Population," *Annals of the American Academy of Political and Social Science*, Vol. 162, July, 1932, p. 198.

[22] Cf. J. D. Black, "Agricultural Population in Relation to Agricultural Resources," *Annals of the American Academy of Political and Social Science*, Vol. 188, November, 1936, p. 206. Black indicates that the highest average output per capita of population is affected by the degree of inequality of the distribution of resources among population groups, and by the average standard of living.

[23] A. B. Wolfe, "The Theory of Optimum Population," *Annals of the American Academy of Political and Social Science*, Vol. 188, November, 1936, p. 244.

definite, limited, understandable (though theoretical) terms. In any case this theory of the optimum population definitely relates the available units of labor to the land resource and acknowledges the far-reaching effects of the technological and societal arts upon the utilization practices and productiveness of man working with land.

Determination of the proper economic population of a restricted area is more difficult than its determination for an entire nation because of potential migration in and out of the area.[24] Nevertheless, governmental efforts in recent years to adapt population more closely to resources necessitate determination of population needs and capacities of limited areas such, for example, as those to be served by the Missouri or the Columbia rivers.

In any case, the theory of the optimum or ideal man-land ratio, although abstract, is very useful in clearing up some of the misconceptions about the effects of declining population. Such misconceptions are caused chiefly by the widespread tendency to consider the size or quantity of the population alone, rather than its quality, its standard of living, and the distribution of its income or purchasing power.[25]

METHODS OF ATTAINING OPTIMUM POPULATION

In modern society, many more ways are available to bring about a closer approach to the optimum population than reliance upon population increase or decrease alone. Every improvement in transportation and communication reduces the handicap of space. Improvements in farming methods and increased production efficiency enlarge the human carrying capacity of the soil and extend the point at which optimum population is reached. Adjustments in human institutions such as local government and adjustments in taxes and credit practices to provide more equitable distribution of tax and credit burdens also extend the point of optimum population in agricultural areas. Improvements in leasing arrangements, irrigation, reclamation and drainage development, and inventions—all such improvements tend to extend the point of optimum population.

Certain methods have been used under specific types of conditions during man's history to bring about a better man-land relationship. These have varied from rather minor changes in the organization of farm and business operating units, or in land utilization methods, to sweeping shifts in types of crops raised or in methods of tillage. When other adjustments seemed inadequate, land abandonment and migration to other areas occurred where the cycle of land settlement and development was begun again.

[24] Wolfe, op. cit., p. 248.
[25] Cf. Frank Lorimer, "Population as a Problem in Quality," in Schultz, Food for the World, op. cit., pp. 58–65.

Man can, of course, take a passive attitude, allowing natural forces to bring about necessary adjustments between population and resources; or he can take the initiative in securing a better man-land ratio through intelligent study and action. The modern age of science assumes that man can play an important part in securing desirable adjustments in the man-land ratio.

MIGRATION

Migration, or movement of people from one area to another, is motivated largely by economic opportunity. People move from areas of low opportunity to areas offering greater economic, social, or cultural advantages. Theoretically, at least, a highly mobile population tends to adjust itself to land resources, by migration, to secure the greatest possible economic, social, and cultural advantages, and this adjustment tends to establish equilibrium of population and opportunity.

Although migration tends to establish a better balance between population and economic resources, it often fails to do so. International migration—that is, movements of peoples from one nation to another—has in many cases failed to achieve more satisfactory man-land relationships. Relatively heavily populated nations have adopted colonization programs intended to absorb their excess population. The emigration had little or no effect upon population numbers and growth, because relieving overpopulation by emigration made life easier for those who remained, and the people left at home tended to have more children, or fewer babies died since there were increased economic opportunities.

It is generally recognized that two consequences of a migration—a lower death rate and a higher birth rate—tend to result in a population increase that offsets the drain of emigration.[26] If the area into which the people have migrated is a rich undeveloped area, the increased population numbers may bring about an increase in total wealth and in total per capita income and higher levels of living. The movement of people out of the older area does not, in itself, bring about a permanent solution of the problem of the ideal man-land ratio, since the older area, having fewer people than before, tends to breed back to its former level. Although migration may bring about some minor and perhaps temporary improvements, it should not be considered an entirely satisfactory long-run solution of the problem of attaining the ideal man-land ratio.

POPULATION POLICIES

Various policies have been adopted by man to influence population numbers. Infanticide, and the killing of the old, sick, or useless members of society, or hastening their death by poverty and neglect were encouraged

[26] Cf. Reuter, *op. cit.*, p. 213.

in some earlier societies. Abortion; sex taboos; passive acceptance of recurring epidemics, famines, and similar catastrophes; war; emigration; and contraceptive practices have all been used to a greater or less degree to reduce population or retard population increase. On the other hand, many societies have inaugurated policies to stimulate increase of their numbers. Princes and political and military leaders have desired large and growing populations for better protection against predatory neighboring rulers or to make possible expansion of their own rule over larger territories. Closely associated with this political stimulation of population increase is the economic motive of having large and growing populations to provide cheap labor for production.

Practically all population policies practiced by social groups have been designed to retard or to stimulate increase, with no attention paid, in most cases, to the improvement or injury of the quality of the stock through such policies. In recent years a number of countries have adopted specific policies to meet population problems that have developed because of the downward trend in birth rates. Practically all these modern policies are designed to encourage births. During the thirties Nazi Germany adopted a comprehensive policy for the promotion of births, and for a time it seemed to accomplish a considerable net increase in the birth rate.

The net effect of modern efforts to increase fertility in various nations has, for the most part, been rather insignificant.[27] Apparently the economic inducements to increase birth rates have not been sufficiently large in the population policies followed by these nations. Cultural factors are greater modifying forces; at least they are sufficiently strong so that they have not been overcome to the point of achieving any significant increase in births.

FUTURE MAN-LAND ADJUSTMENTS

The areas of the world considered most likely for future settlement and emigration include parts of Canada, Africa, Australia, South America, Siberia, and certain islands in the South Pacific. Most of the remaining pioneer lands are considered "marginal" in climate, fertility, and transport.[28] Although there are many political, physical, and economic difficulties to be overcome in settling these areas, modern science has vastly widened the earth's area that is satisfactory for human habitation and

[27] The increase in the German birth rate from 14.7 in 1933 to 18.0 in 1934, and a further increase to 19.7 in 1938 and to 20 in 1940 is the only example of any significant increase accompanying modern population policies effected by any nation. This increase was very temporary, and with the progress of the war the Nazi birth rate declined rapidly.

[28] Isaiah Bowman (ed.), *Limits of Land Settlement: A Report on Present-Day Possibilities,* New York: Council on Foreign Relations, Inc., 1937.

rowth. Facts show that a much greater growth of population has oc-
urred in the four centuries of modern history than in all the thousands
f years before.

Sauer argues that in modern history cultural resources have been
iffused, in contrast with prior history whose cultures were in large
measure self-contained, so that it is difficult to find areas that have not
eceived the cultural goods of other parts of the world.[29]

This implies that the population of the world has become permanently
nactive; that there will not be any extensive waves of emigration and
olonization among the continents; and that the internal shifts in popula-
ion that will occur will be relatively minor in scope. Hence, the prospect
or population redistribution in the future is one in which the man-land
djustments to be made will be primarily by people already inhabiting a
;iven area.

All of this does not mean that there will not be important international
ivalries and conquests of less aggressive, more backward cultures by the
nore advanced, aggressive ones, or attempts by various nations to gain
ontrol of important natural resources for exploitation. However, it does
nean that these conquests and controls that may be established will
)robably involve political and economic changes, rather than wholesale
migration of populations. There will, of course, be important changes in
)opulation density within nations and within continents to bring about
. better man-land ratio; but relative population densities among the
ontinents may not change greatly from those of the present.

The population of the world is increasing by 25 to 30 million persons
innually. About a tenth of this increase is accounted for by the popula-
ion rise in the United States. Such increases cannot be taken lightly.

A sound approach to the problem of future man-land relationships
equires a balanced consideration of the potentialities for increasing
)opulation and for increasing food production. Man does have the ability
o limit his numbers at a point short of the Malthusian survival level.
[n addition, he can take steps needed to provide for the growing land
equirements for living space, and for food, fiber, fuel, minerals, and
)ther land products. New lands may be brought into production, present
ands used more intensively, new techniques of production and processing
leveloped, and many other applications of science and technology em-
)loyed to increase the output of goods and services required by a growing
)opulation.

The big problem is not whether the world population can feed itself
but whether the peoples and nations of the world are willing to make and
iccept the economic, political, and social adaptations that are necessary

[29] Carl O. Sauer, "The Prospect for the Redistribution of Population," Bowman,
Limits of Land Settlement, op. cit., Chap. I, p. 9.

if all the people are to enjoy a richer and more satisfying life.[30] Only time will reveal how man meets this great challenge.

REFERENCES FOR FURTHER READING

Annals of the American Academy of Political and Social Science, Vol. 188 November, 1936, pp. 205–328; Vol. 162, July, 1932, pp. 185–205.

Baker, O. E., "Population Trends in Relation to Land Utilization," *Proceedings of the Second International Conference of Agricultural Economists,* George Banta Publishing Company, Menasha, Wis., 1930, pp. 284–306.

Bowman, Isaiah (ed.), *Limits of Land Settlement: A Report on Present-Day Possibilities,* Council on Foreign Relations, Inc., New York, 1937.

Davis, Darrell H., *The Earth and Man,* The Macmillan Company, New York, 1942, Chaps. II and III.

Davis, Joseph S., *The Population Upsurge in the United States,* Food Research Institute, Stanford University, Stanford, Calif., War-Peace Pamphlet No. 12, 1949.

Ely, Richard T., and Wehrwein, George S., *Land Economics,* The Macmillan Company, New York, 1940, Chap. I.

Hertzler, J. O., *The Crisis in World Population,* University of Nebraska Press, Lincoln, 1956.

Johnson, V. Webster, and Barlowe, Raleigh, *Land Problems and Policies,* McGraw-Hill Book Company, Inc., New York, 1954, Chap. VIII.

League of Nations, *World Economic Survey, 1938–39,* Chap. VI.

Malthus, T. R., *Essay on the Principles of Population,* J. M. Dent & Sons, Ltd., London, 1798.

Mead, Elwood, "Land Settlement," *Encyclopaedia of the Social Sciences,* The Macmillian Company, New York, Vol. IX, pp. 53–64.

National Resources Committee, *The Problems of a Changing Population,* Government Printing Office, Washington, D.C., 1938, pp. 6–73.

Reuter, E. B., *Population Problems,* rev. ed., J. B. Lippincott Company, Philadelphia, 1937.

Schultz, Theodore W. (ed.), *Food for the World,* University of Chicago Press, Chicago, 1945, pp. 36–65.

Sonne, H. Christian, *Crucial Issues in World Perspective—1957,* National Planning Association, Washington, D.C., Special Report No. 43, December, 1956.

Thompson, Warren S., and Whelpton, P. K., *Estimation of Future Population of the United States,* National Resources Planning Board, Government Printing Office, Washington, D.C., 1943, pp. 3–38.

Timmons, John F., and Murray, William G. (eds.), *Land Problems and Policies,* Iowa State College Press, Ames, Iowa, 1950, Chap. III.

Zimmermann, Erich W., *World Resources and Industries,* rev. ed., Harper & Brothers, New York, 1951, Chap. VIII.

[30] Cf. V. Webster Johnson and Raleigh Barlowe, *Land Problems and Policies,* McGraw-Hill, 1954, p. 193.

chapter 6

LAND REQUIREMENTS FOR SPECIFIC USES

AGRICULTURAL LAND REQUIREMENTS

Trend in Agricultural Land Utilization—Capacity to Produce Farm Products—Industrial Markets for Farm Products—The Agricultural Prospect

FOREST LAND REQUIREMENTS

Total Area Available for Forestry—Land Needed for Forest Use—Relation of Current Growth to Drain—Balancing the Timber Budget

RECREATIONAL LAND REQUIREMENTS

Land Needed for Recreational Use—A Program of Development to Meet Recreational Needs

MINERAL LAND REQUIREMENTS

Trends in Mineral Land Utilization—Future Supplies of Minerals—Mineral Control and Peace

WATER REQUIREMENTS

Irrigation—Drainage—Flood Control—Hydroelectric Power

TRANSPORTATION LAND REQUIREMENTS

Prospective Use of Land for Transportation—Unification of Transportation Services

URBAN LAND REQUIREMENTS

The Future of Cities—Improvement of Urban Living

THE PROBLEM of achieving long-range balance between population pressure on the one hand and food supply and needed goods and service from land utilization on the other is primarily one of balancing th economic supply of land for various uses against the demand for variou land products. The first step is to determine the extent and nature of th demand for land in terms of land-area requirements. The second step i to find land adequate to meet these requirements.

In determining land requirements of the world or a nation, all the use to which land can be put to provide the goods and services desired by mar must be considered. These include production of food, fibers, nonfoor crops, forest products, needed watershed and water resources, wildlife an recreation areas, transportation, industry, residential areas, and othe essential uses. Some of these requirements involve multiple land uses still others involve competitive or conflicting uses. In general, land area will be used for those purposes that will return the landowners, operators or the public the greatest profits or want satisfactions.

AGRICULTURAL LAND REQUIREMENTS

There is a tendency in modern nations for agriculture to decline ir relative importance as invention, technology, and industry progress. The United States is no exception. The proportion of the total labor force employed in agriculture, the proportion of the total population living or farms, the proportion of the total national wealth comprised of agricul tural assets, and the proportion of the gross national product and income contributed by agriculture have all declined in the United States during the past several decades.

In view of this trend, what are the prospects for agricultural land utilization in the next four decades? What will be the trend in acreage devoted to cropland? What will be the effect of tray agriculture, or pro duction of foodstuffs and fibers with chemicals? What effect will prospec tive dietary changes have upon the demand for certain agricultural prod ucts? What effect will the sweeping changes in farm technology have on agricultural land utilization practices?

TREND IN AGRICULTURAL LAND UTILIZATION

The acreage of all land in farms in the United States has more than doubled since 1880. The increase has been a continuous one until 1950, but the acreage devoted to the production of crops has not shown any corresponding tendency to increase (see Table 2).

The per capita consumption of food in the United States has been re markably stable since World War I. The per capita crop acreage harvested in the United States has declined during the last half-century (see Table 2), indicating that less acreage is used today than formerly for nonhuman consumption. Prices of agricultural products have varied most, rather than consumption. The relatively constant per capita food and fiber requirement makes the comparative rates of technological advance in agriculture and total population growth of major importance to the occupational role of the farm plant in the economy.[1]

Table 2. United States Population, Number of Farms, Land in Farms, and Cropland Harvested, 1880–1955

			Land in Farms		Cropland Harvested		
Year	Total Population	Number of Farms	Total Acres	Average per Farm	Total Acres	Average per Farm	Average per Capita
1880	50,262,000	4,008,907	536,081,835	133.7	166,186,584	41.4	3.306
1890	63,056,000	4,564,641	623,218,619	136.5	218,705,564	48.1	3.484
1900	76,129,000	5,737,372	838,591,774	146.2	282,218,280	49.2	3.707
1910	92,267,000	6,363,502	878,798,325	138.1	311,293,382	48.9	3.374
1920	107,190,000	6,448,343	955,883,715	148.2	348,548,549	54.0	3.252
1930	123,091,000	6,288,648	986,771,016	156.2	359,242,091	57.1	2.919
1940	131,669,000	6,096,799	1,060,852,374	174.0	321,242,430	52.6	2.440
1945	139,928,000	5,859,169	1,141,615,000	190.1	346,534,000	57.7	2.523
1950	151,683,000	5,382,162	1,158,566,000	215.3	344,399,000	66.0	2.351
1955	165,248,000	4,782,393	1,158,233,000	242.2	332,860,000	69.6	2.014

Sources: U.S. Department of Commerce, Bureau of the Census, *16th Census of the United States (1940)*, Agriculture, Vol. II, Chap. I, Table 4. U.S. Department of Commerce, 1945 Census of Agriculture—Table 1. U.S. Department of Agriculture, *Crops and Markets*, Government Printing Office, Vol. 23, No. 1, and U.S. Department of Commerce, Bureau of the Census, *Statistical Abstract of the United States, 1956*, Government Printing Office, pp. 5, 619, 621.

The decline in the foreign market for United States agricultural products after World War I released some 25 million acres of cropland, much of which reverted to pasture or other comparatively extensive uses under the Agricultural Adjustment Administration program begun in 1933. The change in position of the United States from that of a debtor to a creditor nation, combined with high American tariffs, intense nationalism, high foreign tariffs, and expansion of production in exporting nations, affected our foreign market adversely. The concentration of gold in the United States resulted in reducing, during the interwar period, the purchasing power of many importing nations that formerly bought considerable quantities of American agricultural products. Until international trade is freed from many arbitrary controls and restrictions, American farmers cannot look to the foreign market to use a large portion of their products.

[1] John M. Brewster, "Farm Technological Advance and Total Population Growth," *Journal of Farm Economics*, August, 1945, p. 512.

Under conditions of full employment at home and active foreign trade
per capita consumption of many agricultural products will be higher tha
it was in the interwar years and for some commodities higher than it wa
during World War II. Greatest increases in the demand for food wil
occur among those types of products most needed in American diets from
a nutritional standpoint. Largest increases in per capita consumption
should be registered in milk, citrus fruits, and fresh, frozen, and canned
vegetables. However, if agricultural efficiency continues to increase, total
requirements for all agricultural production can be met by cultivation o
some 330 million acres of cropland, or less, or 30 million or more acre
less than that harvested during World War II.[2]

CAPACITY TO PRODUCE FARM PRODUCTS

It seems logical to conclude, therefore, that the agricultural industry o
the United States, with parity prices, full employment, and active foreign
trade, can produce an adequate and tasty diet for all the people, and
still run the risk of piling up surpluses. If unemployment or general busi
ness depression develops, American diets will be restricted and heavy
agricultural surpluses in several commodities will occur.

About half the farms in the United States account for nearly nine
tenths of the total production, and if the market for agricultural products
were available, present farms and labor in farm areas could produce con
siderably more than current output. Many agricultural leaders feel tha
present output could be produced with about half the current farm popu
lation. There seems to be no doubt about agriculture's capacity to pro
duce; the most important factor determining agricultural land utilization
in the future will be capacity to consume.

If all consumers in the United States were to have diets considered
adequate by nutritional experts, vegetable consumption would probably
be increased at least 50 percent, and consumption of dairy products at
least 15 or 25 percent.[3] The problem of increasing the purchasing power
of lower-income groups is one that should have an important place in
American national policy. However, even if this policy is pursued, it is
likely that increases in domestic consumption will be relatively gradual
and will be much greater for some types of products (particularly vege-

[2] See H. R. Tolley, "Agricultural Adjustment and Nutrition," in T. W. Schultz (ed.),
Food for the World, University of Chicago Press, 1945, p. 170.

[3] Tolley, "Agriculture in the American Economy," *American Economic Review,* Vol.
XXX, No. 5, February, 1941, p. 113. It had been estimated that during the depression
years of 1935 to 1939 per capita food consumption was about 15 percent less than it
would have been under full employment conditions. (See J. P. Cavin, "The General
Food Situation," U.S. Department of Agriculture, Bureau of Agricultural Economics,
Address at 22d Annual Agricultural Outlook Conference, Washington, D.C., November
14, 1944.)

tables and dairy products) than for heavy energy foods (particularly cereals or fats). These increases will undoubtedly necessitate significant shifts in the pattern of agricultural land utilization between various crop or livestock products.

Certain technological changes now in progress may completely offset the increased need for agricultural land resulting from expanded domestic consumption. For example, the labor required on an acre of wheat is now less than half the amount needed in the prewar period, 1909 to 1913. The efficiency of producing livestock products has also increased greatly in recent years.

INDUSTRIAL MARKETS FOR FARM PRODUCTS

The main business of the farmer is production of raw materials for food, clothing, and shelter, less than a tenth of the total farm output being used as industrial raw materials.[4] Some examples of the industrial uses of farm products are the production of leather, glue, gelatin, soap, greases, glycerin, and fertilizers from animal carcasses; starch for sizing and finishing textiles and paper; dextrin adhesive; glucose used in the rayon and leather industries; and a whole list of industrial chemicals and solvents from cereal grains.[5]

Expansion of the industrial market for farm products would not result in any immediate large increase in demand for farm products. Increased industrial use of farm products will be very gradual, and industrial use of some farm products will actually decline in the years ahead because of competition from other raw materials. New outlets for farm products as industrial raw materials appear limited. In the aggregate, nevertheless, and over a period of years, expanded industrial use may be a significant factor in future demand for farm products.

THE AGRICULTURAL PROSPECT

Effects of these changes and trends upon American agriculture will be in the direction of increased governmental control, or group controls of one form or another to bring agricultural output more into line with prospective demand. Present cropland acreage seems to be adequate for decades immediately ahead, and if the rate of population increase declines, or the foreign market improves, or technological advance is checked, the trend during the next few years will be to take some acres

---

[4] Over 80 percent of the entire farm output is used as food, exclusive of tobacco products and beverages of all sorts. Another 5 percent goes into clothing. Probably less than 10 percent is used as industrial raw materials. (See Brewster, *op. cit.*, p. 510.)

[5] For a more complete analysis of present and potential industrial markets for U.S. agricultural products, see W. B. Van Arsdel, "The Industrial Market for Farm Products," U.S. Department of Agriculture *Yearbook,* 1940, pp. 606–626.

out of intensive crop uses and divert them to pasture, forest, or soil-build ing uses.

During these years, there will be excellent opportunities to develop soi conservation practices that will restore much of the former fertility o many agricultural soils and raise the level of productiveness of agricul tural land resources generally. In the more distant future, if full employ ment prevails, nutritional levels rise, the foreign market improves, and population numbers continue to increase, agricultural lands of the na tion will be in a better position to meet resulting increased demands fo agricultural products.

Viewed from the domestic standpoint or that of the world as a whole agriculture will probably not secure any extensive increase in acreage fo producing crops or livestock in competition with other uses for land ir the immediate future. In many nations the agricultural land area wil tend to remain stationary or decline, losing to forests through reforesta tion programs, to recreation, and to other uses, with crop acreages reduced by regrassing programs, soil conservation, and soil improvement; in othei nations, slight increases, and, perhaps in a few cases, significant increase in agricultural land may result.

FOREST LAND REQUIREMENTS

Whether the amount of land devoted to forest use in the future will be more or less than current acreage depends upon a great variety of supply and demand conditions. How many acres under various levels of intensive and extensive management will be needed to meet the demands for forest products in the years ahead? Is the consumption of forest products de clining because of the use of wood substitutes, or is the use of forest products increasing? In order to meet the demands of the future, how much of the total acreage suitable for forest use in the United States will probably be devoted to forestry?

In competition with other uses for these lands, will forestry secure them, or will our domestic requirements be met by importing forest products from other nations that may be able to supply them at a cost lower than that at which we could produce them ourselves? Will we fol low a policy in the years ahead of trying to build up and maintain our forest resources so that the annual drain to meet current requirements will be offset or more than equaled by the annual growth?

There are many unpredictable factors that make appraisal of the future requirements for forest products for any given nation difficult. However, from certain data available showing current trends regarding availability of land for forestry and the probable acreage that will be needed for forest uses, some close approximation can be made of the supply and de mand requirements for balancing the timber budget of any given nation.

TOTAL AREA AVAILABLE FOR FORESTRY

In an absolute sense, the total area available for foresty in any given ation is the total acreage that is physically capable of growing trees. Iowever, the economic supply that will be available for forest use will epend upon the character of the competition among various types of tilization such as agricultural, transportation, recreation, mineral, and rban. As a rule, forestry secures those lands which are not suitable for gricultural production or which, because of competition within agricul- are, are submarginal for production of crops and pasture.

Ordinarily, forestry is the least intensive use that can be made of land nd will, in the last analysis, secure the use of those lands which do not nd their highest and best use in any of the other major use types. Agri- ultural use is ordinarily the next lowest use compared with transporta- ion, recreation, mining, and urban utilization. Consequently, it is fairly afe to predict that within a given nation the area which will be available or forestry will be that which, through competitive processes with other and uses, currently is used for forests, plus the increase or decrease in this rea which is likely to accompany the future use of land for agricultural urposes.

In some countries, the demand for agricultural products is such that the reas devoted to agricultural use will increase at the expense of forest ands in the years ahead. In many areas, clearing of forested areas will ccur and the lands will not be reforested, but used for agricultural pro- uction. In other areas, however, advancing technology, declining popu- ation trends, changes in diet, and associated factors and conditions will esult in a reduced demand for agricultural land. In such cases some land vill be released from agricultural use for forestry.

In a relatively young nation like Canada, considerable cutting of forests vill continue in the future and much of the land will probably be put nto agriculture and other nonforest uses; but in a nation like the United tates, where a considerable amount of agricultural land abandonment as already occurred, where forest areas have already been largely cut over r put into agricultural and other nonforest uses, and where the agricul- ural prospect is such that the future demand for farm products may re- uire somewhat fewer rather than more acres, the forest area will prob- bly expand.

The present forest area of the United States is about 665 million acres, r nearly twice as much as farm cropland. It is estimated that an addi- ional 54 million acres of abandoned agricultural land is available for orest use. The original forest area covered about 900 million acres, or lightly less than half the land surface of the nation, so that even with the nost optimistic estimates for the next few decades, the forest land area

will be considerably less than the original forested area, or the tota
acreage physically suitable for forest production.[6]

LAND NEEDED FOR FOREST USE

Will the above acreages be sufficient to meet the forest needs of th
United States?

A study of timber statistics reveals a rather close relationship betweer
per capita consumption and available supplies of timber. Timber require
ments, as they may determine land requirements, are largely influencee
by the available abundance or scarcity of timber, and of the land avail
able for producing it. The United States is currently failing to balance it
forest budget, not because there is a deficiency of forest land, but becaus
of the failure to maintain forests in a productive or sustained-yield con
dition.

Lumber consumption in the United States reached a peak about 1906
with 45 billion board feet, or 525 board feet per capita, and has been de
creasing since that time, in contrast to the trend of manufacturing and o
population. Lumber consumption declined from the 1906 level to 36¼
billion, or 275 board feet per capita, in 1929, the peak of prosperity anc
business activity following World War I. Consumption to World War I.
averaged about 32 billion board feet annually. This reduced consumptior
is attributable principally to the decline in lumber used directly in con
struction.

The tentative future United States normal lumber consumption, assum
ing that there is an adequate supply of timber to draw upon, is estimatec
to be about 32 billion board feet annually.[7] This amount may be in
creased considerably for several postwar years, because of the government'!
housing program, begun in 1946 to provide low-cost houses for World
War II veterans, and the large housing needs of the nation that accumu
lated during the war when priorities prevented home construction.

The use of wood for fuel has declined in recent decades, but it is
generally felt that a low point has been reached and that the yearly fuel
requirements of the United States may be roughly estimated as approxi
mately 61 million cords, of which 42 million may be charged as a direct
drain on the commercial forests of the nation.[8]

[6] The data given apply only to continental United States. The total area of forests
in Alaska is estimated at approximately 70 million acres, largely unexploited and
representing a potential supply over and above the acreage data cited.

[7] National Resources Planning Board, *Report to the President of the United States,*
Government Printing Office, December 1, 1934, pp. 137–138. See also R. D. Marsh and
W. H. Gibbons, "Forest Resource Conservation," U.S. Department of Agriculture
Yearbook, 1940, p. 488.

[8] Marsh and Gibbons use a figure of 70 million cords as the estimated future annual
drain for fuel wood. The development of farm forestry and improved woodburning
stoves may bring about an upward trend in the use of fuel wood. (*Ibid.,* p. 138.)

The United States imports a considerable amount of its pulpwood for paper production and other pulp products. Ultimate self-sufficiency in pulpwood and a continuing upward trend in paper consumption will necessitate a large increase over present annual consumption. It is estimated that future annual requirements for pulpwood will average 25 million cords annually, or 2500 million cubic feet of timber.[9]

Future requirements for miscellaneous forest products may be estimated at approximately the average consumption of recent years—namely, two and one-half billion cubic feet yearly, because trends in consumption of miscellaneous forest products largely offset one another. Wood is one of the most flexible of organic products and is adaptable to many uses. The uses of wood in a highly industrialized nation are constantly changing. Substitutes and competing materials take the place of wood in many of its uses, but on the other hand, these competing materials may cause increased demand for wood in other forms. In other words, wood loses ground in some uses, but other new uses continually arise that expand the demands for wood. The logical tendency in a modern economy is for the demand for wood, particularly structural timber, to increase; but this tendency is definitely checked as supplies become more limited and prices increase.[10]

The estimated total annual forest requirements are roughly 16½ billion cubic feet, or about 55 million board feet. This amount is approximately equal to the annual drain on United States forests for the period 1925–1929. A margin of safety of from three to five billion cubic feet to provide for possible future calamities, such as the recent chestnut blight, which might wipe out entire species, and to provide for holding or increasing an export trade in forest products, and for new uses, should be added to the 16½ billion cubic feet as the estimated normal timber requirements.[11]

RELATION OF CURRENT GROWTH TO DRAIN

Current annual timber growth on our present forest areas, allowing for the doubtful economic availability of some of the land and the commercial value of some species, is only about three-fifths of the probable future annual requirements. In order to increase the growth to meet future needs, a well-planned program of forest management must be effected. It is estimated that such a program applied to all forest lands of

[9] *Ibid.*

[10] F. J. Hallauer, "Our National Timber Requirements," in *A National Plan for American Forestry*, Government Printing Office, 1933, Vol. I, pp. 245–297.

[11] C. E. Behre and E. N. Munns, "The Area Which Can and Should Be Used for Forestry" in *A National Plan for American Forestry*, Vol. II, p. 1235. Behre and Munns use a billion cubic feet as a reasonable margin of safety; but Marsh and Gibbons use 3800 million as their margin for new uses, for export, and for a safety factor.

the United States would increase the annual growth from the present 11 billion to 21 billion cubic feet.[12]

This program should include a combination of intensive forestry, extensive forestry, and simple protection. Part of the shortage may be made up by natural restocking of available lands now lying idle, part by increasing the productive area by planting, including afforestation of some additional acreage of abandoned farm lands, but most of it will probably have to be brought about by building up the existing growing stock through better fire protection and more intensive management.

Students of forest economics recommend that since the most unsatisfactory aspect of our present forest situation, from the standpoint of timber use, is the tremendous impoverishment of growing stocks in the eastern regions, every advantage should be taken of the existing stands in the East, and they should be developed into adequate growing stock as the beginning and major part of a national forest land policy.

BALANCING THE TIMBER BUDGET

In order to assure an annual production equal to normal estimated requirements, areas available for commercial timber use must be managed in a way that will build up the growing stock. This means considerable intensification of management, even on publicly owned lands. If the 85 million acres of commercial timber now in public ownership are handled according to the plan, intensive forestry must also be practiced on 62.3 million acres of private land, extensive forestry on 243.3 million, and in addition adequate fire protection on another 69.2 million acres. The distribution of these lands is shown in Figure 17.

Heavy emphasis should be placed upon improved management practices to secure sustained yield in the Middle Atlantic and southern regions. The South has many important advantages for forest use. It is an area well adapted to forest production from the standpoint of climate and soil and produces a relatively rapid growth of types of timber that are commercially very valuable. Moreover, forests in the southern regions would be much closer to the large future consuming centers than forest areas on the Pacific Coast, where about a fourth of our present timber supplies are now secured. Moreover, the South has serious land-use adjustment problems growing out of the declining export market for cotton, and the necessity, from the standpoint of soil conservation and erosion control, of developing more diversified land-use programs.

On many of these lands, forestry will probably play a very impor-

---

[12] This is the estimate of the Technical Committee on Forestry and Primary Forest Products of the United Nations Interim Commission on Food and Agriculture. See *News Release of U.S. Department of Agriculture*, Forest Service, Washington, D.C., August 25, 1945.

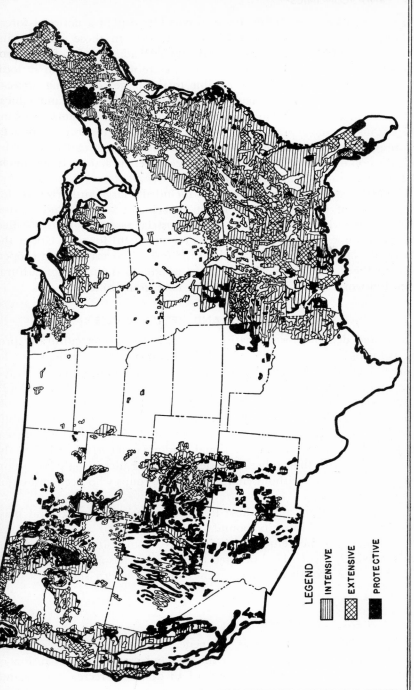

LEGEND

▦ INTENSIVE

▨ EXTENSIVE

■ PROTECTIVE

Figure 17. Recommended Dominant Intensity of Management of Forest Land in the United States. (Source: *Forest Land Resources, Requirements, Problems, and Policy,* National Resources Board, Government Printing Office, 1935.)

tant part in the future. Thus, it seems possible to plan a national fores
program that will increase our forest production in those areas (prin
cipally the South) which are climatically well-adapted for forest pro
duction, where needed land-use adjustments are most acute, and in loca
tions which will be relatively accessible to the large consuming areas.

The forest policy of any nation should include research and educa
tional or extension activities that would look toward the improvemen
of forest-management practices, discovery of new uses for forest products
encouragement of private effort for improvement, forest management by
the diffusion of information concerning best forest practices, tree growth
silvicultural practices, and related matters.

The McSweeney-McNary Act of 1928 included a large authorization fo
the support of the government forest experiment stations and labora
tories, and provision for economic and industrial research greatly needec
to lay the proper economic foundations for successful forestry. Under the
Clarke-McNary Act, authority is given the federal government to coöper
ate with the states in extension work on woodland tracts, as agricultura
extension work is now carried on by the land grant colleges.

RECREATIONAL LAND REQUIREMENTS

Increased demand for recreation is characteristic of a culturally pro
gressive people. Recreation furnished through private enterprise is inade
quate to meet these increased demands, principally because (1) risk is too
great and profit prospects too small in many recreation ventures, and (2)
many recreational opportunities provided by private enterprise are be
yond the financial means of people who may need them most. Public
agencies have therefore taken the responsibility for developing recrea
tional facilities—directly, as recreational land-use enterprises, or indirectly
in connection with their other activities, providing increasingly important
recreational services, without charge, to many groups who need and enjoy
these services most.

Greatest expansion along these lines has occurred in parks and play
grounds created within city boundaries, and national and state parks
forest reserves, game refuges, primitive areas, and similar recreationa
lands. Privately owned land devoted to recreation has also increased con
siderably. The growth of dude ranches in the western states is a good
example.

LAND NEEDED FOR RECREATIONAL USE

In spite of these developments, it is generally conceded that recreational
facilities have not kept pace with the demand created by expansion of
leisure and modern thinking in regard to desirable recreational stand-

ards. Undoubtedly, as shorter working days and increased leisure are made available through the advance of science and technology, the amount of recreational land will increase. Improvements in transportation methods, particularly improvement of the automobile and airplane, will make it possible to use more intensively areas now only partially or slightly used for recreational purposes.

The prospective increase in recreational land use is reflected in estimates showing acreages, which in 1960 will be, or should be, utilized for recreational purposes. These estimates are: national parks and monuments, 32 million acres (more than three times the 1935 area); state, county, and municipal parks, 10 million acres (nearly triple the 1935 amount); bird and game refuges, 38 million acres more than 1935 acreages.[13]

The peculiarities of land in recreational use give rise to the major problems associated with recreational land development and utilization. The following problems are of particular significance: (1) the close interdependence and needed integration of recreational and other important land uses; (2) division of responsibility and control between public and private owners; and (3) division of responsibility and control among local, state, and federal public agencies.

A PROGRAM OF DEVELOPMENT TO MEET RECREATIONAL NEEDS

Areas of primarily recreational value should be designated and conserved unimpaired as such and should not be encroached upon by other commercial uses. Because recreational use of land often must be concomitant with other uses, provision for recreation must be included in an overall national plan of land development and conservation. Accordingly, the National Resources Board in the early thirties drew up a plan for development and conservation of recreational resources in the United States based upon coördination of existing agencies of government and division of responsibility among local, state, and federal public agencies.

This plan advances the following program to meet the needs of recreational lands for the American people in the years ahead: [14]

1. Supplying facilites for the day-by-day recreational needs of the people is primarily a local responsibility. The focal point and foundation of a national recreation plan are within the municipalities and their immediate environs. Essential recreational requirements of any municipality in-

---

[13] National Resources Planning Board, *Report to the President,* p. 109. The authors of "What About the Year 2000?" estimate a probable ultimate need of between 5 and 10 million acres for state parks alone. (Joint Committee on Bases of Sound Land Policy, *What About the Year 2000?* Federated Societies on Planning and Parks, Washington, D.C., 1929.)

[14] National Resources Board, *Recreational Use of Land in the United States, Report on Land Planning,* Government Printing Office, 1940, pp. 17–29.

clude adequate and properly distributed play areas for children and adults, "intown" small landscaped parks, and a few large parks.

In municipalities of 10,000 inhabitants or over, 1 acre of recreation area to each 100 persons is a satisfactory minimum, divided as follows: children's playgrounds, 12 percent, composed of units 3 to 8 acres in extent neighborhood playfields, 15 to 18 percent; miscellaneous recreation areas an undertermined percentage, depending on the kinds of recreation to be provided; the total of these three types amounting to 30 to 50 percent of the whole. The balance would be composed of equitably distributed neighborhood or "intown" parks and large areas characterized by land scape or natural features. To provide communities of less than 10,000 people with the essential components of a city park and playground sys tem, the ratio of recreational area to population should be about as fol lows: 5000 to 10,000 people, 1 acre to each 75 inhabitants; 2500 to 5000 people, 1 acre to 60; 1000 to 2500 people, 1 acre to 50; and communities under 1000 people, 1 acre to each 40 residents.

On the basis of the above standards, the minimum recreational area for cities of 10,000 or more inhabitants would total nearly 600,000 acres for the nation as a whole, and for towns and cities with less than 10,000 people, the minimum recreational acres would total more than 362,000. Thus, nearly a million acres, or about 10 percent of the total area of all lands devoted to municipal uses in the United States, would be devoted to municipal recreation.

2. Provision of parks and playgrounds for the population of metro politan regions comes next in importance in the national recreational scheme. Planning in this sphere should include recreational service for residents of smaller "satellite" cities as well as for those of the principal cities, and for those of rural farm and rural nonfarm areas. Two major zones of development are involved: the area of fairly heavy population surrounding the central city, when the types of recreation area to be pro vided are analogous to those within the municipality; and the more sparsely populated area within approximately two hours of automobile travel of the central city. A number of cities have gone well beyond their borders in acquiring parks. Counties, special metropolitan park districts, and states may all act as agencies for provision of metropolitan parks. Regardless of the agency or agencies involved, however, planning should be on a unified basis for the entire metropolitan region, usually extend ing for some 40 to 60 miles from the heart of the central city.

3. Every state has areas either of such high scenic value or of such high value for active recreation, or both, or of such interest from the scientific, archeological, or historical standpoint, that their use tends to be state-wide in character. Requisition of such areas and their development and operation are primarily functions of the state, but this should not

reclude joint participation by the state and such community or communities as might receive a high proportion of the resulting benefits.

4. Taking the nation as a whole, there are areas of such superlative quality, because of their primeval character or scenic excellence, or historical, archeological, or scientific importance, or because of some combination of these factors, that they are objects of national significance. It is the responsibility of the federal government to acquire and administer these.

Federal responsibility is emphasized especially in the case of primeval wildernesses. Remaining areas of primeval condition are few. A wilderness reserve ordinarily should be large—at least one-quarter million acres, and even two million acres may be too small if its boundaries are not properly located—for example, Yellowstone Park, which contains little natural range for its elk, deer, antelope, and bighorn. It is obvious that the task of saving the primeval must be largely a federal responsibility.

Other fields for federal responsibility are the ocean and Great Lakes beaches. These are sought extensively by people living great distances from them. They are unlikely to be acquired by the states to a sufficient extent, and the federal government should acquire and administer a representative group of them.

It should be evident from the above that a national recreation plan that will be adequate to meet the needs of the nation must have local, state, and federal components.

MINERAL LAND REQUIREMENTS

The mineral output of the world for the past 75 years has closely paralleled the expanding volume of industrial production. Metallic minerals have been produced in increasing amounts to meet the demands of the manufacturing, transportation, and communication industries.[15] The mineral fuels—coal, oil, and natural gas—have been required in increasing amounts to meet the greatly expanded world consumption of power, heat, and light. Uranium production has zoomed following development of the atomic bomb in the mid-forties.

TRENDS IN MINERAL LAND UTILIZATION

Output expansion has not been uniform for all minerals or for all countries. Some nations are still in the expanding stage of production; others are on the decline. For the world as a whole, however, the trend has been upward.

Although the trend is generally toward increased mineral resource utilization, present conditions and prospective utilization may vary greatly

---

[15] C. K. Leith, J. W. Furness, and Cleona Lewis, *World Minerals and World Peace,* The Brookings Institution, Washington, D.C., 1943, p. 8.

among specific minerals. In some cases, the trend of utilization is down ward, because of discovery of more useful substitute products or ex haustion of deposits, or a combination of factors. In the case of some othe minerals, utilization remains about stationary, and there are no importan problems of conservation or economic difficulties involved. In still others consumption is expanding rapidly in line with advancing technology, o reserves are comparatively small, and serious economic problems of utili zation and conservation are developing.

It is thus impossible to discuss future mineral land utilization, excep in very general terms, without going into a detailed analysis of individ ual minerals. Suffice it to say here that some nations have already acknowl edged the necessity of establishing policies in which public control an direction are used to conserve vital resources by reducing wastes involve in controlled exploitation and use.

In the United States, private enterprise has been allowed to exploit ex haustible and irreplaceable minerals freely and, with the increasing impor tance of some of the more strategic and critical of these in domestic an defense activities, it is only common sense to expect increased public inter vention or, in some cases, public ownership, to control the use of man minerals on a less wasteful basis.

FUTURE SUPPLIES OF MINERALS

The geography of mineral production has undergone notable shift in the last three decades because of discoveries, commercial exploitatio of deposits already known, exhaustion of older districts, new technologie of extraction and use, and substitution.

The exhaustion of productive mining districts has caused notable shift in mineral production. Some of the most productive mining districts i the United States have reached near-exhaustion. These include: the Com stock lode and the Goldfield district of Nevada; the Leadville district o Colorado; Lake Superior copper of Michigan; certain oil fields in Penn sylvania, Ohio, Kentucky, Texas, Oklahoma, and California; and man others. The United Kingdom was at one time the world's largest produce of tin, copper, lead, and zinc. Today coal is being mined at more tha 3500 feet underground, some from seams as narrow as 14 inches; yet les than 7 percent of the total reserves of coal of the United Kingdom hav as yet been taken from the ground.[16]

The probable life of most mineral deposits and production districts i now approximately known, according to experts. For example, know copper supplies of the United States are estimated to last about 30 years zinc deposits, 20 years; known oil, less than 20 years, and prospective oi possibly 40 years; Lake Superior iron ores of present commercial grades

16 *Ibid.,* p. 89.

30 years; coal, upwards of 3000 years; natural gas, 33 years; and mercury, 5 years.[17] However, long before the exhaustion period, there will be curtailment of production forced by increasing difficulties of mining.

Technological improvements have greatly widened the range of useful minerals and increased the amounts available for use. The substitution of more abundant materials for scarce minerals helps to ease the problem of supply. Some examples of technological advance include better ventilation methods that permit lowering of the effective depth to which mining can be carried; the flotation process of concentrating ores, making it possible to exploit large tonnages of low-grade copper ores; and purification of smelter and other gases providing important supplies of by-product metals. Whereas the encroachment of substitutes has often been feared as bringing about the end of a given mineral industry, it cannot be proved statistically, at least up to the present time, that any substitutions yet underaken have materially changed world requirements for the principal minerals.

MINERAL CONTROL AND PEACE

A modern war cannot be fought without huge quantities of a few minerals, and smaller amounts of many others. For example, in World War II, nearly a hundred minerals were in use. If accumulation of minerals for war purposes is to be prevented, two essential conditions must be met: (1) There must be preponderant possession of the world's mineral resources by those who elect to prevent would-be aggressors from storing up supplies; and (2) machinery for the control of minerals must be in operation before the actual outbreak of war.[18]

Effective administration of a mineral-control plan would require close coöperation of all mineral-producing nations. Either mineral resources would have to be continuously allocated by the overall governing body to the various nations in the light of peacetime needs or, as a minimum, controls would have to be instituted at any moment when investigation indicated that a certain nation or certain nations might be starting to build up abnormal supplies.

The perfection and use of the atomic bomb by the United States at the close of World War II, and its appalling effectiveness, emphasized the great need of a strong world organization to establish and maintain world peace. Such a world organization with adequate powers and the full coöperation of a majority of the nations, including the great powers, should be able to control the utilization of mineral resources in the interest of peace.

[17] *Ibid.;* L. M. Fanning (ed.), *Our Oil Resources,* McGraw-Hill, 1945, p. 142.
[18] Leith, Furness, and Lewis, *op. cit.,* p. 201.

WATER REQUIREMENTS

About a third of the total precipitation falling upon the earth in the form of rain or snow remains on the surface and runs off toward some lower point; the rest disappears into the soil, or returns to the atmosphere ("flies off") through evaporation. This runoff, in many cases, takes the form of floods, which may be very destructive; or the runoff may wash the soil and cause erosion. Of the total runoff, it has been estimated that less than one-half of 1 percent is needed for domestic or municipal purposes.

About 2 percent of the runoff, or possibly as high as 10 percent in arid and semiarid regions, is used for agricultural purposes. About 5 percent is used for navigation, and less than 10 percent for water power.[19] Thus, less than a third is utilized for these combined purposes—far less than could or should be utilized under well-developed plans.

One of the reasons for this failure to develop fuller use of water resources is that in areas where water is relatively abundant it is accepted as a gift of nature without careful consideration of its economic importance and the need for development programs in the semiarid and arid regions where it is not plentiful. Thus, the public as a whole has not fully appreciated the need and possibility of more complete water control and utilization.

IRRIGATION

Approximately half of the total area of the United States susceptible of irrigation, estimated at 51½ million acres,[20] is now under irrigation. Almost 95 percent of the present irrigated acreage of about 26 million acres lies in the 17 Western states. Irrigation is increasing also in the rice areas of the South and in Eastern truck-crop areas.[21]

Just what proportion of the potential irrigable land in the Western states, about 25 million acres, will be irrigated, and when, will depend upon numerous economic, physical, social, and political factors; but in any case, development will undoubtedly be largely by the federal government, because of the large size, complications, and expense of most of the projects that remain to be developed. The far-reaching benefits of certain large multiple-purpose projects, including control of floods and generation of low-cost power, make some projects that are not economi-

[19] F. H. Newell, "Water," in C. R. Van Hise and L. H. Havemeyer (eds.), *Conservation of Our Natural Resources*, Macmillan, 1930, p. 135.

[20] See National Resources Planning Board, *Report to the President*, 1934, pp. 344-345. Assuming that about 85 percent of the ultimate total irrigable area will be served by surface waters, the total annual draft on surface waters would be 85 million acre feet, or twice the present reservoir capacity in the arid and semiarid areas of the United States.

[21] *Agricultural Land Resources*, U.S. Department of Agriculture, Agriculture Information Bulletin 140, June, 1955, p. 59.

cally feasible for irrigation development only, economically sound and desirable.

Many countries of the world have some irrigated acreage, and certain nations, especially in Asia and Africa, have sizable potentials of irrigable acreage. Joint plans for economic development undertaken by participating countries and the United States, through its technical assistance program for underdeveloped areas, have increased in recent years the acreage of irrigated lands. Many thousands of acres of irrigable lands will probably be developed in the years ahead, especially in Asia and Africa, with the construction of large multiple-purpose and hydroelectric power projects.

DRAINAGE

Too much water may be just as bad as too little. The amount of land in the United States on which drainage is used is nearly five times the irrigated area of the nation. It is estimated that over 100 million additional acres need drainage to be suitable for agricultural use, or nearly as much as the present area on which drainage is used. If drainage development continues at recent rates, it is estimated that the acreage in organized drainage enterprises will be increased by 25 percent by 1975.[22]

Most of the acreage unfit for cultivation without drainage lies in the corn belt and the cotton belt, the latter having about two-thirds of the total acreage. The drained lands of the southern, Atlantic, and Gulf states have been devoted largely to producing corn, cotton, and truck crops, but many other products have been grown on these lands. Whether many or few of the lands needing drainage will be drained in the immediate future will depend largely upon the same economic, physical, social, and political factors that determine future irrigation development. However, drainage has received less public assistance than irrigation, although much the same questions of public policy are involved.

It is undoubtedly true in the case of drainage, as in the case of irrigation projects, that the more easily developed and less expensive projects have been undertaken first, so that future costs of land reclamation through drainage will be greater. It is estimated that a third of the drainable wet land may be drained at an average cost of $30 an acre,[23] compared with an average of about $8 per acre for lands already drained. Total cost to the individual owner, however, will be increased by the cost of clearing the land of trees and related necessary improvements. It has been estimated that about two-thirds of the area yet to be drained requires clearing of trees, stumps, and brush.

[22] *Ibid.*, p. 61.
[23] George J. Miller, "Reclamation of Wet and Overflow Lands," in A. E. Parkins and J. R. Whitaker (eds.), *Our National Resources and their Conservation*, Wiley, 1936, p. 175.

Careful consideration of the proposed areas to be drained should be made before drainage is undertaken. Those projects should be developed first that can be used to produce specialty products for which satisfactory markets are available and that do not interfere with present important uses, such as wildlife refuges, rather than bringing into production those lands that will be devoted to producing crops of which there is a threatened or actual surplus.

It is significant that two-thirds of the acreage needing drainage are in the cotton belt. The United States has had a depressing surplus condition in cotton for many years, particularly the types grown in the Old South, where most of the drainable wet lands are situated. The light, sandy soils of this area are well adapted to truck gardens and small fruit, and the important economic factor determining the acreage of land that can be profitably brought into production through drainage enterprises is the availability of good markets for the products.

In Florida and along the Gulf Coast, much of the drainable land could be used for growing citrus fruits, and in Louisiana and adjacent areas, much of the land needing drainage could also be used for growing sugar cane. The undrained lands of the Lake states and upper Mississippi Valley could be devoted largely to grain, hay, vegetables, and truck crops, although some of them are adapted to the growing of sugar beets.

FLOOD CONTROL

The federal government has taken a very active part in flood control activities ever since the disastrous 1927 Mississippi River flood. Prior to that time, all federal funds for flood control work had to be matched by local contributions. Since 1927, Congress has decided that the federal government should bear the entire expense of new flood control projects, so that today flood control is practically on the same basis as irrigation. This policy of the federal government in taking over the responsibility for flood control work has created some rivalry for appropriations for other water-use programs, including irrigation and navigation, and "rivers and harbors."

Much additional research needs to be done on the relative merits and effectiveness of various control devices. Much study is also needed to establish standards that can be used to appraise the merits of particular projects, the uses to be served, the costs, the benefits, and the manner in which flood control projects may be organized and maintained in order to serve the public interest most effectively. In addition to the technical problems of constructing proper devices, the problem of calculating benefits and contributions to meet the costs of such construction is an important one.

If other meritorious uses can be combined with flood control, they not only help defray expenses, but assist in utilizing the water most efficiently.

In many instances, it is feasible to combine irrigation development with flood control; the two frequently supplement each other effectively. The same can also be said in many instances for combining navigation with flood control, or even of combining navigation and irrigation with flood control. The danger of such a combination, however, is that the most beneficial uses of the water may not necessarily receive proper consideration.

The feasibility of combining power development with flood control has been questioned by many on the grounds that to control floods, reservoirs should be empty when floods start, in order to hold back as much water as possible, whereas power dams must be kept filled to provide a continuous flow of water for the generation of power. However, the two purposes can be combined effectively by providing additional height above the part of the dam used for power, to make for effective flood control.[24] Thus, where wise planning occurs prior to construction, these collateral uses can be combined in many instances in ways that will greatly increase benefits to the general public and simultaneously reduce the net cost of flood control.

HYDROELECTRIC POWER

Water power as a source of energy differs from the mineral fuels in that it is not reduced by use. Water power is wasted if it is not used; consequently, to use it is to conserve it. The power of falling water in streams continues to be available indefinitely for human service.

Total stream energy depends upon how much water flows in a stream and how far it falls in its course. Some idea of the geographical distribution of the water resources of a nation can be secured by comparing the topographic map with a rainfall and drainage map. In the United States, for example, the Pacific Northwest, with its mountain ranges and heavy precipitation, has large water-power resources.

The Federal Power Commission has estimated that the total hydroelectric power potential of the United States is about 105 million kilowatts, with an average annual generation potential of about 478 billion kilowatt-hours. This estimate excludes small sites of less than 2500 kilowatts potential.[25] About a fourth of this total potential is now being utilized.[26] The remaining three-fourths of potential capacity is made up of a great variety of sites, large and small, low-cost and high-cost. The most im-

[24] The Norris Dam in the Tennessee Valley has 137 feet of water for power purposes, and an additional 79 feet for impounding flood water before it flows over the dam.

[25] Federal Power Commission, *Potential Hydroelectric Power in the United States*, May, 1950.

[26] Installed capacity represents nearly 22 percent of the total potential, and average annual generation is about 24 percent of the estimated total potential. (See President's Materials Policy Commission, *Resources for Freedom,* Government Printing Office, June, 1952, Vol. 3, p. 37.)

portant and attractive sites remaining to be developed are those in the Great Lakes drainage area (at Niagara Falls and on the St. Lawrence) and in the Pacific Northwest (the Columbia River Basin).

The use of electricity in the United States increased sharply after World War II and the potential consumption appears tremendous. Installed hydro capacity may be doubled within 10 or 15 years, and by 1975 the output of hydroelectric energy may be three times the 1950 level.[27] An active policy of public and private development of water power is highly desirable since it would contribute to the attainment of three major national objectives: (1) conservation of scarce fuel materials like petroleum, natural gas, and the high-grade coals; (2) strengthening of the national economy by making electricity cheaper and more widely available, and (3) strengthening of the nation through assurance of more ample electrical energy in time of war.

The estimates of feasible undeveloped water power do not include many flood control and irrigation dam sites, which, in the course of their development, may produce a substantial amount of water power incident to the other purposes for which the developments are undertaken. Nevertheless, it seems certain that in a few decades there will be demand for much more electricity than can be furnished through water power, and heavy demands will be put upon other energy sources.

One of the possibilities of the future is that nuclear fission can be used to generate large amounts of electric power. The process has already been demonstrated on a small scale by the Atomic Energy Commission. The most significant aspect of this development is the process by which non-fissionable material may be converted into fuel at a rate more rapid than fuel is consumed in operating the atomic reactor. However, it does not appear that nuclear fission can be regarded as a substantial contribution to electric generation during at least the next 10 or 15 years, and the probability is that the atomic energy industry will remain a heavy net consumer of electricity.[28] But for the more distant future, atomic energy gives great promise of providing large supplies of energy at relatively low cost.

Only about a seventh, or some 75 million kilowatts, of the estimated potential electrical energy of nearly 500 million kilowatts that can be developed by water power on the earth has been developed.[29] Many countries with magnificent water-power sites have failed to develop them, while other countries have taken full advantage of the modest endow-

---

[27] *Ibid.*, p. 38. Cf. also the *Report of the President's Water Resources Policy Commission,* Government Printing Office, 1950, pp. 239–240.
[28] *Ibid.*, p. 39.
[29] U.S. Geological Survey, Department of the Interior, *Developed and Potential Water Power of the World,* Washington, D.C., 1951.

ments of nature.[30] The generation of electric energy in all other free countries combined amounts to roughly the same as that in the United States. With reasonably favorable conditions, the rate of growth in consumption of electric power in these countries as a group should be similar to the growth projected for the United States, with the most rapid growth occurring in the comparatively underdeveloped countries.[31]

Western Europe has scanty reserves of oil and gas, coal reserves that are increasingly difficult to utilize, and comparatively limited water-power sites that can be economically developed. Japan and certain parts of South America also appear to have limited resources for the generation of electric energy. But Canada, much of Latin America, the Middle East, India, and Africa should have ample resources of either fuels or water power.[32]

TRANSPORTATION LAND REQUIREMENTS

Many have believed that, with the elaborate network of roads and railroads already laid out in the United States, future utilization of land for transportation would largely involve straightening some highways and widening others, with no appreciable increase in new roads or new locations. The trend of transportation development accompanying economic progress and rising standards of living over the years indicates that the future will bring tremendous expansion of transportation facilities.

PROSPECTIVE USE OF LAND FOR TRANSPORTATION

Some 70 percent of the present three million miles of roads in the United States are rural roads, or "land-service roads" (roads from main highways to individual farmyards) . It seems safe to say that only to a very limited extent is there any present or future demand for an increase in such roads. Rather, demands will involve surfacing these roads (with gravel, oil, or similar substances) and making them passable in all kinds of weather. It is in connection with the other 30 percent of the roads, which may be termed "highways," as differentiated from land-service roads, that the greatest expansion will occur in response to the prospective doubling of travel. The changes necessitated in highways will expand the acreage of land used for transportation.

Changes in other forms of transportation in the future will probably not equal, in the aggregate, the acreage involved in prospective highway changes, at least for the next two decades. There will undoubtedly be a great expansion in aviation, and more acreage will be devoted to airports and landing and servicing facilities, but these will not equal the acreages

---

[30] Erich W. Zimmermann, *World Resources and Industries*, rev. ed., Harper, 1951, p. 578.
[31] President's Materials Policy Commission, *Resources for Freedom*, p. 39.
[32] *Ibid.*

involved in highway changes. Pipeline and related subsurface uses of land will probably be increased. There is little change in railroad mileage in prospect, at least not an increase. There may be some significant improvements in waterways, but the aggregate surface acres will not approach those involved in constructing modern highways needed for the prospective increased road travel.

UNIFICATION OF TRANSPORTATION SERVICES

Rapid and largely unregulated development of transportation services in the United States has produced a national transportation problem without a national transportation policy.[33] The serious difficulties of the railroads in recent years are part of the general transportation problem growing out of an intensified and economically wasteful competition for traffic among the several types of transportation, partly the result of governmental favoritism in regard to some types to the detriment of others. This is economically wasteful, because transportation facilities have been created that are considerably beyond the ability of the traffic of the nation to support.[34]

Some improvement will come with the increase in the general volume of business characteristic of a young growing nation. A definite national transportation policy, however, should be established to equalize the situation of all types of transportation in regard to regulation, taxation, and subsidies.

URBAN LAND REQUIREMENTS

The normal trend of economic opportunities, as a nation with well-diversified industries and resources becomes more mature, is from the country to the city. The extent to which urbanization will proceed will depend largely upon public policies affecting agriculture and industry.

THE FUTURE OF CITIES

If in the United States, for example, the federal government follows a policy of agricultural subsidies or programs designed to keep the present number of people on farms, urbanization will not increase. If, on the other hand, industrial unemployment can be largely eliminated through governmental or private programs and additional economic opportunities made available in industries, there will be a considerable farm-to-city movement of population. It is impossible to predict which of these two major policies will be followed, but it is estimated that urban require-

[33] See "The Report of the Committee Appointed by the President of the United States to Submit Recommendations upon the General Transportation Situation," December 23, 1938, p. 1.

[34] *Ibid.*

ments in the United States will increase gradually in the future, reaching about 14 million acres by 1960, compared with 12 million acres in 1940.[35]

Regardless of the national policy adopted, there will be great shifts among cities in population growth and development. Although from the strict engineering aspect there is no limit to the size of a city, certain economic, social, and related aspects do limit the size of most cities. Increased costs of living and doing business associated with extreme concentrations of people in small areas tend to check the unlimited expansion of cities.

As economic advantages shift, some cities will grow and others decline. Even during periods of relative prosperity and full economic employment, some cities decline rapidly because of shifts in the resource base. This is particularly true in cities near mining areas or other types of exploitative industries. In the more stable agricultural areas, cities change little even during periods of severe business depression or prosperity. Others experience definite booms. Consequently, it is impossible to predict accurately the pattern of future urban land use.

IMPROVEMENT OF URBAN LIVING

The most optimistic aspect of the future of cities is the growing realization of the modern problems associated with city life. The most important cause of urban land problems today lies in the irrationality of urban patterns.[36] There has been no consistent policy or plan in city development or in urban patterns of land use. As long as urban growth continued at a rapid rate, the basic land-use problems of premature subdivision, overcapitalized landholdings, high assessed land values, and similar situations did not become acute because of booms and new settlement. Neglect to plan for growth of urban areas more intelligently has created many serious economic problems.

It is not likely that the rapid changes that occurred during the past few decades—particularly the tendency to overbuild or construct mechanical monuments—will be continued. One of the great advantages of mechanical standardization is the decrease in the number of variables in the environment. Once constants are established in urban planning, the trend toward higher densities and overbuilding will no longer continue.[37]

[35] National Resources Board, *Report to the President*, 1934, p. 151.

[36] National Resources Planning Board, *Public Land Acquisition in a National Land Use Program: Part II, Urban Lands,* Report of the Land Committee, Government Printing Office, February, 1941.

[37] Mumford believes that, as we design our cities for permanent living and not for impermanent financial exploitation, there will undoubtedly be discovered a whole series of biological and social constants that vary little from generation to generation, and in any case, such variation as is necessary will occur within and not in opposition to the permanent form. (Lewis Mumford, *The Culture of Cities*, Harcourt, Brace, 1938, pp. 445 ff.)

REFERENCES FOR FURTHER READING

Agricultural Land Resources, U.S. Department of Agriculture, Agriculture Information Bulletin No. 140, Government Printing Office, Washington, D.C., June, 1955.

Dorau, H. B., and Hinman, A. G., *Urban Land Economics,* The Macmillan Company, New York, 1928, Chap. XXXIV.

Harrison, J. D. B., "Forestry in a Changing World," in *Land Problems and Policies* (Timmons, John F., and Murray, William G., eds.), Iowa State College Press, Ames, Iowa, 1950, Chap. IX.

Johnson, V. Webster, and Barlowe, Raleigh, *Land Problems and Policies,* McGraw-Hill Book Company, Inc., New York, 1954, Chap. IX.

Lyons, Barrow, *Tomorrow's Birthright,* Funk & Wagnalls Company, New York, 1955, Part III.

Mumford, Lewis, *The Culture of Cities,* Harcourt, Brace and Company, Inc., New York, 1938, Chap. VII.

National Resources Planning Board, *Our National Resources: Facts and Problems,* Government Printing Office, Washington, D.C., 1940.

Pearson, F. A., and Harper, F. A., *The World's Hunger,* Cornell University Press, Ithaca, N.Y., 1945, Chaps. II, III, IV, V, and VII.

President's Materials Policy Commission, *Outlook for Energy Sources,* Vol. III of *Resources for Freedom,* report to the President, 5 vols., Government Printing Office, Washington, D.C., June, 1952, Chap. IV.

Report of the Committee to Submit Recommendations Upon the General Transportation Situation to the President of the U.S., Government Printing Office, Washington, D.C., December 23, 1938.

Report of the President's Water Resources Policy Commision, *A Water Policy for the American People,* Government Printing Office, Washington, D.C., 1950, Chaps. X–XIV.

U.S. Department of Agriculture, *Trees, Yearbook of Agriculture, 1949,* Government Printing Office, Washington, D.C., pp. 715–753.

U.S. Geological Survey, *Developed and Potential Water Power of the World,* U.S. Department of the Interior, Washington, D.C., 1951.

Zimmermann, Erich W., *World Resources and Industries,* rev. ed., Harper & Brothers, New York, 1951, Chaps. XXIII, XXV, and XXXVI.

chapter **7**

THE PROCESS OF RESOURCE ALLOCATION

FUNDAMENTAL PRINCIPLES OF LAND USE

The Principle of Maximization—The Equimarginal Principle—The Principle of Diminishing Marginal Rate of Substitution—The Principle of Diminishing Marginal Productivity—The Principle of Specialization and Comparative Advantage—The Principle of First Choice

OPERATION OF BASIC PRINCIPLES IN LAND UTILIZATION

Popular Interpretations of Basic Principles—Obstacles to Free Operation of Basic Principles—The Highest Return or Best Combination of the Factors—Equilibrium of the Firm—Imperfect or Incomplete Competition

BECAUSE HUMAN wants are insatiable, in the aggregate, and because basic natural resources used to satisfy human wants are scarce rather than superabundant, maximum human satisfaction demands the development of the science of utilizing our resources and our efforts most efficiently. The central problem of economics is the allocation of scarce resources for the fullest satisfaction of ends.[1] In land economics the problem centers around the allocation of land resources and their appurtenances for the fullest satisfaction of the ends of society.

Where resources such as air to breathe are abundant, no problem of

[1] *Economics* means, strictly, proportioning (economizing) to get maximum output with least sacrifice of input factors. The word "economics" is derived from the Greek *oikonomike,* denoting management of the household, *oikos.* In earlier times, the household was the individual producing unit, but as production shifted to the factory, the term "economics" became applied as well to the management of the industrial unit or factory. The concept of management implies proportioning or combining the various factors involved in production and living so as to get the maximum product with a given expenditure of human effort. "Economics is essentially a study of the interrelation of parts, and unless it leads towards the formation of better combinations, it is a dead and useless science." (George M. Peterson, *Diminishing Returns and Planned Economy,* Ronald Press, 1937, p. 103.)

allocation arises; but where they are scarce, and this is the usual situation, choices must be made carefully as to the most desirable use of resources. The allocation process is guided by prices, which are the terms on which alternatives are offered. Prices are the rationing agents rising where scarcity occurs to divide the limited resources among those most urgently needing them on the basis of their ability to pay.

Price is a rationing force whether freely competitive forces are operating in a common market place where buyers and sellers bid with money prices against one another, or at the opposite extreme, where government decrees establish arbitrarily the terms on which the alternatives (prices) are offered. The difference is only in the nature of the market. The institutional structure of the market may differ as well as the technical relations of the persons and products involved.

FUNDAMENTAL PRINCIPLES OF LAND USE

Economically speaking, choices are made as to the use of each resource among alternatives, according to varying motives for achieving maximum results. For the consumer, the maximum results will be in the form of utility or satisfaction; for the businessman, profit; for the government or society, net social benefits determined according to the prevailing political system. Whatever the market, there is a set of principles that explains the economic decisions of people and the consequent allocation of resources to their current and future uses.

Under an economic system where the institution of private property is dominant, the owners of property objects (such as landowners) or those who sell services (laborers) sell their products or services for money with which to buy back products to be consumed. The organization can be classified into two interacting systems of markets and prices. The first is that for the resources of production in which individuals are sellers and enterprises are the buyers; the second is that for the finished goods and services in which the enterprises are the sellers and the individuals the buyers as consumers.

These interrelated markets establish the costs and incomes in the first case and the values and satisfactions in the second case. An example is the simple case of a woodcutter who sells his services to a lumber firm for $1000. His income for that period is thereby determined at $1000 and that much has been added to the costs of the lumber which he cut. At the same time, the woodcutter enters the market for finished lumber for his house and uses a part of his $1000 to buy from the lumber concern a house that he will use as a residence for himself and his family. The price he pays for the lumber is related to the wages he received from the sale of his labor to the concern. In just such a way all markets and all prices are related to one another.

THE PRINCIPLE OF MAXIMIZATION

Direction is given to the allocation of resources and the general production-consumption process through the operation of the principle that *all persons and enterprises tend to maximize their value returns*. The validity of this principle is based on the assumption that economic behavior is rational in the sense that people are motivated by a desire to make the most of the resources at their command. Experience leads us to believe that people act in a manner approaching rational behavior and that their actions are not purely haphazard but reflect an attempt to maximize some particular end.

One of the best examples of the practical application of the *principle of maximization* is the construction of rail fences from excellent sawlumber material, in the pioneer days of the Midwestern United States. Large amounts of good timber were readily available—in fact, the forests were a hindrance to agriculture and the settler had practically no capital or funds with which to buy wire, nails, or other manufactured products for making fences. He did, however, have time to split rails and construct fences. Consequently, timber that would later have had great economic value as lumber was used to build fences to enclose the settler's stock, because this was the cheapest means available for fencing.

Looking backward, this process appears to have been very wasteful, but to the settler, it was the most efficient means of utilizing resources and labor to produce goods he needed in order to survive. In a crude way, he was applying the same principle of maximization that is applied effectively in modern production. The increasing use of farm machinery as wage levels rise reflects the same principle—namely, that the factors of production will be utilized in such proportions that value returns will be maximized.

The practical application of the principle of maximization may also be illustrated by agricultural production in old, densely populated nations and in relatively new, sparsely settled ones. In a country where there is a large supply of labor and a large amount of capital accumulated through generations of saving and thrift, only a very limited amount of land is available for agricultural use. Agricultural production will be characterized by rather *intensive* utilization practices—that is, much labor and capital will be applied to an acre of land, and acre yields will be comparatively large.

In contrast, labor is comparatively scarce in a new, sparsely settled area of rich, abundant, agricultural lands, but capital is even more scarce, with the result that very few units of capital and labor will be applied to a given area of land, and utilization will be *extensive*. In other words, large amounts of land will be utilized in an extensive way, with only small doses of capital and labor per acre. In such areas, the acreage operated by a given individual tends to be several times greater than that operated in an older country.

THE EQUIMARGINAL PRINCIPLE

Maximization is accomplished through operation of the *equimarginal principle*, which may be stated in the following terms: *Assuming effective competition, the division of a fixed quantity of anything among a number of different uses will be made so as to apportion to each use an amount just sufficient so that the increment of gain in one use will be the same as in every other use to which it might be put.*

Transfer of resources from one use to another will occur until the rate of gain from transference just equals the rate of loss from withdrawal. A consumer, for instance, will transfer his expenditure of income from food to clothing at the point where additional units of clothing will yield satisfaction equal to what would have been gained from additional units of food. If additional food would have yielded greater satisfaction than the additional clothing, then the transfer would not be made.

THE PRINCIPLE OF DIMINISHING MARGINAL RATE OF SUBSTITUTION

It is characteristic of consumption and production that as more and more of all goods or services are consumed or produced, the increment of satisfaction or value return diminishes. The same may be said when two goods are substituted for each other. It can be said that, in general, smaller and smaller increments in quantities of a good foregone are necessary to compensate for the substitution of another good. This, in its simplest form, is the *principle of diminishing marginal rate of substitution*.

A consumer will tend to value pork less and less in terms of beef as he substitutes the first for the second. The same applies to an enterprise when machines are substituted for men. The operation of this principle is a condition necessary to *equilibrium* for the individual and also for the economy as a whole. If a diminishing marginal rate of substitution associated with diminishing utility did not apply, once a consumer began to purchase pork he would not stop purchasing it until his whole income had been used for that purpose.

Analogous to consumer choices among alternative goods for the satisfaction of their desires are the choices of firms among alternative agents of production to obtain maximum profit. There is also a similar analogy of the choices of agents among alternative opportunities in different firms or industries to obtain maximum net earnings. According to the equimarginal principle, firms will substitute resources in the production process until the marginal rate of substitution between the agents is equal to the ratio of the prices to the agents.

THE PRINCIPLE OF DIMINISHING MARGINAL PRODUCTIVITY

When Malthus argued that population tended to outrun food supply, he was stating a principle that has become known as the *Principle of Diminishing Physical Returns*. Malthus indicated that the land could not produce food as fast as population could expand. Experience proves it is impossible to add labor, capital, and management to a given piece of land and secure the same proportionate rate of return or increased output indefinitely.

The principle of diminishing marginal productivity applies to each factor of production and determines, in a physical sense, maximum output in units secured from a given combination of productive factors. The economic combination is basically determined by the physical relationships of the factors.

This principle may be stated as follows: If, with productive methods continuing unchanged, successive physical units of one productive factor are added to a fixed physical quantity of another factor (or a constant combination of other factors) the *total physical output* obtained will vary in amount through three distinct phases. (1) It will *increase*, for a time at an increasing absolute rate and then at a decreasing absolute rate, but always at a percentage rate greater than the rate of increase of the variable factor, until finally a point is reached at which the rate of increase of output will exactly equal the rate of increase of inputs of the variable factor; (2) the total physical output will continue to *increase, but at a decreasing absolute rate* and at a percentage rate always less than that of the variable factor, until a point is reached where maximum output is secured; and (3) total physical output will *decrease*, possibly at an increasing absolute rate for a time, but probably at a decreasing rate through most of this phase, until finally a point is reached at which output is reduced to zero.[2]

The principle may also be stated in terms of diminishing *marginal* or additional returns (M) obtained from the variable factor, diminishing *average* returns (A), and diminishing *total* returns (T).[3]

[2] This statement of the principle has been adapted from John M. Cassels, "On the Law of Variable Proportions," in *Explorations in Economics: Notes and Essays Contributed in Honor of F. W. Taussig*, McGraw-Hill, 1936, Part II, Chap. II, pp. 223–236. Cassels points out the more important shortcomings of some common ways of expressing the principle, such as "In a given state of the arts, after a certain point is reached, the application of further units of any variable factor to another fixed factor (or fixed combination of factors) will yield less than proportionate returns." (See also F. H. Knight, *Risk, Uncertainty, and Profit*, Houghton Mifflin, 1921, pp. 97–103; J. D. Black and A. G. Black, *Production Organization*, Holt, 1929, Chaps. V–XI, inclusive; and Peterson, *op. cit.*, Chaps. I and II.)

[3] Black and Black, *op. cit.*, Chap. V. Cassels points out that when the law is stated in these terms alone, it is difficult to distinguish clearly the three important phases, whereas when they are used together the end of the first phase is the point where aver-

These three phases of the principle of diminishing productivity can l illustrated by a typical farm operation. Let us assume that we have a fie of potatoes and two modern potato diggers, and that we wish to find tl best number of men to employ with these machines. If we begin with o1 man and add one at a time, the results might be like those indicated Table 3, in which the point between which the eleventh and twelfth ma is added gives the greatest output per man. This point would be call the point of maximum efficiency of labor, assuming the number of m chines remains fixed at two. Regardless of the wage scale, this point w represent the lowest labor cost per unit of output, if wages are the san for each man hired.

Although output per man falls steadily after the addition of the twelf man, the output per machine continues up to the point at which the si teenth man is added. This point is the point of maximum efficiency machines. As long as the number of machines is limited to two, this is tl point of lowest machine cost per unit of output.

The data in Table 3 illustrate the three phases. It can be seen fro these data that in the third or last phase the amount of the variable fact in relation to the fixed factor is so great as to be actually harmful, whi in the first phase the fixed factor is so excessive in relation to the variab factor that it has the effect of reducing output. In either of these tv phases greater output could be secured by eliminating enough of the e cessive factor to bring the two into a relationship more like that attaine in the second phase.

The preceding behavior of diminishing physical productivity is co1 mon, in general, to all production activities involving the combination two or more factors of production, although the exact character of produ tivity phases varies greatly with different combinations. The stude1 should remember, however, that the principle of diminishing produ tivity is purely physical, as well as strictly static, and is applicable on on the assumption that the factors (or at least the variable factor) can l broken up into small, separable, homogeneous units. This is obvious an abstraction, but it is considered useful in the economic analysis of lar utilization problems if its limitations and assumptions are kept in min

The fact that most production involves combining several producti agents (for instance, barley production may use land, labor, fertilize horses, machines, seed, and other productive agents), and that factors production cannot ordinarily all be divided into minute, separable, hom geneous units, means that the effects of these practical situations mu be analyzed carefully in applying the basic concepts of the principle diminishing productivity to land utilization problems.

---

age outputs attain their maximum, and the end of the second is the point where t marginal outputs become zero. (See Cassels, *op. cit.*, p. 227.)

Table 3. Hypothetical Inputs of Machines and Labor on a Given Unit of Land and Outputs of Potatoes, Illustrating the Principle of Diminishing Physical Productivity

	Inputs				Outputs		
Machines	Man Days	Per Cent Increase of Man Days	Bushels of Potatoes Daily	Per Cent Increase in Potatoes	Marginal Physical Product per Man per Day	Daily Output per Machine	Output per Man Day
2	1	—	35	—	35	17.5	35
2	2	100	90	157.1	55	45.0	45
2	3	50	150	66.7	60	75.0	50
2	4	33.3	240	60	90	120.0	60
2	5	25	350	45.8	110	175.0	70
2	6	20	510	45.7	160	255.0	85
2	7	16.7	651	27.6	141	325.5	93
2	8	14.3	784	20.4	133	392.0	98
2	9	12.5	918	17.1	134	459.0	102
2	10	11.1	1050	14.4	132	525.0	105
2	11	10	1166	11.0	116	583.0	106
2	12	9.1	1272	9.1	106	636.0	106
2	13	8.3	1365	7.3	93	682.5	105
2	14	7.7	1442	5.6	77	721.0	103
2	15	7.1	1485	3.0	43	742.5	99
2	16	6.7	1504	1.3	19	752.0	94
2	17	6.3	1496	−0.5	−8	748.0	88
2	18	5.9	1392	−7.0	−104	696.0	87

[right margin annotations: "a", "b", "c" bracket groups; handwritten notes "out Put falls per man" and "out Put falls machine"]

[a] Range of increasing proportional output per man.
[b] Range of decreasing proportional output per man.
[c] Absolute decline of output.

THE PRINCIPLES OF SPECIALIZATION AND COMPARATIVE ADVANTAGE

One of the entrepreneur's most important problems in utilizing land resources is what things to produce and what to buy. We know that in actual practice some entrepreneurs specialize in certain products, and that certain areas specialize in certain products, while other entrepreneurs and other areas produce others. What determines products produced by individual entrepreneurs or in certain areas or locations? Why does the entrepreneur produce a limited number of products instead of all those he needs or desires? The answers to these questions are found in two principles—one, the *Principle of Specialization*; the other, the *Principle of Comparative Advantage*.

The principle of specialization, applied to persons, is that *each person tends to work at only one task and to sell the product thereof and with the proceeds buy the other things desired or needed.* Applied to areas or locations, the principle of specialization is that *each area or location tends to produce only a few things and to sell its surplus of these and with the proceeds buy the other things desired or needed.* Determination of products specialized in is based upon the principle of comparative advantage or comparative cost. Comparative advantage and comparative cost are reciprocals, because the greater the advantage, the lower the cost, and the lower the advantage, the higher the cost. Consequently, "comparative advantage" and "comparative cost" can be used interchangeably.

A few illustrations will indicate more clearly the meaning and significance of the Principle of Specialization and the Principle of Comparative Advantage. Let us assume that two farmers, Brown and Jones, can grow all the food they need and make all the clothes they need, and that their net outputs per unit of effort at these two occupations, or what might be termed the marginal productivities of their labor, are as follows:

Occupation	Brown	Jones
Clothes	20	20
Food	10	10

Under these circumstances, there will be no specialization, and no trade or exchange of goods between Brown and Jones. One unit of food will be worth exactly two times a unit of clothes to both operators. In other words, there would be no advantage to Brown or Jones in specializing on clothes or food, since their ratio of advantage between clothes and food is the same.

Let us assume that the net outputs per unit of effort, the marginal productivities of labor, at the two occupations for the two operators are as follows:

Occupation	Brown	Jones
Clothes	35	28
Food	15	12

It can be seen that even though Brown's net ouput for both clothes and food is considerably larger than Jones's, the ratio between their two outputs is 7 to 3. Three units of food are worth 7 units of clothes to both operators. Consequently, neither has a ratio of advantage in the production of food or clothes, and specialization on either product would be advantageous to neither.

The following illustration indicates a situation in which specialization would occur, and where exchange of products between Brown and Jones could be made to advantage:

Occupation	Brown	Jones
Clothes	20	10
Food	10	20

Under these circumstances, a unit of food will be worth 2 units of clothes to Brown, but only half a unit to Jones. If Brown specialized in producing clothes, his net output would be 40 units of clothes, and if Jones specialized in growing food, his total output would be 40 units of food. Thus, the combined production of the two operators, by specialization, would be 40 units of clothes and 40 units of food, whereas if neither specialized in clothes or food, Brown's total production would be 20 units of clothes and 10 of food, and Jones's total production 10 units of clothes and 20 of food—a total of 30 units of clothes and 30 of food. By specializing, 10 additional units of both clothes and food are produced, and if the two trade with each other in terms of 1 unit of clothes for 1 unit of food, Brown can have a total of 25 units of clothes and 15 of food, and Jones can have 15 units of clothes and 25 of food, where previously Brown had 20 units of clothes and 10 of food and Jones 10 units of clothes and 20 of food. Thus, by specializing and trading surpluses derived from specialization, each gets 5 more units of clothes and 5 more units of food than he would have without specialization.

It will be noted that Brown has a higher ratio of advantage in making clothes, and Jones a higher ratio of advantage in producing food. Brown's ratio of advantage in making clothes, compared with growing food, is 2 to 1, but the corresponding ratio for Jones is 1 to 2. Consequently, Brown will make the clothes and Jones will produce the food. The principle of comparative advantage is illustrated, since a product tends to be produced by those persons whose ratio of advantage in the production of it is higher.

No attempt will be made here to go into the complex relationships that result when numerous persons and products are considered. The basic principle applies in these more complex cases; moreover, the same principle applies to regions or locations. If, in the preceding illustrations, region A and region B, or country A and country B, are substituted for Brown and Jones, the application of the principle of comparative advantage would be the same. There is, however, a situation not illustrated in the above examples, which frequently occurs in actual practice—the case where one person or region or country is superior to another, or to all others, in the production of both or most products, but not superior in the same ratio.

Let us assume that country A and country B have the following net outputs per unit of effort for the two products, steel and cotton:

Product	Country A	Country B
Steel	36	12
Cotton	24	6

In this case, country A is three times as productive as country B in making steel and four times as productive in producing cotton. In country A 24 bales of cotton are equal in value to 36 tons of steel, or 1 bale of cotton is equal in value to 1½ tons of steel. In country B, 6 bales of cotton have the same value as 12 tons of steel, or 1 bale of cotton is equal in value to 2 tons of steel. Since A has a higher ratio of advantage over B in the production of cotton (4 to 1) than it has in the production of steel (3 to 1) country A will tend to specialize in cotton, in which its advantage is greatest, and B to specialize in steel, in which its disadvantage is least. Consequently, we can modify our statement of the principle of comparative advantage by saying that *a nation will tend to specialize in producing those products in which it has the highest comparative advantage or the least comparative disadvantage.* The same principle applies to individual persons.

THE PRINCIPLE OF FIRST CHOICE

When comparative advantage is measured in ratios of net outputs, as indicated above, demand produces its effect directly by determining selling prices of the various products. Where there are abundant amounts of a product or an abundance of persons well qualified to make it, in proportion to the demand, the product sells at a relatively low price and will tend to reduce output produced more in line with the output of less favored commodities. For example, copper may sell at such a low price that only the richest or most efficiently worked deposits may be used, whereas almost any gold deposit of any significance is likely to be worked

This leads to another statement of the principle of comparative advantage, commonly referred to as the principle of first choice, really a corollary of the first. The principle of first choice states that *any occupation for which only a limited number of persons are qualified, in proportion to the need for it, will be first choice of these persons.* The same principle can be stated in terms of regions or locations. For example, in the matter of factory locations, there is a limited number of areas in which the basic raw materials—such as coal and iron supply, in the case of steel making—are close to each other; and consequently any location of this kind is likely to be used for steel manufacturing.

Areas close to railway and water-terminal facilities and also to the main retailing district are limited in most cities, with the result that such areas are almost certain to be used for wholesaling, coal storage, and related operations. Any land well suited to the production of cotton or corn will robably be used for this purpose, because these crops have very specific imatic requirements, and considerable amounts of cotton and corn are nsumed. There is, on the other hand, an abundance of land well suited the cultivation of wheat relative to the demand for it.

OPERATION OF BASIC PRINCIPLES IN LAND UTILIZATION

The more limited a region or country is with respect to its people and e diversity of its natural resources, the more specialized it will be. A gion will be more highly specialized while it is undeveloped than after becomes more densely populated and has been settled for a considerable eriod. In new countries, people naturally undertake those occupations id industries that produce the greatest net return, and less advantageous idustries are developed gradually. Obviously a nation or region will not ndertake the production of a good if any unit of labor cannot produce 1ough of this good to yield a return equal to the marginal value product f labor employed in producing an alternative commodity.

In some areas, even under the most favorable circumstances, the iarginal productivity of labor in production of a given commodity, C, is ot sufficient to equal the value product of the marginal labor employed a production of commodity B, in which case commodity C will not be roduced. However, if it is assumed that population increases in all egions, the margin of production is pushed down further in each region, nd marginal productivity may be so reduced that while it was uneco- omical to produce commodity C before, it is now possible to do so ecause of the fact that the margin of productivity in commodity B has so eclined as to make the value product of the marginal labor employed 1 producing commodity B as low as that of the marginal labor employed 1 producing commodity C. Thus, with the increase in population, margi- al productivity may be reduced to such an extent that each region would e producing two commodities instead of one, but would still specialize rgely in the commodity in which it has the greatest advantage.

POPULAR INTERPRETATIONS OF BASIC PRINCIPLES

Some popular interpretations of the principle of comparative advantage iclude the rule of buying anything that can be bought more cheaply than t can be produced, and hiring those things done that can be done by hire 1ore cheaply than you can do them yourself. If a manufacturer is trying to ecide whether to buy power or produce it, he decides the question on the asis of which costs less. If others can produce power more cheaply, he 1ould buy power from them and concentrate on manufacturing products 1 which he has a greater relative advantage or less comparative disad- antage than in the production of power.

A country would import any supplies or products that it could buy more cheaply than it could produce. However, in determining what product costs to produce, it is important that all costs be included an weighted properly. Too frequently, accurate comparative measures of th costs of producing the product at home and abroad are not availabl For instance, the United States has in the past exported millions of bal of cotton, and it has been generally assumed that this country had a con parative advantage in the production of this crop. When allowance made for such social costs as soil exhaustion and soil erosion, our re costs of production per bale of cotton may be considerably different fro those usually given in strict, immediate, monetary terms.

Wheat furnishes an example that is rather similar, because to the usu cash costs of operation should be added costs for feed and seed loans, so conservation, protection against grasshoppers, relief of distressed fan families, and other social costs necessarily encountered in many whea producing areas. Similarly, if a nation exploits its people or soil in orde to trade certain products to other nations, it may appear at first glance t have a comparative advantage in such production while in the long ru no such comparative advantage actually exists. However, adequate an accurate cost accounting, including social costs involved, should make possible to determine the comparative cost of producing certain goods i different areas or different countries.

OBSTACLES TO FREE OPERATION OF BASIC PRINCIPLES

Production in true accordance with the principle of comparative ac vantage is economical—that is, it is being done with the lowest possibl expenditure of human effort and natural resources. When it is not s done, human or natural resources are wasted. Using a piece of land i production for which it is not well adapted is wasting natural resources and giving a man a job that many others may be able to do as well, whe he is badly needed for a task which is short of men, is wasting huma resources. Consequently, public policy should concern itself primaril with securing the freest possible working out of the principle of compara tive advantage. Too often in the past it has not done this, and obstacle like the tariff have been placed in the way of the freest possible operatio of the principle.

Such obstacles have often been adopted because one nation or area fear competition from another. However, it should be clearly understood tha even though a nation or area is inferior in many or even all types of pro duction, it may still be able to supply its domestic market and even sel certain commodities to another nation or area. Inferiority in natural re sources will mean that the wage level will be low, but this does not mea that capital and labor will not be employed. Nations with superio natural advantages will not be able to undersell an inferior nation in al

nes, because in the superior nations employers will have to pay higher
ages, with the result that wage levels in those areas may be so high that
ιe inferior area or nation, with its relatively lower wage levels, can
ɔmpete in many lines.

At the same time, high-wage areas or nations need not fear that low-
age areas or nations will be able to undersell them in all lines of en-
eavor, for such countries enjoy high wage levels because of superiority
ι production or higher marginal productivity. Thus, the cost of labor in
ιch superior areas is no higher than that in low-wage areas, on a
ιarginal productivity unit basis. It is not *wages* that determine compara-
ve costs, but relative labor *costs.* If in some cases low-wage countries do
ndersell high-wage areas, the superior areas would inevitably have to
ɛadjust wage levels. However, the fact that many modern nations have
ɛen able to continue high wage scales is proof that their marginal
roductivity is superior to that of some other areas where lower wage
ɛvels prevail.

THE HIGHEST-RETURN OR BEST COMBINATION OF THE FACTORS

The user of land is interested in making the greatest possible net re-
ιrn, or least net loss from his operations. The point at which the product
an be produced for the lowest total cost per unit is not necessarily the
ιme point at which the operator can make the highest net profit. Let us
ssume that an entrepeneur is manufacturing shoes and has the cost con-
ιitions indicated in Table 4. If the market for shoes is a purely competi-
ιve one, demand for the shoes made in this factory will be perfectly elastic,
ᵥhile marginal revenue and average revenue will coincide. That is, ᵣthe
ιumber of pairs of shoes the manufacturer produces and can sell may vary
ιnywhere from zero to the greatest possible output without causing the
ᵥrice of shoes to change. Thus, for each additional pair of shoes the
ᵥperator would receive the same price, and total revenue would always
ιncrease by the price received for the additional unit. In other words,
ιarginal revenue is equal to price.[4]

The above situation is true only under pure competition, where both
ᵥverage costs and average revenue (price) remain constant when a small
ᵥroportionate change in all the factors together yields a proportionate
ᵗhange in product. Under pure competition, the factors are paid accord-

[4] The term "revenue" is more appropriate to use than "value," because the income
f any factor tends to equal its marginal contribution to the *revenue* (or perhaps we
ᵒuld call it "profits") of the firm employing it. Use of the term "value" might be more
ᵉadily interpreted as implying some contribution to a total outside the firm, which is
f social, as compared with individual significance—such, for example, as the total
ᵖroduct or value of the product available to the economic community. For a more
ιetailed analysis of these points, see E. H. Chamberlin, "Monopolistic Competition and
ιhe Productivity Theory of Distribution," *Explorations in Economics,* McGraw-Hill,
ᵉ936, pp. 248–249.

Table 4. Hypothetical Unit Cost Schedule of a Shoe Factory

Output in Hundreds of Pairs of Shoes	Total Fixed Costs	Average Fixed Costs per Pair of Shoes	Total Variable Costs	Average Variable Costs per Pair of Shoes	Total of All Costs	Average Total Unit Cost (per Pair)	Marginal Cost (per Pair)
1	$1000	$10.00	$ 850	$8.50	$ 1,850	$18.50	$ —
2	1000	5.00	1,380	6.90	2,380	11.90	5.30
3	1000	3.34	1,890	6.30	2,890	9.63	5.10
4	1000	2.50	2,380	5.95	3,380	8.45	4.90
5	1000	2.00	2,845	5.69	3,845	7.69	4.65
6	1000	1.66	3,285	5.49	4,285	7.14	4.40
7	1000	1.43	3,695	5.28	4,695	6.71	4.10
8	1000	1.25	4,075	5.09	5,075	6.34	3.80
9	1000	1.11	4,435	4.93	5,435	6.04	3.60
10	1000	1.00	4,755	4.76	5,755	5.76	3.20
11	1000	.91	5,060	4.51	6,060	5.51	3.05
12	1000	.87	5,345	4.45	6,345	5.29	2.85
13	1000	.77	5,595	4.30	6,595	5.07	2.50
14	1000	.71	5,875	4.19	6,875	4.91	2.80
15	1000	.67	6,195	4.13	7,195	4.79	3.20
16	1000	.63	6,620	4.14	7,620	4.76	4.25
17	1000	.59	7,220	4.25	8,220	4.84	6.00
18	1000	.56	8,340	4.63	9,340	5.19	11.20
19	1000	.53	10,870	5.72	11,870	6.24	25.30
20	1000	.50	14,635	7.32	15,635	7.82	37.65

ing to the value of their marginal product; but there is no tendency whatever for factors to be paid in this way when monopoly elements are present. The productivity of any factor must be considered as the total product it creates, less that which its presence prevents others from creating; and under monopolistic conditions, the effect upon price of the increased output must be accounted for, because by definition of monopoly the monopolistic firm's production will influence the price.[5]

It should be realized in the beginning that unless price is at least equal to average variable costs at some level of production, no production will take place under pure competition unless the entrepreneur desires to keep a force of key workers intact or feels that there is a prospect of higher prices or lower costs in the future. With the data in Table 4, if the market

[5] For more detailed treatment of the determination of equilibrium price and the combination of the factors of production under pure competition and imperfect competition or monopoly, see A. L. Meyers, *Elements of Modern Economics*, rev. ed. Prentice-Hall, 1941, pp. 136–174; Chamberlin, *op. cit.*, pp. 237–248; Joan Robinson *Economics of Imperfect Competition*, Macmillan, London, 1933; K. E. Boulding, *Economic Analysis*, Harper, 1941, pp. 455–478; and F. B. Garver and A. H. Hansen *Principles of Economics*, rev. ed., Ginn, 1937, pp. 61–76.

price were $2.50 and 13 units were produced, the total costs would be $6595 and the total revenue $3250 ($2.50 × 1300 pairs of shoes), leaving a net loss of $3345. At this point, net loss is the least possible with any combination of the factors. Consequently, the operator could not continue unless price rose at least to the level of average variable costs, since it would be more expensive for him to operate the plant under these conditions than to allow it to remain idle, thereby losing only the fixed costs (amounting to $1000 per day), or considerably less than the loss indicated above.

If we assume a price of $4.25, what would be the best combination of productive factors in this factory? The principle to keep in mind here is that at any price above minimum average variable cost, the output at which marginal revenue is equal to marginal cost will be the point of least net loss. In Table 4, column 8, a marginal cost of $4.25 occurs with an outpoint of 1600 pairs of shoes. At this output, revenue would be $6800 ($4.25 × 1600 pairs), while cost of producing this volume would be $7620, leaving a net loss of $820. This is the point of least loss if the price is $4.25, but the operator would be better off to produce these 1600 units at this price than to shut down the plant, if we assume that he could save none of his fixed costs by shutting down completely.

In other words, the price of $4.25 covers the variable costs and leaves $180 to meet part of the fixed costs of $1000. The operator could not continue to produce shoes, in the long run, at this price of $4.25, because eventually his plant and machinery would wear out and have to be replaced. They would not be replaced unless prospective prices were sufficiently high to cover costs of constructing the plant and yield a normal rate of return on the investment. Ultimately, therefore, at the price of $4.25 the operator would be forced out of business, so that $4.25 would not be a long-run equilibrium price.

Let us assume a price for shoes of $6 per pair with the production cost data in Table 4. The guiding principle in this case is that at any price above average total unit costs, the output at which marginal revenue is equal to marginal cost will be the point of maximum net profit. At any output less than this point, addition to total revenue (marginal revenue) from a larger output would be greater than the addition to total cost (marginal cost) occasioned by a larger output. In other words, net profits could be increased if the operator carried his inputs in terms of costs to the point where the last addition contributed an increase in output just sufficient to cover its cost at the going market price.

At any point short of this combination, the operator will lose money, because as long as there is even as much as one cent net return over and above the cost of the last increment, his net profit will be increased by the addition; whereas, if he continues beyond the point where the last incre-

ment just pays its cost, his net profit will be reduced, because each add
tional input costs more than it contributes to the net return. Readir
down column 8 in Table 4, it will be seen that a marginal revenue of $
(a price of $6 per pair of shoes) will just equal marginal cost at th
output of 1700 pairs of shoes. At this output, revenue is $10,200, an
cost is $8220, leaving a net profit of $1980. This is true in spite of the fa
that the price of $6 per pair would still be above cost (average total un
cost) for an output of 1800 pairs. At this latter output (1800 pairs
revenue with a price of $6 per pair would be $10,800, but costs wou
amount to $9340, or a "net profit" of only $1460, or $520 less than wit
production of 1700 pairs.

EQUILIBRIUM OF THE FIRM

Following the equimarginal principle, individual firms will reac
equilibrium when marginal costs are equal to marginal revenue; i.e., th
point where the difference between total cost and total revenue will b
at a maximum. The individual firm would be in equilibrium, under th
preceding assumptions, with an output of 1700 pairs of shoes, assumin
that no plant of any other size would have lower costs. However, $6 woul
not be an equilibrium price for the industry if perfect competitio
existed, because any new firm that encountered the same cost condition
would be able to make $1980 net profit, and the industry would probab
attract new competitors.

Increased output would, in the long run, probably force down th
market price because of greatly increased output; but equilibrium for th
industry would be reached at the point where price is equal to minimu
average total unit cost of each firm, assuming that no production facto
are scarce in the industry or firm, and that all firms have the same cos
conditions. Any price higher than this would tend to encourage new firm
to enter the industry, and a lower price would tend to force some of th
operating firms out.[6]

In every industry, some operators are more efficient than others—tha
is, they can produce a greater output with the same costs or produce th
same output at a lower cost than other producers. When an entrepreneu
is just able to cover expenses, he is called a *marginal entrepreneur*, an

[6] This statement is true, assuming that existing firms in an industry are all of opti
mum size. If plants are not of optimum size, an addition to plant and equipmen
might make it possible to increase output at the same variable cost, and with an addi
tion to fixed costs of considerably less than that shown in Table 4. Consequently, it ca
be said that the equilibrium points for the individual firm hypothetically illustrated i
Table 4 are equilibrium points only on the assumption that the firm is already a
optimum size. Otherwise, all equilibrium points shown are what the ultimate output
for the plant at its present size would be at various prices, and they do not take int
consideration the fact that it might be possible to secure lower costs with a plant of
different size. (See Meyers, *op. cit.*, p. 144.)

he unit he operates is said to be a *marginal unit*. *Marginal firms* may be
expected to expand production under the pressure of competition to the
point of lowest total unit cost, and this point tends in competition to
become the prevailing price. Superior operators, who for one reason or
another can produce with lower costs per unit, can carry operations to a
point beyond that of the marginal producer and still meet their costs.

Like the marginal entrepreneur, the superior entrepreneur will continue to employ variable inputs as long as they at least pay for themselves.
In other words, the superior entrepreneur operates on exactly the same
principle and will continue to add inputs until marginal cost just equals
marginal revenue, because at this point he will make his highest possible
net profit. The lower costs of the superior entrepreneur may be attributable to a wide variety of circumstances, but lower costs tend to disappear under the pressure of competitive and price-making forces, and
differences in unit costs result from the failure of production adjustments
to meet promptly the changed conditions continually arising in a dynamic
society.

IMPERFECT OR INCOMPLETE COMPETITION

Various stages of imperfect competition in various industries influence
output and the combination of productive factors used. In imperfectly
competitive or monopolistic situations, the owner of the monopolistic
firm has the same motives and follows the same general process in seeking
the highest-profit combination of factors as does the purely competitive
owner. However, under pure competition the marginal revenue product
consists of the number of units of product added by the last unit of a
factor employed, multiplied by the sale price per unit of the product,
because the individual firm accepts the price as a given condition which it
cannot change, and hence does not consider changes in its own output as a
price-influencing factor.

In contrast, under monopolistic conditions the effect of increased output upon price must be accounted for because, by definition of monopoly,
the monopolistic firm's output will influence price. The marginal revenue
product under these conditions can be computed by the increase in number of units produced by adding an additional unit of input, multiplied
by the price of the product, less the loss in revenue on all previous units
of output caused by the decrease in price necessary to sell the increased
output. Land rent, under certain conditions, and particularly for certain
types of land use, is determined under imperfectly competitive conditions.
Some of the social implications resulting from this situation are discussed
in Part III.

Agriculture is almost perfectly competitive and suffers economically in
relation to industry, which generally is monopolistic and imperfectly com-

petitive. There are some five million farms in the United States, and the individual producer's output is not sufficient to be a price-making factor in the market. In contrast, in many industrial lines a very few firms, sometimes only one or two, produce half or more of the total output. Under these conditions the individual firm has considerable and frequently virtually complete price-making power.

When purchasing power and market demand decline appreciably, such as during a severe depression, industry reduces production, and industrial price levels are maintained or decline relatively little, whereas agriculture maintains production or may even increase total output slightly and prices drop significantly. This is what occurred during the depression thirties, as is portrayed in Figure 18. The resulting economic

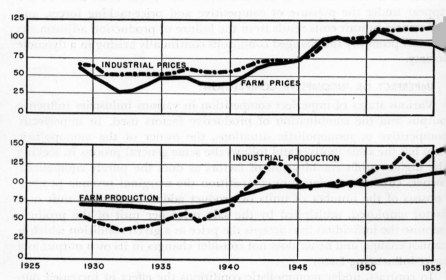

Figure 18.   United States Agricultural and Industrial Production and Prices, 1929–1956. (Source: Compiled from U.S. Department of Commerce, *Business Statistics, 1955,* U.S. Government Printing Office, Washington, D.C., 1955; Council of Economic Advisers, *Economic Indicators,* June, 1957, U.S. Government Printing Office, Washington, D.C., 1957; and U.S. Department of Agriculture, Agricultural Research Service, *Agricultural Outlook Charts, 1957,* U.S. Government Printing Office, Washington, D.C., 1956.)

disparity between agriculture and industry brought forth the domestic allotment plan of the Agricultural Adjustment Administration to reduce farm production, and parity prices and related programs to bolster farm income and purchasing power. In addition, numerous federal agencies were established to provide jobs for the millions of unemployed who were without work because of the greatly reduced industrial production.

REFERENCES FOR FURTHER READING

Baumol, William J., and Chandler, Lester V., *Economic Processes and Policies,* Harper & Brothers, New York, 1954, Chaps. XX, XXI, XXV, and XXVIII.

Black, J. D., and Black, A. G., *Production Organization,* Henry Holt and Company, Inc., New York, 1929, Chaps. V, VI, VII, VIII, IX, X, and XI.

Boulding, K. E., *Economic Analysis,* Harper & Brothers, New York, 1941, Chaps. XXI, XXII, and XXIII.

Ely, Richard T., and Wehrwein, George S., *Land Economics,* The Macmillan Company, New York, 1940, Chap. V.

Explorations in Economics: Notes and Essays Contributed in Honor of F. W. Taussig, McGraw-Hill Book Company, Inc., New York, 1936, Part II, Chaps. I and II.

Garver, F. B., and Hansen, A. H., *Principles of Economics,* rev. ed., Ginn & Company, Boston, 1937.

Johnson, V. Webster, and Barlowe, Raleigh, *Land Problems and Policies,* McGraw-Hill Book Company, Inc., New York, 1954, pp. 99–113.

Meyers, A. L., *Elements of Modern Economics,* rev. ed., Prentice-Hall, Inc., Englewood Cliffs, N.J., 1941, Chaps. IX, X, and XI.

Peterson, George M., *Diminishing Returns and Planned Economy,* The Ronald Press Company, New York, 1937, Chaps. I, II, III, and IV.

Pigou, A. C., *The Economics of Welfare,* The Macmillan Company, London, 1920, Part II, Chaps. VI, VII, and VIII.

chapter 8

ECONOMIC RESPONSES IN LAND USE

THE DEMAND AND SUPPLY OF PRODUCTIVE AGENTS

Demand for the Productive Agents—Supply of the Productive Agents

DISTINGUISHING CHARACTERISTICS OF LAND

Originality or Nonreproducibility—Indestructibility or Permanence—Immobility—Wide Variability or Gradations in Quality

TECHNICAL FACTORS AFFECTING ECONOMIC RESPONSES

Agricultural Enterprises—Forestry—Mining—Recreation—Water Resource Use—Urban Land Use

THE ECONOMICS OF SPACE

Transportation and the Location of Industry—The Theory of Economic Location—Von Thünen's Theory of Agricultural Enterprise Location—Other Factors Affecting Location of Industries—Summary of Location Factors

THE RESPONSE of land in the production of economic goods and services is determined largely by two major groups of factors: (1) man's power to command the land resources of an area or region, which in turn is affected by the state of the arts, the social organization, the character of the institutions (especially property), and the general culture of the people; and (2) the peculiar characteristics of land as a factor of production.

THE DEMAND AND SUPPLY OF PRODUCTIVE AGENTS

The same basic economic principles of demand and supply that determine the economic responses of a production factor, such as labor, capital, or management, also determine the economic responses of land and the consequent allocation of resources to various uses. The emphasis or application of the principles differs, however, because of the peculiar characteristics of each production factor.

DEMAND FOR THE PRODUCTIVE AGENTS

In the short and long run, output is functionally related to both supply (cost derived) and demand (utility derived). Hence, value is also a function of both the demand and the supply. The costs involved must be broken down into the prices of the services of land, labor, loans, etc., which are required to bring them into the firm or the industry, because the prices of these agents are determinants of the prices of the commodities they help produce. All prices or values are therefore interdependent.

According to the equimarginal principle, the marginal cost of the factor must be equal to the marginal revenue from its employment. In pure competition in the agent's market, the price of the agents must equal the marginal revenue productivity, because if the addition to revenue caused by the addition of an agent were less than its price, it would not pay an enterprise to add this agent. If, on the other hand, the addition to revenue were more than the price of the agent, then net revenue would be increased by adding more of the agent until its price just equaled marginal revenue productivity. The firm will be in equilibrium when this condition holds for all agents.

The demand for the services of productive agents is therefore their marginal revenue productivity. The marginal revenue productivity schedule is the addition to product caused by the additional agent times the price of the product in a perfectly competitive market for the product. Where the product is sold in a market where monopoly elements are present, the marginal revenue productivity will be the marginal product times its price minus the revenue lost from a reduction in price of the intramarginal output.

Since it is necessary to recognize that more than one agent may vary in bringing the firm to equilibrium, it must also be noted that the marginal revenue curve of any one agent will be different with every shift in the quantity of other agents employed. The final point of equilibrium will occur where the curve that represents the most profitable combinations of, say, labor with varying quantities of land, intersects the curve that represents the most profitable combinations of land with labor. For every price of labor there will be a corresponding amount that the firm will demand, according to the marginal revenue productivity schedule.

Size of the units into which factors of production can be divided is important in determining how grades (efficiencies and capacities) as well as amounts of the factors will be combined. Breaking down the factors into small doses or units makes possible a more satisfactory fit of th grades or qualities and the amounts of the factors. Use of tractors an combines, in the case of agriculture, makes the doses or applications o capital in the form of machinery relatively large.

In order to use such large machine units effectively, size of the farm unit will be adjusted to the capacity of the machinery. In other words, grain farmer will attempt to operate the number of acres that will utiliz his combine efficiently. In Montana a minimum power unit is a three plow tractor, which will handle about 800 acres; consequently, th minimum desirable size for a dry-land grain-farming family unit (alter nate summer-fallow and crop plan of operation) is 800 acres. If th operator uses a larger power unit, such as four-bottom tractors, he mus increase the size of his operating unit to at least 1100 acres if he is t make efficient use of this equipment. A six-plow tractor unit is capable o handling 1800 acres, and a 12-plow tractor 3000 acres.[1] In the case o sheep ranching, the minimum-sized unit is that which will take care of band of sheep of around 1000 or 1200 head, since a man will be require for herding purposes, and a smaller number of sheep will not make mos efficient use of his labor. It is not possible to hire less than one man, s that the number of sheep that one full-time man can efficiently her determines the practical minimum number of sheep that should b handled by the operating ranch.

In the case of urban land utilization, doses or units of productior factors are frequently very large. When the owner of an office building wishes to increase the size of his building, he must add at least one whole story. He cannot add a few dollars' worth of building, as a farmer car add a few dollars' worth of fertilizer or seed. Inflexibility in size of capital units, in the case of urban, agricultural, and mining land, often deter mines organization and size of the production enterprise. The extent to which the operator will approach the combination of productive factors that will result in the highest possible net profit depends largely on his ability to apply exactly the right amount and quality of each factor in the combination.

SUPPLY OF THE PRODUCTIVE AGENTS

The supply of the agent of production is subject to the same general principles as the supply of any commodity or service. Following the equimarginal principle, agents such as labor or land will be offered in

[1] See E. A. Starch, "Experiments in the Use of Large-Scale Equipment Under Montana Conditions," *Journal of Farm Economics,* April, 1932. The experiments described by Starch show these various sizes of power units at the optimum acreages indicated, and show that when these acreages were operated the best results in low-cost operations were obtained.

service as long as the marginal cost of the service is compensated by the marginal revenue, and each unit will be placed in that service where its marginal rate of substitution is equal to its marginal rate of substitution in every other service. Each person or firm will offer its land for use as long as the cost of the marginal acre returns a corresponding increment in revenue.

In each use to which any grade of land is put, the marginal rate of substitution will be the same as in every other use. If the last acre placed in wheat did not pay returns commensurate with those in some other use, the land would be transferred until the price ratio was proportionate to the marginal rate of substitution in all uses. In so far as the effect of substitution is concerned, if the last acre could not be substituted for an equal value of labor in wheat as in corn, the holder of the land would find it to his advantage to increase the land in wheat and decrease it in corn until the marginal rate of substitution between land and labor was the same in all cases. This is the equilibrium position for the individual controller of the agent, such as a landowner or a laborer.

When we consider the equilibrium of resources or agents as a whole, however, certain other factors must be considered. What, for instance, is the cost of land in its virgin state? What is the cost of a laborer? To the individual who controls his piece of land, the cost is easily computed—it is the opportunity cost, or the next best use to which the land could be put. The landowner knows what he could get in the market for his land if it were in some other use or rented by another tenant; this knowledge sets his *opportunity cost* of placing land in its present use. This opportunity cost establishes, however, only particular equilibrium of the individual firm. When we think of land as a whole, the uses to which it can be put are, in general, the uses to which it is put. Therefore, some determinant of the general supply curve of land and other resources is needed.

There is only one way to find the cost of land and it also must depend on the marginal rate of substitution. Since some of the agents of production must be produced, these become the key to our answer. Produced goods or capital involve the expenditure of time, which people value. The present value of the last unit of capital that is produced determines the amount and value of the last unit of other agents, such as land or labor, at least a part of whose production is a product of nature and involves no cost in the *general* opportunity sense.

Land and labor will be substituted for capital at the social margin until equilibrium is established. The value of the capital at that point will establish the value of the quality and quantity of land for which it may there be substituted. A brief description of certain peculiar characteristics of land and their economic significance is pertinent at this point.

DISTINGUISHING CHARACTERISTICS OF LAND

Land possesses four characteristics of particular interest to land economists: (1) originality or nonreproducibility, (2) indestructibility or permanence, (3) immobility, and (4) wide variability or gradations in quality. These characteristics are important determinants of the nature of competition in the market for land, the rate of use that will be made of it, and the form of enterprise organization tending to exploit it.

ORIGINALITY OR NONREPRODUCIBILITY

Certain aspects of land are said to be *original*, to the extent that they are a natural product, not the result of man's effort. For certain purposes it is useful to consider as land only those resources that are original and a product of nature. This characteristic of land gives rise to serious problems of distribution and use, since claims to the rights to income from original or natural resources cannot be decided on the same grounds as the rights to resources that have been produced through expended effort.

When the supply of a commodity can be increased rather promptly and indefinitely, economic returns from given units of such commodities tend toward uniformity—as, for example, interest rates on capital for loan purposes. In contrast, any increase in demand for a commodity like land tends to widen the spread between the returns from different grades.

In certain societies, as pointed out in the preceding chapter, rights to the original resources of nature accrue to the first claimants and, in other societies, to the nation as a whole, and in still others to the central sovereign. As will be shown in later chapters, serious land problems arise in the American economy over rights to such natural and original resources as water for irrigation and multitudinous other uses. The value of the rights to these original resources is determined according to their relative scarcity in relation to the uses to which they can be put in terms of the economic principles already discussed.

INDESTRUCTIBILITY OR PERMANENCE

A second characteristic of land is the inherent *indestructibility* of certain of its physical features. Site or position in physical space does not change, nor does the general topography or landscape. The economic value of site or topography may change radically with shifts in population, industry, or technology, but the physical permanence of certain aspects of land remain unaffected.

Certain qualities or attributes of land are destructible. The existence of ghost towns in exhausted mining areas indicates that the resources basic to the life and support of the community have been removed. In a strict sense, the mineral was not destroyed, but changed in form, place, and

ther utilities to find its use in modern industry; but certain qualities of
the land from which it was removed were destroyed. Experience has
shown that loss of soil fertility caused by excessive cropping or by wind
or water erosion can destroy the agricultural productivity qualities of
lands.

In the last analysis, the only quality of land that cannot be destroyed
through human use is location, or physical extension, which is most important in urban lands or lands used for transportation. The past emphasis upon the indestructibility of land has misled many land users and
has resulted in short-sighted practices permanently damaging land resources and decreasing the wealth of the nation.

IMMOBILITY

Land lacks physical *mobility* in comparison with other productive resources. The minute fraction of land which has been moved is testimony
to the permanence of the landscape. It is true that the surface layer of the
soil may be hauled away to other points to be used for various purposes;
but this accomplishes nothing except to reduce the surface level. Moreover, the land that was moved away requires space or other land upon
which to place it.

The relative immobility of land prevents its prompt movement from
surplus areas to scarcity areas; consequently, relatively high prices or high
returns can be secured from land in some areas, and extremely low prices
or returns, or none, in other locations. This relative rigidity or fixity of
land means that the owner or user of land is helpless to move it when his
market—for instance, a city—moves away from him, and as a result he
suffers severe losses. On the other hand, if the city moves in his direction
he may find his income and his land values tremendously increased, without any effort on his part.

In other words, the immobility of land accounts for the slowness with
which land use can be adapted to changes in price and demand. The
quality of *situs,* or location, which land possesses has value only when men
collectively, through preference, live in or utilize a certain area of land.
Because land is immobile, different locations take on great value or
become worthless, depending entirely upon the choices made by human
beings. Thus, situs values are socially created values, not physically or individually created ones.

It should not be inferred from this that only land is immobile. In
modern society, more and more of the fixed plants of industry are becoming immovable and highly specialized. Capital invested in land in the
form of buildings, fertilizer applications, and other permanent fixtures
or additions are immobile and cannot be moved in response to changes in
demand and price and profit prospects. The economic effects of this are

far-reaching, since immobile agents tend to have extremely inelastic supply curves and to be highly specialized. The result is a relatively small elasticity of substitution between most kinds of land and other agents. This means, in general, that it requires a large change in the ratio of the prices of the agents to cause any significant change in the ratio of quantities used. Land will be placed in production, in the long run, even if its return approaches zero.

WIDE VARIABILITY OR GRADATIONS IN QUALITY

Land varies greatly in *quality*. Quality may be considered as comprising two major characteristics—*fertility* and *situation*. Variations in situation are, of course, caused by the area, extension, or space aspect of the physical surface of the land. One hundred acres within the boundaries of New York City are equal in physical area to a hundred acres in the semiarid sections of Nevada; but the concentration of population in the city of New York causes a great value to be placed upon the hundred acres lying within its boundaries, while in the case of the hundred acres in Nevada, the sparsity of population in this range country results in a very small and, in some cases, a negative value [2] being placed upon it. In other words, the quality of the situation is not strictly a physical one, but one resulting from a relationship of men to land.

In contrast, the quality of fertility is more strictly physical. Some lands have been blessed with a combination of plant nutrients, soil texture and structure, topography, mineral deposit, forest stand, or other important characteristics that make their ability to produce food or fiber and the minerals and lumber for modern industry much greater than that of other lands. The best grades of land have not been concentrated in certain areas, and the medium and poorer grades in other areas, but all grades of land can be found in practically all areas, interspersed in a checkerboard fashion. This heterogeneous characteristic of land quality has made it difficult to develop uniform practices applicable to most grades or qualities of land. For example, practices found very successful on some pieces or types of soil have been unsuccessful or impractical on others. Consequently, each piece of land becomes somewhat personalized or individualized and methods of land utilization must be adapted to these individual qualities.

[2] Abundant space has many advantages, such as developing vision, allowing freedom of motion, widening the horizon, and so on; but as Zimmermann points out, ". . . an excess of space is one of the greatest luxuries, one of the most expensive possessions of which a country may boast," and the excessive space in North America, while not as extreme as in Australia, is a definite handicap and a weak point in the American resource pattern. (See Erich W. Zimmermann, *World Resources and Industries*, rev. ed. Harper, 1951, pp. 138–140.) In other words, land may have negative value when an excessive amount of space exists, as it does in the more sparsely settled semiarid and arid regions of the world.

The quality of land, whether agricultural, mineral, recreational, transportation, urban, or forest, should not be confused with the mere capacity of the land to absorb units of labor and capital input. Some lands do not justify heavy inputs of labor, capital, or management, but utilize a limited number of such inputs very efficiently and yield a comparatively high net return. Examples of such farming lands are light, sandy soils that warm up early in the spring and whose products bring the best prices and greatest profit through early marketing. Other types of lands, like the heavier loams, may require the incorporation of a large amount of labor and capital, but may be comparatively less efficient than other soils.

In other words, the better land is not necessarily the land that it pays to cultivate more intensively. Productivity is a result of two factors—*capacity* and *efficiency*—and when land possesses both a large capacity and relatively high efficiency, its output will be large. However, the physical qualities necessary for food and fiber production are relatively limited even in the best soils, so that a point is soon reached with most lands beyond which the rate of return decreases when labor, capital, and management are applied.

This tendency of returns to diminish relative to the inputs of labor, capital, and management as the inputs are increased necessitates recourse to additional acreages as demand for the products of land increases. Ricardo believed that because of this tendency the owners of land would grow richer and richer as society developed and the human race increased in numbers. In other words, as the number of mouths to be fed increased, with growing civilization, more acres of land would be necessary to produce the food and fiber to feed and clothe the increasing population. Ricardo contended that the "best" lands were brought into cultivation first and that any increase in population would necessitate going out to the poorer lands, where the costs of production were considerably higher, with the result that the owner of the better grades of land would receive a differential or net return (rent) for his products because of his relatively lower costs of production.

Malthus contended that population tends to increase in geometric ratio and food supply in arithmetic ratio, so that as population increased there would be heavy pressure on the food supply. This would increase food prices and create extremely favorable markets for the products of the land. Yet, beginning in the thirties the United States government embarked upon an agricultural adjustment program to restrict output of farm products in order to prevent or reduce agricultural surpluses, and operated several programs to increase the farmer's returns. Apparently Ricardo's and Malthus' theories have not operated in precisely the manner in which it was assumed they would.

In general, the spread among the various qualities of land is more extreme than among the qualities of other agents. Because of the relative scarcity of certain of the higher quality land, its marginal revenue product is still very high even when it is fully used, whereas the marginal revenue product of the less productive land may readily approach zero. The difference between these returns is the economic rent. The *economic rent* is defined as the return to a factor or agent above its supply price or above the amount necessary to bring it into production.

In addition to the peculiar physical characteristics of land, it will be seen from the above discussion that the economic principles of utilization and valuation of land are basically similar to those for other resources. Nevertheless, the actual application of these principles is sufficiently distinctive to require separate study, especially because of the further difference in institutional procedure surrounding the appropriation of land.

While the original characteristics of land in their current form cannot be separated from the accumulation of investment (capital), the very fact that there are original, permanent, immobile, and highly variable qualities of land leads to serious problems peculiar to the land agent. This applies to problems of taxation, of tenure, of credit, and of conservation.

TECHNICAL FACTORS AFFECTING ECONOMIC RESPONSES

The physical characteristics of land differ in each major type of use and cause unique forms of exploitation. The major technical factors involved in different land uses determine the type of market competition, typical size of the firm, rate of exploitation, and related economic conditions that occur.

AGRICULTURAL ENTERPRISES

Farming is characterized by the use of rather large areas of land requiring the exercise of entrepreneurial decisions that fluctuate daily and hourly, thereby restricting the size of unit generally in terms of labor and machinery input per firm. The extreme dependence on climatic and other physiographic changes that contribute to the flexibility of planning is characteristic of small-scale operation. Labor and machinery are not subject to routine operation as in an airplane factory, and therefore require constant individual supervision and redirection with the result that large-scale assembly-line technique can seldom be applied.

In addition to the daily and seasonal flexibility of farming operations, the annual variations are extreme and the small-scale firm can survive the periods of loss and low income much more readily than the large corporate firms where the annual statement must be presented and the firm must stand or fall on its financial record. The small-scale family unit has almost unlimited capacity to absorb the shock of depression and crop

lisaster through ability of the family to obtain the necessities of food and
shelter from the farm under the worst of circumstances.

The small-scale enterprise in agriculture means large numbers of firms
as found in pure competition. In the market for the final product of the
farm most items can be graded or standardized, thus providing the second
condition, in addition to large numbers, for pure competition and perfectly elastic demand curves facing individual firms. In the market for
and as such, however, the individual parcels of land are immobile, vary
greatly in "quality," and are identified with particular people, schools,
churches, and transportation facilities that differentiate each parcel from
he next. Monopolistic competition results, since there tend to be relatively large numbers of purchasers and differentiated product. The resulting demand curves will therefore be sloping, an indication that each
individual firm has some effect on the price it charges. In some cases only
small numbers of firms are effectively involved as purchasers in the land
market, and the typical competition therefore would be described as
monopolistic *oligopoly*—small numbers and differentiated product.

This can be extended to include the same conditions in the buyers'
market—few buyers and many sellers to be described by the term monopolistic *oligopsony*. Here the supply curves to the buying firms are sloping,
since they can influence the supply to buyers of the land factor. These
economic implications affect greatly the price to be paid for land and the
type and rate of exploitation that results. They explain the great variations in prices paid for individual parcels of land whose physical characteristics may appear similar to most people but vary considerably in the
minds of the actual buyers and sellers.

The fact that individual firms such as wheat farms tend to face perfectly
elastic demand curves from their product means that no individual can
affect the price of wheat and therefore he is much less likely to increase or
decrease production because of price considerations than where monopolistic elements are effective. There is always the hope that others will
restrict production in sufficient quantity to bring prices up to more remun-
erative levels when depressed prices prevail.

Because consumer preferences are relatively stable from year to year for
the products as they come from the farm, and because the farm is usually
operated in close conjunction with the home and family, investments in
land development and equipment are usually for long periods, with the
result that fixed charges are relatively high in agriculture and sensitivity
to price changes relatively low. Variable or marginal costs affect the
short-time decisions and such costs are relatively less in agriculture than in
most classes of industry. Problems of taxation, mortgage foreclosure, and
sporadic income are especially severe as a result of the high ratio of fixed
costs.

⅄ FORESTRY

While a not inconsiderable part of the forests of this country and o
other parts of the world are in farms, by far the greater part is in virgin
areas of very sparse population. The care of forests requires so few indi
viduals per unit area and the harvesting process lends itself so readily
to very large-scale mobile machinery that the size of the harvesting firm
tends to be rather large. Consequently their numbers in any one area are
small and are characterized by various forms of monopoly or oligopoly
Many forest lands are under direct public control because of their long
term public welfare aspects and their multiple uses for forestry, grazing
watershed, and recreational functions. In many areas private exploitation
cannot utilize these resources fully, since certain social benefits accrue for
which no charge can be levied by private enterprise. The price system
thus requires guidance through public ownership. Many forests are har
vested by private enterprise although by contract with the government.

Since much of the forest area of the New World has been subjected to
very rapid and clean-cut harvesting or to fire, maintenance requires very
long-term investment. Many hardwood forests require 150 years or more
for full maturity. As a consequence few individual firms can afford to undertake such long-term investment at prevailing rates of interest. Since
the impatience rate for individuals is too high, much of the development
work in silviculture has been taken over by public agencies. The rate of
interest that a government can use for its calculations is much less than
that of private individuals; therefore public enterprise is able to make
such investments in the forests. The relation of the rate of interest to
conservation is developed more fully in the next chapter.

MINING

In general, mining, including metals, coal, and oil extraction, is one of
great risk in the early stages of prospecting. In the pioneer stage this has
tended to attract foot-loose individuals who are later displaced by large-
scale corporate enterprise operating as monopolists or oligopolists able to
influence the price of their products by the amount of their individual
output. Technical factors in the extraction of minerals, especially the use
of large-scale specialized equipment located in very limited areas, tend to
make monopoly, or at least oligopoly, the prevailing type of competition.
The result of this form of enterprise has been the typical history of
monopoly and oligopoly—rapid technological progress through specialization, and individual restriction of production beyond what would occur
if demand curves for the firm were perfectly elastic, as for instance under
pure competition or maximum fixed prices.

The unique location of minerals and oil results in the differentiation of

he land resources and a type of monopolistic competition in the market
or those resources. With small numbers of firms the result is oligopoly
vith differentiated resources. This type of competition helps to explain
he problems of many oil fields where "cutthroat" competition occurs be-
:ause each individual can affect the price of his product. When any firm
'ails to see its own price changes reflected in the prices and output of other
irms in the "industry," it may drop its price to increase sales, only to find
hat its competitors drop theirs, further leaving the first with a lesser share
of the market than before the original drop in price. This type of price
:utting cannot occur in pure competition where the individual firm
iccepts the price as given and makes his adjustments in output without
iny regard to his own influence on price.

RECREATION

The use of forests, lakes, and mountain areas for recreation seems to
end itself most readily to public ownership and control. Most of the rights
:onnected with the ownership of lands for such purposes cannot readily
be sold to users at rates sufficient to encourage the kind of utilization and
development demanded by people as a social group. In addition, most
recreational areas are very primitive and therefore considered in the mores
and folkways as the heritage of all who wish to use them. The services
of the forests for hunting and fishing, for instance, are sporadic and not
readily valued in the market price. Where this occurs, government ownership and the charge of token fees or licenses is the general rule. Often
recreational areas are multiple-use areas which include forestry, grazing,
watersheds, etc., and the allocation of use rights to each can most readily
be decided by public agencies whose support comes largely from tax
sources rather than from the sale of the rights to use.

The land factor is used very extensively and is combined with very
limited quantities of capital and labor.

WATER RESOURCE USE

Both technically and economically water use represents the extreme
differences between power sites and navigation or irrigation and the use
by humans to quench their thirst. Each of these uses has adapted itself
to a different type of entrepreneurial organization and operates typically
under different forms of competition. Power sites are usually exploitable
only by relatively large-scale corporations under government regulation
or government ownership.

The development of water for navigation consists of channel deepening
and building locks and canals, usually by government enterprise. The
operation of ships is usually handled by private entrepreneurs. These pri-

vate firms may vary from very small companies to huge steamship corpora
tions. Irrigation is being developed more and more by public agencies and
small private firm exploitation. Limited monopolistic competition stem
from the unique rights to water use that the prevailing doctrines of th
society permit—riparian or appropriation, as the case may be.

Watershed protection is usually by government regulation, since pri
vate firms that use the areas for grazing cannot sell their protective serv
ices in the market place. First, the value of avoiding floods in the valle
or maintaining adequate drinking or irrigation water supply cannot b
allotted to a single person or firm. Second, no one person or firm coul
profit by paying for such protection, although the people as a whole or in
coöperative units do find it practicable.

Urban water users are very often served by municipal agencies for th
same reason: only large-scale effort can justify the use of rivers and lake
in the development of drinking-water and sewage systems. If single larg
firms were permitted to exploit these essential services, their strategi
position through monopoly powers would be dangerous to the publi
welfare.

URBAN LAND USE

Land tends to lose much of its strategic influence in the economic or
ganization and processes when it becomes an urban site. In general the
ratio of men and of capital to land is so high in cities that these other
factors can quite readily be substituted for land, and the forms of competi
tion vary widely as they are related to land use, depending on the nature
of the industry involved. It is important, nevertheless, to point out that
land does have unique site value, and the urban market for land, just like
the agricultural market, is one of monopolistic competition with differen
tiation in quality an important determinant of value and use.

THE ECONOMICS OF SPACE

The existence of individuals in time is determined for them, but each
is free to select his location. The place of origin influences but does not
determine our location. Finding the right or best location is essential to
successful enterprise and to the establishment of lasting settlements.

Actual and rational locations do not necessarily coincide. The identify
ing and explaining of existing sites of individuals or enterprises may un
cover numerous considerations that guided or influenced them in choosing
the actual locations. But to concede that such sites are rational or the best
is dangerous. The determination of the *best* location is far more significant
in land economics than determination of the actual ones.

Many theories and explanations for location of economic activities and iterprises have been advanced. Some have transportation costs, some vailability of markets; others labor costs and purely personal considerations. These various approaches or points of view may explain an actual cation, but, except in special cases, no single one shows the correct location. In a free economy the correct location of the individual enterprise es where the net profit is greatest.[3]

TRANSPORTATION AND THE LOCATION OF INDUSTRY ✗

Location is largely a function of transportation. Many unique land ements such as mines, fertile land, or oil deposits derive their value from heir accessibility through transportation channels. The rates charged for oving men and materials greatly affect the value of the products of every ea. Serious problems follow from the fact that most forms of transportation, such as railways, ships, trucks, and airplanes, are operated for the ost part under forms of oligopoly and monopolistic competition. If ansportation firms were given a free hand to charge fees purely in accordance with their own power to affect the market and achieve maximum rofits, the position and profitability of other industries would be subject the whims and fancies of the transporters. This become especially important when it is recognized that transportation charges lend themselves ery readily to a form of monopolistic price policy known as discrimination, which cannot occur where competition is pure.

In order to achieve maximum profits, it is in the interests of any firm to parate the demands of individuals or groups and charge different prices r each. In most industries, even where monopoly is present, discrimination, except on a very limited scale, is very difficult to practice, since the uyers at the lower prices can resell at higher ones and thus bring all rices to a market level. In railroad transportation, however, the services f carriers cannot be resold, and railroads can readily separate their customers into groups, charging varying prices to each. Customers with the ore elastic demand curves, such as those who could use other modes of ansportation if railway fares increased, will be charged lesser rates than istomers whose demand for railroad service is inelastic and vital to their perations such as those who have no alternative means of transportation.[4]

The result of this strategic nature of transportation and its monopoly ower, especially of discrimination between places, commodities, and ersons, is widespread regulation of rates and services and sometimes public ownership, as in certain European countries and Canada, where railoads are wholly or partially government owned.

[3] August Lösch, *The Economics of Location*, Yale University Press, 1954, p. 27.
[4] For a discussion of the theory of discrimination, see Joan Robinson, *Economics of mperfect Competition*, Macmillan, London, 1933, Chaps. XV and XVI.

THE THEORY OF ECONOMIC LOCATION

Alfred Weber argued that location of manufacturing industries is dete mined by the ratio between weight of the localized material and weig of the product (assuming transportation costs to be variable and lab costs constant). This ratio Weber called the *material index*,[5] and it re resents weight loss of the material in process of manufacture. Extractic of gold from its ores requires an extremely high tonnage of material p ton of product, and weight loss is close to 100 percent while the har shoemaking industry has a very low percentage of weight loss, and wou be located close to the consuming areas (centers of population). Mo forest products tend to be manufactured in forest areas, and ores tend be smelted near the mines, if coal or other cheap fuel sources are avai able. On the other hand, products involving addition or use of son product available nearly everywhere tend to be manufactured near are of greatest consumption.

A good example of the effect of the "material index" upon manufa turing locations is the westward movement of the U.S. butter manufactu ing industry. The center of butter production was formerly New Yor State, but eastern dairy farms now produce fluid milk for the inhabitan of the large eastern industrial cities, while creamery butter manufactur has moved to the Midwestern dairy section, where the finished produc butter, can be shipped east with relatively little expense. In other word the weight of the finished product is much less than the weight of mil from which the butterfat is secured to manufacture the butter. Perishabi ity is another important factor. Milk used for fluid consumption must b kept fresh, so that refrigeration costs, as well as transportation costs o the rather bulky fluid milk, are large. A third factor is the large mark for skim milk, a by-product of butter, in the hog industry of the Middl West.

The question of manufacturing location resolves itself into balancin the transport advantages of nearness to materials and nearness to market For each combination of material sources and markets, there must be point, or points, at which total transportation costs involved in assemblin materials and delivering the product to market are less than they woul be elsewhere. In the absence of production cost differentials, the base loca tion for the production process is at the point of minimum transportatio costs.[6] This point, for an industry, may be at some source of material

---

[5] C. J. Friedrich, *Alfred Weber's Theory of the Location of Industries,* University c Chicago Press, 1929, p. 60.

[6] Wilhelm Launhart, *Mathematische Begrundung der Volkswirtschaftslehre,* Leipzi 1885; and Alfred Weber, *Über den Standort der Industrien, Erster Teil, Rein Theor des Standorts,* Tubingen, 1909, translated by C. J. Friedrich as *Alfred Weber's Theor of the Location of Industries,* University of Chicago Press, 1929.

at some market, or perhaps at neither. Consequently, it is essential to
know how important the transportation costs are in relation to differentials in production cost.

An example of the influence upon location of manufacturing enterprises exerted by small changes in relative freight rates on the raw material
and finished product may be taken from the American flour-milling industry, ordinarily referred to as a "material-oriented" industry, because
material transportation costs generally outweigh differentials in production costs, nearly 7 pounds of wheat being required to make 5 pounds of
flour.[7] This fact favored Minneapolis, compared with Buffalo and Roch-
ester, as center of the milling industry after the center of wheat growing
had moved to the Plains states. But in the period 1905–1930, changes took
place resulting in a rise in cost of shipping flour, relative to the cost of
shipping wheat, on the Great Lakes. This and other factors gave the
advantage to Buffalo, and in 1930, for the first time, Buffalo milled more
wheat than Minneapolis.[8]

Weber argued that when labor costs vary, an industry deviates from its
transport location in proportion to the size of its labor coefficient (labor
cost per unit weight of material and product moved). Extent of the deviation caused by varying labor costs is determined by the ratio between cost
of labor per ton of product (the labor index) and total weight of all
goods (product, material, fuels, etc.) transported. This total weight is
called *locational weight*, and the ratio is called the *labor coefficient*.[9] If
transportation costs were constant, all production would go to locations
with lowest labor costs.

Weber draws certain conclusions in regard to location of manufacturing industries. He states that, generally speaking, industries with a high
locational weight are attracted toward material, and those with a low locational weight are attracted toward consumption, because the former have
a high material index and the latter a low material index. He proposes
the formula that all industries whose material index is not greater than 1,
and whose locational weight, therefore, is not greater than 2, lie at the
place of consumption. Pure materials (those entering without weight loss
into the final product, or with a weight loss of zero or practically zero)
can never bind the product to their deposits. (The sum of the component
weight of their deposits is always equal at most to the weight of the prod-

---

[7] "Transport-oriented" industries are those for which differentials in transportation
costs generally outweigh differentials in production costs. Transport-oriented industries
may be further classified into "material-oriented" and "market-oriented" industries,
according to which element of transportation cost is predominant. (Edgar M. Hoover,
Location Theory and the Shoe and Leather Industries, Harvard University Press,
1937, p. 36.)

[8] *Ibid.,* p. 38. See also Hoover, *Location of Economic Activity,* McGraw-Hill, 1948.

[9] Friedrich, *op. cit.,* pp. xxiv and xxv.

uct, and therefore the weight of their material index is never mo
than 1.)

Weight-losing materials, on the other hand, may pull production
their deposits. For this to happen, however, Weber argues that it is nece
sary for the material index which they codetermine to be greater than
and for their portion of the material index to be equal to that of th
remainder, plus the weight of the product. Stated more simply, the
weight must be equal to or greater than the weight of the product pl
the weight of the rest of the localized materials.[10]

VON THÜNEN'S THEORY OF AGRICULTURAL ENTERPRISE LOCATION

In agricultural production, geographical position of agricultural lan
relative to available transportation, cities, and consuming centers pla
an important part in determining types of farm products to be raised i
different areas. The German economist Von Thünen undertook to dete
mine what kind of agricultural production should be carried on at
given place and to analyze the influence of transportation upon localiz
tion of agricultural production.[11]

Von Thünen pictured a city (one consuming center) lying in th
center of an absolutely even plain, without rivers or any means of tran
portation except wagons, with equal transportation rates, equal wage
and equal soil fertility or productivity throughout. He also assumed
limited number of agricultural products, and then proceeded to explai
how production of these would be distributed over the plain surroundin
the city. He concluded that concentric zones of production would b
established around the city, the most bulky and most highly perishabl
products being produced closest to the city, and the less bulky and les
highly perishable products in outer zones. Thus, in zones close to the city
vegetables, berries, and milk (either highly perishable or bulky product
or both) would be produced. In zones farther out would be produce
butter (less bulky and less perishable than milk), root crops (thoug
bulky, not so perishable as fresh vegetables), and grain to be fed to live
stock which would be transported to market on the hoof. In the zone
farthest out would be range for grazing livestock. Von Thünen place
forests in the second zone, comparatively close to the city.

It should be remembered that in Von Thünen's time forests furnishe
fuel and building materials, which are very bulky; and since only wagon
and oxen or horses were available for transportation, the forest had to
be near the city. However, natural forest areas might have no such rela
tionship to points of consumption as the forests of Von Thünen's isolate
state, where it is implied that forests were "man-made" and deliberately
placed in the second zone. Nevertheless, in reestablishing forests in area

[10] *Ibid.*, p. 61.

[11] Johann H. Von Thünen, *Der isolierte Staat*, Jena, Gustav Fischer, 1910.

here forest resources have been depleted, location in relation to population centers should be given serious consideration. It is interesting to note that the great lumber markets in the United States are in the East, where the price is set, while the largest forest resources still available are located in the western part of the country, with the result that transportation costs are a considerable factor in lumber costs.

Von Thünen next assumed a river flowing through this plain and city. The effect of this new transportation method, assuming both upstream and downstream transportation to be available, would be to extend the concentric zones in both directions near the river—but particularly upstream, because transportation downstream would be faster and easier. If water transportation were limited to downstream movement only, the effect would be to extend the zones upstream near the river, but not along the sides of the river below the city.

This situation is well illustrated by transportation of produce down the Ohio and Mississippi rivers to New Orleans during the early development of the Ohio Valley. Produce from this area was loaded on barges and floated downstream to New Orleans, making cheaper transportation available for Ohio Valley producers. However, upstream transportation was impossible, since steamboats were not then available, with the result that products purchased by Ohio Valley producers had to be hauled in overland. Barges piled up at New Orleans and were available there for almost any price, while at the head of the Ohio, a premium was paid for boats or shipping facilities.

If it is assumed that the stream cuts transportation costs to one-fifth that of wagon transportation on the upstream side, the first zone will be extended along the river upstream in such a manner that combined land and water costs will equal costs of land transportation for those parts of the plain not having access to river transportation. The other zones will be elongated similarly upstream. On the downstream side, below the city, the zones will be elongated along the river if upstream transportation is cheaper than land transportation. With modern steam engines, upstream river transportation is nearly as fast and efficient as downstream transportation. In modern economies, streamlined railroad passenger service and fast freight transportation, paved highways, motor truck lines, and airways extend city market areas, or zones, out along these transportation channels. In other words, these transportation lines produce bulges in the zones, and to the extent that modern transportation and refrigeration techniques have overcome perishability and bulk limitations, Von Thünen's concentric circles no longer restrict the market areas that furnish goods and services to modern consuming centers.[12]

---

[12] The extent to which the market areas of the city of New York have been extended by modern transportation facilities is illustrated by the shipment of fruits and vegetables from producing points like Florida and California. This brings the areas

OTHER FACTORS AFFECTING LOCATION OF INDUSTRIES

Land is the only element absolutely fixed in position, and *spatial immo-bility* might be used as a distinguishing definition of land. The economic of location is concerned with spatial adjustment of mobile production agents to land in a way determined by human wants and capacities.[The distribution of natural resources furnishes the basic material for social adaptation. This adaptation is dynamic, because man is able to combine agents of production so that natural resources yield consumable utilities, and the creative effort of human societies to modify action of the geographic environment upon their want-satisfying activities is primarily in technological development.[14] The relationship between the point of consumption and location of natural resources used to manufacture con-sumable utilities gives rise to the transport-cost factor, which limits the extent to which comparative advantage between areas can operate.

If the cost of extraction of each commodity at each source is known, the delivered price at any one point will be cost at the source plus freight charges. The lowest combination of cost plus freight determines from which source any given consumption point will be served. This principle can be represented conveniently by a system of contour lines, or *isotims*, connecting points of equal delivered price.[15] Since price is at a minimum at the source of supply, these isotims will be concentric about the source, but any irregularity in the pattern of transport costs will, of course, dis-tort the delivered price pattern (see Figure 19). The system of contour lines or isotims takes into account all costs of and restrictions on transpor-tation, as well as costs of material, and illustrates rather realistically how the pattern of economic activities is established to adapt mobile produc-tion factors to the immobile agent, land.

While transportation or distance from consuming points to location of raw materials is a very important factor in location of industries, other factors play important parts—for instance, availability of labor supply, supply of capital, climate, or topography. A dense population means an abundant labor supply, which permits more intensive utilization of natu-ral resources. Where population is sparse, farming will be extensive, while

producing vegetables and fruits close to New York City into direct competition with extensive outlying areas. Thus, it would seem that there would be less tendency in the future to construct greenhouses for fresh vegetable production close to New York City and more reliance on fresh vegetables, produced in other areas thousands of miles away, made readily available by modern transportation.

[13] Hoover, *Location Theory and the Shoe and Leather Industries*, p. 3.

[14] W. H. Dean, Jr., *Theory of the Geographic Location of Economic Activities,* Edwards, Ann Harbor, Mich., 1938, p. 1.

[15] Hoover, *Location Theory and the Shoe and Leather Industries*, p. 8. Alfred Weber uses the term *isodapane,* meaning "equal cost" (from the Greek *iso*, meaning equal, and *dapane,* meaning cost).

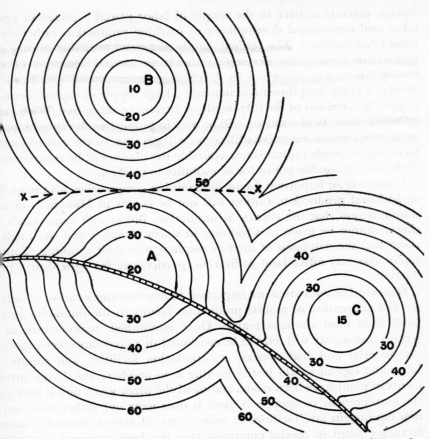

gure 19. Isotims, or Contour Lines Connecting Points of Equal Delivered Price for tractive and Distributive Enterprises. (Based on Edgar Hoover, *Location Theory and the Shoe and Leather Industries*, Harvard University Press, 1937.)

ensely populated areas will grow very little livestock but will produce ops that use a great deal of labor and those which yield a large amount food per acre, like potatoes, rice, corn, and vegetables. Products that ave the greatest comparative advantage in a densely populated area are iose which most need hand labor. Laces, linens, and fine textiles are iade in the more densely populated areas of Europe, as are also high-uality metal goods, jewelry, and toys. In the United States the clothing idustry is located principally in the East and the farm machinery indus-y in the Middle West.

American industry has been slow to develop manufacture of the finest rades of goods, but has instead concentrated on large-scale machine pro-uction, because the supply of natural resources and availability of large

foreign markets relative to the supply of labor placed a premium up
labor and encouraged development of machine production rather th
hand-labor methods. The limited supply of capital available during t
nineteenth century for developing the large natural resources of t
United States was important in developing rather extensive utilizatio
It takes a fairly long time to accumulate a large supply of capital, becau
it must be saved out of the surplus above current consumption. With ca
tal scarce, more land resources will be used in proportion to capital inpu
or, in other words, extensive utilization will develop. In the case of man
facturing, if ample capital is not available the plants will be concentrat
at the most favorable points for accessibility to markets.

Climate is an important factor determining comparative advantage f
agricultural production. Cotton will not be grown in Montana, for t
simple reason that the climate is unsuitable. Butter and many kinds
cheese cannot be made to advantage in warm climates; and the Engli
claim that the dampness of their atmosphere aids their spinning. Topo
raphy also may affect land utilization, particularly for agricultural pr
duction.

Historical reasons are more important in determining location of indu
try and adaptation of mobile production factors to the immobile agen
land, than most students realize. Once established, manufacture of
certain commodity will tend to be continued in a given area, even thoug
raw-material and fuel sources, transportation facilities, and supply
labor and capital would justify moving it to another area. Large inves
ments in plant have been made, and until the plant wears out, it may pa
the entrepreneur to operate it until it does wear out rather than buil
new equipment and facilities in other areas. Moreover, around a man
facturing plant or special enterprise that has been operated in a give
area for any considerable time, a local supply of skilled labor usually d
velops, and being comparatively immobile, tends to remain at lower wag
rather than move to new areas where wages might be higher. Also, th
consumers attach considerable value to goods manufactured in lon
established locations, and it frequently takes much time to convince th
public that products from a new area are as good as those from the ol
Thus, such forces as necessary supply of skilled labor and early develop
ment of the industry exert a strong influence on the location of industr
and may be sufficiently influential on it to offset advantages resulting from
transportation or wage differentiations alone.

SUMMARY OF LOCATION FACTORS

Most analyses of plant location have overemphasized the locational sig
nificance of the transport and processing cost factors. Greenhut maintain
that locating factors are divisible into three main groups: (1) deman

(2) cost, and (3) purely personal considerations.[16] The demand factors include: shape of the demand curve for a given product, location of competition, prejudices and buying habits of consumers, relationship between personal contacts and sales, extent of the market area, and competitiveness of the industry in location and price.

The cost factors include: cost of land (rent and taxes), availability and cost of capital, insurance rates at different sites, cost of fuel and power, cost of labor and management, cost of materials and equipment, and cost of transportation.

The strictly personal factors include: the importance of psychic income, environmental preferences, and the security motive.

In all site selections, there is a balancing of all factors—*demand, cost, and personal.* In a capitalistic economy, maximum profit is the overall motivating and integrating factor in plant location, but *maximum profit* must be generalized by defining psychic income as a part of maximum profits. In any case, it is only by focusing attention on all factors—demand, cost, and personal—that understanding of the basic reality of plant location (spatial economics) is secured.

REFERENCES FOR FURTHER READING

Dean, W. H., Jr., *The Theory of Geographic Location of Economic Activities,* Edwards Bros., Inc., Ann Arbor, Mich., 1938.

Friedrich, C. J., *Alfred Weber's Theory of the Location of Industries,* University of Chicago Press, Chicago, 1929.

Goodrich, Carter, et al., *Migration and Economic Opportunity,* University of Pennsylvania Press, Philadelphia, 1936, esp. Chap. VII.

Greenhut, Melvin L., *Plant Location in Theory and Practice,* University of North Carolina, Chapel Hill, 1956.

Hoover, Edgar M., *Location Theory and the Shoe and Leather Industries,* Harvard University Press, Cambridge, 1937.

Hoover, Edgar M., *Location of Economic Activity,* McGraw-Hill Book Company, Inc., New York, 1948.

Lösch, August, *The Economics of Location,* trans. from the 2d rev. ed. by William H. Woglom, with the assistance of Wolfgang F. Stopler, Yale University Press, New Haven, 1954.

McLaughlin, Glenn E., *The Growth of American Manufacturing Areas,* University of Pittsburgh Press, Pittsburgh, 1938.

Von Thünen, Johann Heinrich, *Der isolierte Staat in Beziehung auf Landwirtschaft und Nationalökonomie,* Schumacher-Zarchlin, Berlin, 3d ed., 1875.

Zimmermann, Erich W., *World Resources and Industries,* rev. ed., Harper & Brothers, New York, 1951, Chap. X.

[16] Melvin L. Greenhut, *Plant Location in Theory and in Practice,* University of North Carolina Press, 1956, p. 279.

chapter
9

LAND CONSERVATION

THE NEED AND NATURE OF CONSERVATION

*The Meaning of Waste—Growing Concern over Waste—
Nature and Meaning of Conservation—The Movement to
Conserve in the United States*

THE ECONOMICS OF CONSERVATION

*The Costs of Conservation—The Principle of Optimum
Land-Use Intensity—Individual and Social Interests in
Conservation—Individual Differences in Conservation
Costs—Limits and Permanency of Destructive Exploitation*

ACHIEVEMENT OF CONSERVATION

Desirability of Social Action—Methods of Achieving Conservation—Conservation Policies

SOIL CONSERVATION

*How Soil Fertility Is Lost—Methods of Controlling Erosion—Suggestions to Improve Soil Conservation—The Soil
Conservation Service—Soil Conservation Districts—Grazing and Weed Control Districts*

CONSERVATION OF NONAGRICULTURAL LANDS

*The Need for Forest Conservation—Recreational Land
Conservation—Mineral Land Conservation—Conservation
of Water Resources—Urban Land Conservation*

THE RAPID settlement of the United States was accompanied by the
waste and depletion of many important basic natural resources which
were so abundant that neither public nor private agencies felt any great

sponsibility for their conservation or protection. In recent years, how-
er, the economic and social consequences of wasteful utilization have
:come more apparent; and the public is now more aware of the desir-
ility—and often the necessity—of using natural resources so as to permit
more permanently prosperous economy.

THE NEED AND NATURE OF CONSERVATION

Public interest in conservation was first aroused by the decline of
heries and forests, but was intensified during the thirties with dust
orms in the Plains, severe soil erosion and fertility impoverishment in
e South and other areas, and by declines in certain types of wildlife,
me, and minerals.

THE MEANING OF WASTE

Conservation means protecting land resources against wasteful exploi-
tion. Waste may be defined as socially uneconomic use of resources re-
lting from failure to combine factors of production to obtain maximum
t returns or from failure to evaluate properly social costs and benefits.
riefly, waste means failure to attain the most economic social use. Waste
sults in a dwarfed realization of the potential want satisfactions in natu-
l resources.

The many forms of waste include failure to utilize natural resources or
ergies when available, to utilize them competently, to arrange them in
propriate forms and combinations at proper times and places, to em-
oy them in quantities indicated by prudent use and needs, to take into
nsideration losses involved in certain uses to balance present against
ture uses, to balance individual against collective use of resources, and
apply human intelligence effectively.[1]

The distinction between waste and loss is not simple. For instance, many
oneers moving westward in the early part of the last centry cut off and
urned much virgin timber in order to use the soil for producing crops.
rom the pioneer's point of view, and that of his contemporary generation,
e immediate result was net benefit or progress and would not have been
nsidered either waste or loss. A generation or two later, however, de-
easing supplies of good timber might have made it appear preferable to
ave preserved the forest in the interests of long-run social benefit.

Certain types of waste, particularly the more obvious kinds and those
sulting from common land utilization practices, can be eliminated with
lanning, concerted effort, and human intelligence. In the past a con-
derable lag existed between the time when better utilization methods
ere developed and the time when they have been put into widespread

[1] For these and other sources of waste see H. S. Person, "Waste," in *Encyclopaedia of
e Social Sciences*, Vol. XV, p. 367.

practice. This educational lag has been a very important cause of wast
and only by greatly increasing the efficiency of the educational syste
can such lags be shortened.

GROWING CONCERN OVER WASTE

In earlier periods, when the threat of famine was very real and scarci
of many goods and services general, thrift was considered a virtue. Such
virtue, however, was regarded as an individual rather than a social matte
It is one of the paradoxes of history that serious concern over waste as
social problem developed only after society entered upon an economy «
potential abundance.

Shortly after the turn of the century a concern developed for waste ;
a social problem, and students of public administration focused the
attention on forests, fisheries, minerals, and other exhaustible natur
resources. The era of rapid economic expansion and development in th
nineteenth century and the increased rate of use accompanying Worl
War I took a great toll of American natural resources.

Waste of resources has not been restricted to the United States, althoug
the rapid development of this country has helped to make consequenc«
of wasteful exploitation more spectacular. Developing agriculture h¡
greatly modified plant and animal life in various parts of the world, an
has usually tended to accelerate the rate of land degradation. Great are«
of formerly useful land—especially in China, North Africa, Asia Mino
and North America—have been rendered unfit for use. This has bee
caused partly by a declining water supply and destructive floods; but so
erosion and fertility depletion on an appalling scale are obvious in mar
older areas. In the United States excellent examples of this can be seen i
longer settled areas like the southern Appalachians.

Extensive depletion of mineral resources is much more recent but m
less obvious. In older districts and nations depletion has frequently ou
weighed the advance of technology; a good example of this is Englan(
which was the largest producer of coal and iron ore and the princip;
source of the world's copper, lead, and tin in the first half of the nin«
teenth century. Today England's copper is all but gone, lead and tin ai
nearing exhaustion, and output of the Cumberland iron mines (the onl
source of rich iron ore in Britain) is steadily declining. English coal mi»
ing has now reached the stage of increasing costs, and output per man pe
year has been declining since 1883 in spite of increased technical know
edge and engineering skill. Competition of lands recently brought int
production, where costs are declining and yields per miner are still goin
up, has contributed to the serious economic difficulties of English minin
in recent years.[2]

[2] Cf. F. G. Tryon, "Conservation," in *Encyclopaedia of the Social Sciences*, Vol. I'

NATURE AND MEANING OF CONSERVATION

Conservation in a narrow and restricted sense means preserving earth resources in unimpaired efficiency, or as nearly unimpaired as wise exhaustion or the nature of the particular case allows. In this restricted sense of preservation," conservation usually involves reduction of the rate of resource disappearance, use, or consumption, and a corresponding increase n unused surplus left at the end of a given period.[3] Conservation should ot be confused with "economizing," since the latter does not necessarily ffect the rate of consumption, but expresses ratio of input to output, or f sacrifice to benefit. Economizing may, of course, result in conservation, epending upon the nature of the industry (whether competitive or mo-opolistic) and the elasticity of demand. In a price system, economizing ncludes all efforts to improve the economic ratio of output to input or, n social terms, to improve the ratio of benefit to sacrifice.

This definition of conservation, which emphasizes curtailment of pres-nt consumption for the future, restricts economic conservation to maxi-nization of social net returns over time. If the term "conservation" is pplied to all kinds of resources, there is no alternative to using this broad definition in its economic meaning, but the definition cannot be used in . physical sense for both fund and flow resources.[4]

The three major types of resource classes (1) *fund*, or *exhaustible*, esources; (2) *flow* resources; and (3) *biological* resources involve differ-nt problems of conservation.[5] *Fund*, or *exhaustible*, resources such as oal and oil, are limited in amount, and conservation may be defined as a lecrease in the rate of consumption which will leave more available for uture use. Conservation of fund resources involves higher prices in the present and may be attained best by monopolistic control.[6] The principal lifficulty in determining the proper rate of use involves evaluation of the lynamic factors of technological changes and the possibilities of substitu-ion.[7] These factors vary for each resource, and consequently, the prob-ems of conservation can be realistically approached only by a careful analysis of the physical and economic factors involved.

Flow resources occur periodically over time—such, for example, as vater flow, sunshine, precipitation, and fertility from the action of solu-ions and organisms in the soil combined with organic matter formed by

---

[3] Zimmermann defines conservation as "any act of reducing the rate of consumption or exhaustion for the avowed purpose of benefiting posterity." See Erich W. Zimmer-nann, *World Resources and Industries*, rev. ed., Harper, 1951, p. 807.
[4] A. C. Bunce, *Economics of Soil Conservation*, Iowa State College Press, 1942, p. 3.
[5] *Ibid.*, p. 4.
[6] Harold Hotelling, "The Economics of Exhaustible Resources," *Journal of Political Economy*, Vol. XXXIX, No. 2, April, 1931, pp. 137–175.
[7] Bunce, *op. cit.*, p. 5.

growth of roots. Conservation means using these resources in such a wa that physical waste (nonuse) is minimized and involves an increase in th rate of use.[8]

Biological resources of plant and animal life have characteristics of bot fund and flow resources upon which they are dependent. They are unlik fund or flow resources in that their annual productivity may be decrease through exploitation, maintained at existing levels, or increased throug human action. Conservation, under these circumstances, may be define as the maintenance of the present level of productivity.[9]

The kind of conservation program established and its success in cor serving land resources will be determined largely by two major force (1) the stage of industrial development of the nation—that is, the statt of the changing quantitative relationships of natural resources to suppli of labor, capital, and management, and the changing economic and soci values of such resources; and (2) the philosophic doctrines that sanctio prevailing economic institutions and culture.[10] The first of these tw major forces involves all the material environment and the machinery (social control.

THE MOVEMENT TO CONSERVE IN THE UNITED STATES

No nationwide appreciation of or movement toward conservation (natural resources developed until the latter part of the nineteenth cer tury.[11] Attention was first drawn to the rapid decline of fisheries and fo: ests, and the national concern caused the creation of the office of Commi sioner of Fish and Fisheries in 1871. The American Forestry Associatio was organized by private citizens in 1875, with the purpose of promotin public appreciation of scientific forestry and timber culture. It began movement that led to a forestry bureau in the Department of Agricultur(

[8] *Ibid.*

[9] *Ibid.*, p. 4.

[10] Cf. R. T. Ely *et al.*, *The Foundations of National Prosperity*, Macmillan, 191! pp. 98–99.

[11] Atwood points out that by 1670 certain towns in Massachusetts were becomin "much straitened" for building timber, and that before another hundred years ha passed, larger cities like Boston and Philadelphia were experiencing a shortage i easily available timber resources. In 1681 William Penn signed an ordinance whic] required that in clearing land 1 out of 5 acres should be left in trees. In 1828 Joh Quincy Adams, recognizing the importance of live oak timber in the construction o battleships, established a naval station in the live oak region of Pensacola, Florid; and set aside 30,000 more acres of land for the cultivation of the live oak trees. Thu a national reservation and careful, if not scientific, forestry were inaugurated; th project was abandoned, however, during the administration of Andrew Jackson (W. W. Atwood, "The Conservation Movement in America," in A. E. Parkins an J. R. Whitaker [eds.], *Our National Resources and Their Conservation*, Wiley, 193(pp. 2, 3.)

nd to the creation of the first national forest reserve in 1891. An irriga-
on division (in the United States Geological Survey) organized in 1888
ter grew into the Reclamation Service. The Geological Survey activities
a classifying public domain resources were expanded into a Bureau of
Iines in 1910. In 1892 the Yellowstone National Park timberland reserve
as created by President Harrison, who set aside 13 million acres as forest
servations before his term expired. President Cleveland, who followed
Iarrison, withdrew 21 million more acres from the public domain and
laced them in forest reserves.[12]

The conservation movement was given considerable impetus by Presi-
ent Theodore Roosevelt, and by Gifford Pinchot, appointed head of the
epartment of Agriculture's Division of Forestry in 1898. Conservation
as first of all applied to forests, under the wise leadership of Pinchot,
nd coal came next with the Ballinger-Pinchot controversy.[13] On March
. 1907, Roosevelt appointed the Inland Waterways Commission, which
uggested a conference of governors of the various states; and on May
3, 1908, such a conference (known as the "White House Conference")
as held.[14] Shortly afterward Roosevelt appointed Pinchot as chairman
f the new National Conservation Commission, which was divided into
our sections assigned respectively to minerals, waters, forests, and soils.
a the 18 months after the White House Conference, 41 state conserva-
on commissions and 51 conservation commissions representing national
rganizations were created.

President Roosevelt also organized the North American Conservation
onference, which was held in Washington on February 18, 1909. Canada,
Jewfoundland, and Mexico were invited to appoint commissioners to
onsider conservation with the United States commissioners. In the same
onth Roosevelt requested the world powers to meet at The Hague for
ie purpose of considering conservation of the earth's natural resources.
n addition to bringing the question of conservation to the foreground
f human consciousness, he withdrew more than 234 million acres of land
rom private entry during his administration.[15]

During World War I the conservation movement was at least mo-
nentarily sidetracked. Many state conservation commissions were not
naintained, although the work they did has branched out into various
elds, and some corporations and private concerns have adopted practices
ending to conserve natural resources. In many states fish and game com-

[12] *Ibid.,* p. 4.
[13] John Ise, *The United States Oil Policy,* Yale University Press, 1926, p. 281.
[14] C. R. Van Hise and L. H. Havemeyer, *Conservation of Our Natural Resources,*
Iacmillan, 1930, p. 6.
[15] *Ibid.,* pp. 10–11.

missions have tended to develop into strong conservation agencies protec
ing scarcer game and limiting the season in which other game can l
hunted. Some states have made significant efforts in building up withi
their departments of agriculture and industry important branches
bureaus for the conservation and development of natural resources. Son
corporations have developed far-sighted policies in utilizing natural r
sources. However, too many private concerns have taken a short-sighte
view, and some resources have been exploited in a wasteful manner.

Almost every President since Theodore Roosevelt has withdrawn lan
from the public domain, and this land has been carefully studied an
classified for its respective uses. In 1920 Congress passed a general leasir
law whereby government lands containing coal, petroleum, gas, oil shal
phosphorus, and sodium salts are to be leased on a royalty basis and n
sold. The National Park Service was organized in 1916, and the nation
parks have been made sanctuaries where certain wild game and wildli
can live and increase undisturbed. These parks today comprise an impo
tant part of the recreational land areas of the nation.

Today the federal government owns a considerable acreage of lan
containing important minerals, as well as a number of irrigation an
power plants, millions of acres of forest lands in its forest reserves, an
many acres of recreational lands, through its national parks and nation
monuments. The conservation movement can be considered quite effe
tive in withdrawing certain important types of land from private explo
tation and waste.

As an emergency depression measure to stabilize employment, Presider
Franklin Roosevelt embarked in the thirties upon various program
many of which were important in the field of conservation. For exampl
the Civilian Conservation Corps made trails, fire lanes, and highways i
the national forests and removed dead timber and debris, replantin
burned-over areas on a large scale in many sections. Large federal appr
priations have been made since 1933 for the study of soil erosion and fc
costs of an action program to eliminate or greatly reduce it. Numerou
areas have been selected for intensive experimentation, with the hope tha
methods would be discovered or developed that farmers could use t
prevent soil erosion and fertility wastage. The National Resources Plar
ning Board was appointed by President Franklin Roosevelt to inventor
the natural resources of the nation and suggest plans of utilization to cor
serve them and stabilize employment. The Agricultural Conservation Pr
gram has tended to encourage, through its benefit payments, agricultura
land utilization practices that prevent soil erosion and maintain or in
prove soil fertility.

Conservation measures fitted in well with the period of depression an
the employment programs of the thirties and the agricultural surpluse

which followed World War II. As a result, the public is much more con-
servation-conscious than in earlier years.

However, on many private lands and some public lands, overgrazing,
erosion, and depletion of soil fertility still occur; shore-breeding species
of fish are diminishing; private forests are being cut over, burned, and
abandoned; wastes in bituminous coal mining average 35 percent, while
if avoidable wastes were eliminated they would average only 10 percent;
and competitive drilling, in the case of oil production, causes formidable
losses of oil and gas.[16]

THE ECONOMICS OF CONSERVATION

It is generally assumed that private or personal sacrifice and postponement involved in any conservation project promise a net economic gain,
or at least sufficient return to cover the costs of such postponement and
sacrifice. Conservation frequently involves not only postponement of possible present income and satisfaction of immediate wants, but a considerable cash outlay for taxes, interest, and upkeep of land resources.

THE COSTS OF CONSERVATION

Unless private proprietors contemplate a net economic gain, or at least
a return sufficient to cover costs of postponement and sacrifice, they will
not postpone or forgo immediate exploitation or use, and consequently
will not conserve. The personal financial conditions of private proprietors,
the present and prospective commercial value of their properties, and the
uncertainties of the future are all important factors in determining
whether the private user will conserve or exploit his property. If the immediate needs are not pressing, and if a sufficient monetary return from
the increase in value (conservation increment) seems assured, it may be
good business to save and wait.

On the other hand, if financial needs are pressing and if the prospective
increase in value within a reasonable time is not inviting, conservation
clearly appears to be undesirable for the individual. For example, from a
private standpoint, the amount that the utilizer of land can afford to spend
to conserve his resources, whether agricultural, forest, mineral, or other
land, is limited by the present value of anticipated returns from the expenditure. If borrowed funds are spent, the rate of interest would be an
important consideration in determination of the present value of future

[16] Tryon concludes that the success of the conservationists in checking wastes attributable to the competitive system is small, but that chemists and engineers have
aided conservation by their improvement of technical processes. For example, in the
production of lead and zinc, selective flotation and recovery of large amounts of those
metals, formerly wasted because they could not be separated, have been made possible. Efficiency of utilizing coal and producing oil has been greatly increased. (Tryon,
op. cit., pp. 228–229.)

returns; while if the land user's own capital is used, the rate of interes
on alternative investments must be considered.[17]

Rationing of credit by credit agencies may cause uneconomic exploita
tion, through limitation of loans or high interest rates. In the case of loan
for personal expenditures, an uneconomic disinvestment may occur becaus
the individual is unable to relate his time preference to the interest rat
by borrowing. In the case of production loans, a high interest rate or limi
tation on the size of the loan may prevent the individual from adjusting
his farming to a more profitable and conservational system.[18]

THE PRINCIPLE OF OPTIMUM LAND-USE INTENSITY

Land utilization, from the entrepreneurial or management point o
view, is governed by the *Principle of Optimum Intensity*. Optimum inten
sity is the point where value of the marginal unit of cost factors put int
land is equal to value of the marginal unit of output from the land. B
this definition, optimum intensity takes account of the economic effects o
fertility or productivity depletion to the marginal increment in volum
of output; or, in other words, a decrease in the present value of futur
income caused by the marginal output is considered part of margina
cost.[19] However, as one author points out, optimum intensity does no
always require maintenance of the producing ability of the land. Onl
if the value of marginal output equals or exceeds the costs of obtaining th
product, plus costs of restoring productive ability lost in obtaining th
product, does land conservation become an economic possibility at th
point of optimum intensity.[20] Thus, the principle of optimum intensit
does not in itself imply land conservation. In fact, it may mean the exac
reverse, because in certain periods and localities, maintenance of produc
tive ability on agricultural, mineral, or any other type of land may b
economically impossible and also socially undesirable. This would be tru

[17] Cf. Eric Englund, "What Price Conservation," *Land Policy Review*, Vol. III, No.
March–April, 1940, p. 1; and Siegfried von Ciriacy-Wantrup, "Soil Conservation i
European Farm Management," *Journal of Farm Economics*, Vol. XX, No. 1, February
1938, p. 88.

[18] A. C. Bunce, "Society and Conservation," *Land Policy Review*, U.S. Department c
Agriculture, Bureau of Agricultural Economics, Vol. IV, No. 6, June, 1941, pp. 15 an
16.

[19] In individual enterprises, assuming free competition and perfect foresight, opti
mum intensity is reached at a point where value of the marginal unit of huma
effort put into the land is equal to value of the marginal unit of output from lan
use. However, these values are not limited to monetary units. A self-sufficient famil
farm, for instance, places certain important valuation or utility upon an increase
supply of food, clothing, and shelter and compares with this utility or satisfaction th
disutility of increasing units of work.

[20] Cf. Siegfried von Ciriacy-Wantrup, "Economic Aspects of Land Conservation,
Journal of Farm Economics, Vol. XX, No. 2, May, 1938, pp. 462–463.

every instance in which conservation diverts productive factors from
:lds in which the present value of their marginal product is higher.
There is some question whether the principle of optimum intensity,
ith due consideration of prevailing interest rate and entrepreneurial
me preference and foresight, determines the economic possibilities of
nd conservation for individual action. For example, although it is gen-
ally held that "maintenance for the plant is a necessity," it is true that
»sts of maintaining "the plant," whether in agriculture or any other in-
ustry, are important before the plant is built or acquired. Costs of main-
ining a fixed plant, however, do not determine the most economic vol-
ne of output at any given time or place. Thus, in the case of individual
rmers or businessmen utilizing land, the interest rate in relation to the
ılue of the expected output would determine the degree of intensity
aintained for the purpose of land conservation.[21]

INDIVIDUAL AND SOCIAL INTERESTS IN CONSERVATION

Even if we assume that the principle of optimum intensity deter-
ines the economic possibility of land conservation for individual action,
ıe question arises whether it leads to desirable results for the economy as
whole. If the classical assumption of free competition and perfect fore-
ght is employed, conservation is achieved when marginal return of a unit
f a production factor invested in land maintenance equals marginal
ıturn from the best alternative use.[22] According to this concept, conser-
ation or exploitation is economic for society when it is economic for the
ıdividual.[23] However, this assumption of harmony has been challenged
n the grounds that, in reality, "we have to deal with conflicting opinions
ınd interests between different entrepreneurs and between the members
f society with regard to land use or anything but harmony."[24] Moreover,

---

[21] For a discussion of this point see W. J. Roth's discussion of Siegfried von Ciriacy-
Vantrup's "Soil Conservation in European Farm Management," *op. cit.,* pp. 115–118,
ıd Ciriacy-Wantrup's reply in "Economic Aspects of Land Conservation," *op. cit.,*
. 463.

[22] Cf. Walter W. Wilcox, "Measures Needed to Achieve Constant and Efficient Pro-
uction," *Journal of Farm Economics,* Vol. XXI, No. 4, November, 1939, p. 864.

[23] "In the case where exploitation is economic for the individual when all costs have
een included, it appears that it is also economic for society." (A. C. Bunce, "Time
reference and Conservation," *Journal of Farm Economics,* Vol. XXII, No. 3, August,
940, p. 542.)

[24] Gunnar Lange, "A Neglected Point in the Economics of Soil Conservation," *Jour-
al of Farm Economics,* Vol. XXIII, No. 2, May, 1941, pp. 467–468. In replying to
ange's theory, Bunce and Wilcox "appreciate that where individual and group
conomic interests diverge, as is conceivable in a number of cases, it would be neces-
ary to have rules and regulations with regard to group action. In case there is a
ivergence of the individual's and group's economic interest, the majority must be
ermitted to dictate to the individual." They also point out four cases where ex-
loitation may occur: (1) when it is economic for the individual, in which case the

when noneconomic considerations are involved, as they necessarily are, economic grounds alone cannot be used in determining the social desirability of conservation. Reliable guidance necessitates consultation of other social sciences as well as economics.[25]

Many argue that the problem of conservation arises because the interests of individual operators and society differ. For example, an individual may not desire to invest in conservation though such action may be desirable from society's point of view, because society and the individual have different time preferences. "Society, which is expected to exist in perpetuity, should have a different standard of values as between the present and future from that of the individual, whose appraisal of the future is governed by his own short span of life, and perhaps by a shadowy allowance for a generation or two of his descendants." [26]

This difference between individual time preference and social time preference indicates a conflict between the social and the individual point of view of conservation. However, time is not the only important factor determining differences in individual and social conservation activities. The concept of individual and social time preference has been used as a blanket rationalization of why society needs to act to conserve resources, but in reality it is a matter of individual judgments, freedom, and economic compulsion as against social values and compulsion. The time preference concept might be replaced with two others to explain the causes of deviation in interests between the individual and society in conservation: (1) differences between prices available to the individual and society, including interest rates; and (2) consumption values of society, which are social choices society makes simply because of what the people want (recreation, scenery, etc.) . Social value judgments are quite separate from individual economizing and may therefore conflict.[27] Many individuals and groups in society have divergent interests; and these conflicts of opinion and interest among the members of society necessitate compromises.[28]

---

problem of determining whether individual and social objectives are compatible must be faced; (2) where all costs are not borne by the entrepreneur, but may be partly transferred to society or to other persons in society; (3) where custom and ignorance are involved; and (4) where rigidities in the price structure and abnormally high interest rates are involved. (A. C. Bunce and W. W. Wilcox, "A Neglected Point in the Economics of the Soil: A Reply," *Journal of Farm Economics,* Vol. XXIII, No. 2, May 1941, pp. 475–477.)

[25] Cf. Bunce and Wilcox, *op. cit.,* p. 476; and Lange, *op. cit.,* p. 468.

[26] Englund, *op. cit.,* p. 2.

[27] These concepts are analyzed in Bunce, "Society and Conservation," *op. cit.,* pp. 15 and 16.

[28] "Such a compromise is in many instances derived from incommensurable objectives," and "seldom allows itself to be expressed in the simple mathematical symbol of a sum of individual plans, as suggested by so many economists." See Lange, *op. cit.,* p. 470.

Society usually has at its disposal superior facilities and instruments ith which to predict the future. Moreover, society by its own action will fluence future events much more than will actions of the individual perator, or even groups of individuals, in most cases; so that society can ake better predicitions as a rule. This has an important bearing upon ajor cost items involved in conservation—particularly prices, the rate interest, and taxes.[29] As a result, economic plans devised by the individ-il and society would often be different. Even if society and the individual ere influenced by the same economic motives and made use of identical counting systems, they might arrive at entirely different land-use recom-endations. The individual might not accept society's recommendations ithout compensation.

Even if we assume a common economic maximization goal, however, ·ivate individuals and society do not use identical accounting systems. hree important differences in the cost accounting include: (1) differ-ices between costs of exploitation or benefits of conservation (apart from pital losses) as these affect the individual and society; (2) capital losses · gains not always impinging upon the individual; and (3) differences prices available to society and individuals.[30] For example, certain cost ems in society's budget—especially labor costs—may be quite different om those of individuals. If there is widespread unemployment, society ay invest in conservation without depriving the people of present en-·yment of their buying power or the advantage of increased resources for iture use. In other words, it could utilize productive power, including bor, which otherwise would be idle and perhaps need to be maintained / public expenditures for unemployment relief. Costs to society of such bor involved in a conservation program would be computed quite dif-rently from labor costs involved in conservation programs of a private itrepreneur.[31]

INDIVIDUAL DIFFERENCES IN CONSERVATION COSTS

There are important differences in time preference among individual perators within a given group in the economy. For example, one farm perator may have much better information upon which to base his ex-ectations or anticipations than his neighbor. As a result, he may adopt nd utilization plans and practices quite different from those of his neigh-ors, even though he may be operating the same type and size of farm. Ioreover, one operator may obtain credit on more favorable terms, and ight therefore be more willing to invest in conservation. Furthermore, ie cost structure and the system of accounting and appraisal differ so

[29] *Ibid.*, p. 471.
[30] Bunce, *Economics of Soil Conservation, op. cit.*, p. 111.
[31] Cf. Englund, *op. cit.*, p. 3, and Lange, *op. cit.*, pp. 471 ff.

much with the type of farm that significant differences would occur in th
land-use plans developed.

In general, family-sized or less commercialized operating units are ord
narily more interested in productivity maintenance and conservation pra
tices than are large-scale commercial units. In agriculture, for exampl
the operator of a family-sized farm does not consider labor supplied k
himself and his family as a variable cost, and therefore does not calcula
net return as a business entrepreneur or the operator of a large con
mercial unit would count it.[32]

Private corporations have several advantages over natural persons, a
proprietors managing natural resources subject to conservation. Some (
these include: (1) the legal attribute of succession, which to some exte
relieves the corporation of the restrictions of a brief and uncertain ter
of life; (2) the relative ease with which property rights may be tran
ferred between individual shareholders and converted into cash (liqui
ity) ; (3) the superior ability of the corporation to borrow funds, whic
removes its investment projects from the limitations of personal financi
ability and from direct competition of private pecuniary necessities; (4
the more centralized control of a considerable portion of the supply (
certain limited resources, which is often sufficient to establish actual (
potential monopoly; (5) the ability of corporations to secure expert ma
agement, which somewhat removes corporate management from the mo
immediate interests of private proprietorship, and should tend to refle
the social interest and public welfare. As a matter of fact, studies reve
that exploitation occurs less rapidly under monopoly than under cond
tions of comparatively free competition.[33]

LIMITS AND PERMANENCY OF DESTRUCTIVE EXPLOITATION

The limit of "economic exploitation" (exploitation justifiable on ec
nomic grounds from an individual point of view) is often the decrease
returns from the land to a zero level. Decrease of return from virgin lar
—or, with most natural resources, including ore deposits and forests, wi
increased use or exploitation—proceeds rapidly at first, declining gradual

[32] Lange states that, in his opinion, "This is a more plausible explanation of t
difference in conservation activities of the European peasants as compared with t
American farmers, rather than a reference to different philosophies of life." (Lang
op. cit., p. 474.)

[33] Hotelling, *op. cit.* This does not mean that private and public monopolies wou
achieve identical results, because private and public output policies would differ wi
differing objectives. However, if private monopolies are compared with numero
competing private firms, the monopoly is in a position to adjust supply more effective
to demand and, as a result, may have an entirely different scale of cost and pri
relationships. In many cases, adjustment of supply to demand involves a holding ba
or restraint on production or use of the resource and the resulting output, compar
with the uncontrolled larger output and faster rate of use of the resource that ten
to occur under competition.

ntil an ultimate standstill is reached. In the case of agricultural land, the .nglish Rothamsted Experiments show that returns are nearly stable /hen fertility depletion reaches a point where accretions of plant food re- ased by climatic environment and natural physical processes of weather- ng just equal the decrease in fertility caused by removing the yearly crop. This may be referred to as the "economic base level of exploitation." Any ncrease in output, or reduction of output decline above this base level, ould necessitate increased input and would be determined by the equi- brium of marginal input and marginal returns.[34]

In actual practice, however, destructive exploitation frequently proceeds uch beyond the "economic base level of exploitation," and has actually esulted in reducing output to nothing, also setting in motion destructive rces that have wiped out "permanently" the possibility of growing rops. In this way both present and future generations are excluded from xploiting soil productivity. A distinction should be made between *fertil- ty depletion* and *soil deterioration*. *Deterioration* implies a loss in the alue of the soil as production capital, permanently reduced rent to the wner, and higher prices to consumers. *Fertility depletion*, on the other and, represents use of resources that can be replaced later at a cost equal o or below the costs of maintaing them, and no permanent decrease of hysical productivity and rent occurs.[35]

ACHIEVEMENT OF CONSERVATION

As a rule, the amount that individual land operators can afford to spend n conserving their land resources is limited by the present value of antici- ated returns from expenditures. Thus, private land operators frequently ind it uneconomic to safeguard future productivity, with the result that 'economic exploitation" prevails.

DESIRABILITY OF SOCIAL ACTION

Social action to achieve conservation is desirable: (1) when it would e economic for the individual operator to conserve but he fails to do so; (2) when conservation is not economic for the individual but is economic or society; and (3) when intangible ends desired by a majority in a de- nocracy can be achieved only by collective action.[36] Under the first con- dition, social action is justified because it will increase both individual ind social net returns. Society could well expend funds so long as they esulted in increasing the social net income—funds that in ordinary times

---

[34] Cf. Ciriacy-Wantrup, "Economic Aspects of Land Conservation," *op. cit.*, p. 468.

[35] See Rainer Schickele, "Economics of Agricultural Land Use Adjustments, 1. Methodology in Soil Conservation and Agricultural Adjustment Research," Iowa Agri- cultural Experiment Station, Research Bulletin 209, March, 1937; and Bunce, *Economics of Soil Conservation, op. cit.*, pp. 14–17.

[36] Bunce, *Economics of Soil Conservation, op. cit.*, p. 105.

would probably be limited to education and perhaps subsidies for spe cific improvements.

Under the second condition, a sound public policy and action program can be formulated only when the basic reasons are understood by indi viduals continuing an exploitive system when it is not economic for them to do so and results in lower net returns than could be obtained from a conservation system.[37] Society is justified in taking steps to eliminate such exploitation, but the action program should be directed at the basic causes operating in the area. Under the third condition, typical examples of intangible ends that have high value to society but have no way of expressing themselves through the pricing system are camping and picnic areas, natural scenic beauty (much of it now destroyed by billboards) virgin forest strips on highways, and recreational values of hunting and fishing. Conservation of such values reflects thinking of the people on broader than solely economic terms.

Society, through wise financial management, may invest in conserva tion without depriving the people of present enjoyment of buying power or increased resources for future use. This could be true particularly during periods in which capital and labor are idle, if public financing of conservation resulted either directly or indirectly in putting to work productive power—including labor, capital, land, management—that would otherwise be idle and necessitate heavy unemployment relief ex penditures. Moreover, certain classes of resources, if not used, are forever lost to society, and public expenditures for development and utilization of these resources are justified.

The question of how much society can afford to spend for conservation ignores the fact that much conservation can be cost-free and implies that whatever is spent for conservation is withdrawn from current consump tion or investment in some productive enterprise; but this condition would exist only if there were no idle funds, idle resources, or idle labor or if all these resources were employed in a way that would be more productive of public good than their employment in conservation work. So long as a conservation program can be financed with public funds so that part or all of these idle resources will be used without diverting pur chasing power from present consumption or, in other words, without necessitating curtailment in present consumption in order to insure a greater abundance of natural resources in the future, there is no limit to the amount that society is justified in spending on conservation.

It is obvious that society can afford to spend much more for conserva tion programs in some periods than in others. It is also obvious that methods utilized to secure public funds to finance conservation programs

[37] Bunce lists some of the more obvious causes of this condition, including custom lack of knowledge, insecurity of tenure, and rationing of credit. (*Ibid.*, pp. 107–111.)

ιre an important factor in determining the point beyond which society
ιs not justified in spending for conservation, since they determine the
ιncidence of the burden for financing such programs. In any case, students
ιf land economics should acknowledge that the price society can afford
ιo pay for conservation is not governed solely by the usual theoretical
ιnalysis of present value of future monetary returns, using some assumed
ιate of interest, but also by the social values which a given society (assum-
ng perpetuity) must take into account, together with the extent to which
ιhe real cost of conservation can be met by using productive resources that
ιtherwise might be wasted through unemployment or nonuse.

METHODS OF ACHIEVING CONSERVATION

The amount and kind of land conservation that would ordinarily de-
ιelop through private initiative in the search for economic gain would
ιot adequately serve the needs of society. Conservation would occur only
ιn areas where it was economic and, because of inertia, ignorance, custom,
ιnd similar forces, might not occur even in these areas; whereas the social
ιnterest, because of social values or the relative prosperity or depression
ιtatus of the economy, might justify much more extensive conservation
ιrograms. Under these conditions, conservation would involve some de-
ιree of government regulation; and where government regulation is in-
ιolved, there is more or less conflict between public and private interests.
Regulative policies may take two main forms—education and compulsion.
Subsidies or benefit payments may be used to achieve desired goals, but
ιhese could be classified as a type of economic compulsion.

Education has important possibilities as a stimulus to conservation. It
ιould tend to make people aware of the importance of conservation and
ιould furnish them information that would assist them in making future
ιlans and commitments. In many cases a strong educational program call-
ιng attention to the need for conservation and the social losses involved
ιn excessive exploitation and waste would cause many people to effect
ιonservation practices that would not necessarily give them an economic
ιeward. They would spend money for conservation as they spend money
ιor other instruments of public welfare. However, for a large portion of
ιhe people, mere knowledge of the facts is not enough to assure establish-
ιnent of a practical conservation program.

In order to overcome ignorance and inertia, the educational program
ιnust be sufficiently strong and long-continued to develop a social philos-
ιophy, so that desire to conserve becomes part of the people's institutions,
ιustoms, and thinking. Moreover, education is essential for enforcement
ιnd maintenance of some of the more compulsory methods of securing
ιonservation, such as statutes, ordinances, rules, and regulations. It is
ιessential that such educational work be accomplished before or at least

simultaneously with the enactment of compulsory regulations if they are to be most effective. If a social philosophy favorable to conservation is firmly established, changes in the rules of the game through changes in statutes and ordinances will follow logically. Without such a social philosophy, passing a law will effect very little sound conservation.

Compulsory regulation to establish and maintain land-use control can be accomplished in many ways, including exercise of the police power and operation of the taxing power of government. Control of land use in the interests of conservation through the police power (the authority vested in the government to restrict certain uses of private property and private contract when their exercise jeopardizes the public health, safety, morals, or general welfare) may be achieved by zoning ordinances or conservation districts. Taxation, although ordinarily considered as a means of providing revenue for the support of government, can effectively control the conduct of persons in the possession, use, and disposition of property.

CONSERVATION POLICIES

Use of police and taxing powers may be inadequate to secure the amount and type of land conservation most desirable for the general welfare. Much can be accomplished under certain conditions by public assistance in the form of economic rewards to private individuals for conservation practices. Such public assistance can be justified on the grounds that private owners are performing a service of public as well as private benefit; and where conservation is not economic from the private entrepreneur's point of view, such public assistance is generally necessary if any widespread conservation is to be effected.

Use of the police power, the taxing power, and public assistance are very important in achieving land conservation; the combined effect, however, of all of these devices may be inadequate. The alternative to private conservation of land resources is public ownership, and many students of land economics feel that some land resources, particularly those which are scarce, necessary, and of potentially great social value, should always remain in public ownership subject to private uses socially feasible at any given time. For certain types of land uses, where conservation is particularly uneconomic from a private entrepreneur's standpoint (especially those in which a long period of time is involved) the government can most advantageously undertake conservation through public ownership. However, public ownership, per se, is no guarantee that land resources will be conserved. For example, tax-reverted lands in many areas are often without any management, with the result that the lands are overgrazed or exploited by private entrepreneurs.

Except for certain types of land, particularly those considered submarginal for uses that would be made of them under private operation, and for certain types of land of strategic importance to the general welfare, most students of land economics agree that public ownership should be considered a last resort, not to be used until police power, taxing power, and public assistance procedures have been exhausted. However, society should always insist that reasonable use of lands be required as a condition of private title.

It should be kept in mind at all times that the central public purpose in using land is to sustain, on a comparatively permanent basis, the highest possible level of living. *Best land use,* therefore, means not only improved living conditions, but improvement maintained on a relatively permanent basis. In order to achieve improvement in living conditions or attain the highest possible level of living, land must be put to its highest and best use. If this is done, the conservation problem will be solved because highest and best use implies attaining the highest level of living possible on a comparatively permanent basis.

SOIL CONSERVATION

The vital importance of the top few inches of soil to successful production of plant growth and to support of human life through agriculture makes it essential that this mantle of soil be utilized so as to prevent serious deterioration. In many parts of the globe, practices followed in cultivating soil or using it for production of plants and animals have not maintained soil fertility or producing ability. In some cases populations have had to move because of declining land productivity; and in many areas, even where settlement has been comparatively recent, ghost communities and ghost farms spot the countryside.

Agricultural land is partly a fund resource, partly a biological resource, and partly a flow resource. This complicates the problem of conserving agricultural land. Agricultural production may utilize the stored-up fertility of thousands of years or the fertility annually renewed through flow resources combined with current receipts of moisture and energy. Agricultural productivity may be built up by man over time. Conservation of agricultural land involves maintenance of fund resources and the present level of productivity of the soil, assuming a given state of the arts.[38]

HOW SOIL FERTILITY IS LOST

Because vegetation is the strongest of the natural forces that produce soils, the type of farming practiced and its influence on the type and character of vegetation are important factors determining the extent of fertility losses. Soil fertility or plant nutrients may be lost or removed from the soil in four important ways: (1) by *erosion*—namely, wearing away of lands by washing or by wind action; (2) by *removal* of crops that have

[38] Cf. Bunce, *Economics of Soil Conservation, op. cit.,* p. 7.

drawn plant food of the soil into themselves in the process of growth;   (3) by *leaching*, or percolating of water downward through the ground carry ing plant food beyond the reach of vegetation; and (4) by *volatilization.*[39]

Ordinarily, erosion and crop removal account for the greatest losses in soil fertility. Certain systems of farming cause a considerable portion of the earth's surface to be exposed in a loose form particularly subject to erosion. Some types of crops require much more plant food than others. Although leaching and volatilization are ordinarily of minor importance and determined mostly by natural forces, leaching is influenced by irriga tion practices in areas where water is applied artificially. If excessive irrigation water is applied on certain types of soils, considerable loss of plant nutrients results because of severe washing out of the mineral salts while in some areas where drainage is particularly poor, excess water may collect in low spots and evaporate, leaving the soil so saturated with addi tional mineral salts that fertility is greatly reduced.

METHODS OF CONTROLLING EROSION

An effective conservation program necessitates a philosophy of conser vation that becomes a part of culture. In the development of such a phi losophy, education and research are extremely important. Education help to remedy some of the conditions chiefly accounting for the failure of farmers to conserve their soil. These conditions require specific remedial measures which, however, to be effectively established and maintained, in turn depend upon a thorough educational and research program.

An adequate soil conservation program involves a wide variety of engineering, cropping, and tilling practices. The amount and kind of engineering work necessary are determined by the type of erosion and the degree to which it has developed, character of the soil and subsoil, amount and distribution of rainfall, vegetative cover, and the use to which the land is put. For example, gully control may require dams of earth, rock, or concrete, and grading between dams may be necessary to check the flow of water and permit vegetation to become established. Contour plowing and terracing may be necessary in some areas to put the land in such shape that runoff will be reduced. Retarding runoff increases water absorption, and horizontal furrows plowed across the slope rather than with it are also effective for this purpose in many areas. On range and pasture lands, contour furrows have been quite successful in reducing or preventing soil erosion. Construction of stock reservoirs in coulees and draws on range areas makes available more readily accessible stock water, and thus tends to reduce the concentration of cattle and consequent over- grazing of certain range lands.

[39] See U.S. Department of Agriculture, "Soil Conservation, Its Place in National Agri- cultural Policy," AAA Bulletin G54, May, 1936, p. 5.

Correct tillage practices are important factors in erosion control because they determine the condition in which land is exposed to forces of
wind and water. For example, in semiarid areas, lands should be left in
a rough, cloddy, open condition during winter and spring, so that as much
water as possible will sink into the ground, and effects of wind erosion
will be reduced to a minimum. In areas of heavier rainfall, serious soil
washing may develop if the surface is left clean, free from crop residues,
and worked down finely. Subsoil porosity may be increased by deep plowing. Applications of humus in soils deficient in organic material will tend
to improve the granular structure of the soil and reduce erosion, and deep
tillage will also increase the water absorption power of many soils and
reduce erosion. Strip cropping, particularly on steep slopes or areas subject to severe blowing, appears to be an effective method of erosion control in many areas.

Improved land-use practices can do much to maintain soil fertility. In
the more humid areas, crop rotations that include intertilled crops, grains,
legumes, and grasses will help to maintain soil fertility by providing
necessary plant nutrients and controlling the more destructive effects of
weeds. Different crops have different food requirements; and certain soils
will be seriously depleted in fertility unless crop rotations are used. Agricultural lands, unlike mining lands, can, if properly managed, produce
indefinitely; for example, in North China, land farmed for many centuries is still highly productive. The fact that there are many areas in the
United States where, after less than 100 years of farming, soils are showing
signs of exhaustion, is a reflection upon human intelligence and judgment. Certain soil-conserving and soil-building practices, including the
use of green manure crops, legumes, and commercial fertilizers, as well
as drainage and reclamation, are important factors in maintaining and
improving soil productivity.

SUGGESTIONS TO IMPROVE SOIL CONSERVATION

It has been estimated that at least two-thirds of all farms are held by
people who cannot be expected to do what needs to be done if they are
merely informed as to the seriousness of soil losses and techniques for
preventing erosion. In addition to a sound educational research program,
three separate, though related, types of action are essential: (1) direct
subsidies to landowners and operators, (2) stabilization of farm prices
and income, and (3) shifts in population and changes in size of farms.[40]

The federal government has subsidized soil conservation through the
United States Department of Agriculture's Agricultural Conservation
Program, which has made direct payments to farmers for certain soil-
building and soil-conserving practices. At the same time, the ACP pro-

[40] *Ibid.,* pp. 19–20.

gram has held up prices of erosive crops such as cotton, corn, tobacco, an wheat. Adjusting the economy to stabilize farm prices and incomes o levels that would make possible a more permanently satisfactory agricu tural industry, without the necessity of resorting to exploitative practice would be the most desirable and effective policy to follow. These adjus ments will undoubtedly come gradually, and not in all parts of the agr cultural industry at the same time or to the same extent. Consequentl such adjustments should be used as a long-time goal of national policy.

It is economically unsound to maintain farm prices and income a levels that encourage utilizing submarginal areas and discourage shiftin operators on such lands into lines of work possessing greater econom opportunities. In many cases farms are too small to make satisfactor agriculture possible without subsidies, and national policy should attemp to develop alternative economic opportunities for operators of these land enabling their lands to be used by remaining farmers who would hav more adequate operating units, or permanently retire distinctly su marginal lands from cultivation. Industrial activity will be an importar factor in creating the alternative economic opportunities so essential f bringing about necessary shifts in farm population with least difficulty c cost.

THE SOIL CONSERVATION SERVICE

The United States Soil Conservation Service was established in 193! as an outgrowth of the Soil Erosion Service established in 1933. In 193! Soil Conservation Service work was enlarged to include erosion contro submarginal land purchase and development, water facilities develop ment, farm forestry, drainage and irrigation, and the agricultural phase of flood control. Thus, the work of the Soil Conservation Service is cen tered around the major objectives of developing better land use to pro mote the general welfare, conserving land resources, and establishing more permanently satisfactory agriculture.

Specifically, the work of the Soil Conservation Service includes: (1 *Soil Conservation:* (a) practical demonstrations to illustrate effectivenes of soil-conserving programs by actual work on the land in coöperatio with landowners, (b) development and improvement of erosion contro and soil-conserving measures through research and field tests, and (c dissemination of information among farm people. (2) *Submarginal Lan Purchase:* (a) purchase of land not suited to cultivation, and (b) man agement of these purchased lands under adapted uses. (3) *Flood Control* development of watershed protection measures to reduce flood hazard and reduce damages that result from silting of riverbeds, harbors reservoirs, and irrigation ditches. (4) *Water Facilities:* (a) assistin farmers and ranchers to plan development of water supplies for bette land use, and (b) constructing water and storage facilities. (5) *Farm Forestry:* (a) production and distribution of nursery stock to farmers, and (b) advising farmers concerning the establishment and maintenance of farm forests. (6) *Drainage and Irrigation:* (a) research in regard to drainage and irrigation techniques, (b) development of specialized equipment, and (c) provision of diversion dams, pumps, and other facilities to make irrigation possible.[41]

SOIL CONSERVATION DISTRICTS

Nearly all the states, with the encouragement of the Federal government through its Soil Conservation Service, have passed state soil conservation district laws. These soil conservation district laws permit farmers to organize soil conservation districts that have the status of governmental subdivisions, and thus combat soil erosion and prevent local misuse of land by coöperative land-use regulations.

The district's board of supervisors formulates a program of erosion control projects and preventive measures and puts it into effect through such technical assistance as it may be able to secure from local, state, and federal agencies, and such equipment as its funds permit and its program requires. Powers granted to a district are of two kinds: (1) authority to engage in coöperative action against soil erosion, and (2) authority to prevent local misuse of land by voting land-use regulations upon the district. The supervisors are empowered to carry out soil conservation operations on the land, including contour cultivation, strip cropping, terracing, ridging of pasture, contour furrowing, etc. They may enter into contracts with farmers, give them financial and other assistance, buy lands for retirement from cultivation and for other erosion-control purposes, make loans and gifts of machinery, seeds, etc., to farmers and ranchers, take over and operate erosion-control projects, and recommend land-use plans for soil conservation. If they feel such action is desirable, they may formulate ordinances prescribing land-use regulations for soil conservation. These regulations, however, as well as changes in the regulations, cannot go into effect until they have been submitted to farmers of the district and approved by referendum.

The use of soil conservation districts to conserve soil resources is an application of the police power. If all the legal requirements are complied with in establishing a district and securing a favorable vote for operation of certain soil conservation ordinances and land-use regulations, "holdouts" who refuse to employ conservation measures called for by the regulations are subject to the same legal procedures as any individual who violates a regularly established statute or ordinance of any other governmental unit. In other words, administrative officers of the district may

[41] *Ibid.,* pp. 29–30.

petition the local court to order the land occupier to observe district ordinances and regulations. The court should, if it issues an order, provide that if an occupier fails to employ the conservation measures required by the regulations, the administrative officers may go to his lands, do the necessary work, and collect the costs from the land occupier. In a few states the court may fine the land occupier for committing a misdemeanor. The laws, however, provide for establishing a board of adjustment in districts that adopt land-use regulations. This board is authorized to permit exceptions and variations from land-use regulations in cases where application of the strict letter of the law would result in "great practical difficulties or unnecessary hardship."

The decisions of this board of adjustment are subject to review in the local courts. Soil conservation district laws also provide that after a district has existed for a certain number of years (five, in most states), farmers may petition to have the district dissolved. The question of dissolution is then submitted to a referendum, and if a favorable vote is secured for dissolution, the district is terminated, so that where procedures followed under the law are impracticable they would not be continued.

GRAZING AND WEED CONTROL DISTRICTS

Grazing districts to conserve range lands have been established in many western states under the federal Taylor Grazing District Act and state grass conservation acts. The purpose of the Taylor Grazing Act (passed June 28, 1934) is to stop injury to public grazing lands "by preventing overgrazing and soil deterioration, to provide for orderly use, improvement, and development, to stabilize the livestock industry dependent on the public range, and other purposes." This act authorizes the Secretary of the Interior to create grazing districts from any part of the vacant and unappropriated public domain that is valuable chiefly for grazing and is located in the 11 western states and North and South Dakota.[42] Within districts, grazing is regulated under a permit system similar to that in use on national forests. Before any district is created, local hearings are held where provisions are explained to stockmen, and administration and enforcement of the law are discussed with them.

Under the Taylor Grazing Act, the Secretary of the Interior may accept title to any private or public lands within the boundaries of a district, and in exchange may issue patents of equally valuable public domain land in the same state or within the adjoining state nearest the district. These exchange lands then become part of the district. Although the Taylor Act applies only to the public domain, its provisions can be applied to

[42] At the time the Taylor Grazing Act was passed, there were nearly 166 million acres of vacant public lands located in these states.

ınd in all types of ownership, provided coöperation of the various types
f owners can be secured.[43]

Many western states have passed legislation providing for establishment
f grazing districts, which are nonprofit coöperative associations of live-
tock operators to control and manage use of range lands within their
oundaries. The first grazing association established was the Mizpah-
'umpkin Creek Association in Custer County, Montana, which required
special act of Congress in 1928 to permit its organization. As an out-
rowth of this experience, the first Montana Grazing Districts Law was
nacted in 1933, amended in 1935, and thoroughly revised in the Grass
Conservation Act passed in 1939. Other states, including North and South
)akota and Wyoming, have passed similar legislation. In general, state
razing district laws empower coöperative associations of livestock opera-
ors to lease or purchase grazing lands, to develop and manage district-
ontrolled lands, and to allocate grazing privileges among members and
onmembers. Thus, state grazing district laws are a form of enabling
egislation permitting the establishment of collective tenure devices for
ecuring and maintaining control over the right to use range lands.

The state grazing districts fill a somewhat different need from that of
Taylor Grazing Districts. State grazing districts seem to thrive most suc-
essfully where there is a checkerboard pattern of ownership (numerous
mall parcels owned by a great variety of absentee and local individual
nd corporate owners), while Taylor Grazing Districts seem to be most
daptable to areas where federal lands comprise a large proportion of the
otal area and the lands are of such low productivity that they have never
•een alienated from the public domain.

Although the provisions of state grazing district laws vary, two char-
cteristics are common to all—voluntary membership and restriction of
nembership to livestock operators. Membership in grazing districts dif-
ers, therefore, from that of soil conservation districts where all occupants
•f the district automatically become members, whether or not they are
•perators.

Another form of coöperative action to conserve land is the creation of
veed control or weed seed extermination districts. For example, a law
)assed in Montana in 1939 provides that when 25 percent of the free-
aolders of any proposed district petition the county commissioners for the
reation of a weed control and weed seed extermination district, the com-
nissioners shall hold a hearing; and if 51 percent of the owners of agri-
ultural land in the proposed district file written consent to creation of
he district, the commissioners may create the weed district if, after the

[43] See Virgil Hurlburt, *Journal of Land and Public Utility Economics*, Vol. XI, No.
, May, 1935, pp. 203–206.

hearing, they deem it desirable.[44] After a weed control district has been established, all landowners within the district must comply with rules and regulations established by the supervisors. If such compliance is not met within a time specified by the supervisors, they are authorized to destroy and exterminate weeds found on the land of noncompliers, and costs of such extermination must be borne by the landowner.

Soil conservation districts, Taylor Grazing Districts, state grazing districts, and weed control and weed seed extermination districts are all uses of the police power. These collective devices have done much in recent years to conserve soil resources and call attention to practices that will increase soil productivity. Each form of control has its particular advantages for special types of agricultural land use, and undoubtedly there will be further developments along these lines as the need arises for special types of collective control and voluntary group action.

CONSERVATION OF NONAGRICULTURAL LANDS

It will be recalled that the establishment of a Forestry Bureau in the Department of Agriculture and the later development of the national forests were the earliest practical examples of conservation in the United States. The extensive root system of trees makes the water-absorbing ability of forest land much greater than that of agricultural grassland. In areas of torrential rains or heavy rainfall, where there are also great slopes and drainage areas, devotion of considerable acreages to forestry is absolutely essential for control of floods. Conservation of wildlife or development of the highest recreational use of land may depend upon maintenance of effective forest cover. Thus, from the standpoint of conservation in general, forests are in certain areas often much more important than agricultural crops or grasses.

THE NEED FOR FOREST CONSERVATION

Important causes of forest depletion include damage by fire, destructive logging, inefficient milling and wood utilization, failure to reforest or replant cutover areas, failure to practice sustained-yield forestry, damage from tree diseases and insect pests, taxation policies that levy burdens on the basis of "wreckage value" and force exploitative forest-use practices, and a tenure pattern of private forest land ownership often resulting in severe competition and exploitative practices. The more important consequences of forest depletion include: (1) increased future prices of forest products, because of decreased supplies and reduced quality of products

---

[44] Twenty-five percent of the freeholders must sign a petition when the proposed district is outside any incorporated town or city of the county, or 25 landowners, when the proposed district is within the incorporated limits of any city or town.

in relation to demand; (2) decline of a great industry engaged in exploiting and manufacturing forest products; (3) injury to transportation systems in cutting down the volume of freight carried by railroads and other transportation units; (4) injurious effects upon water resources and disastrous results from soil erosion; (5) injurious effect on local communities because of depopulation and general impoverishment of extensive areas; (6) destruction of or injury to scenic features possessing significant recreation values; (7) destruction of the habitat of many species of wildlife (particularly fur-bearers and upland game), including game birds and many big game animals; and (8) reduction of the range-carrying capacity or forage production in many forest areas in the Western states.[45]

An adequate forest land conservation program should include: (1) development of effective protection from fire; (2) observance of such minimum logging requirements as disposal of slash and leaving of seed trees to secure conservational logging practices; (3) more efficient milling and wood utilization through use of wood waste, wood preservatives, and some wood substitutes; (4) forest planting and management to secure renewal at a rate commensurate with needs for various forest services ranging from wood supply to game cover; (5) restocking of burned-over or cutover forest lands unsuited to agriculture, particularly in watershed areas; (6) planting trees for windbreaks in some exposed areas; (7) application of sustained-yield principles to as many forest areas as possible; (8) tax revision to adjust tax burdens more closely to the peculiar nature of forest returns and encourage sustained-yield management and conservational logging practices; and (9) increased public purchase of forest lands to make possible more orderly utilization of resources, to relieve the competitive situation in some areas, and enforce conservational logging on the public forest lands through leasing regulations.[46]

In the case of many agricultural lands, economic rewards for conservation practices can be secured within a year, and in some cases less. In the case of forestry, however, many years may elapse before tree crops are ready to be harvested, so that economic rewards are not nearly so prompt. Moreover, returns per acre in forestry are likely to be considerably smaller, since forestry is usually a less intensive use than agriculture; and the uncertainties of a long waiting period help to make conservation programs that may be economic from an individual standpoint unattractive to private initiative. Forest land conservation will ordinarily require programs in which public initiative in the form of subsidies, management,

[45] The first six of these eight economic consequences are cited in Van Hise and Havemeyer, *op. cit.*, pp. 271–272.

[46] For a more detailed statement of measures for adequate forest conservation, see J. R. Whitaker, "Essential Measures in Forest Conservation," in Parkins and Whitaker, *op. cit.*, Chap. XI, pp. 262–286.

or ownership takes a much more active part than in agricultural land conservation.

RECREATIONAL LAND CONSERVATION

Recreational use is characterized by certain peculiar problems and conditions that make sound conservation measures for such lands different from those designed to conserve other lands. The recreational use of many areas is associated with other uses, some of which return owners economic rewards quite apart from the recreational values of such lands. In many cases, the qualities or characteristics that give land value for recreational purposes are comparatively intangible, and this, coupled with the fact that recreational enjoyment does not involve pecuniary reward, makes private initiative unable to provide an adequate conservation program in the case of most recreational lands. An excellent example of this is the conservation of wildlife (an important part of recreational land conservation), which is undertaken almost entirely through public programs.

The demand for recreational land rises with increased leisure, improved transportation, and high living standards characteristic of modern society, but there are serious problems associated with securing and maintaining lands for recreational use in competition with other uses. Only those lands will be developed by private enterprise on which alternative uses are less valuable or satisfactory. The amount of such land is far short of that required to meet current and prospective recreational requirements, so that public development is essential. Public agencies, however, may select for recreational use lands that have alternative uses of great economic importance; they may eliminate competing uses by zoning or other regulatory measures and thus assure the use of the land for recreation; or they may attempt to share use of the land with other uses on some control basis. In many areas conservation is largely a problem of determining the relative importance of different uses for a given piece of land or area.

Much expense is frequently incurred in recreational land conservation to remove economic scars lowering the recreational value of land or to construct facilities necessary to make recreation areas available. Many developments to improve recreational land resources cannot be financed by charges, commissions, or admissions. Thus, the government must act as initiator or manager and undertake the conservation program directly.

MINERAL LAND CONSERVATION

The increasing importance of minerals, combined with the fact that mineral resources are exhaustible and not replaceable, makes conservation of mineral resources peculiarly vital to the general welfare. Where a resource cannot be replaced or grown, the necessity of deciding from day o day how much should be used currently and how much should be saved for posterity is very important.

Two of the most important factors tending to discourage mineral conservation and encourage wasteful exploitation are the uncertainty of discovering new deposits and the uncertain amount of mineral reserves. The chance factor" in discovery has discouraged consistent planning for efficient utilization, because discoveries of deposits have, at least thus far in the United States, provided adequate supplies of most important minerals in spite of wasteful exploitation. Depending upon chance discovery can be a disastrous policy, and the United States should develop a more systematic conservation plan for mining and for utilizing its mineral resources. In addition to the uncertainties of discoveries and of reserves, three other conditions distinguish mineral conservation problems from those of other land resources: localized occurrence, tendency to increasing cost and, to a lesser extent, accumulation of metal stocks.

In general, the chief conservation problem for mineral lands is prevention of resource waste and the associated social and economic disorders caused by destructive competition so characteristic of those minerals in which there is a surplus of plant capacity or production facilities. In this sense the conservation problem is more one of economics than of technology, and the task is to help these mining industries prevent competitive waste, stabilize employment, limit or at least control cutthroat competition, and through increased stability permit those savings in the resource that technology has already made possible. Means of controlling production, capacity, stocks, and, in some cases, prices must be considered. Such control by private industry has been forbidden under the antitrust laws; but it may be wise to permit and even encourage such control, under public supervision, in those industries involving natural resource waste.

The ill effects of destructive competition include more than the waste of irreplaceable natural resources. Such destructive waste also endangers living standards of mine workers, whose isolation, relative immobility, and hazardous life merit special consideration, which may justify provisions for eliminating or at least reducing these ill effects to a minimum through public or private action. Public policies perhaps sufficient to do this would be Congressional legislation authorizing systems for control (by operators within the industry proper) of mining output, mine capacity, or both, and in some cases authorization of minimum and maximum prices. Specific amendment of the antitrust laws may be necessary to permit such action in certain fields—particularly coal, oil, gas, and the nonferrous metals. In some cases public monopolies might be necessary, or the price of the product might be left low and the product rationed by society; which is preferable depends upon the resource.

Experience has shown that a reasonable profit tends to stimulate con servation, because the more valuable an object becomes, the more men tend to save it, and the less valuable, the more carelessly it is used. I mineral reserves are not to be exploited and wasted needlessly, it is neces sary to develop a program whereby reasonable prices can be secured and the industry stabilized so that waste accompanying low prices, overpro duction, and related conditions may be reduced to a minimum.

Manufacturing transforms products from their original character into a multitude of new products, using many otherwise waste products in the process. Because minerals are so important—and increasingly important— in manufacturing, and because so many minerals are of durable character one function of manufacturing is that of conservator of mineral re sources.[47] In many cases, the mining and manufacturing of certain minerals used in industry do not constitute a destructive process, in the true meaning of the word, but rather a change in form [48]—frequently to forms more available for alternative uses.

CONSERVATION OF WATER RESOURCES

Water is regarded by many as a resource so necessary to the genera welfare in its various uses that it should be publicly owned, with private beneficial use.[49] It has been suggested that water rights should be allo cated so that under suitable social regulation the water will naturally accomplish the largest results.[50]

The problem of conserving water resources is mainly one of controlling rights to use water so that beneficial use can be distributed to the greates possible number of people for the longest time. Practically every use o water is important to such a degree that restricted control or appropria tion by selfish private interests might cause widespread suffering and

[47] Helen M. Strong, "Conservation of Natural Resources and the Manufacturing Industry," in Parkins and Whitaker, *op. cit.*, p. 483.

[48] An excellent example of this is the collection of old aluminum pots and pan assembled by local communities in 1941, in connection with the effort to increase aluminum supply for defense needs.

[49] See, for example, Van Hise and Havemeyer, *op. cit.*, particularly pp. 152–161 R. T. Ely, "Conservation Policies," in *Foundations of National Prosperity*, p. 62; and Frank Williams, "Water Power and Its Conservation," in Parkins and Whitaker, *op cit.*, p. 332.

[50] Professor T. N. Carver suggested the system of selling water rights by auction with the idea that he who will pay the most will make the best use of the water Ely points out that shore lands ought to be, in general, publicly owned, and tha although there are occasions when exclusive private beneficial use should be allowed ulimate ownership should nevertheless be public. The experience of cities like New York and Baltimore confirms this position, and failure to recognize earlier the wisdom of such a policy has produced enormous costs and great wastes. (See Ely *et al.*, *op. cit.* p. 62.)

ocial loss. The type of conservation program that will most effectively pportion the rights to use this resource will vary in different areas and or different uses.

URBAN LAND CONSERVATION

The principal problem in conserving urban land is to secure utmost conomy in movement and economic activity of large numbers of people oncentrated in relatively small areas. Experience favors a large amount f public ownership or effective public regulation of urban land uses. The pecific objectives of urban land conservation are chiefly to control private tilization through: (1) Segregating land uses to prevent development of 'blighted" or slum areas and resulting depreciation of land values and oss of utility or buildings. (2) Proportioning land going into various uses o as to prevent too much from going into commercial or industrial uses nd too little into residential use, or vice versa. If this is effectively done, ccurrence of many vacant and abandoned lots will be prevented. (3) Reducing congestion and the consequent economic and social wastes. ntroducing desirable public control or regulation of land utilization hrough zoning, neighborhood unit planning, building, sanitation, lumbing, electrical and other codes, revising tax policies to aid rational rban land use, and in some cases increased public landownership, if ther methods have failed or proved to be ineffective. (4) Lowering costs f expanding the city area through subdivision control.[51]

The quality of land (location, or situs) that gives it its value for urban se is physically indestructible, and many conclude from this that there is, herefore, no conservation problem in urban lands. However, the economic value of situs, or physical location, can be readily destroyed by nwise urban land utilization practices. This is illustrated by the destruction of property values in blighted and slum areas. Urban land is so dependent upon its improvements—dwellings, streets, commercial structures, and factories—that the problems of maintaining the value of improvements are problems of urban land conservation. Consequently, conservation must be built around the central idea of controlling city land se to prevent the development of blighted or unsatisfactory areas and ocioeconomic wastes and distress.

In most instances, using one or more of the various social control devices such as the police power, zoning, eminent domain, or taxation will adequately insure land utilization practices that will conserve urban land values and benefits. Some acquisition of lands by the government, however, may be necessary to adjust present land-use practices to those neces-

---

[51] See Dorau and Hinman, *Urban Land Economics*, Macmillan, 1928, pp. 251–258.

sary to conserve such values and benefits. In general, the cities of the nex generation will differ from today's in proportion to the strength of th dynamic forces of city change, especially those comprising the socia climate and social objectives.[52]

REFERENCES FOR FURTHER READING

Bennett, H. H., *Elements of Soil Conservation*, McGraw-Hill Book Compan) Inc., New York, 1946.

"Building the Future City," *Annals of the American Academy of Political an Social Science*, Vol. CCXLII, November, 1945, pp. 88–162.

Bunce, A. C., *The Economics of Soil Conservation*, Iowa State College Pres. Ames, Iowa, 1942, Chaps. I, V, VII, and VIII.

Ciriacy-Wantrup, Siegfried von, *Resources Conservation, Economics, and Policie.* University of California Press, Berkeley, 1952.

Dana, Samuel T., *Forest and Range Policy*, McGraw-Hill Book Company, Inc New York, 1956, Chaps. X and XI.

Dorau, H. B., and Hinman, A. G., *Urban Land Economics*, The Macmilla. Company, New York, 1928, Chap. XV.

Ely, R. T., Hess, R. H., Leith, C. K., and Carver, T. N., *The Foundations o National Prosperity*, The Macmillan Company, New York, 1918, Part I, Chap: I and V; Part II, Chaps. I, II, III, and IV; and Part IV, Chap. I.

Ely, R. T., and Wehrwein, G. S., *Land Economics*, The Macmillan Compan) New York, 1940, Chap. XIV.

Heady, Earl O., *Economics of Agricultural Production and Resource Use* Prentice-Hall, Inc., Englewood Cliffs, N. J., 1952, Chap. XXVI.

Johnson, V. Webster, and Barlowe, Raleigh, *Land Problems and Policie.* McGraw-Hill Book Company, Inc., New York, 1954, Chap. VII.

Lowdermilk, W. C., *Conquest of the Land Through Seven Thousand Year:* U.S.D.A. Soil Conservation Service, SCS–MP-32, 1948.

Lyons, Barrow, *Tomorrow's Birthright*, Funk & Wagnalls Company, New York 1955, Chaps. VII and VIII.

National Resources Board, *Report to the President of the United States*, Decem ber 1, 1934, Government Printing Office, Washington, D.C., Part II, Sectio) III.

Parkins, A. E., and Whitaker, J. R. (eds.), *Our National Resources and Thei Conservation*, John Wiley & Sons, Inc., New York, 1936, Chaps. I, IV, XI XIII, XVIII, XIX, XX, and XXI.

Stallings, J. H., *Soil Conservation*, Prentice-Hall, Inc., Englewood Cliffs, N. J. 1957, Part III and Chap. XXV.

Timmons, John F., and Murray, William G., *Land Problems and Policies*, Iow: State College Press, Ames, 1950, Chap. VI.

U.S. Department of Agriculture, *Soil Conservation, Its Place in National Agri cultural Policy*, AAA Bulletin G54, May, 1936.

[52] For interesting suggestions of possible future trends in city design by leadin(architects and engineers, see M. D. Meyerson and R. B. Mitchell, "Changing Cit Patterns," *Annals of the American Academy of Political and Social Science*, Vol CCXLII, November, 1945, pp. 149–162.

Van Hise, C. R., *The Conservation of Natural Resources in the United States,* 1910, rev. 1930, Havemeyer, L. H. (ed.), The Macmillan Company, New York, Introduction and Part VI.

Zimmermann, Erich W., *World Resources and Industries,* rev. ed., Harper & Brothers, New York, 1951, Chap. XLIX.

part **III**

LAND INCOME
AND VALUE

LAND RENT AND INCOME DISTRIBUTION
LAND VALUES AND APPRAISAL
MORTGAGE CREDIT AND LAND USE
PRINCIPLES OF LAND TAXATION
TAXATION OF LAND IN DIFFERENT USES

LAND RENT AND INCOME DISTRIBUTION

RETURNS TO each of the factors of production tend to equal their respec-
ve marginal productivities. Thus, the level of wages of a particular kind
[labor under perfect competition is equal to the marginal productivity
[that labor or the addition to total product resulting from the applica-
on of the last unit of the labor force. Similarly, the return to land de-
ends upon its marginal productivity. Under perfect competition the
rice of each productive agent is equal to its marginal product. Our
:onomic system is continually trying to readjust itself to a new set of
mditions necessitated by changes in demand and supply, created as a
:sult of changes in wants, resources, and techniques of production char-
:teristic of a modern, dynamic society. In reality, therefore, equilibrium
1 the economic system is probably never attained.

THE NATURE OF RENT

Any intelligent attempt to improve our economy demands, first of all,
clear understanding of the functional nature of the distribution process
that is, of the forces that determine the returns to the various produc-
ve agents. Under the institution of property, lands used in production

are owned by individuals who maintain the right to receive the incom earned by the lands.

The peculiar physical characteristics of land have led many to conclue that property in land gives greater possibilities of monopolistic gain tha ownership of the other productive agents and that therefore land rent a monopolistic return. What are the causes and nature of land rent? land rent a monopoly return or an unearned increment and, if so, to wh extent? Wherein does it differ in cause and nature from returns to owne of other production factors? Would it be in the interests of society confiscate economic rent? Should land rent be treated any differently fro returns to other factors of production?

RENT AS A SURPLUS RETURN

The word "rent" etymologically means any income or yield from a economic agent, but in economics it has come to be used almost entirely i connection with income from land. Surplus income for any factor of pr duction results whenever any unit is receiving a greater income than th minimum amount necessary to induce that factor to remain in its presel use. Thus, the *surplus* of receipts over the minimum supply price of factor may be called *economic rent*.

Defined in this way, such surpluses or rents can be found in incom received by some units of each factor of production—labor, capital, an management, as well as land. In the case of capital, the amount of func required by borrowers is greater than the amount that would be supplie if no interest were allowed, and so those savers who would be willing lend part of their funds without interest are nevertheless able to charg the full market rate of interest on sums they lend. The difference betwee the amount of interest they actually get and the amount of interest fc which they would have been willing to lend, had the demand been les may be referred to as a *lender's surplus* or *lender's rent*.

The same principle applies to labor. For example, if some workers in trade are willing to work for $20 a week, but the demand for the produ is such that the trade must attract other workers who will not work fc less than $25 a week, the first workers will then be receiving $25 alsc including a rent of $5 a week (the difference between what they woul have been willing to work for and the amount they can actually ge because of greater demand for their services). The same type of surplu may arise in the earnings of the owner-manager of a business. The min mum supply price for his services will be the amount necessary to kee him in business—that is, the amount necessary to prevent him from givin up the business and going to work for someone else or going into anothe business. Any surplus that he happens to receive above this minimur amount may be considered as a rent.

From the above analysis, it will be seen that rent, defined as the surplus receipts over minimum supply price of production factors, can arise ly when the supply of any productive agent is less than perfectly elastic. ✓ definition, if the supply were perfectly elastic, the supply prices of all iits of the factor would be the same. Consequently, no unit would earn surplus that could be called a rent. When the supply of a factor is less an perfectly elastic, the units that have the lowest supply price will be ed first, and there will be no rent so long as only these units are needed f the supply prices of all such units are the same). When demand in- eases to a point where it is necessary to employ additional units, rent will ise on those units of the factor whose supply price is lowest, since in competitive market they will be able to demand the same market price that received by those units which will be offered at the market price. hus, rents constitute a surplus over the normal supply price of a unit a productive agent made possible because the supply of the factor is ss than perfectly elastic and because the demand for the factor is suffi- ent to necessitate use of more units than would be offered at the lowest pply price of any unit.

Many economists have reserved the term "rent" for use in connection ith land only, using terms like "lender's surplus" instead of "lenders' nt," "workers' surplus" instead of "worker's rent," and "excess profits" stead of "rent of management," but this does not mean that the nature land rent is any different economically from that of the rents or sur- uses of these other productive agents. The economic reasons for the cistence of land rent are identical with the causes of lenders' surplus, orkers' surplus, and excess profits. The fact that land resources, in the ;gregate, are fixed by nature and that human efforts cannot change eir amount has been largely responsible for the confusion. From so- ety's point of view, but not from the point of view of the individual ser, any payment for the use of land resources is a surplus over supply ice, and the rent of land cannot be considered as a cost of production. ow is it possible, then, to explain payments to those who happen to own nd?

OCCURRENCE OF RENT ON LANDS OF EQUAL PRODUCTIVITY

Let us assume, first, that all land is capable of producing only one roduct and is of equal productivity or fertility.[1] Under these conditions, ith pure competition, increasing demand for the product will be met y an increasing number of operating units, each producing at the point f minimum average total unit cost of all operating units in the indus-

[1] The analysis of the occurrence of rent on lands of equal and unequal productivity as been adapted largely from A. L. Meyers, *Elements of Modern Economics*, rev. ed., rentice-Hall, 1941, pp. 267–273.

try, and there will be no surplus over cost in the form of rent. The tot income from the product will be distributed as wages, interest, and wag of management. No producer would pay anything to use the land, becaus total cost would likewise equal total revenue and nothing would be lef

If demand for the product increases still further, increased output ca be obtained by adding more units of the other factors of production the fixed amount of land in existence. The *Principle of Substitution* wi then bring about increasing marginal and average costs as an increas in output is attempted. This will necessitate a rise in price equal to th new marginal cost. Each producer will increase output up to the poir where marginal cost equals price, but at this output average total un cost will be less than price, marginal cost being greater than average cos and total revenue will be greater than total cost. Each operating un will be in equilibrium because marginal revenue (which, under pure con petition, is the same as price) is equal to marginal cost, and the industr will be in equilibrium because no new operating units can enter int production to take advantage of the surplus, since there is no more lan for them to use.

This surplus is the economic rent of land, and if the landowner lease the land to others instead of using it himself, competitive bidding for th use of land will force the man who does obtain the use of it to pa the full amount of economic rent. With only one bid, the landlord coul refuse to lease the land for a smaller rent than he could make by usin it himself to produce the product. But even if the landlord decided to rer the land free of charge, tenants would produce to the point where ma ginal cost equaled price and would secure the economic rent for then selves.

OCCURRENCE OF RENT ON LANDS OF UNEQUAL PRODUCTIVITY (DIFFERENTIAL RENT)

In the preceding analysis, all land was assumed to have equal produc tivity or fertility. Let us now make a more realistic analysis and assum that there are different grades of land. Obviously the best (most pr ductive) grade will be used first. If demand for the product is so smal that all the best land is not needed for production of the desired ou put, the situation will be identical with that just described, where it wa assumed that there was only one grade of land and not all of it was used Price will equal minimum average total unit cost, and no rent will de velop. After all the best grade of land is in use, any additional increas in demand for the product will be met by more intensive cultivation o this best land. Price will rise to cover the new marginal cost, which wil be greater than average total unit cost, and rent will occur on the bes land.

The Intensive Margin.   As demand increases still further and output on the best land is expanded, a point will be reached where rising marginal cost on the best land just equals minimum average total unit cost on the next best grade of land. This point is referred to as the *intensive margin* on the best grade of land, or the point at which it does not pay to add further units of capital, labor, and management. At this point, it will not pay to intensify production on the best grade of land, and the second grade of land will be brought into use. The second grade will earn no rent, because price of the product will just equal minimum average total unit cost.

The Extensive Margin.   If demand for the product increases to the point where all the second-grade land is in use, output will be increased on the second-grade land by more intensive methods of use beyond the point of minimum average total unit costs (output on the first-grade land being expanded still further). The new price of the product would then be equal to marginal cost, and greater than minimum average total cost on the second-grade land, with the result that second-grade land would begin to earn a rent, although not as much as the first-grade land.

As demand increases and price rises still further, a point will be found where rising marginal costs on the two grades of land, from increased intensity of utilization, are exactly equal to minimum average total unit cost on a third grade of land. At this point, the third grade will be brought into use, with results similar to those of using the second grade. This process would continue with successive price rises for as many grades of land as there are in existence, and the last grade of land utilized would be referred to as the *extensive margin.*

The concept of intensive and extensive margins in rent analysis should not be in terms of margins for labor and capital. Land has its own marginal productivity, and the intensive margin is not the amount of product added by the last unit of capital and labor, but by the last unit of each quality of land that is available for use. The extensive margin is in reality a marginal productivity of land of zero.

Figure 20 illustrates diagrammatically how economic rent may be measured when different grades of land are utilized, assuming pure competition in the production of any one product. It will be noted from this figure that the difference between marginal cost, which represents the cost of producing the last unit of output as indicated by the curve MC, and average total unit cost, which is the average cost per unit of producing the entire output and which is represented by the curve AC, is the basis for measuring the economic rent secured on any grade of land with a given price. P_1, P_2, P_3, and P_4 are the various possible prices of the product, which in Table 5 are 40¢, 50¢, 75¢, and 90¢ per bushel, respectively; and Q_1, Q_2, Q_3, and Q_4 are the outputs produced at these prices

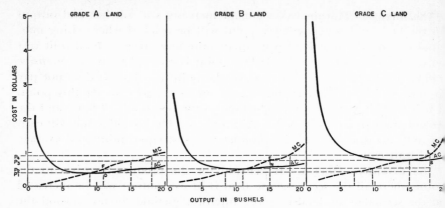

Figure 20. Measurements of Economic Rent on Different Grades of Land. (Based on hypothetical data in Table 5.)

or, as shown in Table 5: 9, 11, 15, and 18 bushels, respectively. It will be noted that at price P_1 (40¢) there is no rent, because at this point grade A land would be the only land in production and marginal cost and average cost on this land would be identical (40¢).

Between prices P_1 (40¢) and P_2 (50¢), grade A land would be the only land in use, price would equal marginal cost, and the difference between marginal and average cost, multiplied by output, will constitute the eco nomic rent on grade A land. At price P_2 (50¢), rent on the grade A land is shown by the area P_2FDP_1, and is found in Table 5 to be 88¢, or 11 units of output multiplied by 8¢, or the difference between marginal cost (50¢) and average cost (42¢). At price P_2, grade B land is brought into cultiva tion, but since at this price marginal cost and average cost are equal, the B land yields no economic rent. Between prices P_2 and P_3, grade B land yields rent, and that on grade A land is correspondingly increased. At price P_3, when grade C land comes into production, the rent on grade B land is shown by the area P_3ENP_2 and the economic rents on grades A and B amount to $3.90 and $3.15 respectively (see Table 5).

At price P_4, grade C land would also yield a rent, and the amount would equal the area of the rectangle P_4LSP_3, or $2.34, as shown in Table 5. A careful analysis of Table 5 and close study of Figure 20 will indicate the method by which economic rent is determined for various grades of land, and the amount of such rent, given the cost and price situations listed in Table 5, and assuming pure competition in the production of any one product.

RENT AS A COST OF PRODUCTION

Economic rent on land that has only one particular use will be deter mined by the difference between the price of the product and the costs

able 5. Hypothetical Average Unit and Marginal Unit Costs of Producing Corn on ., B, and C Grade Lands Illustrating Occurrence of Rent with Different Levels of Corn Prices (See Figure 20)

Output in Bu. of Corn	A Land Average Unit Cost	A Land Marginal Unit Cost	B Land Average Unit Cost	B Land Marginal Unit Cost	C Land Average Unit Cost	C Land Marginal Unit Cost
1	$2.10	$ —	$2.69	$ —	$4.84	$ —
2	1.07	.05	1.42	.15	2.52	.20
3	.73	.10	.99	.18	1.75	.26
4	.58	.15	.79	.20	1.38	.31
5	.49	.20	.67	.25	1.16	.35
6	.44	.25	.60	.30	1.04	.38
7	.42	.30	.56	.35	.92	.42
8	.41	.35	.53	.40	.88	.46
9	.40^a	.40^a	.52	.45	.84	.50
0	.41	.45	.51	.48	.80	.55
1	.42^b	.50^b	.50^b	.50^b	.78	.60
2	.43	.60	.51	.55	.77	.65
3	.45	.68	.52	.60	.76	.70
4	.47	.72	.53	.70	.75	.73
5	.49^c	.75^c	.54^c	.75^c	.75^c	.75^c
6	.51	.78	.56	.77	.76	.80
7	.52	.80	.57	.82	.76	.85
8	.54^d	.90^d	.59^d	.90^d	.77^d	.90^d
9	.57	.95	.61	1.08	.79	1.15
0	.59	1.00	.64	1.20	.82	1.40

^{a} At P_1 (40¢ per bu.) where marginal unit cost and minimum average total unit ost are equal on A land there is no rent on any of the lands.

^{b} At P_2 (50¢ per bu.) where marginal unit cost and minimum average unit cost are qual on B land there is no rent on B land but a rent on A land of $.88 (11 units < difference between average unit cost and marginal unit cost, or $.50 − $.42, or 8 ents).

^{c} At P_3 (75¢ per bu.) where marginal unit cost and minimum average unit cost are qual on C land, there is no rent on C land but a rent of $3.15 (15 units × difference etween average unit cost and marginal unit cost, or 75¢ − 54¢, or 21 cents) on B and and of $3.90 (15 units × 26¢) on the A land.

^{d} At P_4 (90¢ per bu.) all three grades of land would be yielding rent as follows: A, 6.48; B, $5.58; and C, $2.34.

f labor and capital used in producing each unit of output. Under these onditions, rent is not a cost factor that helps to determine output and price. In the competition for use of land that has several uses, a particuar use will have to pay a rental at least equal to that which the land ould earn in its best alternative uses.

Expansion of output accompanying increased demand for the product will necessitate drawing land away from other uses, and the price that wi have to be paid for the use of the land will rise. The minimum suppl price of each piece of land will be the amount that the land could ear in its most profitable alternative use, and may be referred to as th *opportunity* price of the land or *transference cost*. In other words, rem is determined simply by supply and demand, with opportunity for othe uses as one factor limiting supply or increasing demand.

The use that can outbid all other uses to which a piece of land may b put may be considered the *highest and best use*, from a strictly economi standpoint, for this land.[2] The price of the product will be determine at the point where price just equals marginal cost (including *transferenc cost*, or *opportunity* cost of the land) on the highest-cost land to be ut lized in production. The *marginal* land (that land which will leave pro duction first if the price of the product falls, and where price just equal average total unit cost), need not be the least efficient nor the poorest lan in use. Land best suited for the production of corn may also be the bes suited for producing milk. If this were the case, such land might be th first to be withdrawn from corn production and turned to dairy farmin, if the price of corn dropped.

If the transference price of land to a given industry is rising as mor land is used, firms using land with the lowest opportunity price will b able to obtain the same price for their product as firms using the highes cost land. They will expand output to the point where marginal cos equals price, but a surplus return will be secured on the intramargina lower-cost units of output. If the firms using land with the lower oppor tunity prices lease the land outright, they will be able to secure the sur plus; if not, the landlord will be able to secure the full economic ren as soon as the lease expires, through competitive bidding by tenants.

For the individual operator, all rent of all productive agents must be considered a cost of production.[3] If the operator leases land, cash pay

[2] The highest and best use from an economic point of view may not be the highes and best use from a social point of view. Letting crops fight it out for the use o land under a system of *laissez faire*, on the grounds that whatever pays most or bes should have the right to use the land, may result in impoverished soil and distressec families. This policy, which was largely followed by the United States prior to 1933 resulted in the disappearance of forests, which were not replenished, destruction of soi fertility, increased soil erosion, and, in the case of urban land uses, unregulated ane unrestricted competition causing industrial slums and poorly planned cities. The need for social control of purely economic motives in utilization of land resource; under these conditions is obvious.

[3] The consideration of rent as a cost of production by the individual operator shoulc not be confused with the fact that for society as a whole land rent does not constitute a production cost. From the point of view of society, any payment for the use of lanc resources is a surplus over supply price, since the supply of land taken in the aggregate is fixed by nature and man cannot change the total amount of land resources in orde: to secure a price for it. Thus, the elasticity of supply of land in the aggregate can be said to be zero.

nent of the rent is obviously a cost. If the landowner uses the land him-
elf, the full payment he could have received by leasing the land will be
n opportunity cost. While this is not a cash outlay, it should be con-
idered a cost if proper accounting procedures are to be followed with re-
ard to the correct source of the landlord's income because, unless oppor-
unity cost is considered, he may be overlooking a chance to make a greater
ncome. Considering all payments made for the use of land (whether as
money cost, cash rent, or opportunity cost) as a cost of the individual
perator helps to determine which operator is to obtain the land for use
n producing a given good or service.

If costs of production on two pieces of farm land are identical (that
s, if they are equally productive), the one located nearest the market
or the product will command the higher rent, because of the differences
n cost of transportation. The full amount of this difference will be an
ddition to the economic rent of the better-located farm, and may be
eferred to as *location value*. Location value is of particular economic
mportance in urban land utilization, extremely high rentals being paid
or many preferred sites in such cities as New York or Chicago. In other
vords, in the case of agricultural land, rent is paid in order to save trans-
ortation charges, while in the case of urban land, rent is paid in order
o secure a larger volume of sales.

RENT AS AN UNEARNED INCREMENT

The concept of unearned increment was formulated by John Stuart
Mill directly from the Ricardian theory of rent. Ricardo defined rent as
. . . that portion of the produce of the earth which is paid to the land-
ord for the use of the original and indestructible powers of the soil." [4]
The Ricardian theory contends that unequal costs in the production of
gricultural commodities, in the face of equal market prices, as set by
he highest cost producer, yield differential rents, which in capitalized
orm constitute a source of unearned increment for the owner of more
ertile or more advantageously located lands.

All other types of income, such as wages, interest, and profits, under
system of private ownership of the means of production, were consid-
red to represent just compensation for actual services, so that only the
andowner "grows richer, as it were, in his sleep without working, risking,
r economizing." [5] This latter concept grew out of the fact that land
s a natural product, the total physical supply of which cannot be in-
reased by man, and has certain indestructible physical qualities, particu-

[4] David Ricardo, *On the Principles of Political Economy and Taxation*, 1st ed.,
. Murray, London, 1817, Chap. II.
[5] John Stuart Mill, *Principles of Political Economy*, London, Longmans, Green & Co.,
td., W. J. Ashley (ed.) new ed., 1909, p. 18.

larly extension and location. Those who own land secure benefits from these differential returns on better-located or more fertile lands, not be cause of any effort of their own but merely of the fact that they secured natural advantages through control of ownership rights to these particu lar pieces of land.

Application of the differential principle adopted by Ricardo to other economic factors reveals the existence of elements of "unearned incre ment" in virtually all spheres of economic activity. Moreover, land, like capital, is produced, in that it comes into economic use through human activity in the same way as other production agents do. There are certain very definite costs in producing and utilizing land, as we shall see late in this chapter. It is unsound to argue that increment from differentia returns in the utilization of land is unearned, while differential return accruing in the case of more efficient laborers or managers, and superio grades or types of capital are "earned." It is true that land in its raw state is the creation of nature and, in this sense, original. It is also true that many of the costs of "producing" land are not borne by the owner, but the fact remains that before land is a valuable factor in production, man must make specific contributions to it.

As economic theory has turned from the concept of natural value to that of market value, limitation of the concept of unearned increment to one factor of production (land) has become more and more untenable Cumulative experience with cyclical price fluctuations has led economist to conclude that under changing market conditions, equal outlays of cos might yield very unequal returns, and that these might accrue to labor to the entrepreneur, or to the owner of capital, as well as to the owner o land.

Thus, all forms of accretions to the real value of people's property which are not foreseen by them or in any degree attributable to effort made, intelligence exercised, risks borne, or capital invested by them also belong in the category of unearned increment.[6] Moreover, in moderr times when ownership of agricultural and urban land changes hand more frequently, the buyer of land who pays out of his earnings a price reflecting the capitalized value of the rent secures an income from hi land that is no longer unearned increment in the sense in which Mil interpreted it, but rather interest on capital invested.

The treatment of rent as unearned increment led to the formulation of demands for abolishing private ownership of land, which is the source of rent payments, or to methods of socializing rent by taxing the unearned increment 100 percent. The latter plan would retain private property in land, but would enable the state to appropriate part or all of the eco

[6] Cf. C. R. Bye, *Developments and Issues in the Theory of Rent,* Columbia Universit Press, 1940, pp. 77–78.

nomic rent. Henry George's single-tax proposal [7] was advanced as a means of appropriating rent through taxation rather than through nationalization of the land itself.

MODERN RENT THEORY

Many earlier rent theorists attempted to explain rent as a unique return basically different from returns to the other factors of production. Classical doctrine emphasized differing grades of land and differentials measured from extensive and intensive margins. Present-day economists, however, stress fundamental demand-supply relationships, the accompanying principles of marginal productivity, and opportunity cost common to all production factors. It can truly be said that the earlier distinctions between price-determined and price-determining factors disappear. This equilibrium sets the price of the product and, with other forces, determines returns to the production agents. Consequently, neither the prices of products nor the prices of production factors are entirely causes or entirely effects. They are, rather, interdependent parts of the whole complex economic process.

The increasing tendency of modern economists to explain rent in terms of fundamental demand-supply relationships through marginal productivity and opportunity cost is a great improvement over earlier rent theories. This use of general value theory rather than of a unique or peculiar principle is probably the most important recent contribution to the unification of distribution theory.[8] The increasing acceptance of this explanation of rent indicates a general respect for consistency of method and a widespread desire for a single comprehensive principle that can be applied uniformly to all types of income.[9]

This should not be interpreted to mean that conditions of supply and demand are exactly the same or operate in precisely the same way in determining land income or rent as in determining labor income or wages, or the other distributive shares in production. It means merely that the same technique or general approach is applicable and that this approach is adequate to reveal conditions of demand and supply peculiar to individual factors of production, which necessitate some modification in the application of the principles.

CAPITALIZED RENT AND INCOME DISTRIBUTION

Land secures its value for economic purposes because of the net returns or economic rent it will secure for its owner. In this sense, land has value

[7] Henry George, *Progress and Poverty*, Wm. M. Hinton, San Francisco, author's ed., 1879.

[8] Cf. Bye, *op. cit.*, p. 106. According to Bye, "The development reaches fruition when rent is included among the cost manifestations of the equilibrium process."

[9] *Ibid.*

for the same reasons that any other economic good has value. However the greater durability of land as a production factor, compared with many freely reproducible goods, results in peculiar emphasis upon future earn ing capacity of the land for purposes of land valuation. Moreover, be cause of the lack of standardization among different land units, the relative infrequency of sales of some types and grades of land in many localities, and the disorganized local character of the real-estate market individual judgment is more influential in the valuation of land than in that of standardized goods in a better-organized market.[10]

CAPITALIZATION OF RENT INTO LAND VALUES

The buyer of land is actually buying the right to receive a series of annual incomes, and the most tangible basis for judging what these annual incomes will be in the future is what they have been in the immediate past. Studies show that income received from land for a 7-year or 10-year period preceding sale is a most effective gauge of the price the purchaser will agree to pay.[11] The commonly accepted formula for capitalizing the series of expected annual incomes into land values is $V = \frac{a}{r}$ where V is the value of the land, a the annual income, and r the going rate of interest. The values so determined may be referred to as the capitalized "productivity value" of the land.

This formula is a reduction of the more complex one that shows algebraically the value of each expected annual increment discounted to present value.[12] In other words, if the annual net return, or economic rent, of a piece of land is $6 per year and the going rate of interest is 6 percent, the value of the land is $100. This piece of land will yield the

[10] E. W. Morehouse, "Land Valuation," in *Encyclopaedia of the Social Sciences*, Vol. IX, p. 137.

[11] *Ibid.*

[12] The formula for the present value of a given number of dollars (a) due in n years, if the interest is compounded annually at the rate r, can be determined by the formula $\frac{a}{(1 + r)^n}$. This formula is derived from the fact that x dollars compounded at a rate r would be $x(1 + r)^t$, and if $x(1 + r)^t = a$, then $x = \frac{a}{(1 + r)^t}$. Consequently, if the net income or economic rent of a piece of land is a, its value could be expressed by the following equation:

$$V = \frac{a}{(1 + r)} + \frac{a}{(1 + r)^2} + \frac{a}{(1 + r)^3} + \frac{a}{(1 + r)^4} \cdots \frac{a}{(1 + r)^n}$$

The limit of the sum of such a series is $\dfrac{\dfrac{a}{(1 + r)}}{1 - \dfrac{1}{(1 + r)}}$, which reduces to $\frac{a}{r}$, so that the equation showing the succession of expected annual incomes discounted to present value and added reduces to the formula $V = \frac{a}{r}$.

ame annual net return as $100 placed at interest at 6 percent will yield uring the same length of time. Strictly from the point of view of pro- uctivity, therefore, the piece of land is worth $100, or the same as the mount which, at the going rate of interest, would yield $6 annually.

The above formula assumes a constant net income or rent from the and, whereas in reality the net income earned fluctuates considerably rom year to year or from period to period. Consequently, an element of nticipation may have to be included in the capitalization process. The ormula may be altered to include this expectation by adding or subtract- ng a factor that may be referred to as "i," or the amount of expected nnual increase or decrease. For example, if the annual net return or rent rom a piece of land is expected to increase at a constant arithmetical rate, he formula would be $V = \dfrac{a}{r} + \dfrac{i}{r^2}$; whereas if the future net income or ent is expected to decrease at a constant arithmetical rate, $V = \dfrac{a}{r} - \dfrac{i}{r^2}$ An extension of this formula has been suggested to make it more appli- able to practical conditions, because declines in land rent through soil lepletion, changes in market conditions, etc., do not usually reach zero: [13]

$$V = \frac{a}{r} + \frac{i}{r^2}\left[1 - \frac{1}{(1+r)^{n-1}}\right]$$

In this formula, n equals the number of years during which constant ncrements or decrements occur. In the case of decrements, n means he number of years during which constant annual decreases occur, vhether they level out at a positive figure because of shifting the land o some other use, or for some other reason, or to a level at zero or below. At best, however, these formulas can be used in most cases only as rough pproximations or guides, because land incomes ordinarily do not in- rease or decrease at a uniform rate. There will be increases in some ears and decreases in others, or alternating increases and decreases, or hanges in the rate of increase or decrease, and the formula would have o be changed to fit these conditions. Also, it is necessary to have an excellent system of cost accounting to determine net income or economic ent from land, and to separate the return attributable to land from sur- olus wages or excess profits from superior management.

The student should not overlook the fact that the preceding formulas lso assume a constant interest rate. If the interest rate declines, a piece of land earning the same net return as indicated above—that is, $6—would

[13] J. J. Livers and G. H. Craig, "A Note on 'Role of Soil Depletion in Land Valu- tion,'" in *Journal of Farm Economics,* Vol. XXII, No. 4, November, 1940, pp. 773 ff.; D. B. Ibach, "The Role of Soil Depletion in Land Valuation," in *Journal of Farm Economics,* Vol. XXII, No. 2, May, 1940, pp. 460 ff.; and the following chapter gives a more detailed discussion of this problem.

be worth considerably more than $100. In other words, if the intere
rate declines from 6 percent to 3 percent, the value of the land woul
double. Mortgage rates of interest in the United States, for example, var
considerably in different parts of the country, and these variations hav
a significant effect upon the level of land values in these areas.

DISPARITIES BETWEEN LAND VALUES AND CAPITALIZED RENT

The student should not conclude from the preceding discussion tha
land values actually found to exist in various areas at different perioc
will represent strictly the capitalization of the economic rent or net ir
come to be derived from utilization of such lands. There are many reasor
why current land values do not correspond more closely to capitalize
income values, and only a few will be mentioned briefly here. Institutiona
forces play an important part in determining land values and lease rate:
Custom and tradition frequently result in levels of land values or leas
rates considerably above those justified on the basis of economic rent o
net income to be secured from utilization of such lands.

Richard Jones did not believe that Ricardo's explanation of rents o:
the basis of economic forces was realistic. Jones observed that peasan
rents resulted from causes other than strict capitalization of economi
rent, and that competition, being limited by custom, resulted in actua
rents and land values different from those which would have been estat
lished by purely economic forces.[14] Jones divided rents into two classes-
peasant rents and farmers' rents; and he argued that peasant rents ar
determined solely by a bargain between the proprietor and a set of labor
ers who are chained to the soil and who use their small capital to get :
bare subsistence.

Psychological or sentimental values placed upon land, or social pres
tige that may arise from ownership of particular types or parcels of lan
may also determine the level of land values and leases. Many people t
whom land ownership brings a sense of security that ownership of othe
property does not give are willing to pay more for land than the capital
ized net return at the going interest rate would justify. In addition, :
large number of people believe that since land is created by nature an
cannot be reproduced, land values will tend to rise as civilizations matur
and growing population increases the demand for products of the land
This causes land values to rise above the level justified by current eco
nomic returns.

Regardless of the reasons for existing disparities between land value
and capitalized rent, it should be obvious that if the landowner is t

---

[14] Richard Jones, *Peasant Rents*, Macmillan, London, 1895; and discussion of Jones'
criticism of Ricardo in L. H. Haney (ed.), *History of Economic Thought*, rev. ed.
Macmillan, 1920, pp. 473 ff.

secure a reasonable return on his investment or operate the land with a reasonable profit, he should be cautious about overbidding the capitalized net income value in the price he pays for land. This is true whether the operator is purchasing or renting the land. It can be said, therefore, that economic rent is the most important single factor to consider in appraising the level of values of urban, agricultural, forest, mineral, or any other type of land.

COSTS IN UTILIZING LAND

It has been implied that land, while it may be physically free, is not economically free. In other words, land as it occurs in nature is not scarce, but as a factor of production, land is scarce because various costs in the form of money, work, time, and management are required to expand its economic supply. Urban land is not ready for the home buyer until such improvements as streets, sidewalks, curbs, trees, filling, and drainage have been provided.

Except in the case of such extensive uses as grazing or wild hay production, agricultural land improvements must ordinarily be made before the land is ready for man's use. Labor and capital must be expended for clearing, removing stumps, and leveling, draining, or irrigating the land, depending upon its location and character. The cost of clearing cutover stump lands in the Pacific Northwest, with the latest mechanical equipment, is about $15 per acre merely for removing the stumps. The cost of improvements on dry-land areas through the application of irrigation water frequently exceeds $200 an acre. In addition to these improvements to the land itself, considerable outlay must be made in the form of housing, fencing, and related expenditures.

Uses of land in most American communities change from time to time. In the case of urban land, corner lots formerly used for churches or stores may be used for gas stations or garages. Acres formerly tilled or grazed may be used as a landing field for airplanes. Acres formerly mined may be used for agricultural purposes, and so may cutover forest lands. Areas of scenic value, formerly used for agriculture, may be devoted exclusively to recreation.

Lands often mature or "ripen" into higher or more intense uses. For example, when garages or stores supplant homes, or when rather poor agricultural lands develop into highly valuable recreational areas, the land moves from a lower to a higher use. *Ripening costs* arise from the fact that there is a time element involved in the shifting of land from lower to higher uses. For example, near urban areas, farm lands may be subdivided and advertised for sale as city lots for several years, paying higher taxes assessed on the basis of a suburban valuation. It may be several years later that the land is actually developed and urban houses constructed on it. In many cases no income whatever is secured from the land during the period in which it is shifting from agricultural to urban use. Numerous examples of such instances may be discovered on the outskirts of practically every growing city.

Similar situations can be cited in the case of forest lands. Rapid deforestation in the United States produced more cutover land than settlers could take up promptly for agricultural use. Consequently, a period of time elapsed between deforestation and the use of the land for farming, when certain inevitable costs including interest on investment, taxes on the property, and related upkeep charges accumulated.

Costs of shifting land from lower to higher uses are frequently enough to prevent the actual accomplishment of such a shift. These costs may be referred to as *costs of supersession*. A good example is the case of a grain farmer who sees considerable profit possibilities in producing milk and other dairy products, but finds that changing his farm from a grain-producing unit to a dairy farm necessitates heavy costs such as remodeling old buildings or constructing new and adequate ones, purchasing much new equipment, livestock, etc. In urban areas, similar costs of supersession are frequently tremendously large, preventing or postponing the shift from lower to higher use.

It is evident, then, that land as a factor in production is not a free good and that considerable expenditure of human effort and capital must be made before the land will be useful in combination with other production factors. Even the western homesteads given away by the U.S. government, beginning in 1862, were scarcely a gift of nature, so great were the costs to many settlers in hardship and failure. Even the successful homesteader paid a tremendous price in labor and materials before these lands were brought into a state of productiveness. The free homestead policy of the Federal government has been referred to as a program where "Uncle Sam bet the settler he could not last five years." (The settler, under the early free-homestead laws, was required to live on the land five years and make certain improvements before securing title to the land.)

THE FUTURE OF RENT

Certain forces that may decrease or increase the rents of land in the future should be noted. Changes in dietary habits may cause agricultural rents to decline or to rise, for if people consume less food, decreased demand for foodstuffs will lower agricultural rents. Even a shift in dietary habits from animal and cereal to vegetable and fruit products may tend to reduce agricultural rents, since fewer acres are needed to feed a population that uses more vegetables and fruits and fewer animal products and cereals.

It is impossible to prophesy that either agricultural or urban rents will increase over a long period of time; naturally, agricultural rents will increase only if demand for agricultural products increases more rapidly than the rate at which new agricultural production methods are discovered and effected. Urban rents for business sites will increase only if people concentrate more and more of their buying in a given locality. Improved methods of transportation, which cause population decentralization, and new methods of marketing may offset this tendency. It is true that man has many weapons with which to combat the tendency of returns to diminish; but it is important, nevertheless, to remember that there is an absolute limit on land resources and that the *Principle of Diminishing Productivity* is always operating.

The student of land economics should remember that changing techniques and methods of utilizing land, as well as methods and practices of distribution and consumption, will change the proportions of the factors used, but not the basic principles that govern these combinations and determine the amount of rent for different grades of land. We live in a dynamic society, not in a static order. And, while the principles will apply with equal effectiveness under different conditions, the points representing the most profitable combination of factors will result in different amounts of land being used with a given amount of capital, labor, and management, or vice versa, depending upon costs, production techniques, prices, and related conditions.

REFERENCES FOR FURTHER READING

Baumol, William J., and Chandler, Lester W., *Economic Processes and Policies*, Harper & Brothers, New York, 1954, pp. 654–674.

Bye, C. R., *Developments and Issues in the Theory of Rent*, Columbia University Press, New York, 1940.

Chamberlin, Edward, *The Theory of Monopolistic Competition*, Harvard University Press, Cambridge, 1936, Appendix D.

Clark, J. B., *The Distribution of Wealth*, The Macmillan Company, New York, 1931, Chap. XXII.

Garver, F. B., and Hansen, A. H., *Principles of Economics*, rev. ed., Ginn & Company, Boston, 1937, Chap. XXV.

George, Henry, *Progress and Poverty*, Robert Schalkinbach Foundation, New York, 1929, Book III, Chap. II.

Meyers, A. L., *Elements of Modern Economics*, rev. ed., Prentice-Hall, Inc., Englewood Cliffs, N. J., 1941, Chap. XVI.

Mill, John Stuart, *Principles of Political Economy*, Ashley, W. J., ed., Longmans, Green, and Co., Ltd., London, 1926, Book II, Chap. XVI, and Book III, Chap. V.

Ricardo, David, *On the Principles of Political Economy and Taxation*, J. Murray, London, 1st ed., 1817.

Robinson, Joan, *The Economics of Imperfect Competition*, The Macmillan Company, Ltd., London, 1933, Chap. VIII.

LAND VALUES AND APPRAISAL

THE LEVEL of values at which ownership rights in land are exchanged i. a major determinant of the practices and profitableness of utilizing land —particularly agricultural, forest, and urban land. It is, therefore, essen tial to understand the factors that determine land values, and the relation between sound appraisal practices and successful credit experiences tenancy, conservation, wise use of land resources, and related land utiliza tion conditions.

The purposes for which land valuation is undertaken are numerous, particularly in modern complex societies. For example, when land belonging to public utilities is assessed for rate making, its value to the utility is sought, rather than its market value. Another important purpose of valuing land is determination of tax assessments.

Valuation proceedings or land appraisals are also required when property is leased, when securities are issued or business enterprises consolidated, when estates are divided, when loans are made on real estate, when disputes between property owners or between private owners and the government must be decided. While the purpose of an appraisal may determine its technique as well as its results, the selling price of land may be taken as the usual standard from which deviations for special uses or considerations may be made.

DETERMINATION OF THE VALUE OF LAND

The determination of what land is worth is a very complex problem, as are all value determination problems. Land values are determined by demand and supply forces operating in the land market. The value ordinarily sought is the "cash market value," in dollars, under competitive conditions, with voluntary sellers and buyers. Certain specific methods for determining this value have been established and are in use.

A THEORY OF LAND VALUES

Land valuation is subject to all the implications of general value theory, but has certain distinctive features because of the peculiar characteristics of land as an economic good. Land differs from freely reproducible goods in that it is more durable, usually has a negative rate of physical depreciation, has relative immobility, and is not homogeneous.

From the greater durability of land and its resulting inflexibility in economic relations arises the peculiar emphasis in land valuation upon its future earning capacity. Because it is impossible to standardize different units of land, because sales are relatively infrequent, and because the real-estate market in many areas is disorganized and local, individual judgment plays a greater part in valuing land than in valuing standardized goods in a more perfectly organized market. However, the general procedure for evaluating land is similar to that for evaluating other economic goods. First, an attempt is made to appraise accurately the various factors that influence its worth and, second, a general final judgment or appraisal of net worth or value is made.

Some writers insist upon the uniqueness of land value, on the grounds that land value has no connections with production or reproduction, but is based solely upon social pressure, as it expresses itself in the demand for land.[1] However, aside from minor instances, which in the aggregate are not economically significant, land in its virgin or natural state is not very useful to man, and before land as an agent in production becomes economically productive, man must incorporate capital and labor with it. In this process, land has a cost of production and is subject to much the same economic forces of supply and demand as other economic goods.

The point upon which the controversy seems to arise is the difference of origin of land and other economic goods. It is true that land consists of natural resources in all their forms, and that capital is made up of material goods that man has provided by his own effort and sacrifice; but, as an economic good, land is usually a joint product (land and labor) and is in many ways similar to, as well as different from, capital goods.

For purposes of valuation, land may be divided into two major classes —land used for consumption purposes and land used as a production good. Examples of the first class are residential sites or park areas; and the principles of valuing such lands differ considerably from those applicable to land used as a production agent. The two classes merge in agriculture, where farm and home are one. It is essential, however, that in appraising the value of the farm these two classes be kept separate.

The process of determining the value of a piece of land used in production consists of three steps: (1) capitalization of the income yielded or expected from the land in production; (2) addition to or subtraction from "productive value" of the worth of such intangibles as amenities of site, accessibility of social and cultural advantages, and general character of the community; (3) appraisal of the current status of the land market and the local level of values in terms of expected long-time norms. In the process of land valuation, income capitalization procedures will not be emphasized so much in the older nations, where traditional uses and amenities have been established, as they will in newer areas like the United States or Canada, where usages and associations have not been so long or so completely developed and established.

In the previous chapter, we noted that the commonly accepted formula for capitalizing the series of expected incomes into land value is $V = \dfrac{a}{r}$ plus or minus $\dfrac{i}{r^2}$ where V is the value of land, a the annual income, r the

---

[1] "In the case of goods that are reproducible and in which alternative possibilities are present—goods that have a cost of production—both the goods and their values are social products. They are social as instruments and as value-possessing objects. Land value, too, is social value, but land itself is not a social product; it is not a product at all. All value but land value . . . (with minor exceptions, like unique articles such as old paintings) depends upon the fact that supply as well as demand is socially determined. Such values involve more than social demand; they depend in addition upon items like production difficulty and reproduction possibility." (See G. R. Geiger, *The Theory of the Land Question*, Macmillan, New York, 1936, pp. 38–39.)

te of interest, and i the amount of expected annual increase or decrease.
alue so determined is referred to as "productive value." We noted that
is formula is useful only as a rough guide, because incomes from land
dinarily do not decrease or increase uniformly, and in longer settled
ations where population movements and land uses have become rela-
vely stable, the speculative element plays a very small part.[2]

METHODS OF DETERMINING LAND VALUE

It seems perfectly logical to many individuals that in the long run the
ost reasonable basis for determining the worth of land should be its
ility to produce an income. In other words, a reasonable value based
1 productivity is that upon which the land will return, on the average,
fair rate of interest. This statement, however, ignores other factors that
ater into human appraisals. In the first place, how can the intangible
ychological elements of site amenities, community character, and qual-
y of home that the land provides be measured exactly and used in a
recise formula? How can the prestige attaching to land ownership be
lued in dollars and cents?

Moreover, future incomes, not past incomes, indicate what land values
ill be; and the future is always uncertain. Many believe that sales values
etermined in a freely competitive market by voluntary buyers and sellers
ill reflect as accurately as values determined by any other method the
icome-producing ability of the lands, capitalized at the going rate of
iterest. Here again the same criticism applies—that past sales value,
en though based on income, must necessarily be based on past perform-
ice and have serious limitations with respect to determining accurately
ie true long-time net worth or value of the lands.

There are two major approaches to land valuation. There are (1) the
omparison method, apparently dominant in certain European coun-
ies, and (2) the income capitalization method, used widely in the United
ates. The comparative approach uses current sales or market values as
ie basis for determining what land is worth, while the second method
etermines land values by capitalizing the income produced by the land.
ach of these two basic methods has its peculiar limitations and advan-
ges, and a combination of the two appears to be growing in favor as
n accepted appraisal practice. The extent to which either will be empha-
zed in a combination approach depends to a large extent upon local
tuations and conditions.

[2] For example, the value of land in England is expressed in terms of 20 or 25 years'
urchase of the annual rent, the number of years depending upon other elements
esides productivity that enter into the calculations; and in prewar Germany the
alue of land was estimated at approximately 28 times the annual rent. In the United
ates, however, no such close relationship exists between rent and value. (See E. W.
Morehouse, "Land Values," in *Encyclopaedia of the Social Sciences*, Vol. IX, p. 137.)

THE COMPARISON METHOD

There is rather widespread general agreement that the income-produc ing ability of a piece of land used for productive purposes is the maj consideration in determining land value. There is, however, widesprea disagreement in regard to the best method of converting production es mates into value. The sale-price comparison method establishes the val of land according to the known or recognized value of other comparab land, and consists of two parts: (1) the estimate of productivity, and (2 the use of actual sale prices of lands whose productivity is known as basis for evaluating the particular parcel.

This method eliminates the necessity of estimating future income, cos and capitalization rates because, in effect, it accepts the market evalu tion of all of these. Unfortunately, however, market-determined prese values are commonly very poor indicators of future values. During perio of optimism, speculative forces may temporarily so affect the sale val of land that it is not recognized as the reasonable or real econom value of the land. Likewise, during depression periods, future prospec may appear so gloomy that current land values have little relationshi to the real long-time earning ability or economic value of the land.

The land market is profoundly dependent on experiences of the pr ceding few years in its evaluation of future prospects on which, in tur its land value judgments are based.[3] The comparative method, therefor relies upon market values and, because the market is often so serious out of line with long-time earning power or future income-yielding abilit dependence upon this method alone cannot be considered acceptab unless all alternative procedures are equally inadequate. During perio of relative stability in land values, the comparative method is an e cellent way to determine such values. However, land values fluctua widely during depressions, and in these periods the comparative metho will be very unsatisfactory.

Lack of adequate sales data also limits the comparative method. Th small amount of land that changes hands through voluntary sales in ce tain areas is insufficient to establish reliable sales value estimates. Fc example, in areas where owner operation is common and farms are hande

[3] See C. R. Chambers, *The Relationship of Land Income to Land Values*, U.S. D partment of Agriculture Bulletin 1224, 1923; F. L. Thompson, "Factors Affecting Re Estate Values in the United States," *Journal of Farm Economics*, Vol. XVII, No. May, 1935, pp. 379 ff.; L. H. Bean, "Inflation and the Price of Land," *Journal of Far Economics*, Vol. XX, No. 1, February, 1938, pp. 310 ff.; and Conrad H. Hammar, "Th Synthesis of Materials for Appraising," in *Proceedings of the Conference of the Amer can Society of Farm Managers and Rural Appraisers and the Appraisal Institute Canada*, Vol. IV, No. 3, November, 1940, p. 80. Bean indicates that one-half of a give rise in farm land values over a period of years may be associated with prices of far products in the current year.

down generation after generation, very few sales occur. On the other hand, in those areas where serious economic difficulties have arisen, there may be a large number of land sales, though few are voluntary. Consequently, before sales value data can be considered adequate to determine reliable values, there must be (1) an adequate turnover of lands through voluntary sales, (2) an effective means of distinguishing between bona fide sales and those that are not (since many land transactions are made purely for legal reasons and are not strictly transactions between a buyer and a seller), and (3) fairly complete data on land transfer records, showing the sales price of the transaction. (Many times land is sold subject to an outstanding mortgage on which an amount is due, and in many cases the exact amount due is not mentioned in the deed.)

In addition to the scarcity of bona fide sales with complete financial information indicated in the deeds, there is the difficulty of determining what kind of farm or urban property has been sold and how it compares with the farm or urban property in question. The lack of standardization in the land market resulting from the uniqueness of each parcel of land accounts for this added difficulty. Quotations on wheat indicate a price arrived at for a commodity accurately described and labeled according to definite standards; but in the case of land it is extremely difficult to be certain that a given purchase price represents a going market value. The sale price may be unduly low because the two parties are related, or unduly high because an extremely small down payment is made.[4] Thus, it is evident that there are various difficulties involved in the use of sale prices to determine land values, but wherever adequate sales data are available, they should be used fully.

THE INCOME CAPITALIZATION METHOD

The income capitalization method consists of: (1) an estimate of productivity and net income; (2) choice of a capitalization rate; and (3) adjustments to capitalized value to account for the intangible features.[5] In determining net income to be capitalized, the gross income or return from the land is estimated from the best data available, and from these gross returns necessary production costs are deducted. In determining costs of production, typical operation and management are assumed, and the net income is capitalized to obtain the value of the land.

Although capitalized income is considered by many as a cardinal prin-

[4] Murray points out that price is assumed as the actual quotation in sales transactions, whereas value includes not only actual prices but also estimates of price and estimates of worth other than those established in the market. "Sales prices, in this unorganized condition of the land market, may be misleading unless unusual care is taken to make sure what was in the minds of the buyers and sellers." (W. G. Murray, *Farm Appraisal*, Iowa State College Press, 1940, p. 184.)

[5] Cf. *ibid.*, p. 177.

ciple in the determination of land values, its application has some ver
serious difficulties. In the first place, the net income to be derived fro
land cannot ordinarily be estimated accurately from data available. Ther
is still a serious lack of reliable farm management operating cost an
income data upon which to determine net returns to be capitalized int
land values. Where rather complete cost of production and income dat
are available, many estimates and judgments enter into deriving a cap
talized value.[6]

Use of the income approach involves arbitrary choice of a level of price
on which to determine estimated income. In most cases, hindsight i
considered the best basis for foresight, and long-time historical records
rather than current prices, are used as the basis for estimating futur
price levels for purposes of income determination. In areas where much
land is leased, the estimated net income of land can be closely approxi
mated from the lease rates. However, use of the typical landlord or renta
share method has some limitations, including the fact that about as much
estimating is required for determining the landlord's expense items a
is necessary in the cost accounting or operating budget method.[7]

Another limitation of the income capitalization method is that a high
proportion of land value is made up of nonincome factors, or what might
be called "the amenities," which are psychological factors whose income
value can be only roughly estimated. A further difficulty arises in mar
ginal areas where average expenses and average returns so closely approxi
mate each other that a very slight change in yield or expense means a
significant difference in the capitalized land value.

Many feel that under these conditions, present cost accounting and
estimates of net income are too inaccurate to be adequate. There are
numerous other difficulties involved in using the income capitalization
method, particularly in certain types of farming areas and manufacturing
enterprises. For example, in the New England states and the Eastern part
of the United States generally, there is a great diversity of agricultural
enterprises, and tenancy is comparatively small. In these areas, the income
method is at a distinct disadvantage compared with its position in more

[6] See the author's treatment, "Land Classification as an Aid in Real Estate Assess-
ment," *The Classification of Land,* University of Missouri, Agricultural Experiment
Station Bulletin 421, December, 1940, p. 83. A prominent member of the American
Union of Real Estate Appraisers lists 11 estimates involved in the subsidiary estimates
necessary for deriving values on an income basis. (*Property Taxes: A Symposium,* Tax
Policy League, 1940, p. 215.)

[7] Cf. E. C. Hope, "A Discussion of a Paper by Conrad H. Hammar on the Synthesis
of Materials for Appraising," *Proceedings of the American Society of Farm Managers
and Rural Appraisers and the Appraisal Institute of Canada,* Vol. IV, No. 3, November, 1940, pp. 100–101. Hope states that on the average-sized farm, "the landlord's
estimated expense items are as large a proportion of his receipts as the estimated total
farm expenses are of total receipts."

specialized commercial farming areas like the Great Plains or in the one-crop cotton South.

Commercial poultry and dairy farms approximate manufacturing plants and in many cases the soil contributes a relatively small part of the income, the major items being buildings, management, and location. Very small and part-time farm units frequently do not show much or any net savings to be capitalized by strict cost accounting methods, but home and location features and related amenities are involved and make the inflexible allowances for family living used so generally in farm cost accounting techniques seem ridiculous, particularly where a negative return is involved. Use of the income capitalization method must be modified in such cases if it is to be most useful.

CHOICE OF A CAPITALIZATION RATE

Another important problem involved in the income capitalization method is the rate to be used in capitalizing the net income into land value. Choice of a capitalization rate is extremely important, because a shift from 5 percent to 4½ percent adds more than 11 percent to value, so that a tract of land worth $50 an acre would be worth $55.55. Obviously, the higher the risk in the area, the higher should be the interest rate used in the capitalization process, since the interest rate reflects both the productivity of capital and the risk involved in maintaining the principal.[8]

The current method of utilization is an important factor in determining the rate of capitalization, and since the type of utilization may change considerably within a relatively short period of years, serious difficulties are involved in using a constant rate of interest, the usual procedure in the capitalized income technique.

In the case of yields and prices, the use of long-time historical records or averages, or base-period averages, enables certain norms to be established for these items. However, no such norms are established or available for use in selection of the capitalization rate. In determining the specific rate to use, certain alternatives are available: (1) the current average rate on real-estate mortgages in the community at the time, (2) the average rate at which money could be borrowed on real-estate mortgage security at the time, (3) the long-time average rate on real-estate mortgages over the last 25 or 50 years, and (4) other periods or bases.

Use of long-time average rates is not a very sound practice if the trend of interest rates is definitely downward or definitely upward. Moreover,

[8] For example, in the more commercialized and specialized types of farming areas, and in the dryland-wheat-producing areas of the Northern Great Plains, a risk higher than in some other areas is inherent in the existing type of agriculture. The same principle applies on the family-sized diversified farms in more humid areas.

the average rate on mortgages in existence would probably not refle
the capitalization rate accurately, because what the community expec
the rate to be over the long period during which land purchase and sal
contracts normally extend would probably not coincide with the averag
rate on mortgages in existence.

Some students question any use of the borrowing rate as the basis fc
the capitalization rate, on the grounds that the borrowing rate reflec
a response to forces that are quite different.[9] Mortgage rates are als
becoming more and more institutionalized, because of the great share c
mortgage credit held by federal agencies. Loan rates on these mortgage
are determined by Congressional statute and by the investor's rating c
debentures which are quasi-public in nature. Mortgage rates so dete
mined do not necessarily represent prospective risks and returns from lan
purchase or sale.

The mortgage rate has tended to become virtually uniform over all area
of the United States, as the result of the policy of public lending institu
tions, such as the Farm Security, Farmers Home, and Farm Credit admini
trations. However, as previously noted, the capitalization rate should re
flect the great variations in risk among regions of the country. For all thes
reasons, therefore, it does not seem desirable to use the mortgage rate c
interest for purposes of capitalizing land values.

During periods when the appraisal of investment risks is high becaus
of a preceding period of falling land values, numerous bankruptcies, fore
closures, unfavorable weather, and poor economic conditions, the capitali
zation rate would probably approach closely the average land sale an
purchase contract rate. However, during periods when farm and urbai
incomes and land values have been stable for a considerable time, or whei
they are rising, the capitalization rate will closely approximate the aver
age mortgage rate.[10]

In any case, however, the capitalization rate deserves further researcl

[9] Hammar points out that, to begin with, mortgage credit is not extended alon
or even preponderantly for purchase, but is usually employed for refinancing, t
provide buildings and other more or less permanent improvements, to purchase equip
ment and livestock, and for many other purposes. "The forces which determine th
mortgage rate of interest, therefore, are a composite of the lender's evaluations of th
risks and returns of many loans for such purposes, and of the borrower's evaluation
of the anticipations of the marginal efficiencies of the types of capital in which th
money is estimatedly to be invested." (Hammar, *op. cit.*, p. 83.)

[10] Hammar indicates that the most likely capitalization rate of farm income lie
somewhere between the mortgage rate of interest and the land contract rate, anc
points out that in most areas of the United States the land transfer contract rate i
customarily above the mortgage rate by 20 or 25 percent. (Hammar, *op. cit.*, p. 83.
Hope, on the other hand, points out that in Saskatchewan the opposite is usually true
the typical mortgage rate for some years prior to 1931 being 8 percent with practically
no regional variations, and that during this period land contract interest rates rangec
downward from 8 to 6 percent, with nearly all private, Hudson Bay Company, anc
railway land sales contracts at 6 percent. (Hope, *op. cit.*, p. 97.)

nd study, and is one of the items in the income capitalization method of
etermining land values that must be handled with extreme care. The
ind appraiser must in every case seek the average of various extremes
nd support his judgment by comparison with other rates (such as the
ites on long-term federal, state or provincial, or municipal bonds, or the
ites on bonds of local governmental units) typical of the area in which
e is appraising land.

THE VALUE OF IMPROVEMENTS

Determination of the value of buildings and improvements added to
ind is another complicating item in the appraisal process. There are
imes when unimproved land of a given grade is as valuable as improved
ind, because of the fact that unimproved land will fit into the operating
ilans of the renter (lessee) as well as or better than land containing build-
ngs or other improvements. Under these conditions, the value of the im-
irovements (based on productivity or rents that can be secured) will be
ero. However, such cases are the exception rather than the rule; and—
iarticularly in undersettled and underbuilt communities—added improve-
nents increase the value of the property appreciably. The American So-
iety of Farm Managers and Rural Appraisers recommends that buildings
nd other comparable improvements be appraised on the basis of repro-
luction cost less observed depreciation, and acknowledges that obsoles-
ence is frequently a major item of depreciation.

In some of the older parts of the United States, studies have shown that
he size and condition of buildings on farms are a fairly good index of
arm land values. While this may be true in the older parts of the nation,
t certainly would not be a satisfactory way of determining land values in
nore recently settled areas or in regions where rapid adjustments are oc-
urring in land use. Even in the longer settled areas, size and condition
if buildings as a guide to land value should be used very cautiously, and
n any case always supplemented with soils, topography, and related land
lassification data, for the condition of buildings, especially on individual
arms where some money has been inherited or there are sources of income
ither than the farm, can be very misleading.[11]

ADVANTAGES OF THE INCOME CAPITALIZATION METHOD

In spite of all the difficulties connected with applying the income capi-
alization technique to land value determination, it has many advantages,

[11] In many areas, farms which have been foreclosed by insurance companies or other
corporations or agencies have had their buildings given a fresh coat of paint with
corporate funds. Nowell relates the story of the woman who refused to have her
buildings repaired and repainted: "If I do," she said, "the neighbors will think I have
been foreclosed." (See R. I. Nowell's discussion of A. B. Lewis's paper, "Land Classifi-
ation as an Appraisal and Credit Aid," in *The Classification of Land*, University of
Missouri, Agricultural Experiment Station Bulletin 421, p. 77.)

and if used as scientifically as possible and supplemented with good jud
ment, it performs an important function. In the first place, it calls th
land appraiser's attention to the factors and forces that influence valu
The appraiser must understand the conditions that affect income an
living costs, probable future developments in prices and costs, and relate
matters. Moreover, the income capitalization method centers attention o
the developments of the future while the comparative method tends t
emphasize past history of sales values.

The emphasis in the income capitalization method upon forecastin
necessitates a refinement of statistical techniques and studies to make po
sible more accurate prediction. Emphasis upon scientific method i
forecasting helps to offset the swings of the economic pendulum associate
with booms and depressions, which affect the values used in the sales-pric
method. The net results should be more scientific lending and borrowin
policies during rising price periods and more courageous, less pani
stricken policies during depression periods.

In addition to these advantages, use of the income capitalization metho
provides many items and data extremely valuable to borrowers, lender
buyers, and sellers. Accumulation of such data will eventually afford
much better basis for appraisals; and many of the serious consequence
of earlier appraisals—including waves of land speculation, booms, an
panics—will be removed or greatly reduced.

THE COMBINATION METHOD

The limitations of the comparative method and the income capitaliza
tion method of valuation have led many to conclude that a combinatio
of both methods would be a more desirable approach. According to th
American Society of Farm Managers and Rural Appraisers, "the use o
both the income capitalization and comparative approaches to value i
necessary in every appraisal, and one should not be emphasized to th
minimization or exclusion of the other." [12] It further points out that i
the comparative approach is used independently of the income capitaliza
tion method, the income valuation would necessarily be included, and
that it is therefore expedient to use the comparative approach to adjus
the income capitalization value. However, some appraisers reverse thi
procedure and use the income capitalization value as a check. In an
case, both methods should be combined for most effective appraisa
policies.

In areas like the corn belt, where tenancy is common, values are hig
and nonincome factors make up a smaller percentage of value. The in
come approach may be emphasized and sales value used to provide infor

[12] *Journal of the American Society of Farm Managers and Rural Appraisers,* Vol. II
No. 2, p. 91.

mation on the value of the nonincome items and to check the reliability of income estimates. On the other hand, in areas where the opposite is true, sales value may be emphasized and income figures used as a check.[13] The two methods are means to the same end, and since one approach may be better than the other in certain areas, use of both methods, with more weight given to the one better adapted to the specific area, will be the best approach to sound land value appraisals.[14]

FACTORS INFLUENCING LAND VALUES

These methods of determining land values apply generally to land, regardless of its use. However, numerous physical, economic, legal, and other factors also influence the value of land for certain uses. In every case, the appraisal process requires an examination and weighting of these various factors.

FACTORS INFLUENCING FARM LAND VALUES

Physical factors important in determining the value of farm lands include character and chemical content of the soil, variety of crops to which the soil is adapted, number of acres under cultivation, size and condition of fields, amount of woodland, topography, length of growing season, percentage of area tillable, rainfall, drainage, and similar factors. Economic factors include the distance to market or town; the type of road, which obviously influences time and costs involved in marketing and transportation to and from school, churches, meetings, etc.; level of taxes and special assessments; type, size, and condition of buildings and other improvements on the land; and character of title to the land (whether it is clear, or subject to liens or omissions that make the title abstract confused). Certain legal factors, such as legislation in regard to uses that can be made of the land, and the right to sell, bequeath, or otherwise transfer title also have an important bearing on value.

Numerous attempts have been made to determine by statistical measurement the relative importance of various factors determining farm land values. For example, in the corn belt, one study found that four factors—(1) 10-year average yield of corn per acre, (2) percentage of land in corn, (3) percentage of land in small grain, and (4) percentage of land not plowable—explained most variations in farm values.[15] Another survey, in Minnesota, found that six factors—(1) value of buildings per acre, (2) type of land, (3) crop yields, (4) distance from market, (5) size of adjacent city or village, and (6) type of road upon which located—

[13] Murray, *op. cit.*, p. 184.
[14] Cf. *ibid.*, p. 185.
[15] Together these four factors gave a multiple correlation coefficient of .9166. (See Henry A. Wallace, "Comparative Farm Land Values in Iowa," *Journal of Land and Public Utility Economics*, Vol. II, No. 4, October, 1926, p. 389.)

were of major importance in explaining land values.[16] In another study in southeastern Pennsylvania (which is a longer-settled area), Ezekiel found that a multiple correlation of eight factors accounted for 60 per cent of the land value variations, and that buildings are by far the most important of these factors, with land (including fertility, topography, and proportion usable) next in importance, though much less important, general factors of location and type of road being of very minor significance.[17]

Studies such as those cited account for only a part—though a large part —of the variation in land values, and the land value to be explained is itself only a rough approximation, because census reports on the value of land (which were the land values used in these studies) are merely estimates of sale price made by farmers in response to questioning from the census enumerator.[18] Nevertheless, studies along the lines of those cited do give an approximate numerical weight to the various factors that account for sale prices and sale value estimates and, in this way, indicate the relative importance of the factors which influence farm land values in different sections of the country.

FACTORS INFLUENCING THE VALUE OF FOREST LANDS

The fact that 30, 100, or 200 years may be spent in growing the forest crop makes it necessary for the income from the land to cover expenditures accumulated over many years. During the growth period, some income may be derived from supplementary uses like leasing and grazing rights or game privileges. In the United States cleared forest lands have ordinarily been made available for resale for other uses, and land values established under such conditions are determined by these uses.

The determination of forest land values is most useful for tax assessment purposes, and it is extremely important to separate the value of the timber from the value of the land. Moreover, the increasing amount of information available on rate of growth, on costs of cutting and milling the trees into lumber and related products, and on long-time average lumber and wood product prices makes it possible to determine values for forest lands on a capitalized income basis much the same as for agricultural lands. However, the rate of capitalization to use for forest lands is

[16] In this study, a multiple correlation coefficient of .81 was secured. (G. C. Haase, "Sale Prices as a Basis for Farm Land Appraisal," Minnesota Agricultural Experiment Station Technical Bulletin 9, 1922, p. 3.)

[17] The eight factors used are: (1) dwelling value, (2) dairy buildings value, (3) other buildings value, (4) crop index, (5) percentage of area tillable, (6) percentage of area level, (7) type of road, and (8) distance to town. M. Ezekiel, *Factors Affecting Farmers' Earnings in Southeastern Pennsylvania,* U.S. Department of Agriculture Bulletin 1400, 1936, p. 49.

[18] Murray, *op. cit.,* pp. 196–197.

even more difficult to determine than for farm lands, because of the relatively long growth period involved.

FACTORS INFLUENCING VALUES OF MINERAL LANDS

Mineral lands differ significantly from farm and forest lands in that the mineral industry has nothing comparable with a recurring crop. When minerals are extracted from the ground, the future supply is reduced. Consequently, valuation must take into account the factor of depletion or exhaustion and the problem of balancing future needs and present requirements.

The fact that minerals are usually hidden below the surface so that their exact position, amount, and quality are not definitely known leads to a considerable element of speculation in the appraisal of mineral lands. Furthermore, the increasing importance of mineral lands, particularly in connection with international politics and modern warfare, still further complicates the valuation of such lands.

The unpredictability of the future rate of technological advance makes future demand for certain minerals extremely difficult to forecast. In the case of some products, such as uranium-bearing ores, there may be heavy demand increases and resulting appreciable increases in value of lands containing these minerals; whereas demand for others, such as nitrates, may decline considerably or be completely absent because of shifts and substitutes, so that lands containing such minerals would be practically worthless.

FACTORS INFLUENCING URBAN LAND VALUES

In appraising urban land, a distinction must be made between business and residential property. In residential sites, the so-called "amenities"—view, spaciousness, height, light, architecture, freedom from noise, shape of site, and related factors—are highly important. Proximity to schools, churches, and shopping centers is more significant than nearness to traffic, which may be a liability, particularly if there is a heavy flow of traffic. Zoning and deed restrictions in certain urban areas tend to stabilize land values; and cost of utility services and other improvements like sidewalks, paving, and curbing are important influences, particularly on newly subdivided lands.[19]

Factors influencing the value of urban business sites are quite different from those influencing the value of residential property. In business sites (particularly retail business sites) location with respect to pedestrian traffic and the buying power of these pedestrians is of utmost importance. Consequently, front footage is significant, and corner locations command

[19] Cf. Morehouse, *op. cit.*, p. 138.

a premium. In all cases, size and shape of the lot play an important role. If the amount of land available is the proper size for desired development, value will be higher because costs of assembling separately owned small parcels for large building sites are appreciable.[20] The weighting of the various factors that influence value will vary with the type of business to be operated on the site. For example, in the case of factories, nearness to transportation facilities, accessibility, cost of power, and related items are of major importance.

FACTORS INFLUENCING VALUES OF LANDS FOR OTHER USES

The extensive use of land for recreational purposes, particularly in the United States, is a relatively recent development. Consequently, the factors influencing the value of land for this use are not as well known or understood as those influencing the value of lands used for farming, forest, urban, or other purposes. The various qualities that make certain tracts of land particularly useful or valuable for recreational purposes should be given careful consideration in determining their value for recreational use.

Location in relation to the main routes of travel and land settlement is the most important single determinant of the value of land for transportation use. Strategically situated lands will be utilized for transportation and will be able to command a comparatively high price. Often such lands have been procured at the expense of other land uses, through condemnation proceedings. In condemnation proceedings, the appraisal used as the basis for payment to the owner gives first consideration to the personal sacrifice that the owner makes in selling the tract involved.

Condemnation appraisal is the judgment of the state, through the courts, as to the compensation it considers a reasonable reimbursement to the individual for sacrifices involved in giving up his property. The sale price established in condemnation appraisal is ordinarily above the current sale price for comparable property, because the seller would not be willing to part with his property otherwise.

Condemnation appraisals or valuations for highway or street purchase ordinarily involve only a small strip of a given farm or urban unit. However, this strip may be so located that its use for transportation would be particularly embarrassing, unsightly, inconvenient, or detrimental to the owner; and compensation must take these sacrifices into consideration, though they are very difficult to evaluate. One method suggested is to value the unit with and without the tract or strip in question, the difference representing the value of the condemned tract. Even here, however, considerable judgment of the individual case and the many factors involved will be necessary if reasonableness and fairness are to be secured.

[20] *Ibid.*

TRENDS IN LAND VALUES

In most discussions of land value during the past century, emphasis has
en placed upon land value increments rather than land value decre-
ents. This is explained by the fact that during the nineteenth and early
entieth centuries, land values in the United States rose steadily, as a
le. Moreover, classical economic doctrine held that the landowner
nded to become richer and richer, with the passage of time, at the
pense of other groups in society, because of the limited supply of land
ailable to take care of increasing population and to meet the growing
mand for the products of land. This view was held particularly by
icardo, Malthus, and their contemporaries. They did not foresee the
eat scientific and technological advances that were to increase the pro-
ctivity of land and, consequently, increase the economic supply.

One of the most important factors influencing future land value levels
the population. Other forces important in determining future land
lues include prospects for foreign market outlets, the level of domestic
onomic activity, changing dietary habits and consumption trends, sav-
gs and investments, and related factors.

LAND BOOMS AND SPECULATION

Numerous land booms have occurred in various sections of the United
ates during its history, but the best known are the widespread land
oms of 1832–1836, 1854–1857, 1914–1920, and the Florida land boom
the twenties. In the East, more than a hundred years ago, there was a
eat boom in Maine timberlands, caused principally by the feeling that
cessible timber was fast disappearing and that prices would continue to
se with the development of the country. At that same time, there was
uch speculation in western town lots and farm lands, based largely upon
e rapid westward expansion of population. This boom collapsed in
336.

The land boom that reached its peak from 1854 to 1857 was brought
out largely by the great westward expansion of population and by the
latively good prices for grain on the world market, in which the
rimean War (1854–1856) was an important factor. The next big land
oom came during World War I, when unusually high wheat prices,
upled with the knowledge that there was no more free land in the
nited States, gave rise to the belief that the supply of good farm land
as now definitely limited and that increased demand would inevitably
use land values to rise in the future. Apparently it was not realized that
opulation was being curtailed and that, while the West had been settled,
uch of the area in range for livestock production could be plowed up
nd used more intensively for producing wheat.

The Florida land boom, which many people thought was a mushroo growth of the twenties, was nevertheless preceded by a fairly long peri of growth and development in that state. The state's climatic and agric tural resources, together with its increasingly accessible location, creat the psychological basis which, combined with merchandising propogan brought about rapid increases in land values. The rise reached its pe in the late twenties.[21]

Farm land values increased rapidly during and after World War from an index of 82 in 1940 (1912–1914 = 100) to 211 by 1952.[22] Th maintained levels approximating the 1952 peak for a short time and th rose further to 241 at the beginning of 1957.[23]

Land booms have appeared as the culmination of a favorable trend tending over a considerable period, and they are usually accompanied a set of optimistic beliefs not too complex or abstruse to have wide a peal.[24] It is not necessarily true that land booms must always be preced by these conditions, because land values tend to respond promptly pronounced increases in prices and incomes so that any event that caus a rapid upturn in general economic conditions could and probably wou cause a considerable rise in land values. However, the nature of the re estate market makes it seem logical that the rise in land values must ex for some time before it could reach the proportions of a boom.

The real-estate market is naturally comparatively slow, and even boom periods, for example, a relatively small proportion of any co munity's farms or lots changes hands. Consequently, when a considerab number of pieces of land awaiting sale have accumulated during a peri of slowly declining markets, these holdings will not be absorbed for son years. This will necessitate a long-continued upward swing in land valu before the development of an extensive boom.[25]

The important problem connected with land booms is the method controlling or avoiding them. Studies reveal that land booms are general

[21] Cf. R. C. Limber, "Conditions Characteristic of Land Booms," *Journal of Far Economics,* Vol. XX, No. 1, February, 1938, p. 233.

[22] U.S. Department of Agriculture, "Agricultural Finance Review," Agricultu Research Service, Washington, D.C., Vol. XVII, Supplement, May, 1955, p. 32, processe

[23] U.S. Department of Agriculture, "Current Developments in the Farm Real Esta Market," Agricultural Research Service, Washington, D.C., ARS 43–46 (CD-45), Nove ber, 1956, p. 34, processed.

[24] See Limber, *op. cit.,* p. 234.

[25] Cf. *ibid.,* pp. 234–5. As evidence of the tendency for land booms to be initiat by some actual event that appears to offer prospective increases in income for a co siderable period, Limber cites the building of the Chicago Canal, which was assur by 1833, and the consequent Chicago land boom, which got under way immediate This boom collapsed in 1836, with the issuance of Jackson's Specie Circular, and t Canal was not finished until 12 years later, in 1848. This instance shows how spec lative hopes tend to outrun achievement. (See also Homer Hoyt, *One Hundred Yea of Land Values in Chicago,* University of Chicago Press, 1933, pp. 45 ff.)

nanced not by such first mortgage agencies as insurance companies and
he federal land banks but by second mortgage lenders—principally
rivate individuals, former landowners, and others speculating in land.
 study of an Iowa county where the land boom was unusually active
uring World War I reveals that from 1900 to the height of the boom,
isurance companies loaned conservatively and, as land prices rose year
ter year, continued to keep their advances down to a percentage aver-
ing about a third of current value. When the boom was at its peak, only
) percent of the sale price was being lent. In other words, more than 70
ercent of the sale price had to be financed by junior mortgages and cash.
n increase in junior mortgages and in the number of individuals who
ok a mortgage as part payment in the sale of their farms largely supplied
is necessary 70 percent.[26]

CONTROL OF LAND BOOMS

It is evident, therefore, that avoiding or controlling land booms neces-
tates a change in the attitudes and credit policies of private individuals,
rmer landowners, and those who tend to speculate in land, in order
at the financing necessary to create a land boom will not occur. In other
ords, the financing may be considered "the string on the balloon": it is
ot the force that causes the balloon to rise, but it certainly is the factor
at determines how high the balloon will rise. If these people are not
terested in financing land booms, land values will not rise to high boom
vels.

First mortgage agencies (particularly insurance companies and federal
nd banks) are much more cautious and conservative in their lending
olicies; and, while they tend to maintain a fairly constant relationship
tween current sale prices and amounts of loans, the difference in dollars
quired by other financing is much greater in boom periods than during
ormal periods.[27] Unless more funds from other sources are available to
pply the difference (and during most boom periods, purchasers cannot
btain the difference) a great increase in land values cannot occur, be-
use purchases and sales cannot be financed at the high prices character-
tic of boom periods.

It has been suggested that land booms might be controlled or even
revented through changes in the mortgage rate of interest, but it seems

[26] W. G. Murray, "Land Booms and Second Mortgages," *Journal of Farm Economics,*
ol. XX, No. 1, February, 1938, p. 230.
[27] This can be illustrated by the following example: Assume that the current sale
rice of farm land is $48 an acre and that the federal land bank is lending approxi-
ately half of this, or $24. This leaves $24 to be financed by the owner through other
annels—either funds of his own in the form of cash or other borrowings. However, if
nd values rise to $250 per acre and the land bank still continues its 50 percent loan
olicy of $125, a balance of $125 per acre is required from other sources to finance the
rchase of the land.

obvious that unless wide fluctuations in net incomes can be prevented b
some system of taxation, stabilizing the business cycle, or some othe
adjustment, fluctuations in the sale value of lands cannot be prevente
though they might be reduced somewhat through adjustment of the mor
gage rate of interest.

In the United States, up to the present, no technique of controlling th
business cycle seems to have been developed to the point where cycl
fluctuations will not recur. Whether this is caused by use of the wron
method or failure in execution is not important here; the fact remain
that it has not been accomplished, and consequently the major cause
fluctuations in land values—that is, fluctuations in land incomes—sti
exists.

In comparison with the great swings in land income associated with th
business cycle, wars, inflation, population movements, technological a
vances, and similar forces, changes of 1, 2, or 3 percent in the mortgag
rate of interest seem relatively insignificant. During more normal time
the mortgage rate of interest is more important and might be significar
in tending to stabilize land values. A strong credit education program t
convince landowners and lending agencies of the permanent advantage
and mutual benefits to be secured from more scientific lending practice
would probably be more effective, in the long run.

VALUE TRENDS AND LAND USE

The United States has experienced land booms, recessions, and panic
but these periods of high and low price levels have not affected the value
of all lands in the same way. This is amply illustrated by trends in far
and urban land values during World War I. The value of Ame
ican farm land doubled in the 1900–1910 period, and virtually double
again by 1920, while urban land was generally depressed during the wa
period, for the war turned world demand away from housing to produ
tion of war materials and foodstuffs.[28] In 1920, all urban land in Unite
States cities of more than 30,000 was valued at scarcely more than 2
billion dollars—less than half the value of farm land—but a great revers
set in during the twenties, and by 1926 the value of all farm land ha
dropped one-third, while urban land values had doubled.[29] The shrinkag
in demand for foodstuffs to peacetime levels and the great decline i
foreign outlets caused a sharp drop in farm prices; whereas the domesti
demand, centering in the large cities, for manufactured products an

[28] Prices of American farm products more than doubled from 1914 to 1918, whi
average house rents in the United States rose only 9 percent. (Hoyt, *op. cit.*, p. 233.)

[29] The value of all farm land dropped from 55 billion dollars to 37 billion, whi
the value of urban land in American cities of more than 30,000 rose from 25 billio
to more than 50 billion. (*Ibid.*, p. 234.)

arious personal services caused a great expansion in urban housing and pectacular increases in urban land values.[30]

Bean found that the influence of farm commodity prices on farm land alues diminishes through the years and that the duration of the influence epends upon the magnitude of price changes.[31] Consequently, during nflationary periods when price increases are large, farm land values increase significantly and tend to increase during subsequent years, but at a lecreasing rate.[32] This same trend was evident during and following Vorld War II. (See Figure 21.) Obviously, in order to avoid a land boom, nonetary price inflation, or rapid, appreciable price advances must be voided.

Farm land values maintained levels close to or above their post-World Var II peak during the fifties in spite of considerable weakening in farm ommodity prices. Several factors account for the unexpected strength in prices of, and demand for, farm real estate, including the following: (1) he desire of farmers to enlarge existing farms in order to utilize mechaniation more fully and thus reduce costs per unit of output; (2) generally avorable crop yields, which have partly offset lower commodity prices; (3) optimism about the desirability of land as an investment, created by . present buoyant general economy and a favorable outlook for the economy of the future; (4) a strengthened expectation that the long-term lemand for farm land will be favorable because of prospects for a coninued high rate of population growth.[33]

The trend of urban land values in the United States has generally been upward because of the rapid settlement and development of the country. Iowever, there is such a great variation in the stage of development of

[30] For a more detailed explanation of the cause and effect relationships operating luring the early twenties to depress farm land values and increase urban values, see bid., pp. 235 ff.

[31] Bean found that the price factor used was roughly equivalent to the current ncome factor in Chambers' formula, and the varying price lags on land values of ubsequent years is substituted for Chambers' factor of anticipated average annual ncreases in income over a period of years. (Bean, op. cit., p. 313; and Chambers, op. it., pp. 379 ff.) Bean treated land values as the dependent factor in a multiple urvilinear correlation problem and treated prices with different lags as the independent variables. He found that of the total variations in land values associated with prices, about 52 percent are associated with prices in the current crop year, 25 percent with prices in the previous crop year, and 6, 5, 3, and 1 percent in the respective previous crop years. (Bean, op. cit., pp. 313 ff.)

[32] Bean found a lift of 130 percent in the farm price level to be associated with a 17 percent rise in land values during the current year, the following year with an additional rise of 27 percent, and during subsequent years with rises that gradually approached zero after the eighth year. In the case of a lift of only 25 percent, the mmediate effect is a rise in land values of about 8 percent, and in the following year about 3 percent, with practically no additional influence in the subsequent years. Bean, op. cit., p. 317.)

[33] U.S. Department of Agriculture, "Agricultural Finance Outlook," Agricultural Research Service, Washington, D.C., ARS 43–24, November, 1955, pp. 7–8, processed.

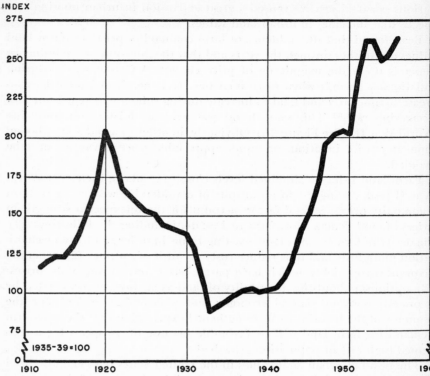

Figure 21. Farm Real Estate Values Per Acre in the United States, 1912–1956. (Source Compiled from data secured from U.S. Department of Agriculture, Agricultural Research Branch, Agricultural Finance Section including selected issues of *Agricultural Finance Review*, especially Volumes 18 and 19, November, 1955, and February, 1957, U.S. Government Printing Office, Washington, D.C.)

different cities that it is impossible to make any accurate statement con cerning national trends for a specific period. Moreover, within each in dividual city there are tremendous variations in land values and trend among different sections and for different types of use.

Land values in the city of Chicago furnish a good example of the di ficulty of making any general statements in regard to urban land valu trends. Chicago has grown from a small hamlet of a dozen log cabins i 1830 to an urban area with millions of inhabitants and thousands o dwellings, skyscrapers, stores, factories, warehouses, and related building The ground value of its 211 square miles has risen from a few thousand t several billion dollars, but this growth has been very uneven.[34] At time there has been feverish boom activity with vertical expansion by means o taller buildings, as well as lateral expansion into the prairie. At othe

[34] Hoyt, *op. cit.*, p. 3.

periods, growth has been so slow as to be imperceptible, or values have declined. Periods of above-normal activity have been much shorter than periods of depression. Absence of adequate data make it impossible to make any sound generalizations concerning the applicability of these real-estate cycles to other cities.[35]

LAND APPRAISAL

Appraisal of land is the process of setting a price or value on it. Factors given major importance in this procedure will vary with the specific use or purpose of the appraisal. For instance, appraisals of land for loans emphasize long-range aspects of income-yielding ability, while appraisals for tax assessment purposes stress present condition instead of long range considerations.

The land appraiser called upon to determine land values for special purposes should first determine "basic value" by the adjusted income capitalization value method in which the comparative approach and income capitalization method are combined. He can then determine values for special purposes or uses by allowing for special factors or influences.

PURPOSES OF APPRAISAL

Land is appraised for many purposes. One author lists 17 purposes, including sale or purchase; reorganizations, receiverships, and mergers; determination of rental value; determination of assets of an estate for inheritance tax purposes or distribution of assets under wills, etc.; determination of values for income tax purposes; determination of rates for public utilities; estimation of cost of an improvement; condemnation purposes; tax assessment; security for real estate loans; and determination of the best utilization of a property.[36]

APPRAISAL METHODS FOR SPECIFIC PURPOSES

An analysis of two or three of these specific purposes is ample to demonstrate the difference in factors and methods used for various appraisal purposes.

Appraisals for Purchase and Sale. An appraisal of land for use in a contemplated purchase or sale is often the deciding factor in the transaction. It is the duty of the appraiser to render the best possible estimate

[35] Studies of land values have been made for a few selected cities, including New York and San Francisco (see E. H. Spengler, *Land Values in New York in Relation to Transit Facilities,* Columbia University Press, 1930; and L. A. Maverick, "Cycles in Real Estate Activity," *Journal of Land and Public Utility Economics,* Vol. IV, No. 4, November, 1928), but there have been no detailed studies of cycles on a comparable basis with Hoyt's study of 100 years of Chicago land values. For a very general account of land speculation in American cities, see A. M. Sakolski, *The Great American Land Bubble,* Harper, 1932.

[36] F. M. Babcock, *The Appraisal of Real Estate,* Macmillan, 1924, pp. 2–11.

of the fair cash market value of the property and to substantiate his esti mate with any supporting facts or available evidence. A man contemplat ing purchase of a farm, for example, is primarily interested in the earning power of the land, based on what he feels will be typical of his manage ment over a period of years.

This emphasis on earnings necessitates a careful inventory of land and buildings, soil characteristics and condition, and other land classification data affecting productivity. The more farm management budget operating data available to purchaser as well as seller, the more sound and satis factory will the value agreed upon be for both parties concerned. Ap praisal for a seller should include all the favorable income and nonincome features.

Appraisals for Tax Assessments.   Appraisals of land made by the tax assessor are ordinarily subject to many influences, some of them political which are not factors in the appraisal of land for purposes such as loans.

The tax assessor is usually elected by popular vote and may or may not have any particular qualifications for appraising real estate. Tax revenue from real estate are determined by the assessed value (taxable value) multiplied by the tax levy or millage rate. This tends to cause assessors to appraise lands on levels high enough to secure the necessary revenue. In many states, legislation has limited the tax rate that can be levied on property, and under these conditions an additional influence is brought to bear upon the assessor to place land values at levels high enough to secure the necessary or desired revenue with the maximum levies allowed

Where there are no legal restrictions on millages, the local assessor may be tempted to lower assessed values, if there is a state property tax levy Through lower assessed values, the local area would benefit by paying less than its proportionate share of the state levy.

The fact that tax assessors are ordinarily elected helps to make the assessor unwilling to take the initiative in revising valuations upward though this might be definitely justified. He follows the line of leas resistance and as a rule would be inclined to lower valuations, if possible or, if not, leave them unchanged. Three major tendencies are usually evident in valuing land for tax assessment: (1) Valuations tend to be come fixed, and undergo little change in later valuations; (2) any actual change is likely to be downward, some properties being reduced con siderably more than others; and (3) there is definite evidence that the poor land is overvalued and that there is an excessive concentration of values about the average.[37] The last characteristic is most easily ex plained by the fact that assessors can measure acres, but not quality. It i impossible for an assessor to distinguish accurately by casual observation among various grades of land, if he has the average amount of training

[37] Murray, *Farm Appraisal*, p. 204.

Appraisals for Loans. Appraisals of farm lands for loan purposes tend to emphasize long-range considerations. The lender who furnishes funds to the borrower in exchange for a mortgage on the farm is primarily concerned with the prospects of loan repayment when the mortgage matures. The major factors that the lender must consider are the quality of security offered and its ability to produce under typical management a net income from which the loan can be repaid.

Because most real-estate mortgages run for a considerable period of time (ranging from 5 to 30 or more years), long-range forecasts of the ability of the security to pay out are essential from the standpoint of the lender. The most difficult conditions to forecast are economic conditions and natural catastrophes. The lender is concerned with the risk from price declines and possible increased production costs, which together reduce the net income from farm operations necessary to retire the loan. Risks from natural hazards must also be considered carefully, risks of floods, drought, insect pests, and hail being particularly important.

In high-risk areas like the Great Plains, it is known that widespread droughts will recur from time to time, but their exact duration and occurence are impossible to predict. In such areas, only those lenders financially able to bear the special risks involved should take the responsibility of furnishing loans for agricultural operations. The fact that interest rates are apt to be somewhat higher in these areas has in the past frequently tended to encourage lenders with limited funds, seeking relatively high returns on investments, to undertake risks that they are not in a position to carry. When making forecasts in regard to agricultural land productivity, such factors as possible soil depletion through erosion or loss of fertility, or through waterlogging because of poor drainage, or formation of alkaline deposits on irrigated land should be given careful consideration.

The borrower is not vitally concerned with the appraisal placed upon his land for loan purposes, provided he can secure the amount of credit he deems advisable and necessary for operating his business, and provided the appraisal is well within the limits of his ability to repay the loan. Both the borrower and the lender are vitally concerned in discovering and using the appraised value that represents the farm's productive value. If the borrower is lent more than he can repay, he may lose his holding or suffer serious embarrassment. At the same time, the lender's funds may be wholly or partly lost, or he may have to go through a tedious and often embarrassing experience to collect what is due him.

Unfortunately, there has been no general understanding and appreciation of this mutual interest of lender and borrower in the case of many loans on farm and city real estate. The results have been numerous farm and city bankruptcies and foreclosures.

A great many recent loan experience studies point out the mistake made in loan practices, many of these stemming from overvaluation (especially overvaluation of the poorer grades of land in certain areas) and from failure to apply the best credit terms, arrangements, or practices. Only the future will reveal whether the lessons learned during the thirties have been learned well enough and widely enough so that repetition of these errors will not occur.

REFERENCES FOR FURTHER READING

Abrams, Charles, *Revolution in Land,* Harper & Brothers, New York, 1939, Chap. VIII.

Babcock, F. M., *The Appraisal of Real Estate,* The Macmillan Company, New York, 1924, Chap. I.

Bonbright, J. C., *The Valuation of Property,* McGraw-Hill Book Company, Inc., New York, 1937, Vol. I, Chaps. VI, VII, XI, and XII.

Dorau, H. B., and Hinman, A. G., *Urban Land Economics,* The Macmillan Company, New York, 1928, Chaps. XXXI, XXXII and XXXIII.

Ely, R. T., and Morehouse, E. W., *Elements of Land Economics,* The Macmillan Company, New York, 1924, Chap. XII.

Hoyt, Homer, *One Hundred Years of Land Values in Chicago,* University of Chicago Press, Chicago, 1933, Chap. VII.

Murray, W. G., *Farm Appraisal,* Iowa State College Press, Ames, Iowa, 1940, Chaps. XVI, XVII, and XVIII.

National Association of Assessing Officers, *Urban Land Appraisal,* Chicago, 1940.

Roberts, Edd, *Land Judging,* University of Oklahoma Press, Norman, 1955.

Sakolski, A. M., *The Great American Land Bubble,* Harper & Brothers, New York, 1932.

Spengler, E. H., *Land Values in New York in Relation to Transit Facilities,* Columbia University Press, New York, 1930.

chapter 12

MORTGAGE CREDIT AND LAND USE

MORTGAGE CREDIT PRACTICES AND LAND UTILIZATION

Influence of Credit Practices on Successful Land Utilization—Credit Arrangements in Marginal Areas

MORTGAGE FINANCING FOR MAJOR LAND USES

Credit Requirements of Agriculture—Credit Requirements of Forestry—Urban Land Credit Requirements—Importance of Credit Policies to Land Conservation—Relation of Credit Policies to Tenancy

IMPROVEMENT OF MORTGAGE CREDIT POLICIES AND PRACTICES

Major Weaknesses of Past Real-Estate Mortgage Financing—Lending on the Basis of Productivity—Flexible Payment Plans—Stabilizing Land Values Through Education—Mortgage Provisions for Better Land Use

Credit has several meanings and shades of meaning in everyday use. We say a man's *credit* is good or that he has *good credit* when he has a good reputation for paying his debts promptly, with the result that others are willing to sell him goods or services, or advance funds to him and wait for their pay until a future date. Another important meaning of the word "credit" refers to the character of the transaction itself. A credit transaction is defined as *a transfer of goods, services, or funds for a promise of a future equivalent.*

An analysis of this definition reveals three important aspects of a credit transaction: (1) Credit contains an element of *time.* (2) The transaction involves *confidence* (*a*) in the *character* and *resources* of the borrower, and (*b*) in the *sufficiency* and *security* of the *goods* he may have pledged to fulfill his promise. (3) A written *evidence of indebtedness* given the lender by the borrower, which constitutes the *instrument of credit*.[1]

Land has numerous advantages over many other forms of security for credit. It is indestructible, immobile, and its services are relatively durable or permanent. Land has one major disadvantage, however, and that is the fixity of investments in land. Once capital is invested in improvements in or on the land, they are ordinarily not easily withdrawn. Consequently land is less marketable than many other forms of investment.

The most common form of credit instrument is the *promissory note* This instrument, or evidence of indebtedness, alone often suffices for short-term credit advances. Middle-term and especially long-term loans on a promissory note are made with the security of a *mortgage*. A mortgage is a conveyance of property, real or personal, for the purpose of securing the payment of a debt.

The literal interpretation of the term *mortgage* is "a death pledge." Originally, if lands were mortgaged, the title and possession of the mortgaged land passed immediately to the mortgagee or lender upon execution of the loan, and he was entitled to all benefits that accrued to it. Ownership of the property could not be recovered by the borrower if he failed to comply with the provisions of the mortgage contract. This concept has been considerably modified in use, but the importance of correct use of mortgage credit cannot be overemphasized, particularly in the case of farms or urban homes, where misuse and abuse of credit have often led to foreclosure and the consequent loss of the farm, home, or business.

MORTGAGE CREDIT PRACTICES AND LAND UTILIZATION

If credit policies are important in determining the level of land values, they are also very important in determining the success of land-use operations. Mortgage credit is important to users of land, primarily because it provides a source of capital with which they can acquire a farm, business, or home before they have accumulated savings enough to finance the purchase themselves.

Adequate mortgage credit, consequently, is an important determinant of the amount of tenancy. Since a relatively large amount of fixed capital is required to finance farm, forest, and many business enterprises, servicing charges (interest and principal payments) comprise a large part of the owner's overhead expense. If satisfactory loan experience is to be achieved and mortgage credit is to fulfill its proper function in the economy by facilitating successful and efficient farm and business operation, the item of overhead debt service charges should be within the earning capacity of the land and its improvements.

[1] Cf. Richard T. Ely and Edward W. Morehouse, *Elements of Land Economics,* Macmillan, 1924, p. 210.

INFLUENCE OF CREDIT PRACTICES ON SUCCESSFUL LAND UTILIZATION

Credit arrangements between borrower and lender have a significant bearing upon successful farm or business operation and upon satisfactory mortgage experience records in any area. Four factors in the credit arrangements are particulary important: (1) amount lent in proportion to the true or productive value of the property, (2) length or term of the loan, (3) method of repayment, and (4) interest rate charged.[2] Many loan experiences have been disastrous because the amount lent was too large in proportion to the long-time productivity value, or the true worth of the land. Such loans were most frequently made during boom periods with high prices.

Studies in some areas of the United States reveal that in the case of agricultural land there is a mortgage debt per acre greater than the long-time productivity value of the land itself, the debt frequently being double the productivity value, or more. In the case of industrial and urban business sites, similar conditions frequently exist.

If real-estate loans are made for too short a term, the annual cost of paying off the loan places an excessive burden on the operator, or the uncertainty of renewing or refinancing the loan upon satisfactory terms at maturity is a source of instability and tends to encourage short-sighted land-use policies. In agriculture, from a third to a half of the farm mortgages outstanding in many areas are for terms of five years or less. In contrast, when many business corporations borrow, they issue bonds that mature as many as 75 or 100 years later and are often refunded at maturity by the issuance of new bonds.

The method of repayment is also very important. If it is a straight-term loan, the operator must pay interest on the entire amount for the full length of the loan, and he is expected to save up a lump sum with which to pay the loan in full at the end of the period. With the lack of control that individual farmers and many small businessmen have over production and prices, and the existence of keen competition, this is a very difficult arrangement, even for the more successful and thrifty operators.

In contrast, if the loan is *amortized* (that is, if an increasing proportion of the equal annual payment goes for principal and a decreasing proportion for interest, so that when the last equal annual installment is paid the loan is paid off in full) it is usually easier for the operator to pay off the principal, and his total interest charge is significantly reduced. In spite of this, studies reveal that from a third to a half of the farm mortgages in effect in many areas are straight-term loans.

The rate of interest is an important item in the total cost of the loan.

[2] See the author's treatment in *Montana Farm Bankruptcies*, Montana Agricultural Experiment Station Bulletin 360, June, 1938, pp. 7 ff.

Money lent at 8 percent compounded annually will double itself in nine years, and the operator who borrows money on a straight-term basis at 8 percent for approximately 12 years pays the full amount of the loan in interest and still owes the full amount of the principal. The fact that the interest rate is fixed or rigid means that a much larger proportion of the farm or business income will be taken to pay interest in low-price or depression periods, when times are hardest, than in prosperous or high-price periods.

CREDIT ARRANGEMENTS IN MARGINAL AREAS

Credit arrangements between borrowers and lenders are extremely significant in marginal areas where natural forces may determine successful operation. For example, in certain parts of the Great Plains where average yearly precipitation is about 15 inches—which is near the critical point for successful crop production without irrigation—there is no natural buffer or cushion of crop dependability, as there is in the more humid areas, to absorb economic stresses and strains resulting from annual variations in precipitation and growing conditions. Without such a natural reserve or margin of crop dependability, a workable substitute or replacement must be established.

The need for such a substitute is further increased by the predominating types of farming. Climatic conditions and present methods of land utilization limit agriculture largely to wheat or range live-stock production—both highly commercialized one-enterprise types of farming. With such a high degree of commercialization and specialization, farmers and ranchers in semiarid regions are peculiarly affected by the highly fluctuating farm prices characteristic of modern economies. With these extreme fluctuations in yield and price, the amount available to meet overhead costs (including principal and interest payments) also varies to a great extent.

Adjustments might be made in semiarid sections to bring about greater flexibility or elasticity in the farmer's overhead to absorb his periodic income variations accompanying weather and price variations, and bring overhead more nearly into line with average or normal weather and price conditions. Debt service charges are one of the most important farm and ranch overhead items; consequently, farm credit practices should be those that will result in bringing the amount lent into line with the long-time productivity value of the farm; and annual loan repayments (including interest payments) should be flexible and adjusted to current production in terms of buying power rather than dollars.[3]

[3] See the author's analysis in *Montana Farm Foreclosures,* Montana Agricultural Experiment Station Bulletin 368, February, 1939.

MORTGAGE FINANCING FOR MAJOR LAND USES

Mortgage credit requirements and practices vary for different types of major land uses. The peculiar characteristics of agriculture, of industry, and of urban properties determine the amounts of credit needed and the lending practices followed.

CREDIT REQUIREMENTS OF AGRICULTURE

Farming is predominantly a small-scale, one-family enterprise with comparatively slow capital turnover, relatively low return on capital, and comparatively little control over production and prices. These characteristics determine the methods of financing best adapted to serve agriculture's credit interests. The fact that American agriculture is made up of millions of small individual interprises makes the credit sources open to large industrial and commercial concerns not readily available to farmers.

A farmer is an individual, and his farm must change ownership and his estate be settled upon his death. This makes debt for the purchase of farms a constantly recurring condition. It has also precluded the extensive application of corporate financing in the form of the long-term bonds used so widely in industrial and business financing; and at the same time, because of the relatively slow turnover of capital in agriculture, farm loans have not been suitable short-term risks for commercial banks where liquidty is of vital importance. This has given rise to the federal land bank system, which provides farmers fairly long-term mortgage credit (for 20 to 34 years).

Since American agriculture is made up of small individual enterprises, there are many debts on small variable units. Handling such debts is expensive for credit institutions, compared with the large credit flotations frequently undertaken or underwritten for industrial and commercial concerns. Consequently, the cost of credit to the farmer, in competition with these large concerns, is greater. Since returns on farm capital are comparatively low and the farmer has little control over production and price, lending on agricultural land, except under the best credit conditions and procedures, is a somewhat more risky venture than lending on many types of industrial or commercial enterprises.

Considerable credit for the purchase of farms is necessary because most purchasers who buy a farm for the purpose of operating it can pay only a portion of the purchase price (often as little as a fourth or less) at the time of sale. In the case of business and commercial enterprises, there is a tendency for individuals to pool their funds, forming a corporate unit so that a greater amount of capital can be collected under one management and used as a means of securing further credit for expanding business operations.

The characteristics of American agriculture mentioned above are merel a few of the more important ones that indicate the need for certain spe cialized financial institutions to furnish necessary credit services. Th Farm Credit Administration furnishes mortgage credit through its 12 farn credit districts, each district consisting of (1) a federal land bank whic makes long-term mortage loans, (2) a production credit corporation making short-term loans, which supervises the production credit asso ciations, (3) a federal intermediate credit bank, which serves as a de pendable source of funds for financing institutions making short-term and intermediate-term loans, and (4) a bank for coöperatives extending credi to farmers' coöperative associations.[4]

CREDIT REQUIREMENTS OF FORESTRY

Need for a comprehensive forest restoration program far more extensive than the relatively small program of the past is generally recognized. Afte nearly half a century of current programs, the annual cut and destruction of forests are approximately twice annual growth. An adequate forest res toration program would require ample credit for prospective investors in forest restoration. In order to provide such credit a proposal has been made to establish a Forest Credit Administration to provide credit for forestry in much the same manner as the Farm Credit Administration pro vides funds for agriculture.[5]

The purpose of the Forest Credit Administration would be to provide investors with direct access to the central money markets through a govern ment-established and government-sponsored credit agency. Specific modi fications from the Farm Credit Administration to meet the needs of forestry would be required for the Forest Credit Administration. For ex ample, loans might be made for as much as 100 years or more, and the beginning of the program of amortization might be delayed until the sixtieth year after the date the loan was made. These and other adapta tions would make possible a much more comprehensive forest restoration program through private efforts than we have had in the past.

URBAN LAND CREDIT REQUIREMENTS

Credit needs of urban landowners are principally of two types: (1) the construction or purchase of homes, and (2) the construction of great office buildings or industrial and business plants. Building and loan associations provide a considerable part of the credit needed for the former; large in-

[4] For a more detailed statement of the organization and operation of the four major types of Farm Credit Administration banks, see the Annual Reports of the Farm Credit Administration, Government Printing Office.

[5] Conrad H. Hammar, "A Proposed Forest Restoration Credit Bill," University of Missouri, Columbia, Missouri, February 15, 1940, mimeographed.

restment and bond firms, through sale of real-estate mortgage bonds, for the latter.

The heavy increase in building costs in recent years, especially since World War II, has intensified the demand of prospective home owners for long-term credit. Building and loan associations are coöperative institutions whose members are either saving members or borrowing members. The former use the associations as a savings bank for the small sums set aside weekly or monthly from salary, wages, or other income. The borrowing members may borrow or get credit, usually through a real-estate mortgage, for purchasing, constructing, or repairing and remodeling a home. They repay their loans systematically with their savings on an installment plan of so much weekly or monthly. The amortization period runs as long as 20 years.

Federal agencies, including the Federal Housing Administration and the Veterans Administration, through insuring or guaranteeing mortgages, provide a considerable amount of the credit needed by veterans to purchase or construct homes and to get established in farming and business. Such credit is provided at relatively low interest rates, and commercial banks, building and loan associations, or other lending agencies make such loans if and when they are underwritten or approved by the federal agencies.

Insurance companies, coöperative credit unions, mortgage and investment bankers, and individuals, along with building and loan associations and federal agencies, provide mortgage credit for the large and growing needs for funds to purchase, construct, and repair homes and businesses in the rapidly expanding American economy.

IMPORTANCE OF CREDIT POLICIES TO LAND CONSERVATION

The operator who assumes a heavy debt obligates himself to make certain definite payments and attempts to plan his operations to meet them. If the debt is greatly in excess of the productive ability of his farm or business, he may be forced to use his land and improvements for the production of products or services that give him the largest immediate cash return, even though this results in depleting the land and the buildings or improvements. Under these conditions, the operator is strictly a credit tenant, and undesirable land-use practices may be the result.

With moderate indebtedness, the economic pressure to deplete the land and use mining practices, which is so common under the worst forms of tenancy, does not exist. Creditors have an equal responsibility with farm and business borrowers to see to it that conservation of land and improvements is facilitated by holding loans closely in line with the productivity of the farm or business.

Tying up management services with the extension of mortgage credit has possibilities, if handled wisely. To improve practices, the mortgage should include specific clauses (1) stating how and for what the land and improvements are to be used, (2) providing some supervision, and (3) stipulating that failure to meet these requirements would make the loan due and payable. Such a course could be successful only if both borrower and lender were in comparatively close agreement about land-use practices and other features incorporated in the contract.

RELATION OF CREDIT POLICIES TO TENANCY

Unwise lending policies resulting in excessive loans not only tend to bring about depletion of land and improvements, but also to increase the number of farms, businesses, and homes operated by tenants. When farmers, businessmen, and home owners lose their property through bankruptcy or foreclosure, it is usually transferred to the creditor, who frequently operates it—at least for a period—through a tenant. Consequently, whereas wise use of credit is distinctly helpful in financing ownership and tending to reduce tenancy, unwise use of credit definitely increases tenancy.

Farm real-estate mortgage debt approximated 10 billion dollars in 1930 and declined steadily to less than half this amount by 1946. Since that time, such debt increased until at the end of the decade the 1930 figure was again approached. The cost-price squeeze that developed after 1951 caused increased borrowing by farmers. Farm real-estate mortgage debt has been incurred increasingly to mechanize and enlarge farming operations and to maintain income by obtaining farms of more adequate size and by reducing costs per unit of production.[6]

About half of the farm real-estate mortgage debt is held by operating banks, individuals, and miscellaneous lenders, about one-fourth by life insurance companies, a sixth by the Federal Land Banks, and the balance by the Farmers Home Administration and miscellaneous agencies.[7]

Urban real-estate mortgage debt is much larger than farm debt. New urban real-estate mortgage debt greatly exceeds new farm real-estate mortgage debt annually.[8]

Less than a third of all farms are mortgaged, and the mortgage indebted-

[6] See U.S. Department of Agriculture, "Agricultural Finance Review," Agricultural Research Service, Washington, D.C., May, 1955, p. 2; and ARS43-30, June, 1956, pp. 1–3, processed.

[7] Ibid.

[8] New nonfarm real-estate mortgages recorded ($20,000 and under) exceeded 27 billion dollars in 1956. New mortgage loans of all savings and loan associations exceeded 10 billions. (See U.S. Department of Commerce, Survey of Current Business, Government Printing Office, Vol. 37, No. 2, February, 1947, p. S-8.) New farm real-estate mortgage recordings average less than two billion dollars annually. Of total mortgage loans in excess of 32 billion dollars held by life insurance companies in 1956, more than 30 billion was made up of nonfarm loans. (Ibid., p. 18.)

ness averages about a fourth of the value of mortgaged farms. Although the average mortgage debt per mortgaged farm in dollars has been increasing in recent years, land values have been increasing faster than debt, so that the ratio of mortgage debt to farm value has declined.[9] Nearly half the urban dwellings occupied by their owners are mortgaged to the extent of more than half their value, and more than two-fifths of those occupied by tenants are mortgaged to more than three-fifths of their value.[10]

Farm and urban mortgage debts generally tend to follow trends in farm and urban land values associated with price and income conditions. However, this is not a hard and fast rule, because a rise in mortgage debt may be associated with depressed conditions in which many owners must borrow to survive temporary low-income periods, or give real-estate security as added protection for non-real-estate loans. Conversely, a drop in outstanding mortgage debt may be associated either with an improvement of the financial position of owners, which enables them to repay debts, or with depressed conditions, which force many heavily indebted owners to give up their properties through foreclosure or bankruptcy or voluntary transfer to creditors in satisfaction of their debts. Changes in outstanding mortgage debt, particularly over short periods, may therefore involve a combination of these various factors.

IMPROVEMENT OF MORTGAGE CREDIT POLICIES AND PRACTICES

Experience has demonstrated that credit, if used intelligently, can be an important factor in successful farm and business operations and can help promote conservation of land resources and reduction of excessive farm and urban tenancy. However, certain fundamental principles should be followed by farm, business, and home owners and those lending on real estate, if loan experience is to be satisfactory to borrowers and lenders, and mortgage credit is to be used effectively.

MAJOR WEAKNESSES OF PAST REAL-ESTATE MORTGAGE FINANCING

The major weaknesses of past real-estate mortgage financing might be summarized as: (1) failure to use scientific methods of land appraisal, so that the poorer lands are usually overvalued; (2) lending a fixed percentage of the appraised value, regardless of the quality of the land; (3)

[9] U.S. Census of Agriculture: 1950, "Farm Mortgage Debt," Government Printing Office, Vol. V, Part VIII, pp. 8–12.

[10] The data showing mortgage status of owner-occupied units are from the 16th Census of the United States (1940), "Housing," Vol. IV, Part I, p. 7. The data for rented properties are based on a sample of 52 cities included in the real property inventory made in 1934. The cities were selected from every state in the Union, and vary in size from a population of 11,000 to more than 1,000,000 (U.S. Department of Commerce, Statistical Abstract of the United States: 1940, Bureau of the Census, Government Printing Office, pp. 908–909.)

using the straight-term method of repayment; (4) making comparatively short-term loans; (5) charging relatively high rates of interest; and (6) requiring fixed annual payments of interest and, in the case of amortized loans, of principal.

These are not by any means all the shortcomings of past lending policies. However, if these six weaknesses were even partially corrected, farm and urban mortgage loan experience would be much more satisfactory, and farm, business, and home operations more successful. The following suggestions indicate how this might be accomplished.

LENDING ON THE BASIS OF LAND PRODUCTIVITY

It cannot be overemphasized that the first and most important step toward more satisfactory credit practices is determination of the productivity value of the land by the income capitalization technique supplemented with the comparative approach. One of the major causes of unsatisfactory loan experience is lending more than the productivity value of the land, so that excessive overhead and a false basis of operations are created.

This tendency is particularly encouraged by the procedure of many lending agencies in lending a given percentage—say 50 percent—of the current value as reflected by current loan appraisals and sales prices. During boom years, when land values are high, the 50 percent lent may be more than the basic value or true productivity value of the land; whereas during depression periods, when land values are extremely low, the 50 percent may be much less than that which could be safely lent, and may be low enough to keep the borrower from carrying out operating plans which, in themselves, may be sound and desirable.

However, after such productivity values have been determined, a concerted effort should be made to lend a smaller proportion of this value on poorer lands or sites than on higher grades. The total income from which debts can be paid is greater in relation to the capital on a good farm or business site than on a poor one.[11] In practice, of course, loans should not equal the full value of the real estate on any grade of land, because there would be no margin of security to provide for contingencies. But if 75 percent were the maximum lent on any grade, average loans on the poorer grades should be proportionately less. These principles apply to urban business and residential sites, as well as to farm lands.

Most lending agencies, including the federal land banks, have in practice lent the same percentage of appraised value on all grades of land in a given area. Loans have apparently been made on the theory that capital

[11] Cf. A. B. Lewis, "Land Classification as an Appraisal and Credit Aid," *The Classification of Land*, Missouri Agricultural Experiment Station Bulletin 421, December 1940, pp. 68–69.

eceives a residual return after labor has been reimbursed at the same rate n all grades of land. Under these conditions, the percentage of loans nat have failed (as indicated by foreclosures and bankruptcies) is natually considerably higher on lower than on higher grades. Changes in rices of products cause greater relative changes in value of land near ne margin than of good land. In some cases, land near the margin delines 100 percent in value.

FLEXIBLE PAYMENT PLANS

Studies have revealed that short-term real-estate mortgage loans (5 to 0 years), loans bearing more than 6 percent interest, and straight-term oans have tended to be the least successful. Farm incomes fluctuate widely rom year to year because of climatic and price conditions, fluctuating coniderably more in some areas of the United States than in others. Under ur economic system business and labor incomes also fluctuate widely, lthough not as much as agricultural income. It is imperative that a speial effort be made to adjust loan repayments to current ability to pay.

Straight-term loans for a relatively short period, at comparatively high ates of interest, are ill-adapted for this purpose. Amortized real-estate oans for a considerably longer period, at lower rates of interest, are now sed much more than in the past, and give the average borrower a much etter chance of paying off the loan. The total interest charges are appreiably less, and the equal annual installments are easier to meet than the ump sum that must be accumulated to pay the characteristic straight-erm loan at maturity.

The equal annual installments of the usual amortized loan, however, re in terms of dollars rather than in terms of purchasing power or actual bility to pay. Such equal annual installments, in terms of dollars, do not onstitute a flexible or elastic overhead. Such flexibility is particularly ssential in the semiarid sections where, as mentioned earlier, the combinaion of climatic conditions and one-enterprise agriculture makes farm perators especially vulnerable to fixed overhead charges. The loan conract might stipulate that the owner would pay back dollars of the same urchasing power as those he borrowed. This would require indexes of hanges in production or yields, changes in the general price level, and hanges in the parity position of commodities the operator produces, so hat the annual loan payments could be adjusted to current ability to pay. ome other alternative proposal might be adopted.

Alternative proposals for flexible payment plans include the following: (1) The amount due each year might be limited to the landlord's rent or hare of the net returns, or a fixed percentage of the returns. A variation f this plan might provide for delivering annually a payment equal to the alue of so many bushels of wheat, pounds of beef, or quantity of some

other product or products. There might be years under this plan when th
amount of the payment would not be sufficient to pay the interest; but
the borrower met the payment provided by the mortgage contract, h
would not be considered delinquent. (2) The amount due each yea
might be limited to the landlord's share of the net returns, or a fixed pe
centage of the returns from a given source, with a minimum paymen
equal to the interest on the unpaid balance of the loan. (3) The amoun
due each year might be determined by adjusting a basic installment a
cording to a predetermined index reflecting changes in the operator
debt-paying ability, including farm prices and production. The basic i
stallment would represent the appraiser's estimate of the average del
service payment the operator could be expected to make over a period o
years.

Under this plan, the total installment called for by the formula eac
year would be due and payable each year; but it would be adjusted to
given relationship to the operator's income annually. Nevertheless,
would be more difficult for operators to make the adjusted payments i
some years than in others. Such installments might or might not be suf
cient to pay interest on the loan. (4) The same as (3) except that th
full amount of the accrued interest would be payable each year. (5) Var
ous other combinations or modifications of the above.[12]

A precedent for variable payment plans has been established in th
Congressional postponement of principal payments on federal land ban
loans. The Farm Credit Act of 1935 stipulated that principal payments o
all land bank loans outstanding on June 3, 1935, need not be met unt
July 11, 1938, if the loans were otherwise in good standing. The feder
land bank policy of encouraging and accepting larger principal paymen
in years when farm income is high, to build up reserves for years whe
farm income is low, is also in line with the principle of flexible repa
ment.[13]

Useful as flexible payment plans are in improving farm mortgage cred
practices, they are of little real value over a long period of time if to
much has been lent on the farm, home, or business property in the b
ginning. In such cases, flexible payment plans would merely postpone th
day of reckoning, since average payments over a period of time would b
in excess of debt-paying ability. However, combined with sound practice
of lending a reasonable proportion of a reasonable value based on pr
ductivity, varying with the grade of land, flexible repayment plans an

[12] Some of these alternatives are listed in F. F. Hill, "Flexible Payment Plans fo
Farm Mortgage Loans," *Journal of Farm Economics*, Vol. XX, No. 1, February, 193
pp. 261–262.
[13] Cf. W. G. Murray, "Prospects for Agricultural Recovery: VI, Farm Mortga;
Policy," Iowa Agricultural Experiment Station Bulletin 315, April, 1934, pp. 143 ff.

ffective in improving real-estate mortgage loan experience and making ossible more successful farm and business operation.

STABILIZING LAND VALUES THROUGH EDUCATION

The preceding practices would do much to stablize land values and real-state investments and improve mortgage loan experience. These two lone are inadequate to do this to the extent desirable, however, because n periods when agriculture and business are relatively prosperous, lend-rs are optimistic in regard to future returns and encourage farmers and usinessmen to expand and take advantage of opportunities for profit. ven with an established, effective policy of lending on the basis of pro- uctivity of the land, serious consequences may result from this optimism.

Too often, what actually happens is that many lenders previously not n the market to lend funds are anxious to lend, and encourage farmers nd businessmen to borrow and expand. Expansion may be so widespread hat the national agricultural and business plant becomes greatly over-xpanded, particularly in certain products, and surpluses, low prices, and arm or business failures may result. In contrast, during periods of rela-ively low prices, lenders are reluctant to make loans, in view of the unsat-sfactory farm and business outlook, and discourage borrowing or expand-ng. Thus, farmers and businessmen are deterred from buying low-priced ivestock, raw materials, land, and improvements; and, since there are few eady buyers, prices are forced down still further.

Prospects for making good investments and achieving satisfactory mort-age loan experience are better when loans are made in the trough of a ow-price phase than in the peak period of prosperity. It is difficult, how-ver, to tell precisely when the trough of a low-price phase has been eached. From a national standpoint, price fluctuations could be smoothed ut considerably and farm or business failures and unsatisfactory loan xperiences reduced by reversing the usual loan policy and making rela-ively more loans during low-price periods and relatively fewer during igh-price periods. The above-discussed stipulations in loan contracts pro- iding for repayment of loans in terms of buying power rather than in erms of dollars would actively encourage this reversal of policy.

This procedure is fair to lenders, because if loans are made when the rice level is down and are paid back when it is up, the lender will actu- lly be repaid more dollars than he lent, but (as in the case of falling price evels) he will receive the same buying power. In effect, this procedure is sed in debt adjustment cases when debts are adjusted downward to make t possible for the debtor to pay out. In sound mortgage credit policies, esponsibility for the soundness of the loan should be the lender's as well s the borrower's.

A strong credit education program will be necessary to bring abou
agreement of thinking along these lines sufficient to have such practice
incorporated in real-estate mortgage contracts. The merits of such stipu
lations, as well as the causes of previous unsatisfactory loan experienc
and the economic and social losses that bankruptcies, foreclosures, an
distress transfers involve, must be thoroughly discussed and understood b
borrowers and lenders in order that they may be fully enlightened in re
gard to the merits of certain credit practices. If this educational work
done effectively, legislation to enable local communities, through con
servancy districts, zoning ordinances, or other methods to control the us
of their land resources in keeping with best land-use principles, woul
probably follow.

Experience and scientific investigation are making available each yea
a greater body of knowledge concerning uses for which land is best fittec
Legislation per se, however, is not the solution of land-use problem
Laws can be repealed or enforcement made difficult or impossible if th
people are not sold and kept sold on the ideas incorporated in the law
Farm and business borrowers and lending agencies must be convinced c
the need of improvements in mortgage credit practices; and if they ar
thoroughly convinced, the necessary legislation and changes will follov

MORTGAGE PROVISIONS FOR BETTER LAND USE

Reference was made earlier to the use of clauses in mortgage contract
to assure improved management and land utilization practices. Both bo
rower and lender must, of course, be in close agreement regarding th
desirability of features incorporated in the contract. Moreover, at leas
a majority of lenders and borrowers should agree on the credit practices t
be followed and on the form of the stipulations in mortgage contracts, o
competition for loans may tend to reduce the effectiveness of this voluntar
means of achieving desirable land-use changes. The need for a widesprea
and thorough mortgage credit educational program, therefore, is eve
more apparent if desired changes are to be effected promptly and with th
least possible waste of human and physical resources.

For the nation as a whole, farm and business borrowers and lendin
agencies are generally in a better position today than in former years t
follow improved credit practices and achieve more satisfactory loan ex
perience. Recent agricultural adjustment programs and related goverr
mental activities, including industrial programs, are increasing annuall
the amount and accuracy of data on the quality and character of the soi
and weather, yield, price, rent, or cost-of-production data upon whicl
more accurate judgments of probable future conditions and long-tim
productivity value can be made.

With the added experience of the past four decades since the great lan

ɔom of the teens, and the lessons learned from the unprecedented rec-
ʳd of foreclosures, bankruptcies, and forced sales of the twenties and
ᴛirties, the fundamental principles of sound credit practices so essential
ɔr improved land use and more satisfactory mortgage loan experience
ᴛould be much more widely applied in the years ahead.

REFERENCES FOR FURTHER READING

ailey, Rex R., "Current Guides as to Safe Debt Loads for Farmers," *Journal of Farm Economics,* Vol. XXXVI, No. 5, December, 1954, pp. 1216–1225.

lack, John D., "Agricultural Credit Policy in the United States," *Journal of Farm Economics,* Vol. XXVII, No. 3, August, 1945, pp. 596–604.

rinegar, George K., "Measuring Risk in Farm Mortgage Financing," *Journal of Farm Economics,* Vol. XXXVII, No. 5, December, 1955, pp. 941–949.

iesslin, Howard G., "A Re-Examination of the Credit Needs of Agriculture," *Journal of Farm Economics,* Vol. XXXVI, No. 5, December, 1954, pp. 1200–1215.

ᴏrau, H. B., and Hinman, A. G., *Urban Land Economics,* The Macmillan Company, New York, 1928, Chap. XXVII.

ly, Richard T., and Morehouse, Edward W., *Elements of Land Economics,* The Macmillan Company, New York, 1924, Chap. XI.

ngberg, R. C., "Reorientation of Policies in Agricultural Financing," *Journal of Farm Economics,* Vol. XXXVII, No. 5, December, 1955, pp. 928–940.

ᴛalcrow, Harold (ed.), *Contemporary Readings in Agricultural Economics,* Prentice Hall, Inc., Englewood Cliffs, N. J., 1955, pp. 331–346.

ᴏhnson, V. Webster, and Barlowe, Raleigh, *Land Problems and Policies,* McGraw-Hill Book Company, Inc., New York, 1954, pp. 347–350.

ᴏyal Commission on Agriculture and Rural Life, *Agricultural Credit,* Lawrence Amon, Regina, Saskatchewan, 1955.

chapter **13**

LAND TAXATION

PRINCIPLES OF LAND TAXATION

Origin of Land Taxes—Bases of Taxing Land—Differentiation of Land Taxes—Importance of Land Taxes—Reasons for Heavy Taxation of Land—Property Classification and the Burden of Land Taxes—Homestead Exemptions—Property Tax Limitation—Net Worth Taxes—Improvement of Property Tax Administration

SPECIAL TYPES OF LAND TAXES

The Single-Tax Proposal—Arguments for the Single Tax—Arguments Against the Single Tax—Land Value Increment Taxes—Special Assessments—Other Special Taxes on Land

SHIFTING AND INCIDENCE OF LAND TAXES

Land Taxes That Cannot Be Shifted—Land Taxes That Are Shiftable—Shifting and Incidence Under Special Conditions—Capitalization of Tax Reductions into Land Values

Taxes are enforced contributions collected from individuals by governments for a public purpose and the common good with no return to the individual in the form of special benefits. Taxes levied on property are charges that must be met if owners are to maintain title to their property. Governments may take property, and frequently do, for failure to pay taxes levied. Widespread farm and urban tax delinquency and reversion of farm and city lands to public ownership reflect the serious problems associated with taxing land.

The tax system is an important force in determining the use and ownership of land. Too frequently tax systems are devised on the theory that

venue should be obtained by "picking the goose where it squawks the
ast," without due regard to the economic consequences of such action.
he amount and kind of taxes levied to obtain funds to operate govern-
ent have a significant bearing upon distribution of wealth and opera-
on of the economy as a whole. Taxes can be used as devices for encour-
ging conservation and proper use of natural resources, or they can be
sed in such a way that the rate of exploitation is increased and extreme
aste of natural resources and soil impoverishment result.

PRINCIPLES OF LAND TAXATION

Many natural resources, such as scenic and climatic advantages or access
) natural transportation systems, are not easily classified. Some resources,
ke forest and agricultural soil fertility, are destructible, but reproduc-
ble; others, like minerals, are destructible and not reproducible; and
till others—urban land sites, for instance—are neither destructible nor
eproducible. This complicates the problem of land taxation if it is to
ontribute effectively toward a program that makes possible the best use
f land resources.

Conservation is important in utilizing natural resources, such as min-
rals, which are destructible and not reproducible, or forests, which are
estructible but also reproducible to some extent. It is generally held
hat certain taxes, such as ad valorem levies (taxes figured in terms of so
nany cents on the dollar, or in proportion to the value of the object) tend
o increase the exploitation rate because owners of mineral and forest
ands try to sell out from under the tax. But it is considered that sever-
nce or yield taxes tend to encourage conservation by decreasing the
ate of exploitation. Taxation, however, should not be regarded as the
nly means of conservation. The police power, eminent domain, public
wnership, and other available methods are used by governments to
ncourage conservation and reduce wasteful exploitation.

ORIGIN OF LAND TAXES

The land tax is probably the oldest form of taxation. There were land
axes in China as early as 2000 B.C., and a tax cadaster (a record of all the
acts necessary for tax assessment, such as area, type of soil, kind of crop,
legree of fertility, etc.) is known to have existed in early Egypt.[1] Primi-
ive forms of the land tax were used throughout the Middle Ages.

The land tax was introduced into England in 1692, spread to most of
Continental Europe, to some countries in the Far East, and to Australia.
After the formation of the republic, the general property tax in the
United States became the major source of state and local governmental

[1] See Karl Brauer, "Land Taxation," *Encyclopaedia of the Social Sciences*, Vol. IX,
. 70.

revenue, but real estate comprised most of the property tax base, an the general property tax became, in effect, largely a tax on land and im provements.

In recent years the land tax has experienced a considerable reviv: (particularly in the new Central and Eastern European states estal lished after World War I). In this process the tax has undergon major modifications in some nations and minor changes in others. A present, land taxes are of major importance (particularly in local go ernmental revenues) in many nations, but provide an insignificant pai of the revenue in others. In the United States, taxes on land and improve ments constitute the major source of local governmental revenue. Th Federal government and some of the states make no direct tax levies o land or improvements.

BASES OF TAXING LAND

The earliest land tax was assessed on the basis of area, but modern taxe are levied on annual revenue or income from land, or on the capital valu of land. Where revenue is used as a basis of assessment, the cadaster assist in estimating average yield for a given parcel of land. For accurate esti mates, the land must be classified according to type of use, degree of pro ductivity, and related characteristics. As a rule, the country is divided into assessment districts, and careful estimates are made of the productiv ity of typical parcels of land in each district. These estimates are then used as the basis of estimating the probable yield of similar parcels i the same district.

In order to determine net yield, production costs are often deducted from gross yield. Since these deductions are usually of a simple or arbitrar nature, the remainder is not the average net yield, but something betwee the gross and the net yield. In countries where tenant farming predomi nates, the determination of yield is simplified by using farm rentals a cadaster values. The land tax, in the form of a tax on revenue, leave land yielding no current returns untaxed, or taxes returns incompletel in periods of rapid appreciation of real-estate values. Because of thi weakness, some nations have adopted increment taxes.[2]

Where assessment is based on the value of land, the usual practice i to capitalize the value of the average annual yield, or assess the tax upor the so-called current or market value. With adequate base periods foi determining average yields to be capitalized, the capitalized productiv

[2] *Ibid.*, p. 71. Kendrick points out certain inequalities resulting from using capita values as a basis of assessment, and suggests that assessment on the basis of the nei rental of the land is the only solution that even borders on completeness, using ne rental to mean the current net annual market rental. If the property is not leased this becomes estimated net rental. (M. Slade Kendrick, *Taxation Issues*, Harper, 1933 p. 72.)

y value is a more accurate index of taxable capacity than current market
r sales value. As we learned in the preceding chapter, if a sufficiently
ong period of market values is taken as a guide, it may be an adequate
ndex of taxable capacity. Usually, however, a combination of the two
methods is most satisfactory for determining land values for tax purposes.

At the present time, land taxes in many European nations are levied
n income derived from land, so that they might be referred to as "land
ncome taxes," while in some other nations (including the United States)
and taxes take the form of levies on the value of the land. For example,
he income method of assessment is used in England, and the taxes (which
re levied on income or rental value instead of capitalized value) are ex-
ressed as the number of shillings in the pound of land rent or income—
hat is, 15 shillings in the pound or a tax of 75 percent of the land rental.
n the United States the tax is expressed as a millage levy assessed against
apital value, or a given percentage of the capital value, referred to as the
taxable value." [3] In spite of the limitations of sales value as the basis for
etermining taxable capacity, most state statutes in the United States
pecify that taxable value is the price for which a property can be sold,
sing the willing buyer-willing seller formula, or what is commonly re-
erred to as "market" or "exchange" value.

DIFFERENTIATION OF LAND TAXES

In earlier times land taxes were strictly proportional—that is, they ap-
lied to all real property and were levied without regard to the taxpayer's
ersonal circumstances. As such, they were strictly taxes in rem (levied in
ccordance with objective characteristics of the tax base, without regard
o personal characteristics of the taxpayer). In more recent years, how-
ver, land taxes have been modified so that they assume more of the
haracteristics of a personal tax.

Some of the methods used to personalize land taxes include differen-
iation according to the type of crop, location, kind of farming, or size
f unit. Tax rates in Japan are differentiated according to the type of crop,
ice fields and truck farms enjoying a lower tax rate than farms devoted

---

[3] The usual tax rate in the United States is from 2 to 2½ percent of the assessment
ased on capital value. In England, the income method of assessment results in much
igher rates, ranging from 40 to 125 percent of assessed value. At times tax rates in
ngland have reached 25 shillings in the pound, or a rate of 125 percent, meaning
hat the government takes in taxes more than the occupier pays the landlord. This
ondition is possible because the rental agreed upon between tenant and landlord takes
nto account the amount of the tax which the tenant has to pay, so that the combined
ayment to the government and the landlord will represent approximately the full
ease value of the land to the tenant. (Rosina K. Mohaupt and Alger W. Lenz, *The
English System for the Taxation of Real Property on an Income Basis*, Social Science
Research Council, Wayne University Report No. 2, Detroit, Bureau of Governmental
Research Report 138, May, 1935, p. 26.)

to other crops. In Australia and New Zealand, differentiation is based on the size of the estate, character of tenure, and residence of owner, absentee owners being taxed at a higher rate than owner-operators.

The major purpose of land tax differentiation may be to influence land use rather than to increase revenue. For example, putting a higher tax on land used for crops when it is more suitable for grazing tends to force it into grass production. In countries like Australia, where agriculture is extensive in character, differential rates have been useful in discouraging the growth of large estates, tenant farming, and absentee landlordism. Differential rates and exemptions may also be used to foster certain types of cultivation and promote land improvements, such as reforestation, reclamation, or forest clearing.

IMPORTANCE OF LAND TAXES

Land is taxed through general imposts levied directly on real estate (particularly the general property tax), and the income tax that reaches incomes obtained from real estate. The increasing use of income taxation has lessened the fiscal significance of land taxes in many of the older European nations and as revenue sources in some states of the United States. In the United States the use of the general property tax (the most important means of land taxation) is reserved to local and state governments. Some states have adopted general sales taxes, and overall tax limitation has been used in order to relieve real estate of part of the tax burden.

Prior to World War II the property tax accounted for more than half of all federal, state, and local tax revenues in the United States; before World War I it accounted for nearly three-fifths. Thus, while the general property tax is of less importance than formerly, it still yields more revenue than any other tax. In contrast, general property taxes in some nations provide only a minor fraction of total tax revenue.[4] The 48 states secure about a fifth of their tax revenue from this source. Local governments (counties, cities and towns, townships, and school districts) rely almost entirely on the general property tax, which accounts for some four-fifths of their total tax revenue.

Theoretically, the general property tax applies equally to real estate, tangible personal property, and intangible personal property, but in practice real estate comprises the bulk of the general property tax base in the United States and Canada. Considerable personal property escapes

---

[4] For example, property taxes in Belgium account for three-tenths of 1 percent of the total tax revenue; in Switzerland, 1½ percent; and in Sweden, 3 percent. In many of the major European nations, the percentage ranges from a tenth to a fifth. Only in Canada is the general property tax approximately as important as it is in the United States. (Adapted from Paul Studenski, "Modern Fiscal Systems," *Annals of the American Academy of Political and Social Science*, Vol. 183, January, 1936, p. 29.)

from taxation, and much of the intangible property is exempted because of the practical impossibility of collecting taxes on so elusive a source.[5]

REASONS FOR HEAVY TAXATION OF LAND

The reliance upon the general property tax, particularly for the support of local governments, and the major importance of land and improvements in the property tax base, have placed a heavy tax burden on real estate in the United States. It is a generally accepted principle that landowners, like other individuals, should be taxed according to ability to pay.

In more primitive societies, where practically all the wealth and sources of income were tangible property (largely real estate) the best single measure of this ability was the amount of property owned. The general property tax was well adapted to such conditions and was widely used. This heavy emphasis has continued through the years in spite of the fact that the nature of income-producing wealth has changed greatly with modern industrialization. Only about a fourth of the national income in the United States is now derived from ownership of real estate.[6]

Many believe that incomes from landed property should pay more taxes than service incomes because landowners receive more benefits from government; and that tangible property is the main beneficiary of government since such property (particularly land and improvements) requires and gains more from protection against fire and theft, foreign invasion, and similar governmental services, than do other forms of property. Furthermore, they argue that governmental services like education, highway construction and maintenance, the development and conservation of natural resources, and the establishment of health and recreational services increase the value of land by making the community more attractive. But the question might well be asked whether these services do not directly benefit persons—professional and wage groups as well as landowners—rather than property as such. Also the risk factor in owning land should not be overlooked. Land values frequently shrink from purchased levels because of changes in population distribution and markets, crop failures, or declining product prices.

[5] Cf. *ibid.*, p. 31. For example, only 13 percent of the Montana property tax base is composed of personal property (including goods, wares, merchandise, and livestock), and only 1.2 percent of intangibles. Montana has a classified property tax law designed, among other reasons, for more complete assessment of all types of property, including intangibles. (R. R. Renne and H. H. Lord, *Assessment of Montana Farm Lands*, Montana Agricultural Experiment Station Bulletin 348, pp. 44 ff.)

[6] For data showing sources of the national income, see H. G. Moulton, *Income and Economic Progress*, The Brookings Institution, 1935; R. R. Doane, *The Measurement of American Wealth*, Harper, 1933; Simon Kuznets (ed.), *Income and Wealth of the United States*, Bowes and Bowes, Cambridge, England, 1952; Kuznets, *Economic Change*, Norton, 1953; and U.S. Department of Commerce, *Survey of Current Business*, Annual Supplements on *National Income*, Government Printing Office, Washington, D.C.

Another reason for heavy taxation of landed property is the belief tha property incomes are more dependable than service incomes, because the are usually more secure and longer lived, and because property constitute a reserve that relieves owners of the necessity of saving. There is also th element of individual effort involved in service incomes compared wit property incomes, which has frequently led to reference to the former a "earned" income and to the latter as "unearned."

PROPERTY CLASSIFICATION AND THE BURDEN OF LAND TAXES

The preceding reasons explain the heavy taxation of landed propert in the United States. In the analysis of agricultural and urban land tax ation later in this chapter, it will be noted that there has been sever tax delinquency and reversion of much private land to public ownershi through tax-deed foreclosures. Many of these undesirable results ar attributable to methods of administering the general property tax. Conse quently, in order to relieve the burden on farm and city real estate, im portant modifications in the property tax must be made.

There has been a movement toward classification and special treatmen of different kinds of property, one purpose of which is to adjust taxe more in accordance with abilities to pay.[7] In general, classification ha taken the form of varying ratios of assessment to true or assessed value for different classes of property. One of the more important reasons fo property classification, in addition to the general purpose of adjustin taxes more in keeping with the respective abilities to pay of the differen kinds of property, is to bring about a more complete assessment of in tangible property like money and credits.

Special classification of intangibles has resulted in a substantial increas in the amount of such property placed upon the assessment roll. However nowhere has the increase been sufficient to constitute a good assessment. In Montana, for example, the very low rate of 7 percent of full and tru value on moneys and credits has made this class of property comprise a smaller proportion of the taxable valuation of all property than before passage of the classification law.[9] Too often, when the classification law went into operation assessors raised assessed value to the point where the new ratio of assessment to full value would result in the same taxable value as before the classification law was enacted.

Although the attempt to personalize the general property tax througl

---

[7] About a third of the states now have a low flat-rate tax on money and credits and Kentucky, Montana, Minnesota, Ohio, and Virginia have fairly complete systems o classification. (H. M. Groves, *Financing Government*, Holt, 1939, p. 99.)

[8] Cf. S. E. Leland, *The Classified Property Tax in the United States*, Houghton Mifflin, 1928, p. 403.

[9] Renne and Lord, *op. cit.*, p. 10.

me system of classification is a step in the right direction, property
assification has in most instances been only partially effective in bring-
g about more equitable assessment of taxes on lands and improvements.
roperty classification is criticized as leading to the use of political pres-
re and abuse; but in spite of this objection most classifications are an
nprovement over assessment of property as an undifferentiated mass.
roperty classification, however, is no substitute for scientific assessment
d better administration, and many improvements in property assess-
ent techniques will be necessary to remove the glaring inequalities that
ow exist within classes of property.

HOMESTEAD EXEMPTIONS

There has been a widespread tendency in the United States to exempt
omesteads from taxation. During the depression of the thirties, when tax-
eed and mortgage foreclosures on farm and urban lands were numerous,
is movement grew. About a fourth of the states have statutes or consti-
tional provisions for homestead exemptions.[10] The state statutes vary
idely in their provisions. The definition of "homestead" varies from
ate to state but, in general, includes any dwelling occupied by the owner
xclusively as a residence, and the site upon which this dwelling is located.
he amount of surrounding land included varies greatly.

The fiscal effects of homestead exemption depend upon a number of
onditions, including the amount of exemption and the units of govern-
ent affected, the degree of home ownership, the ratio of residential
roperty to total property, the average value of the homestead, the extent
) which reliance is placed upon the general property tax as a source
f revenue, and related conditions. Since the general property tax is the
ainstay of local governments, any policy of widespread homestead ex-
mptions will obviously have serious fiscal affects upon local units where
rms and city homes predominate. In many of these local units, tax rev-
nues may be cut by as much as nine-tenths, necessitating serious read-
ustments in the tax base.

At the same time, however, where the state levies property taxes, the
are of local units in county and state property taxes will be definitely
educed. The decrease of the total tax base, because of homestead exemp-
on, will necessitate increase in property tax rates upon the remaining
ase, curtailment of expenditures, or substitution of new revenue sources
) replace that which was lost through homestead exemption.

Homestead exemption is defended largely on the grounds that home
wnership is a community asset and should be encouraged. Excessive ten-
ncy may develop, particularly in certain rural areas and in the slum

[10] Groves, *op. cit.,* p. 101.

sections of large cities. Levying a relatively fixed amount of taxes o homes, regardless of current employment and income conditions, ten to cause serious distress and a larger amount of absentee ownership an tenancy. The homestead exemption program has had a strong politic. appeal in the United States, largely on the grounds that ownership o homes by individual families is both desirable and necessary in a demo racy.[11]

The chief arguments against homestead exemption center around th fact that the benefits attained are inversely proportional to the need that is, one who owns no home gets nothing. In other words, the exem tion program offers nothing to the tenant. As a matter of fact, homestea exemption is likely to increase his burden in so far as increased proper taxes are passed on to him by his landlord. If property tax increases resu from homestead exemption because of the necessity of replacing lost re enue (rented homes would not be tax exempt), the effect of substitu taxes like the sales tax might increase the burden of tenants and also o the poor in general (including the small homeowner).[12]

The further argument has been advanced that it is questionabl whether recipients of low and uncertain incomes should be encouraged t acquire residential property; that homestead exemption measures are e: tremely difficult to administer because there may be no effective imped ment to nominal transfers by which individuals without a bona fid homestead will obtain tax exemption for large landowners; and, finally that the exemption privilege will be capitalized by present owners so tha future owners will pay more for residential property, thus losing whateve benefit an exemption program might offer.

Some governmental units have used property tax exemptions as a mean of encouraging certain types of economic activity. For instance, certai new manufacturing enterprises, residences, farm improvements, hotel and similar economic enterprises have been granted tax exemption for term of years. If encouraging certain kinds of economic activities at th expense of others is assumed to be justifiable, direct bounties would seen preferable to tax exemptions, since the bounty would keep the cost clearl before the public and is a more flexible tool for the purpose than ta: exemption. The political advantages and apparent simplicity of tax ex emptions, however, are evident.[13]

[11] Groves points out that sentiments attached to the word "home" are deep-seate and that most politicians can arouse a following with a slogan proposing to defen the home against "the vicious tax monster." (*Ibid.*, pp. 104–105.)

[12] Only by constructive governmental economies could these undesirable results b prevented; and it is noteworthy that exemption and reorganization have rarely if eve occurred together. (Cf. *ibid.*, p. 105.)

[13] Carl Shoup, "Tax Examption," *Encyclopaedia of the Social Sciences,* Vol. XIV p. 530.

PROPERTY TAX LIMITATION

Property tax limitation has also been used in the attempt to control the tax burdens on farm and urban real estate. Some form of maximum rate has prevailed in most of the states for a long time; but there is increasing emphasis upon this means of controlling the land tax burden.

Limitations upon taxes levied on property are of two main types: (1) maximum rates upon levies for certain specific purposes or by certain levels of government, and (2) overall limits that establish a maximum aggregate property tax rate. The tax limit provisions in the different states vary widely.[14]

In addition to tax limitation provisions, many state governments control local expenditures and debts, usually through a budget system. In some states, the combination of constitutional limitations on tax levies, statutory limitations, and a strong budget system effectively control the amount of taxes levied on property (particularly land and improvements). Most tax limitation provisions permit levies in excess of specified limits by referendum (popular vote) and exempt levies to finance debt payments (principal and interest). These provisions, especially the latter, may reduce the effectiveness of property tax limits.[15]

Recent increased use of property tax limitation is a warning that the property tax system is not all it should be and is a symptom of decadence. In spite of the arguments for and against tax limitation—and there are many—the imposition of all-inclusive, rigid, negative devices from above lacks the constructive quality that should characterize revenue systems.

NET WORTH TAXES

Another proposal offered to adjust land taxes more in proportion to productivity of the resource is to define taxable property not as wealth, but as the rights therein, with deductions of debts from assets. In other words, a landowner's taxable property would be his net worth. Advantages suggested for this method are that everything would be reached once, and only once. There would be no double or multiple taxation and, assuming adequate administration, nothing would escape.

[14] All but about 10 states have some sort of tax limit, although in a large number of these, the limits are too high, either to protect property, or, except in a few instances, to embarrass local finances. About 20 states have constitutional tax limit provisions, 5 of which are of the overall type and were adopted or amended during the depression thirties. In some states, maximum rates are established only for different levels of government or taxing units, while in others, maximum rates for specific levies (as well as a maximum aggregate property tax rate) are established. (Groves, *op. cit.*, p. 461.)

[15] Groves points out that where levies to service all debts are exempted from the limit, a municipality can circumvent the limitation by borrowing freely, even for operating expenses. It can levy such property taxes as it chooses, provided it uses them to pay last year's bills. (*Ibid.*, pp. 464–465.)

Under the present system, a farmer who owns a farm valued at $15,000 with a $7000 mortgage against it is usually assessed on the $15,000 basi though his equity is only $8000. The man who holds the mortgage or the farm is often assessed on the value of the mortgage (which is a form of intangible property usually classified under the heading "money and credits") and is also supposed to pay income taxes on interest derived from such mortgages. Under the net worth basis, the farmer would be assessed on $8000 only, rather than on the $15,000.

Several European countries have adopted the net worth tax as a sup plementary tax, rather than a principal tax, with rates that are usually progressive.[16]

The net worth tax is a personal tax and bears a closer relationship to the anticipated (if not always the actual) annual income from the property of each taxpayer than does the general property tax as now administered in the United States. The net worth tax does not conform to the total ability of the landowner, because total taxpaying ability rests on aggre gate income from all sources, and not only from property; thus, while it conforms to ability more adequately than the general property tax, it is still imperfect. It has the defect of all taxes levied upon capital value— that is, anticipated income, which is the basis for the capital value, may prove considerably different from actual annual income.[17]

IMPROVEMENT OF PROPERTY TAX ADMINISTRATION

It is recognized that the general property tax in its present form and administration has many weaknesses, among which are the following: (1) double taxation (where two or more units of government tax the same source); (2) inequalities in tax burdens among areas and among citizens, owing largely to (a) numerous small, unequal taxing units and (b) exces sive reliance on general property taxes; and (3) expensive duplication of tax administration caused by extreme decentralization of authority.

Improvement of the present revenue system requires (1) broadening the tax base, (2) classifying and assessing property more scientifically, and (3) providing for more effective central supervision and coördinated tax administration. Lack of scientific assessment, combined with too much re liance upon the general property tax, has been the paramount cause of severe burdens laid in many areas on landed property.

The relatively rigid property tax levies must be applied with discretion to certain types of land and must be carefully adapted to the peculiarities

[16] For example, the rate in Denmark is progressive from .65 to 1.6 percent of net value; in Iceland, from 0.1 to 0.7 percent; and in Finland, from 0.015 to 0.8 percent (Jens P. Jensen, *Government Finance*, Crowell, 1937, p. 246.)
[17] *Ibid.*

f each major type of landed property. For example, the classification, ssessment, and administration of the property tax in its usual forms appear to bring undesirable results not only to forest and mineral lands, but lso to agricultural land, where in principle they seem more applicable. hanges that should be effected for forest and mineral land involve alterations in the timing and form of levies (as, for example, from an annual iillage levy on capital value to severance or yield taxes). But the elimination of serious inequalities affecting agricultural land will necessitate iore scientific classification and more centralized or integrated assessient. For urban land, standards for scientific classification and assessment eed to be established.

SPECIAL TYPES OF LAND TAXES

The concept of "unearned" land rent has led to proposals for abolishig private ownership of land. The many instances of landowners who ave profited immensely from community growth (especially the growth f urban communities) and of fortunes acquired overnight through the iscovery of oil or valuable minerals, have encouraged the belief that all and rent essentially represents "unearned increment." Many persons beieve that private property should be recognized in the products of land esulting from man's work or labor, but not in the land itself, since land ; not the product of labor.

THE SINGLE-TAX PROPOSAL

Henry George proposed a tax on economic rent or land values as a neans of providing government revenue. According to this theory, priate property in land would be allowed, but the state would appropriate he economic rent. George's proposal became known as the *single tax*, beause it was assumed that the revenue yielded by the tax appropriating and rent would be sufficient to meet the fiscal requirements of government.

The most orthodox proponents of the single tax believe that the ax rate should equal the full economic rent. Others believe that, along vith heavy taxes on land values, certain other taxes like income and inieritance taxes should be used. Henry George developed his case for the ingle tax from observations of what he considered a mistaken land >olicy in the new and rapidly expanding area of California. George saw hat the free and the rich natural resources enjoyed by a sparse popula-:ion resulted in high wages and high interest which later, through profigate grants to railroads, active private land speculation, and increasing mmigration, narrowed opportunities for labor and capital and finally, with the depression of the seventies, brought the unemployment an bankruptcy familiar in old communities.[18]

He concluded that this sequence of events was the logical culmination of a land policy that permitted private individuals to appropriate eco nomic rent. Such private appropriation caused speculators to hold land out of use and brought about high capitalized land values and accompany ing evils that created poverty, unemployment, and bankruptcy. Henr George found confirmation of his ideas in such basic views of classica economics as the Ricardian theory of rent and the concept of natura value as contrasted with market value.

ARGUMENTS FOR THE SINGLE TAX

Arguments advanced for the single-tax proposal include the following

1. If the tax were levied with such accuracy that only economic ren were appropriated, the tax would not operate to discourage individua initiative or to reduce the total income available to society. At the sam time, it would provide a considerable amount of revenue, which could b used for welfare. In Henry George's own words, "A tax on economic ren would not fall on all land; it would fall only on valuable land, and tha in proportion to its value. Thus it would not have to be paid upon th poorest land in use (which always determines rent), and so would no become a condition of use, or restrict the amount of land that could b profitably used. And so the landowners on whom it fell could not shif it onto the users of the land." [19]

2. The investment necessary to become an owner of a farm or an urba site would be greatly reduced, because the land would be less expensive Government would have the equivalent of a 100 percent mortgage on al land, and the purchase price would not be determined by capitalizec actual or anticipated economic rent, but by competition of users for lan as situs for labor and capital, from which would be obtained all the eco nomic rewards of production except economic rent.

3. Speculation in land values would be almost completely eliminated and certainly reduced. With the knowledge that the government woul take away all the net income or economic rent, there would be no reaso to speculate in future land value increment.

4. Reduction of speculation would tend to stabilize the price of land.

5. Confiscating the economic rent of land would remove possibilitie of great fortunes or speculative gains and therefore reduce inequalitie and mitigate poverty.

[18] Broadus Mitchell, "The Single Tax," *Encyclopaedia of the Social Sciences*, Vo XIV, p. 65; and Henry George, "Causes of Business Depression," Robert Schalkenbac Foundation, New York City, Reprinted November, 1936; and *Progress and Poverty* 50th anniversary ed., Robert Schalkenback Foundation, New York, 1929, Book V.

[19] Henry George, "Not a Tax on Land—or Labor—or Capital," Land and Labo Library, Vol. I, No. 5, Henry George Tract Society, Endsell, N.Y.

6. The single tax would encourage land ownership by actual operators and increase their incentive to improve land, because no taxes would be levied on improvements. The actual operators would be the only ones interested in operating the land, because they would want land as a means of earning returns from their labor and capital—not for speculative gain, which is so frequently the aim of the absentee landlord.

7. The single tax would increase the incentive for land operators to work their land efficiently. Special efficiency would still be entitled to its reward under the single-tax program, because, if administered correctly, the tax would take the economic rent but none of the special rewards of management. As a matter of fact, some argue that the single tax might force some operators to raise efficiency at least to the average in order to pay the tax.

8. The single tax would make it more expensive to hold land out of use. "A tax on land values, instead of enabling the owner to charge that much more for his land, gives him no power to charge an additional penny. On the contrary, by making it more costly to hold land title, it tends to increase the amount of land for which owners must strive to secure tenants or purchasers." [20]

ARGUMENTS AGAINST THE SINGLE TAX

Perhaps the most valid criticism of the single tax is the fact that this levy is limited to the economic rent of land, though much income from many other sources is frequently unearned and should be classed in the same category. For instance, a man's parentage, fortunate qualities, and social environment may more truly account for his success than do his industry and thrift; and in the higher brackets of income, especially, it would seem that there must be a considerable portion of unearned increment to furnish a sound argument for graduated net income taxes.

A second and very important argument against the single tax is the problem of its practical application in an economy where unearned wealth, with the passage of time, has become diffused by exchange inheritance, and similar devices. If, at the time the single-tax proposal were put into operation, the area had not yet been settled and developed, the economic injuries resulting from the use of the tax would not be great. However, in an older country where land has changed hands many times and present owners have bought the land at a price that represented the capitalized actual and anticipated net income, the single-tax levy would work a severe injustice.[21]

[20] *Ibid.*
[21] For example, a piece of land may have been homesteaded, sold after 25 years for $60 per acre, and a decade later sold to another individual for $100 per acre. If the single tax were put into operation, the present owner, who paid $100 an acre for the land, would find that the value of his property would shrink overnight from $100 to perhaps $5 an acre or less. The other two individuals, who secured most of the

A third argument against the single tax is the difficulty of measuring economic rent accurately. In agricultural land many improvements added by the operator's incorporation of labor and capital become part of the land itself. Commons has attempted to isolate "pure site value" or "bare land value" from land value elements like improvements, original fertility, and improved or maintained fertility, each of which, he argues, has a distinctive value.[22] From a theoretical point of view, this objective is sound, but difficult to effect in actual practice. In other words, it is questionable whether the single tax could be levied with such precision that only the economic rent would be appropriated. In any case, if the government did not buy the improvements, it would be a joint owner with the operator and would have the problem of distinguishing the return on improvements from the return on "pure site" or "bare land" value.

Fourth, the single tax flagrantly disregards the principle of ability to pay and substitutes for it another principle. The proportion of land values to total wealth varies greatly in different segments of a modern economy. For example, as much as four-fifths of the real property in a typical rural community is made up of land values, while more than half the modern property values in moderate-sized urban centers are in improvements. Under these conditions, an exemption of improvements from taxation such as that implied by the single-tax proposal would reduce the farm tax base much less than the urban tax base. Under modern financial conditions it is also probable that within certain ranges of income there is an inverse correlation between the size of a fortune and the proportion held in real estate.[23]

Another argument against the single tax is that if the government confiscates "unearned increment" by appropriating economic rent it should reimburse the landowner for "unearned decrement." Finally, it has been argued that the single tax alone would not raise enough revenue to permit the abolition of all other forms of government revenue. But this is not an important criticism, for many proponents have realized in recent years that, with expansion of governmental services, changes in forms of property and economic activity, and slowing up of "community develop-

unearned increment or appreciation in value through "community development," would not be reached by the operation of the single tax. In other words, as Groves puts it, the single tax is an attempt to "pick up spilt milk" (Groves, op. cit., p. 405), and it would seem injurious to put into operation any program which would expropriate the investments of present owners who in good faith had purchased land when economic rent was privately appropriable.

[22] John R. Commons, "A Progressive Tax on Bare Land Values," Political Science Quarterly, Vol. XXXVII, No. 1, March, 1922, pp. 41–68.

[23] A. A. Berle, Jr., and G. C. Means, The Modern Corporation and Private Property, Macmillan, 1933; and A. A. Berle, Jr., and V. J. Pederson, Liquid Claims and National Wealth, Macmillan, 1934; C. F. Ware and G. C. Means, The Modern Economy in Action, Harcourt, Brace, 1936; and other studies of the nature, forms, ownership, and control of wealth in the United States.

nent and expansion," supplementary sources of revenue would undoubt-dly be necessary. Income taxes and inheritance taxes would be particularly acceptable to the less orthodox single-taxers.

If the single tax could be administered in practice as it has been worked out in theory, it would not abolish the institution of private property in land, though it would, of course, seriously modify the rights of the private owner. The social theory of property, however, has always recognized the tax power as a governmental right in controlling land utilization in the public interest; and the single tax is nothing more than a somewhat extreme application of this power. In contrast with the theory of individualism that underlies the single tax, the theory of social control is being used increasingly to support the cause of taxation generally.

The property tax system has in the past served as a heavy tax on landed property in the United States, although in most cases it has not confiscated the entire economic rent. This system has resulted in numerous tax delinquencies and much reversion of private land to public ownership. The single tax, properly administered, would actually result in a lighter tax burden on some lands, notably the marginal and submarginal lands now so frequently overassessed, while some of the higher grades of land (particularly some of the better urban sites) would be taxed more heavily. Disregarding the serious practical difficulties involved in such sweeping tax reform, no new right of government would be involved. Taxing away the entire economic rent is merely an extension of the social theory of property and the governmental right to control private property rights in land through taxation.

LAND VALUE INCREMENT TAXES

In spite of the wide interest aroused by Henry George's writings,[24] efforts to put into practice the entire single-tax program have met with light success. The largest number of favorable acts have been passed in Australia, where the principles of separate valuation of land and improvements, a land tax discriminating against absentee owners, and the almost entire dependence of local revenue on land taxes are widely accepted. England in 1909 adopted a land-value increment tax, under which past increments to land value are ignored and only future increments of rent are appropriated by taxation.

In contrast to George's single tax (which was to be collected annually), this tax was collected only when exchange took place, and the tax base

[24] George's best known work is *Progress and Poverty*, first published in 1879. This book was translated into all the major tongues of Europe and by 1905 (25 years after it was first published), more than two million copies had been printed. With other books that Henry George wrote, some five million copies had been printed by 1905. Thousands of copies have been printed since that date. (See 50th anniversary ed. of *Progress and Poverty*, Robert Schalkenbach Foundation, 1929, p. xii.)

was to be the gain in land value between exchanges. In this sense, the ta
resembles the capital gains features in many income tax statutes, exce
that it applies only to land.

The English land-value increment tax levied a tax of 20 percent of th
increment above a certain exemption. At the end of a decade, howeve
this tax was repealed.

Land-value increment taxes would need to be determined with due r
gard for the fact that future increases have been reflected to a certai
extent in present land values. Properly administered land-value incremer
taxes would not work serious hardship on present landowners and woul
tend to mitigate inequalities and increase funds available for governmer
services or socially desirable programs.

Students of land economics are generally agreed that a substantial pai
of future "unearned increments" could be appropriated by society to it
own advantage, and knowledge of this fact is spreading, as is evidenced b
the tendency of modern municipalities in various nations to levy pr
gressive taxes on increments of private income caused by increasing ec
nomic returns from natural agents and other sources.

SPECIAL ASSESSMENTS

Special assessments are compulsory levies upon property owners to pa
for special services to their property. Special assessments are justifie
largely on the grounds that the improvements, financed by funds obtaine
from the special assessments, benefit the landowner by enhancing land o
property values.

There are many arguments for and against special assessments. Som
students believe that land is a better base for taxation than improvement
and that expenditures in the service of land usually financed throug
special assessments should be considered beneficial principally in makin
land habitable and attractive. Special assessments have a particular valu
from this point of view, but many problems arise in their use.

A major difficulty is the measurement of benefit. Determination of th
portion of an improvement or service that should be financed fron
general taxes and the portion from special assessments, the territory to b
included in the special assessment district, and the methods to be used i
distributing costs among properties within the district, all involve judg
ments which at best are estimates. If benefit is conceived in terms of incre
ment to land value, the increment has to be estimated before it is realized
and events may occur to prevent its realization. Since the fundamenta
justification for special assessments is the equivalent increment to lanc
value, it is extremely important to determine accurately that the improve
ment will increase the value of the lands that are to be specificall
assessed.

In actual use, however, many examples exist where special assessments have been used in spite of the fact that the improvement may not increase the value of the assessed land and in fact may actually result in a reduction in its value.[25] Closer attention needs to be paid in most instances to the amount of the special benefits involved, and where there is also considerable general benefit, special assessments should be supplemented by other more general forms of taxation.[26]

Some argue that land-value increment taxes are superior as a fiscal measure to special assessments. Increment taxes are levied on increments after they arise rather than before, and include land value increases resulting from social (as distinguished from public) improvements. However, the increment tax is hardly a substitute for special assessments, which rest more logically upon the idea of special benefit than upon land-value increments.[27]

Undoubtedly, special assessments will continue in wide use, particularly in municipal finance, though there is a definite tendency (especially in rural areas and in irrigation and reclamation work) to take a broader view of the nature of benefits resulting from such land improvements, and to broaden correspondingly the base of financial support for such improvements. It is desirable that special assessments be maintained to permit certain groups of individuals to effect desired improvements, provided these assessments are administered efficiently, and limited to fields in which the benefits accrue only or almost entirely to the individuals involved.

OTHER SPECIAL TAXES ON LAND

George's single tax has undoubtedly been an important factor in producing certain land reforms and special land taxes effected in some areas.

[25] The fact that a taxpayer receives no benefit at all will not render a special assessment invalid, and the fact that the special assessment is greater than the market value of the property does not make a case for interference by a court of equity. Whatever hardship this position may involve "must be borne as one of the imperfections of human things." *Louisville and Nashville Paving Co.* vs. *Barber Asphalt Paving Co.*, 197430, 434 (1905). (Groves, *op. cit.*, p. 423.)

[26] The headlong rush of cities into unnecessary local improvements during the twenties resulted in reversion of private lots to public ownership during the depression thirties. Creation of overlapping assessment districts is widespread, some cities having imposed as many as 11 simultaneous local improvement assessments upon the same piece of property. The amount of the total assessments that can be levied against a given property should be limited by statute to a fair percentage of market value. (For these and other more glaring abuses of special assessments, together with suggested lines of improvement, see E. H. Hahne, "Special Assessments and Licenses," *Annals of the American Academy of Political and Social Sciences*, Vol. CLXXXIII, January, 1936, pp. 130–135.)

[27] For a more complete statement of the relative merits of the increment tax and special assessments, see E. H. Spengler, "The Increment Tax vs. Special Assessments," *Bulletin of the National Tax Association*, Vol. XXI, No. 8, May, 1936, p. 240.

For example, Sydney, Australia, with a population of a million, relies entirely for its revenue upon a single land value tax, and many smaller municipalities do the same. The land in the Australian capital district of Canberra is leased from the government at its economic rent.[28]

In the city of Pittsburgh, improvements are assessed at only half their true value, while land is assessed in full. The four western provinces of Canada have in varying degrees sought to discourage land speculation by taxation and required cities, villages, and towns to reduce assessments on improvements to 50 or 60 percent of their value. In the United States, unsuccessful attempts have been made in Colorado, Oregon, California, Washington, and Missouri to ratify constitutional amendments permitting exemption of improvements and taxation of land values, but in Oklahoma a measure was passed establishing a graduated land tax with the purpose of breaking up large estates. Australia and New Zealand employ graduated land taxes for this purpose. Denmark has a national tax on the value of unimproved land, and local land taxes which are at least higher than those on improvements.[29]

When all factors are taken into account, there does seem to be a case for special taxation of land. This is particularly true of urban land. Many students agree that it is doubtful whether cities should ever have allowed the sites within their boundaries to have passed entirely from public ownership, and think that if cities do not follow the course of the city of Canberra, "the next best program is to recapture a large amount of urban economic rent through special taxes on land."[30] Any such programs should be put into operation cautiously, however, because of the disruptive influences and inequalities that would result from any drastic increase in land taxation.

SHIFTING AND INCIDENCE OF LAND TAXES

If taxes can be shifted so that their incidence, or "final resting place," is on someone other than the individual on whom the tax was originally assessed, the actual tax burden is different from the apparent one. For example, if land taxes can be shifted to someone else by the owner of the land, the effects of the tax on land use (through land speculation, land values, and related conditions) are substantially nullified.

[28] Mitchell, *op, cit.,* p. 66.

[29] *Ibid.*

[30] It is said that the city of Canberra, Australia, is being built upon land that cost the government nothing, or practically nothing. The land is not sold but leased at 5 percent of its land value. It is revalued periodically and leaseholds for various lengths of time are auctioned off to the highest bidder. "Whether or not one accepts all the philosophy of Henry George, one can applaud this experiment as a sensible city land policy, and an excellent method of financing government, particularly for a young city." (Groves, *op. cit.,* p. 407.)

According to prevailing economic theory, shifting takes place only when imposition of a tax results in price changes. If there is no exchange, or price transaction, therefore, shifting cannot occur; and it is generally assumed that once a tax reaches the final consumer it cannot be shifted further, because no more transactions are involved.

LAND TAXES THAT CANNOT BE SHIFTED

Landlords cannot shift land taxes when they are levied as a percentage of: (1) the income from the land (but not as part of a general income tax), (2) the annual lease value (that is, the amount determined in the market as equivalent to one year's use of the land), or (3) the capital or market value—that is, the amount for which the land would sell on a voluntary buyer-seller basis.

The explanation of the fact that the landlord must bear the tax in these cases is that if the land is marginal, yielding no rent, there is no tax, and hence no motive for taking it out of use, or destroying it, if that were possible. In other words, the tax does not reduce the supply of land. The landlord cannot add the tax to the rent charged the tenant, because the tax does not increase land productivity, or area, nor does it increase the supply of tenants.

If the landlord himself is using the land, he cannot charge an additional imputed rent to take into account the amount of the tax, because he would lose as tenant what he would save as landlord. If he were leasing the land for less than the full economic rent, the tax might tend to force him into charging all that could be obtained, but in the long run, he could charge no more than the maximum economic rent. Neither landlord nor tenant can shift the tax to purchasers of the products of the land, for there is no change in supply of such products or demand for them, and hence no way in which to change the price. To leave the land idle or to operate it less intensively would not shift the tax effectively, for the owner would save less than he lost.[31]

On mineral land or virgin forest land, where there are distinctly destructible properties, an annual tax may tend to increase the rate at which the resources of minerals or timber are removed. Thus, the user removes what might be considered a royalty element or source of future incomes. By immediately removing these elements from the soil and selling them, the operator saves taxes that would have been levied during the next 10, 15, or 20 years, and creates liquid assets immediately.

In a similar way (although much less directly and completely), the fertility of agricultural lands may be removed and sold, in which case utilization yields not rent, but royalty, since the source of future income is gone. Where a royalty element is removed, the removal effects a reduc-

[31] For a general statement of this argument, see Jensen, *op. cit.*, pp. 197–198.

tion in the supply of the given type of land, and will eventually tend to raise the price of the product (a form of delayed shifting). More rapid removal of royalty elements increases the present supply of removed materials and lowers their price, so that a tax on royalty elements may constantly lower present but raise future prices; and shifting is therefore problematical.[32]

LAND TAXES THAT ARE SHIFTABLE

One of the best examples used to indicate the possibilities of levying taxes on land so that they will be at least partially shifted is to assume a tax levied at a set amount per acre on all land in the United States. Land yielding less than this amount annually would become tax delinquent and ultimately revert to public ownership through tax deed. If the governmental unit acquiring title to these lands through tax-deed foreclosures were to leave them unused, the supply of land available for use would decrease. Prices of farm products would rise, and the tax would consequently be shifted.

In actual practice governmental units that acquire lands through tax-deed foreclosures try to sell the lands promptly to private owners and get them back on the tax rolls. However, in many areas and for certain types of land there is a considerable lag between the time such lands come into public ownership through tax-deed foreclosure and the time they can be sold or otherwise put back into productive use. This is true of city and town lots, particularly in areas where excessive platting and subdivision have occurred ahead of the actual demand for building sites, and on the poorer grades of farm land. In some cases such lands have gone to tax deed and remained idle in public ownership for many years.

Obviously, land taxes most likely to be shifted are on marginal lands which they reduce to a submarginal status. In these circumstances the lands are withdrawn from use. The result is a decrease in production and a tendency toward an increase in the price of the product. The tax is thus shifted to the purchasers of these products. When the tax is levied on the rental of land, it is by definition only on land above the margin, and no effect upon the supply of land results. Consequently, there is no effect on price and no shifting.

SHIFTING AND INCIDENCE UNDER SPECIAL CONDITIONS

A distinction should be made between land as such and the improvements that are incorporated into or placed upon it. In urban land, improvements are so important that the problems associated with utilizing these improvements become the major issues of urban land utilization. Buildings and other improvements, considered from the long-time point

[32] *Ibid.*, p. 198.

of view, are destructible, since they wear out in due time. Consequently, if taxes are levied on the value of improvements, the owner can do little to shift such taxes during the ordinary life of the improvement; but when the building or improvement needs to be replaced, the owner will not replace it unless the reward for renewal is sufficient to justify such replacement and unless the investments promise rewards on a basis comparable with those in other alternative endeavors. In this way, the tax may definitely affect the supply, because it encourages failure to replace the improvement or the tendency to increase the price of products or services made possible by such improvements. In either case the tax is shifted. The more durable the improvement, the less adjustable the supply and the less direct and prompt the shifting of the tax. Supply and demand conditions affecting land improvements (especially dwellings, on urban land) at the time the tax is levied will have an important bearing upon the promptness and completeness of tax shifting.

Exempting homesteads from taxation would tend to increase the desirability of all property available for owner-occupier use and would temporarily increase the selling value of land and buildings of this character. Although competitive forces would ultimately tend to eliminate this advantage, homestead exemption would remain a special benefit and privilege for persons who chose to exercise the functions of homeowners. On the other hand, if statutory or constitutional limitation of property tax rates is effective, conditions tend to be more favorable to tax capitalization, since real estate would be a more attractive investment as a result of lower taxes, and its price would therefore be increased.

Under these conditions, present owners are likely to get all the benefit of limitation of rates. Eventually, however, for the reproducible elements of real estate, like buildings and certain improvements, there would be an increase in the amount of building and improvements undertaken, and this increase in supply would tend to cut down the income from improvements. However, to the extent that tax exemption or limitation of rates is applied strictly to land, the tax relief will probably be capitalized.[33]

CAPITALIZATION OF TAX REDUCTIONS INTO LAND VALUES

Many students argue that reduction of the farm tax burden would do American agriculture little good, because farmers would tend to capitalize tax relief into land values, and thus burden themselves with a larger fixed overhead. The question of tax capitalization on agricultural lands cannot be answered so simply.

It should not be forgotten that much of the value of farm land is derived from fertility, which is a reproducible and exhaustible factor. Taxes on fertility operate like taxes on any other reproducible item of

[33] Cf. Groves, *op. cit.*, p. 149.

capital used in production—that is, they tend to be shifted in increase prices of products, rather than capitalized in lower prices for land, or vic versa. Moreover, it should be remembered that in most communitie particularly in less highly commercialized farming areas, a reduction in net farm income because of taxes or an increase because of reduction in taxes may not be reflected in reduced or increased demand for farms and a reduction or increase in the price of land, because other than com mercial values associated with agriculture may predominate.

Finally, land changes ownership slowly in some areas, and without ; fairly active market for sales and purchases, the capitalization theor cannot work effectively. The capitalization process can operate onl through exchange. The owner, new or old, is left with a fixed charge from which he cannot be absolved, and any shift caused by a rise in prices ma destroy enough of the producer's business, through reducing sales, t lower his net return.

Because of the variety of forces operative in the case of each specifi type of tax, the student of land economics must always analyze shifting and incidence carefully to determine direction and extent of shifting.[34]

REFERENCES FOR FURTHER READING

Abrams, Charles, *Revolution in Land,* Harper & Brothers, New York, 1939 Chap. IX.

Brown, Harry G., *The Economic Basis of Tax Reform,* Lucas Brothers, Columbia Mo., 1932, Chaps. III and IV.

Ely, Richard T., and Morehouse, Edward W., *Elements of Land Economics,* The Macmillan Company, New York, 1924, Chap. XV.

Geiger, G. R., *The Theory of the Land Question,* The Macmillan Company, New York, 1936, Chap. V.

George, Henry, *Progress and Poverty,* 50th anniversary ed., Robert Schalkenbach Foundation, New York, 1929, Books VI, VII, and VIII.

Groves, H. M., *Financing Government,* Henry Holt and Company, Inc., New York, 1939, Chaps. III, IV, V, VI, XX, and XXII.

Groves, H. M. (ed.), *Viewpoints on Public Finance,* Henry Holt and Company, Inc., New York, 1947.

Howard, Mayne S., *Principles of Public Finance,* Commerce Clearing House, Chicago, 1940, Chaps. VI–VIII.

Jensen, Jens P., *Government Finance,* Thomas Y. Crowell Company, New York, 1937, Chaps. XII, XV, XVI, and pp. 287–291.

Kendrick, M. Slade, *Taxation Issues,* Harper & Brothers, New York, 1933, Chaps. III and V.

Kuznets, Simon, *Economic Change,* W. W. Norton & Company, Inc., New York, 1953, Chaps. VI–VIII.

[34] For a more detailed analysis of the general theory and application of tax shifting and incidence, see Groves, *op. cit.,* Chap. VI; Jensen, *op. cit.,* Chap. XII; and Kendrick, *op. cit.,* Chap. V.

Scheftel, Yetta, *Taxation of Land Value,* Essays, No. 22, Hart, Schaffner, and Marx, Boston, 1916.

Seligman, E. R. A., *Essays in Taxation,* 10th ed., The Macmillan Company, New York, 1925, Chaps. II, III, XIII, and XX.

Silverherz, Joseph D., *The Assessment of Real Property in the United States,* New York State Tax Commission, Special Report No. 10, Albany, N.Y., 1936.

Tax Policy League, *Property Taxes: A Symposium,* New York, 1940, Chaps. III, VII, IX, XIII, XV, XVII, and XVIII.

chapter **14**

TAXATION OF LAND IN DIFFERENT USES

AGRICULTURAL LAND TAXATION

Causes of Farm Tax Delinquency—Reduction of Farm Tax Delinquency—Improving Farm Land Assessments—Reducing Costs of Governmental Services—Broadening the Tax Base—Achieving Greater Flexibility of Farm Land Taxes—Increasing Agricultural Income

TAXATION OF FOREST LAND

"Wrecking Value" Taxation of Forest Lands—Improvement of Forest Land Taxation—The Principle of the Severance Tax

MINERAL LAND TAXATION

Effects of Ad Valorem Taxation of Mineral Lands—Suggested Improvements in Mineral Land Taxation

TAXATION OF LAND USED FOR TRANSPORTATION

Means of Financing Streets and Roads—"Taxes by the Mile"

URBAN LAND TAXATION

Urban Tax Delinquency—Reduction of Urban Tax Delinquency—Scientific Appraisal of Urban Real Estate—The Graded Tax Plan—Other Improvements

TAXES ON land and improvements in the United States are levied through operation of the general property tax. General property tax levies are the major and in most cases almost the sole support of local governmental units. In the United States, with its thousands of townships and school district units and more than 3000 county governmental units, the total tax bill on agricultural, forest, mineral, and urban lands levied through the general property tax amounts to billions of dollars annually. The machinery of general property tax administration, from assessment through tax computation and collection, is therefore of great importance to land users.

The general property tax as it is administered in most states places a particularly heavy burden on landowners at the very times when net income or ability to pay is comparatively low. During depression periods when prices and incomes are low, public expenditures are usually increased because of unemployment relief. During the period after a war, governmental costs are higher because of heavier debt service charges resulting from borrowing through bond issues to finance the war. In such periods revenue from other types of taxes (especially income and sales taxes) tends to decline in comparison with total revenue required, while property taxes may not be reduced and may even be increased.

Typically, revenues from all other sources are estimated first and the property tax rate is fixed at a level that will provide the remainder of the revenue required by the budget. Since land is a form of tangible property, it is particularly vulnerable during such periods to increased levies by the local governmental units, which rely chiefly upon property taxes for their support. For example, it is significant that farm real-estate taxes in the United States were nearly three times their prewar level in 1930, and two and one-half times their prewar level in 1931, whereas farm prices in these years were only 126 percent and 87 percent respectively of prewar farm prices. Although farm property taxes declined somewhat during the thirties, they were almost twice their prewar level at the beginning of the forties, whereas farm prices were slightly below their prewar level.

Future trends in real-estate taxes will be determined in part by the relative importance of property taxes in the revenue systems of state and local governments, and in part by the amount and costs of services provided. During World War II state and local government revenues from sales and income taxes increased with relatively high prices and incomes. These increases, together with reduced capital outlays and lower relief costs, were responsible for the accumulation of state and local governmental surpluses and the reduction in real estate levies. The marked increase in school population following the upsurge in births immediately after the war, however, has placed very heavy tax burdens on school districts and local governmental units. Since these units rely heavily on the general property tax, real estate taxes have increased tremendously. For example, farm real-estate tax levies were more than four times as high in the mid-fifties as during the pre-World War I period and are rising still further to meet rising school costs.[1]

AGRICULTURAL LAND TAXATION

The great increase in farm real-estate taxes from the beginning of World War I to the end of the twenties and their maintenance of approximately twice the prewar level during the thirties, the continual drop in land values after 1920 to the low point of the depression in the early thirties, and the disastrous decline in farm income after 1929 made it impossible for many farmers to meet tax assessments in the thirties. Continued widespread tax delinquency, increased transfer of farm through tax-deed foreclosure, and related distress in agricultural area have called attention to the need for fairer and more equitable farm land taxation.

CAUSES OF FARM TAX DELINQUENCY

There are numerous causes of farm tax delinquency, many of which grow out of the economic system and the level of general business activity. Property taxes are a fixed and inescapable current cost, and the ability to pay taxes largely depends upon the amount of net income received by the landowner. During the period when American farm tax delinquency increased most, farm income was at a low level. For example, during the severe business depression and droughts of the early thirties, when farm income was low and farm tax delinquency high, farm property taxes equaled approximately a tenth of gross cash farm income, or more than double the proportion of the middle twenties.[2]

In contrast, during the early forties, when farm income was high because of good crops and high wartime food prices, farm property taxes comprised only about 2 percent of the gross cash farm income and farm tax delinquency was exceedingly small. The failure of rigid or inelastic farm real-estate taxes to adjust promptly and completely to changes in farm income is one of the principal causes of farm tax delinquency.

There are other important causes of farm tax delinquency, aside from low farm income. One important economic factor is the tendency of current delinquency to set in motion forces that cause further delinquency.

[1] The index of farm real-estate taxes levied per acre (1909–1913 = 100) was 409 in 1954, compared with 391 in 1953. In 1955 taxes levied on farm property increased about 3.5 percent. (See U.S. Department of Agriculture, "Agricultural Finance Review," Agricultural Research Service, Government Printing Office, Vol. 17, Supplement, May, 1955, p. 17, processed.)

[2] In 1910 farm property taxes comprised only 2.9 percent of gross cash farm income; in 1920, 3.8 percent; and in 1925, 4.7 percent; contrasted with 6.4 percent in 1930 and 9.8 percent in 1932. Farm property taxes averaged around 5 percent of gross cash farm income for the remainder of the thirties. (Eric Englund, "Real Estate Taxation," U.S. Department of Agriculture, *Yearbook*, 1940, p. 779.)

'hen the first lands go delinquent (perhaps because of a drop in farm ices, or crop failures, or low yields), the failure of these lands to pay eir share of current government costs throws a heavier burden upon the maining properties on the tax roll. This in turn causes some of the next oorest lands to go delinquent, throwing a still heavier burden upon the maining properties, and setting in motion a vicious circle of tax-de-nquency and tax-deed foreclosures that tends to grow for a considerable eriod after the original forces causing the first tax delinquency have dis-opeared. Another important economic cause of tax delinquency is higher oerating and living costs in many areas.

An important group of noneconomic factors is a significant cause of rm tax delinquency. The most important of these is the administration f the tax system itself. Unless the tax system operates in such a way as to nd all the taxable property and assess it at a fair and just valuation, juality and justice will not be achieved. Studies reveal great inequalities i the property tax levied in relation to productivity of farms in various arts of the country and within states or local tax jurisdictions. These iequalities result from present assessment methods and the degree of eliance upon agricultural lands in the property tax base.

Tax collection procedures often have an important bearing upon the xtent of farm tax delinquency. In some areas much stricter enforcement iethods are employed than in others, including higher charges for de-nquency in the form of penalties and interest; and because of this variety f procedures, there is great variation in the extent of farm tax delin-uency.[3] There is, in addition to these factors, the noneconomic factor f the "standard of tax compliance," which varies greatly among indi-iduals whose economic circumstances are very similar.[4]

REDUCTION OF FARM TAX DELINQUENCY

In most cases tax delinquency is caused by the inability of landowners o make tax payments, although it must be recognized that some taxes iay remain unpaid as a protest against what the owner regards as an un-iir assessment and an excessive tax burden. Since taxes are a direct out-of-

[3] For a more detailed analysis of the relation of tax collection methods to delin-uency, see Frederick L. Bird, "Relation of Tax Collection Methods to Delinquency," a Tax Policy League, *Property Taxes: A Symposium*, 1940, pp. 254–261.

[4] Differences in tax compliance can be accounted for by one or both of two factors—difference in degree of social responsibility, or a difference in degree of devotion to roperty ownership. Many authors believe that during the early thirties there was a ither widespread change in attitude toward tax payments in many communities, grow-ig out of the critical property tax situation, and that this change in attitude or standard of tax compliance" had an important bearing upon the degree of tax elinquency in many rural communities. (Cf. Joseph Rosa, "Some Causes of Farm Tax elinquency," "Agricultural Finance Review," Vol. III, No. 2, November, 1940, p. 11, rocessed.)

pocket cost that must be met with cash, they are doubly heavy if left unpaid until the following year; and payment must be made comparatively soon to prevent loss of the farm through tax deed. Loss of land through tax-deed foreclosure, together with the discouraging effect of being burdened with disproportionate taxes when acquiring agricultural land, has contributed to a high rate of farm tenancy in many areas, particularly of low-grade farm and range lands.[5]

Adjustment of assessments more in line with capitalized income or productivity value would tend to encourage ownership and conservation of agricultural lands. In many of the more marginal areas—particularly range areas—proper use is the most important single adjustment needed to increase and stabilize farm incomes; and this proper use often involves acquiring larger acreages and using land less intensively. If such land-use adjustments are to be encouraged, assessment adjustments in line with proper use and productive capacity of the land are necessary.

IMPROVING FARM LAND ASSESSMENTS

Lack of uniform assessment standards and absence of land values based on true earning power or productive capacity of the land (capitalized income value), has resulted in much overassessment, particularly on poorer less productive grades of farm and range lands. In most states, sale values based on voluntary buyer-voluntary seller transactions are by statute assumed to be the basis for assessment values for tax purposes, but many inequalities in assessment exist.

Some of the more important reasons why assessments do not correspond with sales value include: (1) failure to use voluntary sales data or any reliable information upon which assessors or deputies can base their valuations; (2) belief on the part of assessors that sales value does not represent the "full and true value" of the land; (3) necessity of making high assessments so that maximum allowable levies (many states have statutory tax limits) will yield the desired tax revenue; (4) other economic or political factors, such as lower assessments for larger and more influential property owners.

One of the first and most important steps toward reducing rural real estate tax delinquency is the determination and use for assessment purposes of capitalized income or productivity values of agricultural lands based on scientific soil surveys and *average* yields and prices. Such a sys-

[5] This tendency is borne out by the fact that in some areas, particularly the low grade range areas of the Plains, many ranch operators would rather lease their range land than own it, because of the disproportionate tax burden. Some operators have allowed all but their headquarters or water-hole sites to go delinquent and revert to public ownership, then leased lands from public agencies, on the grounds that they could lease more cheaply than they could own, and would not, at the same time, have the rigid inelasticity of overhead so disastrous during drought and low-income years.

tem of land classification for tax assessment would tend to reduce dis-
crepancies in tax burdens resulting from present inadequate or unscientific classifications and assessment, particularly in the case of poorer
grades of farm and grazing lands.

Problems associated with classifying land for tax assessment purposes
are numerous, and include those indicated in the preceding chapter on
determining land values. However, the importance of developing a sound
tax structure that will burden taxpayers with the support of government
in proportion to their relative abilities to pay is so great, in view of the
trend toward increased governmental expenditures, that the problems involved should be considered challenges, not insurmountable difficulties.
Modern scientific method, together with realization of the importance of
such improvements, should make possible the satisfactory solution of these
problems.

REDUCING COSTS OF GOVERNMENTAL SERVICES

Undoubtedly, farm tax delinquency could be reduced in many areas by
reducing farm taxes, but such reduction would involve reducing governmental services, or finding new sources of income, or rendering services at
lower cost. All these changes have a place in a reorganized program designed to put local government on a more efficient and economical basis.

One of the first steps toward reducing governmental costs should be the
improvement of the administration and organization of local governmental services, particularly in counties, school districts, and townships.
Much improvement in efficiency of county services generally throughout
the nation might be accomplished by centralizing administration through
inaugurating the county manager, county executive, or county commission form of government. This would centralize executive responsibility
and reduce the number of departments and officers. Coöperation among
counties and with the state to establish a state civil service or merit system
to improve personnel, to centralize purchasing of equipment and supplies,
and to standardize accounting methods and forms would undoubtedly
effect considerable savings in many areas. Some services, such as policing,
now performed largely by individual counties, might be executed more
economically and efficiently on a state-wide basis. Putting school organization and administration on a county-wide or community unit basis in
many areas would reduce costs of school services and improve their
quality.

In addition to these changes, more basic alterations in the character of
governmental services must be made in some areas to reduce costs to a
level adapted to the needs and resources of the community. During recent
years the population of many communities has migrated to other areas so
that the present pattern of local governmental services is now a poor fit.

In some areas, especially those heavily in debt, adjustments in interes charges by refunding indebtedness and even write-downs of principa might be possible by concerted efforts of county officials and coöperatio of creditors.

County consolidation, where population has so declined that the existin county government can no longer be economically supported, might hel to make tax burdens more reasonable. Combining services of variou offices might result in lower governmental costs without sacrificing neces sary services in many communities where consolidation of counties is no feasible. Similar adjustments in school district and township organizatio and administration would be beneficial in many areas.

BROADENING THE TAX BASE

The almost complete dependence of local governments in the Unite States upon the general property tax places the major burden of suppor upon property (farm and home) owners. Broadening the tax base b shifting part of the burden to other revenue sources is desirable not onl for the purpose of bringing about a more equitable allocation of ta burdens, but also to increase flexibility and thereby reduce tax delin quency.

In recent years many state governments have tapped new revenue sources and shifted part of the tax burden away from general property Increased emphasis on certain types of sales, income, and other taxes might help to spread the burden of supporting government to all those who benefit from governmental services, rather than to property owners only. However, unless new taxes are adopted with caution and carefully studied as to incidence and effects, farmers may actually find themselves paying more total taxes than before.

A general sales tax is regressive in its effects and tends to fall heaviest upon persons with small incomes. Moreover, farmers, most of whom buy large amounts of various kinds of products for production and for con- sumption purposes, would pay considerable sales taxes. Many students of public finance believe that farmers pay more than their fair share of consumption taxes. Therefore, unless newly tapped sources of revenue are restricted so as to replace specifically a given amount of property tax revenue, the farmer's burden may be increased rather than decreased. The problem is not as simple as the statement "sales taxes or tax sales" implies.

ACHIEVING GREATER FLEXIBILITY OF FARM LAND TAXES

Present practice is for local governments to collect only enough revenue annually to meet current expenses, avoiding deficits or surpluses so far as possible. Property owners, rather than governments, are supposed to set side cash reserves during good years or borrow to meet tax payments in lean years. However, income fluctuations, particularly among farmers, may be so great and the periods of distress so extended in duration that any such individual savings are rapidly depleted and borrowing becomes difficult and undesirable.

The present organization of American agriculture, with its numerous individual competing units and the general inability of farmers as a group to set prices, makes it practically impossible for most farmers to include taxes as part of their costs of production and reflect them in the selling price of their products. Even if they could include taxes in selling prices, this would be of little benefit during drought and crop-failure periods, when yields are greatly reduced or vanish completely. Consequently, farm tax delinquency is large when prices and yields are low.

Some students of public finance suggest that the responsibility of adjusting finances to fluctuations in income be shifted to governmental units and tax burdens adjusted yearly to taxpayers' current incomes. Under this arrangement, when yields, prices, or wages were high, tax levies would be higher than necessary to meet current expenditures, so that a cash reserve would be built up and taxes might be reduced to less than the amount required to make ends meet when prices, yields, and incomes were at low levels.

With this sliding scale of tax levies, current farm property taxes would tend to be more in line with current farm income, and rural tax delinquency would be reduced.[6] Flexibility might also be increased by supporting services like schools and roads more largely through a combination of local, state, and federal taxes, rather than predominantly through local assessments, as is now so frequently the case. Federal and state governments secure a large portion of their revenues from income, sales, and related nonproperty taxes.

In spite of its many weaknesses, the general property tax will undoubtedly continue for some time to be the major source of local revenue, in many cases furnishing a substantial part of state revenue as well. It is a tax that can be administered more effectively by local governments than can many others. If local governments are to retain any degree of autonomy, it is desirable that they raise at least a substantial proportion of the revenue required to finance their services or completely divorce

---

[6] With such public budgeting and sliding-scale revenues, a high quality of government personnel would be required if pork-barrel methods and wasteful exploitation of surpluses in good years were to be avoided. Improvement of local government personnel through establishment of the merit system of rating and appointment, rather than extreme decentralization and popular election of many officers, would undoubtedly improve the general quality of local government administration and strengthen American democracy as a whole. It would also tend to establish government service at the local level on a professional basis.

the raising and spending of public funds. After all, if every tax were judged only by its faults, none would be acceptable. Consequently, every effort should be made to make the general property tax operate as well as possible.

INCREASING AGRICULTURAL INCOME

The farm tax problem may be attacked from the angle of increasing farm income and, consequently, farm taxpaying ability. Increasing agricultural income would also be desirable because it would increase the income of city and town business and merchandising groups servicing agricultural communities, and consequently would tend to reduce their tax delinquency. It should also help to bring about greater economic equality among farmers and other groups in society, and tend to make the economy operate more smoothly.

Improvement of land-use and farm-management practices would help to increase agricultural income. These require both individual and group action. The individual farmer can increase his farm income by adjusting land use to natural soil and climatic conditions and by organizing his ranch or unit for economically efficient and stable operation. Keeping accurate and systematic farm records and accounts should be encouraged.

Group action is necessary to control effectively the use of land and block it into efficient units in many areas. Group action of farmers, particularly in the semiarid sections, will permit area diversification and enable individual operators to secure higher and more stable returns. Group action is also essential for effective coöperative marketing and more effective control of prices and output.

But a broad educational and research program will be necessary before successful group action on any extensive scale will be assured for American farmers. However, if farm land assessments can be improved along the lines suggested, if local governmental costs can be reduced by more efficient administration and organization, if the tax base can be broadened, and if farmers can improve agricultural income through individual practices and coöperative effort in production and marketing, American agriculture will be more prosperous and, incidentally, the farm tax delinquency problem will be largely solved in the process.

TAXATION OF FOREST LAND

The administration of the property tax is chiefly responsible for problems of forest taxation. Forest land taxation policies have contributed greatly to the increase in public forest land ownership in recent years, because of chronic tax delinquency and abandonment of cutover lands. Forest lands have not been assessed on annual productive capacity or ability to pay, but on the value that would be secured by wrecking the rest and selling the products. In other words the general property tax as been so administered that forest lands usually are assessed at their ill stumpage value (value of the land and standing timber), and annual xes have been assessed against this stumpage or "wrecking" value.

"WRECKING VALUE" TAXATION OF FOREST LANDS

The forest crop does not mature annually, and even in those cases where stematic management has resulted in cutting a given proportion of the rowth each year, so as to sustain the forest on a permanent production asis, taxes have frequently equaled or exceeded annual returns. Under lese conditions private forest owners have "wrecked" their properties by utting off the entire stand, taking their profit, and abandoning the re-ulting cutover tracts.

It is essential in many areas that changes be made in the methods of axing private forest lands, if private forest ownership on a permanently atisfactory basis is to survive. Obviously, in an industry with the eco-omic characteristics of forestry, the tax system, to operate satisfactorily, aust levy taxes more in keeping with current ability of the forest owners o pay.

Under the general property tax laws, timber is assessed as real estate nd part of the land; but if it is to be managed to provide recurring imber crops, it must be taxed as a crop and not as real estate. Assessment, ear after year, of the accumulated timber growth of many seasons does tot make any distinction between the land itself, which remains, and the imber, which does not remain but is the crop or income from the capital the land).

IMPROVEMENT OF FOREST LAND TAXATION

The uncertainty of future tax levies (uncertainty in the sense of a fear of periodical increases without warning) has been one of the greatest obstacles to the practice of good forestry. Assessments naturally increase is trees approach merchantable size; and this puts pressure on the owner o market his product at the earliest possible moment, although his own nterest and the public interest might be served more effectively otherwise. The principle of taxing the land annually and the timber only when it is cut and the income realized is one that students of forest economics recom-mend as most desirable to incorporate in forest land tax policies.

The Wisconsin Forest Crop Law makes such a distinction between land and timber and fixes the annual land tax for 50 years, since entry of lands under the law constitutes a contract for that period between the state and the owner. The Wisconsin law fixes a tax on forest land at a figure that represents the value of the land for growing timber. For ex-ample, an acre of forest land capable of producing 200 board feet of timber yearly at a value of $5 per thousand feet would earn $1 per aci per year. The owner pays 10 cents per acre annually as a tax, which i this case equals 10 percent of the timber produced yearly. When th timber is cut, he pays an additional 10 percent of the stumpage value (the products removed.[7]

The annual rate of 10 cents per acre paid as an annual tax by th private owner averages considerably less than the usual taxes levied b local government on forest lands within its boundaries. However, in th Wisconsin Forest Crop Law, the state also makes a contribution to th local governments, so that the 10 cents per acre and the state contributio comprise a more satisfactory income for local governments than a growin delinquent tax list.[8] Moreover, owners of forest crop land who enter land under the Wisconsin Forest Crop Law must pay up any unpaid back taxe before making entry, so that local governments receive appreciable sum that would have been lost if private owners abandoned their cutove lands and allowed them to revert to public ownership.

THE PRINCIPLE OF THE SEVERANCE TAX

Payment of a given percentage of stumpage value of products removec when timber is cut, as provided in the Wisconsin Forest Crop Law, is ir reality a severance tax. Such severance or yield taxes, in the case of natura resources like forest lands, are generally considered sound by most stu dents of forest economics. Such a plan has distinct advantages from the point of view of the forest owner; certain disadvantages for governments and other difficulties arise from its use.

The principal disadvantages of such a tax plan include the necessity for state-wide administration and distribution of the proceeds among local jurisdictions. This frequently raises serious problems. Lack of a definite method of determining the rate of the yield tax is also con- sidered a serious weakness by many. This, combined with the difficulty of adapting irregular revenue receipts to local governmental fiscal require- ments, has led some students to consider the yield-tax plan distinctly inferior to other possible solutions of the forest tax problem.[9]

Although the Wisconsin Forest Crop Law has not operated long

[7] See Wisconsin Conservation Department, *The Wisconsin Forest Crop and Wood- land Tax Laws*, Madison, Wis., 1938, pp. 4–5.

[8] The Wisconsin Forest Crop Law provides that when funds appropriated for the state contributions to local governments are not sufficient to pay 10 cents per acre on all land, the funds must be prorated. (*Ibid.*, p. 6.)

[9] "The yield tax plan appears distinctly inferior to other possible solutions of the problem, and is therefore not recommended. The fact that after twenty years of experi- ment no state has yet succeeded in setting up a satisfactory yield tax of broad applica- tion is evidence of the difficulties involved." (F. R. Fairchild *et al., Forest Taxation in the United States*, U.S. Department of Agriculture, Miscellaneous Publication 218, October, 1935, p. 638.)

enough for final judgment to be passed upon its success, it has worked sufficiently well to demonstrate the distinct possibilities in such a plan of taxation, given intelligent and sympathetic understanding and support by state and local people. Under the Wisconsin plan the local governments are assured a comparatively regular amount of annual per-acre revenue, approximately half of which comes from the state and the other half from the owner, who finds his annual payment low enough so that he can pay it, and moreover finds it good business under the fixed, 50-year plan to do so, and "grow" his crop of trees on a permanent sustained-yield basis.

In the Wisconsin law, administration of the severance tax is based upon filing with the Conservation Commission regular reports of cuttings made. Certification of cuttings is made by the owner to the Conservation Commission, or the Commission may itself determine the amounts cut. The severance tax is assessed and levied against the owner by the Tax Commission, in accordance with a stumpage schedule determined by it.

Other plans suggested for overcoming present defects of the property tax on forest land generally involve the principle of adjusting annual tax burdens more nearly to the ability of forest owners to pay currently.[10]

MINERAL LAND TAXATION

The utilization of mineral lands is a mining or extraction business, not a crop or genetic business. Consequently, the public has a very vital interest in mineral resources, and many believe the public is entitled to a larger share of the income from mining than from genetic industries. The fact that many large mineral properties are owned by absentee owners also tends to cause relatively heavy taxation of such properties.

Local assessors tend to assess absentee-owned property more heavily than comparable locally-owned property. This is one of the disadvantages of absentee ownership.

Taxation trends, in some cases, also reflect an indirect attempt to reacquire basic natural wealth that has passed into private ownership. Supplementing these philosophical considerations is the very practical fact that deposits are immobile and cannot escape heavy taxation by moving away. Moreover, their per-acre and aggregate value is high in comparison with that of much other local property. The net result is that local taxing units in need of more revenue often tax mineral industries heavily.

EFFECTS OF AD VALOREM TAXATION OF MINERAL LANDS

The heaviest tax burden on mineral industries is imposed by state and local governments. State and local taxes are largely ad valorem on mineral

[10] For an analysis of these plans see *ibid.*, pp. 639–640.

reserves as well as on active mineral properties. Reserves are taxed an nually, perhaps for long periods, before they come into production, an this policy affects exploitation of mineral resources much as the gener; property tax affects forest land. In addition to these property taxes, the is in some areas a group of special taxes on minerals called "tonnag taxes," "severance taxes," "net proceeds of mines taxes," and "royalt taxes."

The ad valorem or general property tax collected annually by state a local governments on all minerals, whether in production or in reserve, the most anticonservational of all taxes. The effects of this type of tax ar viciously cumulative, forcing overdevelopment of mine capacity and gen erally chaotic development and extraction of mineral deposits. It puts premium on use of the least expensive methods of extraction, in spite o the fact that such methods may ultimately lock up or permanently destro important reserves.

In addition to these vicious effects, the valuations on which ad valorem taxes are based vary widely in different localities, causing enormous ta burden disparities among individual properties, among taxing division and among states. Proper valuation of mining properties is a matter re quiring long experience, yet valuations in many states are determined b untrained and unqualified locally elected assessors.[11]

SUGGESTED IMPROVEMENTS IN MINERAL LAND TAXATION

Many students of mineral land taxation argue that the ad valorem ta should be abolished or significantly reduced, in favor of some form o annual production or yield tax. Objections to abandoning the ad valorem tax entirely include the fact that it would favor concentration of minera reserve ownership in very few hands and hence put a premium or monopoly.

One solution of present mineral land tax difficulties might be to asses such taxes on a scale that would make it possible for operating mines to carry reserves essential for prudent investment in plant and yet to dis courage accumulation beyond this requirement. One possible solution might be reduction or elimination of ad valorem taxes on reserves held by operating companies in amounts representing a reasonable ratio to their production. For reserves held beyond this ratio, ad valorem taxes might be maintained or even increased.

This procedure might result in reversion to public ownership of many important mineral reserves that cannot be used until the distant future State and local governments might suffer temporary loss of revenue, but this loss would be made up by various yield taxes on active mines, reason-

[11] National Resources Board, *Report to the President of the United States,* Govern- ment Printing Office, December 1, 1934, p. 427.

ble ad valorem taxes on the limited reserves retained by mining com-
anies, and later might be more than equaled by collection of royalties
om reserves under state ownership.[12]

Regardless of the revisions that are ultimately worked out, policies of
ineral land taxation, like those of forest land taxation, need to be
noroughly revised to secure wise use of these vital resources. Certain
ypes of mineral lands will need to be treated differently from others.
he specific taxation policies adopted should be such as will fit the
eculiar requirements of the particular mineral resource to achieve wise
tilization.

TAXATION OF LAND USED FOR TRANSPORTATION

Streets and roads are public property and are not taxable. In the case
f railroad rights-of-way, ownership is private and consequently these
ights-of-way are taxable. Railroad rights-of-way cover some four million
cres, having a value of some three billion dollars, while street and road
ights-of-way combined, covering more than 21 million acres, have an
stimated valuation (based on investment in road construction and right-
f-way) of more than 11 times as much as the valuation of railroad rights-
f-way.

MEANS OF FINANCING STREETS AND ROADS

With this large valuation of highway and street rights-of-way eliminated from property taxation, the amount of revenue raised by local
governmental property taxes for roads and streets is appreciably reduced.
n the absence of this property valuation as a source of tax revenue, other
neans must be provided for financing the cost of constructing and main-
aining the ever-growing network of streets and roads. Gasoline taxes and
notor vehicle registration fee taxes have already been raised to compara-
ively high levels in many states.[13] County, township, and city property
axes for construction and maintenance of streets and roads are also
depressingly high in many areas.

The use of special assessments on contiguous property holders, to
finance paving or other street improvements, places heavy financial
ourdens on many city dwellers. Increases in property taxes can be made
in some areas, but for the nation as a whole the financing of the increasing
annual burden of support of roads and streets must be borne by more
widespread taxation of property or increased federal appropriations (fed-

[12] *Ibid.*

[13] In some of the Southern states, total gasoline taxes amount to as much as 12¢ per
gallon—1¢ for the federal government, 6¢ for the state, 3¢ for the county, and 2¢ for
the city in which the gas is purchased. The total price of gasoline in many of these
areas is less than twice the tax, or in other words the taxes represent more than half
the total cost of gasoline.

eral aid to cities and counties, as well as to states) to reduce inequalitie in tax burdens in various areas for support of the highway system.

"TAXES BY THE MILE"

In recent years, diversion of revenues collected specifically for highwa construction and maintenance to other uses than for highway purpose has been a serious factor in reducing the amounts available for street and roads. It has been estimated that around 20 percent of special-use taxes, largely gasoline taxes and motor vehicle registration fees, ar diverted to other purposes than roads. "Taxes by the mile" are funda mentally sound, because they constitute special service charges agains motor transportation for road construction, maintenance, and admini tration. The registration fee has been generally regarded as a "readines to serve" charge, while the gasoline tax is a charge based on the measur of use.

Diversion of these revenues to other than highway purposes bring about far-reaching detrimental effects, including encouragement of highe motor taxes, endangering road bond indebtedness of states, jeopardizin the large investment in highways, subjecting motorists to double taxation imposing on them as a class a disproportionate share of the cost of gov ernment, and many other serious consequences.[14]

URBAN LAND TAXATION

General property tax assessment procedure is one of the most significan causes of delinquency on urban as well as agricultural lands. The rea property tax is the chief source of most municipal revenue in the Unitec States, as it is in most rural local governmental units. Thus, methods o levying and administering general property taxes significantly affect th development of urban property.

URBAN TAX DELINQUENCY

Urban tax delinquency reached alarming heights during the depressior thirties. Many cities had more than 40 percent current tax delinquency and in some, accumulated tax delinquency exceeded the current levy.[15]

[14] See Roy F. Britton, "Taxes by the Mile," *Proceedings of the 32nd–33rd Annua Conference of the American Roadbuilders' Association, 1935–36,* National Press Build ing, Washington, D.C., pp. 226–236.

[15] The median year-end tax delinquency for 150 cities of over 50,000 population reached 20 percent in 1932, rose to 25 percent in 1933, and fell back gradually to 1 percent by 1938. The 20 cities showing widest fluctuations in tax receipts had a median delinquency of 40 percent in 1933. In 1938 the ratio of back taxes to current levies for 118 cities of over 50,000 population was 48.6 percent (nearly one-half). In nine of these cities, the ratio was more than 100 percent, and only six cities had a ratio of less than 10 percent, averaging 7.2 percent. Even arrears as low as 7.2 percent of current levies are serious—for example, the city of Birmingham's whole health and sanitation pro-

heavy tax delinquency, particularly the chronic delinquency in blighted and slum areas, partially explains the fact that in February, 1933, more than 1100 local governments in 42 states had defaulted on their bonds or other obligations.[16]

An important cause of high urban real-estate tax delinquency is the lack of intelligent planning in development of urban patterns. This results in conditions that create high costs of rendering necessary services by the city government and makes for high tax levies. For example, traffic congestion requires heavy expenditures for municipal services to direct and regulate traffic.[17] Blighted areas are unable to bear their proper share of the tax burden, with the result that a greater tax burden is laid upon other areas of the city. Moreover, the cost of providing new facilities required by people who have moved to escape from decaying or blighted areas is large.

Population movement from such areas often leaves behind unused schools, libraries, and other public utilities that must be supplied at considerable cost to the new suburbs. Large apartment houses, skyscrapers, or industrial buildings that are allowed to invade residential areas require installation of high-pressure water mains for fire control, larger sewers, and more expensive streets. Slums usually constitute great fire hazards, which increase the city's protection costs and raise insurance premiums of property owners. "There is hardly a single manifestation of the inefficient urban pattern that does not add its mite to the cost of municipal servicing." [18]

Another significant cause of urban tax delinquency is found in property tax assessment and administration procedures. Numerous investigations of the ratio of assessed value to market value of urban property reveal great inequalities.[19] Urban property assessment generally is very unscientific and nonuniform. Assessment is much worse in some states than in others, but a high degree of variation and regressivity is found in all states. One of the most important reasons for this is the small size of many assessing units, which justify only a part-time official and, combined with

---

gram represents only 7.1 percent of its annual budget, while San Francisco finances all its library and recreational facilities with 7.1 percent of its budget. (National Resources Planning Board, *Public Land Acquisition in a National Land Use Program, Part II,* Government Printing Office, 1941, p. 4.)

[16] Evans Clark, "Internal Debts of the United States," Macmillan, 1933, quoted in National Resources Planning Board, *Public Land Acquisition.*

[17] It has been estimated that traffic congestion in Manhattan costs $500,000 per day and in Cincinnati, $100,000 per day. (National Resources Committee, *Urban Planning and Land Policies,* Report of the Urbanism Committee, Government Printing Office, 1939, p. 222.)

[18] National Resources Planning Board, *Public Land Acquisition,* p. 3.

[19] Joseph D. Silverherz, *The Assessment of Real Property in the United States,* New York State Tax Commission, Special Report No. 10, Albany, N.Y., 1936.

the practice of electing assessors for compartively short terms, serious reduces assessment efficiency.[20]

Special assessments are levied rather generally in American cities, an extensive use of this form of tax is an important factor accounting fo severe real-estate tax delinquency in a great number of cities. In man cases use of special assessments has brought about extravagance in urba improvements, excessive debt, and extreme hardships for some proper owners. Although special assessments have proved useful in many area they should be supplemented by other taxes that will not place the entir burden of certain public improvements on owners of property contiguou to or near these improvements. In many cities, a general levy would be more just and equitable way to defray the costs of a public improvemen

REDUCTION OF URBAN TAX DELINQUENCY

Permanent reduction of urban real-estate tax delinquency requires planned program of land-use control and development, as well as specifi revisions in the tax system. Such control is being increased through zonin ordinances and related police power and eminent domain procedure Some specific changes in the tax system that would improve assessment and reduce delinquency include more scientific appraisal of urban rea estate and use of a graded tax plan which would assess land and improvements at different rates.

Scientific appraisal of urban real estate requires the use of soun methods and adequate appraisal tools. Development of the unit rule i land valuation has been important in securing more accurate appraisals The standard physical unit is a strip of land 1 foot wide and of ordinar lot depth—usually 100 feet. Front-foot values based on sales data and othe information are assigned for various blocks. The front half of the strip i considered more valuable than the back half and is ordinarily valued a two-thirds of the whole. Adjustments can be made by the use of a formul. for lots of greater or less than standard depth, allowing certain adaptation for corner lots.

THE SCIENTIFIC APPRAISAL OF URBAN REAL ESTATE

The unit rule removes much of the guesswork from land assessment, bu it is not equally applicable to all kinds of land, and supplementary

[20] There are nearly 16,000 assessing units in the United States, almost 2000 of whic are in the state of Minnesota, 1600 in Iowa, nearly 1600 in Pennsylvania, etc. Wher the county is not the assessing unit, the borough, ward, town, precinct (or even in som cases a special tax district) may be the unit of assessment. In 40 of the 48 states, assessor are elected. In six of these, the assessors of certain towns or cities are appointed; in 1 states, the assessor's term of office is limited to one or two years, but he may b re-elected to succeed himself. In only one state is the term longer than four year (Georgia, which has a six-year term). National Resources Committee, *op. cit.*, Vol. II pp. 295–296.

ethods must be developed to secure scientific appraisal of certain types
urban property. Zoning ordinances unthought of when the unit foot
les were first established have been adopted in recent years to stabilize
nd use and strengthen resistance to undesirable change. Certain modifi-
tions will be necessary in the unit-foot rules of value first developed
uring the period when full convertibility of land was universally
sumed. It is possible that the unit-square-foot basis may become the
andard for assessment of suburban residential real estate, whenever
ning has established protection and some degree of stability.

With permanence of development as much assured as possible under
odern zoning ordinances, every part of a spacious lot becomes just as
nportant a part of the whole landscape frame of the dwelling as any
her part, and the theory that the front half equals in value two-thirds of
ie whole is not valid. The general tendency to consider corner resi-
ential sites more valuable because of the gain in light secured by such
cations may also be outmoded, because loss of privacy, sidewalk repairs,
low removal, noise of traffic, and related considerations make it a grave
uestion whether the corner site in a properly planned and effectively
ned residential area really confers any benefit or not. In the case of
idustrial properties, the square-foot measure is already applied even in
ities where the unit-front foot is used as the basic measure for all other
roperty.

THE GRADED TAX PLAN

In the case of city sites, where mere space is the most important attri-
ute, land is genuinely nonreproducible, although it may to a slight extent
e made more available for urban use by clearing, draining, grading, etc.
he purchaser of an urban site buys an irreproducible good, and he will
ay for it according to its anticipated future income. If heavy taxes detract
rom the prospects of his anticipated profits, he will pay less for the land
ecause of them. In contrast, a tax on buildings (which are reproducible)
ends to raise rents and therefore also their selling price.[21]

Out of this situation grows the important social consideration that taxes
n improvements discourage building by reducing profits, whereas land
axes stimulate building by decreasing the price of land so that it becomes
asier to acquire, and by penalizing the holder of vacant land.[22] This
ifference in incidence warrants a distinction between the tax treatments
f urban land and of improvements.

The problem of tax administration on urban real estate would be
onsiderably reduced if taxes were levied on the land alone, and the tax-
aying ability represented by income-producing improvements reached

[21] Cf. H. M. Groves, *Financing Government*, Holt, 1939, p. 135.
[22] National Resources Committee, *Urban Planning and Land Policies*, p. 305.

through an income tax. Building would be doubly encouraged becau
the tax on land would keep values down and make land easier to acquir
and elimination of taxes on improvements would also make building le
difficult. Moreover, speculation in land values would be discouraged, an
such procedures would be much more justifiable and equitable tha
present homestead exemption and related measures of granting relief i
urban homeowners.[23]

The most outstanding example of differential taxation in the Unite
States is found in Pittsburgh. Land is taxed at rates twice as high as tho:
on improvements. Proponents of the graded-tax plan claim that the ta
has stimulated building and decreased the burden on homeowners, whi
opponents claim that the large volume of construction in Pittsburg
during the interwar period cannot be attributed to the graded-tax la\
and that the city has no advantage over other cities. Furthermore, the
claim that rents in Pittsburgh have been higher than in other cities.
Similar differentiation of taxes on urban land and improvements is foun(
in varying degrees, in numerous cities of western Canada, Australia, Ne
Zealand, South Africa, and other countries.[25]

OTHER IMPROVEMENTS

Numerous other improvements should be made in the assessment an
administration of urban real-estate taxes. For example, the number (
assessing units should be reduced, assessors should be appointed on
qualified basis, and more scientific and uniform methods of apprais:
should be established. Improvements in organization and administratio
of city government, along the lines of the city manager plan, would d
much to improve the efficiency and to reduce the cost of municipal ser\
ices. These improvements, together with elimination of the abuse (
special assessments, use of the graded-tax plan, well-planned, effectivel
administered zoning ordinances, building and sanitary codes, and relate(
land-use control devices, would do much to make cities better places i
which to live and would reduce urban tax delinquency to a minimum.

REFERENCES FOR FURTHER READING

Barlowe, Raleigh, *Administration of Tax-Reverted Lands in the Lake State*
Michigan Agricultural Experiment Station Technical Bulletin 225, 1951.
Dorau, H. B., and Hinman, A. G., *Urban Land Economics,* The Macmilla(
Company, New York, 1928, Chaps. XXII and XXIII.

[23] *Ibid.,* p. 306.
[24] Thomas C. McMahon, "Pittsburgh Graded Tax on Buildings," *Proceedings of th
National Tax Association, 1929,* pp. 133–140; and Edward F. Daume, "A Critical Analy
sis of the Operation of the Pittsburgh Graded Tax Law," *Annals of the America(
Academy of Political and Social Science,* March, 1930, pp. 145–156.
[25] National Resources Committee. *op. cit.,* Vol. II, p. 307.

Fairchild, F. R., et al. *Forest Taxation in the United States,* U.S. Department of Agriculture, Miscellaneous Publication 218, Government Printing Office, Washington, D.C., October, 1935.

Groves, H. M., *Financing Government,* Henry Holt and Company, Inc., New York, 1939, Chap. XVII.

National Resources Committee, *Urban Planning and Land Policies,* Report of the Urbanism Committee, Government Printing Office, Washington, D.C., 1939, Vol. II, pp. 283–311.

U.S. Department of Agriculture, *Taxes Levied on Farm Property in the United States,* Agricultural Research Service, Washington, D.C., Statistical Bulletin 189, August, 1956.

Wehrwein, George S., and Barlowe, Raleigh, *The Forest Crop Law and Private Forest Taxation in Wisconsin,* Wisconsin State Conservation Department, Madison, Bulletin 519.

part **IV**

PROPERTY IN LAND

LAND APPROPRIATION
SOCIAL CONTROL OF LANDED PROPERTY
AGRICULTURAL LAND TENURE AND TENANCY
TENURE IN NONAGRICULTURAL LAND

chapter 15

LAND APPROPRIATION

SOCIAL STRUCTURES AND PROCESSES OF LAND APPROPRIATION

Human Ecology—Social Interaction—Property as an Institution—Characteristics and Attributes of Property—Types of Property—Property and Other Institutions

EVOLUTION OF PROPERTY RIGHTS IN LAND

Theories of the Origin of Private Property—Landed Property in Primitive Societies—Landed Property in the Ancient World—Landed Property in the Feudal-Manorial System—The Enclosure Movement—Landed Property in Modern Societies

LAND AS PROPERTY

Surface, Subsurface, and Supersurface Rights in Land—Waning Social Importance of Modern Land Ownership—"Land Hunger"—The Landowner's Role in Modern Society

MEN SHARE land for use and profit according to the prevailing culture. Some cultures permit completely free and uncontrolled use of land by all who express a desire for it, and others strictly regulate all actions that affect land.

SOCIAL STRUCTURES AND PROCESSES OF LAND APPROPRIATION

Groups have survived only when they have defined expected individual behavior rather specifically, achieving order in their societies through communication, imitation, suggestion, and other processes of social interaction. The ecological processes that establish through competition the relation of man to his habitat help to shape the structure of society. These

315

two types of processes are of great importance in determining the relation of man and his culture to land.

HUMAN ECOLOGY

How men and their cultures assume characteristic patterns of distribution in space and time is the field of human ecology.[1] Because of relative scarcity, the selective distribution of men and their cultures on land is highly competitive. An impersonal competition for existence occurs among human bengs just as it does among plants and animals. Competition also occurs between man and other forms of life in his environment, but it is most ruthless between man and man.

The ecological distribution of men is distinguished from that of animals by the development of a social structure. This structure can be built only by human beings, because no other form of life has access through language to a social heritage. Man's relation to his environment is therefore characterized by both a biological and social motivation. The first operates through ecology; the second, through processes of social interaction.

The ecological processes through which competition operates are dynamic forces of change causing continual adjustment of population numbers and forms, and adaptation of the institutional structure. A knowledge of these processes is very useful in explaining the migrations of people and their distribution on the land.

Sociologists suggest five major processes of human ecology: *concentration, centralization, segregation, invasion,* and *succession. Concentration* is the process by which certain areas become densely populated. This may occur where natural sources of food supply are readily won through a minimum of effort. Huge concentrations of people have occurred in India, where the soil provides year-round food for large concentrations of people. On the other hand, there are many regions of active concentration such as the maritime coasts in northern countries where the climate and soil are less bountiful.

Here the rigors of climate and the frugality of nature originally required much ingenuity on the part of those people who were to survive. Passive enjoyment of the resources was not sufficient for such folk: they developed an intricate system of transportation, food storage, and distribution that eventually freed large numbers of the group for other pursuits. Urban communities of England, such as London or Birmingham, to which food is shipped from all corners of the world, illustrate active concentration. Areas of active concentration can use land in highly specialized ways, increasing the total productivity immensely.

Development of focal points dominating the hinterland is called *cen-*

[1] See especially R. D. McKenzie, "The Scope of Human Ecology," *Publications, American Sociological Society,* Vol. XX, pp. 141–154.

tralization. The focal points are the most active and sensitive spots where basic institutional services are located. They are the centers of transporation and communication to which other points look for leadership and direction. In the capitalistic world the metropolitan cities of New York, London, and Paris have long been the centers of dominance. Trade and the financial and cultural movements of subservient areas are channeled through these cities.

Every community exhibits the process of centralization—sometimes by the growth of cities, towns, or villages at a crossroads, and sometimes by a nodal string of towns along a railroad, like those so common in sparsely settled prairie or plains areas. The same process occurs in metropolitan areas where financial and downtown areas become centers of activity, and subcenters establish themselves in little knots through the city's periphery. The central sections are characterized by the highest land values, the greatest mobility of people, the most rigorous competition, and the most rapidly changing institutional patterns.

The clustering of like units is the process of *segregation*. Homogeneity in ideals, customs, and institutions promotes similar uses of land within these units. This is impressively illustrated by the segregation of ethnic groups into homogeneous communities such as the Black Belt of Negroes, "Little Italy" in Chicago, or the Mennonite communities of North Dakota and western Canada. Segregation occurs in areas of occupational specialization around specific resources, like the mining sections of the intermountain United States, or New England's small-scale manufacturing communities with miniature water power facilities.

When people are on the move, or new resources, methods, or products are discovered, the process of *invasion* occurs. Communities and institutions are living, growing things, subject to new movements at all times. A dramatic illustration of invasion was the phenomenon of the gold rush, where people from all walks of life moved rapidly into the gold fields. The same general pattern is exemplified by the development of new resources in the Columbia River Basin of the State of Washington, where the building of the Grand Coulee Dam attracts settlers and permits the establishment of intensely farmed irrigation units.

The process by which the original land use is displaced by a new one is that of *succession*. It is the equilibrium occurring after invasion, which establishes the pattern of distribution of men and their culture on land. In a gold rush, for instance, the entering people displace old structures and land uses with new ones, in the process of finding temporary shelter, setting up mining machinery, hotels, gambling houses, and new communication and transportation systems.

Several stages of displacement and succession can be discerned in the Columbia River development. A temporary city grew up overnight to house workers at the dam site. When the dam construction was completed, the intensely active mobile population catering to the needs of engineers and laborers disappeared, and the needs of an irrigation agriculture were supplied by fewer people and a more stable set of institutions. The outlying agricultural population, the transportation network, and the whole landscape were changed in type and distribution. Such a process of succession realigns the social structure and especially affects the institutions of property in ways of great interest to the land economist.

These ecological processes, the result of human competition for the appropriation and use of land resources, help to explain the past changes in the temporal and spatial relations of men and to indicate changes likely to occur in the future. Through the interaction of these dynamic elements, man and his institutions are continually driving toward an equilibrium. The processes of human ecology explain the migration, density, and distribution of men and give direction to many human aims and ideas.

SOCIAL INTERACTION

The ecological framework is given life and consciousness by the processes of social interaction in which the common practices and experiences of men give rise to the loyalties, the hates, the conflict of ideas that are characteristic of society. Ecological action, largely unconscious and impersonal, distributes men and their institutions, but social interaction is responsible for group adaptation, invention, and "progress." Social interaction builds a society out of folkways, customs, mores, and institutions, through the penetration of mind by mind and the interchange of group attitudes.

Institutions (one of the most primary of which is property) may be defined as well-established social structures within which men do collectively the things that seem right and proper, in regard to some fundamental interest of life. Institutions can be distinguished from other forms of long-established practices by the following four characteristics: (1) a common set of *attitudes* held by all persons in the group, which are directed toward gaining satisfaction for basic needs; (2) *symbols,* which arouse interest and by which people can be made to do things as a group that they would not do as individuals; (3) *physical objects,* which tend to give it reality; and (4) *rigidity, permanence,* and *form,* which are attained by written or oral documents, laws and creeds.[2]

A *social structure* is a set of behavior patterns, accepted within a society, which individuals in that society learn to use. Legal codes, the leader-follower relationship, and respect for the rights of others are examples of

[2] Cf. F. Stuart Chapin, *Contemporary American Institutions,* Harper, New York, 1935, p. 15. For various definitions and explanations, see particularly E. C. Hughes, *The Chicago Real Estate Board: The Growth of an Institution,* The Society for Social Research of the University of Chicago, Series II, monograph No. 1, 1931.

LAND APPROPRIATION 319

ıch patterns. No one structure determines the entire behavior of any ıdividual. For each fundamental interest he has, the individual's action ₃ guided by a different institutional mechanism. It would be highly im-.robable that a group of students would begin a dance in the middle of n afternoon class in land economics, but quite probable that they might .repare after class to attend a dance in their student union building; for ach institution developed around education and around recreation has unique code of behavior recognized and conformed to by the individual.

Institutions tend to be relatively permanent; they draw upon particular ndividuals but are not dependent on them. The particular individual is he "carrier" of the institution, for his own mind retains institutional be-ıavor patterns, either consciously or unconsciously; but the pattern is so .mnipresent in the group that particular persons are unnecessary to the :ontinuance of the institution. Persons cannot belong to an institution,)ut they can belong to a group or an association, the objective counter-)arts of institutions, like the church or the family.

Knowledge of the development of institutions is essential to an under-tanding of their functions. Living in groups forces men to develop rules)f behavior. Early in the history of society, sheer force gave place to folk-vays, or behavior that was "proper." Certain folkways eventually became ?ssential to the welfare of society and grew more rigid. For instance, pre-ıistoric hunters had to hide or guard their meat. Groups that formed the ıabit of respecting individual rights to the hunt or the harvest survived. These rights later became sanctified into mores; and those who failed to respect the mores were eliminated from the group. Finally these mores ?volved into the institution of property, under which each member of the group well knew how he should act with respect to the tools of other men ınd the fruits of other men's labor.[3]

In "high civilizations," institutions may seem to have been rationally ınvented or intended. They may be partly enacted by common consent or the power of government. Many characteristics of modern property are a part of the social heritage, but many others are the result of current effort to force certain desired habits upon the social group through legislation or rules of procedure. The recognition of this fact is essential, if we are to achieve a social system that can adapt itself to the most desirable aims of society.

[3] ". . . Institutions . . . take shape in the mores, growing by the instinctive efforts by which the mores are produced. Then the efforts, through long use, become definite and specific. Property, marriage, and religion are the most primary institutions. They began in folkways. They became customs. They developed into mores by the addition of some philosophy of welfare, however crude. Then they were made more definite and specific as regards the rules, the prescribed acts, and the apparatus to be employed. This produced a structure and the institution was complete." William Graham Sumner, *Folkways: A Study of the Sociological Importance of Usages, Manners, Customs, Mores, and Morals*, Ginn, 1906, Chap. I.

PROPERTY AS AN INSTITUTION

Property is the most important institution conditioning land utilization. Land cannot be a limiting or strategic factor where there is a super-abundance of it, and property in land exists only where there is an economic scarcity of land. Property therefore is the one all-inclusive institution conditioning the economic processes of land utilization. It determines the rights and duties of the individual in utilizing a given parcel of land or in dealing with others who may utilize land.

Property, marriage, and religion are considered the primary institutions, but emphasis is placed on property in this chapter, for the reasons given, although it is true that other institutions help to shape the institution of property itself and to make up the cultural environment within which man operates. Even though property is influenced by this institutional and cultural environment, the situations and relationships with which land economics is concerned are those which arise directly or indirectly out of the relationships of rights and duties occurring within the institution of property, as it exists in the cultural environment. Moreover, most social improvement projects involve the substitution of some more consciously social form of control over private property and individual freedom of contract. Thus, the possibility of improving human living through changes in the organization of want-satisfying activity in the utilizaiton of land resources centers around changes in the property institution.

Lands of certain desired production or location qualities are scarce enough so that protected rights and duties must be established in connection with their use if order is to exist. The concept of *property,* which gives persons or groups a protected right in land, thus "personalizing" it, has been found essential under conditions of scarcity where human labor is incorporated into land to produce economic goods and services. Property rights in land are the basis of other rights—the right to lease, the right to use, or the right to sell—and in this sense condition land use and the value, price, income, cost, and related economic and social considerations involved.

The word "proprietas" is adopted from the Latin noun *proprietas* ("in accordance with custom"), but property has passed beyond the stage of mere custom. Like other institutions, it has been modified from time to time, when necessary, in order to meet successive crises. Institutions that do not or cannot change with changing times are said to be coated too thickly with the "cake of custom"—that is, to have lost their capacity to act or to be useful in the world of reality. Property today, therefore, especially as it applies to land, implies certain things and implies action patterns which property in ancient times did not.

Because of the predominance of property as an institutional force conditioning land utilization, it is essential that the student of land economics understand the characteristics and attributes of property and the stages through which landed property has evolved to its present status. The nature and scope of the problems in land utilization with which land economics is concerned arise out of the property institution, because it determines how and when men will utilize land.

CHARACTERISTICS AND ATTRIBUTES OF PROPERTY

The property institution regulates relationships of men to material things, distinguishing the belongings of one man from those of another. A man may utilize or dispose of his property, or of the products of his property, under the right of contract (the means by which a property owner enters into transactions with others, pledging to do or abstain from doing certain things in accordance with laws and regulations); or his property rights may pass to the next generation by *inheritance*.

Value is a universal attribute of property, because economic goods or services (which must possess utility and scarcity) are valuable, and exclusive property rights in such goods have value to the owner. Such rights may be sold or leased "for value received," or they may be used and controlled to secure to the owner a flow of income or benefits; and these rights may be restricted by the governing power, or may be very broad. The concept of property varies as widely as the societies where it is found; that is, its meanings depend upon its use and the current cultural development of the people who use it.

During medieval times, "property" came to mean "a feudal privilege or relationship." This emphasized the essential nature of property as a reflection of the dealings of men arising from their relations to things.[4] Property does not exist until human control is established over things, and only a thing that has three essential characteristics can be made property. (1) It must be capable of satisfying a human want, in which case it is called a good or service; (2) it must be capable of appropriation; and (3) it must be so limited in supply that some human wants must go unsatisfied—that is, there must be a scarcity of the good or service, otherwise it would be a free good. Property rights are established only in economic goods or services, since there would be no reason to appropriate a valueless thing.

A good definition of property is the right to control (use, lease, and dispose of) an economic good or service subject to the limitations established by laws and regulations.[5] There are three components of this con-

[4] R. T. Ely, *Property and Contract in Their Relations to the Distribution of Wealth,* Macmillan, 1914, Vol. I, p. 96.

[5] Property has been defined as "a conditional equity in the valuables of the community." (*Encyclopaedia of the Social Sciences,* Vol. XII, p. 529.) Definitions given by Blackstone and Ely emphasize the feature of exclusive dominion. For example, Blackstone once called property "that sole and despotic dominion which one man claims and

cept of property—the *owner*, who exercises control over the good or service, subject to limitations established by laws and regulations; the *object of property*, which is the thing controlled; and the *sovereign state*, community, group, or other social organism protecting the owner in his rights over the property object. Property is, then, *a conditional control existing at the pleasure of the governing group*, which may be the state or, in less formally organized societies, the family, community, or tribe.

If rights to control or use an economic good or service were absolute or exclusive, they would prevent any limitations or qualifications upon such control or use. A social aspect of property rights implies a certain social control and an evolutionary flexibility in the property concept for the purpose of meeting changing needs.

Each group develops its unique and changing ways of using natural resources, of organizing production, of appropriating wealth, and of carrying on the other activities that satisfy its needs; and property as an institution exists because it fulfills one of the primary human needs—the desire for security.[6] The owner's equity in a property object, however, remains definitely conditional. It is conditioned by current conventions, attitudes, and group habits, changing with cultural, technological, and biological variations in the society, whether such changes occur in a few years or over a long period of time.[7]

---

exercises over external things of the world, in total exclusion of the right of any other individual in the universe." (Blackstone's *Commentaries on the Laws of England*, Book II, Chap. 1.) Ely defines property as the exclusive right to control an economic good (see his *Property and Contract*, p. 101). However, these definitions must be modified because neither property rights (see *Munn vs. Illinois*, 94 U.S. 113, 124, 125) nor contract rights (see *Allgeyer vs. Louisiana*, 165 U.S. 578, 591) are absolute or exclusive. "Government cannot exist if the citizen may at will use his property to the detriment of his fellows or exercise his freedom of contract to work them harm. Equally fundamental with the private right is that of the public to regulate it in the common interest." (*Nebbia vs. New York*, 291 U.S. 502.)

[6] Sociologists have grouped the major human wants into four kinds: (1) desire for new experiences, (2) desire for security, (3) desire for recognition by one's fellow men, and (4) desire to achieve a response from others in order to develop one's personality and ego. A society's way of satisfying these major needs fixes the conditions under which wealth (material objects that have economic utility) may be appropriated. R. E. Park and E. W. Burgess, *Introduction to the Science of Sociology*, University of Chicago Press, 2d ed., 1924, pp. 489–490.

[7] "The power to promote the general welfare is inherent in government, and according to the Constitution, the United States possesses the power, as do the states in their sovereign capacity, touching on all subjects jurisdiction of which is not surrendered to the Federal Government. These correlative rights, that of the citizen to exercise exclusive dominance over property and freely to contract about his affairs, and that of the state to regulate the use of property and the conduct of business, are always in collision. No exercise of the private right can be imagined which will not in some respect, however slight, affect the public; no exercise of the legislative prerogative to regulate the conduct of the citizen which will not to some extent abridge his liberty or affect his property. But, subject only to constitutional restraint, the private right must yield to the public need." (*Nebbia vs. New York*, 291 U.S. 502.)

The Fifth Amendment, in the field of federal activity, and the Fourteenth, in connection with state action, condition the exercise of the admitted power to regulate private property by providing that the end shall be accomplished by methods consistent with due process. The guaranty of due process is that laws shall not be unreasonable, arbitrary, or capricious, and that the means selected shall bear a real and substantial relation to the object sought to be attained.

Regulations valid for one sort of business or in any given circumstances may be invalid for other sorts or for the same business under other circumstances. The reasonableness of each regulation depends upon the relevant facts.[8] Although the Fourteenth Amendment extends protection to aliens as well as to citizens,[9] a state may for adequate reasons of policy exclude aliens altogether from the use and occupancy of land.[10] There is no closed class or category of businesses affected with the public interest. The phrase "affected with the public interest" merely means that for adequate reason the business or property is subject to control for the public good.

There can be no doubt but that on proper occasion and by appropriate measures the state may regulate a business in any of its aspects. The legislature is primarily the judge of the necessity of a given law or regulation, and the courts merely decide whether the laws passed have a reasonable relation to a proper legislative purpose and are neither arbitrary nor discriminatory. Under these conditions, the requirements of due process are satisfied provided there are no constitutional restrictions. Thus, a state is free to adopt whatever economic policy may be reasonably deemed to promote public welfare and to enforce that policy by legislation adapted to its purpose.[11]

The peculiar importance of property rights lies in the fact that they are the basis of other important rights. However, none of these rights can be final, irrevocable, and "inalienable," especially in a modern highly commercialized machine civilization. Through social control, property rights must be modified from time to time, so that property may improve the general welfare rather than enrich too greatly the fortunate or aggressive few.

The limitation of property rights by society affects both their *quantity*

---

[8] *Ibid.*

[9] *Yick Wo* vs. *Hopkins*, 118 U.S. 356, 369.

[10] *Terrace* vs. *Thompson*, 263 U.S. 197; *Webb* vs. *O'Brien*, 263 U.S. 313.

[11] "With the wisdom of the policy adopted, with the adequacy or practicability of the law adopted to forward it, the courts are both incompetent and unauthorized to deal. . . . Times without number we have said that the legislature is primarily the judge of the necessity of such an enactment, that every possible presumption is in favor of its validity, and that though the court may hold views inconsistent with the wisdom of the law, it may not be annulled unless palpably in excess of legislative power." (*Nebbia* vs. *New York*, 291 U.S. 502.)

and *quality*. What goods can be owned privately, and which are reserved for public ownership? What may an individual do with his property? What a man may do with the property which he is permitted to own is as important as the type of property he may own.

Society has usually not desired to abrogate the right of private property in order to reduce the waste and dangers of uncontrolled private property in land, but has preferred to exert necessary control through modifying property privileges. Though in some cases abrogation of private property rights in certain goods has been necessary, in others more restrictions upon utilization, lease, and sale practices have been sufficient, for the time being, to achieve the desired ends.

TYPES OF PROPERTY

Property may be divided into classes of owners (property subjects) or of property objects. By subject, property may be classed as *private, public, group,* and *qualified*. By object, it is divided into *realty* (real estate) and *personalty* (personal property); by law, on the basis of relative mobility. Since land is the most immobile property object, landed properties are called "real estate," and most things attached to the land—buildings of a permanent and fixed character, trees, minerals, etc.—are also classed as realty.[12]

Private property exists when the right to an economic good or service is vested in a private person, either "natural" or "artificial." A corporation is legally an "artificial person," with the same property rights as a "natural person" or ordinary private individual.[13] The property of quasi-public corporations like privately owned railroads and utility companies should not be confused with public property, since it is only private property

[12] Property objects may also be classified as (1) rights of control over corporeal things (tangible, material commodities), (2) rights of control over personal services, and (3) property in relation to persons and things—what might be termed intellectual property, such as patents, trademarks, copyrights, and good will (Ely, *op. cit.*, p. 274). Commons classifies property objects into (1) corporeal (tangible), (2) incorporeal (credits, including proprietary stocks or equity shares in modern corporations), and (3) intangible ("the present value of future bargaining power of capitalists"—that is, good will and associated property values). H. M. Groves, "Commons' Theory of Reasonable Value as Applied to Taxation," in *Property Taxes*, Tax Policy League, 1940, p. 175.

[13] In recent years, the development of corporate business in the United States has caused an increase in the amount of property owned or controlled by corporations. Partnership property is intermediate between strictly individual property and corporate or collective property, and this step has been omitted in the United States in most instances. The economic complement of the mass production factory or machine is the corporation which, through the issuance of stock shares or equities, accumulates under one management the large amounts of capital needed to finance such large-scale, commercialized production; and technological processes have developed too rapidly, under modern finance capitalism, to allow as much use of partnership property as might be logically expected in a more gradual evolution of business organization and production toward corporate enterprise.

subjected to strict government regulation because of the peculiar position of such enterprises in relation to the public welfare.

Public property exists where the right to control an economic good or service is vested in formally organized governmental units (which are classed as legal or artificial persons), such as school district, township, city, county, state, or Federal governments. The rights of Federal and state governments to own property are established in the Federal Constitution. Political subdivisions of the states, however, such as counties, cities and towns, school districts, and townships, may also own property under authority granted them by state governments representing the people of the state. A wide range of variation exists among the states in degree of control granted to political subdivisions.

Group property occurs when the exclusive right to control an economic good or service is vested in an association of individuals or in a community, tribe, or family bound together by some common loyalty or interest. Such associations or communities or groups must be distinguished from and are usually smaller than a formally organized governmental unit, as we understand government.

Common property is a well-known form of group property. In the case of common property, individuals can use the property "in common," or to the exclusion of others who are not members of the group or do not meet qualifications established by the group who have "rights in common" to the property. Modern public property differs from common property in that no individual has exclusive rights to use or control such property except as authorized or granted by governmental officials elected, as representatives of the people, to operate the government.

The common pastures of early New England, best known of which is the Boston Common, were examples of common property. Ordinarily, those owning land and cattle in the surrounding township area had the right to use the common; those who did not own such surrounding lands could not graze cattle with their neighbors' on the plot designated as the common.

Common property, in the strict sense of the word, does not exist in the United States today, because of the widespread tendency to establish ownership in some natural person or to develop an artificial legal entity such as the modern corporation. The old New England commons cannot today be classed as common property, since they are owned by the town and are therefore public property. Where a formally organized unit of government exists, property rights common to the members or residents of that political unit must now be classified as public property, not common property.

Grounds and buildings of a private corporation, such as a golf club, which are used in common by the members of such clubs, cannot properly be classed as common property, since the club itself is legally merely a private corporation or "artificial person." This form of private property may be referred to as *property in severalty*.

The term "joint property" has been used by various writers to distinguish a form of collective ownership by partners, families, clubs, religious fraternities, or sibs.[14] In those cases where the landholding group and the economic group coincide, there is no distinction between joint property and common property, but where they do not coincide, the difference in territory and membership involved distinguishes them. Basically, however, they are similar types of property under the general heading of group property.

The term "qualified property" is sometimes used to denote "a temporary or special interest liable to be totally divested on the happening of some particular event" [15] in contrast with full property, which denotes a "full and complete" title and dominion over the property object. This term has been found useful because of the special difficulties pertaining to private appropriation of certain kinds of property objects. Fish and game are frequently classed as qualified property on the grounds that, while they are generally considered the property of the state, they are really controlled by the state "in trust for the public," not owned by the state.

This quesion of ownership is primarily an academic one, and of little practical significance; and to define "qualified property" as that which is somewhere between free goods (in which individuals have no legal rights at all) and full property (in which individuals have many rights) does not clarify the question. All private property rights are conditional and not absolute, since society may at any time abolish certain privileges of private property and may even remove property objects from the domain of private property. Literally, then, all property is "qualified."

In a modern economic society with formally organized governmental units, only private property and public property have much economic significance, though at various stages of civilization the terms "common," "joint," and "qualified" property have been very useful. There are all grades and qualities of private property and various degrees of public regulation short of outright public ownership. Even in the case of publicly owned property, great variation occurs in the use that private individuals may make of such property.

PROPERTY AND OTHER INSTITUTIONS

In a great many ways, the appropriation of land through property rights is significantly influenced by such other institutions as the family and the church. Agricultural land appropriation is especially influenced

[14] R. H. Lowie, *Primitive Societies*, Liveright, 1920, p. 206.
[15] Kent's *Commentaries on American Law*, 14th ed., Vol. II, p. 348.

y family relationships, though urban or forest land appropriation is ominated much less by these factors. Family loyalties are often identified ery closely with farms; and the resulting inertia to migration materially ffects land use, size of operating units, and sensitivity to price response.

Where family bonds are strong, and where custom demands that certain nembers of the family shall inherit the property rights of the father, the mall units that result from splitting farms among successive heirs give ise to serious problems. Programs of directed resettlement have often been eriously impeded by the unwillingness of families to seek new economic pportunities when the original farm has become submarginal.

Religious codes are responsible for the growth of many unique uses of and. Even in the modern cultures, where religion has been least influ- ntial in land appropriation, may be found block-settled communities of hakers, Dukhobors, Mennonites, or Mormons. Each of these groups has special pattern of land use. The last three are characterized by a village ype of agriculture entirely unlike that in adjacent and similar areas.

Closely related to the institutions of the family and religion is the insti- ution of education, whose primary function is the transference of aims, deals, and common practices from one generation to the next. Education s therefore an important means of maintaining the continuity of society nd keeping the rights of property in land within fairly predictable ounds from period to period.

In contrast to its continuity function, modern education provides a nedium of social interaction in which invention and innovation are leveloped and problems are met and solved. Education is an ideational rossroads, from which civilization advances to meet its new problems.

EVOLUTION OF PROPERTY RIGHTS IN LAND

Property, as we have noted, is the most important institutional influ- nce upon land utilization through its effect on distribution of income or eturns from land. Obviously, property in land did not arise until methods f utilizing land were such that incorporation of human labor was in- olved, or until there was a scarcity of lands of certain location or pro- luction qualities. When this stage was reached, the forms taken by property in land varied with the culture and the stage of social develop- nent of the people involved. Moreover, the nature of property rights in and has varied considerably during its evolution among different peoples, nd the privileges that property in land now conveys to the owner are quite different in various parts of the world.

Because of the basic place that property holds in land economics, the tudent should be familiar with the explanations which have been made f the origins of private property in general; with the stages in the evolu- ion of landed property, from primitive to modern times; and with the

present status and trend of private property rights in land, compared wit
those of property in capital goods. This historical treatment gives th
student a more comprehensive understanding of the important cha
acteristics of the property institution, of the problems arising because c
the utilization of land resources within such an institution, and of a
proaches that might be used in solving such problems.

THEORIES OF THE ORIGIN OF PRIVATE PROPERTY

Much has been written to justify private property on philosophical c
natural grounds, and many theories have been propounded to explai
how private property originated.[16] In appraising these theories, it shoul
be pointed out that private property is a man-made device, related t
group survival and demanded by expediency. Since property is a cond
tional grant by the state or the sovereign unit, giving the owner certai
protected although not absolute rights, private property must serve som
desirable ends or the state would withdraw its assent and abolish it. Cons
quently, any adequate explanation of the origin of private property mu
justify it on social grounds. The general welfare theory is now general
considered the correct theory of the origin of private property.[17]

LANDED PROPERTY IN PRIMITIVE SOCIETIES

It is generally conceded that private property developed first in certai
personal possessions, and later in certain types of land, often buryin
grounds, wells, and springs. Burying grounds often had special religiou
importance to primitive peoples, and wells and springs in arid areas wer
strategic and relatively scarce.

Intensive specialization or cultivation of the lands seldom develope
in the earliest stages of civilization. Hunting tribes tended to regard lan
as held by the local group in a vague sort of common or joint tenur
though tribal boundaries were often defined rather exactly and protecte
against outsiders. In some parts of Australia, an especially strong sens
of group proprietorship strengthened by religious precepts bound th
tribe in "indissoluble bonds" to its native soil; and ancient Hebraic la

[16] Ely lists and discusses in some detail nine theories, in the following order: (1) th
natural rights theory, (2) the social contract or social compact theory, (3) the huma
nature theory, (4) the occupancy theory, (5) the labor theory, (6) the theistic concep
of property, (7) the robbery and violence theory, (8) the legal theory, and (9) th
general welfare theory. See Ely, *op. cit.*, Vol. II, Chap. XXII.

[17] As Ely says, "The very words of this theory point to the permanent basis of prop
erty in social utility, and they indicate the nature of its evolution. . . . Propert
exists because it promotes the general welfare, and by the general welfare its develop
ment is directed. . . . It is a theory of social evolution, because as society is in flu
property can accomplish its ends only by a corresponding evolution. It is a legal theor
because property in itself implies law. . . . At the same time, the words used t
describe the theory show that law cannot be arbitrary." (*Ibid.*, p. 456.)

taught that land belonged to God and temporary human "ownership" should be considered in the light of a lease.

Some pastoral peoples, feeling that land itself had only "derivative values,"[18] concentrated private property rights in their animals. Tillage societies varied widely in their ideas about property, but many (especially in the Americas) felt the land to be a common "inalienable" possession of which the tribe members enjoyed only the usufruct for a set term or during use. A form of feudal tenure existed in Africa, where the rulers usually had some sort of superior right in the land.[19] In so far as a trend can be observed, land tenure seems to have evolved from tenures in common or by groups, with extensive cultivation, to more individual tenures and more intensive cultivation.[20]

LANDED PROPERTY IN THE ANCIENT WORLD

In the ancient world, forms of landed property known in primitive societies were modified, rather than discarded. Usually they became more regularized into formal systems, sometimes with great complexity and variation. Poorly integrated "village economies" were customary, with here and there a city functionally more like an oversized town than the modern financial metropolis. The most important trend of the period was the Roman change from small farms to large slave-run estates, and then to estates with free tenants, an innovation that foreshadowed later European feudalism.[21]

LANDED PROPERTY IN THE FEUDAL-MANORIAL SYSTEM

The chief reason for the rise of the feudal-manorial system was the feeling of insecurity that the average individual experienced because of the lack of a well-established system of law and order after the decline of Roman civilization. In this new system the individual gave up many of his personal rights in exchange for the physical and economic protection afforded by group or village life and the self-sufficing activities of the manors.

The feudal system set up a complex pattern of interdependent rights

[18] Carl Brinkman, "Land Tenure," in *Encyclopaedia of the Social Sciences*, Vol. V, p. 76.

[19] Much of this discussion of property rights among primitive peoples has been adapted from Lowie, *op. cit.*, Chap. IX.

[20] Much has been written on the subject of the development of property rights in land among primitive societies. Much vague terminology—for instance, in regard to such terms as "common" or "joint"—has been used, and accurate records of these early societies are not available, so that generalizations are difficult to make. It is probably true in most cases that ideas of property acquired increasing refinement, detail, and complexity, or underwent "progressive particularization," just as man's goods and machines and literature grew more complex with increasing civilization and culture.

[21] For a more complete discussion of this period, see N. S. B. Gras, *A History of Agriculture in Europe and America*, Crofts, 1940.

and duties of protection and obedience affecting landholders. There ar
three chief types of tenure—(1) possessions in *allodium* (lands outside th
feudal system, passed down in the same family from early times, throug
inheritance); (2) possessions in *villein* or *servile* tenures (where th
usufruct was enjoyed on condition of rent or service payments to the lor
of the manor); [22] or (3) possession in *fief* (enjoyment of usufruct on cond
tion of knightly services, as distinguished from *villein* service).[23] Comple
overlapping tenures developed, with the land belonging, in the last ana
ysis, to the king, though in fact each domain or "seigneury" resembled
petty state, with little actual centralization of power or ownership i
the kingdom.

The variety and complexity of these tenure arrangements gave rise to
managerial or bailiff class, especially in Germany.[24] In this period th
Church became a great landed proprietor; and church lands, generall
exploited like lay lands, were managed by the *advocatus* (similar in fun(
tion to the bailiff or manager on lay lands). Servile or villein tenants o
church lands possessed fewer rights, ordinarily, than those on lay lands
but the powers of most lords were very broad.

The term "exploitation," originating in this period, signified the lord'
right to take revenue and services from the peasants, yielding them i
return only possession and a measure of protection. Furthermore, as cen
tral sovereignty became weaker or fell into partial disuse, property right
in a measure replaced it, and most types of tenure became hereditary.

The manorial-feudal system began to decline in strength after 130(
The rising town economy afforded a market and offered tenants altern

[22] These rent or service payments have been classified in various ways. Rights t(
payments or services that the lord might claim were classified by Herbert as (1) servi
tudes, (2) payments or services rendered in money or in kind, (3) seigneurial monop
olies, and (4) jurisdictional rights. (Sydney Herbert, *The Fall of Feudalism in France*
Stokes, 1920, Chap. I.) Another classification of rents demanded of manorial tenant
included (1) *redevances*, (2) *banalities*, (3) *prestations*, and (4) *corvees*. *Redevances* wer(
general or recurrent charges paid either in money or produce; or they might be charge
on certain acts—that is, toll and commerce fees, or inheritance charges. *Banalitie*
(actually a form of redevance) were monopoly charges originating in the lord's powe
of proclamation (the "ban"), and included charges for the use of the lord's mills, forests
or weights and measures, and certain court charges in connection with his power o
justice. *Prestations* included the lord's right of seizure, his right of credit (usuall
limited) and his right of demanding food and shelter from his tenants for himself anc
his attendants. *Corvees* were rights to the labor of the tenant. (Charles Seignobos
The Feudal Regime, Holt, 1926, Chap. I.)

[23] There were various types of fiefs. One might be a "tenant-in-chief," holding lanc
direct from the king, or a "mesne tenant," holding it from some intermediate lord
Tenants might perform "knight-service," or under "free socage" tenure perform peace
ful services or pay money rents. Special duties (often trivial or nominal) at the king'
court were assigned to tenants in "grand or petty serjeanty"; and a church might be a
tenant by "frankalmoign" or free alms, performing services for the welfare of the
donor's soul. (H. W. C. Davis, *Medieval England*, Clarendon Press, 1928.)

[24] J. W. Thompson, *Feudal Germany*, University of Chicago Press, 1928.

ive opportunities in the form of the professions, trade, and, later, in
manufacturing. The lords of the manors found returns growing insuffi-
ient to meet disbursements, and desired cash, rather than payment of
oods in kind. This caused an increase in the use of *quit rents* (rents paid
by the tenant to be quit of a given service). A decline in the value of
money made the old fixed rentals and other fixed dues insignificant. Mili-
ary obligations were generally abolished, and the other obligations that
emained were so slight that "virtual free proprietorship was imper-
eptibly established." [25]
The Black Death greatly reduced the labor supply in the fourteenth
entury and caused a rise in wages and prices. While the manorial lords
were becoming more and more unable to meet competition, the peasants,
with increasing alternative ways of earning a living, revolted against the
manorial system. Serfdom diminished and wages remained higher. These
developments were accompanied by the enclosure movement.

THE ENCLOSURE MOVEMENT

The enclosure movement was a process of consolidating the small,
scattered plots of land in the open unenclosed fields of the manor into
more efficient fields. The manor had been characterized by the fact that
each tenant's holdings were usually distributed over various fields, often
separated from the holdings of other men by nothing more than a small
ridge of earth. In order to offset higher wage costs resulting from development of towns and industrial economy, to initiate new cultivation and
production methods, and to reduce disputes, these strips were consolidated and hedged or fenced.[26] However, the dispossessed serfs were forced
to migrate to the towns or add domestic weaving to their ordinary activities in an effort to make ends meet.

Prices and rents continued to rise, and manorial lords sold lands to the
more capable serfs or to people of the towns who desired land for speculative purposes. In this way a system of free proprietorship came into
existence, and owner operation or a system of renting was established.
Meanwhile, as trade and manufacture continued to develop and a commercialized system of production for sale and profit became established,
land tended to lose the status as the most widespread form of material
wealth, or the sole source of wealth production, which it had held during
the manorial period.

LANDED PROPERTY IN MODERN SOCIETIES

Changes and transitions in modern forms of landed property have
varied greatly among the different nations. In general, the privileges that

[25] Gras, *op. cit.*, p. 261.
[26] Chapter VII in Gras's *History of Agriculture* gives a rather detailed analysis of
the enclosure movement in England.

property in land give the owner correspond rather closely to the stage of economic development of society. In more backward or conservative regions, feudal principles of land tenure tend to resist the dissolving tendencies of modern finance capitalism and tend to establish complicated systems of exploitation by middlemen, and intricate credit relationships. The struggle for political influence between large estates and small units with more independent cultivators seems to have been fairly continuous.

From time to time, attempts to communalize land have been made, parallels usually being drawn between such attempts and the supposed "primitive communism" of early societies. However, in nations where modern capitalism has achieved its greatest development, free proprietorship has developed and landed property has, in general, been put on the same basis as personal property. In other words, the owner is a proprietor free of the necessity of paying rents to anyone; and he may sell the land, mortgage it, lease it, or do with it what owners of personal property may do with their possessions. This is the kind of land ownership so familiar to American students.

In Europe free proprietorship in land developed from the semi-manorial system. France set up a free proprietorship system at the time of the French Revolution. In Russia the Communist Revolution of 1917 offered the peasants an opportunity for private proprietorship in land, but in the following year all private property in land was abolished and the land passed to the use of those who would work it. Title was vested in the Soviet Republic and the use and management of the land was entrusted to the soviet organization of the district.[27] A later law, while maintaining state ownership, established the family's right to withdraw from soviet control and use the land, therefore, more or less as they desired.

Among primitive German tribes, land ownership carried with it certain responsibilities to the social group and to the family, which were above the rights of the individual owner. When a peasant died, it was understood as a matter of course that his estate was an indivisible whole and that it belonged to one child—either to the oldest or, where *ultimogeniture* (inheritance by the last-born, or the opposite of primogeniture) prevailed, to the youngest. Though the development of commerce and technology emancipated landowners from the earlier traditional views, giving the landowner legal freedom to dispose of his land as he saw fit, he continued to effect arrangements to assure the alliance of blood and soil from generation to generation.[28]

[27] *Ibid.*, p. 265.

[28] Heske states that this concept, which persisted into the nineteenth century, arose from traditional beliefs concerning the essential basis for a permanent existence of the race and the state. When it became legal for the peasant to dispose of his farm as he saw fit, he entered into a contract with his heir, turning the farm over to him and

Land systems might be divided into free and unfree proprietorships. Unfree systems are characterized by the fact that some group or individual stands between the individual cultivator and the state. In the case of an allodial holding, it was the undivided family; in communism, the village group; in the manorial-feudal system, the lord and, to some extent, the family and the village group.[29] Family and village are no longer strong land-tenure institutions in the more advanced nations, where the only rivals of free proprietorship are the landlords, who possess great economic strength, under modern finance capitalism.

Landlordism has undergone great changes in recent centuries. When the tenants of the manor became free proprietors, lords became landlords by retaining their demesne holdings (the lord's special property on the old manors), by purchasing more lands to rent out to tenant farmers, and by family marriages to build up huge estates. The Scully estate is a modern instance of this landlord concept transplanted from Ireland to the central United States. A detailed scheme of tenant obligations and landlord relationships has been worked out and stipulated in the leases.

In Mexico the attempt to substitute free proprietorship for the landlordism that had developed was the issue in the revolution which overthrew the Diaz government and brought about legislation limiting the size of holdings in some areas, according to the nature of the land.[30] In several European nations after World War I, and in numerous Southeast Asian nations after World War II, many land reforms were undertaken which had as their main purpose expropriation of the lords' estates and the distribution of these estates among small farmers, tradesmen, peasants, and others. For the most part, the tendency toward small proprietorships has been dominant and the landlords have had a rather serious time of it.

The landlord system, small proprietorships, and public holdings are at present contending for the dominant position in different parts of the world. Study will indicate that each has its merits as well as demerits, but different peoples may favor one or another, and undoubtedly each of the three systems, or modifications and combinations of the three, will continue to be used. Together they provide the basic alternatives for social change.

LAND AS PROPERTY

The relative permanence of land has caused the development of certain legal arrangements concerning property in land, such as inheritance of

---

determining what the residuary legatees were to receive, in this way assuring the continued alliance of family and land. (See Franz Heske, *German Forestry*, Yale University Press, 1938, pp. 231–233.)

[29] Gras, *op. cit.*, p. 265.

[30] *Ibid.*

land through *bequest* by will, *entail* (cutting off the heirs general an conferring the inheritance right on some particular heir or line descent), and *primogeniture*. Deed restrictions that bind future users the land for indefinite periods, and consequently reduce the land's us fulness, have been upheld as legal and proper rights of landed proper by the courts.

The perpetuity of land has given peculiar significance to the recordir of deeds or titles and the transfer of titles, mortgages, leases, liens, an other instruments pertaining to property rights in land. Because of th legal requirements for securing a clear title, these records have becom voluminous after the passage of many years, in the longer-settled cou tries or, in the United States, the older New England or Atlantic seaboar settlements. Even in the western United States a modern abstract of titl may be more than a hundred pages long, in spite of the relative youthfu ness of the area, since in this region mobility in land ownership has bee pronounced. The problem of maintaining an accurate record of all deed or contracts affecting title in lands becomes increasingly serious as th nation grows older.

SURFACE, SUBSURFACE, AND SUPERFACE RIGHTS IN LAND

Although property in land is measured, purchased, and sold on a spac basis, in terms of surface measurement, it does not always convey to th American owner all surface, subsurface, and supersurface rights. Owner ship of the surface of the earth may be quite different from ownership o minerals below the surface or of the air or space above. In fact, differen strata of the soil may be owned by different individuals. In China, fo example, where tenancy prevails in one form or another, the land i owned in partnership between the landlord and the tenant, the landlor owning the so-called "farm bottom" or space of the field (the land exclu sive of the surface), while the tenant possesses the farm surface or fertil soil, comprising improvements made or labor spent in developing th land into a cultivated farm.[31]

Separation of ownership of the land surface from ownership of under lying strata often gives rise to conflicts when the property owners attemp to enjoy their individual rights. Both the surface owner and the sub surface owner have certain overlapping or joint rights to the surface land

---

[31] Traditionally, in China all farm lands are supposed to be barren and are brough to life and fertility by gradual development and cultivation by the farmer. This explains why the farmer is entitled to the surface of the farm. In other words, the fertility of the farm is the sole property of the tenant who cultivates it. This concept represents a definite modification of the traditional classical concept of the "original" quality of land, in an economic sense. (A. Kaiming Chiu, "The Division of Rent Between Landlord and Tenant in China," *Journal of Farm Economics*, Vol. VI, No. 4, October, 1929, pp. 651–653.)

such, for example, as the right of ingress and egress and trespass at all times, or the right of partition.[32] Separation of surface and subsurface fee is a relatively recent development in the American land system, and the courts have not yet fully agreed on the nature of the legal interest created by subsurface conveyances or numerous other points of conflict that arise in the splitting of the fee.

Modern aviation has necessitated modifications in the old English law which held that ownership of the surface carried with it rights to the soil down to the center of the earth and indefinitely upward, above the surface. In the United States, the Federal government has the right to control aviation as part of its power to regulate interstate commerce. Frequently rights to the air over land crossed by planes are purchased; and this form of air right has also been used by skyscraper owners who do not want other high structures to shade or interfere with their buildings. In other words, land has become a commodity that can be divided into numerous surface, subsurface, and supersurface rights.

WANING SOCIAL IMPORTANCE OF MODERN LAND OWNERSHIP

In early times, a man's wealth and social position were closely related to the amount of landed property which he held. In the early American colonies, only landowners were allowed to vote, and in many places today the same rule applies, particularly where an issue involving the raising of revenue through property taxation is involved. In World War I, the political privileges and social advantages historically connected with land ownership caused Russian soldiers to abandon their positions at the front and return home, to secure a small acreage allotment promised them by the revolutionists.

The explanation of why landed property has historically carried with it certain political or social privileges may be found in the fact that in the earlier, more primitive agricultural societies, land was more directly the basic factor in production. In other words, the production process was a simpler one of incorporating labor with land to produce directly the things for the household.[33] Today, industrial technology has made such astounding strides that land as a factor in production has become relatively less direct. For example, the use of fertilizers may lessen, to some extent, the importance of the climatic characteristics and natural productive qualities of the land.

With every successful advance in agricultural technique, the number and importance of uncontrollable variables diminish, so that there is an

[32] James Salisbury, Jr., and Leonard A. Salter, Jr., "Subsurface Resources and Surface Land Economics," *Journal of Land and Public Utility Economics*, Vol. XVII, No. 3, August, 1941, p. 278.
[33] Charles Abrams, *Revolution in Land*, Harper, 1939, p. 201.

increasing proportion of mobile capital (such as machinery and other investment costs, excluding site cost) in the total. Landed capital and the operating conditions tend more and more to approach the ideally controlled and predetermined conditions of the laboratory experiment or modern large-scale industrial production. The growing of hothouse vegetables is an example of the tendency, and some of the implications of the modern farm chemurgic movement illustrate the possible dwindling importance of land, in the more primitive sense.

These developments have reduced the relative direct importance of land as a factor in production, and account for the waning social prestige and privileges associated with modern land ownership. In fact, the rise of modern finance capitalism and the pyramiding of economic power accompanying the methods of financing and managing modern industrial corporations, through the mechanism of paper stock equities, have caused land to lose its privileged position.

There is a widespread tendency to avoid ownership of land because of the economic burdens of land taxes and the inflexibility characteristic of capital tied up in land. Liquidity is the new key word of modern corporate industry and is represented by an increasing proportion of stocks and bonds—that is, intangible property. Intangible property is ordinarily not taxed directly or, if so, very lightly, leaving the burden of property taxes to be borne largely by land, both urban and rural.

The concentration of economic power in industry has given more and more price-making influence to the more potent interests. "Sticky" industrial prices have accompanied the rigid control inherent in modern large-scale machine production, which is in sharp contrast to the highly variable farm prices that accompany fluctuations in output caused by weather and the large number of individual competing farm operating units.[34] There has been a widespread tendency for rural youth to move to the cities to get jobs in industry or to go into the professions. Investors have preferred putting their savings in more liquid forms of property, such as stocks and bonds, than in farm and urban real estate.

The social implications of these shifts which have accompanied the technological advances initiated by the Industrial Revolution, and their economic complement, the modern corporation, are far reaching. In a rural agricultural economy, primary or face-to-face relationships pre-

[34] Corporate farming has not developed along with the development of the corporation in industry, primarily because the family-sized farm unit seems to be comparatively efficient in producing food and fiber at low cost, so that the commercialized large business unit has not found the agricultural field economically enticing. Another reason is found in the fact that production in agriculture cannot be concentrated on a small city lot or block, story upon story, but requires for a large-scale output a comparatively large area in acres, which increases the difficulty of managing this extensive area as efficiently as a small concentrated factory can be managed.

dominate and certain social customs, taboos, and attitudes maintain relatively stable communities. In modern industrial economies, secondary group relationships predominate, and the personalized social ties and bonds of rural communities are lost in the highly impersonalized large modern city.

Ownership of tangible property carries with it a personalizing element that has a stabilizing social effect. Ownership of impersonalized, intangible property like stocks and bonds does not carry a similar active interest and concern of the owner. Agrarian unrest has been greatest where attachment to the land through owner operation has been least, or where ownership has been associated with such heavy economic burdens of mortgage debt or taxation that the economic advantages of property are practically destroyed.

"LAND HUNGER"

These phenomena are often cited as evidence of an "instinctive" trait in man, referred to as "land hunger." It is true that where custom and long and close association with the land have created a respect, understanding, and love for the soil, man will often cling to the land even though he has other more lucrative alternatives.[35] Thousands of individuals who have lived in cities all their lives probably have little real desire to own land, either rural or urban, as such, and do not feel any innate desire to live on the land. However, many of those closely associated with the soil under economically and socially satisfactory conditions do feel a very close affiliation and loyalty to the land, which few capital goods can command. This is particularly true among peasants of the older nations, especially in Europe.

In America the higher percentage of farm ownership among foreign-born whites than among native-born whites is evidence of the psychological, social, and economic importance that these people place upon land, and their resulting desire for it. This desire has been increased, in many cases, by the fact that although they have been associated closely

---

[35] In Greek mythology, the story of Antaeus, son of Poseidon and Ge (symbolic of water and earth, respectively), and his combat with Heracles is an interesting example of the earlier reverence for the soil as a foundation for human life. Heracles, the powerful, was unable to overcome Antaeus in combat until he discovered that Antaeus had to touch the earth periodically in order to retain his strength. By holding him off the ground, Heracles was able to win the fight. The formation of Antaeus clubs or societies, with invitations for membership extended only to those who are practical or "have their feet on the ground" is a modern interpretation of the Antaeus story. In modern impersonalized society, the complexities of life in a scientific and technological world have made many professional workers appear theoretical or academic in the eyes of the average businessman or farmer, who feel that these men have no solutions for present-day problems. The Antaeus clubs are attempts to call attention to the necessity of more realism and practicality, which a deeper appreciation of the soil and the simpler type of life on the land can give.

with the land, they could not satisfy their desire for land ownership i
their native land, or could do so only with great difficulty and sacrific
This was particularly true in the case of Russia before World War I.

THE LANDOWNER'S ROLE IN MODERN SOCIETY

Two main types of value account for the worth of land, namely *us*
value and *scarcity value*. Of these two, the landowner asserts his greate
influence over scarcity value.

Use value of land depends upon two qualities—*fertility* and *situs*. *Ferti*
ity is primarily dependent upon the natural physical characteristics of th
land as endowed by nature, although the landowner, by skillful manage
ment and enterprise, can improve this fertility or destroy it by poor mar
agement. *Situs* is that quality of land resulting from its location relativ
to the preferences of society, and site value can only be created by societ
not by the landowner.

In the creation of scarcity values through an alternation in the deman
and supply relationships of land, however, the landowner has certai
reservation prices for his land that cause him to withhold given tracts o
land. This establishes a supply curve and influences the final price of th
land. The landowner also usually holds land out of production or us
until demand for it has developed, and in this intermediary stage th
landowner stands the costs involved in the land's *ripening* into use
Society, in a systematic and organized way, could do all of the things don
by the landlord or private owner; but the fact remains that it has not don
so, preferring to leave them to be accomplished by the landowner throug
the institution of private property.

John Stuart Mill, Ricardo, Henry George, and others predicted tha
landlords in time would become increasingly wealthy and powerful; bu
these men did not foresee the development of our modern corporatio
and monoply capitalism and the consequent decrease in the relative im
portance of land in production. In other words, in modern economie
land has become less important because of the great substitution of capita
for land in the roundabout production process. Ironically enough, mos
agricultural programs in modern nations deal with subsidizing or bolster
ing farm incomes, rather than devising ways and means of extracting
large "unearned increments" from landowners. As a matter of fact, public
ownership of agricultural and urban land through tax and mortgage
foreclosures has increased in many areas, not because of excess profits
from the land but because of excessive losses incurred by landowners with
resultant reversion of landed property to public ownership.[36] This reflects

[36] For example, in Montana more than four million acres of agricultural land were
taken by county governments from private ownership through tax-deed foreclosures
during the thirties. This is the equivalent of one-twelfth of the total taxable acreage in
the state.

ιe distressed condition of many landowners and their inability to con-
.nue to meet the social costs involved in private ownership of these lands.
The social effectiveness of permitting land to be owned by private
ιdividuals cannot be questioned on the grounds that experience has
ιown that it has given landowners generally a strangle hold on society
·hich they have used to exploit the masses and make great fortunes for
ιemselves. There have been instances, however, of excessive exploitation
f the public welfare by landholders in all types of land resources and
·articularly in certain minerals.

The present distressed condition of landowners in many leading nations
; evidence that in general they have not fared as well as many of those
·ho have secured property rights in some other forms of property in
ιodern society. The question of whether land should be owned by private
·ndividuals should be decided on one basis—that is, whether or not such
·wnership tends to secure the socially most efficient and desirable utiliza-
ιon of land resources.

REFERENCES FOR FURTHER READING

ιbrams, Charles, *Revolution in Land,* Harper & Brothers, New York, 1939,
Chaps. I, II, III, and IV.

ιerle, A. A., Jr., and Means, G. C., *The Modern Corporation and Private
Property,* The Macmillan Company, New York, 1933, Chap. I.

ιooley, C. H., *Social Organization,* Charles Scribner's Sons, New York, 1929,
Chaps. XXVIII and XXIX.

ιly, R. T., *Property and Contract in Their Relations to the Distribution of
Wealth,* The Macmillan Company, New York, 1914. Volume I. Bk. I, Chaps.
III, IV, V, VI, VII, X, and XI; Vol. II, Chaps. XXII and Part III, Appendix
1, "Vested Interests."

ιly, R. T., and Wehrwein, G. S., *Land Economics,* The Macmillan Company,
New York, 1940, pp. 74–98.

ιeiger, G. R., *The Theory of the Land Question,* The Macmillan Company,
New York, 1936, Chap. III.

ιras, N. S. B., *A History of Agriculture in Europe and America,* F. S. Crofts
& Co., New York, 1940, Chaps. IV, V, VII, and XI.

ιughes, Everett C., *The Chicago Real Estate Board: The Growth of an Institution,* University of Chicago Press, Chicago, 1931, pp. 1–5.

ιaidler, H. W., *Concentration of Control in American Industry,* Thomas Y.
Crowell Company, New York, 1931, Chap. I.

ιational Resources Committee, *The Structure of the American Economy,* Government Printing Office, Washington, D.C., 1939, Part I, Chap. I.

ιumner, W. G., *Folkways: A Study of the Sociological Importance of Usages,
Manners, Customs, Mores, and Morals,* Ginn & Company, Boston, 1906,
Chap. I.

ιare, C. F., and Means, G. C., *The Modern Economy in Action,* Harcourt,
Brace and Company, Inc., New York, 1936, Chaps. I, II, and III.

chapter **16**

SOCIAL CONTROL OF LANDED PROPERTY

THE MEANING OF SOCIAL CONTROL

The Quasi-Social Character of Governmental Control—
Essentials of a Good System of Social Control—Social
Control Procedures

INFORMAL CONTROLS

Custom — Tradition — Public Opinion — Education and
Propaganda—Religion—Codes of Ethics of Business and
Professional Groups—Informal vs. Formal Controls

POLICE POWER

Use of Police Power as a Formal Control—Zoning as a Use
of The Police Power—Urban Zoning—Rural Zoning—
Zoning Procedure—Taking Property by "Due Process of
Law"—Coördination of Police Power Use

EMINENT DOMAIN

Distinction Between Police Power and Eminent Domain
—Excess Condemnation as a Use of Eminent Domain—
Eminent Domain Procedure

TAXATION

The Tax System as an Instrument of Social Control

PRIVATE LEGAL CONTROLS OF LAND USE

Deed Restrictions—Mortgage and Lease Restrictions—
Easements—Extralegal Procedures

RAPID TECHNOLOGICAL developments in recent years have changed methods of producing and living and have caused problems and conflicts necessitating continual adjustments of rights and privileges in the use of land resources. These adjustments have involved an increasing number of social controls to secure well-being and maximum harmony among various economic groups.[1] While government action in many cases does facilitate the necessary adjustments, it may prevent or delay readjustment to changed economic conditions, depending upon the type of program effected.

Land is fixed, immobile, and the source of the foods and fibers necessary for life. Furthermore, since so many of our resources (like minerals) are exhaustible, it is particularly dangerous for any society to allow unregulated, unbridled private property rights in land. These points emphasize the desirability of directing the modern social control movement toward more effective control of landed property. It is, therefore, important to consider the meaning of social control, to analyze the formal and informal controls that are available for this purpose, and to appraise their relative effectiveness as instruments for such control.

THE MEANING OF SOCIAL CONTROL

The word *control* means to "exercise restraining or directing influence over or, more briefly, to coerce." This coercion is usually applied by means of orders or accepted, established procedures backed by irresistible power ("irresistible" in the sense that the agency or group that has such power is in a position to make the penalty for violation of the orders or procedures so severe as to make anything but obedience economically undesirable or unwise). One may choose to break the law, if willing to take the consequences; but the state—the sovereign power in modern societies—sets penalties for violations so high that anyone who wishes to survive economically or physically, with any degree of freedom, must abide by its orders.

Control may be direct, consisting of legislation with stated conditions of enforcement and penalties for violation, or indirect through less obvious, but effective, inducements like the use of example, custom, and opinion.

Social control is that control exercised by or in behalf of the entity we

[1] The trust movements and antitrust laws; developments in irrigation, reclamation, and flood prevention; labor legislation, social insurance, minimum wage laws, and compulsory arbitration of industrial disputes; and growing control over public health, markets and marketing, city planning and zoning, and agricultural production have developed within the structure of modern industry. The many-sided movement toward control "must be guided and directed, its movements made more informed and enlightened, but it cannot be stopped and no one group can dictate its course." (For a more detailed statement of developments along these lines, see J. M. Clark, *Social Control of Business*, 2d ed., McGraw-Hill, 1939, pp. 4 ff.)

call society. The concept of "society," however, is not too clear. Societ is, of course, an aggregate of individuals, interests, and groups whicl though organically bound together, are still distinguishable.[2]

Control by pressure groups or specific interests within the social orde should not be confused with "social control." Where such group contro causes no serious conflicts of interests or standards among different group it may be regarded as part of the entire system of social control. Th nation itself is not really the whole of society, because some of its interes conflict with those of other nations; but for the most part the nation is grouping adequate for most purposes. In the United States, the townshij city, county, state, and Federal governments exercise among themselve the formal legal powers of control in economic life.

To question whether governmental control in such a society is reall social is to question whether the government is truly representative o the various interests and groups in the nation. Of course, the more ir clusive the group, the more nearly socialized is the control it exercises but it is only fair to say that in modern, highly complex, interdependen societies like ours, all controls are imperfectly comprehensive or impei fectly representative, or both, and therefore imperfectly social.[3]

THE QUASI-SOCIAL CHARACTER OF GOVERNMENTAL CONTROL

The expressions, "We are the government" and "The government i the people taken en masse" are survivals of the classical concept of th state as the sum total of individuals within it. Modern states, even in th most democratic nations, are separate entities—abstractions apart from the group of individuals within them.

When the modern state acts, some official really does the acting. Thi person has his own particular prejudices and loyalties; he is an agent whe executes the orders of his superiors, and his superiors have other superiors and so on, up to the heads of departments who interpret and enforce laws passed by state or national legislatures, or enforce rules or regulations o county or city councils and commissions. Moreover, these laws, rules, anc regulations may have been established by some pressure group throug logrolling, compromise, and related political techniques.

In any case, there is a considerable margin of discretion within whicl the official or administrative agency acts to interpret and enforce the law; and within this margin, the official or agency *is* the state—at least for al practical purposes. Officials in action constitute the state in action, and relations between officials and private citizens determine relationships among the citizens themselves.[4]

---

[2] *Ibid.*, pp. 7–8.
[3] *Ibid.*
[4] John R. Commons, *Legal Foundations of Capitalism*, Macmillan, 1924, pp. 122–124.

It would be logical to believe that private property would be abolished through the usual social processes if it did not serve the general welfare. However, this assumes a smoothly-working, efficient government that promptly and completely reflects the will of the whole people. We have seen how half-social governmental or state action may be, and we have seen that this characteristic is inherent in our modern representative government. Consequently, it is possible for an institution like private property to continue for some time without abolition or significant modification, because the "social control" may not be truly social.

After a time, however, this situation should correct itself, although we may find that other forces, controls, or pressures may cause the continuation of private property in land or other objects, even though this might not produce the best results for a given period. In these circumstances, general welfare in the broadest sense would not be achieved. However, confidence and participation in modern social living demand the view that public interest will ultimately carry the day.

ESSENTIALS OF A GOOD SYSTEM OF SOCIAL CONTROL

Controlling landed property in the interests of the general welfare is a complex and difficult task. The major social purpose of controlling landed property is to secure just, wholesome, efficient, and generally satisfactory utilization of natural resources. In deciding whether to employ formal or informal control, positive or negative pressure, and to command or prohibit, three things must be considered: (1) the nature of the ultimate source of control, (2) the nature of the resistance to be overcome, and (3) the amount of independent discretion that can be safely entrusted to the official agents.

Clark lists 11 characteristics or tests of a good system of social control.[5] One of the most important of these is that it be capable of progressively raising the level of mankind. In a democracy where the mass of mankind does the ultimate controlling, this really means that social control must somehow rise higher than its source. This is possible, through the occasional power of enlightened leadership, but not easy.

SOCIAL CONTROL PROCEDURES

In brief, private property is a social trust, and the individual is nothing more nor less than a steward taking care of the property during the period

---

[5] These 11 are that it must: (1) be democratic, (2) know what it wants, (3) be powerful (powerful enough to make an unwilling minority obey the will of the majority), (4) be efficient, (5) economize coercion, (6) utilize all the strongest and most persistent motives of human nature, both generous and selfish, (7) impose duties simple enough to be understood (which means that social control must follow precedent much of the time), (8) be guided by experience or be wisely experimental, (9) be adaptable, (10) be farseeing, and (11) be capable of progressively raising the level of mankind. See Clark, op. cit., pp. 16–17.

when society approves and permits such stewardship. The social right to regulate and confiscate private property is basic to the institution of property itself. Society always has the last say in determining the limitations and the privileges that property bestows upon its owner. The instruments for such control available to society constitute the *safety valve* in modern economic development and progress.

Society uses controls of two major types—*informal* and *formal. Informal* controls are those developed by economic groups out of their own needs and qualities, but not formalized through governmental machinery as are statutes or laws. These informal controls, including custom, tradition, religion, education, public opinion, propaganda, and the whole temper or point of view of a class, an organization, or a profession,[6] are important forces determining attitudes toward property and practices developed in utilizing it.

Formal controls, comprising those formalized by governmental action through legislation in the form of laws or statutes, may be divided into two types: (1) those which the courts develop during the settlement of disputed cases, through their interpretations of and decisions in regard to statutes and legislation, and (2) those which are the direct result of legislation changing men's relations with one another in the use of property and natural resources.

Legislation is greatly influenced by informal controls, through the process of judicial interpretation and development, as well as through the legislative process of making the laws. The effective enforcement of formal controls (particularly of legislation) is greatly enhanced when formal controls are supported by a sympathetic set of informal controls. Thus, informal controls are the foundation of modern control systems because of the necessity of relying on voluntary obedience in most cases, and because of the lack of social solidarity and the importance of minority attitudes.

INFORMAL CONTROLS

Though informal controls have many advantages over government action in the guidance and direction of rights and duties pertaining to ownership, they possess some disadvantages and weaknesses. Among their advantages are: (1) cheapness—no monetary support in the form of governmental taxation is ordinarily required; (2) promptness; (3) discrimination among cases according to numerous circumstances that would be irrelevant in a court but which affect the equities of a particular dispute; (4) efficiency—for example, the pressure of public opinion is felt even by those whose misconduct is still their own secret.

The more important disadvantages of informal controls may be

[6] *Ibid.,* p. 201.

summed up thus: (1) when, for any reason, informal controls cannot act promptly, they often do not act at all; (2) informal controls, like public opinion, are often swayed by the spectacular, and discriminate on personal or sentimental grounds that have little to do with the economic implications of the case. They need formal institutions to give them consistency, persistence, rational regard for consequences, and the advantages of expert knowledge.[7] Furthermore, where the social group is large, solidarity or uniformity of attitudes does not prevail, and minority attitudes, because of their vociferousness and ability, may be more influential in affecting the direction and extent of social control than the attitudes of the majority, who may be passive or poorly organized.

CUSTOM

The unwritten rules, the habits, or the whole body of practices or conventions which become the usual practices or usages regulating the social life of a group are so familiar that their significance is frequently underestimated or escape observation altogether. However, custom is one of the most important of all forces exerting informal control.

Customary ways of using natural resources and habitual attitudes toward the privileges and duties of land ownership are potent aids or handicaps in regulating the use of the resources of any system. This depends, of course, upon whether regulation represents an attempt to prevent a change in present practices or to develop a new practice.

TRADITION

Unwritten transmission of information, opinions, practices, customs, etc., from ancestors to posterity also control land utilization practices and attitudes toward the social control of landed property. They may be distinguished from custom largely because of the fact that traditions are considered longer established.

While traditions have been handed down from previous generations over a long period of time, customs may be habitual or usual courses of action, usages, or practices developed within a given generation or followed merely because they are practices of the older generation currently living and active. A certain amount of sentimentality and emotional allegiance centers upon traditions, which may also cause actions or attitudes less justifiable or desirable than those usages or practices established through custom.

PUBLIC OPINION

"Public opinion" is a term used to express the thought or belief of the social group, or at least of the effective majority. It represents the view,

---

[7] An analysis of the principal merits and defects of the major informal controls is presented by Clark. *Op. cit.*, Chaps. XII and XIII.)

judgment, impression, notion, or idea of the dominant social group. An opinion has less definiteness or certainty than a settled conviction, and a weaker hold upon man's activities or thoughts than a custom or a tradi tion. Public opinion is flexible and easily molded through the use of such devices as education, religion, or propaganda.

Public opinion is a composite of many conflicting and varied interests within the social body, and it is sometimes difficult to determine just what public opinion is in regard to some subject or to be sure that it will func tion so as to meet the true needs of society. However, public opinion, at least in a democracy, has the ultimate right to say what the true needs of society are and how they should be satisfied, and no one individual or group idea of the public welfare should presume to control it. Moreover though informal forces such as education, religion, and propaganda have their place in harmonizing group interests within a society and in broad- ening and unifying public opinion, final judgment of what constitutes true social control rests with public opinion itself.

EDUCATION AND PROPANGANDA

Though education and propaganda are both important means of regu- lating informal and formal controls, they differ widely in character. Edu- cation tries to serve the general welfare, while propaganda is usually the expression of some group interest. Where education strives to be disin- terested, accurate, and fair, propaganda tends to be defensively belligerent or prejudiced, its excesses often encouraging the growth of counter- propaganda or violent social disorder.

Education, at least in a democracy, must furnish a fairly equal oppor- tunity to acquire factual and other information as a basis for desirable adaptation to life through intelligent and responsible judgment and de- cision. On the other hand, propaganda materials are arranged to promote or justify some special doctrine, system, theory, or practice. Propaganda appeals to the emotions for an unqualified acceptance, but education im- plies a certain comprehension and choice. In borderline cases it is difficult to distinguish between education and propaganda; sometimes, where propaganda approaches the breadth and sociality of education, it may be a helpful corrective force in shaping public opinion.

RELIGION

From time to time in history, religious ideals have been uniquely sig- nificant social controls. The appeal that religion makes to man's most vital and enduring emotions, ideals, and inner convictions furnishes him with an especially strong incentive to accomplish religious ideals in prac- tice. Moreover, the religious mechanism of most societies has typically been more highly organized and more unified, within the limit of the social organism, than such controls as evanescent, often self-contradictory public opinion, which lacks the long-range view, the long-time program, and the relatively constant pressure in one direction that religion affords to social control.

Religion has succeeded to a large extent in combining abstract, ideal aims with concrete, practical, secular action. Besides striving to modify the individual with a view to his personal salvation, religious organizations have attempted to lessen his egocentricity by inculcating qualities desirable for the good of society as a whole, and by motivating him to act with unselfishness, coöperation, and some sense of social responsibility.

CODES OF ETHICS OF BUSINESS AND PROFESSIONAL GROUPS

Codes of ethics, or formal statements of conduct made by business and professional organizations, are powerful forces for those who live under their influence. These codes are private rather than public in character. However, they are given statutory force by the organization propounding them, and in this sense are as formalized as the statutes and laws of political units or governments, for members of the organizations in which such codes are established are coerced by these codes. Whether they comply or not, the attitudes and feelings of their fellows toward the codes constitute a definite source of social pressure.

In our modern society, where so much of our economic life is carried on through economic organizations or special interest groups, the codes of ethics or conduct drawn up by the many business and professional organizations are very frequently contradictory. Many are antisocial, yet some are comparatively broad in their social aims.[8] In any case, this body of codes constitutes a force inflencing the actions, attitudes, and practices of owners and users of property.

These informal social controls of a society combine to make up its collective attitudes; and it is these collective attitudes that determine the direction and amount of social control exerted over landed property.

INFORMAL VS. FORMAL CONTROLS

Among more primitive folk, where a legal system of statutes and laws was not known, the control of property was embedded within the mores of the society. Slow development of government in response to the increasing need of peace, order, and security of contract accompanying more social complexity caused the previously informal controls to be embodied in formal statutes and laws. This trend has been fairly continuous, resulting in an ever-increasing body of statutes and laws. Legis-

[8] Clark refers to these codes as "a most curious mixture of the more presentable phases of intelligent private interest, class interest, community obligation, and natural human sympathy, wherein altruism is upheld one moment and apologized for the next, and virtue and expediency are inextricably interwoven." (Clark, *ibid.*, p. 215.)

lation is never entirely original or impromptu, but is rather the expression of public opinion developed through custom, tradition, education, and other informal controls.

Formal control of landed property is exercised by the state or sovereign through the legal framework within which price forces operate. That is, the state formally controls the use made of landed property, the quality of ownership and the number of rights that pertain to it, through laws and statutes which determine how the land may be used or how much profit may be derived from such use. This legislation influences the cost and profit aspects of land utilization which, in turn, determine values attached to land ownership. Formal social control of landed property may be exercised in various ways, but is generally exercised through some form of the *police power, eminent domain,* or *taxation.*

POLICE POWER

The police power is the right of government to control property for the use of society in the interests of public health, safety, morals, and the general welfare, without compensation to private owners for any limitations or restrictions so imposed upon private property rights. In the case of the United States, it is that power of the state through legislation interpreted by the courts (this interpretive power is transmitted to the courts by federal and state constitutions) to shape property and contract to existing social conditions by determing what burdens may, without compensation, be imposed by society. Perhaps "police power" should be called "community power" or "public power," since it seeks to serve the public welfare most effectively by preserving a satisfactory balance between the individual and social sides of private property.

USE OF POLICE POWER AS A FORMAL CONTROL

In the United States, several levels of government, ranging from federal to municipal, must deal with some aspects of the control and regulation of landed property. This is because the American system of government vests sovereignty in the 48 states, except for federal governmental powers delegated specifically by, or implied in, the Federal Constitution; moreover, local governments (such as city, town, or county governments) are administrative units established under state laws, exercising only those powers of sovereignty granted or delegated to them by the state constitutions and acts of the state legislatures.[9] There are more than 3000 of these county governments in the United States, and more than 17,000

[9] This division of powers between the states and the Federal government is stated in the Tenth Amendment: "The powers not delegated to the United States by the Constitution nor prohibited by it to the states are reserved to the states respectively, or to the people."

incorporated cities and towns, on both of which the states may depend for the execution of certain land-use regulations, controls, or plans; but coöperation among the states is essential if any national plan of land utilization is to be effective, since only the states can use the police power and levy property taxes.

Division of powers has an important effect on utilization of agricultural as well as urban land. In contrast to the United States, where sovereignty is vested in the 48 states and only delegated or implied powers are given the Federal government, Canada vests police power largely in the Dominion government. Since Canadian sovereignty rests in the Dominion government, except for certain powers exclusively assigned to the province legislatures, authority is much more centralized in that country.

Use of the police power varies widely, especially in the United States. For instance, in specifically enumerated cases the Federal government has essentially the same powers as the states, which are really the sovereign governmental units. The Federal government controls property primarily through the admiralty, navigation, and commerce clauses of the Federal Constitution, the entire field of interstate commerce being under the regulatory control of the Federal government.

Other examples of use of the police power type of control by the Federal government include plant and animal quarantine, livestock inspection, and food inspection. These controls, particularly under the commerce clause, increase in importance as our society becomes more complex, so that the Federal government influences the regulation of private property more and more. However, the states have used the police power primarily in zoning legislation so far as land-use control is concerned.

ZONING AS A USE OF THE POLICE POWER

Adoption of zoning ordinances is one important means of utilizing the police power. The area to be controlled is divided into districts, in each of which certain uses are prohibited. Most zoning ordinances are telescopic in their classification of different kinds of districts, uses not allowed in more restricted districts being successively allowed in each of the less restricted districts.

In an ideal zoning ordinance, however, uses of the several districts would be mutually exclusive.[10] That is, residence, business, and industry would each be limited to a particular district. Ordinarily, residence districts or zones are the only ones protected against mixed buildings, and only in a few cases are residence buildings excluded from industrial zones. In no case are they prohibited in the business zone.

It would seem logical that if it is undesirable or unhealthful for people

[10] National Resources Committee, *Urban Planning and Land Policies*, Report of the Urbanism Committee, Government Printing Office, 1939, p. 329.

to live near an isolated factory in a residence area, it is equally or more unhealthful or undesirable for isolated dwellings or tenements to be situated in a heavily industrialized zone. Certainly, wholesome homes are not possible when surrounded by chemical plants, steel mills, tanneries, railroad yards, and slaughterhouses. In spite of the many advantages and the great desirability of exclusive zones, most cities have telescopic zoning. As a result, though zoning has prevented many undesirable uses in certain sections, it has not accomplished the maximum benefits possible in urban land-use planning and control.

Zoning is also used, in some instances, to control rural land uses. In cities the grounds for zoning are the public health, safety, and morals. For example, placement of billboards at intersections has been prohibited to protect the public from the dangers of automobile accidents under modern motor traffic conditions. Sanitation or public health and safety have been important bases for limiting the height or bulk of buildings. In the case of rural zoning, economic grounds are frequently used to justify regulation of rural property. For example, in the cutover Lake states, the necessity of reducing local governmental expenditures for schools, roads, and related services in order to reduce tax delinquency, tax deeds, and corresponding distress has given rise to zoning for the control of settlement and land use.

URBAN ZONING

Zoning ordinances are used extensively as a means of controlling urban land use. The positive effects of zoning ordinances in bringing about changes in urban land use are usually of necessity very gradual, because most zoning ordinances are not retroactive in their effects. No community seems to have been able, through zoning, to meet the difficult problem created by the erection of flimsy buildings and shacks on the fringe of the city.

Most zoning ordinances require a minimum lot area for a house, a maximum height for the buildings, limitations upon the percentage of lot occupied, a certain setback of buildings from the street, and similar regulations. Most of these are not applicable to the cheap shacks built on city fringes during depression periods or for summer use, because most of these requirements are met. Insistence upon a minimum lot area per house has sometimes helped to prevent the development of shack areas, because, through increasing the land area required, construction of a house becomes so expensive that it is uneconomic, considering the investment in land, to erect a mere shack.[11]

[11] It has been argued that increasing the required amount to be invested in the lots leaves a smaller amount for constructing the dwelling, so that poor houses result. However, it is a matter of common observation that the best dwellings are usually located on the most expensive lots, and not the reverse.

Some ordinances now include a statement setting forth the minimum standard of construction that new buildings must attain, and zoning thus effectively excludes inferior buildings from the community. Building, sanitation, plumbing, electrical, and related codes, while sometimes abused for graft by interested trades, are primarily designed to protect the safety and health of the people by preventing cheap, jerry-built structures of inferior materials and shoddy construction. In spite of the importance of such codes in a comprehensive urban land policy, hundreds of fair-sized municipalities have no building codes at all, and many more very poorly devised codes.[12]

It is essential that reasonable standards of construction be provided for, so that building costs do not become excessively high and jerry-building is not permitted. Adoption by the central city of a code that does not apply to suburbs, which may have no codes, or codes of varying adequacy, raises certain competitive situations with serious implications. County codes or state-wide codes would standardize construction over areas large enough to eliminate ununiform competitive conditions in the building field. To effect such codes, however, would require closer coöperation between city and county governments or more active participation on the part of state governments than has generally prevailed.

Zoning is being effectively used to control open space about residence buildings, to eliminate dark rooms, land overcrowding, rear dwellings, blighted areas, congestion of population, and constant shifting of residence centers. Regulation of inner courts, setbacks in courts, minimum window areas, percentage of lot occupied, location of accessory buildings, congestion of population, garden apartments, country estates and green belts, front yard requirements, setback of buildings from street centers and on corner lots, setbacks in commercial zones, and height of buildings are contained in many zoning ordinances which, in the aggregate, are improving city living conditions.[13]

One of the difficulties in zoning that is characteristic of many cities is the failure to revise zoning ordinances promptly as occasion requires. Mistakes will in all probability be made in the original regulations and in the boundaries delimiting initial zones.

RURAL ZONING

In rural zoning, control of land use is not so detailed as in the case of urban zoning, and generally only broad types of use are regulated. In Wisconsin, for example, the enabling act provides for zoning land for agriculture, forestry, and recreation. In Michigan, however, the enabling

---

[12] National Resources Committee, *op. cit.*, p. 272.

[13] For an analysis of the use of zoning ordinances for each purpose listed, see National Resources Committee, *op. cit.*, pp. 334–349.

act has been broadened to include soil and water conservation, and all-year residents may be zoned out of certain areas.[14] Zoning as a land-use control measure is fairly effective where patterns of land use are changing rapidly, as in the urban-rural fringe or the forest-farm fringe.

Zoning appears to be least effective on already developed, relatively stable agricultural areas, because (1) land-use practices and conditions under which land may be used for crops or grazing vary so greatly, even from farm to farm, that it is difficult to set up districts within which uniform regulations apply, (2) the major need in these areas is for specific land-management practice regulation, which is handled by soil conservation districts, and (3) there is no great need in most of these areas for protection from encroachment of other uses.[15] Moreover, if the nonretroactive feature were continued, zoning would not be effective in changing a land use established before the ordinance was passed.[16]

Rural zoning began in 1929 with an amendment of the Wisconsin county zoning law. The law had previously limited county regulation to urban land use. Since the adoption of rural zoning in Wisconsin, several other states have permitted local governments to zone land for strictly rural purposes. State-wide enabling acts for municipal zoning have been adopted by all the New England states, and although they have been designed principally to meet urban and suburban problems, it is believed that rural zoning is possible under their provisions.[17]

Although soil conservation districts may technically be given limited districting and use regulation powers comparable to zoning powers through broadening their present scope of action by statutory amendment, it would be inconsistent to broaden such powers in view of the original purposes for which soil conservation districts were established, unless zoning is limited to the prevention of erosion. Where the problem is one of preventing continued high cost of public services in cutover

[14] G. S. Wehrwein, "Rural Zoning," U.S. Department of Agriculture, *Yearbook*, 1938, pp. 241–245.

[15] Virgil Hurlburt, "Rural Zoning for Missouri?" *Journal of Land and Public Utility Economics*, Vol. XVI, No. 2, May, 1940, pp. 155–158, and Conrad Hammar, "Regulation or Development for the Missouri Ozarks," *ibid.*, pp. 159–164.

[16] Courts have considered retroactive urban zoning legal, but in most states rural zoning is not expected to be retroactive. However, in Pennsylvania, provision is made for termination of nonconforming uses over a period of time. (See Virgil Hurlburt, "Pennsylvania Planning and Zoning Enabling Acts," *Journal of Land and Public Utility Economics*, Vol. XIII, No. 3, August, 1937, p. 315; and U.S. Department of Agriculture, "Rural Zoning and Land-Use Planning," County Planning Series, No. 7, Bureau of Agricultural Economics, 1940.) Chapter I, pp. 1–16 of "State Legislation for Better Land Use," a special report by an interbureau committee of the USDA, Washington, D.C., April, 1941, gives a thorough analysis of rural zoning, including preparation of zoning ordinances, zoning procedure, administrative regulations, and types and current rural uses of zoning.

[17] For a statement of the development of rural zoning in the United States, see "State Legislation for Better Land Use," *op. cit.*, p. 2.

areas, rather than one of erosion, zoning has certain advantages as a land-use control technique.

Under Michigan statutes, zoning may attempt to counteract soil and water loss, but its techniques are so limited that it cannot be expected to do the same work as a soil conservation district. Grazing districts are obviously limited to a particular type of land use, as are weed control and related types of districts.

ZONING PROCEDURE

Before local governments can pass zoning ordinances to regulate the use of property, authorization must be given them through an enabling act passed by the state legislature. This is done because of the provisions of the Fourteenth Amendment to the Federal Constitution, which states, ". . . nor shall any State deprive any person of life, liberty, or property without due process of law." This is interpreted to mean that zoning must be effected democratically through legal procedure such as state enabling acts and local discussions and decisions. The enabling act is nothing more than a legislative act specifically granting municipalities or counties the right to zone. Under the enabling act, local governments may proceed to establish zoning ordinances, usually with provision for free discussion and full comprehension of proposed zoning ordinances through public hearings before they go into effect.

Zoning may protect and promote proper utilization or may restrict improper utilization. Zoning should be regarded as a dynamic science and a continually evolving process. Zoning regulations are neither in perpetuity nor for a fixed term of years, but continue only as long as they remain unchanged. This elasticity and flexibility have been considered a weakness, because zoning regulations can be changed very quickly with any change in public opinion. However, with proper education and intelligent planning, this elasticity and flexibility are the very characteristics that permit zoning regulations to be promptly adapted to changing conditions. Failure to revise zoning regulations promptly in accordance with changes or new conditions in the utilization of urban or rural land will seriously hamper their effectiveness.

TAKING PROPERTY BY "DUE PROCESS OF LAW"

The Fifth Amendment states that no person shall "be deprived of life, liberty, or property without due process of law; nor shall private property be taken for public use without just compensation." The courts must decide just what constitutes "taking" private property.

Any regulation or restriction imposed through the police power upon the utilization of landed property may be literally considered as "taking" property for public use. For example, zoning may restrict the utilization of a given piece of land or may even prohibit entirely its use for certain purposes. This reduces the income potentialities of the land and diminishes its value. Literally, this is a taking of property, although change is more complete in a complete transfer of the property from private to public ownership.

No sharp line clearly indicates the place where use of the police power ends, beyond which any further regulation or "taking" of property would require compensation. As a matter of fact, in extreme cases the police power may be used actually to remove land from private ownership and withdraw it to public ownership. The term *confiscation* may be used to indicate such taking of property without pay. This practice is sometimes referred to as "robbery by the state."

Ordinarily, however, confiscation implies forfeiture of individual rights because of the owner's failure to comply with certain specified legal requirements, so that a taint of illegality is usually associated with it. An example of this is confiscation of automobiles transporting bootleg whisky during the Prohibition period of the twenties in the United States. The confiscation of American-owned and English-owned oil fields by the Mexican government (1928) has also been considered an act of Mexican confiscation, because the property was seized without fair, prompt, and adequate compensation, although the oil lands may have been secured originally by bribing Mexican officials. Had such fair, prompt, and adequate compensation been made, the term *expropriation* would have been used.

The individual property owner has only one recourse when he feels that he has been unjustly deprived of his property. He can take his case to the official board that may have been set up for the individual to appeal special cases, or to the court, where the legality of the government ordinance or action can be scrutinized to determine whether it constitutes "due process of law." If the court feels that the procedure in establishing a zoning ordinance, for example, was undemocratic, or the ordinance was not really concerned with public morals, health, safety, or the general welfare, and that the individual was actually deprived of his property either partially or entirely, it will decide in favor of the individual and against the governing body attempting to enforce the ordinance.

The decisions of the court will, of course, depend somewhat upon the economic philosophy and point of view of the court. A conservative court will lean in the direction of protecting individual rights, while a progressive one ordinarily tends to protect the public welfare at the expense of private rights.

Although the police power is usually considered applicable only to the control of future land use, and not retroactive, there is no reason why it should not be sufficient to prevent continuance of previously established nonconforming uses. If a certain newly established nonconforming use affects public health, morals, safety, or the general welfare, so would a long-established use of the same type. Theoretically, the police power is broad enough to permit ousting all nonconforming uses, but the courts would undoubtedly prevent such sweeping action.[18]

Few cases have come before the courts involving the ousting of existing nonconforming buildings, but zoning ordinances ousting nonconforming cases have been upheld in the courts.[19] While much can be said for zoning ordinances that provide for ousting existing nonconforming uses, retroaction is not a usual feature of zoning. Nevertheless, most state enabling acts do not provide that no regulations shall be made retroactive, and the future development of zoning may show that this power to oust existing nonconforming buildings and uses in certain instances is very important.

COÖRDINATION OF POLICE POWER USE

Various types of state and local measures have been adopted to control or direct land use through application of the police power in one form or another. These include urban zoning, rural zoning, coöperative grazing associations, soil conservation districts, and weed control districts.

Much debate has arisen in recent years concerning the relative merits of these different forms of social control of land use through the police power. Many argue, for example, that soil conservation districts can be used exclusively to control and direct the utilization of land in rural areas and that rural zoning or grazing districts are not necessary. Each of these types of social control has particular advantages or disadvantages for given situations; but the organization of grazing districts, soil conservation districts, zoned areas, and other types of controlling authorities has given rise to numerous overlapping jurisdictions, so that there is a definite need to reorganize land-use control functions. Every time a new special unit is created to serve some limited purpose, another community of interest has the force of its public attention diverted from the principal task of securing responsible and responsive local self-government.

[18] Pennsylvania was the first state to include the retroactive principle and under Pennsylvania statutes the discontinuance of nonconforming uses may be attempted, providing certain guides are followed. Bassett contends that "theoretically the police power is broad enough to warrant the ousting of every nonconforming use, but the courts would rightly and sensibly find a method of preventing such a catastrophe." (Edward M. Bassett, Zoning, Russell Sage Foundation, 1936, p. 112.)

[19] As early as 1913 the California Supreme Court upheld the Los Angeles Ordinance, ruling that a brickyard established in a residence district before the ordinance was adopted must be removed. (Ex parte Hadachek, 165 Cal. 416.) The U.S. Supreme Court also upheld the ordinance. (Hadachek v. Sebastian, 239 U.S. 394.) This case really involved nuisance abatement, which is always legal and was not decided on bases of retroactivity. In two more recent New Orleans cases a zoning ordinance was upheld ousting nonconforming cases. (La-Dema Realty Co. v. Jacoby, 168 La. 752, 123 s. 314, 1929; and Dema Realty Co. v. McDonald, 168 La. 172, 121 s. 613, 1929.)

A rough coördinating statute has been drafted which, it is believed illustrates how zoning and soil erosion control powers can be consolidated This coördinating statute attempts to consolidate the police power necessary for the various types of local rural land use regulation now in operation, providing for suburban-type zoning, strip zoning along high ways, soil conservation, flood control, and other local land-use adjust ments.[20]

The draft of the proposed statute in the article cited incorporates only the main aspects of a complete legislative bill, and reads that "The governing body of any and every county is hereby authorized and empowered within its nonincorporated portions, to regulate, control and restrict land utilization practices and the use and occupancy, including the condition of use and occupancy, of land for trade, extraction of subsurface resources industry, residence, recreation, agriculture, forestry, grazing, soil and water conservation, flood control, and other purposes; and the location size, character, and use or conditions of use of buildings and other struc tures." It is obvious that this broad grant of powers would permit applica tion of the police power in all its various forms and for all the major land uses, and would greatly simplify administrative machinery to effect such social control.

EMINENT DOMAIN

Eminent domain is the right of government to claim private property for state use, if compensation is made to the private owner for property so claimed. In other words, the government may convert private property into public property without consent of the owner, but with compensation. In the United States, eminent domain is an inherent power of the state governments and an implied power of the Federal government. The use of eminent domain is limited by the "due process of law" clause in the Fourteenth Amendment to the Federal Constitution, just as is the use of the police power.

DISTINCTION BETWEEN POLICE POWER AND EMINENT DOMAIN

One important distinction between police power and eminent domain is the fact that, as a rule, application of the police power is *general,* while eminent domain affects specific property for some *particular* public purpose. Under the police power, private property may be regulated and restricted in the interest of the public welfare; in the case of eminent domain, private property is taken from the owner for fair compensation

[20] V. W. Johnson and H. Walker, Jr., "Centralization and Coördination of Police Power for Land-Control Measures," *Journal of Land and Public Utility Economics,* Vol. XVII, No. 1, February, 1941, pp. 24–26.

and appropriated to some particular use designed to promote the public welfare.

The distinction frequently made between eminent domain and police power on the grounds that compensation is made in the former and not in the latter is not entirely correct; because indemnification or compensation is frequently made, though title to the property is not transferred from private individuals to the public, when the police power is invoked as it is when eminent domain is used. For example, if property is destroyed while a fire department is fighting a conflagration, or if exposed bands of live-stock are killed to check the spread of a contagious disease, there is no expropriation—that is, no transfer of title to the public—and therefore no exercise of the power of eminent domain giving rise to a claim to compensation.

Nevertheless, although such instances involve only exercises of the police power, legislatures may be induced to provide for compensation as a matter of equity; and this has been done frequently in connection with cattle diseases, fires, and similar cases. But since the right to compensation is not a constitutional right, as it would be under eminent domain, adjustments may be made more equitable toward those who have to bear the burden of compensation, and recognition of the difference between police power and eminent domain is then an important advantage.[21]

The fact that the use of eminent domain, or expropriation, requires compensation to the private owner whenever it is used, while compensation under the use of police power is discretionary and, in most cases, nonexistent, makes eminent domain a more expensive means of social control than police power.

In the United States, the power of eminent domain belongs to the Federal government as well as to the states. Furthermore, the states may delegate the exercise of eminent domain to local governmental units like counties and cities, and even to private corporations—particularly railroads, telephone and water companies—if the public welfare is best served thereby. Railroad rights-of-way and power company easements are examples of the exercise of eminent domain by private agencies in the interests of the public welfare.

EXCESS CONDEMNATION AS A USE OF EMINENT DOMAIN

The use of eminent domain is theoretically limited to the purchase of land for public purposes. However, some difference of opinion exists in regard to what constitutes a public purpose. The opening of a new street in a city is obviously for a public purpose. But governments may condemn

[21] Ernst Freund, "Eminent Domain," in *Encyclopaedia of the Social Sciences*, Vol. V, p. 495.

more property than actually necessary to create a public improvement and subsequently sell or lease the remainder.

This policy, known as *excess condemnation,* may be used to accomplish one or more of the following purposes: (1) To solve the problem of lo remnants. For instance, where construction of a new city street would have lot remnants on certain parts of the street that would injure nearby owners as well as the city itself, the city might take more than the exac footage required for the street. Ordinarily, the excess area taken under eminent domain not needed for the street proper would be resold to adjacent lot owners, although it might be used by the city for beautifica tion of the area. (2) To protect the beauty and usefulness of public im provements so made. (3) To make money.

The last purpose seems like a rather improper use of eminent domain but taking more than absolutely necessary for creation of a public im provement in order to make money by selling or leasing the remainder may be justified on the grounds that the public improvement made greatly enhances the value of adjacent private property, or value of the private property of the city as a whole, and that condemning in excess and using part of the condemned property to make money would substantially offset the cost of the improvement.

Another use of excess condemnation is illustrated by cases in which cities buy up from private owners a large number of water rights, not then needed for the present city water supply, but which may be needed 10 or 20 or 30 years later, as the city grows or dry years come. In other words, this is a protective device, which is a means of securing a very vital commodity for the public use.

EMINENT DOMAIN PROCEDURE

Eminent domain, or expropriation, is not limited to purchase of land for public purposes, though it is in land sales that this type of social control has its chief use. Ordinarily, the use of eminent domain does not necessitate actual condemnation and appraisement to transform a piece of land into public property. The usual procedure is outright purchase by the public agency from the private individual, in the same way that all voluntary sales are executed. However, where voluntary agreement cannot be reached between the private owner and the public agency, proper legal procedure has been established to effect the transfer of the private property to public property.

General legislative acts provide appropriate procedures for exercise of the power of eminent domain in most states. A condemnation proceeding instigated by the expropriating agency places the matter with the judiciary, making the case a common lawsuit. In other words, the court intervenes to carry out expropriation. The judiciary is the only authority ompetent to order occupation of private property, and the judgment or decision of the court in regard to proper valuation of the property and payment to be made the private owner is final. The court may appoint an individual, a board, or a committee to appraise the property, or may itself determine the proper amount to be paid.

It has been customary in the United States to fix the amount at not less than the fair market value of the property. This has been interpreted by the courts to mean the amount that would be paid voluntarily by someone purchasing in good faith a piece of property which another wants to sell. The private owner can, of course, appeal his case from a lower court to a higher court; but in the last analysis the judiciary (either the higher or the lower court) finally determines the amount to be paid by the expropriating agency for the property taken. The expropriating agency can likewise appeal the case to a higher court, if it feels that the amount of payment established by the court is unreasonable.

TAXATION

The tax system is usually thought of as a means of securing revenue to defray costs of rendering certain essential or desired governmental services, but it can be a very important instrument of social control, particularly over landed property. Careful planning and efficient administration make it possible to achieve two important purposes of the tax system—to secure adequate revenue for governmental services and to encourage most efficient and desirable utilization of land resources.

THE TAX SYSTEM AS AN INSTRUMENT OF SOCIAL CONTROL

Used as an instrument of social control of landed property, the tax system must be so constructed and administered that it will place on different types and grades of land, relative burdens closely approximating their relative productivities. In other words, since assessed valuation is the base upon which tax levies are made, quality or productivity of the land must be carefully considered in assessment. If this is not done, an excessive burden is placed upon poorer lands, with the result that private ownership is untenable and the lands revert to public ownership through tax delinquency and tax deed. The heavy increase in rural and urban tax delinquency in some areas of the United States in recent years is a good example of the forced transfer of private landholdings to public ownership.

Any changes made in taxation of land, either for purposes of social control or to secure more revenue for the support of governmental services, should be made slowly, because of the relatively fixed and immobile nature of land as a factor in production. Nevertheless, if made intelligently and slowly, changes in the tax system can be one of the most

important peaceful means of securing better land use and effective control of land ownership in the interests of the general welfare.

PRIVATE LEGAL CONTROLS OF LAND USE

Formal controls of land use are of three major types—namely, public
ownership, private control of private land, and public control of private
land. Public ownership requires no explanation, since, where the government owns the land, it can utilize the land as it wishes, although government agencies ordinarily can purchase or acquire land only for certain
specific purposes. We have seen how society formally controls private land
by means of various forms of the police power, eminent domain, and taxation. Formal private controls of private land take the form of deed,
mortgage, and lease restrictions and easements.

DEED RESTRICTIONS

Deed restrictions are encumbrances on property limiting the future
uses that can be made of it by the individual who buys it. The restrictions
may apply over a limited period or over a very indefinite period. They are
frequently used by real-estate development companies to insure a certain
homogeneity of development or the erection of high-quality buildings in
a given subdivision. Deed restrictions have been used almost exclusively
on urban land, but they have been used to some extent in the development of recreational land. The deed restriction may be applied to single
parcels of land or to an entire subdivision. With such restrictive measures,
details of setback, density, use, and related developments can be controlled more easily than in a zoning ordinance or subdivision regulation.

The weakness of deed restrictions is that the regulation may be applied only by the owner, so that they are not of general use unless the city,
an individual, or a corporation owns most of the area involved. Unless a
public agency owns property that it wishes to sell, it cannot effect land-use
control by this means, but may work out some agreement or understanding with owners under which they agree to include certain restrictions in
deeds when they sell their properties. In the case of sale of county or
township land acquired through tax delinquency, a clause could be in-
serted in the tax deed setting forth certain desirable use restrictions on
the property. The Federal Housing Administration uses this method and
insures loans for development of new areas only after they have been
covered by suitable deed restrictions.[22]

Use of deed restrictions is further limited by the fact that the more
stringent the deed restrictions, the lower the value of the land, as a rule,
except in the case of high-quality urban development. There is also the

[22] National Resources Planning Board, *Public Land Acquisition, Part II, Urban
Lands*, Government Printing Office, February, 1941.

very serious difficulty of enforcing the deed restrictions, because if the restrictor dies, and the next owner has no specific interest in the restriction provisions, there is no one to bring suit to achieve enforcement.

MORTGAGE AND LEASE RESTRICTIONS

Limitations on the use of land by mortgagors and lessors are more generally used than deed restrictions. Almost no land, urban or rural, is actually leased or mortgaged without some restricting provisions. These are, however, designed to protect lenders and landlords, not, ordinarily, to insure social values and costs in the use of land.

At the present time, society has no technique whereby it can insert desired restrictions into private mortgage contracts or leases, although if this could be done it would be a very useful means of controlling land use. The increase in public land ownership in many areas through tax reversion, federal land purchase, foreclosure of state land mortgages, and reversions through delinquency of irrigation and drainage district levies is increasing the sphere of influence of social control, since where a public agency is a landlord, it can use mortgage and lease restrictions to achieve desired land-use practices.

There has been a tendency thus far for few public agencies outside of the Federal government to take full advantage of these opportunities. However, with greater coördination of land-use policies among different public and private agencies, more effective use may be made of mortgage and lease restriction techniques.

EASEMENTS

An *easement* is a right to make use of the land of others, whether it be that of the public or of individuals, for a precise and definite purpose not inconsistent with a general right of property in the owner, especially where it is for the public use. Easements include the right of pasture on other land, of taking game on other land, of fishing in the waters, of taking wood, minerals, or other produce of the soil from other land, of receiving or discharging water over other land, and many others.

Easements of every kind must originate in a grant or agreement, express or implied, of the owner. One of the most common easements is the granting of a right-of-way by the owner to permit use of his land by someone else for a road, or to construct a power or telephone line on his property, or for some similar purpose. The right-of-way may involve only the use of the air over the land, or it may involve surface or subsurface or supersurface rights. Access rights to streams and woods for hunting and fishing are another use of easements. Such easements frequently bring appreciable sums and may not interfere with the regular use made of the land by the owner.

EXTRALEGAL PROCEDURES

There is another type of social implementation or group control of landed property that alert public or private agencies occasionally use known as *extralegal procedures*. These actions are within the law, yet slightly stretching the law. In other words, action occurs that was not contemplated in the law yet is not specifically prohibited by it. For example, in tax delinquency foreclosure procedures, the cost of the foreclosure process may be so high that on low-valued properties the county or township cannot afford to foreclose. Consequently, the local governmental unit may get some of the owners of the delinquent properties to deed the land to it. Thus, no foreclosure cost.

Another example of the use of extralegal procedures is that of a hunting club that wanted exclusive hunting rights to a 10-mile square area so that its members could get a deer each fall. The club canvassed the area and gave each occupant landowner a membership in the club. In return, all the landowner had to do was post his land. The state law prohibits hunting on posted property and provides a stiff fine for violations. Thus, the hunting club has good hunting territory—all within the law, yet stetching the law slightly.

In the adoption of zoning ordinances, public officials may hold extra meetings (uncalled for by statute) in explaining zoning, getting it accepted, and consequently decreasing significantly the enforcement and administration problems later. This is more than good local government administration—it is using extralegal procedures to good advantage in achieving improved land use.

REFERENCES FOR FURTHER READING

Bagley, William C., "The Task of Institutionalism," Chap. II in Solo, Robert A. (ed.), *Economics and the Public Interest,* Rutgers University Press, New Brunswick, N.J., 1955.

Bassett, Edward M., *Zoning,* Russell Sage Foundation, New York, 1936, Chaps. II, III, IV, and V.

Clark, J. M., *Social Control of Business,* 2d ed., McGraw-Hill Book Company, Inc., New York, 1939, Chaps. I, V, XII, XIII, and XIV.

Commons, John R., *Institutional Economics,* The Macmillan Company, New York, 1934, Chap. II.

Ely, R. T., and Wehrwein, G. S., *Land Economics,* The Macmillan Company, New York, 1940, pp. 99–111.

Johnson, V. Webster, and Barlowe, Raleigh, *Land Problems and Policies,* McGraw-Hill Book Company, Inc., New York, 1934, Chap. XIII.

Landis, Paul H., *Social Control,* J. B. Lippincott Company, Philadelphia, 1939, Chaps. I, II, XVII, and XIX.

Penn, Raymond J., "Public Interest in Private Land," Chap. XIII in Timmons,

John F., and Murray, William G. (eds.), *Land Problems and Policies,* Iowa State College Press, Ames, Iowa, 1950.

Rowlands, W. A., Trenk, F. B., and Penn, R. J., *Rural Zoning in Wisconsin,* Wisconsin Experiment Stations Bulletin 479, November, 1948.

Rural Zoning in the United States, U.S. Department of Agriculture, Agricultural Research Service, Government Printing Office, Washington, D.C., Agricultural Information Bulletin 59, January, 1952.

State Legislation for Better Land Use, Special Report by an Interbureau Committee of the U.S. Department of Agriculture, Government Printing Office, Washington, D.C., April, 1941, Chap. I.

chapter 17

AGRICULTURAL LAND TENURE AND TENANCY

FOUNDATIONS OF LAND TENURE AND TENANCY IN THE UNITED STATES

America's Traditional Land Policy—Legal Background of Land Tenure in the United States

EXTENT AND TREND OF FARM TENANCY

History of Farm Tenancy—Extent of Farm Tenancy in the United States

FACTORS IN THE GROWTH OF FARM TENANCY

Land Ownership in Fee Simple Absolute—Disposition of the Public Domain—Speculation and High Land Values —The Cropper System—Recurring Economic Depressions —Credit and Tax Policies—Natural Hazards

LANDLORD-TENANT RELATIONS

Forms of Rent Payment—Length of Leases—Written vs. Verbal Leases—Insecurity of Occupancy—Compensation for Improvements and Penalties for Deterioration—Remedies for Nonpayment of Rent—Kinship Between Landlords and Tenants

STRENGTHS AND WEAKNESSES OF FARM TENANCY

Arguments for Farm Tenancy: A STEPPINGSTONE TO FARM OWNERSHIP, FARM MORE CLOSELY APPROXIMATES OPTIMUM SIZE, MISCELLANEOUS ADVANTAGES OF TENANCY—*Arguments Against Farm Tenancy—Status of Farm Tenancy in Europe*

IMPROVEMENT OF FARM TENURE AND TENANCY

Economic Foundations for Farm Tenancy Reform—Programs to Improve American Farm Tenancy—Farm Tenancy Programs in Other Nations—The Future of Farm Tenancy

EVERY INDIVIDUAL enjoys a claim, right, or form of tenure with respect to some land, varying from the right of passage over it on a street, highway, or trail to ownership in fee simple. No one enjoys absolute ownership. Society entrusts certain rights in the use of land resources to private individuals as long as such trusteeship best serves the social interest. Governments have taken away many private rights in land through use of the police power, eminent domain, and taxation. Thus, landowners share their property with the state to some degree, often being greatly restricted in uses that they can make of their lands, while in other cases they are restricted little, if at all.

Land *tenure* is a broad term covering all those relationships established among men that determine their varying rights in the use of land. It deals with the splitting of property rights, or their division among various owners, between owner and occupier, and creditor, and between private owners and the public; and it includes assessment of taxes on private rights, and regulation of land use through various social control devices. Land tenure also refers to the period of time for which rights in land are held.[1]

Tenancy is a much more limited term than tenure and refers to the occupier's or land operator's practice of renting the land from other individuals (known as "landlords") who own it. Thus, tenancy is merely one phase of the general field of land tenure, dealing with the splitting of rights between owner and occupier.

A complete analysis of land tenure includes land credit, land taxation, police power, eminent domain, and other social controls, since all these involve the division of property rights in land—either between owner or occupier and financier, or between private individuals and public bodies.[2] However, only those aspects of tenure involving tenancy, or the division of rights between owner and occupier, those involving division of title among various private owners, and those involving division of ownership between private owners and public owners—or extensivity, rather than intensivity—will be discussed on the following pages and in the next chapter.

[1] Harris states that the concept "land tenure" refers to the manner in which and the period for which rights in land are held. (See Marshall Harris, *Origin of the Land Tenure System in the U.S.*, Iowa State College Press, Ames, Iowa, 1953, p. 1.)

[2] Salter divides those aspects of human behavior in which property rights in surface units are the dominant directing factor into two groups, as problems arising from (1) land exchange, and (2) land tenure. Under the first group, he lists land ownership, land values, and land transactions; under the second, tenancy, land credit, title splitting, land taxation, and land regulation. (See L. A. Salter, Jr., "The Content of Land Economics and Research Methods Adapted to Its Needs," *Journal of Farm Economics*, Vol. XXIV, No. 1, February, 1942, pp. 226–247; and the author's comments, *ibid.*, pp. 249–251.)

FOUNDATIONS OF LAND TENURE AND TENANCY
IN THE UNITED STATES

The rights and privileges of the public and of private individuals i all classes of land are established by law and custom. Consequently, tenur is more a phase or function of cultures, laws, customs, and societal ir stitutions than is land utilization; but it is not necessarily independent c physical backgrounds and foundations. Land tenure, of course, affect land utilization because production may be increased or reduced by th laws, customs, and institutions associated with land tenure.[3]

AMERICA'S TRADITIONAL LAND POLICY

Early plans for disposal of the public domain emphasized the need c revenue to operate the new Federal government. It was also the avowe purpose of early American land policy to establish family-sized farms o the public domain, owned by those who operated them. The method used to dispose of the public domain, including the credit system, th cash sale system, and the preëmption procedures followed in the early par of the last century, as well as the later policies of giving the land outrigh to settlers under homestead laws—all were designed to accomplish thi purpose.

The feeling was widespread that unlimited freedom of disposition o property in land would best serve to attain the major aim of establishin; family-sized farms owned by those who operated them. It was arguec that this freedom of disposition of property in land had the advantages o elasticity and readiness of adjustment to changing conditions, so tha under it each individual was free to acquire and own the size and type o farm unit he was best fitted to handle.

This belief rested on the assumption that the majority of individual: will act continuously in their own interest, and that the individual inter est coincides with the social or public interest.[4] The extent of farm tenancy in the United States today, and the problems associated with it are ample evidence that in practice the principle does not work out alto gether in this way and that a number of socially undesirable results have stemmed from our traditional policy of complete freedom of disposition of landed property.[5]

[3] For example, medieval agricultural production was relatively small, because of the system of feudal land tenure and the lack of scientific farming knowledge. See Social Science Research Council, *Research in Agricultural Land Tenure: Scope and Method,* Bulletin 20, New York, April, 1933, p. 2.

[4] L. C. Gray, "Our Major Land Use Problems and Suggested Lines of Action," U.S. Department of Agriculture, *Yearbook,* 1940, Government Printing Office, p. 405.

[5] After title passed to private owners, there were no restrictions on the right of the owner to dispose of the land in any way or at any time he might desire, although state

LEGAL BACKGROUND OF LAND TENURE IN THE UNITED STATES

American land law springs largely from English common law. In eleventh-century England, the king assumed supreme right over all land, and as lord sovereign divided the land among his vassals, who had no original rights in the land, but only those rights deriving from the king's grant. The mesne lords in turn transferred the land to their tenants; but all land, in the last analysis, belonged to the king. Each individual in the chain, below the rank of lord, held or used the land on condition of performing certain services or duties. Thus, all land was "feudal" land, as contrasted with "allodial" land, which the owner possessed in his own right; and "tenure" concerned the relationships between the grantor and the grantee in regard to rights in land.[6]

This feudal relationship between lord and overlord has given rise to court controversies in the United States. Some courts have held that there were no limits to the extent to which the common law was adopted in the Colonies, while others have insisted that only that portion was adopted which was applicable to colonial conditions. The fact remains that in colonial times oaths of fealty to the lord were taken, and services (often nominal rents) rendered. Some authorities argue that after the Revolutionary War the feudal position of lord sovereign, previously occupied by the king, passed to the state with other sovereign rights. Statutes or judicial decisions have declared restricted tenure nonexistent in some states—that is, the last vestige of feudal import has been removed, and individual title derived from the government involves the entire transfer of ownership of the land; or in other words, ownership is purely allodial.[7]

Regardless of the relative merits of these arguments, in the United States the people traditionally consider ownership as assigning absolute control. Consequently, various schemes of land reform, like the proposal of land nationalization, which had a wide following in England, would not be received to the same extent in the United States, where the people are not accustomed to regard the right of the landowner as limited.[8]

The almost unlimited freedom of disposition of property in land, developed in the United States through our traditional land policy of rapidly settling the public domain, has created a widespread feeling on

laws were passed to determine the direction of ownership, in case the owner died intestate.

[6] Cf. H. W. Spiegel, *Land Tenure Policies at Home and Abroad*, University of North Carolina Press, 1941, p. 8; and Marshall Harris, *op. cit.*, p. 3.

[7] These states are Connecticut, New York, Maryland, Virginia, Ohio, Wisconsin, West Virginia, Minnesota, California, and possibly Kentucky. Spiegel, *op. cit.*, p. 8.

[8] Spiegel indicates that in England, where the doctrine of "feudal" or limited tenure was never given up, various schemes of land reform, and even the proposal of land nationalization, found a wide response because the people were accustomed to regard the right of the owner or occupier as limited. (See *ibid.*, p. 10.)

the part of most Americans that the rights of individual owners are not limited. But society always reserves at least three specific sticks out of the bundle of rights in land, namely the rights to *tax,* to *condemn,* and to *police.* The fee simple owner holds the largest possible quantity of rights under our system of private property. He holds these rights for the longest period of time, and his rights are effective immediately. All other estates are conditioned by some limitation as to quantity of rights, as to permanence, or as to how soon the rights are effective.[9]

EXTENT AND TREND OF FARM TENANCY

Public ownership has not been generally recommended, nor has it been a major issue in the United States for agricultural land, as it has been for certain other major types of land. American agriculture consists of millions of small, family-sized, generally diversified units; and many of the more serious economic and social problems associated with private ownership and exploitation (particularly in mineral and forest lands) have not arisen in agriculture.

Farm tenancy in the United States has received a great deal of attention, as reflected in the report of the President's Committee on Farm Tenancy (1937), the passage of the Bankhead-Jones Farm Tenant Act (1937), the passage of some state legislation dealing with landlord-tenant relations, and the appointment of state farm tenancy committees. The depression thirties, which were accompanied by severe drought and crop failure, aggravated the problems associated with farm tenancy and helped to focus public attention upon the nature of farm tenancy and its place in the economy.

The Census of Agriculture defines farm tenants as farmers who rent all the land they operate. This would include all croppers, cash renters, standing renters, and various kinds of share renters who rent all their land. Sharecroppers are listed separately and are defined as tenants who own no work stock. The laws of some states define sharecroppers as tenants, while others hold that sharecroppers are laborers.[10]

The census classifies farmers who rent part and own part of the land they operate as part owners, although the problems that arise in connection with the rented portions of these farms are in many respects similar to the problems associated with full tenancy and sharecropping. The census makes a separate listing showing farms operated by hired managers, and these operators should be considered as employees or laborers rather than as tenants.

[9] Harris, *op. cit.,* p. 5.

[10] See U.S. Department of Agriculture, *Farm Tenancy,* Bureau of Agricultural Economics, County Planning Series No. 9, p. 4.

HISTORY OF FARM TENANCY

Farm tenancy has existed in one form or another for thousands of years; even in early historic times farmers rented land, paying a share of the crops, cash, or personal services. In the United States some farmers have always rented land, but only after the Census enumerated tenants for the first time in 1880 did we recognize that farm tenancy has assumed major proportions. In 1880 a fourth of the four million farmers in the nation were tenants, and during the next 55 years the number of tenant farms increased from a million to nearly three million (a gain of 180 percent), while the number of farms increased only 32 percent. Thus, in 1935, 42 per cent of the 6¾ million farmers were tenants. From 1935 to 1955, the total number of tenants, as well as the number of tenants in proportion to the total number of farmers, declined. The 1954 Census of Agriculture revealed that the percentage of farm tenancy had declined to 24 percent, the lowest on record.

Farm tenancy increased in every decade from 1880 to 1930, but declined steadily after that. The greatest increase in the percentage of tenancy occurred during the decade from 1890 to 1900 (28.4 percent to 35.3 percent), and the greatest percentage decline occurred from 1940 to 1945 (38.7 percent to 31.7 percent) During the next five years, to 1950, the percentage decreased to 26.8 and declined still further to 24.0 in 1955.

The relatively large increase in tenancy during the decade of the nineties may be in part accounted for by the fact that free land in the United States substantially disappeared after 1890. All figures on tenancy must be used with care, because of the limitations of census data. How many croppers were counted as tenants in 1880 and what the rate of increase was before 1920 in the number so counted will never be known. It is generally recognized, however, that many were not counted as tenants at the outset, and that the count has increased as the enumerators have learned better how to follow instructions. It is also known that during these years more and more plantations were being broken up into cropper holdings.[11]

EXTENT OF FARM TENANCY IN THE UNITED STATES

Approximately three out of every five farmers in the United States own all the land they operate, and nearly two out of every five rent all or part of their operating units.

Farm tenancy is more pronounced in the South than in any other major section of the United States. (See Figure 22.) Nearly a half of all farmers in the 16 southern states are farm tenants. This number (which includes croppers) comprises almost two-thirds of the total tenants and croppers

[11] Cf. J. D. Black and R. H. Allen, "The Growth of Farm Tenancy in the United States," *Quarterly Journal of Economics*, Vol. LI, May, 1937, pp. 399 ff.

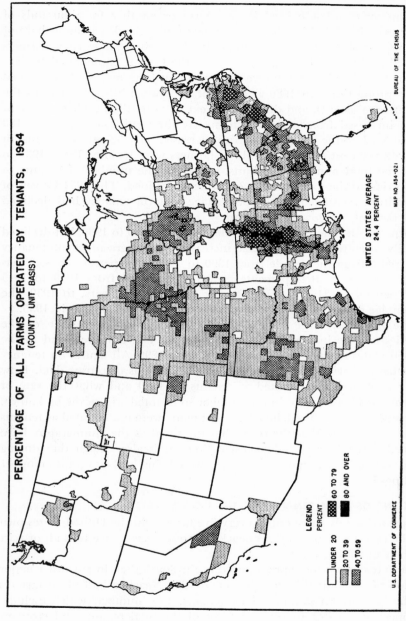

Figure 22. Percentage of All Farms Operated by Tenants, 1954. (Source: U.S. Department of Commerce, Bureau of the Census.)

n the nation. Tenancy is lightest in the 11 western states, only about an eighth of the farmers being tenants.

The proportion of land in farms under lease is considerably different from the above figures. For example, in the western states where tenancy is lowest, large acreages of rented grazing lands make up more than a third of all western land in farms operated under lease. (See Figure 23.) These figures do not include some of the federal, state, railroad, and absentee-owned land rented to ranchmen for grazing purposes, so that the actual proportion of rented land is even greater.

Another factor accounting for the difference in proportion of rented land and proportion of tenant farmers is the fact that farming corporations are extensive renters in the specialized cash crop areas where much of the work is done by migratory agricultural laborers. Moreover, there are a number of "pockets" in these cash crop areas (and also in the semi-arid dry farming areas) where the tenancy rate is comparatively high.[12]

There is a close correlation between the amount of farm tenancy and the type of farming practiced. Areas of high tenancy are predominantly those of specialized cash crop production—especially the production of cotton, tobacco, wheat, and corn. Rental contracts are usually made for one year, without specific assurance of renewal. Moreover, most leases provide for payment of rent as a share of the crop.

One-year leases and share rentals tend to encourage production of annual staple crops for sale, and are not readily adaptable to livestock farming, fruit growing, dairying, or similar types of farming, which do not complete one cycle of production for several years. The highest rate of tenancy exists on cotton farms, where about half of all the operators are tenants. Tenancy in tobacco, corn, and wheat farms is also high, and in areas where rice and sugar cane predominate. In contrast, tenancy is lowest in dairy regions and in general farming areas.

FACTORS IN THE GROWTH OF FARM TENANCY

The rapid growth of farm tenancy from 1880 to 1930 in the United States, where a federal policy of encouraging operator ownership has been diligently followed, raises many questions as to how and why a high proportion of tenancy developed.

LAND OWNERSHIP IN FEE SIMPLE ABSOLUTE

One of the most important factors—considered by some the most important—in the growth of tenancy is our policy of permitting land to be

---

[12] In some of the western states where Orientals make up a significant portion of farm operators, state legislation prohibiting them from owning land has been a special factor tending to increase tenancy rates. However, purchase of land by American-born children of Oriental parents is tending to offset the effect of these laws. (See *Farm Tenancy*, Report of the President's Committee, Government Printing Office, 1937, p. 36.)

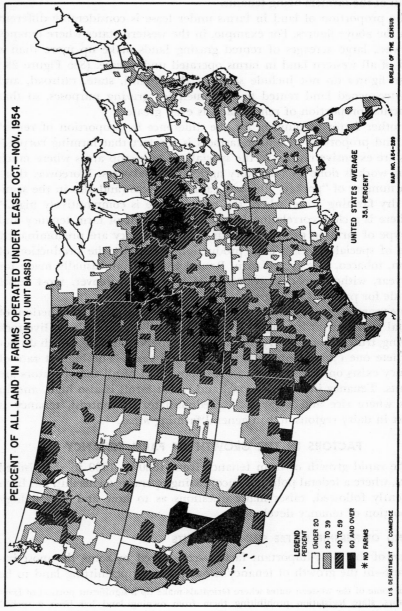

PERCENT OF ALL LAND IN FARMS OPERATED UNDER LEASE, OCT.-NOV., 1954
(COUNTY UNIT BASIS)

UNITED STATES AVERAGE
35.1 PERCENT

MAP NO. A54-289

BUREAU OF THE CENSUS

LEGEND
PERCENT
UNDER 20
20 TO 39
40 TO 59
60 AND OVER
* NO FARMS

U.S. DEPARTMENT OF COMMERCE

Figure 23. Percent of All Land in Farms Operated Under Lease, October–November, 1954. (Source: U.S. Department of Commerce, Bureau of the Census.)

made private property in fee simple absolute.[13] This policy permits property accumulation and transfer with practically no restrictions on its use or disposition. It is undoubtedly correct to say that our ancestors, who struggled so long to free themselves from the restraints of a feudal tenure system, went too far in the opposite direction in their zeal to create conditions that would eliminate such restraints. For example, primogeniture and entail were abolished early in the history of the United States, to discourage retention of large tracts in the hands of one family and to impede development of a landed aristocracy like that which had developed in Europe.

The American system of land ownership in fee simple absolute makes land freely salable and easy to mortgage. This freedom of use and disposal of land has made it possible to treat land much the same as any other commodity. The most undesirable results of complete freedom of disposition of landed property were postponed in a young pioneer society where there was a rapid expansion of economic activity and profit opportunities through various speculative and financial devices.

DISPOSITION OF THE PUBLIC DOMAIN

Another important factor in tenancy growth was the procedure followed in disposing of the public domain. For nearly three-quarters of a century before 1862, when the first homestead act was passed, public domain tracts were sold at public auction, with practically no limitations on the amount of land acquired or purposes of acquisition. Moreover, these sales continued until 1890, and homestead policy was then modified to permit money commutation of part of the required period of occupancy.

The rapid disposal of much of the public domain in small units of 40-, 80-, or 160-acre tracts through sale and homestead entries has resulted in division of the western lands into numerous small holdings. The dry farming and ranching practices adapted to the arid and semiarid regions require considerably larger acreages than these for satisfactory operating units, or even larger than the maximum of 640 acres which the amended Homestead Act of 1916 granted.[14]

[13] Cf. *ibid.*, p. 39; and Gray, *op. cit.*, pp. 404 ff.

[14] Studies show that some 4000 acres of average range land are required for a small family ranch operating unit without irrigation. If irrigated lands or wild hay meadows are available for hay production, the acreage of range land necessary for a satisfactory family unit can be reduced in the ratio of about 12 acres of range land for each acre of hay land. Thus, if a ranch family operated 100 acres of hay and about 2500 acres of grazing land, it would be a fairly adequate family-sized ranch unit. (See M. H. Saunderson, "A Method for the Valuation of Livestock Ranch Properties and Grazing Lands," Montana Agricultural Experiment Station Mimeographed Circular 6, March, 1938.) In the case of dry farming lands, at least 800 acres, and with increased acreage restrictions through the Soil Bank and other federal grain output control programs, between 1000

One of the most serious land-use problems of the arid and semiarid regions in the thirties was that of blocking the numerous small ownership tracts into units of economic size controlled for maximum productivity. These numerous small tracts were scattered in shotgun fashion among many types of owners, including railroads, investment and mortgage companies, commercial banks, insurance companies, land banks, nonresident individuals, nonoperating residents, resident operators, county, state, and Federal governments, and others (see Figure 24). The thousands of separate properties, combined with absentee ownership, made the problem of working out effective utilization difficult.

The numerous small absentee-owned, scattered parcels necessitated farmers and ranchers leasing from several owners residing in various parts of the nation. This placed the operator in an uncertain position because he had no assurance from year to year that he could maintain his operating unit intact. This insecurity encouraged misuse and abuse of the land.

Considerable progress in blocking out the small tracts and establishing more secure occupancy and use of farm and ranch lands has been made in recent years by: (1) consolidation of farms and ranches by the more successful ranchers taking over lands abandoned by their less successful neighbors; (2) voluntary grouping of ranchers to form coöperative grazing districts and acquire effective control of a given area (collective tenure); [15] (3) establishment of adequate control of the public range in areas where federal lands are a significant portion of the total through the Taylor Grazing Act; and (4) outright purchase of the numerous small privately owned tracts in selected areas by the Federal government to block out adequate operating units.

SPECULATION AND HIGH LAND VALUES

A third important cause of tenancy growth in the United States was speculation and resulting high land values, which were closely associated with the two preceding factors. A considerable amount of land speculation resulted from the rapidity with which the public domain was disposed of, and the expanding market for agricultural products accompanying rapid increase in population. Many believed that, since land is physically limited in amount, it would not be many years before con-

---

and 1600 acres are more generally considered necessary for fairly efficient operation of modern production and harvesting equipment. With this size of unit on the better dry farm lands of the semiarid sections, the average operator can earn a satisfactory labor income for the year for family living expenses. (See R. R. Renne and H. H. Lord, "Assessment of Montana Farm Lands," Montana Agricultural Experiment Station Bulletin 348, October, 1937, pp. 53–56.)

[15] See M. H. Saunderson and N. W. Monte, "Grazing Districts in Montana: Their Purpose and Organization Procedure," Montana Agricultural Experiment Station Bulletin 326, 1936.

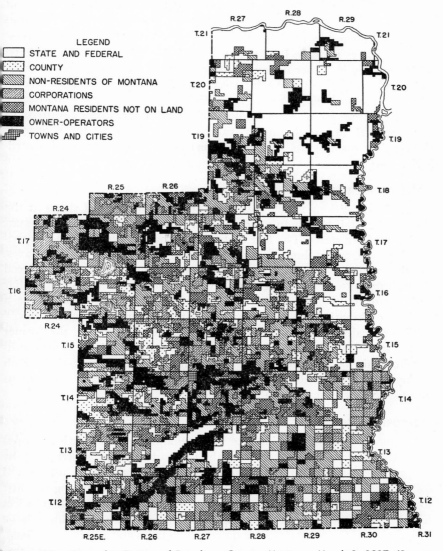

Figure 24. Ownership Pattern of Petroleum County, Montana, March 1, 1937. (Source of data: Montana Agricultural Experiment Station.)

tinued population increase would result in a scarcity of agricultural lands and an increase in agricultural prices.

Land values rose almost continuously until 1920, and this upward trend caused a widespread practice of anticipating in advance further increases in land values and capitalizing these anticipated rises into current values. The result was to force land values out of line with land productivity, with resulting increases in taxes, interest, and related overhead charges.

Agricultural prices in the interwar period (the years between World War I and World War II) were not sufficient to support these high costs, and large numbers of farm bankruptcies and foreclosures resulted. In most cases, these forced transfers caused ownership to be taken over by the creditor (usually an absentee owner) and tenancy increased accordingly.

THE CROPPER SYSTEM

Certain conditions which developed from the freeing of slaves at the close of the Civil War help to account for the high proportion of tenancy in the southern states. The fact that planters had ample land and experience in management, but no funds for paying wages to their former slaves, together with the availability of hundreds of thousands of recently freed slaves, unaccustomed to wages, uneducated, impoverished, and familiar with cotton cultivation under rigid supervision and direction, made a perfect combination for development of the cropper system of tenancy.

Theoretically at least, the cropper system tended to give the former slave a greater interest in his work and to force him to share losses resulting from his own neglect, at the same time that it minimized the cash outlay of the landlords who furnished the land, teams, and implements and usually secured half the crop.

RECURRING ECONOMIC DEPRESSIONS

Economic depressions stimulate farm tenancy growth. During depressions there is a tendency for wealth, particularly that represented by property in land, to concentrate in the hands of the more astute and financially fortunate. Prices of farm products tend to be among the first to decline during depressions, and drop faster and farther than prices of other commodities. At the same time, charges that make up a large proportion of the farmer's cash expenses (like taxes and interest) are fixed, or decline very slowly. Heavy reliance upon the general property tax, combined with the fact that farm real estate constitutes about five-sixths of the farm investment, indicates how important fixed charges like taxes and interest can become during depression periods of greatly reduced farm income.

The increasing commercialization of agriculture through mechaniza-

ion and specialization increases the amount of farm bankruptcies, foreclosures, and poverty accompanying depressions.[16] The absence of any
major business recession after 1935 and the higher level of business activ-
ty accompanying the post-World War II period have resulted in a
ignificant decrease in farm tenancy since the mid-thirties.

CREDIT AND TAX POLICIES

Credit and tax policies played important roles in farm tenancy growth.
n earlier years, farm loans were made for very short periods of from
hree to five years, with high interest charges running from 8 to 12 per-
ent, or more, and loans were made on high appraised values. Under these
onditions, a high proportion of farm bankruptcies and foreclosures was
nevitable.

The tax system of the United States, with its predominant emphasis
upon general property, placed a particularly heavy burden upon farm
ownership. Inequalities in land assessment, heavy local tax levies, and
elated tax factors contributed significantly to increased farm tenancy
hrough forced transfers of land ownership by tax deed and mortgage
oreclosure especially in the semiarid Great Plains.

NATURAL HAZARDS

Droughts, floods, and other natural hazards which were particularly
pronounced in the thirties discouraged farm ownership in some sections.
High ownership risks and resulting economic vulnerability in marginal
areas like the Great Plains and similar semiarid sections, where natural
hazards are particularly great, have caused many farm operators to regard
enancy as more desirable than ownership, particularly with existing
credit and tax policies.[17]

LANDLORD-TENANT RELATIONS

The arrangements effected between landlord and tenant regarding the
rights and duties of each have a marked effect on land utilization and the
economic and social status of farm tenancy.

[16] Three-quarters of a million farms changed ownership through foreclosure and
bankruptcy sales during the five depression years, 1930–1934. Large numbers were also
transferred to creditors or sold to avoid foreclosure. (See *Farm Tenancy*, Report of the
President's Committee, pp. 44–45, for a more detailed statement of the depression forces
that operated to increase farm tenancy.)

[17] It is significant that in some areas of the Great Plains in the thirties owners
voluntarily allowed their lands to go to tax deed, on the grounds that they could rent
the lands from public agencies after tax-deed foreclosure more cheaply than they
could own the lands and pay the high taxes charged. For a brief statement showing
the economic significance of fluctuating farm prices and relatively high taxes in areas
where natural conditions create a high degree of uncertainty in crop production and
range carrying capacities, see R. R. Renne and H. H. Lord, "Montana Farm Price
Variations," Montana Agricultural Extension Service Circular 93, June, 1938, and
"Montana Farm Taxes," Montana Agricultural Extension Service Circular 94, June, 1938.

FORMS OF RENT PAYMENT

Various forms of rent payment include cash, livestock share, crop share, crop share cash, sharecropping (where the tenant supplies labor only, the landlord supplying land and equipment), standing rent (where a stated amount of the principal crops is paid as rent), or stated price renting (where there is an agreement to raise crops or stock and deliver them to the landowner at a stated price per unit). Under the livestock share and crop share forms of rent payment, the share that goes to the landlord varies in different areas of the country. The most usual arrangement under livestock share leasing is for the landlord and tenant to share the ownership of all, or a large part, of the productive livestock, usually sharing receipts and expenses on a half-and-half basis, except that the tenant supplies all the labor.

Crop share renting is the most common method of leasing for the United States as a whole, and in many areas a half-and-half share basis is common, although there is a tendency for the share rent paid to be smaller on very intensive crops like cotton and tobacco than on less intensive crops like small grains and corn. Livestock share leasing usually grows out of or results in a close association between the landlord and tenant. Crop share renting is particularly well adapted to areas in which a single cash crop is produced. It has a very important weakness in that it provides little opportunity for the production of livestock and tends to emphasize the sale off the farm of most of the crops produced, which tends to deplete the soil. Moreover, studies indicate that there is no necessary relation between the landlord's share and the yield or productivity of the soil. In many areas, division of the share between the landlord and tenant seems to be established and continued more by custom than by yield or productivity rating of the lands.[18]

Under cash renting, the tenant ordinarily has the greatest degree of freedom in the utilization of the land of any form of renting. Cash renting tends to lead to less soil exploitation than crop share renting, because livestock enterprises are more intensively developed, security of occupancy is greater, and the cash tenant is usually in a much stronger financial position than the share tenant. This is the typical picture where cash renting is common, although in some share renting areas only the smallest and poorest farms are rented for exorbitant cash rates to highly insecure

---

[18] It would seem logical to assume that on the more fertile and productive lands the share which goes to the landlord would be greater than that in the case of very poor or unproductive lands, because on the latter the proportion of the total return required for producing the crop—the tenant's labor, cash expenses, etc.—is greater and the tenant would have to have a larger share of the total product to meet his expenses. In some preliminary studies in Montana by the author, no correlation seems to be found between the division of the share and the productivity rating of the soil.

and financially weak tenants. Under these conditions, results of cash renting are decidedly unfavorable.

LENGTH OF LEASES

A great variation also exists in the length of lease periods and in the form of leases. Many leases are for only one year, others are for periods of five to ten years, or even longer.

The year-to-year lease is prevalent throughout the United States, and the most common plan is for the lease to run indefinitely and to close only by a termination notice given several months before a specified date. A less common arrangement is for landlords to grant relatively long-term leases, usually from three to five years, but reserve the right to terminate the lease by notice some time in advance of a set date. This does not give the tenant much more security of tenure than the year-to-year lease, and makes it impossible for him to plan his farming operations over a period of years.

On the other hand, fixed leases of three to five years, or longer, have many disadvantages from the landlord's point of view, although such fixed-period leases can be written to give the landlord an option of terminating the lease at the end of any crop year, provided that the tenant is definitely unsatisfactory, as indicated by his doing certain things prohibited in the lease.

The relationships between tenant and landlord, however, cannot be improved merely by signing the landlord and tenant to a fixed contract for a period of years. Harmonious working relations between the two must be built upon a sound basis approximating the character of a business partnership, and this requires an intelligent and sane attitude on the part of both. Tenancy conditions can be made quite satisfactory and socially constructive without the landlord's coöperation, through legislation placing more managerial freedom and responsibility in the hands of the operator—as has been done in some other countries.

The use of provisions in leases that either party must give the other notice a specified period in advance of the date of termination, if he plans to terminate the contract (providing that this period is sufficiently long to assure the tenant time to arrange for another place), is about the most effective way of dealing with the farm lease problem, so far as term of leases is concerned.

WRITTEN VS. VERBAL LEASES

Most farm leases in the United States are merely verbal agreements or understandings between landlord and tenant. In many areas written contracts are relatively few or practically nonexistent. The oral lease is convenient for making changes, but is likely to give rise to misunderstandings that would be less likely with a specific written contract, and i may cause difficulties or failures to renew leases at the end of the year.

INSECURITY OF OCCUPANCY

Most farm tenants do not have any security of occupancy from year t(year.[19] Without such security, tenants are not likely to use farm practice that look further ahead than the present year. The likelihood of moving combined with the fact that upon departure tenants cannot ordinaril) obtain compensation for improvements made, restrains them from makin§ improvements on the farm where they are temporarily located. Statute in many states, as well as the common law, cause an improvement affixec to the soil by an agricultural tenant to become the property of the land lord at the termination of the lease.

Some states have already changed their statutes to allow tenants to tak(away removable fixtures and improvements, while other states have changed the common-law rule by requiring landlords to make all repair: and improvements; but neither of these adjustments covers improvement: that cannot be removed. Farm tenants do make many such improvements including application of lime and fertilizer, construction of fences, ditches and roads, and terracing.

If productivity is to be maintained, tenants must make improvements Consequently, plans should be worked out that will encourage them tc do so. This involves incorporating into the written lease, plans for com- pensation to the outgoing tenant for the unexhausted value of such improvements. Although, at present, the number of written farm lease contracts is comparatively small, there has been some tendency toward the increasing use of written leases.

Compensation for improvements made by the tenant may be of two main types, (1) improvements that the tenant cannot make without prior consent of the landlord, and (2) improvements that he is free to make without consulting the landlord. More permanent types of improvements (buildings, permanent fences, commercial fruit and vegetable enterprises, and the like) are usually included in the former, and items like the application of fertilizer and manure, lime, and related improvements in the latter.

COMPENSATION FOR IMPROVEMENTS AND PENALTIES FOR DETERIORATION

The amount that the landlord should pay the outgoing tenant for un- exhausted improvements should ordinarily be agreed upon in advance.[20]

[19] Marshall Harris, "Compensation as a Means of Improving the Farm Tenancy System," U.S. Resettlement Administration, Land Use Planning Publication 14, 1937, mimeographed.

[20] Amount of compensation need not always be determined in advance. For a discus- sion of statutory regulations see Marshall Harris, Albert H. Cotton, and Rainer

The tenant should agree to keep a complete cost record of improvements he makes, so that the amount of his compensation at termination of the lease can be equitably determined. In case the landlord and tenant disagree on the amount of compensation, an appeal should be made to an arbitrative board selected by the parties concerned. This procedure should work out satisfactorily in most cases, though there will be instances when the temperaments, personalities, and characters of the two contracting parties may make satisfactory settlement impossible.

Although there has been an increased tendency in recent years to incorporate compensation provisions in lease contracts, the practice is still not very general. Only the more farsighted landlords appear to have adopted this practice. Failure to use such compensation provisions more generally is an important factor accounting for some of the more significant shortcomings of farm tenancy in the United States, partly accounting for the low economic and social status of farm tenants in many sections.[21]

Many written leases specify that the tenant must treat the property in a good and proper manner, or return the farm in as good condition as when he first rented it, ordinary wear and depreciation of course being excepted. As a matter of fact, considerably more written leases contain this provision than provisions for compensation for unexhausted value of improvements made by the tenant. It should be added, however, that in cases where the farm deteriorates by wasteful or negligent practices, the only recourse available to the landlord is usually to terminate the contract.

In more glaring or obvious cases, of courses, the tenant can be sued in the courts; but the most serious types of deterioration caused by wasteful and negligent practices of tenants are so gradual and so difficult to measure for a single year that the landlord ordinarily does not find it easy to make a strong case against the tenant. Moreover, unless reciprocal provisions are incorporated in the lease contract to allow the tenant compensation for improvements, more liberal courts, at least, would not be inclined to consider the landlord's case in deterioration instances too favorably.[22]

Schickele, *Some Legal Aspects of Landlord-Tenant Relationships,* Iowa Agricultural Experiment Station Bulletin 371, April, 1938; and Iowa State Planning Board, *Report and Recommendations of the Farm Tenancy Committee,* Des Moines, Iowa, October, 1938.

[21] Studies conducted in various parts of the United States substantiate census data which indicate that homes of tenant farmers have fewer fixed conveniences of all kinds than homes of owner farmers, but that tenants' homes are much more like those of owners with reference to movable equipment. (Cf. Margaret G. Reid, *Status of Farm Housing in Iowa,* Iowa Agricultural Experiment Station Research Bulletin 174, September, 1934; and *Some Factors Affecting Improvement in Iowa Farm Family Housing,* Iowa Agricultural Experiment Station Bulletin 349, June, 1936.)

[22] The Report of the President's Committee on Farm Tenancy lists four important reasons why, in spite of statutory provisions, common-law rule, and contractural stipulations, a large proportion of tenant operators' farms not only are unimproved but are

If many of the greatest evils of farm tenancy in the United States are to be removed, lease contracts must contain provisions for compensation to tenants for improvements, as well as provisions for penalties for deterioration.

REMEDIES FOR NONPAYMENT OF RENT

When granting possession and control of his land to another, the landlord is ordinarily protected in his right to receive payment for such temporary surrender of control, and the foregoing of benefits which he might have secured from personal operation of the land. Such protection usually arises in legal form from the *right of distress, the right of attachment,* or the *landlord's lien.*[23]

As a remedy for nonpayment of rent, the landlord can take and hold, under the right of distress, any goods and chattels found upon the land, if by such action he does not cause undue hardship on the tenant. The right of distress exists in the United States in a number of areas, particularly in the East, although in some areas distress has become impersonalized and the approved remedy is identical with or closely similar to the ordinary process of attachment. A statutory lien upon crops or chattels has come to be the most common remedy for nonpayment of rent.[24]

KINSHIP BETWEEN LANDLORDS AND TENANTS

Where tenants are related to the landlord, farm tenancy may serve as a desirable working arrangement when the father or father-in-law or relative is retiring from active operation of the farm and the son or son-in-law or relative is assuming full responsibility. About a fifth of the tenant farmers of the United States are related to their landlords, being brothers, sisters, children, or grandchildren of their landlords, or married into the

allowed to deteriorate year after year, until the soils are seriously depleted and eroded, and buildings and fences dilapidated: (1) A large proportion of landlords are interested in their farms only as temporary sources of income or for speculative gain; (2) much deterioration is so gradual and so difficult to measure for a given year that the landlord finds it difficult to make a case of deterioration against the tenant; (3) many tenants are negligent about maintaining the farm in its original condition, to say nothing of improving it, because they are not assured that they can continue their occupancy; and further, they know it is improbable that they will be held responsible for deterioration; (4) tenants realize they will receive no compensation for any improvement added to prevent deterioration. (See *Farm Tenancy,* Report of the President's Committee, p. 52.)

[23] *Ibid.*

[24] Some 29 states have adopted the statutory lien, including all southern states and most of those in other areas of high tenancy. In general, the law fixes definitely the amount of lien to which the tenant is subject, and the length of time for which it is valid. Ordinarily the language of the lien restricts its operation to the current year's crop. In the southern states, the landlord's lien for rent is usually attended by a statutory lien for advances and supplies. In such cases, these liens are usually balanced by the mechanics' lien, which aims to assure the cropper of payment for his labor. (*Ibid.*)

landlord's family. The percentage of tenants related to their landlords is comparatively low in the South and the drier portions of the Great Plains, where many farms are fairly new. In the South it is lowest in areas where colored farmers are most numerous. In many northern counties in Wisconsin, Minnesota, Nebraska, Kansas, and Utah, more than a third of the farm tenants are related to their landlords.[25]

It has been observed generally that tenants who are related to their landlords are more inclined than other tenants to use farming practices aimed at conservation of the land and maintenance of improvements, because many of the related tenants expect to become owners, and many of them work under general supervision of their landlord. This is not always the case, however, and there are numerous examples of depleted farms operated by one of several heirs, who has the task of obtaining the consent of three or four brothers and sisters in distant cities before he can turn a hand in operating the farm. Moreover, despite kinship, the landlord may have only a transitory interest in maintenance of soil fertility and upkeep of improvements, because he looks forward to early disposition of the property by sale.[26]

Another important aspect of kinship between landlords and tenants is the fact that when farm estates are settled, a great deal of farm wealth is transferred to cities, because many of the children or relatives have migrated from the farms. O. E. Baker has estimated that from three to four billion dollars were drained from farms to cities by inheritance during the decade 1920–1930.[27] The division of the farm property among the heirs of deceased farm owners tends to require the farm operator, who may be one of the heirs, to buy out the other heirs at prices often above strict market values, or necessitates his sharing the annual returns from the farm each year with the various heirs who have an interest in it. This aspect of inheritance or transference of property through decease places a heavy burden on the farm, through the necessity of practically repurchasing it every generation.[28]

STRENGTHS AND WEAKNESSES OF FARM TENANCY

Some of the economic and social effects of farm tenancy as it has operated in the United States can be seen from an analysis of the characteristics of tenant families.

[25] "A Graphic Summary of Farm Tenure: 1950," U.S. Department of Commerce, Bureau of the Census, and U.S. Department of Agriculture, Bureau of Agricultural Economics, Government Printing Office, Coöperative Report, Vol. V, Part 5, 1952, p. 76.

[26] *Farm Tenancy*, Report of the President's Committee, p. 47.

[27] O. E. Baker, "Rural-Urban Migration and the National Welfare," *Annals of the Association of American Geographers*, Vol. III, June, 1933, pp. 59–126.

[28] For some aspects of this problem, see E. D. Tetreau, "The Location of Heirs and the Value of Their Inheritance: Farm and City Estates," *Journal of Land and Public Utility Economics*, Vol. XVI, No. 4, November, 1940.

The average annual net income of tenants in the northern and western states is not particularly different from that of farm owners, while in the South the tenant incomes are considerably lower than those of operating owners.[29] The level of living of tenants probably does not seriously handicap them in their social, educational, and religious activities and relationships. However, tenants have costs of moving that owners do not have or do not have so often, and these in the aggregate are appreciable.[30]

Tenancy is generally more prevalent in the highly commercialized farming areas, and the proportion of products produced on the farm used by the farm family is considerably less in tenant families than in owner families. This means tenant families purchase a considerably higher proportion of their food than owner-operator families, and it is acknowledged that, generally, foods purchased lack many of the important health qualities of the fresh fruits, vegetables, meats, and dairy products produced on the farm. The lack of gardens on tenant farms is mainly a matter of insecurity. This situation undoubtedly has a bearing on the health of farm tenant groups compared with that of owners.

Tenant families are generally at a disadvantage in regard to education and literacy, because of their relatively great mobility. Studies indicate that children of less frequent movers make more rapid educational progress per school-age year than those of more frequent movers, and that excessive mobility of tenant farmers is important in hindering proper educational development and utilization of educational facilities.[31] Participation of farm tenants in religious activities is ordinarily lower than that of owners. Tenants also show a lack of interest in or failure to participate in community and group activities and coöperative enterprises, largely as a result of their high mobility and insecurity. These characteristics have serious implications because many improvements in the economic and social status of farm tenants can be achieved most effectively through local coöperative effort and group participation.

ARGUMENTS FOR FARM TENANCY

The unfavorable aspects of farm tenancy, revealed by landlord-tenant relationships and characteristics of tenant families in the United States,

[29] For a more adequate treatment of planes of living and incomes of tenant and cropper farmers on southern plantations, see A. F. Raper, *Preface to Peasantry*, University of North Carolina Press, 1941; and T. J. Woofter, Jr., *et al.*, "Landlord and Tenant on the Cotton Plantation," Work Projects Administration Research Monograph 5, 1936.

[30] J. T. Sanders, *Economic and Social Aspects of Mobility of Oklahoma Farmers*, Oklahoma Agricultural Experiment Station Bulletin 195, 1929, p. 3; and W. D. Nicholls, *Farm Tenancy in Central Kentucky*, Kentucky Agricultural Experiment Station Bulletin 303, April, 1930, p. 152.

[31] Sanders, *op. cit.*, p. 41; Nicholls, *op. cit.*, p. 176; and J. O. Rankin, *The Nebraska Farm Family*, Nebraska Agricultural Experiment Station Bulletin 185, February, 1923, p. 28.

should not be considered as a blanket condemnation of farm tenancy per se. Tenancy of the right type is a useful and important institution in many ways; but, like many other institutions, it has bad features as well as good, depending upon the conditions surrounding it.

A Steppingstone to Farm Ownership. Tenancy has played an important role in the welfare of American farmers and in the growth of agriculture. The tenancy system has enabled young and inexperienced farmers to begin as tenants when they lacked the knowledge or capital to assume the responsibilities and hazards of farm ownership. As a rung in the ladder to ownership of agricultural land this is one of the most useful aspects of tenancy as a form of land tenure. But how much tenancy is necessary to fulfill this function properly? Naturally, if there is too little tenancy, it will be impossible to have an uninterrupted movement up the ladder from the status of laborer to tenant to part owner to owner.[32]

The effect of too little tenancy is similar to that involved in climbing a ladder on which one of the rungs is missing or placed much further up the ladder than the previous rungs. On the other hand, if there is too much tenancy, the effect is to jam up a large proportion of the farm operators on a particular rung, or a group of rungs spaced close together, making it difficult for them to move on up to ownership.

A working hypothesis set up in the late twenties was that 30 percent tenancy is perhaps about the right amount to give young farmers a chance to climb the agricultural ladder from the status of hired laborer, through tenancy and mortgaged owner debt, to the free ownership of land.[33] The United States average is less than this. In Denmark, farm tenancy is about 5 percent, and is considered too little to give many aspiring farm youths opportunity to achieve farm ownership.

Farm More Closely Approximates Optimum Size. Another important argument for tenancy as a form of land tenure is the fact that with the customary practices of credit institutions and the rationing of capital that farmers are permitted to borrow in the capital market, a tenant farmer who does not have to tie up a large portion of his capital in the form of land, as do owners, may be better able than an owner to operate a farm unit more closely approximating optimum size. With prevailing farm prices, interest rates, and rental rates, Schultz found that when a corn belt farmer with restricted assets goes from tenancy to ownership,

---

[32] The agricultural ladder refers to the steps through which a farm operator passes in attaining farm ownership. In some cases, through inheritance, purchase, etc., the operator begins farming as an owner; but the great majority of farm operators who become owners begin either as laborers or tenants. Some jump from the status of laborer to that of owner, or laborer to part owner, skipping the tenant rung, but it is most usual to proceed from laborer, either on the home farm or a neighbor's farm, to tenant, to owner, and in many cases an intermediate step—namely, part ownership.

[33] H. C. Taylor, "What Should Be Done About Farm Tenancy?" *Journal of Farm Economics*, Vol. XX, No. 1, February, 1938, p. 145.

economic effects are either (1) lower rewards to the farmer and his family for their labor and management inputs, or (2) higher costs reflected in higher prices for farm outputs.[34]

In other words, if a farmer is not allowed to secure the use of as much capital as is necessary to permit him to add resources up to the point where marginal cost equals marginal revenue, the average cost per unit of output is necessarily increased, or the best combination of production factors is not achieved. If a farmer has a given amount of capital, a significant portion of which must be tied up in land at the expense of other operating capital, this result is very likely to occur. The landowner may have a higher social status in the community which ownership bestows, and he has the "privilege" of large prospective windfalls and losses; but too frequently ownership is bought at the expense of returns to the farmer and his family.[35]

Tenants have an advantage over owner-operators wherever they can secure farm lands in sufficient quantity and quality at reasonable rental rates to make efficient use of their larger operating capital. In many northern and western areas, tenant farms average appreciably larger than owner farms, and in these areas the process of capital rationing works to the advantage of tenants. In the South, however, because of the existence of certain racial, economic, and social conditions, tenant farms are much smaller than owner farms, and this advantage in favor of tenancy disappears. There are other disadvantages of current rental practices, such, for example, as the lack of compensation for improvements made by the tenant, which tend to offset and in many cases to outweigh the unfavorable implications of ownership incurred in usual capital rationing practices.

The disadvantages of ownership noted tend to encourage farm tenancy, particularly with increasing mechanization of agriculture. To offset this, adjustments must be made in farm credit practices to allow owner-operators to acquire sufficient capital to achieve as effective combinations of land and other production factors as are now achievable by tenants who do not have to allocate a considerable portion of the limited capital available to them to land purchase.[36]

---

[34] T. W. Schultz, "Capital Rationing, Uncertainty, and Farm Tenancy Reform," *Journal of Political Economy*, Vol. XLVIII, No. 3, June, 1940, p. 317.

[35] *Ibid.*

[36] Essentially, the farm credit adjustments that would be required would involve granting landowners more total capital than tenants, on grounds that the land is complete security for the loan against it and does not detract from the amount of capital which can be reasonably loaned the operator, as an operator. Most credit agencies, particularly the Federal Land Bank, insist that their loans be based both on the man and the land. Lending agencies are adopting more scientific methods of appraising, and the amounts loaned are being based primarily upon security represented by the land itself, regardless of the operator. Although the establishment of farm credit practices

Miscellaneous Advantages of Tenancy. Other less important advantages of tenancy include (1) providing the farmer a temporary arrangement or opportunity to become thoroughly acquainted with the farm before purchasing it, if for any reason he doubts the desirability of the particular place he has in mind for purchasing; (2) providing a period of apprenticeship for an inexperienced farmer under an experienced landlord; (3) providing convenient alternatives for those who have become owners and who for one reason or another cannot or do not desire to operate their holdings directly.

ARGUMENTS AGAINST FARM TENANCY

Arguments against farm tenancy grow largely out of the character of the landlord-tenant relationships that have developed in the United States. In this young pioneer capitalistic nation, where rugged individualism and ruthless exploitation of natural resources have predominated, and where land has been treated much the same as any other economic good, there has not been the proper cultural attitude or regard for the land by either landowner or tenant, on a plane commensurate with its proper status as a storehouse of life, requiring careful husbandry for continuing productivity.

Too often the landlord's ownership or intent of ownership of a given farm is quite transitory. He may not be a farmer or interested in agriculture as such and may have acquired a farm through inheritance, or for speculative purposes, or by foreclosure of a mortgage, and may be looking for an opportunity to sell the place advantageously at his earliest opportunity. Under these conditions, the tenant's outlook is uncertain, and this influences his management plans and his attitudes toward making improvements and conserving the soil. The general environment, which has been so prevalent in the American economy, combined with failure to utilize more generally such contractual and related devices as compensation for improvements and written rather than verbal leases, has been largely responsible for unsatisfactory farm tenancy conditions in the United States.

Americans generally have come to regard tenancy as a social disease and an inferior form of land tenure compared with ownership. The notorious conditions associated with farm tenancy in the South have also contributed to the disrepute in which farm tenancy is generally held. Moreover, Americans are inclined to overlook the fact that the alternatives are not farm tenancy or farm ownership, but farm tenancy or a larger quota of hired men and indebted owners.[37]

based upon the land as the sole security for the loan tends to impersonalize farm credit, it is apparent that something along these lines must be done if landowners are not to be penalized at the expense of tenants.

[37] Black and Allen, *op. cit.*, pp. 402 ff.; and Spiegel, *op. cit.*, p. 61.

STATUS OF FARM TENANCY IN EUROPE

Evidence that farm tenancy under the right conditions has many advantages in an economy can be seen from the social esteem in which it is held, and its importance and meaning in Europe. In many European nations, farm tenancy has been the pacemaker of agricultural progress and is regarded as a sound and necessary component of the tenure system.[38] It has been recognized in many of these nations that in times of depression the position of tenant is often superior to that of owner-operator; and in England the function of the landlord as a shock absorber is widely appreciated. In other nations the most striking instances of poor tenancy conditions have been improved by various agricultural reforms effected after World War I.[39]

Tenancy has been used as a means of land settlement in various countries, including England, Italy, Holland, Estonia, and Yugoslavia. In general, the policy in land settlement programs in European nations has been to establish a state tenantry from whose prosperity the whole community would profit.[40] Some European nations have developed over many decades a body of practical legislation and administrative arrangements that have eliminated most of the major evils associated with farm tenancy in the United States. Undoubtedly one of the prerequisites for achieving the necessary legislative and administrative arrangements to make for more satisfactory farm tenancy conditions is the basic concept that tenancy has an important role and a proper place in an economy, and that ownership of the land by every farm operator is not necessarily a desirable goal. In those nations where tenancy has been so acknowledged, and clear-cut tenant rights established, the greatest advancements have been made in establishing satisfactory farm tenancy.

IMPROVEMENT OF FARM TENURE AND TENANCY

It would be an overstatement to say that an improvement in land tenure policies alone could be expected to stabilize American argriculture or to change habits of ruthless exploitation into habits of conservation. It would not be an overstatement, however, to say that the effecting of policies that would make for greater security of occupancy would contribute greatly toward such ends.

During recent years American agricultural policy has apparently involved three major objectives: (1) conservation, (2) adjustments to bring about a better balance between agriculture and industry through parity

[38] Spiegel, *op. cit.*, p. 62.
[39] Spiegel indicates that at present there are no farm economists in Europe who would generally and unconditionally condemn farm tenancy. (See *ibid.*, p. 62.)
[40] *Ibid.*

prices, and (3) help for the underprivileged classes. Obviously, if the major objective of agricultural policy is to help underprivileged classes, it would seem that the position of the farm tenant in the United States would be strengthened so that he could become an owner; or that landlord-tenant relations would be so improved that many existing economic and social evils associated with farm tenancy would be removed.

The improvement of the position of farm tenants might involve programs and activities conflicting with another current objective of American agricultural policy—that of securing a better balance between industry and farming. More diversified southern agriculture, to be achieved by shifting large cotton acreages to other crops, is considered basic to any fundamental improvement in conditions of southern tenants and sharecroppers. This worries Middle Western farmers, because of the prospective increase in competition that might result from this more diversified agriculture. Also, if tenant conditions are improved appreciably, their farms should be more productive, and in many cases the tenants would stay in agriculture rather than shift to other occupations.

These developments would tend to offset or work against the objective of bringing agricultural production more nearly into line with demand conditions, so that farm prices will be more on a par with industrial prices. Widespread unemployment and the lack of alternative economic opportunities in industry in the thirties, however, encouraged improving conditions of tenants, many of whom were involuntarily forced to remain in agriculture.

Activities to improve the condition of farm tenants fit in well with the other of the major objectives of American agricultural policy—conservation. If changes can be made so that the farmer can secure compensation for his improvements and can look forward to a considerable period of occupying the same farm, he will be encouraged to follow those management practices that maintain and improve soil productivity. In this respect, conservation and tenure policies can be said to be complementary, as well as compatible with each other.[41] However, conservation cannot be achieved through laws or a tenure system, but only by the establishment in the mind and spirit of the farmer of a proper philosophy of use of the land. Just as laws cannot make people good, but can strengthen the

---

[41] Cf. Spiegel, *op. cit.*, p. 3. Spiegel goes on to say that it is doubtful, however, whether the land-tenure policies propounded so far in the United States will ever result in that degree of conservation which the European peasant applies to his land. European peasantry is preserved by tariff fences and receives prices much higher than those received by American farmers, with the result that, since the government conserves the peasant, it need not conserve the land. Spiegel adds, however, that while the European peasant is financially able to practice conservation because of the high price of agricultural products secured for him through tariff fences, restrictions on the alienation of land, on its devisability, inheritance, and utilization tend to confirm the peasant in his conservation practices.

tendency of people to behave in their dealings with their fellow men, so can tenure laws and customs help bring about conservation of the land, even though they cannot create the spirit of conservation itself.

In a nation as commercialized as the United States, if a tenure system can be established that will assure farm tenants of securing adequate rewards for their conservation practices, a considerable amount of conservation will be effected. The rewards of conservation practices are frequently intangible or deferred, however, and unless fundamental reforms in land tenure can accompany provision for compensation for improvements, American farm tenants may not be inclined to undertake desirable long-run conservation practices. Fundamental changes in land tenure, together with restrictions on the alienation of farms, and related adjustments that are probably essential for an effective conservation program of a continuing and permanent nature, require a fundamental change in the traditional attitude, thinking, and culture of American farmers. In Europe present attitudes toward conservation, which are so much in contrast to those in the United States, are the result of ancient traditions.

ECONOMIC FOUNDATIONS FOR FARM TENANCY REFORM

The actions of public bodies in pursuing farm tenancy policies designed to improve tenant conditions can be justified on strictly economic grounds, as well as on social or other bases. Individual farm operators are largely concerned with the private net product of their actions, and they attempt to equalize the values of marginal private net products of resources that they utilize in their farming operations. There is no tendency, however, toward equalization of the values of the marginal social net products, unless the marginal private net product and the marginal social net product are identical.[42]

When there is a divergence between these two types of marginal net products, the self-interest of the farm operator will not, therefore, tend to make the national dividend a maximum. As a result certain definite acts of interference with normal economic processes may be expected, in order to increase the national dividend.[43]

Those types of primitive contracts between landlords and tenants in which nothing is said concerning the condition of the land at the end of

[42] Cf. *ibid.*, p. 69.

[43] This is the argument advanced by Pigou in his *Economics of Welfare*. Pigou states: "The marginal social net product is the total net product of physical things or objective services due to the marginal increment of resources in any given use or place, no matter to whom any part of this product may accrue. . . . The marginal private net product is that part of the total net product of physical things or objective services due to the marginal increment of resources in any given use or place which accrues in the first instance . . . to the personal responsibility for investing resources there." (A. C. Pigou, *Economics of Welfare*, Macmillan, London, 4th ed., 1932, p. 172.)

he lease or about compensation for improvements tend to maximize the lifference between the private and the social net product. In other words, he contract merely provides for the return of the land to the owner at he end of the lease, in whatever condition it may be at the time. Thus, he difference between the private and social net product amounts to almost all the deferred benefit that would be conferred upon the farm hrough any improvements made.

But, as Pigou points out, the private net product is not less than the ocial net product by the whole of this deferred benefit, because a tenant vho is known to leave the farm in good condition is likely to secure farms hrough leasing more easily and on better terms than one who is known 1ot to do this. To this extent, good tenant farming yields an element of orivate as well as social net product.[44]

PROGRAMS TO IMPROVE AMERICAN FARM TENANCY

The widespread belief in the advantages of land ownership in the Jnited States has made public opinion particularly favorable to measures hat facilitate ownership of farms by tenants. The most widely prevalent dea has been to make easy credit available to tenants, but obviously, this s not always desirable. It too frequently results merely in exchange of an obligation to pay rent for an obligation to pay interest, combined with he added risks and vulnerability accompanying ownership.

Unless the tenant can pay down a substantial part of the purchase orice of the farm, permanence of occupancy may be less assured rather han more assured. Improved farm mortgage credit policies would be of nuch benefit to many tenant farmers who are capable of responsible ownership and who would benefit by arrangements that would make it oossible for them to purchase under more suitable conditions. The Federal government, through its land bank system and the Bankhead-Jones Farm Tenant Act of 1937, is attempting to bring about significant improvements in farm credit.

The Farmers Home Administration is supplying a combination of credit and technical guidance to numerous tenants who lack the funds or who are as yet unable to look forward to early purchase of a farm, even under the Bankhead-Jones Act. But many of these clients are gradually building up to where they may be able to climb onto the higher ungs of the agricultural ladder. Measures to prevent excessive speculation n farm lands, particularly in view of recent tendencies growing out of the

[44] The practice in many European nations of making separate contracts, often at onsiderable intervals of time, makes this qualification practically insignificant. Pigou rgues that compensation for improvements should be based not on the value of the mprovements to an incoming tenant, but on the value to the landlord. (See *ibid.*, p. 175 ff., for shortcomings of compensation schemes and their effects upon the rela- ion of the private net product to the social net product.)

war, would help to prevent heavy reversion of farmers from ownership to tenancy.

In certain states various laws designed to improve farm tenancy conditions have been passed but, for the most part, they fall far short of bringing about any extensive reforms or of securing adequate protection for tenants.[45]

The Federal government has largely followed a policy of converting tenants into owners or preventing reversion from ownership to tenancy. Efforts to improve the character of the tenant-landlord relationship which is as important as converting tenants into owners or preventing increased tenancy, have been limited primarily to federal supervision of leasing arrangements of Farmers Home Administration rehabilitation clients. There is a great need for more effective federal and state legislation dealing with landlord-tenant relationships along the lines of providing compensation to tenants for improvements or for unwarranted and arbitrary termination of lease contracts or for refusal to renew. In the end, such provisions should benefit both landlords and tenants. Certain constitutional difficulties and public attitudes retard more rapid development, but the trend seems unmistakable.

FARM TENANCY PROGRAMS IN OTHER NATIONS

Improvement of farm tenancy in England, Scotland, and Wales has been based principally on revision of leasing arrangements. The more important of these changes have given the tenant the right to take movable improvements with him on termination of the lease and to be compensated for the unexhausted value of other improvements he leaves behind; the right to receive compensation for disturbance; and the right to bring differences regarding right of compensation before the arbitral committees.[46] In addition to these improvements, Scotland has spent considerable effort to enlarge holdings, relieve poverty in heavily populated areas, and increase ownership for certain groups of operators.[47]

Improvement of farm tenancy in Ireland was tried, but shortly aban-

[45] Joseph Ackerman, "Status and Appraisal of Research in Farm Tenancy," *Journal of Farm Economics*, Vol. XXIII, No. 1, February, 1941, p. 277; and Spiegel, *op. cit.* pp. 75–76.

[46] For a more detailed analysis of British landlord-tenant relations, see Marshall Harris, *Agricultural Landlord-Tenant Relations in England and Wales*, U.S. Resettlement Administration, Land Use Planning Publications No. 4 and 4a, July, 1936; also *Farm Tenancy*, Report of the President's Committee, pp. 72–74; and Spiegel, *op. cit.* Chap. V. This latter reference gives a particularly thorough analysis of English land tenure policy, including developments in connection with the British war effort beginning in 1939.

[47] For a more detailed statement of agricultural land tenure reform in Scotland, see Marshall Harris and Douglas F. Schepmoes, *Scotland's Activity in Improving Farm Tenancy*, U.S. Resettlement Administration, Land Policy Circular, February, 1936, pp. 13–21.

doned in favor of a program to give tenants full title to the land through purchase. Farm tenancy in Ireland has been reduced from 97 percent to 3 percent since 1870. This policy of purchase and resale to Irish tenants was adopted as a definite policy of the British Government with the passage of the Ashbourne Acts of 1885 and 1886; and passage of subsequent acts made possible the undertaking of a land purchase program on a large scale. By 1921 two-thirds of the area of Ireland had been brought under the land purchase acts. Money to finance this large program was raised through issuing bonds at a low rate of interest.[48]

Because of a highly developed farm credit system, farm tenancy in Germany is not nearly as general as it is in many other countries, only about a tenth of all land in farms and forests being rented.[49]

In 1937, a series of model lease contracts was prescribed by the powerful Reich Food Corporation. Under the model contracts, the lease term has been greatly lengthened and the tenant has the right to claim compensation for improvements. Compensation is compulsory for improvement which, according to the principles of good husbandry, is a helpful amelioration like reclamation of wasteland and swampland, change of grassland into cropland, and similar changes that increase output. The model lease contracts contain other provisions, including stipulations concerning the rent rates, and any deviation from standard conditions laid down in the contracts results in increases in or reductions of the standard rent.[50]

For a long time the German Government has sponsored an almost continuous program to promote owner-operated farms among farm laborers and rural youth. Many owners who had farms too small for economical operations have been aided in obtaining additional lands, and in many cases large estates have been divided or sizable tracts of land have been reclaimed, and village-type settlements established. In recent years, a type of development intermediate between the closed village and the scattered farm type of settlement has been emphasized. Also, the average size of newly established holdings has risen considerably in an attempt to increase efficiency and output.

Denmark, by the end of the nineteenth century, had done much to increase the proportion of farmers owning holdings. By 1895 the proportion of all Danish rural properties operated by owner occupants was 87.4 percent; [51] and with liberal credit, reclamation, and land purchase programs effected later, tenancy has been reduced to about 5 percent.[52]

[48] *Farm Tenancy,* Report of the President's Committee, p. 71.
[49] Spiegel, *op. cit.,* p. 119.
[50] Spiegel, *op. cit.,* p. 129.
[51] Elizabeth R. Hooker, *Recent Policies Designed to Promote Farm Ownership in Denmark,* U.S. Resettlement Administration, Land Use Planning Publication 15, p. 2.
[52] *Farm Tenancy,* Report of the President's Committee, p. 71.

Through coöperative action, individual farms, even though small, have been able to achieve much of the efficiency and many of the economies enjoyed by large estates, and the technique of group action acquired through these coöperative societies enabled farmers on small holdings to become an effective influence politically in securing legislation to improve their condition.

Many nations, including Norway, Sweden, Egypt, Mexico, and others, have also made important changes in legislation to improve farm tenancy and land tenure.[53] In Egypt during the last 30 years, agricultural land tenure conditions have been much improved through legislation that has equalized land taxes, increased the amount of cultivable land through irrigation and reclamation projects, and greatly enlarged and improved agricultural credit facilities. In Mexico,[54] the states have the duty of destroying the large plantations, because conditions in the different states are so varied that a general program is not feasible. Each state determines the extent of the area an individual may own. The states have also assumed the functions of developing small holdings by creating zones around the villages within which only small properties may be held. Local laws also govern the extent of the family patrimony, which may not be mortgaged or attached in any form.

The ultimate land tenure system in most nations will be neither complete ownership by those who till the soil, nor a system that eventually results in reducing farm tenancy to a social status of peasantry based upon capitalistic farm enterprise. In the nations that have been most active in doing something about agricultural land tenure, three major tenure types have been proposed or adopted: (1) ownership, (2) tenancy, and (3) mixed tenure, or a form combining the elements of ownership and tenancy. On a number of occasions, land settlement laws for various reasons authorized the application of a variety of tenure types; but absentee, private, unrestricted ownership has not been created in any of the European nations discussed above, and restricted tenures have played an important part in their land settlement activities.

THE FUTURE OF FARM TENANCY

The use of restricted tenures has met with considerable success in many land settlement undertakings, in warding off important dangers such as the inefficient use or abuse of the land, undesirable subdivisions or enlargement, overindebtedness, speculation, and similar undesirable de-

[53] For a brief statement indicating the changes effected in Norway and Sweden, as well as in Denmark, Germany, England, and Scotland, see Erich Kraemer, *Tenure of New Agricultural Holdings in Several European Countries,* U.S. Department of Agriculture Social Research Report II, September, 1937.

[54] The statements concerning land tenure in Mexico are condensed from *Farm Tenancy,* Report of the President's Committee, pp. 85–86.

velopments. Obligations imposed on the owner in such matters as compensation for unexhausted improvements, determination of rent payments, and determination of the lease contract have done much to improve conditions prevailing under tenancy and mixed tenure.

In the future, valuable results may be expected from the use of special arbitration and adjustment machinery to adjust outside the courts disputes between the contracting parties. Kraemer indicates from his study of selected European nations that further simplification of agricultural land tenure will take place in the future, by emphasis on mixed tenure, and he holds that instability of land tenure policies in the field of land settlement is likely to continue as long as the problem of finding an adequate pattern of landed property in agriculture remains unsolved.[55]

In the United States, although national policy is somewhat confused and indecisive, the general intent on new holdings made available principally through irrigation, seems to be to have units of an adequate size to support a family. However, legislation adequate to curb effectively both speculation and many of the evils associated with complete freedom of disposition of landed property has not been enacted.

The necessity of developing opportunities for considerable numbers of unemployed may arise in the coming years, and an adequate small-holdings program may be developed. Efforts to diversify agriculture in the South, accompanied by efforts to enable tenants to become owners, along the lines of the Bankhead-Jones Farm Tenant Act, may substantially reduce the percentage of farm tenancy in the United States in the years ahead.

It is not likely, however, that the percentage of farm tenancy in the United States will be reduced below that proportion required for effective operation of the agricultural ladder system, although the disrepute in which farm tenancy is rather universally held in the United States may cause public opinion to swing to extremes in efforts to encourage farm ownership to the point where many who may not be ready for or capable of assuming responsible ownership may be encouraged to become owners, with resulting reduction of the general welfare.

Programs to improve landlord-tenant relationships should parallel programs seeking to convert tenants into owners. Special efforts will have to be made to secure sufficient appreciation of the place of tenancy in its right forms in the economy, if any significant improvements in landlord-tenant relations are to be effected.

It would seem that for the next few years, in the United States at least, greater improvements in the farm tenancy situation can be made by improving the character of the relationship of tenants and landlords, rather than in any wholesale attempt to convert tenants into owners.

[55] Kraemer, *op. cit.*, p. 80.

The achievements of some of the older nations along these lines, particularly those arrangements dealing with compensation for unexhausted improvements and compensation for disturbance, should furnish a good guide for improving American landlord-tenant relationships.

At the same time, however, such desirable adjustments as more scientific assessment and taxation of farm lands, or more adequate and sound land valuation and credit policies, and reform of the land transfer system to incorporate some of the better points of the Torrens or some similar system, together with related adjustments encouraging farm ownership, should not be overlooked. These programs can effectively improve the agricultural land tenure system of the United States and make American agriculture more attractive and prosperous.

REFERENCES FOR FURTHER READING

Clawson, Marion, *Uncle Sam's Acres*, Dodd, Mead & Company, Inc., New York, 1951, Chaps. 1–3.

Ely, Richard T., and Wehrwein, George S., *Land Economics*, The Macmillan Company, New York, 1940, pp. 192–210.

Farm Tenancy, Report of the President's Committee on Farm Tenancy, Government Printing Office, Washington, D.C., 1937.

Farm Tenure, A Graphic Summary, 1950, U.S. Department of Commerce, Bureau of the Census, and U.S. Department of Agriculture, Bureau of Agricultural Economics, Government Printing Office, Washington, D.C., Vol. V, Part 5.

Harris, Marshall, *Origin of the Land Tenure System in the United States*, Iowa State College Press, Ames, 1953, Chaps. I, II, III, XVI, XVII, XVIII, and XXI.

Harris, Marshall, "Compensation as a Means of Improving the Farm Tenancy System," U.S. Resettlement Administration, Land Use Planning Publication 14, 1937, mimeographed.

Harris, Marshall, Cotton, Albert H., and Schickele, Rainer, *Some Legal Aspects of Landlord-Tenant Relationships*, Iowa Agricultural Experiment Station Bulletin 371, April, 1938.

Hibbard, Benjamin Horace, *A History of the Public Land Policies*, The Macmillan Company, New York, 1924, Chaps. XVII, XVIII, and XXVII.

Johnson, V. Webster, and Barlowe, Raleigh, *Land Problems and Policies*, McGraw-Hill Book Company, Inc., New York, 1954, Chap. XI.

Kraemer, Erich, *Tenure of New Agricultural Holdings in Several European Countries*, U.S. Department of Agriculture, Social Research Report II, September, 1937.

National Resources Planning Board, *Public Land Acquisition in a National Land Use Program*, Part I, Report of the Land Committee to the National Resources Planning Board, Government Printing Office, Washington, D.C., 1941.

Parsons, Kenneth H., Penn, Raymond J., and Raup, Philip M. (eds.), *Land Tenure*, Proceedings of the International Conference on Land Tenure and

Related Problems in World Agriculture, University of Wisconsin Press, Madison, Parts XIII, XVI, XVII, and XVIII.

Raper, A. F., *Preface to Peasantry,* University of North Carolina Press, Chapel Hill, 1941, Chaps. I, IV, V, and VI.

Salter, Leonard A., Jr., *A Critical Review of Research in Land Economics,* University of Minnesota Press, Minneapolis, 1948, Chap. VII.

Spiegel, H. W., *Land Tenure Policies at Home and Abroad,* University of North Carolina Press, Chapel Hill, 1941, Chaps. I, IV, V, and VI.

Woofter, T. J., Jr., *et al.,* "Landlord and Tenant on the Cotton Plantation," Work Projects Administration Research Monograph 5, Washington, D.C., 1936.

TENURE IN NONAGRICULTURAL LAND

FOREST LAND TENURE

Advantages of Public Ownership—Federal Ownership of Forests—Management and Use of National Forests—State Ownership of Forests—County Ownership and Management of Forests—Recommended Expansion of Public Ownership—Forest Areas That Should Remain in Private Ownership—Public Regulation of Private Forest Lands—Forest Policies in Other Nations—Future Forest Land Tenure

RECREATIONAL LAND TENURE

Public vs. Private Ownership and Control of Recreational Lands—Recommended Increased Public Ownership of Recreational Lands—Division of Responsibility for Recreational Land Administration

MINERAL LAND TENURE

Sale and Leasing of Public Domain Mineral Lands—Petroleum as an Example of Tenure Problems in Mineral Lands—Recommended Future Mineral Land Policies—Mineral Land Policies of Other Nations

OWNERSHIP OF WATER AND WATER RIGHTS

Water Rights for Irrigation—Public Control of Water Power—Government Control over Water Resources

OWNERSHIP AND CONTROL OF TRANSPORTATION LAND

URBAN LAND TENURE AND TENANCY

Home Ownership and Tenancy—Title Insurance and Registry—The "Ground Rent" System, or Long Leasehold Tenure—The Neighborhood Unit (Pooling and Replotting Land)—"Lex Adickes"—Public Ownership of Urban Land

SOME OF the more difficult and serious economic and social problems associated with private appropriation and exploitation of natural resources have arisen in connection with nonagricultural lands. Problems associated with private ownership and use of mineral and forest lands and water resources have frequently attracted widespread attention and public consideration. Scandals, political corruption, and wars have resulted from struggles to attain or keep control of strategic minerals or water rights. Each of the major land resources requires thorough study and individual consideration because of its peculiar tenure problems.

FOREST LAND TENURE

Tenure problems in forest land are concerned primarily with public versus private ownership, rather than with the division of property rights between owner and occupier (tenancy) as in agricultural land, or among various private owners, as shall be seen in the case of water rights. Private ownership is held largely responsible for forest devastation and deterioration on the grounds that, because of the nature of forest as an industry, it is less effective in maintaining the forest resources than public ownership.[1]

Many students of forest economics recommend the increasing acquisition of forest lands by the Federal government and a systematic plan of reforestation and development on these lands. Others contend that it is not public acquisition that is needed, but a higher degree of social control in the interests of the general welfare. Many would concede that some systematic plan of resource use in the interests of the general welfare could have prevented much of the social wastes and losses of unrestricted exploitation.

ADVANTAGES OF PUBLIC OWNERSHIP

The growing of forests and the kind of care required to maintain forest productivity are longtime propositions that require, for most effective operation, programs and activities which may not show any significant return for many decades. Ordinarily, private capital is not anxious to undertake such ventures because of the piling up of investment in standing timber at a relatively high rate of interest. It is more interested in types of investments where returns will be more quickly received. Another

---

[1] Of the 83 million acres of devastated or poorly stocked forest land, 74 million (nine-tenths) are privately owned; and of the 850,000 acres devastated annually, about 95 percent are in private hands. It is further estimated that fully 95 percent of the private cutting is probably made without any conscious regard for future productivity, while nearly all the cutting on publicly owned forests is designed to perpetuate the forest. (See *A National Plan for American Forestry,* U.S. Sen. Doc. 12, 73d Congress, First Session, Government Printing Office, 1933, Vol. I, p. 12; and Barrow Lyons, *Tomorrow's Birthright,* Funk & Wagnalls Company, New York, 1955, pp. 102–106.)

argument for public ownership is that forestry is a large-scale proposition running into hundreds of thousands of dollars on single operating units.

The development of the modern corporation has made it possible for private individuals to secure the amount of capital necessary to operate such large-scale businesses, so that this is not an insurmountable difficulty. However, combined with the type of risk that forest production involves, the size or scope of operations does tend to discourage private investment. Still another advantage of public ownership is that public lands are tax free, and high taxes are one of the principal causes of the present difficulties of private ownership and operation.

At the present time the federal government gives 25 percent of the direct gross revenue from national forests to the state treasurers and to the counties in which such national forests are located, to be spent by the counties for schools and roads. However, such contributions are quite different from tax assessments on private lands. Contributions vary with the amount earned from the national forests, and are consequently flexible. On the other hand, tax assessments on private land are based on assessed valuation of the real estate (land and trees) and are comparatively rigid.

Another advantage of public ownership is that the Federal government, state, or county agency can devote a considerable amount of funds to developing scenic and recreational forest values without the necessity of making these activities pay a profit. Private owners cannot afford to put in a considerable sum of money for developing trails, campsites, and similar facilities for the benefit of tourists or vacationists unless they are reimbursed for such activities.

As yet, the policy of paying for the right to camp or picnic, particularly in forested areas, is not established. Most citizens feel free to use such facilities without paying for them, and public agencies have developed many facilities for the free use of these lands by vacationists, tourists, and others. The same situation holds in regard to the development of hunting and fishing facilities.

Fire burns over many millions of acres of U.S. forest and potential forest land annually, and records show that the cost of providing fire protection, based on the burn record, is very high in some areas. These high costs make it very difficult for private owners to protect their forest lands adequately.

Similar conclusions in regard to the advantages of public ownership have been reached by students of forest economics in connection with protection from insects and forest tree diseases—that is, that public agencies are in a much better position to give the attention and funds necessary for adequate protection, while private owners are not able to protect their properties, or at least do not do so adequately.

FEDERAL OWNERSHIP OF FORESTS

The national forests are an example of federal ownership and administration, and demonstrate what can be accomplished by this means. National forests, first called "forest reserves," were established in 1891 by an act of Congress, which provided that the President might from time to time set apart as public reserves public land bearing forests, whether of commercial value or not, in any state or territory having such land; and that the President by public proclamation should declare the establishment of such reservations and the boundaries thereof. The forest reserves were placed under the jurisdiction of the Department of Agriculture in 1905, and in 1907 the name was changed to "national forests" as being more descriptive of the fact that they contain a variety of resources whose greatest possible value to the public lies in management that will integrate the development and use of these resources for the largest possible net public benefit.

Under this theory of management has been worked out a program benefiting the local population contiguous to the national forest area, by the annual payment of a fourth of the gross receipts to the counties to help defray the costs of schools and roads. Federal expenditures for roads in and adjacent to the national forests have also contributed much to local employment and local payrolls, so that local areas first prone to oppose the establishment of national forests, on the grounds that their taxable resources would be reduced, have almost universally come to be the strongest supporters of such a program.

The timber stands of most of the present national forest areas are poor or inaccessible, since private owners had acquired the choice timberland under the public homestead and other laws. Most of the public land available since 1891, when the first national forest was created, has been located in the mountainous portions of the West. Even in the western country, however, private ownership had acquired significant areas within what have later been established as areas within the national forest boundaries. Moreover, the checkerboard land grants made by the Federal government to aid the railroads created many private holdings within present national forest boundaries. In addition to these private holdings, there are within the national forest boundaries private lands obtained under mining and townsite laws, and agricultural homesteads in the narrow valleys running up into the national forests or situated in the surrounding timbered areas.[2]

[2] Consequently, while there are 186,215,256 acres of land within the national forest boundaries, 24,854,565 acres are in ownership other than federal, leaving 161,360,691 acres of federally owned national forest lands. (*A National Plan for American Forestry*, Vol. I, p. 560.)

The passage of the Weeks Law in 1911 marked a definite step toward national ownership and operation of forest lands. This law provided for the acquisition of forest lands by the federal government for the protection of the flow of navigable streams. The Clarke-McNary Act of 1924 extended this policy to lands within the watersheds of navigable streams necessary for the production of timber. Under these acts, national forests have been created east of the Mississippi River (except those created from the public domain in the states of Michigan and Florida). Figure 25 shows that there is a very small acreage in the eastern two-thirds of the nation, reflecting growth of national forest areas by federal purchase

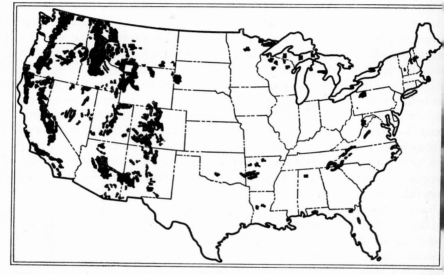

Figure 25. National Forests of the United States. (Source: *Forest Land Resources, Requirements, Problems, and Policy,* National Resources Board, Government Printing Office, Washington, D.C., 1935.)

MANAGEMENT AND USE OF NATIONAL FORESTS

The dominating thought in the management and use of the national forests is to balance the multiple uses against one another in such a way that maximum public benefit will result. Frequently this means excluding some use, or reducing in intensity the particular use in order to enable a more intensive or more widespread appropriation for other uses. Wherever it is possible, by suitable compromise, to enable two or more uses to occupy a given area, concessions are made by each. For example, timber cutting on watersheds is usually permitted, but regulated to avoid impairment of the watershed value. Or, timber growing and livestock grazing may use the same area, as long as the grazing does not prevent or unduly damage forest production.

Selective timber cutting may proceed with very little, if any, interruption of the nonconcentrated forms of recreational utilization of the forest. Properly administered, the national forests constitute a large variety of overlapping uses so harmonized as to avoid any significant conflict—for instance, timber sale cutting, water supply for domestic irrigation and power uses, livestock grazing, game conservation, and recreation. This harmonizing has been more complete in some areas than in others. In any case, the principle of controlling the extent of various uses to prevent serious conflict among them is definitely established.

Timber management plans on the national forests are built around the principle of obtaining a steady, continuous yield of wood products best suited to the public need, so as to contribute the maximum to stabilizing industries and communities wholly or partly dependent on operations based on national forest stumpage. The disposal of national forest timber is controlled by formal statements of policy that define the markets to be served, the policy for the sale of the timber, and the general silvicultural methods for the private buyer to follow in cutting. Disposal has been controlled in such a way that the annual cut has been kept well within the sustained-yield capacity of the national forests.

The work of the U.S. Forest Service in developing recreational values on forest lands, particularly in the West, is becoming increasingly well known. The thousands of miles of forest trails, the numerous campgrounds, and the related recreational facilities in forested areas are excellent examples of what may be done under public ownership and control without reducing the economic value of the forests or creating abandoned cutover lands, unsightly scenes, and unstable industries. Similarly, in wildlife preservation and improvement (including both fish and game) the work of the Forest Service is an excellent example of the possibilities of making more complete use of forest lands.

Perhaps public ownership and operation have been most effective in the field of forest protection. Fire hazards, particularly in drought years, have been rather general throughout the western states and have increased in severity. Yet the practical and educational programs effected by the Forest Service have been important in keeping fire losses to a minimum. The control of forest insects and tree diseases in the national forests has been much less outstanding than that of fire protection, largely because of the lack of adequate funds to meet the problems.

STATE OWNERSHIP OF FORESTS

State lands consist largely of lands granted to the states by the federal government, principally for the support of schools, or tax-reverted lands and lands acquired through gift, exchange, or purchase. It is significant that three of the seven leading states in state forest land acreage are th cutover Lake states of Michigan, Minnesota, and Wisconsin, and tha two others in the first seven—Washington and Idaho—are in the cutove areas of the Pacific Northwest, where tax reversion has been large.

This is further evidence of the breakdown of private forest land owner ship and the trend toward abandonment of cutover lands by privat owners. In 29 states title reverts to the counties or towns in tax for feiture proceedings, so that the amount of state-owned forest lands in some states would not reflect the extent or trend of forest land tax rever sion. In these 29 states, as well as in several of the others, the acreage o state forest lands represents principally acreages that were received through federal grants to the states.

Millions of acres of land unsuited for agricultural use, which hav been cut over and cleared of forest growth, are awaiting return to publi ownership. Some steps have been taken by federal agencies to purchas certain areas of such lands under a varied program of acquisition, but large acreage is still left to be rehabilitated by the state in which it i located. For the most part, ownership and management of the smalle blocks of from 10 thousand to 100 thousand acres, which are too larg for smaller local governmental units to handle, must be assumed by th states themselves.[3]

COUNTY OWNERSHIP AND MANAGEMENT OF FORESTS

County governments become owners of forest lands principally throug failure of private owners to pay taxes assessed. In two states—New York and Wisconsin—encouragement has been given to the county forest move ment by special legislation providing for state participation in the ex pense of operating county forest lands. In New York, the legislature pro vides for contributions to counties for land purchase, reforestation, and protection.[4] Title is vested in the county, but state law provides that th area must be forever devoted to watershed protection, production o timber and other forest products, and recreation or related purposes Lands owned or acquired by the county under these provisions are exemp from state and county taxes. The board of county supervisors may sel trees, timber, or other forest products from the county forest lands, upor terms considered to be for the best interests of the county, and under rule and regulations prescribed by the State Conservation Commission.

The Wisconsin Forest Crop Law of 1927 was amended in 1929 to per

[3] All but 9 of the 48 states now have state forests with a total area of about 13½ million acres, divided into 732 units. (U.S. Department of Agriculture, *State Forests fo Public Use*, Miscellaneous Publication 373, Government Printing Office, pp. 1–2.)

[4] *A National Plan for American Forestry*, Vol. I, p. 848.

it the counties to list tax-reverted land as "forest crop land." For every cre of land listed, the state pays 10 cents each year to the township in hich the land lies, to be divided among the school districts, the town, nd the county in a manner similar to private forest cropland payments. s a further encouragement, the 1931 Wisconsin legislature ordered the onservation Department to pay the counties an additional 10 cents to e used for reforestation, administration, and maintenance under the pervision of the Conservation Department. Thus, every acre of county rest land in Wisconsin draws 20 cents of state money annually. When he timber is cut, the state receives 50 percent of the stumpage value, ur-fifths of which is restored to the State Forestry Department fund for rther encouragement and development of county forests.[5]

RECOMMENDED EXPANSION OF PUBLIC OWNERSHIP

Only a fifth of the forests of the United States are now publicly owned, ut students of forest economics insist that this percentage should be increased. The National Resources Board, in its *Report to the President* in 934, presented a recommendation by the United States Forest Service hat the public forest land area should be increased from 180 million cres, to 358 million acres, or practically doubled. This recommended ncrease is principally in national forests and state forests. These recommendations are the summarization of recommendations made by local and-use planning, forestry, and conservation agencies.

In the minds of many students, public acquisition offers the only sound nd workable solution of the forest problem in areas: (1) where growing tocks have been wholly or largely depleted by destructive logging, fires, nd other causes; (2) where profitable operation for timber production nay be impossible or very difficult for private enterprise, but where public nterest in watershed, wildlife, and recreation values can be served only y organized management; (3) where acreage might be operated profitbly by private owners but the public need for recreation and related ses makes public ownership highly desirable; (4) where privately owned orest lands are so interspersed with existing public forests and public cquisition units that management and development would be facilitated y public ownership; (5) where lands are submarginal for agriculture nd the highest and best use is for forestry and related uses; and (6) where tands of timber are likely to be exploited destructively in private ownerhip because of excessive overhead or operating costs and other reasons.

The interstate character of the dependency upon forest resources, and ther benefits from the use of forest lands make it desirable that a large

[5] *Wisconsin Forest Crop and Woodland Tax Laws,* Wisconsin Conservation Department, Madison, Wis., 1938.

part of the acreage recommended for public ownership be owned an operated by the federal government through the Forest Service. Thi seems logical because many states that are the most important source c timber for neighboring states are unable to finance the entire or majo portion of the recommended forestry program within their boundarie: The 60-million-acre increase recommended for state forests by 1960 i believed to be a very liberal estimate of the ability of the states to financ desirable forest programs. The recommended increase of more than twic this number of acres for national forests reflects the widespread belie that the federal Forest Service is in the best position to finance an administer the forest development and maintenance program desirabl in the public interest.

FOREST AREAS THAT SHOULD REMAIN IN PRIVATE OWNERSHIP

It is not only impractical, but probably undesirable for public agencie to acquire all the forests of the country that should be under permanen productive management. Forests favorably located in relation to markets with good growing conditions, and with growing stocks not seriously de pleted by fire, cutting, and lack of silvicultural treatment, and not over burdened with taxes and interest payments on borrowed capital tha cannot be readily liquidated (see the next two chapters) have a very goo possibility of being so managed under private ownership that they cai realize their economic and social potentialities, provided there is ade quate industrial self-regulation or sufficient public control.[6]

Experience with private forestry in the United States indicates tha under favorable conditions reasonable returns from businesslike manage ment of forest lands are fully possible, and the public interest also ma be well served. The qualifications noted indicate that continued privat ownership is recommended for those areas on which private enterpris appears to have the best chance.

For the most part, farm woodlots are a very satisfactory means of privat ownership and operation of forest lands. They contribute, in most cases to a more balanced farm operating unit. In certain local areas, however public interest will be served better by placing groups of farm woodlot under public ownership so that they may be used for public recreation wildlife, watershed, and erosion protection and control, and as demon strations of organized management of scattered holdings of timber ii highly developed agricultural sections where premium prices for timbei make it profitable to follow intensive forms of silviculture.[7]

[6] National Resources Board, *Report to the President,* 1934, Government Printing Office, p. 211.
[7] *Ibid.*

PUBLIC REGULATION OF PRIVATE FOREST LANDS

Public regulation of private forest lands to prevent excessive exploitation and encourage sustained-yield management should constitute an important part of national forest policy. Along with such regulation should go greater public aid to private owners in protecting their forests against fire, insects, and disease; in forest credits; in more reasonable taxation; and in development of better production and marketing techniques.

A plan has been suggested by which private owners would retain ownership but the government would manage the forests, pay a proportion of the income to the forest owner at the time of cutting, and pay local governments a stated yearly amount in lieu of taxes for support of these local governmental units. This plan recognizes the fact that a large proportion of our forest land will continue for many years in private ownership, and it seeks to avoid interference with private property beyond what is necessary to safeguard the rights and welfare of the public.

This plan may be considered one of public regulation, which would secure all the advantages of public ownership and at the same time maintain private ownership. Public agencies would be responsible for enforcing sustained-yield management practices. Another important advantage of the plan would be that public treasuries would not be drained by enormous outlays for land purchase. Moreover, local governments would have a definite and dependable annual income with which to pay the cost of their services. However, the author of this plan states that it is not advocated as a general substitute for eventual public ownership of a large proportion of the nation's forest land.[8]

FOREST POLICIES IN OTHER NATIONS

Forest policies differ widely among nations, both in extent and method of public control over private forests. In practically every case, however, the accepted solution of the destruction resulting from unfettered private or commercial ownership and operation is some form of public intervention and public control, which is now practiced in nearly every civilized country of the world.

Briefly, the essential features of forest land policies, taking foreign nations as a group, are as follows: [9] (1) Ordinarily, an owner is free to manage and utilize his forest as he pleases, so long as his utilization practices do not directly or indirectly injure others or the public welfare. (2) The public exercises sufficient control over forests, where destruction

[8] W. N. Sparhawk, "A Possible Program of Public Regulation," in *A National Plan for American Forestry*, Vol. II, pp. 1343–1353.

[9] *A National Plan for American Forestry*, Vol. I, p. 1037.

or mismanagement are said to result in injury to others, to insure that their protective functions (stream flow, sanitation, water conservation, holding of soil in place to prevent erosion, etc.) are not jeopardized. Since maintaining these protective functions requires a continuous forest cover, public policies frequently involve reforestation, or engineering improvement works, or even afforestation of hitherto nonwooded land, either by public agencies or by the owner. Except where reforestation is required by law, the public pays part or all of the cost and usually indemnifies the owner for any loss of income resulting from restrictions on the use of protection forests. As an alternative, the public may acquire the land, either at the owner's request or by condemnation. (3) Protection forests are classified as such by a governmental agency, upon the recommendation of some public body or upon application of interested individuals or groups after appropriate investigations and hearings.

(4) Cutting in classified protection forests can be done only with permission of competent public authorities. Methods of cutting and utilization of forage and other products are specified in some detail, either by law or through regulations promulgated by the supervisory authority. Reforestation of cutover areas is compulsory. (5) The object of public control over forests other than protection forests is generally not to compel owners to produce any particular kind or quantity of material, but to insure that the land will be kept in a productive condition. Sustained-yield management is usually not required, and a minimum of control is exerted over methods of management and utilization on privately owned forest lands not classed as protection forests. (6) Public control in many nations is democratized and decentralized by vesting general supervision in local or provincial boards or commissions on which forest owners, technicians, and administrative officials—and in some instances the local population—are represented. Some of the very small nations have only one central commission for the entire country.

FUTURE FOREST LAND TENURE

The need for some form of public regulation or control of timber cutting in commercial forests of the United States is generally conceded, but there is not complete agreement as to the best method to follow. One report draws the following conclusions: "No one knows how effective the states will be in preventing future destructive practices, nor does anyone know how satisfactory federal legislation would be. Pertinent considerations regarding the control of cutting include these: It is not so difficult to move in the direction of public ownership and control as it is to reverse the process; the implications of federal control are far-reaching; the efficiency of financial aid in stimulating adequate state regulation has never been tested. For these reasons, it would appear wise for us to make a fair trial of federal financial aid to states which will undertake the control of cutting. If this fails, then it may be necessary to place increased reliance on federal control and public ownership and management of forests to insure adequate and sufficient supplies of timber." [10]

There are some who feel that the above conclusions are inadequate and that more definite steps should be taken at once toward increased federal control and public ownership. There are others, however, who feel that by making adjustments in the forest land tax system along the lines of taxing the land annually and the timber only when it is cut, and preventing future destructive practices through state legislation and state programs, the necessity for greatly expanded public ownership can be avoided. The arguments on both sides should be considered very carefully in working out a future forest land-tenure policy. Certainly where state or local governments or individuals will undertake to do the job, every effort should be made to effect the necessary adjustments through these channels.

RECREATIONAL LAND TENURE

Two major types of tenure problems are associated with the use and development of recreational lands. These are dividing responsibility and control (1) between public and private ownership, and (2) among public agencies—that is, among local, state, and federal bodies.

PUBLIC VS. PRIVATE OWNERSHIP AND CONTROL OF RECREATIONAL LANDS

Many forms of recreation are outside the field of public action. However, public regulation of private or commercial recreation and public provision of recreational services are increasing. Many forms of private recreational activity require public regulation in the interests of the general welfare, along the lines of preventing stream pollution, controlling billboards, and preventing private appropriation and exclusive use of resources in which the public has a definite interest. Open spaces and recreational facilities at minimum cost should be provided for the large groups who have neither means nor leisure to get out of the great industrial centers, since recreation for these groups is necessary for national welfare. Public bodies can also establish and maintain park areas and monuments.

Private enterprise, by its very nature, cannot provide adequately for many of these services because (1) they require comparatively large outlays for development and maintenance, and (2) it is not desirable to charge admittance fees. Also, private enterprise is not well adapted to

[10] *Postwar Agricultural Policy,* Report of the Committee on Postwar Agricultural Policy of the Association of Land Grant Colleges and Universities, 1944, p. 47.

undertake the restrained use and continued protection and development from generation to generation which certain types of recreational land require for most beneficial use.[11]

Since more than half the traffic over our public highway system is recreational traffic, it is important to develop trafficways with recreational value as well as efficiency for commercial use. To do this, some control over private lands on either side of the highway must be established. This may be achieved by outright purchase or by certain regulatory measures. To purchase such land, even for small distances on both sides of the highway, would be extremely expensive and unnecessary. Sufficient control can be established through such regulatory devices as zoning, which restrict the uses of lands lying along highways in regard to type, size, and location of billboards for outdoor advertising, size and distance from the highway of residences and industrial buildings, or similar activities.

Another problem of recreational land ownership arises in connection with game animals. The preservation of certain big game animals is now considered the duty of the federal government—at least, federal agencies are active in this work. In the case of small game such as rabbits, squirrels, other furbearers, and upland game birds, no such clear-cut division of responsibility has been developed.

Public agencies can accomplish certain desirable results by establishing demonstration areas, but could probably do much more by promoting the establishment, through coöperative action, of practices that would best conserve small game in farming areas. These public programs might even provide for paying farmers small sums for such recommended practices.

RECOMMENDED INCREASED PUBLIC OWNERSHIP OF RECREATIONAL LANDS

There are selected areas throughout the nation that are submarginal for farming and should be put to other uses. Some are in the national forests, and federal purchase of such lands, combined with resettlement of families on better areas and in more compact communities, would help to solve the game-protection problem and at the same time assist in getting the lands into their best use.

A heavy drain upon wildlife resources is caused by the large number of submarginal farmers in forest areas, who, because of their economic circumstances and isolation from law enforcement agencies, use these wildlife resources rather freely. In addition to retiring submarginal farms in the national forests and resettling on better areas the families involved, the federal government should purchase certain essential winter range

[11] For a brief statement concerning the place of public and private recreational activity in a nation, see National Resources Board, *op. cit.*, pp. 217–221.

areas within and adjacent to the national forests. Other selected areas should be purchased to expand the system of public wildlife refuges.[12]

Although expansion of the land area devoted to wildlife conservation is an important phase of developing the nation's recreational land resources, a well-balanced national recreational program should be the concern of municipalities and their immediate environs. The major problem is to provide places for active recreation and enjoyment within easy reach of inhabitants of these large cities. This means including in urbanized areas adequate and properly distributed play areas for children and adults, in the form of small landscaped parks and playgrounds and, in the case of large cities, a few comparatively large parks. Recreational areas in most American cities are very inadequate, underdeveloped, and far below the minimum standard (1 acre to every 100 persons) recommended for municipalities of 8000 inhabitants or more.

This increase of public ownership at the expense of private land is recommended because, for certain types of recreational land development and use, public ownership and control are considered more effective in the public interest than private ownership and operation. For many types of recreational land, private development and operation are adequate especially in certain areas; and here private ownership and operation should continue. In the aggregate, such services are extremely important in fulfilling the recreational needs of the nation, although public regulation may be necessary to prevent abuses and private gain at the expense of the general welfare. One of the most important problems in connection with private recreational land is premature development and resulting overexpansion, and poor land use. Some kind of public regulation or control over rate of use or settlement is essential in such cases, if these disastrous consequences are to be reduced or eliminated.[13]

DIVISION OF RESPONSIBILITY FOR RECREATIONAL LAND ADMINISTRATION

The division of responsibility for effective development and control of recreational lands among various levels of government is a serious problem. Provision of "in-town" park, playground, and related recrea-

[12] *Ibid.,* pp. 150 and 226.

[13] A good example is valuable lake shore property. Wehrwein and Parsons found that more than half of the 16,000 registered lots in three northern Wisconsin counties, subdivided during the period 1902 to 1930, were laid out between 1923 and 1928. Each of these 16,000 subdivisions had to be carried on the tax rolls as a separate taxable description, and when the boom collapsed, over 9000—more than one-half of all these lots—remained unsold and became tax-delinquent. The cost of advertising and selling these delinquent lots was more than the counties received in taxes on the rest of the plots. (G. S. Wehrwein and K. H. Parsons, *Recreation as a Land Use,* Wisconsin Agricultural Experiment Station Bulletin 422, 1932, pp. 19–20; and Ely and Wehrwein, *Land Economics,* Macmillan, 1940, pp. 348–349.) This speculative development in private recreational land indicates the extent to which the private search for profit causes overexpansion and premature subdivision.

tional areas is primarily a municipal responsibility or, where the city covers almost the entire county, a city and county problem. This does not mean that other agencies, particularly state and federal governments, or local governments like the town or township, should not help to create and develop such recreational facilities; these agencies can do much to support and sponsor educational programs for the development of an interest in such projects. However, city officials must take the lead in initiating, developing, and administering them.

Most city governments have been very slow to accept responsibility for furnishing "in-town" recreational areas. In too many cities, development has been unplanned, with the result that many sites most convenient and useful for playgrounds, parks, and related recreational use have been developed for private residences or commercial use. Even if certain areas have been set aside for recreational purposes, leadership or supervision may not have been provided.[14]

Distribution of responsibility for provision of parks, playgrounds, and related recreational areas for metropolitan regions outside city boundaries is a more complex problem. Some cities have acquired parks well beyond their borders. Counties, special metropolitan park districts, and states may all serve as agencies for providing metropolitan parks; and the federal government, without any particular plan, has established recreational areas of various types within metropolitan regions. However, there is yet no definite policy with respect to division of responsibility among the agencies involved, nor are there any specific standards regarding the area, types of recreation to be established, or administrative methods used. The state may well accept a considerable measure of responsibility for the large outer zone parks, while the metropolitan park board or the county may function satisfactorily for parks in the inner, more heavily populated zones.

The following program for state governments in recreational land policy is recommended: (1) that state recreation systems be based upon comprehensive surveys by qualified persons; (2) that factors to be considered in selection of areas include (a) unusual or unique natural features, (b) scenic quality, (c) probable adequacy of obtainable lands for expected kind and quantity of recreation, (d) variety and quantity of active recreational yield, (e) probable ability to produce legitimate income, (f) location with respect to population and to competitive areas, and (g) relative significance of historic, prehistoric, or scientific values; (3) that any outstanding natural features be included completely within

---

[14] Out of 6000 towns and cities in America, only 1204 (approximately one-fifth) reported recreation under leadership. In 75 percent of those reporting parks, the park acreage is below accepted standards. (See U.S. Department of the Interior, *Yearbook,* National Park Service, Government Printing Office, 1939.)

the boundaries, and that a satisfactory year-round habitat for wildlife be furnished; (4) that adverse types of occupancy or use near recreational properties be prevented by the use of scenic easements; (5) that all values involved be carefully considered in determining kinds of public use to be encouraged; (6) that intensive uses be limited to one location or, at best, a small number of locations; (7) that state administrative agencies be equipped to render advisory service on the recreation problems of political subdivisions of the state, (8) that part of the cost of operating state recreational holdings be borne by users on a fee basis; (9) that a liberal portion of the total area in every state park be left completely undisturbed, free from roads, and with only a limited amount of trails. Similar considerations are suggested in the case of development of state forest and game lands.[15]

The federal government is now providing and will undoubtedly continue to provide much of the recreational land area available for public use. Preservation of outstanding scenery and historical or archeological sites of national importance is properly a responsibility of the federal government, and in recent years this agency has done much to preserve and develop such recreational lands. Many historic and archeological sites and scenic areas are not limited to one state. The construction of parkways, involving improvement of scenic beauty along great trunk highways, involves expenses and legal difficulties that can more easily be handled by the national government. The complex problems and extensive areas associated with wildlife management and conservation (particularly in the case of migratory waterfowl) and the administration of great national park areas are best handled by the federal government.

Adequate management of big game in the national forests presents particular difficulties because, while the Forest Service is in general charge, states in which forests are located claim jurisdiction over the game. The legal status of game on nationally owned lands has never been definitely settled. Under the present system of divided authority, it is difficult to work out an effective system of administration and conservation; but state game commissions, even when most competent, are obviously unable—subject as their policies are to changing political expediency—to equal the efficiency of the federal government, whose activities can be extended to national forests under federal plans of coordinating all forest uses.[16]

Aside from developing and administering specific types of recreational land, which involves either extensive area, interstate legal problems, or special technical difficulties, the recreational activities of the federal government should largely supplement state and local, public and private recreational programs, rather than compete with or replace such services.

[15] National Resources Board, *op. cit.,* p. 218.
[16] *Ibid.,* p. 223.

The federal government should furnish a well-coördinated recreational land-use program, coöperating with state and local public agencies and private individuals and organizations to bring about increased interest in and better use of recreational land. Only through such democratic development and widespread public use can recreation be a vital force in a nation where it takes such a variety of forms as it does in the United States.

MINERAL LAND TENURE

Society's major problem arising from the peculiar nature of mining and minerals is conservation or wise use of these exhaustible and non-replaceable resources. In general, the United States has followed an "open door" policy of rather free individual exploitation under private initiative; and this has been associated with waste and depletion of many important minerals.

SALE AND LEASING OF PUBLIC DOMAIN MINERAL LANDS

Many areas of the more than one billion acres of public domain land disposed of to private individuals contained mineral resources, but federal policy has usually been to allow private owners securing title to these public domain lands to exploit minerals found, unless the deposits were discovered prior to the disposition of such lands. It is quite easy to designate land as principally useful for farming, grazing, or forestry; but how can the existence, extent, or commercial value of mineral deposits be ascertained? Even after these problems are solved, there is still the question of the policy to follow in disposing of or in utilizing mineral lands. The Northwest Ordinance of 1785 (which dealt with the public lands of the Northwest Territory) reserved to the federal government one-third of all gold, silver, lead, and copper discovered. In 1796 an act was passed providing for the sale of public lands northwest of the Ohio River and reserving all salt springs and licks to the federal government.[17]

These provisions, made early in the history of the United States, indicate that Congress intended to treat mineral resources differently from agricultural or forest lands. Gradually a policy of leasing came to be followed. In 1800 Congress authorized the Surveyor General to lease reserved saline lands, and in 1807 extended the lease provisions to include lead mines on the public domain of Indiana territory. In 1816 leasing of public domain mineral lands was made general by the indirect method of forbidding mining on public lands without approval of the President.[18]

[17] Hibbard, *A History of the Public Land Policies*, p. 512; and C. J. Hynning, *State Conservation of Resources*, National Resources Committee, Government Printing Office, 1939, p. 37.
[18] Hynning, *op. cit.*

With the exception of opening lead mines and lands in Missouri to sale in 1829, the policy in regard to minerals on public lands was one of reservation and lease till 1846, when the Government embarked upon a new program of sale after the President's report that the reservation and lease program had proved unprofitable and unsatisfactory to the lessees. This policy of sale, inaugurated in Arkansas, Illinois, Iowa, and Wisconsin lead mines, was extended to other areas soon afterward, and to coal mines in 1864.[19]

Discovery of gold in California in 1848 led to a change in mineral-land policies on the public domain. By 1866 nearly a billion dollars in gold and silver had been produced from western public lands in accordance with local customs which came to be recognized by courts and legislatures. In that year Congress recognized and validated equitable rights acquired in accordance with such local customs and provided that mineral lands of the public domain should be free and open to exploration, occupation, and acquisition, in general conformity with established local customs. Thus (with the exception of coal, which remained under the policy of sale and purchase established in 1864) mining law in the United States usually followed the rule of "possessory occupation." [20]

The principle of sale and purchase was extended in 1872 to mineral lands generally, and the mining act of May 10, 1872, amended the 1866 act by constituting mineral lands a distinctive class subject to special conditions of sale and set prices specifically applicable to mineral lands.[21] This principle of sale and purchase was based upon the general theory that anyone has a right to keep minerals in such lands.

This wide-open-door policy has been one of the major reasons why United States mineral production has been so difficult to control. In 1914 Congress revised the leasing system by passing a coal leasing law for Alaska; and in 1917 Congress extended the policy to potash on all public lands of the United States. In 1920 a general leasing law for coal, oil and gas, phosphate, oil shale, and sodium was passed. This was extended in 1927 to cover sulphur; and the principle of leasing was also applied to gold, silver, and mercury to be reserved in certain existing land grants.[22]

---

[19] National Resources Board, *op. cit.,* p. 421. President Polk reported in 1845 that although more than a million acres of public lands had been reserved from sale and numerous leases made, only some $6000 were collected for the years 1841 to 1844, while administrative expenses were $25,000, and the mines were carelessly and wastefully worked. On these grounds, President Polk recommended abolishing the lease system and placing mineral lands on the market, for sale on terms approved by Congress. (Hynning, *op. cit.*)

[20] National Resources Board, *op. cit.,* p. 421.

[21] The 1872 act provided for survey and sale of mineral lands, fixing the price of placer lands at $2.50 per acre, and lode claims at $5 per acre. (Hibbard, *op. cit.,* p. 517.)

[22] National Resources Board, *op. cit.,* p. 421.

Numerous federal acts passed during the history of the United States dealt with minerals on the public domain, recognizing two main types of mineral deposit—metalliferous and nonmetalliferous. Generally speaking, metalliferous mineral deposits may be acquired in fee under the lode or placer acts, and nonmetalliferous deposits may be developed under lease. Metalliferous mining claims may be filed on the remaining unappropriated and unreserved public lands, on areas in the national forests, and on some of the 35 million acres disposed of with reservation of mineral rights to the United States.[23] The maximum acreage that may be included in any single permit or lease, in the case of nonmetalliferous minerals like coal, oil and gas, phosphate, potash, sodium, sulphur, and oil shale, is usually 2560 acres (four sections).[24]

Metallic minerals are substantially unaffected by any mineral conservation program of the state governments, and even in the case of the mineral fuels the problem has been largely economic rather than conservational. The urgent need has been for governmental intervention to stabilize mining operations by preventing or controlling surplus production and plant capacity.[25] The authority of the states to act under the police power gives them great opportunities to conserve their own resources; but in only a few cases has mineral conservation been a definite policy, and in most states the problems have hardly been considered at all.

PETROLEUM AS AN EXAMPLE OF TENURE PROBLEMS IN MINERAL LANDS

Oil is one of the best examples of private exploitation of a major mineral resource to the point where U.S. reserves are dangerously low in face of prospective increased demands.[26] The owner of oil land does not own the oil in his land, but owns the right to capture and appropriate oil

[23] In case of lands in Indian reservations, the Secretary of the Interior may lease any part of the unallotted lands within such reservations in the states of Arizona, California, Idaho, Montana, Nevada, New Mexico, Oregon, Washington, or Wyoming, in the case of both metalliferous and nonmetalliferous minerals, except oil and gas. This procedure was established by act of June 30, 1919, and amended December 16, 1926, to provide for the collection of 5 percent of the net value of mineral output as royalties. (Ibid., pp. 419–420.)

[24] No person, association, or corporation may hold coal, phosphate, or sodium leases or permits aggregating more than 2560 acres in any one state, or more than 7680 acres in any one state under oil and gas lease or permit. The original lease term is usually 20 years, with provision for renewal by successive 10-year periods. These leasing laws apply to unreserved public domain and to national forest (excluding the lands reserved under the Appalachian Forest Act, which may be leased under a special act) but do not apply to parks and monuments (see ibid., p. 420).

[25] It is significant that the 19 investigations or hearings before Congress or by specially created commissions between 1913 and 1935 were largely concerned with price and labor problems of the coal industry rather than with conservation of coal resources. (Hynning, op. cit., p. 42.)

[26] For an analysis of this problem, see John Ise, The United States Oil Policy, Yale University Press, 1926.

from the common pool through wells drilled on his land. As a consequence of this peculiarity of ownership and lack of capture regulations in the oil industry, destruction and waste of United States oil resources have been excessive.[27]

Among the essential needs of the oil industry is the development of a standard of individual ownership rights so that every owner will participate in a just proportion of the reservoir content, and preservation of ownership control,[28] perhaps through some form of collective tenure or group control like that developed in grazing districts. In order to do this, unit operation of oil pools (the opposite of the present wasteful competitive development of pools) would have to be introduced. By unit operation is meant development of a whole geologic unit according to a definite program supervised by the state, with royalties to be shared by the individual owners on the basis of acreage, oil in place, or some generally equitable arrangement, regardless of the location of producing wells.[29]

Accompanying unit operation should be the establishment of certain minimum engineering standards by state and federal regulatory bodies; and restrictions on abandonment of old oil wells as long as they are still in a state of production should accompany unit production. Abandonment may occur because of physical circumstances or because of economic difficulties in the industry.

Premature abandonment of producing wells because of economic changes may be limited by regulatory measures. Restriction of production to current needs might be accomplished by federal determination of production quotas for each state and by state allocation of these quotas. Proration on the basis of allocated production quotas may result in operating wells at much less than their most efficient rate, although many geologists say that pinching down the production of oil wells increases final oil recovery. The best way to stabilize the oil industry is to control drilling so that oversupplies and extreme price fluctuations can be avoided.

[27] Earl Oliver, "United States Oil Industry," in C. K. Leith (ed.), *Elements of a National Mineral Policy*, The Mineral Inquiry, New York, 1933, p. 141.

[28] Oliver also lists as essential needs: (1) balancing supply and demand so that oil production and consumption will be brought into reasonable balance, and (2) securing the greatest possible recovery of oil at the lowest cost. (*Ibid.*, pp. 145–146.)

[29] Effective unit operation obviously requires compulsory pooling of operating and leasing interests. Voluntary unit operation schemes have demonstrated that they are inadequate for the achievement of major gains in oil conservation on a nation-wide or state-wide basis. Advantages of compulsory unit operation are considered so great that England provides for coöperation among lessees of a geological unit to be effected voluntarily, failing which the government (through the Board of Trade) has the power to require unit operation subject to the right of arbitration. (Glenn E. McLaughlin, "Proposals for Petroleum and National Gas Conservation," in *Energy Resources and National Policy*, National Resources Committee, Government Printing Office, 1939, p. 216.)

Unless some such arrangement can be established voluntarily by owners and operators with a minimum of government regulation, government ownership and operation will be necessary to prevent the continuation of wasteful exploitation of a very limited, irreplaceable, and useful resource. It is significant that complete nationalization of all oil rights in the United States, in line with the procedure followed by Germany and other nations, has been discussed from time to time in Congress. The federal government has acquired the important helium reserve in the Texas Panhandle by outright purchase. In many states, courts have already modified the rule of capture so that the landowner can recover only a certain portion of the oil within a given period.[30]

RECOMMENDED FUTURE MINERAL LAND POLICIES

In spite of the fact that the open door policy of private ownership and exploitation followed in the United States on most mineral lands has been an important factor in the serious economic and social problems associated with the mining industry, and in spite of the many arguments in favor of public ownership of mineral lands, the 1934 report of the National Resources Board's Committee on Mineral Policy did not recommend general extension of public ownership of minerals now in private hands, with the exception of purchasing and retiring part of the coal reserves and some submarginal coal mines, and retaining tax-reverted mineral deposits in public ownership until the minerals are needed, when the deposits should be leased and royalties paid to the government.

The committee states, "Whatever the abstract merits of public ownership may be, private ownership is so inherently a part of the American genius and tradition, and is so firmly entrenched, by law and custom, as a national policy, that the practical difficulties alone of any general reversal of the status quo at this late date would appear insuperable. However, future conditions cannot be foreseen, and the committee recognizes the possibility that restoration to public ownership of minerals now privately owned may sometime become a desirable feature of national policy." [31]

MINERAL LAND POLICIES OF OTHER NATIONS

Relatively few nations follow the American open door policy in utilizing their mineral lands. The degree to which the door to unrestricted

[30] For a more complete analysis of proposals for petroleum and natural gas conservation, see *ibid.*, pp. 214–236.

[31] The Committee argues that many of the recognized ills of our domestic mineral industries—particularly excess capital investments, variable and uncertain market demands, and irregular tenure and labor, combined with the problems peculiar to the mining industry, which center around exhaustibility and irreplaceability—can best be dealt with by private ownership and operation, with public supervision and control. (National Resources Board, *op. cit.*, p. 423.)

private exploration and exploitation is closed extends through a wide range, from compliance with a few simple regulations in some nations to absolute prohibition of mining by certain classes in others.[32] In Canada exploration and exploitation are carried on through a system of license and lease, traceable largely to the fact that mining rights exist or had existed in favor of the Crown. A fundamental characteristic of Canadian mining laws is that development, once projected, must be pursued, particularly on state lands.

Most mining laws are based upon the theory of concession, prospecting in almost all countries being free and open to citizens or aliens, with regulations restricting the class of individuals who can engage in prospecting. Such regulations prohibit prospecting by impecunious persons, but would not ordinarily affect activities of any well-organized company. Africa is nowhere freely open to prospecting. For example, in Portuguese possessions ownership of mineral right is vested in the state, and the government may restrict prospecting rights on any land. Egypt claims exclusive ownership of all mineral substances and will not sell or grant term leases on them. Petroleum is subject to preëmption or preferential purchases. Foreigners operate on the same basis as subjects if they have secured licenses or leases from the proper governmental agency or office.

In the Transvaal mining is not free and open, and no land can be prospected until declared open by the Ministry of Mines. In Guiana the government has a prior right to oil, and in both Northern and Southern Rhodesia, mining rights are vested in the British South African Company. Several countries in Asia have definite closed door policies. Japan is closed to all but Japanese subjects. In China free exploration is not permitted, and all ordinary minerals (aside from building materials) theoretically belong to the state, though considerable bodies have been alienated in actual practice. Fee simple ownership is not possible.

In order to secure the right to prospect in India, one must secure a certificate of approval and a prospecting license. In the Federated Malay States, regulations require the tin produced to be smelted in the British Empire. In Europe mineral land policy varies considerably, As a rule, the closed door policy exists unless other rules seem expedient. Spanish mining is on a decree basis, which means that power to grant mining rights reposes ultimately in the ministry. Foreigners and citizens are subject to the same treatment under the many mining regulations in Belgium. In Rumania several salines are state monopolies, and the state has established oil reserves.

This brief review indicates that in most cases private exploration and

---

[32] The brief statements concerning different national mineral policies are taken from J. W. Frey, "The Open Door Policy of Mineral Developments," in C. K. Leith (ed.), *Elements of a National Mineral Policy*, pp. 72–78.

exploitation of mineral resources have been considerably restricted. In some nations special restrictions prevent aliens from participating in exploitation; but in most of these nations, similar restrictions and public control hold for nationals as well. The conditions growing out of unrestricted exploration and exploitation, which most nations have experienced, are such that these nations have learned their lesson and are taking a more intelligent view of future policy by establishing public controls and restrictions that will tend toward a wiser use of natural resources in the public interest.

OWNERSHIP OF WATER AND WATER RIGHTS

Tenure problems associated with water resources vary with the type of use involved. In the case of irrigation water, tenure problems are largely those of dividing property rights among various private users. In the case of water power, they are largely those involving division of ownership and control between private and public agencies.

WATER RIGHTS FOR IRRIGATION

The first generation of western settlers gave little thought to their right to use creeks and rivers for irrigation. When settlements were small and widely scattered, the few users on each stream had the entire supply; but as settlement increased, competition increased and the *doctrine of priority* was evolved. According to this doctrine, water rights were established according to the order in which utilization had been made by the settlers.

But complications arose in applying this doctrine, and the *doctrine of relation* was adopted.[33] This doctrine holds that the right does not date from the time the water is used, but from the time of beginning construction work,[34] although the proving of the water right is not completed until water has been actually diverted and used.

Neither of these doctrines, however, defined the quantity of water that could be used; for this purpose, *beneficial use* was made the measure. That is, each appropriator has a right to continued use of the quantity of water put to beneficial use at the time a later right was acquired.[35]

---

[33] Since many ditches were built about the same time, it became necessary to determine what constituted first use. For example, should the water right date from the time of actual water use, or from the time when construction of canals or ditches began? If the right were to date from time of actual use, a premium would be placed upon poor construction, since it might happen that during the construction of a large canal, more easily built or smaller ones might be completed, and appropriate all the water, leaving the larger canal a total loss to its builders.

[34] To prevent abuses, the doctrine of relation has been modified in actual practice by providing that construction must be carried on with due diligence. (See Elwood Mead, *Irrigation Institutions*, Macmillan, 1903, pp. 65–66.)

[35] What constitutes beneficial use, and the determination of the quantity so used, are left to the courts in most of the states. Decisions on these points have been hotly

The appropriation doctrine of water rights for irrigation can be summed up as a right limited to the amount of water that can be beneficially and continually used for the purpose for which the right is acquired. In spite of the fact that the appropriation doctrine has important weaknesses,[36] it does enable arid and semiarid regions to develop more nearly to their maximum producing ability through utilization of their coördinated resources. Since an individual does not have to live on the stream to utilize its waters, he may operate land at a considerable distance and transport the water through canals or ditches to the spot where it can be most beneficially used. He is not required to return the water, or any part of it, to the stream in any manner, so that great flexibility is possible in determining the lands upon which the water will be used.

Under the appropriation doctrine, the right to water use is a separate property right distinct from property in land, and can be sold separately from the land, so that an individual could purchase a water right to apply to already-owned acreage that cannot be utilized effectively because of the absence of water. The public interest is served by utilizing waters on nonriparian lands, so that economic and social conditions are better than when homes and irrigated lands are confined to stream banks.

However, the appropriation doctrine does not necessarily bring about the best use of water. If earliest appropriators are, for the most part, at the lower end of the stream, there may be much less efficient total use of water than where most of it is appropriated upstream near its source, and use is made progressively downstream for other operators. This is attributable to the fact that, in mature irrigation projects, as much as 30 percent of the water, on the average, returns to the streams as seepage and can be utilized on lands lying downstream.

The doctrine of riparian rights grew out of the common law of England and was transplanted to the eastern United States. According to this doctrine, the owner of land along a stream has the right to use the waters thereof, provided he returns the water to the stream undiminished in quantity and unimpaired in quality. The right of a riparian owner to

---

contested, and many controversies have arisen that show the practical difficulties of applying the theory, as well as the keen competition for use of limited water supplies in arid and semiarid regions. (*Ibid.,* pp. 66–67.)

[36] In most states, posting and recording notice of water use is required in acquiring an appropriation right, but there is no limitation upon the amount of water that might be claimed. As a result, the sum of all notices claiming water in a given stream is in many cases much greater than the total flow of the stream, and often several times as large. (See T. S. Harding, *Water Rights for Irrigation,* Stanford University Press, 1936, pp. 35–36.) Notices are useful in determining priorities, but they are of limited assistance in determining the size of the rights. Courts are often called upon to *adjudicate* the rights of a stream—that is, to hear all the testimony, get all the records and information available, and allocate the water in the given stream to various claimants on the most just and equitable basis.

the continued natural flow of the stream is enforceable by judicial process.[37] Obviously, irrigation consumes most of the diverted water, and in many cases that which is returned is muddy, and, in a strict sense, "polluted." However, irrigation with reasonable regulation has been recognized as permissible among riparian owners in early English and eastern cases where such use was involved in riparian right litigation.

Modified riparian rights are recognized in the semiarid states of North and South Dakota, Nebraska, Kansas, Oklahoma, and Texas. Washington and Oregon have placed various limitations on the application of the riparian doctrine. In California riparian rights have been recognized to a greater extent than in these states, while the remaining eight western states recognize only the appropriation doctrine.[38] It is significant that in the eight western states that recognize riparian rights, the climate is partly humid and partly arid. The riparian doctrine has a climatic fitness in the humid parts of these states, and where riparian rights have been recognized, they will probably not be abandoned.

In most of these states, however, the courts have so changed the character of the common law doctrine of riparian rights that it can hardly be recognized. In California recent decisions have practically extended riparian privileges to all the lands within the drainage basin of a stream, instead of restricting them to the owners who live along its banks.[39] The riparian doctrine has been modified in other states to make it possible for the waters of western streams to be utilized for irrigation, while strict adherence to the riparian doctrine as such would make this practically impossible.

Water rights are real property and their loss can be decreed only by proper legal procedure in courts having jurisdiction over such property titles. *Abandonment* of an appropriation right is the voluntary releasing of use and right to use, while *forfeiture* is the loss of water rights because of nonuse for a period long enough to represent intention to abandon. The period of nonuse that constitutes forfeiture varies, and is generally defined by statute. Failure to assert one's water rights may under certain conditions result in their loss. For example, the failure of lower users to assert their rights against an upper appropriator may result in his acquiring rights adverse to those of the lower owners. Rights acquired under such conditions are called "rights by adverse use or prescription." [40]

---

[37] *Water Resources Law,* Vol. III of *Report of the President's Water Resources Policy Commission,* Government Printing Office, 1950, p. 156.

[38] See Harding, *op. cit.,* p. 55.

[39] See Mead, *op. cit.,* p. 323.

[40] In order to establish a right by adverse use, the diversion must be (1) continuous for the statute period, (2) open, (3) notorious, (4) peaceable, (5) under claim and color of right, and (6) to the damage of the one against whom the right is acquired. (See Harding, *op. cit.,* p. 86.)

PUBLIC CONTROL OF WATER POWER

Water power is subject to public control either through direct government ownership or through regulation by various state and federal bodies. Most notable of such federal agencies is the Federal Power Commission. The numerous requests for permission to construct power dams and the work involved in determining whether or not the interests of the United States would be affected adversely by the proposed construction led to the creation of the Federal Power Commission in 1920, to relieve Congress of this burden and to establish a more general determination of policy in such matters.

Federal authority granted by the Constitution over navigable waters has been extended over nonnavigable streams that affect the capacity of navigable streams. Perhaps more control is exercised over certain phases of power use and development than is required strictly for navigation purposes; in any case, the courts have upheld the 1920 act on the ground that its principal purpose is the protection of navigation.

Each of the larger states has also established a bureau or commission charged with duties relating to state control of water power. Most states have created regulatory commissions with jurisdiction over electrical utilities. These commissions have established for the utilities accounting systems to be maintained, upon which rates for power sold to consumers may be based. Regulation of rates for services and securities involved in producing and distributing power generally falls wholly within state lines, and is consequently within state jurisdiction; but where electrical energy is transmitted over state lines, such transmission becomes interstate commerce and in most cases is a matter for federal jurisdiction.

Increasing use of electricity makes an active policy of public development of water power highly desirable. There are many reasons why the federal government should be given primary authority over and responsibility for such a policy. The Energy Resources Committee of the National Resources Planning Board points out that private business firms cannot be expected to undertake the several important nonpower functions that cannot yield salable products. It states, moreover, that private business firms cannot even be expected to bring about the most economic development of water power, because the necessary storage does not seem to be generally justifiable for power alone.

State and municipal projects may fit in well with federal plans, but the interstate character of most major streams and the international character of some of them make state jurisdiction too limited for the drainage-basin plan. Modern developments in terms both of the characteristics of modern power supply systems and of river basin programs require the federal government to undertake an increasing responsibility in the development and marketing of power. The President's Water Resources Policy Commission concludes that the country's expanding power requirements can be best met by coöperation between federal, local, public, coöperative, and private power systems, all committed to the same objectives.[41]

GOVERNMENT CONTROL OVER WATER RESOURCES

The nature of government control over the utilization and conservation of water resources will be affected greatly by the status of intrastate and interstate water rights, and by the statutory and constitutional provisions relating to them. The states in general claim and exercise control over the appropriation and use of waters within their respective boundaries, while the federal government has been exercising a steadily increasing control over the waters of the nation through Congressional action based upon its constitutional power to control navigable waters. This increasing federal control over vital water resources has created intense feeling on the part of the states (particularly in the West), which have bitterly resisted it.

Flood control projects of the federal government have involved the protection and promotion of navigation, which affords unquestionable constitutional authority for this type of work. Furthermore, the federal government undoubtedly has the power to build flood control projects to protect interstate commerce over highways and railroads, the postal service, etc. It has also been able, through its authority on rights-of-way over public lands, to exercise considerable control over the use of water in the public land states, especially where its interests are involved, because of irrigation or similar projects. Interstate compacts require the approval of Congress, which may interject conditions it deems necessary or desirable.

The states of the arid region contend that control of the waters within their boundaries lies exclusively with them, and many such states have by constitutional provision or legislative enactment declared that their waters are their property, or the property of the public. These rights in the state are subject not only to the principle of equitable apportionment among the states on an interstate stream, but also to the power of Congress over interstate commerce and navigation. However, the question of ownership of the water of nonnavigable western streams has not been definitely settled by the Supreme Court.

The controversy between the federal government and the states over the right to control utilization and conservation of water resources is largely limited to the western arid region. In the states east of the Missis-

[41] *A Water Policy for the American People*, Vol. I of *Report of the President's Water Resources Policy Commission.*

sippi River, there has never been any question as to the power of the state to control the waters within its boundaries, because little public land and no federal interests are involved, except in connection with navigation, diversions from one drainage basin to another, or control of runoff waters to prevent widespread floods.

The eastern states were sovereign entities when they came into the Union, and reserved to themselves all rights and privileges except those specifically granted to the federal government. In these states the major purpose of water-conservation activities is to *prevent* damage; and these states, where runoff waters constitute a liability, are anxious to get rid of this menace. In the western states, however, the major purpose of water conservation is to store and hold the waters for irrigation in order to *develop* the semiarid lands for more beneficial, stable, and profitable uses—and floodwaters are a very valuable natural resource. In the states east of the Mississippi, state control of water resources varies from practically none in some southern states to complete control over all water uses and developments in the case of New York.[42]

One of the most important arguments for increasing federal control over water resources is the interstate controversies that arise in the increasing competition for water of certain streams, and the lack of any well-coördinated plan or program of multiple-purpose development. Without any central or regional agency authorized and equipped to consider the development and effectuation of a unified multiple-purpose program for major rivers or streams, competition among the states is inevitable.

Interstate compacts are one means by which interstate water problems might be settled; but as yet they are a relatively new and unproved method. All such compacts must be authorized and approved by Congress, and in each case of a compact involving western states, Congress has provided that a representative of the United States be appointed to participate in the negotiations. If for no other reason, federal interest and Congressional power could be upheld under the "commerce clause" of the Constitution, on the grounds that all waters of the country affect the navigation of some stream, and this would give the federal government a constitutional right or interest in every stream.

Congress undoubtedly has the power to authorize a federal agency or agencies to make plans for the complete, coördinated utilization of the water resources of each important river system of the country, and to make an equitable apportionment of the use of said waters. However, to enforce the plans and findings of such an agency might be difficult, without clear constitutional authority, or a Supreme Court decree.[43]

---

[42] National Resources Board, *op. cit.,* p. 379.
[43] *Ibid.,* p. 381.

Singstad, who observed methods of administration and control over water resources in Austria, Czechoslovakia, England, France, Germany, Italy, and Switzerland, states (1) in all seven countries there is more or less complete governmental control of all water resources; (2) three out of seven countries have a department of public works controlling conservation and utilization of water resources; (3) hydroelectric power plants, are, except in Italy and England, largely in public ownership; (4) all countries have a highly developed forestry; (5) land drainage and irrigation are ordinarily done by local districts under government concessions; and (6) all governments exercise rigid control over stream pollution.[44]

OWNERSHIP AND CONTROL OF TRANSPORTATION LAND

Highways, waterways, and airways are publicly owned in the United States, while railroads and pipelines are privately owned. Federal, state, and local governments own and administer the highways, and the federal government regulates the use of navigable streams and waterways.

Highway tenure problems largely concern control of the use of roadsides in the interest of recreational development and traffic safety. This problem has already been discussed in the section on recreational land tenure. Public ownership or extensive public regulation and control of practically all land used for general transportation in the United States is now considered to be in the interests of public safety and the general welfare.

The peculiar characteristics of pipelines have aroused much discussion, and many contend that pipelines are not, in a strict sense, common carriers; [45] nevertheless, they are now subject to regulation by the Interstate Commerce Commission and various state commissions, and all rates and charges are subject to regulation prohibiting injurious and unreasonable charges and practices.[46]

[44] See Ole Singstad, "Government Control over Water Resources in Certain European Nations," National Resources Board, *op. cit.*, 1934, pp. 374–387.

[45] The purpose for which pipelines in the United States have been built is a single purpose, in a single industry—to transport only one commodity, in one direction. The typical pipeline is built from a refinery or terminal to an oil field to secure a supply of crude oil for that refinery. Functionally, a crude oil pipeline bears more resemblance to the aerial tramway and belt conveyor used in mining than to the common carrier railroad except, perhaps, where a railroad is used for the lumber industry in a logging district. See *Hearings before the Temporary National Economic Committee*, 76th Congress, Second Session, Part 15, "Petroleum Industry," Section 2, October 2–7, 1939, Government Printing Office, 1940, p. 8594.)

[46] The Hepburn Act of 1906 changed the Interstate Commerce Act of 1897 to make it applicable to pipelines. The status of pipelines as common carriers has been affirmed by the Supreme Court of the United States. (See the pipeline cases, 234 U.S. 548; and *Temporary National Economic Committee Hearings*, pp. 8543, 8595.)

It is the duty of pipelines as common carriers to receive and transport oil and petroleum products for all shippers alike regardless of the identity or affiliations of the shippers, and unjust discrimination among shippers, receivers, or localities is prohibited.[47] The law has never been carried out fully. Pipeline rates have not been regulated effectively, and independent oil companies complain considerably about the difficulty of getting oil transported in them.

The Mann-Elkins Act of 1910 made telegraph, telephones (wire or wireless), and cables subject to regulation by the Interstate Commerce Commission; also express companies, sleeping-car companies, bridges, and ferries. Since the Federal Communications Act of 1934, communication facilities are regulated by the Federal Communications Commission.

URBAN LAND TENURE AND TENANCY

The concentration of large numbers of people in small areas, characteristic of modern urban development, makes the problem of housing and conditions affecting home ownership and leasing of major importance.

HOME OWNERSHIP AND TENANCY

A little more than half the houses in American cities are occupied by the owners, and about 47 percent are occupied by tenants.[48] The percentage of houses occupied by owners has been increasing in recent years. More than a million houses yearly have been constructed since World War II, and with liberal financing by federal agencies, especially for veterans, urban tenancy has declined.

The problem of adequate housing for low-income urban families is a very serious one. High rentals in large cities create particularly severe hardships for low-income families because of the large percentage of family income required to meet monthly rental payments. Rents definitely tend to rise as urbanization increases, and the percentage of income spent for rent increases correspondingly. During such depression periods as the thirties, when unemployment increased greatly and thousands of wage incomes declined, the urban housing problem became acute in many sections.

[47] All but about 10 percent of pipeline mileage is owned and operated by companies that are affiliated with other companies engaged in producing or refining petroleum, or both. This small percentage of unaffiliated lines is represented largely by eight pipeline companies which were at one time subsidiaries of the Standard Oil Company of New Jersey, but which were separated by the dissolution decree in the Standard Oil Case. (See *Temporary National Economic Committee Hearings,* p. 8589.)

[48] The 1950 Census lists nearly 36 million urban dwelling units, of which 19 million are owner-occupied and 17 million renter-occupied. (See U.S. Bureau of the Census, *Census of Housing; 1950,* Government Printing Office, Vol. II, Part I, pp. 1–7.)

Low-income families and the families of the unemployed tend to con centrate in low-rental areas too frequently consisting of inadequate hous ing facilities. In many cases slum or blighted areas have been created by families on the outer edges of cities, where they have attempted to earn part of their living costs by tilling small pieces of land, and to get ou from under the heavy overhead of high rentals by building make-shif shacks in which to live. On the outskirts of almost every city, during the thirties, such blighted areas could be seen. In the bigger cities, slum areas exist in the older sections. Half the dwelling units in some citie are physically substandard.[49]

In addition to a high degree of urban tenancy, particularly in the tenement house and slum sections, problems arise from short-term lease and rapid turnover of tenants. In one study, it was found that nearly a fourth of the tenant-occupied units are occupied for less than 6 months and an additional 27 percent for a term from 6 months to a year and 11 months. More than half the tenant-occupied units are occupied for les than two years.[50]

This brief period of occupancy, which is partly a reflection of job in security, tends to discourage landlords from making desirable improve ments and to reduce the general level of urban housing facilities. A viciou circle usually develops in which areas of short occupancy cause landlord to offer poor housing facilities, resulting in even shorter terms of tenan occupancy. The general result is the creation of unsatisfactory residentia districts, inadequate housing, substandard units, and generally unsatis factory living conditions.

TITLE INSURANCE AND REGISTRY

The cost of title examinations and insurance is an important element in delaying free transfer of real property. This is particularly true of home ownership—in the case of purchases, as well as loans on houses already owned. Under the present United States recording system, a title search must be made every time a specific tract of land is transferred. Abstracts are prepared that contain all the important matters affecting title; and with each new transfer or mortgage the abstracting company brings the abstract up to date.

In recent years a system of title insurance has made considerable head-

[49] Nearly half the dwelling units in the city of Butte, Montana, were found to be physically substandard, in a survey in 1938. A dwelling unit is rated as substandard in regard to physical characteristics if any one or more of the following conditions exist: (1) need for major repairs; (2) unfitness for use; (3) lack of private flush toilets; (4) lack of a private bathing unit; (5) absence of running water; (6) absence of in stalled heating; (7) no electricity or gas for lighting. (See R. R. Renne, *A Preliminary Report of the Butte Economic Survey*, City of Butte, Mont., October, 1939, p. 79.)

[50] *Ibid.*, p. 86.

way in some parts of the United States, particularly in urban areas. Title companies with records, abstracts, indices, maps, etc., guarantee the holder of a title against loss resulting from title defects, with certain specified exceptions. The lack of certainty in title under the title search and abstracting systems has made title insurance a practical necessity where the Torrens system of title registry has not been adopted.[51]

The basic principle of the *Torrens system,* originated by Sir Robert Torrens in South Australia (where it was enacted into law in 1858), is registration of title to the land rather than registration of mere evidence of such title. Major characteristics of the system are (1) creation of truly indefeasible titles warranted and guaranteed by the state; (2) provision for special proceedings by which validity of title is established and a governmental certificate attesting that fact is issued, and transfer of title to registered land by entry, to the exclusion of all other methods; and (3) creation of an indemnity fund to compensate those who may suffer damages through the operation of this system. The Torrens system has been adopted in a number of foreign countries and is at present a permissive method in 17 states, Hawaii, and the Philippines, though it is not mandatory in any state.[52]

In the case of mortgage foreclosures, serious problems are raised by the necessity of extinguishing the mortgage and producing a perfect title. Foreclosure proceedings in the various states of the United States exhibit a great diversity—particularly in connection with the enforcement of remedies available to the mortgage after the mortgagor's default. Usually, foreclosure procedure is by action in court. It is generally considered that a simpler method of foreclosure than the ones generally used would be very desirable.

The costly and cumbersome features of present foreclosure procedure and the uncertainties in title so characteristic of present foreclosure methods should be removed. The Uniform Real Estate Mortgage Act, drafted in 1927, would make the mortgage a lien upon instead of an estate in the premises, leaving the right of possession in the mortgagor until foreclosure is complete. It also provides a simple, inexpensive, and efficient method of foreclosure without resorting to the courts, with ample protection to later lien holders, leaving the title clear, specific, and unclouded. The method is "foreclosure by sale," and provides for a substantial period of redemption after foreclosure sale.

There are merits in making foreclosures more, rather than less, difficult in order to protect occupancy. Refinancing of overcapitalized property

[51] National Resources Committee, *Urban Planning and Land Policies,* Report of the Urbanism Committee, Government Printing Office, 1939, p. 243.
[52] For a more detailed statement in regard to the Torrens system and the use of this method of land title insurance, see *ibid.,* pp. 245–247.

and deferred payment plans are important means for reducing disturbance of occupancy.

THE "GROUND RENT" SYSTEM, OR LONG LEASEHOLD TENURE

Long-term leases are a form of urban land tenure that was known in Greek and Roman times. Ecclesiastical and other corporations were required by law to keep the fee simple of their lands in their own hands, and consequently adopted the device of leasing the lands for a fixed term of years. The practice has gradually been taken up by private landowners who recognized the system as a means of retaining land as a source of income for their families and heirs.[53]

Tenure for a period of 99 years or more is considered to be long leasehold tenure. (Some leases recorded in Detroit, Michigan, in 1834, were for 999 years.) Distinctive features of long-term leases are ordinarily the provision requiring tenants to erect improvements, pay taxes, manage the property, and pay a fixed rent to the landlord. The chain store type of merchandizing has recently tended to increase the number of long-term leases.

Too often the advantages or disadvantages of long-term leases have been judged strictly from the point of view of the parties to the lease. Too little consideration has been given to the effect of such leases upon the community. Numerous advantages are obtained by the landlord, as well as the tenant; but long-term leases are not always for the good of the public. Tenants often refuse to make improvements, because buildings on leaseholds revert to the landlord toward the end of the lease term. Thus, buildings and neighborhoods are often neglected.

The value of the land in or near important business districts may be so great that it would strain the city's financial resources to cope with this problem through condemnation proceedings. Moreover, owners or trustees of estates may refuse to sell their reversionary interest in the property, thus retarding important business or neighborhood developments.[54]

Long-term business leases have undoubtedly helped to advance large real-estate projects; but if such leases are permitted, they should be drawn with some regard to public improvement as well as private tenure; and if the public interest requires certain leaseholds, the law should provide for proportionate compensation according to some specific plan. Without such provisions, leases of more than 99 years, irredeemable leases, and those providing for renewals in perpetuity are detrimental to the public interest and should be forbidden by statute where no such legislation exists.

[53] *Ibid.*, p. 255.
[54] *Ibid.*, p. 257.

THE NEIGHBORHOOD UNIT (POOLING AND REPLOTTING LAND)

Numerous problems, including blighted areas and slums, overuse and underuse of land, high cost of municipal services, tax delinquency, mortgage foreclosures, inadequate housing, and increased tenancy are associated with unplanned and rapid city growth. Greater powers of control than those currently in use are desirable and necessary to insure the maintenance of more satisfactory urban living conditions.

As a mean of achieving this control by private initiative rather than by government regulation or ownership, the neighborhood unit plan has been proposed.[55] One form of this plan is the formation of a private corporation in which the owners in a block or area voluntarily pool their interests. They convey title to their properties to the corporation, in return for the corporation's stocks or bonds. Or there may be a voluntary conveyance of all the interest of the owners in an area to a trust company, which issues certificates of interest in a trust to the owners. Another form is incorporation of a neighborhood protective and improvement district, upon the initiative of a large percentage of the owners in a given area. This district becomes a new political subdivision in the city, with the power of eminent domain, taxation, and police powers subject to municipal regulation and control.

"LEX ADICKES"

An interesting example of pooling and replotting land as a means of correcting defects in urban land utilization resulting from crooked streets, dead-end streets and alleys, poorly shaped lots, and lack of adequate open spaces is the *Lex Adickes,* which refers to a law passed in Frankfurt-on-Main, Germany, in 1902, and named after the mayor, Dr. Adickes. This law was the first of several statutes and ordinances that eventually applied the principle of compulsory pooling and replotting of land to almost all German cities.

The initiative may be taken by the municipality or by a stated portion of the property owners (ordinarily one-half), provided they own at least half the area scheduled for replotting. A commission appointed by owners and public authorities is authorized to carry out the work. After the land has been pooled, a layout of planned streets, squares, parks, and other public spaces is prepared. After the public spaces have been dedicated, the rest is redistributed as building sites in a proportion as close to the

---

[55] A neighborhood unit has been defined as an area of a town usually bounded by main traffic roads, without any main traffic routes passing through it. The school is its basic feature, together with all neighborhood recreational and shopping facilities necessary for a self-contained residential unit. It may be considered as a satellite form of government, either within or outside the town itself. (*Ibid.,* pp. 274–275.)

original area and value of the owners' holdings as possible. Holdings too small for buildings sites are sold to owners of adjacent plots, if possible and unavoidable differences in value are adjusted by money payments with the right of appeal to the courts. However, the important point is that, whether initiative comes from the owners or from the municipality the procedure is compulsory. It can be employed in built-up areas, but no instance of such application has been discovered.

This procedure deserves careful consideration as a means of improving urban land utilization and living conditions. Voluntary reorganization of vacant or sparsely built subdivisions is a most desirable means of effecting needed adjustments, but involves many difficulties. In the case of German cities, the mere threat of compulsion has frequently been sufficient to in sure the coöperation of all owners. In urban areas (already solidly built up in most cases) a procedure such as that in *Lex Adickes* appears to be impracticable; and only in the event of catastrophes such as widespread fires or earthquakes, where large-scale rebuilding of slums and blighted areas is necessary, would these procedures be particularly applicable.[56]

PUBLIC OWNERSHIP OF URBAN LAND

In the United States public ownership has been viewed rather generally as a last resort in controlling urban land use and development, when other methods, including pooling, replotting, and regulatory activities like use of the police power through zoning or through building, sanitation, and other codes have failed or are inadequate. Only in recent years has public ownership been used to any considerable extent in urban land. It has been found in many instances that only by public ownership could governments secure the degree of control necessary for proper land utilization and development. In 1937 Congress passed the Housing Act to assist local public housing agencies to construct low-cost dwellings, apparently on the grounds that it is "probably neither sound business nor good social policy for very low-income urban families to put all their savings into one rather uncertain and unliquid investment." [57]

Land acquisition by city governments may be used to supplement other land-use control measures. Also, public purchase of land may exercise an influence on land use beyond the limits of the public tract. The whole character of a neighborhood may be changed by establishing parks or playgrounds, by filling a swamp, or by some similar improvement made

[56] After the great earthquake and fire that destroyed a large part of Tokyo and Yokohama, a national act was passed embodying the principles of *Lex Adickes,* under which the urban areas were replanned. (For a more detailed statement of the application of this procedure, see *ibid.,* pp. 280–281.)

[57] For a more detailed statement concerning the arguments for publicly owned "projects" instead of individual "owned homes," see Catherine Bauer, *A Citizen's Guide to Public Housing,* Vassar College, Poughkeepsie, N.Y., 1940, pp. 57–63.

through public land purchase. A new highway can materially affect surrounding land values.

National policy in the United States until recently has been so definitely one of getting as much land as possible into private ownership that today few American cities own land beyond their immediate public needs. In contrast, municipalities in European nations often own large holdings, many of them dating from feudal times.[58]

The principal arguments for public ownership of urban land are: (1) In many cities a great deal of land is not profitable in some type of private ownership and generally reverts to public ownership through tax delinquency. (2) Land is often necessary to carry out a particular program; and when the city government has decided to provide playgrounds, clear slums, or acquire water supply systems, the city government must purchase or secure land in one way or another. (3) Although many argue that private ownership will put land into its highest use, it should not be forgotten that this means the *most profitable* use.

A careful distinction should be made between uses that bring financial profit to shrewd or fortunate developers, and uses most beneficial to the taxpayers or the community as a whole. Private ownership, forced through competition to extract the highest possible yield, is ordinarily considered ill-equipped to usher land through a descending scale of intensities and values, and this process will probably be necessary in the future in many cities. In these cases, governments may be forced to take over the adjustment from intensive to extensive urban land use. In other words, public ownership should be considered in conjunction with current needs, rather than on the theoretical basis of the merits or demerits of public ownership compared with private ownership.[59]

REFERENCES FOR FURTHER READING

A National Plan for American Forestry, Senate Document 12, 73d Congress, First Session, Vols. I and II, Washington, D.C., 1933.

A Water Policy for the American People, Vol. I of *Report of the President's Water Resources Policy Commission,* Government Printing Office, Washington, D.C., 1950, Chap. XV.

Dorau, H. B., and Hinman, A. G., *Urban Land Economics,* The Macmillan Company, New York, 1928, Chaps. XXIV, XXV, and XXVI.

Harding, T. S., *Water Rights for Irrigation,* Stanford University Press, Palo Alto, 1936.

Hibbard, Benjamin H., *A History of the Public Land Policies,* The Macmillan Company, New York, 1924, Chaps. XIX, XXI, and XXV.

[58] See National Resources Planning Board, *Public Land Acquisition in a National Land Use Program,* Part II, Urban Lands, Report of the Land Committee, Government Printing Office, 1941, p. 11.

[59] *Ibid.,* pp. 12–13.

Huffman, Roy E., *Irrigation Development and Public Water Policy*, The Ronald Press Company, New York, 1953, Chap. IV.

Ise, John, *The United States Forest Policy*, Yale University Press, New Haven, 1920, Chap. XI.

Ise, John, *The United States Oil Policy*, Yale University Press, New Haven, 1926, Chaps. XX–XXVII.

Leith, C. K. (ed.), *Elements of a National Mineral Policy*, The Mineral Inquiry, New York, 1933.

National Resources Committee, *Energy Resources and National Policy*, Report of the Energy Resources Committee, Government Printing Office, Washington, D.C., 1939.

National Resources Committee, *Urban Planning and Land Policies*, Report of the Urbanism Committee, Government Printing Office, Washington, D.C., 1939.

National Resources Planning Board, *Public Land Acquisition in a National Land Use Program, Part II, Urban Lands*, Report of the Land Committee to the National Resources Planning Board, Government Printing Office, Washington, D.C., 1941.

Water Resources Law, Vol. III of *Report of the President's Water Resources Policy Commission*, Government Printing Office, Washington, D.C., 1950, pp. 154–167.

part V

DISTINCTIVE FEATURES
OF MAJOR LAND USES

AGRICULTURAL LAND
NONAGRICULTURAL LAND
LAND AND WATER

chapter 19

AGRICULTURAL LAND

THE IMPORTANCE OF AGRICULTURE

Agricultural Trends in Modern Economies

TYPES OF FARMING

Commercial Farms—General or Diversified Farming—Part-Time Farming

AGRICULTURE IN ARID REGIONS

Dry Farming—Ranching—Irrigated Farming—Land Use Practices Adapted to Arid Conditions

DISTINGUISHING CHARACTERISTICS OF AGRICULTURE AS AN INDUSTRY

Farmer Has Little Control Over Production—Agriculture Not Highly Commercialized—Agriculture a Relatively Small-Scale Industry—Agriculture a Highly Competive Industry—Agriculture an Industry Characterized by Relatively Slow Turnover—Demand for Agricultural Products Relatively Inelastic—Agricultural Population Widely Scattered—Great Importance of Fixed Charges in Agricultural Industries

PECULIARITIES OF LAND IN AGRICULTURAL USE

Importance of the Spatial Element—Importance of Fertility—Absorption of Investments or Improvements in Agricultural Land

AGRICULTURE is an occupation, a business, and a land use. It is regarded by many as the most important or essential occupation, the keystone of economic and business life, and the highest and most desirable use to which land can be put.[1] This point of view is commonly referred to as "agricultural fundamentalism." Its proponents argue that the importance of agriculture in the economy cannot be measured in terms of the relative proportion of the population or the relative value of capital (land and improvements) in agricultural production.

THE IMPORTANCE OF AGRICULTURE

Some 60 percent of the total population of the world is engaged in agriculture, but in the United States only about a tenth, or 11 percent is so engaged. In the 17 years from 1940 to 1957, the proportion of the U.S. population engaged in agriculture decreased from a fourth to one-tenth During this same period, output per man-hour in agriculture doubled and total production of agricultural products increased more than a third reflecting the rapid advances in science and technology during and following World War II.

Agriculture furnishes an important part of the materials for manufacturing and commerce. Many farm products must be processed and transported to the points of consumption, and many occupations, such as transportation, manufacturing, banking, retailing, merchandising, and the professions, find their prosperity dependent upon volume and value of agricultural output. Mining and forestry likewise furnish a considerable part of the materials for manufacturing and commerce, but agriculture may be said to produce a more essential type of product than these in the last analysis, because it produces the foodstuffs necessary to sustain life itself. In some areas, however, the forest products are essential for heating and shelter, and human living at its present level would not be possible in many areas without forestry or mining. Moreover, for the maintenance of our modern level of living, the automobile manufacturing plants of Detroit are just as fundamental as the cotton fields of the South or the wheat farms of the West. Only when we think of levels of living in terms of the most primitive kind of economy can we conclude that agriculture is strictly the most fundamental enterprise.

AGRICULTURAL TRENDS IN MODERN ECONOMIES

In spite of the emphasis that many leaders have placed upon the fundamental nature of agriculture, and in spite of the fact that for the world as a whole more people are today engaged directly in agriculture than in any other occupation, history reveals a trend, most conspicuous in the more advanced nations, toward a smaller place for agriculture in national

[1] For numerous citations from addresses and writings of many agricultural leaders in regard to the fundamental character of agriculture, see J. S. Davis, *On Agricultural Policy, 1926–1938*, Food Research Institute, Stanford University Press, 1939, Chap. II.

economies [2] as invention proceeds and commerce, industry, the arts, and the professions are expanded.

This trend has been noticeable since 1850, and more particularly after World War I. In George Washington's time, three-fourths of the population of the United States lived on farms, while today only a tenth are farm people. Many believe that it is unwise to maintain an unnecessarily large farm population, and that from the standpoint of long-time maximum satisfaction of human wants, it is desirable to devote the smallest possible proportion of total national energy to providing for the essential wants of food, shelter, and clothing. In this way, a maximum is available for leisure activities and for satisfying human wants for the wholesome nonessentials.[3]

TYPES OF FARMING

In discussing agricultural land utilization and the economic problems of farming, most people think in terms of the type of agriculture with which they are most familiar. There are many types or systems of farming, and the type that is used will determine to a large extent the amount of land and the practices followed in utilizing it within a given farm.

In the United States the census lists all land in farms as farm acreage, although this land in farms includes in addition to cropland harvested, acres upon which crops were planted but failed, cropland that is lying idle or fallow, plowable pasture, pasture that is not plowable, and all woodland. In other words, all farm woodlots are included in farm acreage and are generally included in the figures showing the acreage of agricultural land. On the other hand, some of the area not included in the land in farms is used for farming—such, for example, as very small tracts in gardens in urban areas. Only about two-fifths of the land in farms in the United States is actually used for cultivated crops (approximately 400,-000,000 out of more than 1,060,000,000 acres), and about half the land in farms is devoted to pasture; the remainder, or about a tenth of the land in farms, is in the form of farm woodlots, and in reality should be classed as forest rather than agricultural land.

There are numerous bases upon which types of farming can be classified. One author lists 12 bases.[4] The U.S. Bureau of the Census classifies

[2] This trend seems so pronounced that Davis ventures to state, as a law of economic history, "Economic progress, broadly viewed, tends to be accompanied by a decline in the relative importance of agriculture." (*Ibid.,* p. 27.)

[3] See the author's treatment in "On Agricultural Policy," *Journal of Farm Economics,* May, 1940, pp. 484–492, a critical review of Davis' book, *On Agricultural Policy.*

[4] Gray lists 12 bases for classifying systems or types of farming, as follows: (1) characteristics of natural resources, (2) kind of enterprises, (3) variety of enterprises, (4) kind of field system, (5) size or scale of operation, (6) proportion of labor and capital to land, (7) kind of power used, (8) effect on soil resources of the type of farming, (9)

farms into two groups: *commercial* farms and *other* farms. Commercial farms are those with a total value of $1200 or more of farm products sold during one year, and those farms with a value of $250 to $1199 of products sold, provided the farm operator worked off his farm less than 100 days and the total value of agricultural products sold from the farm was greater than the income received by him and members of his family from other sources.[5]

Other farms comprise *part-time, residential,* and *abnormal* farms. Part-time farms are those with a value of $250 to $1199 of farm products sold, provided that the farm operator reported 100 or more days of work off the farm during the year, or that the income received by him and members of his family from other sources was greater than the total value of agricultural products sold from the farm. Residential farms include all farms, except abnormal farms, with a total value of less than $250 of agricultural products sold. Abnormal farms comprise public and private institutional farms, community enterprises, experiment station farms, and similar types of units.[6]

Commercial farms make up more than two-thirds of all farms in the United States, and the proportion of commercial units to total farms is increasing.[7]

COMMERCIAL FARMS

The census divides commercial farms into 10 major types: cash-grain, cotton, other field crop, vegetable, fruit and nut, dairy, poultry, livestock other than dairy and poultry, general, and miscellaneous. The largest of these 10 is livestock farms other than dairy and poultry. Livestock farms comprise approximately one-seventh (14.5 percent) and nearly 700,000 farms of the total of approximately three and one-third million commercial farms. Dairy, cash-grain, and cotton farms rank next in number, each type comprising more than a half million farms and better than a seventh of total U.S. commercial farms. These four types combined comprise about two-thirds of all commercial units. The remaining third are divided among the other six types in this order: field crops other than

---

character of business organization, (10) tenure of operator, (11) kind of labor, and (12) motives of farming. (L. C. Gray, *Introduction to Agricultural Economics,* Macmillan, 1924, pp. 7–8.)

[5] See U.S. Bureau of the Census, *U.S. Census of Agriculture: 1954,* Vol. II, Type of Farm: General Report, Government Printing Office, 1956, Chap. XII, p. 1269.

[6] *Ibid.*

[7] The 1954 Agricultural Census reported 4,783,021 farms in the U.S., of which 3,327,-617 or 69.6 percent, were classified as *commercial,* and the remaining 1,455,404, or 30.4 percent as *other.* In 1950 the total number of farms was 5,379,250, of which 3,706,412, or 68.9 percent, were classified as *commercial* and 1,672,838, or 31.1 percent, as *other.* (*Ibid.*)

cotton or cash-grain, general, poultry, fruit and nut, miscellaneous, and vegetable.[8]

There are various degrees of commercialism in farming, but when the farm family produces some products for sale to secure funds with which to purchase other necessary goods or services which it cannot supply from the farm, it is no longer a strictly self-sufficing farm. On this basis there is very little strictly self-sufficing agriculture in the United States or in other recently settled agricultural areas. The highly commercialized character of southern agriculture was an important factor creating the serious economic difficulties in which the South found itself at the outbreak of the Civil War. Southern plantation owners sold their cotton and tobacco in an unprotected world market in England, but had to purchase the products they needed in a protected domestic market at an entirely different price level. This selling in an unprotected market and buying in a protected one was an important factor contributing to the economic distress of southern agriculture, not only prior to the Civil War but until recent years, when governmental programs have been designed to secure benefits for southern farmers.[9]

During severe business depressions, when the commercial farmer finds his prices declining heavily without any corresponding decline in his overhead costs, a system of self-sufficing or "subsistence" farming is advocated by many as the solution. However, the proponents of commercial agriculture argue that commercial farming enables the farm operator to take advantage of the principle of specialization or division of labor and enable a higher level of living to be secured by farm people as well as urban folks, through the greater productiveness resulting from specialization. Such proponents argue that the solution to the farm problem is not a return to self-sufficing or subsistence farming, but rather a removal of the forces in the economy that create violent price changes, or adoption of governmental or other programs which will compensate for these price changes.

In modern societies proposals to have farmers follow a type of agriculture largely self-sufficient in character are not generally popular. This type of program not only is in opposition to the recognized principles of comparative advantage and specialization, but it is a difficult program to pursue in many areas, because of climatic, topographical, soil, or other

[8] *Ibid.,* pp. 1284 and 1285. For an explanation of what is included in each type, see p. 1270.

[9] The AAA program inaugurated by the New Deal in 1933 was an attempt to secure parity prices for agricultural products. Cotton and tobacco, two of the South's most important farm products, were included in this parity price program, "parity price" meaning that farmers would secure prices for their products that bore the same relationship to prices of things farmers must purchase as the relationship that existed between these two types of goods in a given base period (1910–1914, in the case of most products under the AAA program).

limitations. American farmers have looked upon a strictly self-sufficing type of farming as "peasant" agriculture, characteristic of the older nations of Europe, where farmers have operated relatively small units, largely with hand labor, and have been able to secure only a relatively low level of living. Chinese agriculture also is largely of a self-sufficing or subsistence type. American farmers have insisted upon following a combination of enterprises and practices which would enable them to attain a higher standard of living than that achieved through this peasant type of farming.

GENERAL OR DIVERSIFIED FARMING

General farming ordinarily refers to a type of highly diversified agriculture in which, although the farmer produces a great variety of products, both of crops and of livestock, he nevertheless produces a considerable amount of products for sale and is not on a strictly self-sufficing basis.

For various reasons the principle of diversification, or not putting all of one's eggs in one basket, has been widely followed, even though it may seemingly be in opposition to the principle of specialization or comparative advantage. The most important reason for diversified agriculture is that it has been necessary in most areas in order to permit a balanced labor load through the year for the farm operator and his family, and the use of a system of crop rotations combined with livestock enterprises to maintain or improve soil fertility.

The areas in which general diversified farming has been practiced are mostly those in which soil erosion and fertility wastage have been least. The two major agricultural problem areas in the United States are the South, where a one-crop system of cotton production has predominated, and the Great Plains area, where dry-land wheat production has predominated. General or diversified farming is a fairly intensive type of land use, because a comparatively large amount of labor is utilized with a given area of land. Moreover, the investment in capital in the form of machinery is relatively large, for the great variety of enterprises requires many different types of machinery. In some areas farmers have grouped together to use coöperatively certain types of the larger, more expensive machines, so that the same amount of capital is spread over a larger land area. The proportion of U.S. farms classified as general is declining and now comprises only 1 out of every 14 farms.

PART-TIME FARMING

In this type of agriculture, the family lives on a farm, and the operator or head of the family works at least 100 days elsewhere during the year for wages or a salary. There are more than a half million part-time farms in the United States.[10]

Part-time farming is greatest in areas where population centers are close enough to make commuting to and from employment practicable. Part-time farming is considered especially desirable by industrial and agricultural leaders who believe that industry should decentralize. During the early thirties the federal government embarked upon a subsistence-homestead program designed to give stranded or migratory families an opportunity to live on a few acres of land and secure part-time work in a neighboring town or industrial area.[11]

AGRICULTURE IN ARID REGIONS

The United States may be divided agriculturally into two parts—the East and the West—on the basis of whether the land is chiefly used for crops or pasture. The dividing line is close to the 100th meridian, the area east of this line having a subhumid or humid climate, and the area west of it having an arid or semiarid climate except in parts of the Columbia Plateau, the Pacific Coast area, and at the higher altitudes in the mountains (refer to Figure 5). The East is divided into eight regions, excluding the forest and hay belt, on the basis of the dominance of a certain crop or type of farming, the result primarily of latitude and temperature conditions. The West is divided into four large regions on the basis of the use of the land for grazing or crops, determined in turn principally by altitude and rainfall (see Figure 26).

Nearly 1200 million acres, or more than three-fifths of the land area of the United States, are classed as arid. These lands are situated in the western half of the nation, and it is here that the more spectacular land-use problems of dust storms and widespread farm abandonment and migration have occurred. The characteristics of the arid regions are so different from those of the humid areas that special adaptive practices must be devised if they are to be successfully used.

Generally speaking, an average yearly precipitation of about 18 inches seems to be the marginal point for successful crop production without special adaptive procedures to conserve or add water. The farther south, the higher must the precipitation be to be equally effective, because of

[10] The 1950 Census reported 639,230 part-time farms, but the 1954 Agricultural Census reported data by type of farms only for commercial farms. (See *ibid.*, p. 1269.)

[11] M. L. Wilson, "The Place of Subsistence Homesteads in Our National Economy," *Journal of Farm Economics*, Vol. XVI, No. 1, January, 1934, p. 73; and W. W. Wilcox, "Planning a Subsistence Homestead," U.S. Department of Agriculture, *Farmers Bulletin, 1933*, April, 1940. For an analysis of studies of part-time farming, see L. A. Salter, Jr., and Larry F. Diehl, "Part-time Farming Research," in *Journal of Farm Economics*, Vol. XXII, No. 3, August, 1940.

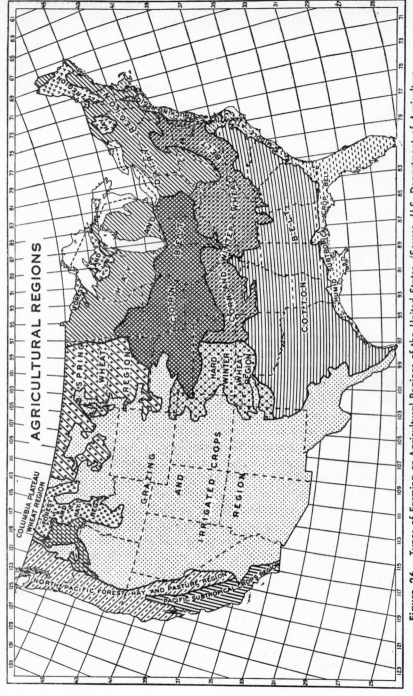

Figure 26. Types of Farming or Agricultural Regions of the United States. (Source: U.S. Department of Agriculture, Bureau of Agricultural Economics.)

greater evaporation and more torrential rains. The lands of the South-west, with less than 10 inches of rainfall, are considered definitely arid, and no attempt is made to farm them without irrigation.

In the Middle West and the East, on the other hand, natural precipitation is such that crop production can be undertaken without danger of complete crop failures caused by lack of rainfall in any period. However, the semiarid and subhumid regions, which receive from 10 to 20 inches and from 20 to 30 inches of precipitation respectively, are definitely "in-between country," neither strictly arid nor strictly humid. Since the average precipitation in this section is so near the critical point required for the successful production of crops, any deviation therefrom is extremely important.

Tree ring growth studies and studies of lake beds and other Great Plains geologic formations indicate that the history of the region has been one of recurring droughts causing complete crop failures for several succeeding years, followed by periods of above average precipitation and yields. It is the relative certainty of successful crop production without special adaptive land-use procedures that is the outstanding characteristic distinguishing humid areas from semiarid and subhumid regions (see Figure 27). Note from this figure that precipitation in humid Iowa fluctuates around an average of 31 inches yearly, while precipitation in semiarid Montana fluctuates around an average of about 15 inches annually, or less than half as much. Thus, Iowa has a natural safety margin of moisture. Without this natural margin of safety to absorb economic

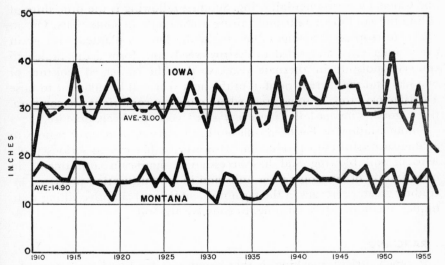

Figure 27. Average Annual Precipitation in Iowa and Montana, 1910–1956. (Source: U.S. Department of Commerce, Weather Bureau data.)

stresses and strains resulting from the yearly precipitation variations common in humid areas, farm operators in semiarid and subhumid regions like the Great Plains area must organize their farms and ranches so as to furnish a workable substitute for this natural buffer or cushion.

DRY FARMING

Three types of agriculture have been developed in the arid regions: dry farming, ranching, and irrigation farming. Before 1910 most of the Great Plains had been utilized primarily for livestock grazing, but after that date the area in tilled crops increased greatly and dry-land farming became the major type of use. Grain, especially wheat, has been found to be the most drought-resistant crop, and most of the dry-land agriculture of the arid regions is devoted to producing this single cash crop.

The combination of comparatively favorable precipitation, high wheat prices in the war years, temporary large yields from the virgin sod, and availability of free land permitted the establishment of farms very similar in size and operation to those characteristic of the more humid areas from which the settlers came. However, with return to more normal price levels, more normal, and in some years below-average, precipitation, settlement of most of the formerly free land, and the decline in yields after the virgin sod had been cultivated for a time, farm operators in the arid regions soon realized that they would have to adapt their land utilization practices to these conditions in order to survive.

One of the first adaptations made in the arid areas of the United States and Canada was summer-fallowing. Summer-fallowing is the procedure of tilling the land every year and raising a crop only in some years. On an alternate crop and summer-fallow basis, the land is planted with grain every other year, and tilled to destroy weeds and form a dry mulch to conserve moisture in alternate years, so that the conserved moisture of one year and the current rainfall of the next year will be sufficient to raise a satisfactory crop. In some areas where moisture conditions are comparatively good, summer-fallowing every third year has been practiced.

Summer-fallowing has been sufficiently effective in many arid regions to enable successful crop production. However, it has caused serious problems of soil blowing and has necessitated significant adjustments in organization of farm operating units and in land-utilization practices, including greater acreages in the farm unit, additional adaptive tilling techniques, including strip farming, to conserve the soil.

RANCHING

A ranch, strictly speaking, is that amount of land and equipment devoted to production of livestock through grazing, occupying most of the time of one or more operators. In other words, ranch land is not utilized by tilling or raising crops; instead, livestock graze the natural vegetation. Stock farming is a combination of farming and grazing; on stock farms, crops are raised to feed the livestock.

Formerly, ranchers raised no crop, not even tame hay, for livestock feed; and even today, many areas in the western arid regions, where ranching is the major type of land utilization, raise no crops of any kind, but cut wild hay or native hay or grasses and feed this to livestock during the winter when the range is covered with snow and cannot be grazed. Failure to produce supplemental feeds or hay for winter use in the early days was one of the most important factors contributing to disastrous failures of many ranches during severe winters. More and more ranchers in the arid areas are coming to appreciate the desirability of putting up a considerable amount of native or tame hay for winter feed. Wherever irrigation water is available for economic use in ranching areas, it is being used to produce hay for livestock feeding.

Ranching units in western arid regions are necessarily relatively large, causing a sparse population and high per capita costs of schools, roads, communications, and related services. In addition, ranching is characterized by relatively slow turnover. Moreover, the ranch directly supplies very little of the total living of the ranch family, and this high degree of commercialization means that ranchers are particularly affected by price fluctuations.[12]

The western range produces annually a large number of feeder cattle for the feed lots of the corn belt. About one-sixth of the cattle and calves of the United States are located in the 11 western states, Texas leading all states, with an average of between six and seven million head. The 11 western states contain nearly half the United States total of sheep and produce approximately half the wool clip.[13]

IRRIGATED FARMING

The artificial application of water to arid lands may make many otherwise unproductive lands very productive. For successful irrigation farming, water must be available, the user must be able to control the water supply and apply moisture when and where it is needed, and the supply must be capable of being utilized in economically feasible ways, so that costs are not excessive. In addition, the soil must possess certain qualities

[12] See Roland R. Renne, "Range Land Problems and Policies," Chap. VII in *Land Problems and Policies* (eds. John F. Timmons and William G. Murray), Iowa State College Press, 1950, p. 106.

[13] Cf. Mont H. Saunderson, *Western Stock Ranching*, University of Minnesota Press, 1950, p. 125; and Marion Clawson, *The Western Range Livestock Industry*, McGraw-Hill, 1950, p. 163.

if irrigation efforts are to be profitable. Land that is too porous and drains easily will absorb excessive amounts of water without correspondingly adequate returns; while land that has extremely poor drainage will tend to waterlog, and, in the high-evaporation areas characteristic of arid regions, alkali will tend to accumulate in the top few inches of soil.

The value of irrigated land in connection with dry farming and ranching has been mentioned. Although the acreage irrigated will never be a large percentage of the total acreage of the arid regions, the production of the irrigated lands far outweighs their proportionate acreage. Irrigation farming is usually an intensive method of utilizing land, and yields per acre are several times those from comparable lands.[14] The greater intensity of land use in irrigated areas permits adequate farm units to be smaller, so that population density per square mile is much greater than in dry farming or ranching areas.

Some 20 million acres of irrigated land, mostly in the 11 western states, are used for agricultural production. In the aggregate, irrigated farming is a significant factor in American agriculture; but in certain specific local areas, it is particularly important in stabilizing production and furnishing necessary winter feed reserves for stable and successful ranch operation. It permits production of a greater variety of crops and enables many operating units to produce a major portion of the foodstuffs used by the family, with a salable surplus of many of these products to supplement operating incomes. Since irrigation farming must compete for the use of water with all other alternative uses to which water can be put, including generation of hydroelectric power, recreation, and transportation, as well as land drainage, it can more logically and adequately be treated in connection with the larger field of the economics of water utilization in Chapter XXI.

LAND-USE PRACTICES ADAPTED TO ARID CONDITIONS

Because of the natural characteristics of arid regions, and especially of the semiarid regions where dry-land agriculture is practical, farm operators must devise methods of adaptation to anticipated variations in growing conditions. People who settled the Plains from humid eastern areas, from the western seaboard, or from foreign nations (particularly the British Isles and the Scandinavian countries, which are extremely humid) transplanted the culture of these humid areas to the Great Plains, postponing necessary adaptations. Such adaptations were not immediately neces-

---

[14] For example, in Montana only about 2 percent of the total land area is irrigated, but of the people on farms in the state, about a third are on irrigated farms or ranches, and the value of the irrigated land in farms (including buildings) amounts to 36 percent of the value (including buildings) of all land in farms in the state. (P. L. Slagsvold and J. D. Mathews, *Some Economic and Social Aspects of Irrigation in Montana,* Montana Agricultural Experiment Station Bulletin 354, January, 1938, p. 3.)

sary, because the arid regions experienced relatively heavy rainfall during the period of heaviest settlement and fabulous wheat prices during World War I. However, with more normal rainfall and the inevitable droughts that occurred later, the consequences of an unadapted culture became evident.[15]

The cardinal feature of a farm economy adapted to the variations of growing conditions characteristic of semiarid regions is flexibility, or as one writer has put it, the ability to "roll up and unroll," much after the manner of some plants that have structural provision for living through unfavorable growth periods in order that they may later take advantage of suitable growing conditions.[16] In order to achieve this flexibility, the farm operator needs a combination of enterprises that will allow him to take advantage of good growing conditions when they occur, and to cut down during unfavorable periods to avoid dissipating his accumulated reserves.

This process of expanding promptly in certain periods and shutting down drastically and suddenly in others is not consistent with usual conceptions of good farm management practices, because most budget items in the farm management account require continuous and steady operation for highest efficiency. However, such "rolling up and unrolling" procedures are essential in areas where precipitation variations occur in an irregular and unpredictable manner above or below a norm which is so close to the margin of successful crop production that bumper crops or complete crop failures occur from time to time.

Achieving a diversification or combination of enterprises that will give the flexibility needed for the "rolling up and unrolling" practices essential in the arid regions is extremely difficult within the boundaries of an individual farm or ranch operating unit. *Area diversification,* rather than diversification by specific farm units, may be an adaptive procedure that will be useful.

With area diversification, the farm headquarters would be located in

---

[15] Many settlers were poorly equipped, from the standpoint of background and experience, to understand and effect the land-utilization practices that would work most efficiently in the arid regions. In a study of the Triangle Area in North Central Montana, Wilson found two deep-sea divers, six musicians, two butchers, two milliners, two draymen, two wrestlers, two blacksmiths, two schoolteachers, two physicians, and one bartender. (M. L. Wilson, *Dry Farming in the North Central Montana Triangle,* Montana Extension Service Bulletin 66, June, 1923.) For a comprehensive analysis of the consequences of an unadapted culture in the Northern Plains, see C. F. Kraenzel, William Thomson, and G. H. Craig, *The Northern Plains in a World of Change,* Gregory-Cartwright, Ltd., Canada, October, 1942; C. F. Kraenzel, "New Frontiers of the Great Plains," *Journal of Farm Economics,* Vol. XXIV, No. 3, August, 1942, pp. 571–588; and Carl F. Kraenzel, *The Great Plains in Transition,* University of Oklahoma Press, Norman, 1955.

[16] E. A. Starch, "Type of Farming Modifications Needed in the Great Plains," *Journal of Farm Economics,* Vol. XXI, No. 1, February, 1939, p. 115.

the irrigated area along streams where feed crops and a large garden for the operator's family could be grown; wheat could be grown upon good nearby land extending back to the benchlands above the irrigated valleys; and, finally, livestock could be run on grazing lands lying beyond the wheat-producing benchlands in the foothills or near the mountains. Modern rubber-tired machinery permits operating wheat lands several miles from the farm headquarters without much loss in efficiency. Grazing areas could be handled coöperatively and cattle cared for by coöperative grazing associations during the grazing season.

Thus, a farm operator could have a few acres of irrigated land surrounding his headquarters, additional wheat-producing acres on the benchlands within a radius of 10, 20, or 30 miles from headquarters, and an allotment of a number of animal units of sheep or cattle in the grazing district on the range lands beyond the wheat lands.

But achieving flexibility in arid regions to the extent necessary for successful farm operation requires more than flexibility through diversification; it requires flexibility in overhead costs—particularly debt service charges and taxes, the two major fixed operating costs in agricultural land utilization.

DISTINGUISHING CHARACTERISTICS OF AGRICULTURE AS AN INDUSTRY

Each major land use has distinguishing characteristics caused by the interplay of numerous physical and human forces peculiar to it. An appreciation of these is essential for an adequate understanding of the problems associated with utilizing land for each major purpose.

FARMER HAS LITTLE CONTROL OVER PRODUCTION

Changes in production of agricultural commodities are much influenced by weather conditions and natural forces, unlike the production of most other industries. Insect pest ravages and weather conditions affect crop yields, carrying capacity of grazing lands, and the quality of soil products. Consequently, farmers exert much less control over output in any year or any brief period of time than operators in most other industries; and the volume of agricultural production may not respond promptly to changes in demand.

Unless the weather coöperates perfectly, prices of farm products are likely to rise more quickly and to higher levels with a demand increase than prices of manufactured goods. Although the farmer may respond to increased demand by increasing his acreage, it may yield a smaller output than a larger one, so that there is no increased supply to help hold down rate and extent of price increase. Manufacturers are in a better position to respond promptly to price increases resulting from increased demand by expanding volume of production, since weather factors are much less important.

During periods of declining demand and falling prices, agricultural prices are likely to decline most because, even though farmers may decrease acreages planted somewhat, exceptionally favorable weather may result in an output which is just as large as before, or larger, so that the heavy volume tends to depress prices relatively more than the shrunken volume of manufactured goods. Thus, it may be said that farm prices tend to react more vigorously than nonfarm prices to upswings and downswings of the general price level accompanying changes in purchasing power and demand. This tends to result in serious disparities between prices of things farmers buy and prices of things they sell.

Many agricultural land-utilization problems, particularly problems of soil erosion and declining fertility, have resulted from the economic difficulties facing farmers as a result of these disparities. These disparities associated with physical conditions in agricultural production are increased by the economic conditions of pure competition characteristic of agriculture, as contrasted with imperfect competition characteristic of manufacturing enterprises. Farmers attempting to make economic ends meet find it necessary to tighten their belts or exploit the soil. Frequently both are involved, and the soil is exploited, or utilization techniques are faulty, or producing ability is lowered. It is much easier for farmers to follow land-use practices that maintain and improve soil fertility and producing ability when they have a satisfactory income and can meet necessary expenses without too much difficulty. It is under the stress of economic poverty and the urge to secure more dollars with which to meet necessary operation and living costs that most serious exploitation of land resources occurs.

AGRICULTURE NOT HIGHLY COMMERCIALIZED

Agriculture generally is much less commercialized than most industries, and consequently reacts differently to price and income changes. In farming, home and business are one, and the family is usually the principal source of labor. Consequently, when prices decline rapidly, the farmer can seldom save by curtailing his individual output, because (1) he hires little labor and cannot fire his own family, and (2) his variable expenses constitute a relatively small percentage of his total. Correspondingly, expansion of farm production, when prices rise in response to increased demand, is much less prompt and complete, even assuming uniform weather conditions.

In some areas, where agriculture has become highly commercialized—such, for example, as the spring and winter wheat belts of the United

States—"suitcase farmers" are numerous.[17] Such highly commercialized one-crop farming frequently results in land-use practices that do not prevent soil erosion and maintain productivity. Such operators frequently fail to follow recommended summer-fallow and water conservation practices, and try to make a killing whenever weather conditions seem favorable, letting the land lie idle or go to weeds in less favorable years.

The economic and social consequences of such "suitcase farming" are numerous and serious. Similar criticism could be made of other highly commercialized agricultural undertakings in which the land is exploited when profit prospects are good and allowed to deteriorate or become foul when profit prospects are poor. The continuity of attention and husbandry necessary to secure most consistent and satisfactory production from the utilization of land is lacking in highly commercialized enterprises, with the result that basic natural resources are frequently permanently dissipated.

AGRICULTURE A RELATIVELY SMALL-SCALE INDUSTRY

The fact that most farm operating units are on a family basis, operated largely with family labor, means that the size of the business is limited to an acreage that can satisfactorily be handled with family labor under the given system of farming followed. For example, in the United States the average farm contains about 215 acres, and although much farm machinery is used and a considerable investment is often made in farm buildings and dwellings, the average investment is small compared with that of modern large-scale industries and factories. Though many have criticized family farms on the grounds that they do not permit the farm operator to combine the factors of production most efficiently or use his managerial ability most fully, the family-size farm has remained the dominant type of farm unit throughout the world.

The advantages alleged for corporation farming include economies in buying and selling, in management, and in use of machinery and man power. However, these are apparently more imaginary than real, because such factors as the seasonal nature of work on most farms, the uncertainties of weather, the difficulties of overseeing laborers when they are scattered over a large area rather than concentrated in one or two floors as they are in a factory, have made it difficult for corporation farms to meet the competition of the smaller family-size units. Moreover, the large corporation or "bonanza" farms do not possess any of the self-sufficing features of the family units, and are fully exposed to the vagaries of price cycles and weather, which determine the success or failure of farming.

[17] Suitcase farmers plow the land and seed the wheat in the spring with extensive equipment, and return to town or to some other area where their regular residences and jobs are located. At harvesttime, they return and harvest the crop with a large combine and tractor outfit.

Mechanization of agriculture has resulted in an increase in the average size of farms in the United States, from about 155 acres in 1935, to 215 acres 20 years later. This increasing mechanization will promote an agriculture that is more commercialized and more exposed to the vicissitudes of nature and the price cycle. The resulting effects upon land utilization practices will be far-reaching.

The desire to secure the most satisfactory combination of productive factors in agriculture has caused much study of the most economic sizes of operating units. What constitutes an economic or adequate unit will depend largely upon the type of farming. In a self-sufficing type of agriculture, the economic unit will be of that size which utilizes most efficiently the entire family labor available for work. Such a size of unit would enable the farm family to produce the largest possible amount of goods that it will need for its living. On the other hand, if the type of farming is highly specialized and commercialized, the economic unit will be of that size which utilizes the operator's managerial ability and capital most efficiently and enables him to make the highest possible net return.

There is no one ideal economic or adequate size. The most desirable size will depend largely upon what the farmer is trying to do with his farm and under what circumstances he is trying to do it. Nevertheless, budgets worked out by farm management specialists for different types of farms in various areas, which show the minimum-sized operating units that will use certain types of machinery efficiently or produce a certain minimum net family income under average conditions, are useful guides in determining the general pattern of farm operating units for most satisfactory land utilization.

AGRICULTURE A HIGHLY COMPETITIVE INDUSTRY

The dominance of small, family-sized diversified farms creates many individualistic, competitive operating units. Agriculture is the last large segment of modern economies in which such units predominate. In many manufacturng and industrial plants, competing units have combined until a few large units control most of an industry's output. Such combinations and concentrations of control have never occurred extensively in agriculture, and its highly competitive nature generally means that changes in demand bring about price changes. On the other hand, because of its characteristic concentration of economic control, or monopoly, modern industry adjusts to decreased demand chiefly through output changes, not through price changes. This is substantiated by the record of industrial and agricultural production and prices in the United States during the depression of the thirties.[18] Thus, industrial product prices tend to be

[18] Industrial production in the United States declined from 115.2 in 1929 (1924–1929 = 100) to 60.7 in 1932, while agricultural production during the same period increased

more rigid and output more elastic than prices and market supply in agriculture, where competition operates more completely.

The land-utilization practices of farm operators are largely determined by the effects of the competitive nature of the agricultural industry upon them, and the disparities between prices they receive and prices they pay. Economic disadvantages resulting from these price disparities tend to force users to exploit the soil and fail to maintain productive capacity of their lands, particularly during periods of generally declining prices and falling demand, when price disparities are most pronounced.

AGRICULTURE AN INDUSTRY CHARACTERIZED BY RELATIVELY SLOW TURNOVER

A large portion of the farmer's investment is in land and buildings. Opportunities for substituting one crop for another are limited because of soil, climate, plant diseases, technical factors, and others. It requires from 12 to 20 years to get a good stand of native grass established on Great Plains land formerly used for grain production, and some 10 to 12 years to establish a good orchard in most areas. A farmer's decision to expand or curtail output must be made many months, or sometimes years, in advance of marketing his product.

There is less possibility of extensive mechanization in agriculture than in most nonagricultural fields, because the seasonal nature of agriculture and the technical production conditions for many types of crops and livestock make the efficient use of machinery impossible. Consequently, agricultural production is ordinarily a matter of combining labor with land and limited capital inputs, so that the investment ratio is fixed, in comparison with circulating capital, and is greater than in most nonagricultural industries. All things considered, therefore, agriculture is more rigid and less able to adjust quickly and completely to rising or falling prices than most nonagricultural industries.

DEMAND FOR AGRICULTURAL PRODUCTS RELATIVELY INELASTIC

Consumer demand for most agricultural products is relatively inelastic compared with the demand for many nonagricultural products. Human wants for farm products are comparatively satiable. The human stomach can consume just so much and no more. However, there is considerable elasticity in the wants of consumers for different types of food. This is another way of saying that the total importance of farm products is very

---

from 101 in 1929 to 107 in 1931, but declined to 100 in 1932. During these same years, prices received by farmers declined from 146 to 65, whereas prices paid by farmers for commodities they purchased declined only from 153 to 107. (See *1941 Outlook Charts—Demand, Credit, and Prices*, U.S. Department of Agriculture, Bureau of Agricultural Economics, Agricultural Marketing Service, October, 1940, pp. 2, 7, and 14.)

great, while their marginal importance is modest. We might eliminate more than 40 percent of our farmers and still be able to supply our population with basic foods and fibers, but it would be impossible to eliminate all farmers.

Demand for many types of farm produce can be quickly satisfied, and beyond that volume a definite surplus arises. This is true of all commodities, to a certain extent, but the amount wanted at different price levels will fluctuate much more with respect to the wholesome nonessentials than to necessities of life such as the foodstuffs, which comprise such a large proportion of the agricultural output.

AGRICULTURAL POPULATION WIDELY SCATTERED

In longer-settled nations, farm people often live in villages and travel to and from their farm lands. In the United States, Canada, and many of the more recently settled nations, operators live on their farm units; and since area is so important in agricultural land utilization, farm populations under this pattern are widely scattered. The population density of many farm communities (particularly in the western range areas) is less than one per square mile; and even in the more densely settled agricultural areas of the Middle West, population density in farm communities in some states averages only 16 persons per square mile.

The relatively low population density of agricultural areas increases per capita costs of such necessary services as schools and roads, or communication facilities, and is an important cost factor in agricultural land utilization.

GREAT IMPORTANCE OF FIXED CHARGES IN AGRICULTURAL INDUSTRIES

Fixed charges are generally more pronounced in farming than in nonagricultural industries. Some of the principal reasons for the relative importance of fixed charges in agriculture are: (1) Differences between agriculture and other industries in the methods by which outside funds are secured. In agriculture, outside funds are obtained largely through mortgage instruments that call for a fixed money payment of principal and interest regardless of farm income, whereas industrial enterprises obtain a large portion of their outside funds through the flotation of common stocks or ownership equities, which are exchanged for a share of the net income, if any. (2) Real estate (land and buildings) comprises a much larger percentage of the total capital investment in agriculture than in other industries, and consequently property taxes fall heavier on agricultural enterprises than on nonagricultural. Property taxes are relatively rigid and do not vary with price changes as do the income, sales, or similar taxes which are more important for nonagricultural industries.

During periods of price declines, public expenditures ordinarily increase because of unemployment and relief expenditures, and after a war public expenditures increase to service debt incurred to finance the war During such periods, the amount of revenue secured from income and sales taxes tends to decline in relation to the total revenue required while property taxes are not reduced and may even be increased. This occurred in the United States during the severe deflation following 1920,[19] and the resulting serious consequences to agriculture were factors that contributed to agricultural land tenure, credit, taxation, and conservation problems.

PECULIARITIES OF LAND IN AGRICULTURAL USE

The preceding section has pointed out several characteristics of agriculture that distinguish it from nonagricultural pursuits, and lead to some of the more important problems involved in utilizing land for agricultural purposes. This section discusses some of the more significant peculiarities of agricultural land growing out of these distinguishing characteristics of agriculture.

IMPORTANCE OF THE SPATIAL ELEMENT

One of the most important characteristics of agricultural land is the spatial element. In urban land use, if the demand for apartment space or for commercial use increases, it can often be met by more intensive use Adaptation may be made largely by building upward or expanding vertical use. It is impossible to increase the output of agricultural land by this method. If demand for vegetables increases, more acres must be brought into production, because it is not possible ever to increase vegetable production by raising vegetables in stories or crowding them together, after a certain point is reached, even with tray agriculture. In other words, a certain amount of space, sunlight, and plant nutrients must be provided for each individual plant.

The importance of the spatial element in agricultural production may cause a nation to adopt an imperialistic policy if demand for agricultural products increases. Imperialistic policies of some modern nations, including the *lebensraum* ("living space") policy of Nazi Germany, have been

[19] Indexes of farm real estate taxes per acre rose steadily during the twenties to 281 in 1929 (August, 1909–July, 1914 = 100). Although farm property taxes declined during the thirties, the index in 1938 was 186, while the index of all commodity wholesale prices was 115, and the index of prices received by farmers, 95 (U.S. Department of Agriculture, *The Agricultural Situation*, Bureau of Agricultural Economics, March, 1940, Vol. XXIV, No. 3, p. 24). See also Siegfried von Ciriacy-Wantrup's "The Relation of War Economics to Agriculture, with Particular Reference to the Effects of Income and Price Inflation and Deflation," *American Economic Review*, Part 2, Supplement, March, 1940, Vol. XXX, No. 1, pp. 366–382, and the author's treatment in "Effects of the War on Agriculture," *Proceedings of the Fourth Annual Pacific Northwest Conference on Banking*, State College of Washington, Pullman, April 4–5–6, 1940.

planned to secure control of more agricultural land to feed and support growing industrial-urban populations. The technological economies of modern nations have resulted in greater desire for lands containing basic raw materials—particularly oil and such minerals as coal and iron—rather than purely agricultural lands.

IMPORTANCE OF FERTILITY

David Ricardo referred to the "original and indestructible" properties of land. Location or extension, or physical area, is the most indestructible of all characteristics of land. The qualities of the soil commonly referred to as "fertility," which give it the ability to support plant life, are not indestructible. It is true that some soils are heavily endowed with the qualities that support productive plant growth, and that man has been able to utilize some of these lands year after year, with little regard for scientific soil management, and yet continue to secure good crops. On the other hand, some soils less richly endowed fail to yield satisfactory crops after a few years, unless commercial fertilizer is added to supply necessary plant nutrients, or crop rotations and proper soil management practices are followed.

Results of the Rothamsted experiments in England furnish data on the indestructibility of fertility. At this famous experiment station there is a plot that has been sown to wheat continuously since 1839, with no fertilizers added. During the first 18 years production declined, but for the last four or five decades yields have remained practically constant.

Fluctuations have resulted from character of the season, corresponding closely with yield fluctuations on fertilized plots. The test plot seems to have reached a stationary condition, yielding a crop that averages 12½ bushels to the acre, which will probably continue or be reduced only slightly in the future. The yield on this plot corresponds closely with crop yields throughout Europe during the Middle Ages, when no fertilizers were used and crop rotations were practically unknown. For more than a thousand years, this stationary yield supported the European population.[20]

Apparently natural soil processes each year make available enough plant nutrients to produce about 12½ bushels, so that ordinarily crop yields will not be reduced below this amount. Therefore, it may be said that reduction of fertility below this point in appreciable amounts is usually impossible. However, the fact that the land produced much more than this in the beginning and could produce much more than this with proper soil practices, including desirable crop rotations, indicates that fertility or producing ability is relatively destructible.

[20] See C. R. Van Hise and L. H. Havemeyer, *Conservation of Our Natural Resources,* Macmillan, 1930, pp. 377, 378.

Fertility may be destroyed in ways other than by overcropping or by land-use practices that use up most of the essential plant nutrients (particularly nitrogen, potassium, and phosphorus). Improper land use may produce serious wind or water erosion, which removes much of the solid matter in the top few inches. It has been estimated that soil erosion annually removes fifteen hundred million tons of solid matter in the United States, wasting 126 billion pounds of plant food, which is 21 times the annual net loss attributable to removal of crops.[21]

In many areas where the top few inches have been removed through erosion, several years are required to bring back productivity, because organic matter and necessary plant nutrients must be reëstablished or applied to the eroded surface before satisfactory plant growth can be achieved. In some areas absolute failures result during the first two or three years crops are attempted on badly eroded soils that have lost their top few inches.

It seems obvious that while the fertility of most lands cannot be destroyed to the extent that the lands will produce absolutely nothing, fertility can be reduced significantly by land-use practices. Man is unable to destroy the extension or physical area of land itself; and consequently, from the standpoint of urban land use or even the use of land for transportation purposes, man cannot destroy to the same extent the most important and basic qualities of the land. Fertility, therefore, is an especially important characteristic of agricultural land, and agricultural land-use programs and policies must be developed and effected to maintain and, if possible, improve the ability of the land to produce agricultural products.

ABSORPTION OF INVESTMENTS OR IMPROVEMENTS IN AGRICULTURAL LAND

One of the principal ways in which land varies from other production goods is in fixity of investment. In agricultural land, improvements in the form of fertilizer, lime, green-manure crops, and related labor and capital inputs are absorbed by the land and become so definitely a part of it that it is impossible to distinguish land from improvements.

In the case of urban land utilization, much of the investment takes the form of buildings or structures which, although they are attached to the land, considered immobile, and classed as real estate, are nevertheless readily distinguishable from the land itself. For purposes of taxation, improvements can be assessed as improvements and land can be assessed separately on the basis of its bare land value. In the case of agricultural land, such separation is difficult and usually impossible. The implications of this ability of agricultural land to absorb and destroy the identity of

[21] *Ibid.*, pp. 361–362.

much of the investment in it are particularly significant in taxation, especially when proposals are made to tax "unearned increments."

REFERENCES FOR FURTHER READING

Clawson, Marion, *The Western Range Livestock Industry*, McGraw-Hill Book Company, Inc., New York, 1950, Chaps. I–XIII.

Davis, J. S., *On Agricultural Policy, 1926–1938*, Food Research Institute, Stanford University Press, Palo Alto, 1939, Chap. II.

Doane, R. R., *The Measurement of American Wealth*, Harper & Brothers, New York, 1933.

Ely, Richard T., and Wehrwein, George S., *Land Economics*, The Macmillan Company, New York, 1940, Chap. VIII.

Klimm, L. E., Starkey, O. P., and Hall, N. F., *Introductory Economic Geography*, Harcourt, Brace and Company, Inc., New York, 1937, pp. 66–75.

Kraenzel, Carl F., *The Great Plains in Transition*, University of Oklahoma Press, Norman, 1955.

National Resources Planning Board, *Our National Resources: Facts and Problems*, Washington, D.C., 1940.

Renne, Roland R., "Range Land Problems and Policies," in Timmons, John F., and Murray, William G. (eds.), *Land Problems and Policies*, Iowa State College Press, Ames, 1950, Chap. VII.

Saunderson, Mont H., *Western Stock Ranching*, University of Minnesota Press, Minneapolis, 1950, Chap. I.

Schultz, T. W., *Agriculture in an Unstable Economy*, McGraw-Hill Book Company, Inc., New York, 1945, Chaps. I and II.

Zimmermann, Erich W., *World Resources and Industries*, rev. ed., Harper & Brothers, New York, 1951, Chaps. XI and XII.

chapter
20

NONAGRICULTURAL LAND

FOREST LAND

Importance of Forestry in the Economy—Types of Forests —Costs in Forest Operation—Returns from Forest Operation—Forest Management—A Multiple-Use Resource— Time Element in Production—A Large-Scale Business— Flexibility of Operations—Demand Factors and Substitutes for Forest Products

RECREATIONAL LAND

Increasing Importance of Recreation—Place of Recreation as a Land Use—A Partial and Often Noncompeting Land Use—Waste and Submarginal Lands Often Useful for Recreation—Benefits Difficult to Measure for Private Operation in Competition with Other Uses—Economic Effects of Developed Recreational Resources

MINERAL RESOURCES

Importance of Minerals in the Economy—Competition of Mining with Other Land Uses—Irreplaceability of Minerals—Highly Localized Resources—"Hidden" Nature of Most Mineral Resources—Durability of Many Minerals— Interchangeability of Minerals—Mining a Large-Scale Operation—Peculiar Labor Situations in Mining—Diminishing Returns or Increasing Costs in Mining

TRANSPORTATION

Transportation as a Land Use—Factors Determining Use of Land for Transportation—Effects of the Freight Rate Structure on Land Use

URBAN LAND

Importance of Urban Land in the Economy—Competitive Uses for Urban Land—The Location of Cities—The Structure of Cities—Intensity of Situs Utilization—Im-

*portance of Transportation to Urban Land—Doses of
Labor and Capital Inputs Relatively Large—Large Fixed
Overhead—Slow Capital Turnover—Separability of Value
Improvements from Land Resources—Production Costs
in Urban Land Utilization*

THE MAJOR nonagricultural uses of land are forestry, recreation, mining, transportation, and urban. Each of these has its own peculiar characteristic which differentiates it physically and economically from other
land uses. An appreciation of these is fundamental for an adequate
understanding of the land-use problems associated with each and the most
effective ways of dealing with such problems.

FOREST LAND

Forestry accounts for a larger acreage of the earth's surface than any
other major use. Forest requirements are ordinarily enough less exacting
than crop or pasture requirements that the forest acts as a residual use for
land that agriculture and pasture cannot profitably utilize. Certain lands,
of course, are not suitable even for forests. The settlement history of the
United States is an excellent example of the encroachment of agriculture
upon forest land, though this process has to some extent characterized
settlement in every continent.

Next to agricultural crops, forest crops have contributed most to human
progress and security and, like agricultural crops, they are renewable.[1]
Wood is the world's most versatile raw material. No other material provides fuel, fiber, food, and chemical derivatives while also serving a great
variety of structural uses. Wood has played a significant role in the development of modern living standards, because of its almost countless variety
of uses, including paper for the spread of knowledge throughout the
world.

IMPORTANCE OF FORESTRY IN THE ECONOMY

The importance of forests in modern economies varies greatly. Nearly a
third of the area of the United States is forest land of one sort or another,
estimated to be worth from 8 to 10 billion dollars. Of the major land uses,
forest lands rank fourth in importance, being exceeded by urban land,

[1] See *Third Report to the Governments of the United Nations by the Interim Com-
mission on Food and Agriculture,* transmitting report of the Technical Committee on
Forestry and Primary Forest Products, Charles Lathrop Pack Forestry Foundation,
Washington, D.C., 1945, p. 9.

land used for public highways, and agricultural land.[2] In spite of forest depletion for purposes of agricultural use, and heavy consumption of forest products in modern industry without reforestation to maintain the supply, the forest industry as a whole easily accounts for a tenth of all railroad revenue freight. U.S. forests support the fifth greatest manufacturing industry of the nation, being exceeded only by iron and steel, machinery, food, and textiles. In addition to these contributions, forests are particularly important in the conservation of water and soil, as recreational environment, as a natural habitat for many wild game and bird species, and in the production of forage and livestock grazing.

In nations like Finland, Norway, and Sweden, forests comprise a much greater proportion of the total land value, making a much larger contribution to the total income of the nation. Moreover, in nations where a sustained-yield policy has been established over many decades through controlled cutting and systematic reforestation, forest land resources have not decreased in value as they have in the United States and other nations where more exploitative forest practices have been followed. At the turn of the century, forest lands comprised more than a tenth of the total value of land in the United States, while now they comprise about a twentieth.

Forests cover approximately seven and one-half billion acres, or about a fourth of the total land area of the earth. Thus, forestry uses much more of the earth's surface than agriculture (about an eighth), but it does not furnish employment to nearly as many of the population. The proportion of total land area in forests varies from as much as 60 percent in Finland to less than a half of 1 percent in Italy. In the United States, forests now use about a half billion acres, or a little more than a fourth of the total land area, which is about the average for all nations.

TYPES OF FORESTS

Forests may be divided into *natural* and *cultivated* or artificial forests. The best examples of natural forests are the primeval or virgin forests, while the best examples of artificial or cultivated forests are those that have been planted and cultivated by man. There are, of course, many variations between these two extremes, all of which are influenced more or less by man. For example, second-growth forests (or third-, fourth-, or other growths) are frequently the result of spontaneous reseeding and natural growth where man has established sufficient corrective and protective measures to bring back a forest cover. Thus, the forest is a joint product of natural forces and human efforts. However, natural reproduction after clean cutting often results in dominance of other and less desirable species than those dominant in the original forest.

In areas where natural conditions do not favor natural reproduction,

[2] R. R. Doane, *The Measurement of American Wealth*, Harper, 1933, p. 199.

artificial replanting and careful cultivation must be employed for successful reforestation. This is frequently the case in many regions of Europe, and is attributable not only to the character of natural conditions predominating in these areas, but also to economic and institutional factors. In the United States, very few forest areas can be considered cultivated or artificial.

In many forest areas where the trees represent the natural stand and frequently the orginal or virgin forest, good forestry practices involve selective cutting of mature trees and piling of brush and slash for disposal. Good harvesting practices, which permit securing the greatest possible amount of timber from each tree by cutting low stumps and using as much of the tops as possible, also increase efficiency of forest use.

Nearly four-fifths of the commercial forest area of the United States is owned privately; and of this privately owned land approximately one-third is in farm woodlots, the remaining two-thirds being owned principally by private corporations. Most of these privately owned commercial forests have been and are being exploited rapidly without any program of sustained-yield management. This applies not only to virgin forest areas, but even to second-growth forests. The one-fifth owned publicly consists largely of lands in national forests, with relatively minor areas owned by state, county, and municipal governments.

COSTS IN FOREST OPERATION

If virgin forests or forests where growth has already matured are handled on an exploitative basis, no costs are involved, aside from cutting or harvesting expenses, except interest, taxes, and protection costs. Where land is being reforested and young trees are growing on the land, or where sustained-yield management has been effected for an area already covered with mature trees, additional costs are involved. Costs of intensive forestry on a sustained-yield management basis vary considerably. As a general rule, a minimum of about 50 cents per acre may be taken as fairly representative; ordinarily, costs will not exceed a dollar even for the higher cost forests.[3] However, interest is not included in these figures, and interest charges are usually a large cost item.

Interest should be figured not only upon the estimated per acre value of the forest stand, but also upon the amount invested in bare land values and funds invested in taxes, protection, and timber management. It can readily be seen that interest charges are a very significant item in forest operations, particularly when it is recalled that more than 50 years, and sometimes as many as 200 years, are ordinarily required to mature a stand of trees.

[3] See *A National Plan for American Forestry*, U.S. Sen. Doc. 12, 73d Congress, First Session, Government Printing Office, 1933, Vol. 2, p. 1320.

Assuming an average $300 per acre stumpage value (which would not be excessive for many forests), interest charges alone would amount to $15 per acre annually, with an interest rate of 5 percent. To these interest charges must be added interest on investment in the bare land itself and on forest improvements.[4] The main elements of the fixed capital investment in forestry are soil, forest improvements, and growing stock or standing trees. The proportions of capital investment that these elements represent vary, but average about as follows: soil, 0–5 percent; forest improvement, 5–15 percent; and forest growing stock, 80–95 percent.[5]

RETURNS FROM FOREST OPERATION

Income from forest operation may be from: (1) sale of saw logs or timber; (2) sale of pulpwood; (3) sale of posts and poles; (4) grazing; (5) recreation; (6) miscellaneous products such as turpentine, game, etc. Timber is ordinarily the principal source of revenue to forest owners, although the recent development of the pulpwood industry makes the sales of pulpwood the major source of income for southern forests. For the United States as a whole and for most other nations which have commercially important forests, lumber production is the most important single source of revenue.

In the United States, forest properties held especially for timber (either as virgin forests, second-growth, or artificially grown stands), have appeared unattractive as sustained revenue producers. The competitive marketing of forest products resulting from overrapid exploitation of virgin stands has done much to prevent conservative cutting on many privately owned forests, and in public forests has prevented relatively inaccessible timber from coming into production, thus deferring financial returns from it.[6] Overrapid exploitation has been attributable largely to the relatively heavy carrying charges that must be deducted from income from privately owned forests. Heavy interest and tax charges have made it unprofitable to hold forest properties for any considerable period.

Recent studies of forest yields and average incomes which can be secured on a sustained-yield basis indicate that in many areas carrying costs (protection costs, taxes, interest charges, and timber management expenses) are so great that little, if anything, is left from receipts. In some cases, taxes assessed annually against the land are practically equal to the entire average annual forest income, and occasionally exceed it.[7] Under

---

[4] F. R. Fairchild, et al., *Forest Taxation in the United States*, U.S. Department of Agriculture, Miscellaneous Publication 218, October, 1935, pp. 239 ff.

[5] *A National Plan for American Forestry*, Vol. I, p. 893.

[6] *Ibid.*, Vol. II, p. 1321.

[7] For example, in Flathead County, Montana, the U.S. Forest Service estimates that the average stand of timber will produce from 10,000 to 15,000 board feet an acre. If it is assumed that this timber could be grown in a 60-year period, the annual

these conditions, the forest owner will cut off his timber stand, secure what income he can, and abandon the barren, cutover stump land, letting it go tax-delinquent and eventually revert to public ownership or become a part of submarginal "stump" farms.

In some areas private forest owners may be able to secure additional revenue through grazing their forests. In the case of private farm woodlots, the value of grazing per head of stock reaches its highest level. It is true that excessive grazing will reduce timber returns from forests, but under proper management, grazing constitutes a very legitimate and appreciable source of revenue. In some areas recreational use of private forests is increasing and can be made to yield some revenue, with proper management. Revenue may also be possible from development of hunting and fishing facilities on some private forest land, and revenue from naval stores and minor forest products is large in some localities.

Forced liquidation of commercial timber stands caused by excessive carrying costs has been rather general in many areas in the United States. This same situation has precluded private production of new timber crops on cutover lands, which would take from 60 to 100 years. High carrying costs have been an extremely significant factor accounting for forest depletion in the United States during the past several decades.

FOREST MANAGEMENT

In recent years there have been significant improvements in management of privately owned forest lands. Important gains have been made through fire protection organized with federal and state coöperation. The example of good forest management set by the national forests, the research and extension efforts of federal and state governments, and the general influence of the conservation movement (which grew stronger during the depression thirties) have also been important factors contributing to improved management practices on privately owned forest lands. Many private owners are sincerely attempting to manage their forests like a crop instead of a mine, despite serious economic handicaps.

Publicly owned forest lands do not operate under difficulties of overhead costs, particularly heavy taxes and interest charges common to private owners, and generally have had some form of effective forest manage-

---

average yield or growth would be approximately 250 board feet. Stumpage values for fir, larch, and western white pine in this area range from about $1 to $1.50 per thousand board feet of log scaled on the stump, so that the average annual growth would yield a return of about 25 or 30 cents. In other words, under sustained-yield management, the forest owner could, over a period of years, afford to own the land as a private individual or corporation only if annual costs of operating the land were less than 25 or 30 cents an acre. Timber lands in Flathead County are assessed taxes at an average of approximately 25 cents per acre. Thus, tax charges are such as to consume practically the entire average annual return from timber sales in this area.

ment, varying from intensive sustained yield to fire protection. Much of the national forest area has been placed on a sustained-yield basis, and many community forests (owned by counties, cities, towns, hospitals, or schools) have had excellent sustained-yield management. Most state forests are protected against fire and trespass, and on many cutting is permitted, with or without restrictions.

A MULTIPLE-USE RESOURCE

A forest is something more than a mere group of trees. It is a highly organized community of plants and animals in close association, and with varying degrees of interdependence.[8] As a result, forest land serves at least five major purposes, each of which is essential for human living in modern economies. These major purposes are: (1) timber production, (2) watershed services, (3) recreation, (4) support of wildlife, and (5) forage production.[9] In addition, forests produce food and many products useful to man, including camphor, turpentine, rosin, and cork.

These major uses are not necessarily mutually exclusive, and in many cases forest land is used simultaneously for two or more of them. Forest land is thus distinctly different from agricultural land, where each major crop or enterprise use is mutually exclusive. Some idea of the nature and extent of the multiple-use quality of forest land in the United States can be obtained from the following acreages useful for different purposes.[10] (1) Commercial timber can be grown on some 462 million acres out of 630 million acres of forest land in the United States. (2) Approximately three-fourths of all forest land exerts a favorable influence on watershed protection and soil erosion control. (3) More than half (342 million acres) of the forest area, chiefly in the West and South, is grazed by domestic livestock. (4) Almost all the area is suitable for wildlife. (5) Eleven million acres of land naturally suitable for timber use have been set aside exclusively for scenic purposes and recreation in the form of parks, monuments, and other reservations; much of the rest can also be used for recreational purposes.

The multiple-use aspects of forest land make forests particularly beneficial to man; but, on the other hand, competition between uses for control of the forest may likewise create serious economic problems. Use of the forest for game and wildlife may compete with its use for grazing livestock. Properly managed, competition between wildlife use and grazing use can be reduced so that sportsmen and ranchers may both benefit significantly from forest lands. The most important factor determining

[8] M. F. Heisley, *Our Forests: What They Are and What They Mean To Us,* U.S. Department of Agriculture, Miscellaneous Publication 162, July, 1940, p. 2.
[9] R. D. Marsh and W. H. Gibbons, "Forest Resource Conservation," U.S. Department of Agriculture *Yearbook,* Government Printing Office, 1940, p. 461.
[10] *Ibid.*

he competitive nature of these various uses is the character of the forest ownership; but regardless of who owns it, different types of use must be coördinated and adjusted if optimum benefits are to be secured.

Except in areas where forest tracts are used to protect municipal watersheds (watersheds supplying water for human consumption in urban areas) forest land need not be withheld from other use for the sake of the watershed protection function. Most forest lands have some recreational value, but some have such exceptional recreational value that they should be withdrawn from timber or grazing use. The U.S. Forest Service has, in recent years, excluded all other uses from certain "primitive areas" and devoted them exclusively to recreation. However, many forests producing timber under proper management also constitute excellent recreational areas.

TIME ELEMENT IN PRODUCTION

Perhaps the most significant feature of forestry is the long time required to bring a forest to maturity or to profitable production. The time element does not enter into the utilization of virgin timber stands—which even now are responsible for most of the world's supply of commercial forest products—except to influence the size of trees and the general character of the forest itself. For the most part, virgin forests consist of mature trees. However, in determining the general desirability of devoting a given piece of land to forests or some other use, or in determining the relative desirability of public or private ownership, the time element is very important.

The length of time required to mature a crop of trees depends on many factors, most important of which are the climate, the soil, and the species of tree (some trees grow much faster than others). Trees are a crop, and depend upon much the same basic soil and climatic factors for their rate of growth as does agriculture. Softwoods mature in 30 to 50 years, while some of the hardwoods require more than 200 years to mature to saw-log size (18-inch trees). This long time factor helps to determine the types of tenure, taxation, and use-control policies and programs that are best adapted to forest land.

A LARGE-SCALE BUSINESS

Another very important characteristic of forestry is the size of the area that constitutes an efficient minimum-sized operating unit. A forest is usually thought of as much larger in size than an acre or a few acres, and is composed of trees crowding each other in such a way that uniformly shaped trunks result. Trees in a forest crowd each other and kill out the weaker members; lower branches are also killed, because of their inability to get sunlight; and a long, straight trunk free from knots, almost cylin-

drical in shape, and sometimes more than a hundred feet long is produced
The lumberman can use logs of this type most efficiently.

A real forest, to produce the best lumber, must be one of considerabl
area, and efficient use of sawmills requires large tracts. These facts hav
important economic consequences. The average individual is not able t
handle the financial obligation of operating such a large area, and thi
combined with the length of time required to mature a forest, make
public or corporate ownership much more general than private, indi
vidual ownership and operation.

FLEXIBILITY OF OPERATIONS

Forest industries possess a fair degree of flexibility, because forests hav
no one harvest period as do most agricultural crops. Trees may be har
vested when very young for Christmas trees, fence posts, or firewood, o
harvested later for telegraph poles, railroad ties, or building logs, or har
vested at a still later stage for saw logs and lumber production. In othe
words, the forest operator has a considerable range of time over which h
can harvest his "crop" of trees.

The flexibility which this choice gives the forest operator is evidence
by the behavior of the lumber industry during the world-wide economi
crisis that began in 1929. Lumber manufacturers were better able to adap
output to declining demand than were the operators of the great majorit
of staple industries. Lumbering can be suspended altogether for a year o
so without any significant damage to the forest, which simply goes or
growing. Mature trees may stand for several years, in many cases, before
beginning to decay or depreciate in value. If the forest operator has the
financial resources, he has an unusually favorable natural situation that
enables him to adapt production to a fluctuating demand. However, like
most commercial production, the lumber industry is ordinarily interested
in maintaining a fairly uniform production level.

The flexibility of forest production is increased by the fact that the
forester can store his products "on the stump," as it were, without the
storage costs, depreciation, and risk of price changes that affect most agricultural crops. When forest operations are largely of a mining character—
that is, when virgin forests are cut without any effort at regeneration or
maintenance—this flexibility is particularly pronounced. However, under
sustained-yield management, cutting quotas are computed as a definite
proportion of forest stand annually, but cutting quotas for several years
may be grouped to meet market conditions. It is this situation that has led
forestry students to believe that a lower rate of return is justified for forest
investments than for business investments generally.[11]

[11] Franz Heske, *German Forestry*, Yale University Press, 1938, pp. 91–93.

DEMAND FACTORS AND SUBSTITUTES FOR FOREST PRODUCTS

No adequate substitutes are readily available for many agricultural products, particularly certain foods and fibers. The competition of forest products with other products is much more acute. Rising industrialism and progressive mechanization have caused a decided shift from organic to inorganic substances, especially from wood to metal.

In spite of the increased use of metal products, however, there is still a heavy demand for forest products throughout the world, and particularly in the United States. The use of wood for paper production in the United States is now three times as large as it was a quarter of a century ago. The important thing about the demand for forest products is its dynamic nature, in comparison with the more stable demand for certain agricultural products which are necessities of life.

The more dynamic the demand for forest products, the less stable, less predictable, and more sensitive to certain economic and social changes it will be, with the result that greater economic risks are involved in successful marketing of forest products than in marketing products for which the demand is more stable. The fact that the annual supply of forest products can be adjusted more easily to changing demand conditions is an important offset to the economic disadvantages of the more dynamic demand for forest products.

RECREATIONAL LAND

Recreation, or the creative use of leisure, takes a great variety of forms among modern peoples. These forms express the needs, desires, qualities, interests, powers, and instincts of individuals. Recreation may be *passive,* such as complete rest and relaxation without action; *mildly active,* such as viewing a beautiful landscape, walking or strolling, witnessing sports or games, or attending a dramatic performance; *active,* such as hiking, riding, hunting, fishing, camping, traveling, swimming, and participating in games and sports. Recreation brings immediate personal satisfaction or happiness and must always permit freedom of individual choice and freedom of individual action. Recreation may have and usually does have far-reaching beneficial results, both individual and social.[12]

Americans spend a considerable portion of their time and wealth on leisuretime activities. It has been estimated that the people of the United States spend more than 10 billion dollars a year for recreation.[13] The desire for the kinds of recreation that lands of various types may provide

[12] See National Resources Board, "Recreational Use of Land in the United States," *Report on Land Planning,* Government Printing Office, 1938, Part XI, p. 3.
[13] Jesse Frederick Steiner, *Americans at Play,* McGraw Hill, 1933, p. 183.

is a natural and legitimate one, and amply justifies public and private agencies and individual owners assigning lands to recreational use.

INCREASING IMPORTANCE OF RECREATION

Recreation plays a much more important role in society today than ever before. This increased importance stems from a variety of causes, beginning with the Industrial Revolution which ushered in the age of leisure. Within the past century the hours of labor have been reduced from 72 per week to 40 per week. The increasing division of labor and specialization, while expanding the productive efficiency of the average individual, restricts employment of his faculties. In the preindustrial era, a worker found use for a wide range of his faculties and opportunity to stamp the product with his own genius. Man's creative impulses are usually thwarted in the modern factory, and his physiological balance is upset by the constant use of the accessory and the neglect of the large skeletal muscles.

The growth of cities has accompanied modern factory production. Life is more artificial under urban than under rural conditions, and naturally there is greater demand for outdoor recreation to offset the more sedentary indoor work of urban living. It is significant that public recreation has had much greater growth in cities than in rural communities.[14]

The need for recreational land under modern urban conditions has resulted in (1) setting aside public lands for recreational use, such as national and state parks, forests and game refuges, and municipal playgrounds, and (2) an increase in privately owned land devoted primarily to recreation, such as dude ranches, summer camps, picnic grounds, commercial beaches, summer cottages, and country estates.

PLACE OF RECREATION AS A LAND USE

Recreational land is important not only because it brings in a considerable revenue but because it makes effective use of idle lands or wastelands and lands submarginal for agricultural purposes. Furthermore, recreational use of forested or mountainous districts unsuitable for agriculture does not prevent their use for forest purposes. Thus, recreational land uses in general may be considered complementary to agricultural and forest use, although lands with excellent scenic or location qualities may be utilized for recreation even though they possess unusually productive soils

The recreational needs and demands of a progressive people cannot be met by certain prescribed areas specifically and primarily devoted to recreational use. They can be met only if all the resources of the country as a whole which are susceptible of use for recreation are developed and utilized. Resources of recreational value may be found almost anywhere

---

[14] For a more complete discussion of reasons for the rise of recreation see George Hjelte, *The Administration of Public Recreation,* Macmillan, 1940, pp. 4–8.

and if these resources are to be used most effectively, their use must be coördinated with other land uses. Consequently, the recreational function of the various forms of land use must be analyzed, evaluated in relation to other functions, and provided for by the various public and private agencies and individuals of the nation according to their different capacities and responsibilities.[15]

Like all other natural resources, recreational resources occur where nature has scattered them, and without any orderly relationship to human demand. Physical factors play an important role in determining suitability of land for recreational use just as they do in the case of agricultural and forest lands; but the relative importance of the various factors is considerbly different and they operate within more definite limitations of geographical factors than in the case of agricultural and forest lands.

The major characteristics peculiar to recreational land are that (1) *use of land for recreation is, in many cases, only partial and often a noncompeting use*; (2) *lands which would be waste lands and strictly submarginal for any other major use are often very useful for recreation*; and (3) *the benefits of many types of recreational lands are difficult to measure and consequently hard to operate on a private business basis in competition with other major uses.*

A PARTIAL AND OFTEN NONCOMPETING LAND USE

Many examples could be cited to demonstrate that recreational use is often a partial and noncompeting land use. Utilization of forest lands is an excellent example. In the national forests, the construction of trails for hiking, establishment and maintenance of picnic grounds, and hunting are all examples of the partial use of forest lands for recreation. Each of these uses can be considered noncompetitive with the forest, since they do not appreciably reduce timber yields or the value of the forest. As a matter of fact, good trails frequently facilitate getting into and out of a forest for inspection trips and fire-control activities.

The use of water resources for recreation usually constitutes partial and noncompeting use of this resource. For example, the lakes and bodies of water created by reservoirs and dams for power and irrigation provide fine recreational resources in the form of fishing, boating and canoeing, swimming, and skating. These recreational uses do not reduce the value of the resource for its primary uses—hydroelectric power and irrigation water for crop production.

Agricultural land resources are frequently used partially for recreation without reducing the value of the lands for agricultural production. For example, on the east shore of Flathead Lake in northwestern Montana the lands bordering the lake are used largely for sweet cherry orchards. The

[15] Cf. "Recreational Use of Land in the United States," *op. cit.*, p. 1.

area is a beautiful scenic and recreational area, in the heart of the Rockies with Glacier National Park nearby. Many tourists and summer vacationists use the area for recreation—fishing, boating, swimming, and restful relaxation. A cherry producer with several cottages on his property to house cherry pickers during the brief picking season, can rent them to vacationists for recreational purposes the rest of the summer. These vacationists provide an important market for locally grown produce such as cream, milk, eggs, broilers, fryers, and small fruits; excellent prices are usually obtained. Thus, the recreational land uses, rather than being competing uses, call forth and make profitable complementary agricultural land uses.

WASTE AND SUBMARGINAL LANDS OFTEN USEFUL FOR RECREATION

Lands unsuited to agriculture and forestry because of physical conditions may be very useful for recreation. The badlands of South Dakota with their bare, rough terrain are practically valueless for farming or foresty and have very little value for grazing. The same physical conditions that make them of so little value for these purposes make them valuable for recreational uses. Much the same can be said for the Painted Desert country in the Southwest. High mountaintops, deep colorful canyons like the Grand Canyons of the Colorado and the Yellowstone, and similar lands are unproductive for farming, grazing, or forestry, but are excellent for recreational purposes.

Recreation, therefore, makes effective use of many areas that would otherwise make little or no contribution to the general welfare.

BENEFITS DIFFICULT TO MEASURE FOR PRIVATE OPERATION IN COMPETITION WITH OTHER USES

Many of the benefits to individuals and the public generally from wise use of land for recreation are difficult to measure in dollars and cents. For example, provision for adequate recreational facilities and qualified leadership serves to cut down the cost of police, prisons, and courts. There are also savings in hospital bills and maintenance of insane asylums, because of the better physical and mental health resulting from adequate recreation.

The impossibility of measuring these benefits accurately, combined with the prevailing American notion that outdoor recreational facilities such as campgrounds, picnic spots, and areas for hunting, fishing, hiking, etc., should be free, makes it extremely difficult to operate such recreational facilities satisfactorily through private ownership on a cost charge basis. Where exclusive occupancy and special services are involved, special charges can be made as an equitable means of sustaining private ownership costs. The modern campground, in point of facilities offered, is just one step below the tourist cabin. It ordinarily provides safe water supply, safe sanitary facilities, and often shower baths; a place to cook meals, a table and benches; very often daylight shelter in case of bad weather; and police protection.[16]

Similarly where exclusive occupancy or use is given for hunting and fishing privileges, specific charges can be levied to meet private ownership costs. This is occasionally done.

ECONOMIC EFFECTS OF DEVELOPED RECREATIONAL RESOURCES

Establishment of town and city parks raises the value of properties near and adjacent to them, particularly when these properties are devoted to residential uses. An attractive outlook from a home and the availability of a place to rest or engage in physical activity raises the monetary value of property. Purchasers or renters of residence property recognize this value.

An important achievement resulting from establishment of recreational parks is the increased emphasis placed upon logical planning and development of lands surrounding them. This is particularly true in townships surrounding county park lands.[17] Because of the parks, lands have taken on new values as residential sites, and the towns, appreciating the fact that this growth must be guided, have created zoning boards.

The increased desirability of adjoining lands for residential use is similar in the case of state parks and municipal parks, although this residential use is largely of the summer home type. Most of the effects on values are attributable to commercial opportunities which result from the use of the parks. The tendency of parasite commercial ventures to establish themselves as close to the park entrance as possible depreciates the value of the park by crowding in on it with architecturally ugly and heterogeneous structures. Examples are the gasoline station, the "hot dog stand," the dance hall, etc. Such economic developments may be controlled by establishing areas of concentrated use well inside the park or by providing parking approaches on which complete public control of the roadside exists; by zoning; or by acquiring easements limiting use of lands within a certain distance of the park entrance.

The part that recreation plays in preventing juveniles from becoming criminals and in helping to reform them is generally recognized by sociologists. Funds invested in playgrounds and recreational lands are far more productive of beneficial results to society than those spent in building a prison or reformatory. Studies of the effects of playgrounds and community centers on the extent of juvenile delinquency show that the

[16] *Ibid.,* p. 59.
[17] *Ibid.,* p. 60.

existence of active play areas reduces the amount of juvenile delinquency in the neighborhood.

MINERAL RESOURCES

The types of land utilization previously discussed—agriculture, forestry, and recreation—are genetic or reproductive in character. Mining, however, is an extractive industry. Minerals are formed so slowly, that for all practical purposes they are not replaceable.

Within the mineral industry itself, however, there are marked differences in the amount and degree of destruction that comes from use. The fuels like coal and oil, once burned, are gone. In contrast, most of the metals are only partly destroyed by use and a high percentage of the scrap is recoverable. Eventually, the stock of scrap may be so large as to affect appreciably the annual demand for new metal.

The nonmetals are between the fuels and metals as to recoverability. The chemicals, like nitrates, once used are so changed in form that recovery is often unprofitable. On the other hand, most building stones can be used over and over again almost indefinitely.

The problem of furnishing and maintaining an adequate supply of minerals is recent. Until the Industrial and Mechanical Revolutions created a demand for fuels to operate the new machinery, coal was used only in small quantities for household use. The development of mechanical equipment made it possible to mine coal more rapidly and deeply and thus increase coal production for expanded industrial use. The accelerating rate of advance of technology in recent decades has made a heavy drain on mineral resources generally. As a result, the world has produced more minerals since 1900 than in all previous time.

IMPORTANCE OF MINERALS IN THE ECONOMY

The most striking characteristic of modern civilization is its widespread use of power machinery, which depends for its source of energy upon the mineral fuels. Most of the energy used in the United States is derived from the fossil fuels (coal, oil, and natural gas). The actual human energy involved in mining, refining, and transporting these fossil fuels is only about 3 percent of the energy realized from them. Consequently, they are an unusually efficient energy source.

Minerals are extremely vital in modern economies, since they furnish the metals for all the mechanical contrivances in daily use and the fuel to operate most of them. They also furnish the metals and energy for armaments. The importance of coal and iron in making the steel used in modern armaments, and of the petroleum used as fuel, creates an intense public interest in these products. If modern nations are to enjoy a rising level of living with the wealth of mechanical contrivances and energy sources such a level demands, the supply of minerals, particularly the fuels and metals, must be assured for the future, or new techniques or substitutes developed.

COMPETITION OF MINING WITH OTHER LAND USES

Much mining is done underground, so that the surface, in many cases, can be used for other purposes. In some instances, only the subsurface rights are purchased, to permit extraction of the underground mineral deposits, while surface and supersurface uses continue unmolested. For example, the city of Butte, Montana, is built directly over many of the mining shafts, some of which go down to ore bodies a mile below the surface, so that the land serves a double use—for urban residences and also for mining.

In other cases, however, serious conflicts may arise between mining and the surface and supersurface uses of land. In the strip mining of coal or open copper mining, the land is made useless for any concurrent use. The fact that mining lands ordinarily require very little surface area minimizes the competition of this use with other land uses.

IRREPLACEABILITY OF MINERALS

The most important peculiarity of mineral resources is their irreplaceability. We have seen that forest resources are exhaustible, but not irreplaceable. When a tree is cut down, another can be planted to take its place. Soil resources, which are the product of the last few hundred thousand years, are also exhaustible, and it is true that we cannot build a new soil in the same sense that we can grow a new tree. Yet it is possible, by proper management, to rebuild or rejuvenate old, wornout soils.

It is still easier, of course, through proper cropping, rotation, and related soil management practices, to prevent soil from becoming worn out. In other words, soil productivity can be maintained or even improved as it is used. Water resources are neither inexhaustible nor entirely irreplaceable. The hydrologic cycle causes a continuous flow of water in the larger streams of the land, but proper utilization and maintenance of existing water resources demands proper attention to methods of use.

Mineral resources, however, are exhaustible and irreplaceable. In other words, mining is a completely extractive industry, not a genetic one like agriculture or forestry. Consequently, the use of minerals is of peculiar importance to society as a whole, and wise use of such exhaustible and irreplaceable resources is particularly desirable.

HIGHLY LOCALIZED RESOURCES

Mineral resources are unequally distributed among the nations and occur in strictly limited areas. Agricultural crops and forests can be grown over much of the earth's surface, and most nations possess some fairly productive or good soils and water resources. However, mineral resources are so highly localized that many nations have none of some minerals basic to modern machine technology. Concentration of mineral resource control or ownership in a limited group of nations is facilitated by this extreme localization.

For the world as a whole, mineral supplies are large enough so that there is little need for concern about early exhaustion, but for each individual nation there is definite danger that particular minerals may soon be exhausted.[18] This makes it essential that each nation utilize its minerals efficiently in the public interest.

"HIDDEN" NATURE OF MOST MINERAL RESOURCES

Forest, soil, and water resources usually involve surface use, but most mineral deposits are hidden below the surface. Their discovery is largely a matter of chance, so that mining is ordinarily a highly speculative enterprise.

There are far-reaching economic implications of this "hidden" characteristic of most minerals. (1) The "accidental" discovery of rich mineral deposits may change overnight the utilization of the land and permit the acquisition of great fortunes. (2) Entire populations may be disorganized because of the uncontrolled, frantic effort to "get rich quick" by exploiting newly discovered minerals. (3) The extent of the deposit, or the length of the period during which operations can be continued is always unknown or uncertain, since there is no accurate way of determining just how great the hidden deposits may be, or of judging the quality of the ore at lower levels.

This uncertainty or indefiniteness colors the entire economic and social life of the mining community. Popular thinking usually assumes an inevitable decline into a ghost town for all types of mining communities, largely because of the exhaustibility, irreplaceability, and uncertainty typical of mineral deposits. However, there are significant differences in types of mining, just as there are in types of farming, and some deposits will last for many decades at present rates of use. Moreover, the development of science has enabled mining engineers to estimate the nature of deposits more accurately, though their appraisals can at best be only good estimates.

The unpredictability or uncertainty of mineral deposits is particularly pronounced where the mineral is in a liquid form, like oil, which is called the "fugitive resource." A fairly scientific appraisal of such mineral deposits or concentrations may be made at a certain time, yet many be-

[18] C. K. Leith (ed.), *Elements of a National Mineral Policy,* The Mineral Inquiry, 1933, p. 4.

come valueless if, at a later date, the mineral shifts its location or is withdrawn by operations at another point.

DURABILITY OF MANY MINERALS

Since most metals are durable, stocks of metal tend to accumulate and create problems peculiar to the mining industry. For example, the annual amount of iron available for industrial use is not merely the volume currently mined and produced, but all scrap and old iron made available by discarded or worn-out machinery, tools, and structures in which iron or iron products were used. As a result of this "competition" from scrap or "secondary" metal, the price of currently produced iron is lower than it would be if the metal were used up permanently and its form destroyed in its first industrial use.

The durability of some metals, however, possesses certain advantages. The current supply of gold, silver, or similar durable metals is the accumulation of generations, and any great fluctuations in output from year to year do not seriously affect the total quantity available, because of the great previous accumulations. Consequently, the supply is much more constant in relation to demand, and price tends to be much more stable. This durability is one of the most important reasons for the long use of gold and silver, the precious metals, as the monetary standard of many nations.

The durability of most metals should not lead the student to believe that minerals are inexhaustible. In their native state, mineral deposits are definitely exhaustible through mining (because it is an extractive and not a genetic process). The form of the metal is changed through its use in industry, and it may not be destroyed in substance; but the mining industry, built upon the process of extracting the mineral from the earth, is destroyed through the exhaustion and irreplaceability of the mineral deposit.

The many ghost towns scattered over former mining areas are mute evidence of the exhaustibility and irreplaceability characteristics of minerals and should not be confused with "durability." Accumulation of metal stocks suggests one way by which modern economies can meet the problem resulting from the increasing difficulties that arise from the necessity of mining deeper and poorer ores.

INTERCHANGEABILITY OF MINERALS

Another important characteristic of minerals and the mineral industry is interchangeability. Some minerals possess unique characteristics enabling them to meet certain industrial demands and prevent the substitution of others. Many of the metals have uses peculiar to them—copper, lead, zinc, nickel, and chromium, for instance—as do the nonmetal mineral products like brick, lime, cement, and asbestos. Yet metals may be substituted for each other in many instances, and though actual substitution frequently involves economic loss because of the sacrifice or nonuse of the product that would be most completely or peculiarly adapted for a given use, this substitution is nevertheless of great economic significance.

The characteristic of interchangeability or substitutive quality is very important, because of the exhaustibility and irreplaceability of many minerals. Pressure of demand on scarcer minerals can be relieved by the use of substitutes. It may be said, therefore, that the scarcity of many minerals is relative rather than absolute; geologic occurrence and economic availability are not the same thing.

MINING A LARGE SCALE OPERATION

Much has been written about the placer mining activities of gold rush days, where individuals panned out gold by hand and in some cases made small fortunes. However, this type of individual enterprise is not applicable to modern mining, which is generally a large-scale enterprise. Mining has become highly mechanized, and with this mechanization the size of operating units has increased.

Even the mining of precious metals, particularly gold and silver, is now on a large scale and is usually operated in connection with the production of metals like zinc, lead, or copper. Modern large-scale, highly mechanized operations make it economically possible to recover the small traces of gold and silver often found in copper, lead, and zinc ores. The greater abundance of low-grade ores made economically available through mass production and modern chemical methods is one of the more important reasons for the large operating units increasingly used in mining.

PECULIAR LABOR SITUATIONS IN MINING

Labor conditions in mining areas have been notoriously bad. Large amounts of unskilled labor were formerly used for mining operations, and mines were usually located where there were practically no alternative economic opportunities for laborers. Unionization of mine workers in many areas has contributed much to the improvement of miners' living conditions and incomes, but even where unionization prevails many problems peculiar to mining operations still exist.

Many types of mining are injurious to the health of laborers. Explosions, floods, high temperatures, excessive humidity, harmful dusts and gases, and falling rocks are also common hazards of mining. The accident rate in mining is about double that of any other industry. In addition to these may be mentioned the economic hazards of a shifting or uncertain industry, and the fact that the industry is a temporary one because of its extractive nature and the irreplaceability of the deposits, which in most areas are relatively soon exhausted. For these reasons, the level of economic and social well-being of miners is usually considered below average, particularly where unionization has not occurred.

DIMINISHING RETURNS OR INCREASING COSTS IN MINING

The exhaustibility of mineral resources is the most important single factor tending to cause an increase in operating costs as mining continues. Obviously, richer and more readily accessible deposits are mined first; and as these become exhausted, operations proceed to poorer and less accessible deposits. In some instances, development of mining techniques and modern machinery make it possible to overcome these conditions without any increase in unit costs; but more frequently a point is soon reached where production costs tend to increase. More efficient management, improved techniques, new machinery, discovery of new bodies of rich ore, expansion of transport facilities, and similar factors may interrupt this tendency; but the trend toward increasing costs is unmistakable. However, technology has advanced more rapidly than discovery or transport during the present century.

This success of man-directed forces in offsetting or overcoming the increasing natural difficulties involved in continued mining should not cause the student to overlook the fact that the Principle of Diminishing Returns is particularly applicable to extractive industries, and that, in the long run, the tendency toward increasing costs because of ultimate exhaustibility and irreplaceability is a force that should encourage wise and economical use of mineral resources at all times.

The student should also remember that technological advance, discovery, and improvement in transport facilities do not occur in all nations at the same rate or reach the same level at the same time. Within a nation like the United States, much migration from old to new mining fields has occurred, which is quite as much a sign of increasing costs in the old areas as it is of abundant and more economically available resources in the new. In the United States many once famous districts have already been exhausted, and production is continued by turning to new fields or to sources of lower-grade or that can be operated efficiently with modern techniques. For example, petroleum pools ordinarily reach their peak in a few years—often a few months—after discovery of the well. Then follows a rapid decline, and ultimate abandonment and migration to new fields or pools.[19]

[19] The interval between discovery and the telltale appearance of salt water in the marginal oil wells is said to be, characteristically, from 18 months to 3 years. (See

TRANSPORTATION

A good or service in a given place may have little or no value; made available at another place, it may be very useful and valuable. From the standpoint of efficiency of operation, the smaller the amount of space in which economic and social activities occur, the less energy and costs necessary to provide place utility. Too much space requires that a large proportion of the population devote its time to getting from one place to another, or to moving goods or materials from one location to another.

Railroads and highways, automobiles and pipelines, telephone and power transmission lines, airways, canals, inland waterways—in short, all means of efficient land, water, and air transportation—are used to overcome the space problem. The automobile industry, whose large expansion in the United States in the twenties was considered a sign of great prosperity, is in reality designed to overcome America's greatest handicap, namely excessive space.

No great civilization has ever been built without some well-defined system of transportation. As the standard of living of a people rises, transportation fulfills an increasingly important place. A high standard of living is one in which a great variety of goods and services are available to the people quickly and at various seasons of the year. Improved transportation facilities are essential to bring a great variety of food products and related goods and services to consumers who may live thousands of miles from the source of these products.

As technology advances, the means of overcoming space are increased both in number and in speed. Modern aviation is a good example of improved transportation facilities resulting from advancing technology. Highway construction must be adapted to provide safe driving for modern high-speed motor vehicles as must also roadbeds for modern streamlined railroads.

These changes increase the cost of construction per mile and require the use of much more land per mile of highway or roadbed than formerly. Superhighways like the Pennsylvania or Ohio turnpikes or the New York Thruway require 50 to 60 acres of land per mile. Ordinary first-class highways require 25 acres or more per mile. Many acres are required for expanding airfields to take care of increased airplane transportation. Large union railroad terminal facilities, warehouses, bridges, wharfs, and harbors use a great deal of iron and steel and other mineral resources, as well as a large amount of power resources.

F. G. Tryon and Margaret H. Schoenfeld, "Utilization of Natural Wealth," *Recent Social Trends*, Report of the President's Research Committee on Resource Trends, McGraw-Hill, 1933, p. 83.)

TRANSPORTATION AS A LAND USE

From the standpoint of area used, transportation ranks considerably below agriculture and forests, but in terms of wealth in the form of fixed capital, it exceeds them.[20]

Transportation bids high for the services of land, in competition with other uses. Transportation is a higher or more intense land use than agriculture, forestry, or recreation, and it is ordinarily a higher use than urban residence, and frequently than urban industry. Only in the case of very rich ore deposits would a given piece of land be utilized for mining rather than for transportation, if the land were situated in the line of transportation development.

The student of land economics should not conclude that density of population is the only remedy for excessive space and consequent heavy transportation expenses, for excessive population density results in heavy transportation expenditures. For example, in New York City great expense is involved in overcoming the space factor in getting from lower to higher floors of office buildings, apartment houses, and similar buildings. The concentration of several million people in such a limited area necessitates expensive overhead and underground transportation facilities. Traffic consumes much time and requires policing and regulatory measures. Thus, solution of the problem is not excessive population density, but optimum population density.

FACTORS DETERMINING USE OF LAND FOR TRANSPORTATION

Historically, topography has been one of the major factors determining the location of transportation routes, and most trails, roads, and railroads ran along river valleys, mountain passes, and generally level areas, avoiding mountains and steep hills. In spite of modern technology, the cost of highway construction in mountainous areas, where roadbeds must meet minimum grade requirements for modern sustained speed, is often great enough to compel the use of more level routes.

Aside from topography, natural factors are of minor and usually insignificant importance in determining the transportation route. It is true that some soil characteristics in association with more important factors like strategic location are more desirable than others, but they are not generally so significant as to be the limiting factor. For instance, it may cost more to construct a roadbed in very rocky or clayey soils than in sandy ones, but the difference is a very minor factor in deciding where the road will be built.

[20] The total wealth involved represents the current value of all transportation equipment facilities, including terminal buildings and repair shops, and all steam and electric railroads, taxis, waterways, drydocks, pipelines, and airways. (R. R. Doane, *The Measurement of American Wealth*, Harper, 1933, p. 15.)

Human forces are of major significance in the determination of transportation routes. Land whose principal use is for upholding or supporting strength can hardly be considered as destructible physically through utilization or nonuse, and the value of transportation land is acquired through *situs*. Situs has been defined as the "consensus of human choice and convenience, or the quality aspect of situation." [21] Like all economic utilities, situs is a social product created by man collectively, through preference or choice, and this value may be destroyed by the human choice that created it. Improvements on the land, in the form of roadbed preparation and surfacing, are so large that maintenance of the improvement constitutes the major problem of transportation land use. In this respect, transportation land more nearly resembles urban land than any of the other major types.

Many argue that if street and highway systems were properly planned and constructed to eliminate traffic congestion at various points in larger metropolitan areas, and to facilitate rapid and economic movement of goods and people from point to point within the nation, increased efficiency from time saved would greatly increase the productiveness of the economy as a whole, and this increased productiveness would help defray the major portion of the costs of financing highways. In addition to these savings—from increased efficiency and elimination of lost time and cost of "stop-and-go" driving—travel would be much safer and the cost of injury and fatal accidents should be considerably less with the improved traffic conditions resulting from the improved highways.

In the interests of securing increased widths of highways, and to promote safety at intersections, setback ordinances and related legislation are desirable. Roadside improvements help stabilize the roadside against erosion, control snow drifting, and gratify the esthetic sense. It is also essential to have public control of land abutting on the highway right of way, as well as control of the right of way itself, if development of the lands the roads serve is to be in the best public interest. Land-use problems which affect highways are simply the ones that are most conspicuously visible from the highways.

EFFECTS OF THE FREIGHT RATE STRUCTURE ON LAND USE

When economic forces have established a price for a commodity in a central market, the amount received by the individual producer will equal approximately the market price less the costs of transportation. In an area of surplus production, the price is approximately equal to the primary market price minus the costs of moving the product to the market; while in the case of a deficit area the price is roughly equal to that in the most distant area of surplus production from which the supply

[21] H. B. Dorau and A. G. Hinman, *Urban Land Economics*, Macmillan, 1928, p. 167.

is secured, plus the cost of transportation and handling.[22] Since agriculture produces about two-thirds, measured by cost, of the raw materials used in American industry, freight rate differentials are particularly important to farmers in determining the agricultural land-use pattern.

Transportation charges are a cost of production, and like other production costs they must be met by the price paid by consumers if production of the goods and services is to be continued. If the transportation haul is long, so that transportation costs are appreciable, the operator must have certain other conditions of production that make his costs of production relatively low; otherwise he will not be able to compete with other producers in areas nearer to market, where the transportation costs are appreciably lower. Thus, transportation charges are an important factor determining comparative advantage or disadvantage of various regions in the production of different goods and services.

Competition of low-cost water transportation on through traffic from Atlantic seaboard ports to Pacific coast ports results in lower transportation rates to these points than to inland points where no through competitive rates are effective. The relatively high freight rates to and from points in Rocky Mountain states and in the South are an important obstacle in the industrialization of these areas.

Land values represent in general the capitalized net return to be secured from the lands. The lower the transportation costs, other things being equal, the greater the amount that can be capitalized into land values, and vice versa. As a general rule, therefore, land values are higher in areas close to central markets or located near transportation facilities that provide prompt and cheap transportation to central markets.

URBAN LAND

The tremendous growth of cities in recent years has concentrated large numbers of people in comparatively small areas. This process, referred to as *urbanization,* accompanying advancing machine technology and the associated shift from farms and villages to urban manufacturing areas, has brought about a fundamental change in the occupational structure of the country and has revolutionized ways of living and making a living.

More than half the population of the United States lives in urban areas (cities, towns, boroughs, or villages of 2500 or more people). Urban lands total about 12 million acres, of which 3 million are in public streets, parks, and parkways, the other 9 million being devoted largely to residential and industrial sites.[23]

[22] *Prices of Farm Products Received by Producers,* U.S. Department of Agriculture, Statistical Bulletin 17, and *Reliability and Adequacy of Farm Price Data,* U.S. Department of Agriculture Bulletin 1480, Government Printing Office, 1927.

[23] National Resources Board, *Report to the President of the United States,* 1934, Government Printing Office, p. 151.

IMPORTANCE OF URBAN LAND IN THE ECONOMY

The estimated value of urban real estate (land and improvements) in the United States is more than two and one-half times that of farm real estate, and more than that of any other type of real estate in the nation. Urban real estate alone comprises more than a fifth of the entire wealth of the country.[24]

Geographically, as well as economically, urban land is dependent upon agricultural, forest, and mineral land. The growth of cities causes an increased demand for land for urban use. This increased demand may be met in two ways—by extending the urban area, or by using the present urban area more intensively. Ordinarily an expanding town will meet its need for additional land area by outward extension from the center into the adjacent countryside. At the same time land in the center of the city becomes more valuable, and if the city expands sufficiently it may be more desirable, or less inconvenient, to build taller buildings rather than to increase area by extension. Thus, the city may expand both up and out. In any case, the surrounding hinterland is a potential supply of urban land. Thus it can be seen that while urban uses and other land uses are complementary, they are in another sense competitive.

COMPETITIVE USES FOR URBAN LAND

There are six major types of urban land utilization: (1) residential, (2) retail, (3) financial and office, (4) wholesale, (5) industrial, and (6) public and quasi-public. Consequently, to determine the highest use for a tract, it must be analyzed on the basis of the factors or conditions that are advantageous and detrimental for each of these six major uses. The competition of these various types of use of urban land tends to utilize more of the earning power of the land, and thus brings in greater net returns than would occur without this competition of uses. This is on the assumption that intelligence and good judgment govern the competition, because the principle of competition implies that if the new use is able to displace the told one, it must be able to produce a higher net income.

Obviously, when land, through this competitive process, reaches its highest use, the land is earning its maximum profit. The wastes of supercession involved in the competition of uses in urban land are more than offset by the increased earning power of the land in being stepped up to a higher use. Consequently, this process of supercession through competitive uses represents a net economic gain in the utilization of urban land. However, where intelligent planning and good judgment have been lacking, economic losses rather than economic gains have resulted from wastes of improvements through supercession.

[24] See R. R. Doane, *op. cit.,* pp. 11 and 15.

Urban land cannot be fully utilized except with an investment in improvements which in most cases is considerably larger than that in the land itself; it is not uncommon for the improvements to be worth several times the value of the land. Urban land value is so dependent upon its improvements that the problems of the improvement are land problems. Consequently, in urban land utilization some of the most important problems—such, for example, as the ratio of improvement value to site value, building height limitation, rent regulation, and housing—are inconsequential in the utilization of other types of land. Because of the comparatively high use value of urban land, particularly in the larger metropolitan areas, the urban use will ordinarily have a competitive advantage over other uses of land, with the possible exception of transportation uses.

THE LOCATION OF CITIES

The concentration of people in urban areas is very definitely localized, as can be seen from Figure 28, showing the percentage of urban population by states. This raises the question as to what made cities locate where they are.

The oldest cities were for the most part those which were strategically situated from the standpoint of military defense. The ancient city of

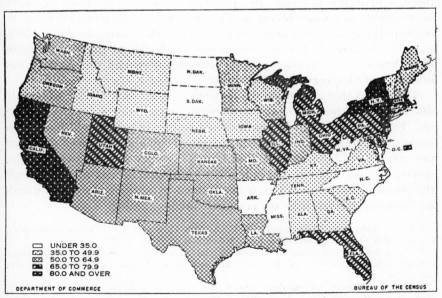

Figure 28.   Percent Urban Population, by States, 1950. (Source: U.S. Department of Commerce, Bureau of the Census.)

Petra, for example, was accessible from only one direction. The hilltop cities of Rome and Athens were located where they could be easily defended. In very early times, defense was the primary factor in locating cities.

Probably the most important factor in determining the location of cities is commerce. The opportunity for trade, which is the lifeblood of urban areas, is the deciding factor in the choice of urban sites in the majority of cases. Where trade routes follow watercourses, cities develop at the points where ocean and rivers meet, or where rivers and creeks meet, or where transportation ceases, or at the junction of trails and highways with water routes. An excellent example of the development of cities at such points is the string of eastern cities in the United States— Philadelphia, Baltimore, Washington, Richmond, Raleigh, Augusta, Macon, Columbia, and Montgomery—which, because of their location at the head of navigation on the major streams flowing into the Atlantic (the "Fall Line"), possess important commercial advantages.[25]

Good harbors, fords in rivers, passes in mountain ranges, and similar locations are important commercial choice sites for cities.[26]

Industry is an important city-building factor, and consequently the force or forces that locate industries are important in determining the location of cities. The weight-losing industries tend to be located near the sources of the raw materials, while those in which the weight loss of the raw materials is minor and perishable commodities tend to locate near centers of consumption. Steam tends to be "agglomerating," concentrative, or centripetal in its influence, while electricity, the automobile, and the airplane tend to be centrifugal, dispersive, or decentralizing in their action on the location of industry, since they tend to shift factories into the outlying regions of the cities.[27]

The factors that determine the location of cities today are considerably different from those which were of major importance a century or two ago. For example, a hill or peninsula or mountain pass would have been important two centuries ago as a matter of defense, but now their importance would be perhaps one of health or of scenery. In any case, the specific site for a city is determined by physiographic features, although the general location of a city is determined by various economic, social, and political factors, with the economic predominating.

[25] G. S. Wehrwein, "The Land," in C. R. Van Hise and L. H. Havemeyer (eds.), *Conservation of Our Natural Resources,* Macmillan, Part IV, p. 323.

[26] For a detailed statement of the commercial advantages of sites upon which these and other important cities of the world are located, see Dorau and Hinman, *op. cit.,* pp. 51–55.

[27] National Resources Committee, *Our Cities: Their Role in the National Economy,* Government Printing Office, June, 1937, p. 30.

THE STRUCTURE OF CITIES

Modern economic forces encouraging development of urban areas cause cities to become roughly star-shaped, as a natural result of what has been called axial and central growth. All cities illustrate both forms, but central growth occurs first in some, and axial growth first in others. Central growth (the clustering of utilities around a given point of attraction) is based on proximity, while axial growth results from transportation facilities and is based on accessibility.[28] The normal result of axial and central growth is a star-shaped city with the growth extended first along the main thoroughfares emanating from the center, and later filling in the parts between. Physiography and other influences, such as avenues of transportation, nuisances, private restrictions, and public control may modify this tendency in any given city.

The land-use patterns of cities vary greatly in detail, but certain characteristics or tendencies are common to all cities. The usual city has a denser business district or core around which its economic life revolves. In this center are tall buildings (numerous in large cities) and skyscrapers, appearing irregularly at various points and indicating the location of subcenters. Around the edges of the business district are located light manufacturing and warehouse areas, and along railroad tracks or waterfronts the heavy industries are located. Within the light manufacturing and warehouse area are sprinkled blighted areas and slums; and contiguous to this belt are tenements and workmen's homes. The rest of the city consists principally of residential sections, in which are interspersed stores, parks, playgrounds, schools, churches, and similar structures. There is great variety, however, in the proportion of the city's total area included within these various types of land use, as well as in their locations within the city proper. In a great majority of cities, physiographic forces (including topography, or location of rivers and lakes) will individualize the land-use pattern.

Along main transportation lines radiating from the center of the city are usually located numerous residences of families who work in the city or are employed directly or indirectly in the economic life of the area. These suburban areas often form uninterrupted extensions of the city proper, and become satellite towns which in many cases contain some industries as well as residences. The country estates, country clubs, and open farm lands located between the settled areas or suburbs are all part of the metropolitan region which has as its center the principal city in the locality.

An important characteristic of city structure is the extensive network

[28] Dorau and Hinman, *op. cit.*, p. 64.

of streets and alleys used for transportation purposes. There are usually a number of radial streets connecting the heart of the city with the outlying area; and since traffic congestion is likely to develop on these radial streets, circumferential streets usually arise to handle part of this.

INTENSITY OF SITUS UTILIZATION

Indestructibility and immobility are the two physical characteristics of land most significant in urban land utilization. Agricultural and forest lands are not truly indestructible, since they can be appreciably worn out and depreciated, while mineral land can be completely destroyed. However, land whose principal function or service is to afford standing room can hardly be considered destructible through utilization or nonuse, in a physical sense. There is no maintenance or depreciation problem in the case of urban land, therefore, corresponding to the need for conservation of agricultural soil, maintenance of forests, or depletion of mineral lands.

Land is physically immobile and a given location may become extremely important economically, although transportation improvement may significantly alter this situation. In the case of urban land (and land used for transportation), certain locations acquire economic significance out of all proportion to that of particular locations in other land uses.

Those sites singled out by human choice for most intensive industrial or residential use are ordinarily of higher value than those utilized for other purposes. The owner of an urban site has little control over situs. If human choice shifts so that his particular site is in an unfavorable situation, there is little he can do about it; his only alternative is to hope that he can influence human choice so that demand forces will change in such a way that they benefit him rather than cause him further loss.

Modern skyscrapers reveal the extent to which capital and labor can be profitably spent upon a given tract of urban land. This intensive utilization of situs makes the urban landowner extremely vulnerable to the vicissitudes of the business cycle. A site containing an investment as fixed and permanent as a skyscraper has little adaptability to other uses. In types of land utilization where smaller amounts of capital and labor are invested, or where the land is used in its natural state, opportunities are greater for shifting the land into other uses in accordance with changing economic conditions.

There is a wider range in the intensiveness of urban land use than in any other form of land utilization. Lands may be used for great skyscrapers and large office buildings, or for comparatively small residences, small shops, or corner gasoline stations involving but a few hundred dollars. Significantly, this range usually prevails within the confines of an average city, investment being heaviest in the heart of the business district and decreasing outward from this center to the city's fringes. The numerous failures in urban real estate development are evidence of the complexity of urban exploitation and investment problems.

IMPORTANCE OF TRANSPORTATION TO URBAN LAND

The great importance of situs and the intensity of its utilization is closely related to the availability of efficient transportation. In other words, transportation is more significant in urban land utilization than in most other types of land use (particularly agriculture, forestry, and mining). A distance of two or three blocks from a car or bus line is a significant factor in determining city land values, while the same distance in the country is relatively unimportant.

DOSES OF LABOR AND CAPITAL INPUTS RELATIVELY LARGE

The intensive utilization of urban land is also characterized by applications of capital in comparatively large units or doses. An additional floor in a building may cost many thousands of dollars, increasing appreciably the amount of capital investment in the given parcel of land. A farmer can approach the margin of intensive utilization gradually by adding a little more or a little less seed, fertilizer, or livestock; but in most types of urban land the applications in arriving at the intensive margin are very large, so that it is more difficult to approach precisely the point of maximum utilization or profit.

LARGE FIXED OVERHEAD

The investment in fixed, durable capital (buildings and permanent fixtures) in urban land use is large, compared with the annual operating investment. This necessitates use of a large part of the annual revenue to cover the return to invested capital, and the use of a relatively small part to cover operating expenses. Operating expenses on agricultural land relative to fixed capital investment are more than twice as much as those on urban land.[29] Any industry that has a major portion of its total costs recurring annually instead of at long intervals (30 to 50 years, in the case of urban land utilization) can better adapt itself to current market demand conditions.

SLOW CAPITAL TURNOVER

The turnover on capital invested in urban land is relatively slow compared with some other major land uses. For example, capital turnover in urban land averages about once in 8 to 10 years, compared with once in

[29] Dorau and Hinman, in a sample study of Cleveland office buildings, estimate that the annual investment to cover operating expenses is about 44 percent of the fixed capital investment in the case of agricultural land, compared with an estimated 20 percent for annual operating investment in urban land. (*Ibid.*, pp. 194–195.)

4 or 5 in agriculture. The slower the capital turnover in an industry, the more vulnerable is that industry to fluctuations in economic activity.

Although all modern economic endeavor is rather speculative because of specialization and the roundabout process of production, urban land utilization is relatively more speculative than many other types of land use. A modern building has an engineering life of 40 or 60 years, or longer; and anticipation of future demands for these facilities extends forward over this period. Obsolescence often destroys the value of improvements before their engineering life has been exhausted. The occurrence of numerous "ghost towns" evidences the great risks and uncertainties involved in the effort to anticipate future demands for urban land.

SEPARABILITY OF VALUE OF IMPROVEMENTS FROM LAND RESOURCES

An important peculiarity of urban land utilization is the ease with which the value of improvements can be separated from that of the land itself. In cities, improvements added to the land ordinarily do not become inextricably merged with the soil itself, as they do in agriculture. This makes it easier to gauge the effect of a particular tax, or to adjust the tax system so as to influence land utilization in certain desired ways.

PRODUCTION COSTS IN URBAN LAND UTILIZATION

The several types of production costs in urban land utilization may be classified as direct and indirect. Direct costs are actual expenditures or out-of-pocket costs incurred; indirect costs are alternative incomes foregone by the owner. Direct costs include (1) expenditures for clearing, draining, filling, and grading to make the land fit for use; (2) taxes and special assessments on the land; (3) interest on borrowed money, if the owner did not have sufficient capital to pay cash for his land; and (4) miscellaneous costs, including sales commissions to real estate dealers, abstract charges, title insurance, and related expenses usually involved in transferring land ownership.

Indirect costs include (1) the loss of income that might be secured if the capital or effort were used in some alternative form of investment; (2) the losses unavoidably incurred when the land is not in its highest and best use; (3) the loss in interest that could be obtained from the above two lost incomes, were they available and invested; and (4) the loss of interest that could have been secured, in other forms of investment, from the funds actually spent as direct costs.[30]

Because of the direct and indirect costs involved in urban land utilization, land should not be held out of urban use too long, nor brought into such use too quickly. There are many evidences, particularly in suburban

[30] *Ibid.*, p. 207.

areas, of the tendency to bring land into urban use too soon. Oversub-division has occurred, and heavy expenses for sidewalks and other special improvements have been incurred without corresponding increases in population to utilize the subdivided tracts for dwelling sites.

As a result, annual special improvement assessments have accumulated during the years, and in many cases have resulted in allowing tracts to go to tax deed and revert to public ownership. In such cases, the owner and society would have been better off had the land remained in a less inten-sive use (such as agriculture or forests) where annual improvement and carrying costs were lighter, until the time when an effective demand was established for dwelling sites on this land. Subdivision and corresponding improvements to fit the land for urban use would then have been op-portune.

REFERENCES FOR FURTHER READING

Clawson, Marion, and Held, Burnell, *The Federal Lands: Their Use and Man-agement,* The Johns Hopkins Press, Baltimore, 1957, Chap. II.

Dana, Samuel Trask, *Forest and Range Policy,* McGraw-Hill Book Company, Inc., New York, 1956, Chap. VII.

Davis, D. H., *The Earth and Man,* The Macmillan Company, New York, 1942, Chaps. XVIII and XXXII.

Dorau, H. B., and Hinman, A. G., *Urban Land Economics,* The Macmillan Company, New York, 1928, Part I.

Dewey, Ralph L., and Nelson, James C., "The Transportation Problem of Agriculture," U.S. Department of Agriculture *Yearbook,* 1940, Government Printing Office, Washington, D.C., pp. 720–739.

Ely, R. T., and Wehrwein, G. S., *Land Economics,* The Macmillan Company, New York, 1940, Chaps. IX, X, XII, and XIII.

Heisley, Marie F., *Our Forests: Whaty They Are and What They Mean to Us,* U.S. Department of Agriculture, Miscellaneous Publication 162, Washington, D.C., July, 1940.

Hjelte, George, *The Administration of Public Recreation,* The Macmillan Com-pany, New York, 1940, Chaps. I and II.

Klimm, L. E., Starkey, O. P., and Hall, N. F., *Introductory Economic Geography,* Harcourt, Brace and Company, Inc., 1937, Chaps. XXV through XXVIII, XXIX, and XXX.

Leith, C. K., Furness, J. W., and Lewis, Cleona, *World Minerals and World Peace,* The Brookings Institution, Washington, D.C., 1943, Chaps. I, VI, and XII.

Mumford, Lewis, *The Culture of Cities,* Harcourt, Brace and Company, Inc., 1938, Chap. VII.

National Planning Association, "A Ten Year Program for Metropolitan Areas," in *Looking Ahead,* Washington, D.C., February, 1947, Vol. 5, No. 1.

National Resources Board, "Recreational Use of Land in the United States," *Report on Land Planning,* Government Printing Office, Washington, D.C., 1938, Part XI.

National Resources Committee, Report of the Urbanism Committee, *Our Cities, Their Role in the National Economy,* Government Printing Office, Washington, D.C., 1937.

National Resources Planning Board, *Planning for Wild Life in the United States,* Government Printing Office, Washington, D.C., 1935, Part IX.

National Resources Planning Board, *Our National Resources: Facts and Problems,* Government Printing Office, Washington, D.C., 1940.

National Resources Planning Board, Report of the Land Committee, *Public Land Acquisition in a National Land Use Program,* Government Printing Office, Washington, D.C., Part II.

Peterson, Elmer T. (ed.), *Cities Are Abnormal,* University of Oklahoma Press, Norman, 1946, Chaps. I, II, III, IV, XII, XIII, and XIV.

Report of the Committee to Submit Recommendations upon the General Transportation Situation to the President of the United States, December, 23, 1938, Washington, D.C.

Steiner, J. F., *Americans at Play, Recent Trends in Recreation and Leisure Time Activities,* McGraw-Hill Book Company, Inc., New York, 1938, Chap. IX.

Timmons, John F., and Murray, William G. (eds.), *Land Problems and Policies,* Iowa State College Press, Ames, 1950, Chaps. IX, X, and XI.

Trees, U.S. Department of Agriculture *Yearbook,* 1949, Government Printing Office, Washington, D.C.

U.S. Senate Document 12, *A National Plan for American Forestry,* 73d Congress, First Session, Government Printing Office, Washington, D.C., 1933, Vol. 1, pp. 2–57.

Van Hise, C. R., and Havemeyer, L. H., *Conservation of Our National Resources,* The Macmillan Company, New York, 1930, Part V.

Zimmermann, Erich W., *World Resources and Industries,* rev. ed., Harper & Brothers, New York, 1951, Chaps. XXII, XXIII, XXIV, and XXV.

Zon, R., and Sparhawk, W. N., *Forest Resources of the World,* McGraw-Hill Book Company, Inc., New York, 1923.

Zon, R., and Sparhawk, W. N., *America and the World's Woodpile,* U.S. Department of Agriculture Circular 21, January, 1918.

WATER AND LAND

USE OF WATER FOR IRRIGATION

Extent and Importance of Irrigation—Types of Irrigation Enterprises—Federal Irrigation Laws—Recent Federal Legislation—Allocation of Responsibilities Among Federal Agencies—Irrigation in Humid Areas—State Irrigation Policies—Major Irrigation Problems—Evaluation of Feasibility of Irrigation Projects—Acreage Limitations

DRAINAGE

Extent of Drainage—Federal Drainage Policies—State Drainage Policies—Major Drainage Problems

FLOOD CONTROL

Causes of Floods—Control of Floods—The Headwater Land-Use Approach

WATER POWER

The Role of the Federal Government—Undeveloped Resources—Water-Power Resource Problems

DOMESTIC, MUNICIPAL, AND FOOD USES OF WATER

Domestic and Municipal Water Supplies—Transportation of Waste—Water for Food Production

NAVIGATION

Early Navigation—Federal Land Grants for Canals and River Improvements—Oceanic Navigation—Great Lakes Transportation — Coastwise Transportation — Inland Waterways: Rivers and Inland Streams—Canals—Waterways in an Overall Transportation Program

INTEGRATED DEVELOPMENT AND USE OF WATER RESOURCES

Interrelationships of Land and Water—Upstream Watershed Management—Downstream Watershed Management —The Need for Coördinated Action—The River Basin Approach

WATER IS used in a great many ways to satisfy man's wants. Major uses made of water are: (1) for domestic and municipal water supply for human consumption or use, (2) for transportation of waste, (3) for food production (production of fish and similar seafood), and for agricultural production through irrigation, (4) for water power, through hydroelectric development, (5) for recreation, and (6) for navigation. The use of water for some of these purposes does not necessarily prevent its use for another.

Beneficial uses of water are of two main types—*usufructuary* and *proprietary*.[1] Under the former are water power, navigation, and fisheries, in which only rights in the water as it flows past—in the *use* of the water—exist. Under the latter, ownership tends to be in the *substance* of the water itself, as in domestic, municipal, or industrial uses, and irrigation. Drainage and flood control activities are attempts to overcome destructive or harmful effects of water.

The use of water has been increasing rapidly in the United States because of a growing population and higher per capita consumption. Per capita consumption for domestic purposes exceeds 200 gallons per day. The expanding industrial economy requires increasingly large amounts of water. For example, some 65,000 gallons of water are required to make a ton of steel, and about five times this much to produce a ton of aluminum.

The way in which land is used is an important factor determining the quantity, quality, and timeliness of water flow. Land-use practices that tend to retard runoff and place a maximum of the water in the soil will result in the greatest possible uniformity of stream flow throughout the year. Obviously the water retention ability of soils with grass or forest cover is higher than soils used for crops.

Land is a two-storied reservoir: (1) a plant cover at and above the surface, and (2) a soil and rock mantle at and beneath the surface. These two components, plant and soil, individually and collectively perform many water receiving and dispensing functions. Each is subject to change by land use, and these changes not only have a direct bearing on how much useful water the land reservoir will provide, but also what production from the land can be achieved.[2]

These interrelationships of water and land emphasize the importance of proper management and wise use of soil and water resources to the prosperity and survival of a nation. Abundant and low-cost water supplies are indispensable to our highly industrialized, urban way of life. At the same time this way of life is peculiarly vulnerable to an overabundance of

---

[1] R. T. Ely and G. S. Wehrwein, *Land Economics*, Macmillan, 1940, p. 361.

[2] President's Water Resources Policy Commission, *A Water Policy for the American People*, Government Printing Office, 1950, Vol. I, p. 125.

water in the form of destructive floods. Poor management and misuse of soil and water resources may well lead to poverty. We do not know why many of the great civilizations of the past vanished, but there is ample evidence that some of them failed because their water resources failed. It appears that some civilizations broke down because of a failure to recognize the basic interrelationship of water and land.

The increasing demands on water supplies suggest the desirability of an objective appraisal of the alternative uses for a given supply of water. How much of the available water supplies should be used for domestic, industrial, agricultural, or recreational uses? Full consideration must also be given to situations in which there is too much water with resulting destructive effects on other resources. Fortunately the same land-treatment practices and engineering structures that serve to control water and reduce its destructive effects (erosion, flooding, sedimentation) also are important in increasing the usable supply of water.

USE OF WATER FOR IRRIGATION

In arid and semiarid regions water is so scarce that it is the strategic or limiting factor in the agriculture of these areas, and its wise use is of the greatest importance. In the United States, irrigation acreage is largest in the 17 western states and more particularly in the area west of the 98th meridian (see Figure 29). Irrigation in the humid areas east of the Mississippi River has increased significantly in recent years.

EXTENT AND IMPORTANCE OF IRRIGATION

The total irrigated acreage of the United States is less than 2 percent of the land area of the nation and only slightly over 2 percent of all land in farms. In the 17 western states irrigated land approximates 4 percent of all land in farms. California, Texas, Colorado, Idaho, and Montana are the five leading states in irrigated acreage.

The number of irrigated farms amounts to about 6 percent of the total farms of the country. Most (over four-fifths) of the irrigated acreage is devoted to production of crops for harvesting, about one-sixth for pasture, and the remainder (2 percent) for other purposes. Alfalfa is the leading crop on irrigated land, with cotton second, rice third, wild hay fourth, orchards, vineyards, and nuts fifth, and barley sixth.

Hay and barley are grown extensively on irrigated lands in the western states. Most of the hay is used for feeding livestock (largely beef cattle and sheep). Much of the grain raised on irrigated land is also utilized by the livestock industry for winter feed. Thus, irrigated land is very important to and is an integral part of the livestock industry of the western arid and semiarid states.

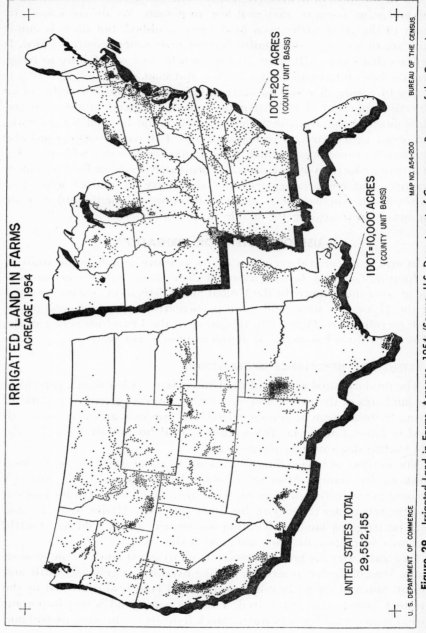

Figure 29. Irrigated Land in Farms, Acreage, 1954. (Source: U.S. Department of Commerce, Bureau of the Census.)

TYPES OF IRRIGATION ENTERPRISES

About half of the total irrigated area of the United States is in enter-prises undertaken by individuals or single farms. These are, for the most part, small undertakings where very little construction and development work was required to get the water onto the land. Consequently, these irrigation enterprises are in general the most inexpensive, and therefore were developed first. Less than a tenth of the total is in enterprises under-taken through coöperative associations. Some of these are comparatively large undertakings, but most of them are small and did not require any large construction or development efforts. Of the remainder or nearly a half, more than half the necessary construction and development work has been undertaken through organization of irrigation districts, and the rest principally through commercial or private corporation undertakings, or the federal government.

In recent years the federal government has been active in financing additional irrigation enterprises. Since the U.S. Bureau of Reclamation was established in 1902, it has placed irrigation works in operation to serve nearly five million acres of land.

The increased activity of the federal government in irrigation projects has been closely associated with its public works and employment pro-grams designed to furnish economic opportunites for unemployed and dislocated workers. Some of these projects, like the Grand Coulee Dam on the Columbia River in Washington, the Boulder Dam Project on the Colorado, and the Fort Peck Dam on the Missouri in Montana, are very large undertakings involving hundreds of millions of dollars—sums that could not be readily financed by individual, coöperative, or state and local governmental action, and projects not likely to be undertaken by private concerns. In many cases, production of hydroelectric energy is an im-portant part of the project.

FEDERAL IRRIGATION LAWS

The first federal legislation in the United States on the subject of irriga-tion or use of water from streams for this purpose was recognition of local customs, rules, and court decisions, in the act of July 26, 1866. By this act, together with an amendment approved in July of 1870, the federal gov-ernment surrendered any control it might have had over the nonnavigable streams of the arid region, by reason of its ownership of the lands of that area.[3] This law is usually considered the "Magna Charta" for state control of nonnavigable streams in the arid regions. Whether the rights of the states are based on this act or merely recognized by it, it does represent

[3] R. P. Teele, *The Economics of Land Reclamation in the United States,* Shaw, 1927, pp. 61–62.

a distinct and important policy, and one that has been much discussed in recent years with the increasing activities of the federal government in irrigation development.

Passage of the *Desert Land Act* on March 3, 1877, provided for granting title to 640 acres of arid land (reduced to 320 in 1890) to an individual in consideration of his conducting water upon it, paying $1.25 per acre, expending at least $3 per acre in improvements, and actually reclaiming at least an eighth of the land. The Desert Land Act had a very important weakness, in that the land could not be made security for the cost of irrigation. Thus, unless the individual could do his own irrigation development work or have it done by agencies that could provide the funds, irrigation development was impossible. Compliance was completed on less than nine million acres under the act, although nearly four times this much was originally entered for settlement.

Congress tried to remedy the weakness of the Desert Land Act by making the cost of irrigation development a lien on the land in the *Carey Act,* passed August 18, 1894. Under this act, the federal government ceded to each state containing arid land a limited acreage (one million acres, additional acreage being granted to Wyoming and Idaho in 1908 and to Colorado in 1911) on condition that the states provide for the development of irrigation on these lands. The federal government did not furnish any funds to assist in this development. It left the details to the states themselves, except that they were forbidden to lease lands or dispose of them in any way except so as to secure their irrigation, cultivation, and settlement. In addition, they could not sell more than 160 acres to any one person.

Under the Carey Act the states contract with construction companies for building the irrigation works to develop specific areas of public lands to be claimed by the states. The construction companies may sell water rights to reimburse themselves for the construction cost, while the states sell the land (agreeing to sell the land only to parties who have contracted for the purchase of water rights). In this way, the land and the water are brought together for more effective development and use of the irrigation works.

In spite of numerous amendments since its original passage, the Carey Act has fallen far short of its anticipated goal. There are several reasons for this: First, state officials elected for political reasons, without any necessary ability or particular interest, were generally overloaded with routine duties and could not or did not take the time or display the far-sighted vision needed. Second, corporations formed to irrigate and sell these lands were essentially speculative. Third, the supply of water was inadequate in many areas selected for development. Fourth, constitutions of many states in the arid region forbade them to extend credit to private undertakings, so that they could not undertake actual irrigation development or even lend their credit to communities of settlers or companies to accomplish it.

Fifth, the act fixed 10 years from passage of the law for completion of any project undertaken, and although this was amended in 1901 to a possible 15 years from date of approval of the project by the Secretary of the Interior, the time is still too short to undertake a job of irrigation development of any magnitude. Sixth, the most important and fundamenal cause was that there was not a real need for more farm land.[4]

Passage of the *Reclamation Act* of June 17, 1902, definitely committed the federal government to a program of irrigation development. The act provided for government construction of irrigation works, with provision for repayment of construction cost by those who use the water. It established a revolving fund for irrigation enterprises from receipts from the sale of public lands. Costs of construction of irrigation projects were to be repaid by settlers who took up irrigated land, but costs were not to include interest. Subsequent legislation has enlarged the scope of the act [5] and enlarged the sources of additions to the reclamation fund; but the principles of repayment and reinvestment in further irrigation development have been retained.

The original Reclamation Act of 1902 spread repayment over a period of 10 years, without interest on deferred payments, but the repayment problem became so acute that numerous acts have since been passed to extend the period and change the plan of payments. In 1914 passage of the *Extension Act* increased the time of repayment from 10 years to 20 years, with allowance of a grace period of 5 years before payments had to begin, with payments to be completed in 15 annual installments.

The Extension Act also prescribed that each man's holding was to represent a "farm unit," the exact size to be determined for each project by the Department of the Interior. This flexibility in size of unit was an attempt to shut out speculators and also to make operation of the act more adaptable to varied conditions of soil, enterprises, markets, and production costs peculiar to various federal irrigation projects. Unfortunately, on some projects the acreage set by the Department as constituting a "farm unit" was too small and resulted in serious problems.

During the general business depression and low agricultural price period that prevailed immediately after World War I, settlers on fed-

---

[4] Thomas, Teele, and Newell each stress one or more of the above reasons, although none lists all of them. See George Thomas, *The Development of Institutions Under Irrigation*, Macmillan, 1920; Teele, *op. cit.*; and F. H. Newell, "Water," in C. R. Van Hise and L. H. Havemeyer (eds.), *Conservation of Our Natural Resources*, Macmillan, 1930, p. 135.

[5] Passage of the *Warren Act* in 1911 authorized the sale of surplus water from federal project works to provide supplemental water for lands already irrigated.

eral irrigation projects had increasing difficulty in making their payments. On May 17, 1921, Congress passed a public resolution permitting the Secretary of the Interior to furnish irrigation water during 1921 to water-right applicants who were delinquent in operation and maintenance payments, in spite of the fact that the Extension Act provided that any settler who was more than one year in arrears in his payments could not secure any irrigation water services from the government.

Continuance of unsatisfactory conditions led the Secretary of the Interior to appoint a committee in 1923 to go over the whole problem of federal irrigation development and repayment and make recommendations for improvement. This committee, known as the *Factfinders Committee,* made the following recommendations in 1924: (1) That the 20-year limit for making payments be abandoned, and that repayment of construction costs be changed from an annual payment of a percentage of the total cost to a percentage of average annual returns. (2) That if, after a careful survey of construction costs and soils, it were found that present construction costs per acre were more than the lands could bear, a fair and equitable adjustment be made to fix the charge per acre at a sum the land could reasonably bear. (3) That justifiable temporary relief be provided by Congress. (4) That construction costs apportioned to land that could not repay them be suspended and ultimately charged off. (5) That a credit fund be established from which settlers could borrow funds at a low rate of interest to make permanent improvements or buy livestock and equipment. (6) That agricultural advisors be employed to give sound agricultural and business advice to enable settlers to increase their farm incomes.[6]

In 1924 Congress passed an act adopting the first four of the six major recommendations of the Factfinders Committee. The acceptance of the new repayment basis (percentage of the value of the crop) was optional with water users. The act of May 10, 1926, renewing appropriations for new projects, provided for repayment periods of not more than 40 years on new projects and left details to the Secretary of the Interior. On May 25, 1926, Congress passed the so-called *Omnibus Reclamation Act,* which repealed provision for the crop plan of repayment, except as to contracts already in force or being negotiated at the time, and the 40-year plan was established for both old and new projects.

RECENT FEDERAL LEGISLATION

The repayment situation on many federal irrigation projects again became acute during the thirties; and on May 31, 1939, Congress passed an act authorizing the Secretary of the Interior to extend relief to water

[6] The report also made other recommendations. For a more detailed statement, see Teele, *op. cit.,* p. 78.

users who were unable to pay construction charges without great hardship for the calendar year 1938 and for prior years. The *Reclamation Project Act* of 1939, enacted into law August 4, 1939, extends the provisions of the act of May 31 for each of the years 1939 to 1943, inclusive, and provides specific measures for adjusting economic and financial problems on federal irrigation projects. It makes possible the drafting of new contracts gearing repayments to ability of farmers to make payments year by year, and the accomplishment of other needed reforms.

The act provides for extending the time for payment of construction charges, where justified, to not more than 40 years from the date of the first installment, or not to exceed double the number of remaining years. It also reëstablishes the principle of the crop payment plan for repayment by providing for adjusting annual charges on the basis of current crop values. If these two provisions are not adequate, new contracts can be negotiated providing for fair and equitable plans of repayment after approval has been given by Act of Congress.[7]

Congress has shown its continued interest in encouraging further irrigation development in arid and semiarid regions by additional legislative acts. The *Water Facilities Act,* approved August 28, 1937, authorizes the Secretary of Agriculture to construct new water facilities, acquire any necessary lands and water rights, sell or lease water facilities, or enter into agreements with or furnish financial or other aid, if he feels it is warranted, to any agency or person. The facilities included within the program may be located on private or public lands.

The act represents a broad program to encourage and assist in developing water facilities, including small reservoirs, dams, wells, etc., in range areas or dry-land farming areas of the arid and semiarid regions, on the ground that these smaller water facilities play an important part in the wise use of an area's land resources, in cases where large irrigation dams are neither feasible nor desirable.

The *Case-Wheeler Act,* approved August 11, 1939, and amended October 14, 1940, provides among other things, that expenditures for construction, maintenance, operation, rehabilitation, or financial assistance of any one project undertaken in pursuance of the Water Facilities Act shall not exceed $50,000 of federal funds. Moreover, contracts entered into between the United States and water users for lease, purchase, or employment of these lands are to provide for annual or semiannual payments in number and amounts fixed by the Secretary of Agriculture; but in no case shall they exceed 50 years from the time the land is first settled upon.

Also, expenditures from federal appropriations to meet construction

[7] Annual Report of the Secretary of the Interior, *Annual Report of the Commissioner of the Bureau of Reclamation,* Government Printing Office, 1940, p. 103.

costs allocated to irrigation cannot exceed one million dollars for dams and reservoirs in any one project undertaken under the provisions of the Case-Wheeler Act. These provisions reflect the tendency of the federal government to encourage construction of smaller irrigation projects and related water facilities to stabilize individual farms and ranches, rather than to construct only monumental dams, like the Grand Coulee project, which bring into production large tracts of new land.

The *Flood Control Act* of December 22, 1944, provides that the use of water for navigation in states lying wholly or partly west of the 98th meridian shall be for only such use as does not conflict with the beneficial consumptive use of water for domestic, municipal, stock water, irrigation, mining, or industrial purposes. This declaration of policy settles the question of priority of use of water in the arid and semiarid west. In addition to providing a water "bill of rights," the act charted a new course for multiple-purpose development of river basin areas for the nation by defining the duties and coördinating the work of various federal agencies, and providing for state participation in the development of land and water resources.

Under the Flood Control Act, Congress recognizes the interests and rights of the states in water utilization and control to preserve and protect established and potential uses for all purposes. Provision is made that investigations which form the basis of development plans shall be conducted by federal agencies in such manner as to give the affected states the information developed and the opportunity for consultation and coöperation in the investigations with the federal agencies in charge. If there is disagreement on plans among the federal agencies or between the federal agencies and the states, federal agencies must submit to Congress the views of those disagreeing with them along with their own recommendations.

ALLOCATION OF RESPONSIBILITIES AMONG FEDERAL AGENCIES

When in the West, the Army Engineers and the U.S. Bureau of Reclamation and other interested agencies are required to coöperate in their investigations and plans. Investigations of watersheds, undertaking measures for runoff and water flow retardation, and soil erosion prevention on watersheds are under the jurisdiction of the U.S. Department of Agriculture.

The Army Engineers are authorized to construct, maintain, and operate public park and recreational facilities in reservoir areas. They are also assigned the duty of prescribing regulations for use of storage allocated for flood control or navigation at all reservoirs constructed wholly or in part with federal funds.

The Secretary of War is authorized to make contracts with states, municipalities, private concerns, or individuals for domestic and industrial uses of surplus water available at any reservoir under control of the War Department. The Secretary of the Interior, in whose department is placed the Bureau of Reclamation, is authorized to build reclamation works to utilize surplus water of flood control reservoirs after making a report of findings as provided in federal reclamation laws.

Federal irrigation policies might be briefly summarized as encouraging, over a period of many years, the development of additional irrigation enterprises. The policy of irrigation development has been based largely on the belief that these lands would provide homes for new settlers, and that production of additional farm products would make possible a more profitable economy generally. Integrated industrial and agricultural development is one of the basic prerequities for orderly economic growth of the West. During World War II, federal reclamation projects paid big dividends by helping to provide the needed electric power to operate airplane factories, aluminum and magnesium plants, shipyards, and other industries that made fighting equipment, and to produce the needed food and fiber for the armed forces, civilians, and allies.

IRRIGATION IN HUMID AREAS

Farm irrigation in humid areas provides supplemental water for growing crops to assure more uniformly favorable moisture during the growing season, with resulting higher yields. Irrigation in humid areas generally requires the use of pumps, some kind of power, and sprinkler equipment. A few farmers use gravity flow from lakes, streams, and artesian wells and require very little equipment.

The activities of the Bureau of Reclamation and the U.S. Department of the Interior are limited to the 17 western states plus Arkansas and Louisiana. Irrigation development in humid areas has been almost entirely by private effort. The role of public agencies is likely to be in the directions of aid to private developments in the field of education and technical assistance.[8]

STATE IRRIGATION POLICIES

With increased federal activity in irrigation and control and development of water resources, many western states have passed legislation permitting fuller cooperation with the Federal government and permitting construction or sponsoring irrigation enterprises with the assistance of federal appropriations. Although few states have attempted to plan com-

[8] Cf. Roy E. Huffman, *Irrigation Development and Public Water Policy*, Ronald, 1953, p. 242.

prehensively for water uses within their boundaries,[9] several of them began to undertake this important work in the late thirties in coöperation with the National Resources Planning Board and its consultants.

The proposed creation of several river basin authorities patterned after the Tennessee Valley Authority for such western areas as the Missouri River Basin and the Columbia River Basin has made the states in these areas more conscious of the need of sound irrigation development and wise use of water resources. Active state reclamation associations and state water-conservation boards are operating in several of these states. Consequently, more effective coöperation of federal and state agencies should be possible in future years in development and utilization of water resources.

MAJOR IRRIGATION PROBLEMS

Some of the more important problems associated with the existing water utilization pattern for irrigation include: (1) Development of additional storage at reasonable cost (since many lands now irrigated require additional water for an adequate supply). (2) Limitation of areas to be irrigated to available water supplies. Many irrigation enterprises have been developed in which irrigated acreage is overexpanded so that during dry years serious losses, troublesome litigation, and urgent requests for public assistance occur. (3) Existence of too many small irrigation organizations on a given stream. Pooling a complexity of water rights would simplify administration, reduce operating costs, and eliminate much of the litigation which would otherwise result from attempts to preserve priority of individual water rights.[10] (4) Failure to utilize water for its highest and best use in many areas. In many regions of the West, irrigation is the highest and best use for much of the water, but in some instances water-use projects constructed for navigation and flood control have hindered irrigation development. (5) Failure to apportion irrigation costs properly. In the past there has been little use of the principle of apportioning costs of irrigation development on the basis of benefits received from such development. Arguments advanced for government irrigation enterprises are based largely on benefits to communities where projects are located, rather than merely on benefits to settlers who are to operate the irrigated lands. Businessmen of the communities that service

[9] Hynning states, "State attempts at the comprehensive planning of water uses are few in number at the paper stage, and obviously fewer or perhaps nonexistent at the stage of administration. Only a handful of instances have come to the attention of the writer, after extensive investigation and conferences with water specialists." (C. J. Hynning, "State Conservation of Resources," National Resources Committee, 1939, p. 61.)

[10] Cf. National Resources Board, *Report to the President of the United States*, 1934, p. 344.

such irrigation areas benefit not only from the construction of the irrigation works, but from the expenditures of the settlers in bringing land into cultivation and of operating the lands.

On irrigation enterprises developed by private initiative, the settler is expected to repay the entire cost of the irrigation development, with interest. Spreading cost of the irrigation development over all property to be benefited directly or indirectly, rather than merely over the property to be reclaimed, is a much more sound and equitable policy of irrigation development.[11] Cost of construction, operation, and maintenance could be made general obligations of districts, to be met by a general property tax, while water users could be charged rates fixed on the basis of the value of the water to the farmers, and not of a return on the investment. Such rates might be fixed as a percentage of the returns from the land, and the revenue thus secured might be applied to the cost of the irrigation enterprise, thus reducing the amount to be raised by taxes.

EVALUATION OF FEASIBILITY OF IRRIGATION PROJECTS

In projects involving irrigation and other purposes, such as generation of power, flood control, navigation, or furnishing of municipal water supplies, costs of development should be apportioned as accurately as possible to those various uses in terms of estimated benefits. Both direct and secondary economic benefits should be considered in evaluating proposed multiple-purpose projects involving irrigation. Primary or direct benefits include: (1) prevention of flood damage, (2) increase in net income of farm families from land reclamation, (3) savings in transportation costs by waterways as compared with alternative means, (4) value of electric power from power installations, (5) increases in net land income from watershed treatment, (6) increases in value of fish and wildlife resources, (7) value of water supply for municipal and rural areas, (8) savings in water treatment costs through abatement of water pollution.[12]

Secondary or indirect benefits represent the more general efforts on regional and national economics as contrasted to strictly individual benefits. Secondary benefits are very difficult to evaluate in precise dollar values. Nevertheless, such gains as higher national productivity, higher national income, improved levels of living, increased economic stability, and more ample supplies of basic goods whose production is dependent on water, either directly or indirectly, are just as real as the material considerations involved in primary benefits. In reality they are more real and

[11] Teele points out that spreading the cost over property other than the land to be reclaimed will tend to check the demand for irrigation when it is not needed but, at the same time, should not seriously retard irrigation development if there is a real need for such an undertaking. Private enterprise would still be free to reclaim land when it appears that the land itself can pay the cost. (Teele, *op. cit.*, p. 327.)

[12] *A Water Policy for the American People*, p. 65.

more vital because they constitute the motivation for social action and the ultimate test of social survival. A uniform procedure for evaluation of such benefits for the use of federal agencies should be developed jointly with the approval of a National Board of Review.[13]

In determining the feasibility of a given project, the *total net benefits* must be considered and not merely the *benefit-cost* ratio. A project with a very high ratio of benefits to costs would not necessarily assure the greatest total net benefits. In the case of multiple-purpose projects, each phase of a project having a benefit-cost ratio of at least 1 to 1 will pay off in monetary terms. But when extra market or indirect gains and losses are considered, it becomes obvious that projects may be justified at some level other than the marginal point in benefit-cost analysis. If extra market values are judged to be of sufficient importance, public expenditures for water resource development can be carried beyond this point because the benefit-cost ratio includes only market values.[14]

ACREAGE LIMITATIONS

Numerous attempts have been made to change the acreage limitations on federal irrigation projects. The original Reclamation Act of 1902 limited the irrigable land holdings to be furnished water by any Bureau of Reclamation irrigation project to 160 acres for any landowner. This was construed to permit 320 irrigable acres to be held jointly by man and wife. Moreover, the law does not preclude coöperative farming by any number of owners, members of a family or otherwise, so long as each owns no more than the acreage limit for any one owner.[15]

The purpose of this limitation is to make family-sized farms available for settlement and to prevent large landholders from monopolizing the benefits of federal irrigation projects. Many concepts of the "family farm" exist, but it is generally considered to be an economic unit which a family can operate. Promotion and preservation of the family farm is the generally stated and avowed policy of the nation.

The matter of relaxing acreage limitation on federal irrigation projects is a highly controversial one. Some projects have been exempted from acreage restrictions by Congressional action.[16] Opposition to acreage limitation arises not so much in cases of public development to benefit nonirrigated private lands as in cases of public development to benefit private lands already irrigated.[17] The most serious opposition comes from

[13] *Ibid.*

[14] Huffman, *op. cit.*, p. 200.

[15] *A Water Policy for the American People*, p. 170.

[16] Huffman, *op. cit.*, pp. 58–59.

[17] For various explanations of opposition to acreage limitation, see Marion Clawson, *Uncle Sam's Acres*, Dodd, Mead, 1951, p. 194; and Mont H. Saunderson, *Western Land and Water Use*, University of Oklahoma Press, 1950, pp. 158–159.

areas where provision of supplemental water is proposed for lands now irrigated but with an inadequate water supply.[18]

In view of technological progress in American agriculture, very serious questions may be raised as to whether the acreage limitation is too rigid. Consideration can well be given to what constitutes an adequate farm unit under varying conditions of irrigation agriculture without necessarily abandoning the long-standing policy of the family farm as the major objective of public development. The acreage that comprised a family farm at the turn of the century is inadequate in the mid-fifties, especially in irrigation areas of extensive agriculture. Nevertheless, providing opportunities for family farms is the justification for using interest-free public funds in irrigation projects. In any case, the 160-acre limitation should apply only to the irrigated portion of a farm.

In projects designed to deliver supplemental water to areas already under irrigation, the existing acreage limitation provision should be modified to make it possible to supply an equitable share of the supplemental water to existing farms exceeding the limitation. Charges for water supplied to such excess lands should be fixed on the basis of full costs, including amortization with interest of the full investment allocable to this purpose.[19]

DRAINAGE

In some areas too much water causes serious damages through floods, erosion, or waterlogging of the soil. This makes successful crop production impossible. Too much water is harmful to plant growth, and means must be devised to remove this excess.

In many parts of the more humid areas, lands are so poorly drained that they are unsuitable for crop production. Often these swampy areas are comparatively fertile, because of the accumulated decay of aquatic vegetation, but this is not always true. Millions of acres of productive land have been made available for crops in the United States, particularly in Illinois and along the tributaries of the Mississippi River. The low-lying Everglades of Florida also constitute an area where drainage may be utilized effectively.

Much of the water applied to lands in the arid and semiarid regions carries in solution considerable amounts of earthy salts or alkalies. The water that disappears through evaporation leaves behind it salts carried in solution, which may accumulate at such a rate as to cause the soil to become alkaline or "sick," so that crops grown do not thrive. To remedy this situation, an excess of water considerably greater than that of the theoretical needs for plants must be used to wash out and keep moving

[18] Huffman, *op. cit.*, p. 60.
[19] *A Water Policy for the American People*, p. 171.

the salts in solution. This excess water must be drained off the cultivated fields by carefully constructed drains.[20]

There is considerable evidence that prehistoric cities were abandoned because of the accumulation of salts in farm fields. Apparently the failure or inability to provide drainage for the irrigated land on which the towns and cities depended was the cause of abandonment in many cases.

EXTENT OF DRAINAGE

More than 100 million acres of land are included in organized drainage enterprises in the United States. Of this acreage some four-fifths are improved. In addition, about 50 million acres outside organized districts have been improved by farm drainage. It is estimated that about 21 million acres of suitable undeveloped land might be made available for agricultural production by drainage at moderate costs compared with probable returns. More than 30 million acres need supplemental drainage.[21] Two-thirds of the land in drainage enterprises is located in the glaciated portions of northwestern Ohio, northern Indiana and Illinois, southern Michigan, and north-central Iowa and Minnesota. The glacial deposits obstructed many former stream courses, forming numerous shallow lakes, marshes, and swamps. Most of the other third is in the bottom lands of the Mississippi River and its tributaries, in the Everglades of southern Florida, and in the irrigated districts of the West (see Figure 30).

Drained lands in the United States extend through the heart of the hay and dairy region, the corn belt, and the cotton belt. Drained lands, to a greater extent than irrigated lands, are devoted largely to standard farm crops rather than to special products that have peculiarly advantageous market situations.

FEDERAL DRAINAGE POLICIES

The Federal government has followed actively a policy of encouraging swampland reclamation for many years. Its earliest effort was the passage of the *Swamp Land Act* of 1849. This act granted to Louisiana all swamps or overflowed lands unfit for cultivation, and the policy was made general in an act passed September 28, 1850. These acts provided that the proceeds to be secured from the ceded lands should be applied, as far as necessary, exclusively to the purpose of reclaiming these lands by means of levees and drains.

---

[20] In the Salt River Valley of Arizona, and on the lands in Southern California near the Salton Sea, it is estimated that each year there are brought to the fields by canal systems deriving waters from the Colorado River and its tributaries upwards of two tons of salt per acre. (See Newell, *op. cit.*, p. 171.)

[21] U.S. Department of Agriculture, *Agricultural Land Resources*, Agriculture Information Bulletin No. 140, Government Printing Office, June, 1955, pp. 56 and 61.

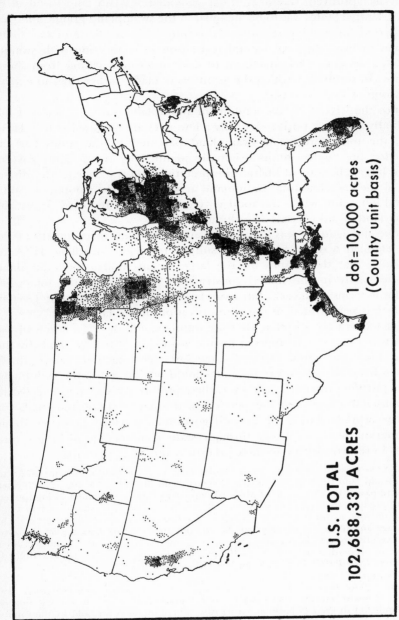

U.S. TOTAL
102,688,331 ACRES

1 dot=10,000 acres
(County unit basis)

Figure 30. Land in Drainage Enterprises, Acreage, 1950. (Source: U.S. Department of Commerce, Bureau of the Census.)

An act approved March 12, 1860, provided that no land disposed of by the United States was to be included in the swampland grants, and that the period for making selections of swamplands in all states was to be limited to two years. All federal legislation in connection with swamplands passed since 1860 has been to settle questions arising from shortcomings of statutes by which the grants were made, rather than to extend the scope of these grants.[22]

Since the Civil War the amount of swampland annually selected has gradually declined, until today only a few acres are patented yearly. However, the total acreage of swampland patented to the states has far exceeded the modest limits originally planned by the Federal government, largely because of liberal interpretation and fraudulent administration of the law. The total swampland acreage patented amounts to some 64 million acres, while the total covered by claims reported under the swampland grants exceeds 83 million.

Time and again, it was found on examination that three-fourths of the land claimed was not swampy or subject to serious overflow. Hibbard concludes that the reasons for the large patents under the swampland acts lie partly in the liberal construction placed upon the somewhat indefinite terms of the acts, but more largely "in the persistent and extensive frauds perpetrated in the administration of the law." [23]

The acts did not stipulate that the improvement or reclamation of the lands was a necessary condition for the acquiring of title to lands by the states. In a few states, plans of some sort were made by which funds derived from the sale of swamplands should be devoted to the fulfillment of the purposes intended. However, these proceeds were later deflected to other uses until the funds expended in drainage became too small for effective work.[24] Thus, the Federal government's effort to bring about reclamation of swamplands through state construction of levees and drains in return for title to these lands was very disappointing.

[22] In 1866 measures were passed to "quiet land titles in California"; in 1872, "to quiet certain land titles in the State of Missouri"; and in 1874, 1875, and 1877, further laws were passed for the benefit of Missouri, supplementing these statutes as interpreted and enforced by the Land Office. Numerous bills have since been introduced in Congress proposing to quiet swampland titles, but Congress has tended, in general, to discourage any further legislation, on the grounds that existing laws are adequate to guide executive officers in deciding claims. According to Hibbard, this stand has been effective in preventing any increase in the potential source of conflicts. (B. H. Hibbard, *A History of the Public Land Policies*, Macmillan, 1924, p. 272.)

[23] *Ibid.*, pp. 274–287.

[24] For a more detailed analysis of the disposition of swamplands, see *ibid.*, pp. 281–287. Hibbard indicates that open fraud was practiced not only in the selection of these lands but in their disposition, citing cases where the land was sold by the county commissioners to themselves for nominal considerations or, in some instances, where states bargained with an emigration company, selling the land to the company for 25 to 75 cents an acre with the provision that the company was to put settlers on the land.

Since the beginning of the present century, various proposals have been advanced in Congress for the Federal government to take an active part in reclaiming swamplands through construction of drainage enterprises, but so far they have been unsuccessful. However, since World War II the Agricultural Conservation and Soil Conservation programs of the U.S. Department of Agriculture have been active in clearing and drainage activities. Land in drainage enterprises increased from about 87 million acres in 1940 to nearly 103 million acres in 1950. If drainage development continues at recent rates, it is estimated that by 1975 as much as 125 million acres may be in organized drainage enterprises.[25]

STATE DRAINAGE POLICIES

In general, the states have made swamplands and wet lands pay for their own reclamation. The means used for accomplishing this have been adoption of legislation authorizing drainage districts with power to incur indebtedness and assess benefited lands in order to meet construction and maintenance costs of levees and drains. The first states to pass such legislation were Michigan and Ohio in 1847, and more than three-fourths of the states now have statutes authorizing establishment of drainage enterprises.

Drainage laws of the various states differ considerably, but there are two main types of organization: (1) the *corporate,* which is organized by landowners under public supervision, and (2) the *county drain,* established and constructed like any other local improvement, and managed by county officials. About 95 percent of organized drainage enterprises are included in drainage districts and county drains, and the cost of drainage is thus almost universally met by assessments against the lands benefited.

Ordinarily, state laws provide that districts may be organized only when benefits will exceed costs. Both costs and benefits are estimated, of course, and there is a tendency to underestimate costs and overestimate benefits. However, benefits of drainage enterprises have generally exceeded costs, and defaults on payments are not numerous. The cost of draining swampland is ordinarily only a fraction as large as the cost of providing a water supply for irrigation, and it is much less difficult for landowners to meet drainage district assessments than to meet assessments in irrigation districts.

MAJOR DRAINAGE PROBLEMS

Where wet lands are flooded by water of interstate origin, there is a definite need for a clarification and unification of national and state policies. One of the first needs in this connection is the classification of projects in which waters of interstate origin are involved.

Drainage for the prevention of malaria is an important aspect of na-

[25] U.S. Department of Agriculture, *op. cit.,* pp. 61 and 69.

tional drainage policy. The transmission of malaria has been traced to night-biting mosquitoes whose breeding habits have been learned; and the methods of preventing reproduction of the mosquito are largely through drainage, combined with house-screening and medical elimination of the acute disease from infected persons who are carriers. In areas where malaria is prevalent, largely in the southern states, drainage must follow a special technique, and usually must supplement drainage for land reclamation.[26]

Drainage for reduction of pest varieties of mosquitoes not involving public health considerations also requires a special technique. Ordinarily, only very shallow lowering of the ground water horizon is necessary or economically justifiable. The preservation of area values for wildlife refuge and breeding is in many cases a major economic and esthetic consideration too often overlooked. Some of the areas already drained were formerly very fine wildlife refuges and breeding grounds. Their present agricultural use is insignificant in comparison with their value in their natural state.

In periods of expanding domestic and foreign markets for agricultural products, new lands can be brought into production through drainage enterprises without creating any serious economic difficulties; but in periods of distressing agriculture surpluses and widespread unemployment, expanding agricultural acreage through reclamation by drainage can be justified only if national policy dictates that the impacts of unemployment and lack of alternative opportunities in industry can be met best by furnishing farm operating units for the unemployed or stranded families. The same considerations apply to future irrigation policies. Both irrigation and drainage are means of increasing the productive agricultural area by reclaiming lands not suitable for crop production in their normal state, or unable to produce the amount and types of crops which they can produce through irrigation or drainage.

FLOOD CONTROL

Man is interested in water because of its destructive as well as its beneficial aspects. No year passes without floods, some of them very serious, somewhere in the United States. The aggregate direct damages caused by floods have been estimated roughly at 35 million dollars yearly,[27] and in some years this amount is greatly increased by the occurrence of widespread floods, such as the Mississippi River flood of 1927.[28] In addition to

[26] National Resources Board, *Report to the President,* 1934, p. 341.

[27] National Resources Board, *Report to the President,* 1934, p. 325.

[28] In the 1927 Mississippi River flood, it is estimated that 250 people lost their lives, 700,000 were driven from their homes, and property and crops valued at hundreds of millions of dollars were destroyed. The Red Cross alone spent $17,000,000 in rescue and rehabilitation work. (See Van Hise and Havemeyer, *op. cit.,* p. 126.)

these direct damages, there are indirect and intangible losses for which no allowance is commonly made, and which are far more widespread.

CAUSES OF FLOODS

It is generally conceded that flood losses, both direct and indirect, have been increased greatly by unwise encroachment of settlement and industry upon lowlands subject to inundation, and the denuding of forest areas in the upper reaches of drainage basins. Floods have occurred for many years, however, and it is not correct to imply that floods in many areas in recent years are attributable entirely to human occupancy and exploitation of natural vegetation, including forests.

Evidences of great floods in certain areas like the Mississippi Valley, prior to the time these areas were settled, are available to show that floods have occurred through strictly natural forces. It is obvious, of course, that the damage done by floods is much greater after settlement, if for no other reason than the fact that human life and property were not there until after man had settled on these lands. In many areas, however, man has by his use of the land destroyed the natural cover and increased the possibilities of soil erosion and flood damage.

CONTROL OF FLOODS

In many areas improved land-use and soil-conservation practices in agricultural and forest land use are sufficient, if followed generally, to reduce floods and erosion to a minimum, but in others special measures and structures are necessary. Flood control structures are of four general types: (1) storage reservoirs to impound flood waters for release at a later time; (2) retarding basins that automatically retard and smooth out flood peaks; (3) channel improvements designed to increase capacity or facilitate stream flow; (4) levees to protect the bottom lands behind them from the overflow waters of the rivers.

In general, storage reservoirs are most satisfactory, particularly if the impounded waters can be put to multiple uses, as in the Boulder Dam project on the Colorado River. The best example of complete protection involving the use of retarding basins is found in the Miami Conservancy District of Ohio.[29] Channel improvements are seldom an adequate protection by themselves, but combined with other means of flood control, they are an important contributing control factor.

The use of levees is the traditional method of controlling floods. The use of levees has many advantages, although a policy of "levees only" is not always adequate to control floodwaters. Levees are a direct and very visible form of protection that serve as a standing warning against the

[29] National Resources Board, *Report to the President*, 1934, p. 325.

occupation and use of the part of the flood channel that remains exposed, but they are not always enough. To confine a river like the Mississippi, which normally spreads over 50 miles of flood plain, between dikes only a mile or more apart, simply "sets the river on edge." Moreover, the cost of building levees so high and so strong that they would be entirely safe would be so enormous that the results might not justify the expense.

Rivers like the Mississippi, which carry large amounts of soil, are continually building up their stream beds so that they tend to become higher than the surrounding land, making it increasingly difficult and expensive to hold the water in check by levees. In addition, during the years required to carry out such a gigantic scheme, the annually recurring breaks in the completed system would be even more destructive than in the past. There may also be a physical limit to the height to which the walls or dikes can be built, because the delta soil, as in the case of the Mississippi River, may not be able to support the weight of high earth structures, especially on the wet grounds of old sloughs and lake beds.

Most critics agree that there is no one entirely effective means of controlling floods, but rather a combination of activities and methods that may tend to keep dangerous flood waters in check. An important method is to use practices that will tend to prevent floods from occurring, rather than merely to construct mechanical and other devices, like levees, to hold the floodwaters in check.

The prevention of floods involves headwater control. Construction of dams or reservoirs to catch and temporarily hold the waters at the heads of the streams and their tributaries is the only effective way of preventing floods. By this means, the waters can be gradually released so as not to flood the lands and cities below. The failure of these dams to hold, as in the case of the Johnstown and Conemaugh rivers in Pennsylvania on May 31, 1889, results in very serious damages.

Forests at the headwaters of streams are important in controlling floods. The natural forest cover of litter and humus has great absorption and percolating capacity, which mechanically retards the rate of runoff of water, and thus slows down the stream flow. The removal of standing timber alone, however, has only moderate, if any, unfavorable influence on the absorption and percolating capacity of the underlying humus and soils and on the mechanical retardation of runoff; but the related conditions that have been associated with lumbering operations—such as completely clearing the forest area and cultivating the soil, forest fires which have devastated cutover land, etc.—destroy the underlying humus and vegetative cover, which does have a significant effect upon the absorption capacity and mechanical retardation of runoff. Conservationists urge that forests be protected and extended not only throughout the headwaters of streams but, where practical, all along the watercourses, particularly in the lower areas where great uninhabited sections are needed to retain the floodwaters temporarily.[30]

THE HEADWATER LAND-USE APPROACH

Proper land use in the headwater areas is the soundest approach to flood control and one that ultimately must gain ascendancy over reservoir building. The headwater land-use approach to flood control must include a wide range of activities and alternatives from land acquisition for restoration of reclaimed upstream natural "sponge" or absorption areas, and afforestation of badly eroded farm lands, to influencing of farm practices and land use by coöperative management, subsidy payments, or regulation.[31]

Floods in the humid areas have been influenced greatly by the use of land. In the arid and semiarid western areas, floods result principally from a combination of brief but intense summer storms, steep upland watersheds above a settled agricultural valley or plain, and denudation of range and forest cover from an upland watershed area. Western flood control is primarily a matter of good land management in the uplands— good range management, good forests, and conservation of the upland soils.[32] Flood plain zoning resulting in enforced evacuation in some areas might save many lives and much property, because in spite of all flood control works and the best land-use management practices, there is always the possibility of unusual floods for which the maximum of protection would prove inadequate.[33]

WATER POWER

The use of falling water as a source of power occurred early in the history of the United States. From early Colonial beginnings until late in the nineteenth century, the power could be used only at the site of the waterfall. Consequently, industries using such power developed around the water wheels of New England, New York, and Pennsylvania, and along the "Fall Line" (the source of the rivers flowing into the Atlantic) southward.

In the 1880's, with commercial use of electricity as a source of power, hydroelectric power became available anywhere within reach of electric transmission from the power site. During the past five decades installed generating capacity of hydroelectric plants has increased 17 times, with the largest increase occurring in the latest decade.[34]

[30] H. S. Person *et al.*, *Little Waters,* Soil Conservation Service, Resettlement Administration, November, 1935, pp. 25–26.
[31] Saunderson, *op. cit.*, p. 181.
[32] *Ibid.*, pp. 184–186.
[33] *A Water Policy for the American People,* p. 146.
[34] Robert W. Hartley, *Land and Water Conservation Development,* The Brookings Institution. Washington, D.C., August, 1955, Reprint No. 7, p. 550

THE ROLE OF THE FEDERAL GOVERNMENT

The Federal government has played an increasingly important role in the expanding development and use of hydroelectric power. Dams and related structures for generating hydroelectric power affect other uses of a river. Consequently, as early as 1890 the national Congress, through passage of the Rivers and Harbors Act for that year, forbade their construction on navigable water without its consent and the approval of plans by the Chief of Engineers and the Secretary of War.

By a series of steps, the Federal government broadened its interest in water-power development until, in the *Federal Water Power Act* of 1920, it established a licensing procedure for encouraging private enterprise to undertake such projects. At the same time, it left the way open for possible ultimate public ownership of the projects. The act also required that water-power development be undertaken as a part of comprehensive multiple-purpose plans for the improvement or development of river systems.[35]

In the meantime, the Federal government began constructing hydroelectric plants in connection with irrigation projects of the Bureau of Reclamation. Passage of the *Boulder Canyon Project Act* in 1933 marked a new step in the evolution of federal power policy as related to water resources. Under this act Congress established for the first time a single agency with responsibility for the comprehensive development of a river basin for all purposes, including maximum development of electric power consistent with flood control and navigation.[36]

Whether future decisions provide for more valley authorities, or for improvement in the interagency river basin committee technique, or otherwise, the Federal government will play a major role in water-power development. More than a tenth of all electric energy produced in the United States is now generated by federal plants.

UNDEVELOPED RESOURCES

Only about a fifth of the potential hydroelectric power in the United States has been developed. The Federal Power Commission estimates undeveloped hydroelectric power at about 88 million kilowatts, or about five times the installed capacity of existing projects, with annual generating capacity nearly four times the annual output of existing installations. More than half of our undeveloped water power is west of the Continental Divide. More than a third of the total undeveloped power is in the Columbia River Basin alone, and a tenth is in the Missouri River Basin.[37]

[35] *Ibid.*, p. 551, and *A Water Policy for the American People, op. cit.*, pp. 221–224.
[36] *A Water Policy for the American People, op. cit.*, pp. 225–226.
[37] See the *Thirty-first Annual Report of the Federal Power Commission*, 1951, Government Printing Office, 1952, pp. 72–75.

The figures on undeveloped water power do not include many flood control and irrigation dam sites which, in the course of their development, may produce a considerable amount of water power incident to the other purposes for which the development is undertaken. This may bring many additional sites into the field of economic feasibility and increase the estimates of potential water power. Technological developments, such as long-distance transmission of electrical energy, may also increase the amount of water power that is feasible for development.

WATER-POWER RESOURCE PROBLEMS

Production of power from streams must be handled with proper regard for the other important purposes of control of water resources, such as flood control, navigation, soil conservation, water supply, pollution abatement, irrigation, and other special uses of water. Not all these problems are found in every stream, but two or more are likely to be found in minor streams, and most or all are likely to occur in the great rivers.

In this group of water problems, there is both complement of purpose and conflict of purpose. For example, water storage in rainy seasons for release in drier seasons may reduce destruction by flood, increase power, maintain depth of water for navigation, assure continuity of public and industrial water supply, and, by limiting the relative pollution of streams in dry seasons, maintain a better quality of water. In contrast, use of too much of the possible water storage space to facilitate continuous deepwater navigation or to increase the acreage irrigated will leave an insufficient storage for control of floods. The major problem of water resources for water-power production is to fit this use in with these other complementary and conflicting uses in such a way as to maximize the total benefits to the public.

The most obvious and most debated conflict of purpose in the use of water resources deals with flood control and power. Even in the case of use of water resources for irrigation, there may be serious conflicts with the use of the same waters for water power.

It would not seem possible that there would be any conflict of purpose in running public water supply, irrigation water, or navigation water through a turbine during periods of release from storage, but if the demands for these uses are so great that most of the water is used, there will be too little left in storage for development of water power later in the season. The only effective way by which these conflicting uses can be handled adequately in the public interest is on the multiple-purpose plan, in which due allowance is made for the various uses of the water resources, including production of power.

Three examples of successful operation of storage facilities to produce the multiple benefits for which they were designed are the Hudson River

Regulating District, which is an agency of the State of New York; the Tennessee Valley Authority, which administers the overall water utilization, control, and development program in the Tennessee River Basin; and the Boulder Canyon project of the U.S. Bureau of Reclamation.[38]

Multiple-purpose plans are recommended for stream development aimed at several important purposes, including direct or incidental power production, and these multiple-purpose plans should be designed and executed in terms of drainage basins, or major subbasins. The Federal government should have primary authority and responsibility for designing and executing these multiple-purpose drainage basin plans. Also, the design of the power system in any drainage basin development should include, in accordance with the best technology of power transmission, the best practicable interconnection (1) of the several plants within a basin system, (2) with neighboring basin systems within the reach of economic transmission, and (3) with the steam capacity built or acquired to balance capacity.[39]

DOMESTIC, MUNICIPAL, AND FOOD USES OF WATER

Use of water resources for domestic and municipal purposes and for transportation of waste are the highest uses to which water may be put. In the competition of uses, these two, in the order mentioned, should secure the water to the exclusion of the others if the supply is limited.

DOMESTIC AND MUNICIPAL WATER SUPPLIES

Water can command a higher price or justify a greater expense or cost of production for domestic and municipal consumption than for any other use. There is relatively little conflict over the utilization of water for these purposes, because of the small amount needed; and in most areas of the world, supplies are sufficient to meet these uses.

Practically every farm in the United States has its own well or pump, which is the source of its water supply, and in the urban areas, heavy outlays are made to develop safe and adequate municipal water supplies. The declining water table in the Great Plains states, the Southwest, and other areas in the United States associated with droughts, heavier consumption and demands accompanying settlement and agricultural uses of the soil,

---

[38] For an analysis of each of these three undertakings, see National Resources Committee, *Energy Resources and National Policy*, Government Printing Office, 1939, pp. 310–313.

[39] The British "grid" system is a network of interconnected transmission lines operated by the central electricity board and so planned that almost all the generating and distributing interests in the nation can effect a connection. The recommendation of the Energy Resources Committee for the best practicable interconnection of transmission lines is along the same channels as the British "grid" system. (See *ibid.*, pp. 279–280.)

and other conditions have created serious problems of providing adequate water supplies for human, livestock, and related needs.

In some cities the water supply system is operated by the city government itself, whereas in others a private corporation provides water. In any case, water for drinking and domestic purposes in cities is sold at a price that covers the costs of engineering enterprises which must be developed to pipe the water to the homes and to assure a safe and adequate supply. The problems associated with this use of water are largely engineering or technological ones, and are not primarily economic, there being in almost all cases an ample supply of water from one source or another to meet these needs if the proper construction and facilities can be provided at reasonable cost.

TRANSPORTATION OF WASTE

The second most important use of water is the transporting of human and industrial wastes away from human habitations. In many large urban areas, streams or water bodies constitute means of sewage disposal. In recent years, through experimentation and research, treatments have been devised to recover much of the waste materials in sewage; but most modern sewage treatment systems leave a large quantity of fluid which, although harmless, must be disposed of in natural drainage channels.

The problems associated with the use of water for transporting sewage and industrial wastes are primarily those of pollution, or of securing the proper engineering facilities and equipment to purify the sewage or wastes at reasonable costs. Frequently the utilization of streams for transporting sewage and industrial wastes so pollutes them that they cannot be used as sources of public water supplies or for the supporting of fish life or for recreational purposes.

Taxpayers often find it impossible to assume the expense of complete purification, in spite of the recommendations of state boards of health, sanitary engineers, and others urging the great importance of restrictive measures to prevent unnecessary pollution of streams. In small cities, or where the costs of other governmental services are high, or the average per capita income is relatively low, a compromise between theory and practice will usually be effected, whereby the expense of complete purification will not be incurred, but the cheaper means of waste disposal, such as dumping into a nearby stream, will be utilized, with all the possible dangers that such pollution incurs.

WATER FOR FOOD PRODUCTION

All bodies of water of any considerable size which have not been polluted or poisoned by sewage, mine drainage, or some form of industrial waste have some value as producers of fish for food. In recent years one of the most important efforts of conservationists has been to stress or encourage the increased use of such waters by preventing pollution and by stimulating fish culture. This use is also closely related to the recreational uses of water resources, because fishing is a very important sport or recreational activity in many areas. However, from the engineering and economic standpoint, the most important use of water in the production of food is irrigation and drainage.

The value of the total catch of fishery products in the United States and Alaska exceeds a hundred million dollars annually and in the canned or manufactured state the value of these products is much greater. Fishery products include clams, oysters, shrimps, crabs, sardines, salmon, cod, and fishes of all kinds. The oceans, bays, gulfs, Great Lakes, and many rivers and smaller streams produce in the aggregate a great variety of sea food, which has an important place in modern commerce.

NAVIGATION

The least important use of water is navigation. From the standpoint of law, however, navigation has a preferred position, being practically the only use recognized in the Constitution of the United States. In the early days, when the Constitution was being considered, about the only safe way of communication between the settlements in the Colonies was by water. In spite of modern more speedy and efficient methods of transportation by highways, railways, and skyways, water transportation still plays an important part in the trade and life of communities within nations and between nations.

EARLY NAVIGATION

Transportation by water has been a means of moving goods and people from place to place from time immemorial. The Egyptians, as early as 2000 B.C., were building vessels larger than those in which Columbus sailed to the New World. Rome depended so much upon wheat imports that the Empire subsidized the merchant marine.

For a long time navigation was largely a matter of utilizing water near shores, and navigation techniques were extremely crude, involving a considerable amount of guessing. A classic example is that of Columbus, who, in searching for a route to the East Indies, discovered America. Early navigation used sails, and when the wind failed, the galley system (human muscles). The wind was an important factor in determining transportation dates, ports, and routes. Arabian and Phoenician merchants kept close to the shore line all the way to Calcutta until they discovered the regularity of the monsoon winds, which would blow them directly across the Indian Ocean to the desired Malabar Coast in about half the days the shore route required.

Early navigation was slow. Seasonal winds required a certain amount of waiting, and the ships themselves were slow. Protection of sea lanes after the Egyptian period was only sporadic. On inland waters, tolls flourished and ports were largely natural. A fairly good canal system had been developed by the Egyptians near the present Suez Canal, and during the Middle Ages the Italians invented the lock system for canals.

FEDERAL LAND GRANTS FOR CANALS AND RIVER IMPROVEMENTS

Similar to its policy of granting lands in aid for wagon road and railroad construction were the Federal government's grants for canal and river improvements. On March 2, 1827, lands were granted to Indiana and Ohio for the construction of a canal on the Wabash River to Lake Erie; and from that time until 1866, nine other grants were made to various states for canal construction and improvement. In these 10 grants, a total of four and one-half million acres was granted.[40]

The federal government made four main grants for river improvements, Alabama being awarded land on May 22, 1828, Wisconsin in 1846, and Iowa in 1846 and 1862. River improvement grants totaled approximately two and one-quarter million acres.

OCEANIC NAVIGATION

Oceanic navigation is concerned with foreign commerce (exports and imports). This foreign commerce is handled largely through a few ports, the principal one New York City. The quantity handled is governed largely by depth and safety of the harbors, handling facilities, communications, and nearness to large centers of population and industry.

Ocean transportation is much less expensive than transportation on land, largely because the right of way on the ocean is usable in its natural state. There are no construction costs, no taxes, no maintenance or upkeep. In areas where the use of water for transportation necessitates certain expenditures such as surveying, dredging, and lighting, as in restricted bays, rivers, or canals, the expenses are much higher; but even under these conditions water transport is ordinarily much less expensive than land transport.

In addition to the fact that the ocean is a free highway, water transportation is cheaper because the capital invested in the carrier is less per ton of freight than in any form of land transportation. Terminal charges,

[40] These canal grants were made to the states of Indiana, Ohio, Illinois, Michigan, and Wisconsin, during the period 1827–1866, and totaled 4,597,678.22 acres, the largest grant being the first one (in 1827) for construction of the Wabash and Erie Canal to the state of Indiana, totaling 1,480,418.77 acres. (U.S. Department of Interior, *Transportation*, General Land Office, Information Bulletin 5, 1939 series, Government Printing Office, 1940, p. 4.)

labor, insurance, and power used per unit of freight volume and weight are also less.

GREAT LAKES TRANSPORTATION

The Great Lakes are the most important group of inland waterways in the world. They are international in character, since both Canada and the United States utilize them for transportation. The channels between the lakes were originally only a few feet in depth and could be navigated only by small vessels, but these channels have been increased in depth in recent years so that freighters of large capacity (some drawing as much as 25 feet of water) can be successfully operated. With development of the St. Lawrence-Great Lakes Waterway, it is possible that the Great Lakes may be used by ocean-going vessels.

Movement of freight on the Lakes is largely eastbound, and more than half of the total tonnage consists of iron ore from the Lake Superior region to Ohio ports where it is transshipped to Pittsburgh and other iron-manufacturing centers. Westbound freight consists largely of coal taken to the head of the Great Lakes for distribution to the interior. About four-fifths of the total ton mileage of freight carried on the inland waterways of the United States is transported over the Great Lakes.

The use of the Great Lakes for transportation has developed complications through competition of other uses for these waters. Increasing the depth of the connecting channels between the lakes reduces the height of the water and makes efficient transportation more difficult. The city of Chicago, which has been diverting upwards of 10,000 cubic feet per second from Lake Michigan and turning it into the headwaters of the Illinois River, has caused an additional permanent lowering of the lake level.

During years of extreme drought, the annual losses to shipping interests are said to be several hundred thousand dollars for every inch of decrease in height of water, so that reduction of the lake levels by such diversion is an important economic factor influencing the efficiency of the Great Lakes for transportation. These and other losses have resulted in controversies between Illinois and other states and in the prosecution of suits in the United States Supreme Court. The most important point established is that the United States has full jurisdiction over the use of waters of the Great Lakes by American interests, and may prevent the sanitary district of Chicago from diverting water. At the same time, Canada has set up claims of interference with its riparian rights and has brought pressure through diplomatic channels, bringing up important international as well as interstate relations.[41]

[41] For a more detailed analysis of Great Lakes transportation, see Newell, *op. cit.*, Part II.

COASTWISE TRANSPORTATION

The coastwise trade of any country that has a long coast line is of great importance. Coastwise traffic is slow, but so cheap compared with land routes that a nation that can take advantage of a large amount of coastwise traffic has an important economic advantage over one that cannot. The United States has long coast lines on two great oceans, in addition to a considerable coast line on the Gulf of Mexico, and its coastwise traffic is of tremendous importance not only in total volume of trade involved but in reducing rates on land transportation in many parts of the country.

The Panama Canal has made United States trade between the Atlantic and Pacific coasts so cheap that the transcontinental railroads have felt the competition keenly. The Interstate Commerce Commission has allowed the railroads to quote rates for a through haul from coast to coast lower than those for much shorter distances between inland points. The freight rate schedules for the United States resulting from the competition of low-cost coastwise water transportation, as has been noted earlier, is an important factor determining the location of industries and land utilization patterns for the nation as a whole.

INLAND WATERWAYS: RIVERS AND INLAND STREAMS

Transportation on inland waterways differs significantly from ocean transport or transportation on such large inland bodies of water as the Great Lakes. In the first place, the rights of way for inland waterways are often not "free." Most inland waterways require some dredging, straightening, and lighting before they can be used most effectively, and many require the construction of canals with locks and similar expensive equipment. However, in many cases these costs are not recovered through the freight charges, as is often the case with railroads or highways, but are borne by the government, thereby enabling inland waterway transportation rates to be comparatively low.

Transportation on inland waterways has several important disadvantages, compared with overland routes, which tend to offset their lower freight rates. In the first place, transportation on inland waterways is slower than most forms of land transportation, and many waterways are too small to admit large ships, so that the economy of power that is used in proportion to cargo is reduced. Moreover, the use of large ships on restricted inland waterways with narrow channels increases the danger of collision or grounding. But the outstanding handicap of inland waterways is that they are relatively fixed in direction, while overland routes are much more adaptable to changes in location of freight.[42]

[42] L. E. Klimm, O. P. Starkey, and N. F. Hall, *Introductory Economic Geography*, Harcourt, Brace, 1937, p. 275.

In spite of the limitations of inland waterways and the frequently appreciable costs involved in making them usable for transportation, they play or have played a rather important role in the opening up of new regions for land settlement and development in many areas. Small boats can frequently navigate unimproved waterways, if certain precautions are used, and this type of transportation in areas like the Amazon Valley, or the Mississippi Valley before the Civil War, is far cheaper than building roads or railroads. In this way, inland waterways play important parts, particularly in the pioneer stages of land settlement and development.

CANALS

In the United States over 4500 miles of canals were built, largely before the days of the railroads, and of these over half have been abandoned. Today, few canals are in active use, and even those which are being used, with the exception of the artificial waterways connecting the Great Lakes, and those which may form part of the great system of intercoastal passages are of doubtful economic importance, since the services they perform could be rendered by the railroads or by other means of transportation at possibly less cost.[43]

Some canals are icebound during the winter, and all are subject to unfavorable conditions of low water caused by drought, or dangerous water caused by floods. Few canals have been provided with proper freight terminals, and all are maintained at public expense, directly or indirectly. The most notable canal in the United States now in operation is the New York Barge Canal, built by the State of New York at a cost of some 170 million dollars. However, the tonnage carried on this canal is only a very small fraction of that carried on the New York Central Railroad, which approximately parallels it.

In the old days, when navigation had practically no competitor in transporting passengers and goods, it was the surest and often the quickest way of getting from place to place, and involved the least discomfort; but the revolution brought about by steam and the steam engine and the greater flexibility possible in reaching distant points by highways, railroads, and skyways has brought about a gradual abandonment of inland waterways in favor of these more modern transportation methods.

In order to utilize what might be cheap water transportation, however, it is necessary to have a highly developed system by which freight may be brought by rail or truck to the boat, and in turn removed from the boat and distributed by rail or truck throughout the city or nation. To do this requires coördination and coöperation between railroad and water carriers which, although theoretically possible, involves many practical difficulties.

[43] Newell, *op. cit.*, pp. 211–212.

Development and use of canals has been more extensive and effective in Europe than in the United States. The industries and centers of population in certain parts of Europe developed early in the delta country of the Rhine and the Rhone; and in such countries as Holland and Belgium, the navigation canals connecting the channels of the rivers with important cities have been built in part to control floods and drain the lowlands. Under these conditions, the development and use of canals for transportation have been most favorable. Moreover, the distances involved are not great, so the time factor plays a less important role than in the United States.

WATERWAYS IN AN OVERALL TRANSPORTATION PROGRAM

In an economical and efficient coördinated transportation system including railroads, motor transport, waterways, and airways, all forms of transportation should be considered as complementary rather than competitive with each other. The United States should continue to improve its inland and intracoastal waterways to standard depths as an important objective of comprehensive multiple-purpose basin programs.

Waterway charges should not be considered as yardsticks for railroad rates, but rather as rates for traffic which, in a coördinated transportation system, can move more economically by water than by rail. To assure the maximum overall contribution of the transportation system to the nation's welfare, railroads paralleling waterways should not be permitted to establish discriminatory rates.

User charges or tolls for all forms of transportation should be based on full costs. Under such conditions an interconnected system of modern waterways, coördinated with land transportation, should be able to sustain itself, yield returns on the public investment, and contribute to most economic use of the nation's resources.[44]

INTEGRATED DEVELOPMENT AND USE
OF WATER RESOURCES

The multiple uses made of water by man complicate the problem of allocating a scarce supply of water in many areas. But whatever the particular competitive water-use situation, there must be complete understanding and appreciation of the fundamental relationships of water and land, and the need for integrated development and use of water resources if maximum well-being is to be achieved.

INTERRELATIONSHIPS OF LAND AND WATER

Every square foot of land in a drainage basin plays a part in the water runoff that creates flood-control problems and affects the supply of water

44 Cf. *A Water Policy for the American People, op. cit.,* p. 217.

for economic use. This is the case whether the lands are part of the head-waters of the stream or drainage area, or whether they are part of a lower agricultural watershed. The way in which land is used, whether for crops, grazing, or forests, is important in determining the quantity, quality, and timeliness of water flow.

The problem of water control through land management in a drainage basin falls naturally into two geographic areas: (1) the *headwaters* portion of the basin consisting mainly of forest lands and grazing lands, and (2) the agricultural or lower portion of the watershed consisting mostly of cultivated croplands with some pasture and hay areas. Much, but by no means all, of the headwater lands of most major streams are in public ownership or subject to public supervision and control. Much of the forested parts of the upstream watersheds is under the general supervision of the U.S. Forest Service, especially in the western states, and much of the range areas is subject to supervision by the Soil Conservation Service and the Bureau of Land Management. The national forests of the 11 western states occupy but a fifth of the total land area of the West, but supply over half the total stream flow in these states.

UPSTREAM WATERSHED MANAGEMENT

It would appear that federal agencies are in a very strategic position to accomplish a sound pattern of use and management for upstream water-shed lands. Upstream watershed management differs very little from forest and range management, except in objectives. In the case of forest and range management the principal objectives are maximum sustained yields of highest quality timber and forage, while in the case of upstream water-shed management, the basic objective is production of maximum quantities of usable water. However, private owners have little incentive to follow recommended land-use practices on upstream watershed lands, because such practices yield little direct or immediate revenue to them and are largely beneficial to others downstream. Consequently, very strong and continuing educational and incentive programs are essential to achieve maximum coöperation of private owners and users in carrying out upper watershed management practices promulgated by the federal agencies most directly concerned.

Moreover, very sharp conflicts arise over the relative emphases to be put on timber production and livestock forage on the one hand, and adequate forest and range cover to prevent erosion and maintain water-shed values on the other. Obviously, the ideal is to strike a nice balance between these two conflicting objectives, which will give due consideration to the relative values of timber, grazing, and water yield. Sometimes the conflict becomes very difficult because a watershed may be so eroded and the cover so depleted that it becomes necessary to exclude all livestock until a satisfactory forage cover is reëstablished. In such situations much patience and an effective educational program are essential for satisfactory solutions.

Since the benefits of water yield are less direct and less apparent in many cases than returns to competing uses, there is a tendency to overlook or subordinate upstream watershed services to other uses, to the detriment of the public welfare. In the arid and semiarid West, where water is the strategic and limiting factor in the economy, the public interest in watershed services is especially pronounced.

DOWNSTREAM WATERSHED MANAGEMENT

In contrast to upstream watershed areas, downstream watershed lands are held by numerous independent farm and ranch operators. As a rule, the further downstream the more the watershed lands are cultivated for production of crops. Agriculture in many areas is practiced in such ways as to decrease appreciably the ability of the land to absorb precipitation. The result is an increase in runoff, serious erosion and soil fertility losses, and damaging floods (see Figure 31).

The use of agricultural lands in ways that will provide adequate water control is not easy to achieve. The number of land users that must be dealt with is usually considerably larger than that in upstream watershed areas. Moreover, farmers are dependent on their operating units to secure a living for themselves and their families. Yet some very effective soil conservation devices or techniques are quite simple and inexpensive to utilize. For example, contour furrowing does not require great financial subsidies, major amounts of government assistance, or large capital investment.

The educational and demonstrational efforts of the Agricultural Extension Service and the Soil Conservation Service and the incentive payments of the Agricultural Conservation Program Service of the U.S. Department of Agriculture have resulted in much progress in recent years in achieving more adequate soil conservation and sound agricultural land-use practices. Much yet remains to be done, however, and especially in low-income or one-crop farming areas.

THE NEED FOR COÖRDINATED ACTION

Rivers and major drainage areas do not follow man-made political boundaries, such as counties or states. The problems involved in proper use of the lands and waters of a river basin are ordinarily interstate in character. The same is true of the benefits to be derived from such proper use. If maximum benefits are to be realized, it is obvious, therefore, that the development and use programs devised for such drainage areas must represent the coördinated efforts of local, state, and federal agencies, and private users and citizens.

The delegation of power to Congress by the Constitution to regulate commerce has placed the Federal government in a powerful position in water resources development. In exercising the commerce power, Congress has jurisdiction over all navigable waters, and the courts have taken a broad view of the determination of navigability. In addition, the commerce power of Congress includes flood protection and watershed development.

The federal government has in recent years played a major role in the development, utilization, and conservation of water resources, and undoubtedly will continue to do so in the future. Federal responsibility has been expressed in many statutes, passed at different times, devoted to separate phases of development, and administered by separate agencies.[45] In earlier years, a fragmentary approach was sufficient for construction of small, single-purpose projects. But in recent years, as the magnitude of river structures increased, the potentiality of their use for many integrated uses has become apparent, and there has been a growing awareness of the need for comprehensive development. This has been reflected gradually in changes in law and administrative practice.

Steps have been taken to allocate primary responsibility for each of the functions served by any reservoir project among the agencies traditionally responsible for various functions, regardless of which was the constructing agency. Congress has declared its policy to facilitate the consideration of projects on a basis of comprehensive and coördinated development. Certain requirements have been imposed for interagency consultation in planning. But no provision has been made for reconciling conflicts in agency recommendations; nor has provision been made for eliminating interagency duplication in undertaking basin surveys.[46]

Comprehensive development necessarily affects both federal and state activities. Congress has recognized this and has repeatedly declared its policy to recognize the rights and interests of the states in the development of water resources. Federal agencies are instructed to coöperate with or work through state agencies in administering many of their responsibilities, especially in agricultural and land-use activities, forest practices, and power distribution. Nevertheless, results achieved in many instances fall far short of what is possible with complete coördination of action by all interested local, state, and federal agencies, and private owners, users, and citizens.

[45] *Ibid.,* p. 295.
[46] *Ibid.,* p. 297.

Figure 31. Wind and Water Erosion. Serious soil losses are caused by wind and water erosion. The upper picture shows wind erosion in the Northern Plains, and the lower picture shows small gullies and sheet erosion in fallowed land, formed after a single heavy half-hour rain. (Soil Conservation Service photo.)

THE RIVER BASIN APPROACH

A river basin is an entity and the river is its common denominator. The river basin consists of all the land that drains to the river. It includes all the resources of that drainage area up and back to where the divide breaks over and down into another drainage basin. The term *watershed* is frequently used synonymously with *river basin* or *drainage basin*, but most often it refers to smaller drainage areas within a major river basin. The river is a product of its drainage area, and it is on the drainage area or basin that people live and work. The river and the drainage area go together, as a unit, to comprise the natural resources of the region.

Few would not agree that we should have some form of organization for basin-wide planning and for unification of programs in the development of land and water resources of the main river basins or drainage areas. But there is a wide difference of opinion as to the precise form the organization should take. The *valley authority* or federally created public corporate entity is one form. This form is now in operation in the Tennessee Valley.

Another form is a federal-state *basin interagency committee,* consisting of representatives of the area involved and the federal bureaus most concerned in the development program. The Missouri Basin Interagency Committee has been organized to help coördinate the program for these federal agencies in their Missouri Valley program.

Still another form of river basin organization is the planning and programming that grows out of *interstate compacts* for development and use of the water and power of a major river. The Colorado River Compact defines the functions of federal agencies in the management of reservoirs constructed under provisions of federal and state legislation growing out of the compact.[47]

Another possible form of river basin organization might be creation of a *federal-state commission or board* with full authority to coördinate the functions, within its territorial jurisdiction, of all federal agencies in so far as they relate to resource development. All federal agencies would be *authorized* and *directed* to comply with all coördination requirements that the Commission might prescribe.[48]

There are 14 major river basins or drainage areas in the United States (see Figure 32, facing p. 540). Some are very large, such as the Missouri River Basin, which is 1300 miles long and 700 miles wide. In some cases it

[47] Saunderson, *op. cit.,* p. 194.
[48] For details of this proposed river basin organization, see *Draft Bill Entitled Water Resources Act of 1951, submitted to the President in February, 1951, designed to carry out principal recommendations of the President's Water Resources Policy Commission Report, sent to Congress by President Truman, January 19, 1953,* The Public Affairs Institute, Washington, D.C., May, 1955.

may be desirable to subdivide some river basins for development purposes. In others, several may be found to constitute together areas of common regional interest for which water and land resources programs may be coördinated.[49] The President's Water Resources Policy Commission recommended that there be not more than 15 river basin commissions to plan and coördinate all federal participation in resource development within the 48 states.[50] But, regardless of these variations, the river basin provides the natural unit for planning, programming, and developing the water and land resources of the nation.

REFERENCES FOR FURTHER READING

Ackerman, Edward A., "Questions for Designers of Future Water Policy," *Journal of Farm Economics,* Vol. XXXVIII, No. 4, November, 1956, pp. 971–980.

Carbut, Arthur H., *Water or Your Life,* J. B. Lippincott Company, Philadelphia, 1951.

Ciriacy-Wantrup, S. V., "Benefit Cost Analysis and Public Resource Development," *Journal of Farm Economics,* Vol. XXXVII, No. 4, November, 1955, pp. 676–689.

Ely, Richard T., and Wehrwein, George S., *Land Economics,* The Macmillan Company, New York, 1940, Chap. XI.

Hartley, Robert W., *Land and Water Conservation and Development,* The Brookings Institution, Washington, D.C., Reprint No. 7, August, 1955.

Hibbard, B. H., *A History of the Public Land Policies,* The Macmillan Company, New York, 1924, Chap. XIV.

Huffman, Roy E., *Irrigation Development and Public Water Policy,* The Ronald Press Company, New York, 1953, Chaps. V, X, and XIV.

Klimm, L. E., Starkey, O. P., and Hall, N. F., *Introductory Economic Geography,* Harcourt, Brace and Company, Inc., New York, 1937, Chaps. XXIX and XXX.

Mead, Elwood, *Irrigation Institutions,* The Macmillan Company, New York, 1903, Chaps. IV, XIII, and XIV.

Moreell, Ben, *Our Nation's Water Resources—Policies and Politics,* University of Chicago, 1956, pp. 13–188.

National Resources Committee, *Energy Resources and National Policy,* Government Printing Office, Washington, D.C., 1939, Section 2, Part III; Section 3, Part I.

Parkins, A. E., and Whitaker, J. R. (eds.), *Our National Resources and Their Conservation,* John Wiley & Sons, Inc., New York, 1936, Chaps. IV, VI, VIII, and XIII.

President's Water Resources Policy Commission, *A Water Policy for the American People,* Government Printing Office, Washington, D.C., 1950, Vol. I, Chaps. I, VII, and IX–XV.

President's Water Resources Policy Commission, *Ten Rivers in America's Future,* Government Printing Office, Washington, D.C., 1950, Vol. II.

[49] President's Water Resources Policy Commission, *Ten Rivers in America's Future,* Government Printing Office, Vol. II, p. 17.

[50] *Draft Bill Entitled Water Resources Act of 1951,* p. 4.

Saunderson, Mont H., *Western Land and Water Use,* University of Oklahoma Press, Norman, 1950, Chaps. VIII, IX and X.

Steele, Harry A., and Regan, Mark M., "Organization and Administrative Arrangements for an Effective Water Policy," *Journal of Farm Economics,* Vol. XXXVII, No. 5, December, 1955, pp. 886–896.

Stegner, Wallace, *Beyond the Hundredth Meridian,* Houghton Mifflin Company, Boston, 1953, Parts II, III, V and VI.

Teele, R. P., *The Economics of Land Reclamation in the United States,* A. W. Shaw Company, Chicago, 1927, Chaps. II–VI.

Thomas, George, *The Development of Institutions Under Irrigation,* The Macmillan Company, New York, 1920, Chaps. XIV, XV, and XVI.

Timmons, John F., and Murray, William G. (eds.), *Land Problems and Policies,* Iowa State College Press, Ames, 1950, Chap. VIII.

U.S. Department of Agriculture, *Yearbook of Agriculture, 1955: Water,* Government Printing Office, Washington, D.C., pp. 161–340, and 478–576.

Van Hise, C. R., and Havemeyer, L. H. (eds.), *Conservation of Our Natural Resources,* The Macmillan Company, New York, 1931, Part III.

Widstoe, J. A., *Success on Irrigation Projects,* John Wiley & Sons, Inc., New York, 1928, Chaps. I, V, VI, and IX.

Zimmermann, Erich W., *World Resources and Industries,* rev. ed., Harper & Brothers, New York, 1951, Chap. XXXVI.

part **VI**

IMPROVEMENT OF
LAND USE

LAND USE PLANNING
LAND REFORM

chapter **22**

LAND USE PLANNING

THE PLANNING PROCESS

The Nature of Planning—Social vs. Individual Planning —Goals of Planning—Methods of Planning—Problems of Planning

CONDITIONS ESSENTIAL FOR SUCCESSFUL PLANNING

Basic Requirements for Successful Planning—Attitudes That Should Be Changed

LINES OF PUBLIC ACTION

Lines of Federal Action—Lines of State Action—Lines of Local Governmental Action

LINES OF PRIVATE ACTION

Individual Action—Coöperative Effort—Corporate Action

THE PROBLEM OF COÖRDINATION

Methods by Which Effective Coördination Can Be Achieved—Coördination of Research and Education— Integration of Plans

THE EXPLOITATION and waste of natural resources (particularly mineral, forest, and certain agricultural lands) that has occurred through private appropriation in the United States reflects the trend of rapid resource development accompanying advancing technology and commercialized production typical of the times. Private property lent itself to such exploitation because it gave much freedom to the large number of individuals with property rights in land resources.

The rapid rate of development and utilization has permitted a higher material level of living for the present generation than a system of public ownership would have allowed. Under public ownership, land would have been withheld from use, or the rate of development and use would have been restricted to immediate needs rather than determined by prospective, often speculative, demands developed by profit-seeking private interest; nevertheless, most Americans would probably agree that in spite of mistakes made in utilizing land resources through private ownership, its advantages have more than offset its disadvantages except possibly in timber and minerals.

Consequently, the best program to follow is to restrict or control private practices instead of removing land resources completely from private hands. In other words, continuance of private property in land is generally approved with the understanding that the dwindling of many basic land resources and the complexities of modern life necessitate an increasing degree of social control and regulation to prevent excessive abuses or wastes.

It is generally conceded that some systematic plan or policy guiding resource utilization in the interests of the general welfare could have prevented many of the social wastes and losses of unrestricted exploitation. Far-reaching recent economic and social changes have shaken the very foundations of civilization and have centered attention upon planning use of land resources to prevent the dangerous consequences of unplanned exploitation.[1] The harnessing of nuclear energy in the form of the atomic bomb during the latter part of World War II and rapid strides in peacetime adaptations of such energy since the war, presages great technological changes ahead, with corresponding far-reaching impacts upon the economy and the social and institutional structure.

THE PLANNING PROCESS

The practical justification for the study of land economics is a belief in the possibility of improving the quality of human living through changing the organization of want-satisfying activity in land resource utilization. Most attempts to improve human living involve substituting for private property and individual freedom of contract a more consciously social form of control. Such attempts will have more chance to produce significant improvements if the character and tendencies of the system to be modified or controlled in the interests of the general welfare are clearly understood.

The degree of social unity necessary to achieve the highest possible level of living can best be brought about by organizing the economy so

[1] According to Galloway, we are living at the end of an epoch, and "if the nineteenth century was the Age of Planlessness, the twentieth century is certainly the Plan Age." (George B. Galloway, et al., Planning for America, Holt, 1941, pp. 3–4.) See also Lewis L. Lorwin, Time for Planning, Harper, 1945, Chap. I.

as to make the fullest use of productive capacity, and prudently conserve, develop, and utilize its material and human resources. This necessitates a plan to guide all segments of the economy toward the desired goal. The first problem, therefore, is to formulate a policy and plans; the second, to effect them by means of those instruments of social control best adapted to the situation.

THE NATURE OF PLANNING

The word "planning" is used in many ways, and means different things to different people. Generally speaking, however, planning is a conscious effort to direct human energy to secure a rationally desirable end. Every plan has two major elements—a goal and a method.[2] Planning is the opposite of improvising. In simple terms, it is organized foresight plus corrective hindsight.[3]

The concept of planning is nothing new. Each individual businessman —farmer, banker, industrialist, or whatever he may be—plans operations on the basis of future expectations and past experience. As long as men are confronted with problems, a certain amount of planning will be done; but planning in the past has not been complete or coördinated enough to bring about balance and unity within the whole economy.

In a well-planned economy, responsibility for production organization is centralized; but individual planning is decentralized, the spontaneous decisions of private citizens being assumed to serve in the aggregate the general welfare. But as one writer has put it, "The evident failure of individual planning in recent years to promote the public good is leading the visible hand of the State to replace the 'invisible' hand of Adam Smith." [4]

SOCIAL VS. INDIVIDUAL PLANNING

The history of the United States affords examples of special-interest or pressure group planning for labor, agriculture, or industry, but little of overall social planning in the interests of the whole nation. Individual or group-interest plans have often advanced selfish interests, to the detriment of the general welfare. Furthermore, when the automatic self-regulating mechanism of the market place fails in its traditional function of harmonizing and synchronizing the various individual plans of men, a social plan or overall blueprint is necessary as a coördinating or synchronizing agent. The question is not a matter of *whether* to plan, but of *how* to plan.

[2] Lorwin, *op. cit.*, p. 5.
[3] Galloway, *op. cit.*, p. 5.
[4] *Ibid.*, p. 6.

Social planning may be distinguished from individual planning, and plans designed to protect or promote group or sectional interests, by six essential characteristics: [5] (1) Social planning is concerned with dynamic things and deals with change and variability. (2) It is continuous and flexible rather than occasional and intermittent. (3) It is a function of collective activity, achieving a collective objective or solving collective problems. (4) It relies upon research and experiment, rather than guess-work. (5) It is concerned with coördinating specialized activities. (6) It is a specialized service function requiring the temperament and analytical powers for fact-finding, logical synthesis, and perfection of arrangements to achieve its objective.

Planning, conceived of as a process, can be said to embrace the following steps: [6] (1) determination of the objectives sought; (2) research leading to an understanding of the problem; (3) discovery of alternate solutions; (4) choice of alternatives (including the frequent choice of doing nothing), or what may be termed "policymaking"; (5) detailed execution of a chosen alternative which may be referred to either as the "blueprint" or the "design."

Many people feel that planning tends toward regimentation, with rigid rules compelling individuals to conform; but they forget that compulsion exists whether operations are planned or unplanned, because chance compels conformity in line with certain events even if there is no planning. It has been argued that, on the whole, planning probably reduces regimentation by eliminating some of the uncertainty and inhibiting force of chance in a situation.[7]

GOALS OF PLANNING

A planned economy without definite social goals is a contradiction in terms, for "it must lead to a series of concrete destinations, expressed economically as a standard of living, and morally and socially as a way of life.[8] Planning is nothing more, in the last analysis, than collectivism applied to the major processes of the economic system. It may be used by any society, and may be partial or complete, restrictive or expansive,

---

[5] Harlow S. Person (ed.), *Scientific Management and American Industry*, Harper, 1929.

[6] Galloway, *op. cit.*, p. 6.

[7] Cf. *ibid.*, p. 7. This same thought is expressed by many other students of social planning.

[8] Lewis Mumford, "Forward" in Findlay MacKenzie (ed.), *Planned Society Yesterday, Today, and Tomorrow*, Prentice-Hall, 1937, p. ix. Mumford points out that, without definite social goals, industrial production will expand in one direction if the social aim is exploitation and conquest of other people, and in other directions if the aim is new housing and new communities for the population as a whole. Even competitive industry attempts to fix standards, in terms of goods, which will produce the maximum opportunity for profit.

democratic or authoritarian, militaristic or pacifist, and so on, depending entirely upon the aims of society.[9]

The goals of planning, then, vary with the type of planning and the agency undertaking it. In general, the aim of planning in a democratic nation is to promote a progressive rise in material and cultural levels of living for all the people, through reasonably full use of the nation's productive resources. Full, balanced, and efficient use of resources has been called "optimum use of resources." [10]

According to the classical economists, the free play of competitive forces would automatically harmonize private plans and the optimum use of resources. The fact that this harmonizing did not occur, however, has resulted in the modern planning movement designed to implement plans of private enterprise and supplement them, if necessary, by public activity.[11]

Supplementing private enterprise by public activity, however, implies an expansion of governmental activity in modern economies. The part that technicians and public officials will be called upon to play as guides and advisers in a constantly changing social order should not be underestimated, but it should be realized that all they can do is to provide society with a choice of certain alternatives or routes. Society itself must make the ultimate decisions.[12] The role of governmental agencies, therefore, is one of coördinating various conflicting interests and attempting to secure effective coöperation among groups by agreement upon certain fundamental goals.[13]

[9] Max Lerner, *It Is Later Than You Think,* Viking, 1938, Chap. VI. Galloway points out that planning employed by great corporations is apt to be oligarchic, partial, and restrictive; by totalitarian states, dictatorial, militaristic, and authoritarian; while planning employed by democratic societies operates by democratic procedures toward social objectives set by representative bodies. (Galloway, *op. cit.,* p. 8.)

[10] "If a country were using its resources to the optimum, there would be no unemployment of men or machines except the minimum unemployment necessitated by seasonal production, transfer from one activity to another, and similar causes. The resources going into different uses would be in balance with each other and in relation to consumers' wants . . . and, finally, in doing any particular job, the minimum amount of resources, would be used or consumed consistent with the job to be done. Thus, effective use of resources could be said to consist of full, balanced, and efficient use. . . ." (Gardner C. Means, "Basic Structural Characteristics and the Problem of Full Employment," in National Resources Planning Board, *Structure of the American Economy,* Part II, June, 1940, p. 4.)

[11] Cf. Galloway, *op. cit.,* p. 9.

[12] MacKenzie, *op. cit.,* p. 16.

[13] Many writers point out that the difficulty of agreeing upon the really fundamental goals may not be as difficult as it appears. "The exciting, the exalting, idea in our minds is that there are very considerable possibilities of knowing better and more precisely, and of bringing together into more effective coöperation a great multitude of aims in life that are at present, merely through lack of lucidity, divergent and conflicting." (H. G. Wells. "What All Men Seek," Part I of "The Anatomy of Frustration," *Harper's Magazine,* April, 1936, p. 499.)

METHODS OF PLANNING

Naturally, methods used in planning vary with type of planning, scope of the geographic, social, or economic area involved, objectives sought, agency of government to be the main coördinating or initiating agency, culture of the people involved, and related factors. *Laissez faire* and planning may be found side by side in modern economies. The American economy is a heterogeneous mixture of large and small private enterprise, public and private competition, coöperation, and government ownership; but the basic mechanism relied upon to coördinate the entire economy is market price, increasingly modified by private administration, restrictions and controls used by monopolistic business units, government intervention, and some collective ownership.

The numerous techniques used to effect social planning include zoning, excess condemnation, public purchases, quarantine, taxation, eminent domain, soil conservation, and others. City and regional planners have developed techniques of land use, zoning, traffic control, building codes, land subdivision, and highway development (see Figure 33). Land conservationists have devised methods of soil conservation, sustained-yield management of forest lands, development and effective utilization of water, grazing control and management, and proration and unit operation of petroleum fields.

PROBLEMS OF PLANNING

Social planning involves all the problems—political, economic, social, psychological, technical, and legal—of human relations in modern industrial societies. Some of the more important political problems include (1) securing capable, intelligent, and efficient government personnel through use of Civil Service or merit selection, rather than popular vote; (2) obtaining coöperation of local, state, and federal administrative officials in planning effectuation over areas involving more than one political unit; (3) obtaining legislative and judicial coöperation; (4) overcoming inertia or lack of interest among citizens and securing coöperation in the routine of administration; (5) securing public support in the form of funds and official interest to execute the planning program properly; (6) counteracting misuse of democratic rights by holders of key positions who may be working chiefly for private gain or advancement; and (7) administrative management of the increasingly difficult functions imposed upon the modern national unit.[14]

The major economic problem in social planning is to organize resource utilization and production and distribution to obtain a smoothly operating economy, yielding the highest levels of living possible with modern

[14] Galloway lists problems, 1, 3, 4, 6, and 7. (Galloway, *op. cit.*, pp. 34–35.)

Figure 32. Major Drainage Basins of the United States. (Source: U.S. Department of Agriculture, Guide to Agriculture, U. S. A., Agriculture Informaton Bulletin, No. 30, U.S. Government Printing Office, Washington, D.C., revised September, 1955, inside cover page.)

Figure 33. Aerial View of Nahalal, Israel, Showing Concentric Circles of Land Use. (Courtesy, Mrs. Dvora Elon, Tel Aviv, Israel.)

science and technology. Waste of resources because of ruthless exploitation, idle men and machines, and failure to use the most effective available technology is estimated to have caused the loss of 200 billion dollars' worth of goods and services during the depression thirties.[15]

People must be taught to think in terms of working together, and more coördinated and desirable use of resources must be developed to prevent wastes of unemployment, depression, war, and exploitative practices. Such modifications in the culture of a people which has thought, acted, and lived for generations under a philosophy of rugged individualism is not simple, but is essential to a sound land-use planning program.[16]

CONDITIONS ESSENTIAL FOR SUCCESSFUL PLANNING

The success of planning efforts will be conditioned by numerous social, legal, psychological, economic, and technical forces. In many cases, statutes must be changed by new legislation, and some constitutional provisions must be modified if best use of resources is to be secured. A program that would be most effective now in one region of the nation might not be most effective at another time in the same region or at the same time in another region. However, certain basic requirements must be met by any planning program that is to be successful in the United States.

BASIC REQUIREMENTS FOR SUCCESSFUL PLANNING

An effective planning program must meet the following requirements: (1) It must be *economically sound*. In the confused state of contemporary economic thinking, it is not easy to determine just what may be economically sound or unsound, and only one thing is certain—that many concepts of classical economics need to be modified if they are to be useful under modern conditions. Keeping the objective clearly in mind may be the most important single factor helping to determine the economic soundness of any given plan. (2) It must be *administratively workable*. (3) It must be *politically acceptable* to public opinion—a very important requirement in

[15] National Resources Planning Board, *Structure of the American Economy*, Part I, "Basic Characteristics," June, 1939, p. 2.

[16] Galloway lists several factors conditioning the kind of planning undertaken or advocated—the scheme of institutions and habitual modes of thought, the propensity to identify the common welfare with the interests of groups to which one happens to belong, and ideals which are the "frames of reference." There are three such frames of reference in modern thought—the *competitive*, the *coöperative*, and the *collectivist*. Galloway points out that the competitive has been traditionally dominant, both ideologically and empirically, but that the material conditions that gave birth to this body of thought are rapidly passing. The coöperative ideal is now a powerful factor affecting thought and land utilization practices in many countries; but, according to Galloway, collectivisim appears to be the "wave of the future" because, in one form or another, it is coming to dominate government and economy in the western world. (Galloway, *op. cit.*, pp. 37–40.)

a democracy. (4) It must be *constitutional* in the eyes of the Supreme Court. (5) It must be *compatible with the American tradition and democratic principles,* and take account of geographic, political, cultural, and economic differences among various regions. (6) It must also be *capable of being symbolized and dramatized* so as to evoke more willing coöperation on the part of labor, agriculture, business, and government interests.[17]

The psychological and social difficulties involved in cultural changes necessary to insure effective planning are numerous and varied. Essentially, they involve a change of mental attitude—establishment of a philosophy of planning instead of a philosophy of "rugged individualism" or competitive exploitation. In most cases, technical problems involved are insignificant in comparison.

ATTITUDES THAT SHOULD BE CHANGED

Destructive land utilization practices can be corrected only by changes in the attitudes of land users, since practices are the outward expressions of controlling attitudes of mind. Many of these attitudes are deep-seated, and some have been prevalent for many generations. In the course of time, however, these mental patterns tend to crystallize, and fail to take account of new conditions. Frequently they become so inflexible that desirable or necessary adjustments are prevented. Consequently, if land utilization practices are discovered to be ill adapted to the basic physical conditions, a satisfactory solution must include revision of some of the traditional ways of thinking as well as the encouragement of better land-use practices.

The desires for security, stability, higher levels of living, and more opportunity for leisure, self-expression, and creative work are universal.[18] Methods of attaining these objectives must be continually revised with the economic and social changes caused by technical, physical, institutional, and social forces. The increasing tempo of economic life characteristic of modern machine technology has made these changes particularly numerous and far-reaching in recent years, and many attitudes hindering necessary adjustments in land utilization must be revised before land-resource planning can be fully effective. Some of these attitudes are listed below.

1. *That free competition accomplishes the necessary coördination of economic activities for various groups in society, and that planning is therefore unnecessary.* Under the assumptions of the traditional free market system, it is held that automatic forces promote increased productivity

[17] For a more detailed analysis of these requirements, see *ibid.*, pp. 44 ff.
[18] Cf. Great Plains Committee, *The Future of the Great Plains,* Government Printing Office, December, 1936, p. 63.

and interchange of goods among groups in society, so that the greatest possible gains for all the people result. As demand declines, prices are reduced until demand is restored, and the volume of production and exchange remains substantially the same.

We have noted, however, that free price competition no longer functions automatically in many segments of the economy, and that agriculture, for instance, is handicapped because it cannot establish the price-fixing or price-determination conditions characteristic of many other types of modern industry. The flexible price system of agriculture and the relatively inflexible or "sticky" price structure of industry promote exploitation of raw materials (particularly of agricultural lands) and restrict industrial output. The result is great disparities between prices of raw and finished products.

Thus, effective planning in the form of price control and output restrictions by certain industrial groups necessitates effective overall planning to secure more equal economic advantages for other groups where such planning through individual action is impossible. For example, the prosperity of agriculture depends partly upon adjusting agricultural output and partly upon adjusting industrial prices. To assume that free competition automatically accomplishes the necessary coördination is naïve. The fact that free competition no longer exists is in itself evidence that democratic overall planning is necessary for the general welfare.

2. *That what is good for the individual is good for society.* Classical economic doctrine held that society is merely the sum total of the individuals within it; that if each individual is allowed to pursue his own interests freely, he will naturally pursue those activities that will bring him the most returns or satisfactions; and that, since society is merely a sum total of individuals, the greatest social wealth possible will thus be achieved. Recent decades show that this does not hold true in actual practice. In the first place, society is more than the sum total of its individual parts; and the second, an individual pursuing his own particular interests may interfere with the efforts of others to pursue their interests. When these individual interests conflict, some agency must reduce conflict and friction to a minimum so that all may satisfy their wants within certain limits, instead of permitting a few (to the exclusion of many others) to pursue their efforts toward achieving the greatest potential satisfactions.

3. *That any public or group planning action is "dictatorship," "socialism," or "regimentation," and the antithesis of democratic living.* Many feel that the proper role of government is that of agent, arbitrator, or "reasonable umpire" for the different groups in society, and that government umpiring is quite a different proposition from national economic

planning.[19] The increased specialization of knowledge characteristic of the extended application of scientific methods is to improve man's life instead of bringing about serious maladjustments and chaos.[20] Planning of the right type—that is, democratic planning, as opposed to authoritarian planning—is the one effective means of preventing dictatorship. It is class or special-interest group planning that brings about dictatorship. Overall planning essential for democracies is implied in the kind of planning required for social control of land utilization.

4. *That public expenditures or public activity cannot be as efficient or desirable as private spending and private activity.* Nothing about private spending, per se, makes it better than public spending; the efficiency and desirability of public activity depend entirely upon institutional arrangements, quality of personnel, and type of work undertaken. If planning is to be effective in the future, particularly in periods when economic activity stagnates and unemployment and depression occur, there must be no deep-seated prejudices against governmental public works and employment-stabilization activities if they are aimed at the prevention of chaos and economic disintegration.

5. *That the owner may do with his property as he desires.* Ownership carries with it definite duties or obligations, as well as rights or privileges. One of the duties of ownership is that property be utilized in ways not harmful to the rights of others; and unless this rule is followed, the owner's property may be taken from him, or his rights in it definitely restricted. Ownership should not confer an unlimited right to exploit, to waste, or to spoil; it is merely tenure at the pleasure of society, depending upon good behavior.[21]

6. *That habitual practices are best.* There is a natural tendency for most people to be conservative, to follow customary practices that have proved satisfactory, to fear novelty and cling to the old or the familiar. In other words, there is a tendency to endure known evils rather than

[19] Cf. Galloway, *op. cit.*, pp. 68–69.

[20] According to Dewey, the idea of a preëstablished harmony between the existing "capitalistic regime" and democracy "is as absurd a piece of metaphysical speculation as human history has ever evolved." (See Dewey, *Freedom and Culture*, 1939, p. 72.) Ortega y Gasset points out the grave dangers of specialization resulting from extensive application of scientific method in *Revolt of the Masses* (tr. from the Spanish), Norton, 1932.

[21] For a more detailed treatment of the question of whether the rights of property carry with them the right to waste, see A. A. Bruce, *Property and Society*, McClurg, 1916 (particularly Chap. V, "The Doctrine of Public Necessity vs. The Principle of Feudal Relationship," and Chap. VI, "The Right to Waste"). Under the social theory of property, society has the right to insist upon beneficial use, and beneficial use implies not only prevention of destruction or harm to the property of others, but of waste destructive to one's own self or one's own property. The right to suicide has never been acknowledged, for instance, on the grounds that society, not the individual himself, is the one to decide whether the loss of a given human life is harmful to it.

risk the consequences of a change. "Be not the first by whom the new is tried nor yet the last to lay the old aside," may be good advice, but it is extremely difficult to get society to assume a reasonable middle ground. Allegiance to the general principle, "Habitual practices are best," creates a serious social lag in effecting desirable and necessary adjustments.

7. *That professional planners or "experts" are highly impractical.* Universal education, extensive specialization, science and technology, and a democratic form of government create a general tendency to distrust "experts." Each individual who has mastered some limited field of knowledge feels free to criticize the fields of others, with the result that distrust of specialists or highly trained "experts" is apt to be general.[22] Under such conditions, allegiance to an overall plan is difficult to secure.

8. *That man conquers nature.* The term "rugged individualism" has often been referred to with considerable reverence, on the grounds that it represents the self-help, aggressive, individual initiative that has developed a great nation of free men. However, rugged individualism, strictly speaking, means ruthless exploitation of natural resources. In a pioneer settlement, it is logical to assume that nature is something to be conquered if man is to survive. However, ". . . civilization is not . . . the enslavement of a stable and constant earth. It is a state of mutual interdependent coöperation between human animals, other animals, plants, and the soil, which may be disrupted at any moment by the failure of any of them." [23] The concept that man can conquer nature will not lead to relationships that are as harmonious and satisfactory as those developing from a concept of coöperation with nature based on mutual dependence.

9. *That the individual must make his own adjustments.* In the settlement of the United States, a man who failed in one occupation or became dissatisfied with his status in a given locality could move to a new area and begin over again. Migrating and beginning again were comparatively simple, because readily available free land resources were

---

[22] For a very interesting analysis of this problem the student is referred to Jose Ortega y Gasset's *The Revolt of the Masses, op. cit.* Gasset indicates that development of scientific method and more specialization of knowledge have made it increasingly easy for an ordinary individual to master a given segment of knowledge. By so mastering this small segment, he develops the illusion that he is a true scientist or scholar and competent to appraise or pass judgment on other fields of knowledge. In earlier times, when knowledge was not broken down into such small fields, a scholar had to master a great body of knowledge cutting across various fields. The fact that an ordinary individual now usually masters a given specialized field, combined with democratic forms of government, has, according to Gasset, developed the "mass man" or "mass mind," which is an extremely dangerous force in modern society. See also Harold J. Laski, "The Limitations of the Expert," *Harper's Magazine,* December, 1930, pp. 101–110.

[23] Aldo Leopold, "The Conservation Ethic," *Journal of Forestry,* Vol. XXXI, No. 6, October, 1933, p. 635.

abundant.[24] Such a situation no longer exists, and the individual who suffers reverses or misfortune is now, for the most part, permanently handicapped.

Obviously, the only alternative is for the community, the state, and the nation to coöperate in controlling the conditions that bring about such calamities, so that they will be eliminated or at least substantially reduced, and so that, where they do occur, these larger bodies will stand ready to assist in rehabilitating and reëstablishing the individual. Widespread calamities occurring with little warning, and affecting thousands or millions of families at once, have necessitated a great expansion of community, state, and national activities and programs since 1930, and have caused much fear that such increased governmental activities will completely destroy self-interest and individual initiative. However, over a longer period of time society should be able to adjust so that individual initiative and public help and support can work harmoniously to bring about a more balanced, stable society.

LINES OF PUBLIC ACTION

In order that the use of land resources can be controlled in the interests of the general welfare, full coöperation of private and public agencies is necessary. Each level of government—federal, state, and local—as well as private individual, corporate, and coöperative action, has a particular sphere of operations in which it can effectively further the necessary social control of land use. It is not a question of one agency rather than another agency, or of public versus private agencies, but of securing the joint coöperative effort of all.

Public land-use control may take an almost endless variety of forms, and may serve a great variety of purposes. It is generally conceded, however, that adjustments between individual and social rights must be attained without the discouragement or destruction of private initiative. Some of the older European nations have attempted to develop an optimum of individual freedom combined with social control, on the grounds that public ownership or operation means political instead of economic control of production, and that, while the process of reconciling private control with social control is tedious and time-absorbing, it is desirable, in the last analysis.[25]

[24] The same concept is implied in the phrase that the western lands were "a landing net for the unemployed."

[25] Cf. Karl Brandt, "Public Control of Land Use in Europe," *Journal of Farm Economics*, Vol. XXI, No. 1, February, 1939, p. 70. Brandt states that in Europe "For three generations the philosophy behind the scores of laws referring to land use has been that adjustments between the rights of the individual and of society as a whole must be attained in a manner which does not discourage or destroy private initiative." According to M. M. Kelso, discussing Brandt's paper, "A great deal of education and

LINES OF FEDERAL ACTION

Powers not specifically granted to the Federal government nor prohibited by the Constitution to the states are reserved to the states. There is much overlapping of authority, and in many instances the Federal government has undertaken activities that have not been specifically granted to it, but have grown out of more specifically delegated powers. The courts have upheld the constitutionality of these acts under general provisions such as the navigation or commerce clauses and the related implied "necessary and proper" powers.

The complex problems accompanying a more mature, highly specialized and technical machine economy, however, have given rise in the United States in recent years to a definite trend toward increased centralization, and the Federal government has undertaken an increasingly large number of activities. In a few instances, these activities have been held unconstitutional and a usurpation of authority; but the seriousness and extensiveness of existing problems have usually caused the courts to interpret the law very liberally and to uphold most federal legislation, particularly that dealing with land use.

Because of its position as central authority of the nation, the Federal government has definite advantages over state and local governments in certain activities associated with land-use control. Financially, it has the entire wealth of the nation behind it and is therefore much more powerful fiscally than any individual state government. Moreover, the increasing interdependence of economic groups makes the Federal government the most logical agency for programs where group interests must be harmonized for the general welfare. However, certain dangers are associated with increased centralization of authority and expansion of federal activities; and there are many fields of land-use improvement in which state and local government action or individual and group coöperative action are most effective.

Perhaps the most important field of federal activity in connection with land-use adjustments and social control is that of making studies or conducting research needed to provide the factual basis for better practices. The rapid changes—physical, as well as economic and social—in man's environment have increased the need for intensive investigation and study, particularly in marginal areas of cutover and semiarid regions. Facts upon which to base sound adjustments in resource use, operating units, land tenure, cultural practices, and institutional arrangements are often inadequate or entirely lacking. The Federal government can,

'trial by fire' will be needed before a web of land-use controls in the public interest will exist in this country in any degree approaching what now exists in Europe." (*Journal of Farm Economics*, Vol. XXI, No. 1, February, 1939, p. 73.)

through coöperative research agreements and financial support of educational programs operative in the different regions, increase the effectiveness of research and investigations conducted by state and local institutions.

LINES OF STATE ACTION

State governments have in recent years become alarmed at the increasing expansion of federal activities and authority, but the activities of state governments should often be complementary to federal activities. State governments can play important roles in effecting desirable land-use adjustments. In the case of investigations and surveys, state research agencies and federal research agencies must coöperate fully to secure necessary facts and other details for sound control and land-use adjustment programs.

There is also need for each state to consider thoroughgoing legislation necessary for a comprehensive program of resource use. Laws, both permissive and mandatory, are required to implement many measures suggested by lines of federal activity, and many existing laws hinder achievement of the purposes of new specific legislation. The states should survey, simplify, and consolidate or codify all their legislation relating to resources (land and water use). This need is particularly apparent in the western states in regard to legislation affecting water use.

Some of the more important land-use legislation that each state should adopt include: (1) A state-coördinated zoning enabling act authorizing counties and other local governments to adopt rural as well as urban zoning ordinances. (2) Statutes to promote efficient and conservational use of water, especially in the West. These statutes should provide for minimum standards of design and construction, simplification of procedures for adjudicating water rights, and establishment of state agencies like state water conservation boards to coöperate with federal agencies and farmers in studying, planning, and financing new enterprises. (3) Soil conservation district laws to permit formation of such districts in states where such legislation has not already been passed, and similar legislation to permit organization of coöperative grazing districts, weed control districts, and related types of collective tenure for the control of land use. (4) Revision or amplification of farm tenancy laws, including lease provisions for compensation for improvements and penalties for deterioration, in coöperation with federal agricultural conservation and farm tenancy programs. (5) Statutes offering a procedure for revising structure of rural governmental units. (6) Legislation to simplify existing procedures for collecting delinquent taxes and acquiring reasonably sound state or county title to chronically tax-delinquent lands. (7) Provision for state purchase of lands in the interests of land-use adjustment. (8)

Authorization of an appropriate state agency to survey and classify lands that come into public ownership through tax delinquency or other involuntary routes to make such lands available for private use and administration in accordance with best use. (9) Legislation providing for conservation and proper utilization of private forest and mineral lands, in coöperation with federal legislation establishing coöperative sustained-yield units (in the case of forest lands) and more stabilized and rational utilization of mineral resources. (10) Legislation to provide for proper development and utilization of recreational lands, including active coöperation with the federal government, through the Pittman Act, in wildlife management and development. (11) Legislation requiring scientific classification and assessment of private farm and city real estate to reduce inequalities in tax burdens. (12) Legislation revising state tax systems for a more equal distribution of tax burdens and consequent reduction of tax delinquency, improper land use, and related maladjustments.[26]

Many of the above-mentioned types of state land-use legislation will complement existing or necessary federal legislation to bring about more effective social control of land use. The Federal government is in a position to give financial assistance and guidance along many of the lines indicated above but, because of constitutional limits, the states alone can adopt such land-use measures as those listed.

In addition to these types of legislation and to increased research and extension activities dealing with land-use problems, including establishment of state planning boards to integrate research, educational, and action programs within the states, state governments can do much to bring about improved land use through increased appropriations for types of development such as provision of wells and small reservoirs for farm units in semiarid regions, and specific appropriations for drainage and similar land improvement activities. In many instances, state governments could increase the effectiveness of land-use adjustment programs by establishing state agencies with adequate appropriations to work coöperatively with similar federal agencies already operative.

LINES OF LOCAL GOVERNMENTAL ACTION

County, city, township, and school district governments are agencies of the state in which they are located, and do not possess sovereign authority except so far as it is delegated to them through state legislation. In those states where considerable authority has been delegated to local governmental units by state legislatures through home rule and related

[26] Eight major types of state land-use legislation needed are listed in *State Legislation for Better Land Use,* Special Report by an Interurban Committee of the U.S. Department of Agriculture, Government Printing Office, April, 1941, p. 17; see also Great Plains Committee, *op. cit.,* pp. 80–84.

laws, local units can take the initiative in starting as well as operating many important land-use adjustment programs. Even in these states, however, local units have been slow to take such initiative.

Local governmental units should be the most active ones, since they are nearest to the people and feel most acutely the immediate effects of land-use maladjustments. But the increasing impersonalization of modern society and the traditional hangover of antiquated forms of structural organization in local governments have made these agencies the least active or effective in adopting some of the more important and badly needed land-use adjustments. This is a particularly serious weakness, because local units of government are frequently most practical for dealings with the land users or residents of an area.

No doubt one of the reasons why local governmental units have been slow to develop more intelligent and effective land-use policies and programs is the structural organization of county government, which is characterized by absence of any effective coördinating head, many independent, elective administrative offices, general lack of any special qualifications or training for office, short terms of office, and numerous small counties with small valuations. Some of the same weaknesses apply to municipalities and township and school district units. Township and school district units are ordinarily so small that they lack the vision and financial capacity to initiate or operate any far-reaching or adequate land-use adjustment programs.

In those states where enabling legislation has not been adopted to permit various reforms and improvements in structural organization of local governmental units, or to permit these local units to initiate and administer various land-use adjustment programs, such state legislation is obviously the first need. However, in many states where such legislation has been adopted, local governmental units have not taken advantage of the authority so granted. Counties—particularly in more marginal areas like the cutover sections and the semiarid Plains—should undertake reclassification of land for assessment purposes, revise organizational structure, and lower operating costs. Consolidating many of the smaller units of local government (such as the numerous small school districts in some areas) would do much to increase the effectiveness of local government, and improvements in city government along the lines of the city manager or centralized executive system would improve urban government and reduce its costs.

LINES OF PRIVATE ACTION

The types of public action outlined above would do much to improve utilization of land resources. However, it must be recognized that, in the last analysis, adjustments must be effected by the individual land user, on his individual holding. In other words, these public programs will be effective only in so far as they are incorporated into the thinking and actions of land users.

INDIVIDUAL ACTION

Unfortunately, a very small percentage of all operators ordinarily adopt recommended practices voluntarily and promptly, and there is a relatively long lag between the time when recommendations are made and when their adoption and use become widespread. This lag is a very serious factor in securing improvements in the use of land resources and tends to force the imposition from above of more extensive and aggressive public programs.

Some specific examples of what individual land users can do can be observed in agricultural land. Farmers can do much to improve the productive ability of the soil by following approved soil conservation practices like contour plowing, terracing, rock tillage, use of cover crops, recommended rotations, and related practices. Often small stock reservoirs or small dams to supply water can be built by the individual operator to furnish water supplies for garden products and supplementary feed. Through proper stocking of the range and systematic provision of feed and seed reserves in good years, to be used as protection against the poor years, the farm economy can be made more stable, particularly in semi-arid regions or areas where great variations exist in growing conditions.

COÖPERATIVE EFFORT

In many agricultural areas, individual operators can, through coöperative grazing districts, soil conservation districts, weed control districts, and related units, help to bring about a more properly balanced use of the land and more adequate farm and ranch incomes. Coöperative action of land users is essential in most instances to obtain improvements in assessment and land taxation practices by local and state tax officials.

It has been too widely assumed in recent years that expansion of governmental activity has made it unnecessary and undesirable for the private individual to take any initiative in starting or operating various desirable practices. It is more, rather than less, true that in these days full responsibility of each private individual is essential for the effective utilization of resources. The many local, state, and federal programs merely help the individual, through coöperation with his neighbors, to increase the effectiveness of his efforts. If he fails, through ignorance, inertia, or lack of initiative, to take advantage of these opportunities, land-use control programs are more and more likely to be initiated and administered from the top down, rather than from the roots up.

CORPORATE ACTION

Large private corporations have exerted a strong influence toward certain methods of utilizing land resources in recent years. These agencies are in an increasingly effective position to be an influence for improved land use, if they so desire, and possess many advantages over the private individual. They operate on a relatively large-scale basis, have a continuing management, are longer-lived, and have greater financial reserves.

The greater use by such large private corporations of policies working in harmony with the social interest rather than purely for selfish or temporary gain, is particularly desirable, and would be a most effective way of preventing too rapid expansion of governmental activity (particularly of the federal agencies) in land-use control efforts. Unless private agencies, both individual and corporate, can work out effective land-use control programs by employing information and opportunities made possible through public legislation and public support, governmental activity in the social control over land use will expand at the expense of private activity.

THE PROBLEM OF COÖRDINATION

The large number of federal agencies, in addition to the many other public and private agencies concerned with land acquisition, land administration, and land planning tends to create confusion, since many of the agencies have been guided by different ideas and conflicting policies, and their efforts have lacked close coördination.

In general, the concept of coördination apparently followed is that all that is necessary is to form a committee representing different bureaus or agencies and have them accomplish "coördination." The problem is not so simple, however, but is one of the "most complex and difficult problems both of policy-making and of administration." Effective coördination in a democratically organized nation necessitates a more general understanding of the true meaning of coördination and methods by which it can best be achieved.

Coördination means *adjusting* or *harmonizing,* while coöperation means *working together.* Coöperation is necessary for effective coördination, but coördination is a step beyond coöperation. Correlation is the establishment of mutual relationships and represents a step in the consideration of coördinating procedures. To *integrate* means primarily to unite separate parts into a whole; and as correlation is the beginning, integration is the end or objective of the coördinating process.[27]

[27] Cf. Carleton, R. Ball, "Coördination of Agricultural Activities," a lecture before the School for Extension Workers, Kansas State College, Manhattan, Kan., April 13, 1939, mimeographed.

Since coöperation is the basis on which coördination must be built, it is important to have a comprehensive understanding of the basic principles underlying successful coöperation.[28] Coöperativeness is, of course, primarily a mental attitude, and is much more highly developed in some individuals than in others. However, most people are reasonable and are willing to undertake coöperative activity if they recognize its advantages.

It is generally realized that coöperation is not a remedy for all problems, but that it does offer specific personal, technical, and financial advantages, under proper conditions. It should be borne in mind that coöperation is encouraged and advanced by mere association and conference of individuals, institutions, and organizations on problems of common concern. The advantages of coöperation lie in three major fields —promotion of better institutional and individual spirit, more effective advancement of knowledge, and important savings of time, money, and materials.[29]

METHODS BY WHICH EFFECTIVE COÖRDINATION CAN BE ACHIEVED

Since coöperation is the foundation for effective coördination, and since coöperativeness is primarily a matter of mental attitudes, the problem of coördination is to a large extent a problem of personnel and psychology. However, important as the matter of personnel is, other problems involved are also important. In the first place, a sincere effort must be made to organize and to obtain agreement on objectives and methods. In other words, there must be some common objectives or goals to which all agencies, institutions, or individuals can give common allegiance.

The rapid rate at which the United States has been settled and developed and the emphasis upon resource exploitation and material gains have not contributed to a careful consideration of ideas concerning common objectives. The emphasis on individual initiative in a pioneer stage has served to develop the nation rapidly; but effective coördination requires a series of intermediate stages or points at which ideas, policies, procedures, and activities can be brought together into a working relationship. Group action, discussion, and thinking are essential; and these have not been the primary methods by which the American economy has operated.

Merely bringing together committees or representatives of specialized groups, agencies, or institutions is not enough to achieve effective coördination. Too often, these individual representatives are too busy or absorbed in their own specialized problems and programs to give adequate attention to the achievement of effective coördination. It is neces-

[28] Ball sets forth 10 principles for successful coöperation. (*Ibid.*, pp. 5–6.)
[29] Ball points out in some detail the distinctive ways in which coöperation accomplishes these objectives. (*Ibid.*, pp. 6–7.)

sary to make coördination a full-time job for specially qualified men, and to set up structural organization or arrangements through which the work of such individuals can be effected.

Personnel problems are, of course, in the last analysis, matters of mental attitudes. Human relationships vary all the way "from active antagonism, through self-centered indifference, to free interest, and finally, to planned coöperation. . . . One type of relation may prevail at one time or in one place while another prevails at the same time in another place or in the same place at another time. Attitudes precede action." [30] By and large, however, free interest generally prevails among individuals; and human progress is characterized by an increasing recognition of social values and responsibilities.

Although the many new agencies and programs established in recent years have tended to produce confusion, it is generally recognized that coöperation among individuals and groups in society has increased. Effective coördination or harmonious adjustment of individual group programs within the economy can be accomplished, is in a small way being accomplished, and ultimately must be accomplished completely. Personalities are the single largest factor in coöperation, and therefore in coördination.

COÖRDINATION OF RESEARCH AND EDUCATION

The securing of sound information concerning forces, problems, and trends is basic to long-time effective coördination of social control and land-use planning activities. It is essential, therefore, that research and educational agencies coördinate their work in such a way as to make the best use of funds, personnel, and resources.

Some of the factors that are considered to be most responsible for lack of fuller coördination in research programs are: (1) geographic isolation; (2) inability of workers to confer frequently; (3) cost; (4) conflict with local obligations; (5) lack of coördinating leadership; (6) institutional pride and professional jealousy; and (7) problems of personnel relationships.[31] However, most leaders would agree that the situation is improving and has been distinctly better in recent years than formerly. The acknowledged lack of coördinating leadership is a definite challenge to achieve more effective education in the entire field of social obligations and human relationships.

One of the purposes of education is better adaptation of the individual to his environment; and in a democracy it is particularly vital that

[30] Ball, *op. cit.*, p. 9. See also Max Lerner, *Ideas Are Weapons—the History and Uses of Ideas*, Viking, 1939.

[31] L. E. Call, "The Planning and Coördination of Research Projects," *Proceedings of the Annual Conference of the Association of Land Grant Colleges and Universities*, November 18–20, 1935, Washington, D.C., 1936, pp. 91–95.

an efficient system of universal education and equal educational opportunities be established at all educational levels. Studies reveal great inequalities in educational opportunities and facilities at grade and high school levels among local units within a state, and among states. In recent years efforts have been made to achieve a more equal distribution of the burden of school costs through increased federal and state aid. Considerable progress has been made within some states, but there is much room for improvement.

INTEGRATION OF PLANS

Obviously, there should be some central federal agency with which state, county, and community planning agencies could implement their programs. Several state planning boards have been established, but the failure of many of these to survive has been partially due to lack of interest in communities and counties to make the work of such state boards significant. In many cases, organization of state boards was premature, and efforts should have been concentrated upon establishment of local planning rather than on attempts to bring about planning from the top down. The uncertainty of the World War II period, however, diverted attention in many areas from some of the longer-time and less dramatic land-use adjustments that should be made.

No doubt, as planning work proceeds, local committees will be forced to consider more carefully the ways in which their goals or objectives may be achieved. The question of private or governmental action will no doubt be important. However, those most closely associated with the land-use planning program believe it entirely logical that coöperative planning may make its greatest contribution by "helping people to help themselves" through private action, rather than by mere coördination and unification of the programs of governmental agencies.[32]

Obviously, achievement of many of the goals and objectives that will undoubtedly be set up will require combined private and public action. However, the possibility that private action alone may be able to deal with many problems of our modern world presents a major challenge to planning committees. Prophesying is dangerous; but students of planning hope that the land-use planning process will develop individual initiative and increased participation in coöperative procedures among farm and other groups to deal with many difficult problems.

It should be kept constantly in mind that the purpose of all planning and social control of land use can be summed up in a single aim—a better life, attained through sounder land-use practices and better adjustment of institutions and man-land relationships. More than the ma-

[32] E. A. Foster and H. A. Vogel, "Coöperative Land Use Planning—A New Development in Democracy," U.S. Department of Agriculture, *Yearbook*, 1940, p. 1155.

chinery of democratic planning is needed for the achievement of a better life. Beyond economics, beyond politics, beyond material satisfactions, must be ". . . some motivating force or driving quality, a social conscience or a common mortality, a sense of social solidarity or a consciousness of kins, a spirit of social service or *noblesse oblige,* some spiritual force or a finer faith . . . to animate the hearts and minds of men." [33]

REFERENCES FOR FURTHER READING

Adams, Thomas, *Outline of Town and City Planning,* Russell Sage Foundation, New York, 1935, Introduction and Chaps. XI and XII.

Annals of the American Academy of Political and Social Science, "Government Expansion in the Economic Sphere," Vol. CCVI, November, 1939, pp. 1–34 and 121–160.

Banfield, Edward C., "Organization for Policy Planning in the U.S. Department of Agriculture," *Journal of Farm Economics,* Vol. XXXIV, No. 1, February, 1952.

Berle, A. A., Jr., *New Directions in the New World,* Harper & Brothers, New York, 1940.

Council of State Governments, *Planning Services for State Government,* Chicago, 1956, 63 pp.

Doob, Leonard W., *The Plans of Men,* Yale University Press, New Haven, 1940.

Galloway, G. B., *et al., Planning for America,* Henry Holt and Company, Inc., New York, 1941, Chaps. I, II, III, and XXXIII.

Great Plains Committee, *The Future of the Great Plains,* Government Printing Office, Washington, D.C., 1936, Chaps. V and VI.

Hayek, Friedrich A., *The Road to Serfdom,* University of Chicago Press, 1944, Chaps. II–X and XIV.

James, Harlean, *Land Planning in the United States for the City, State, and Nation,* The Macmillan Company, New York, 1926, Introduction and Chaps. V and XXV.

Johnson, V. Webster, "Planning the Use of Land Resources," Chap. XIV in *Land Problems and Policies,* J. F. Timmons and W. B. Murray (eds.), Iowa State College Press, Ames, 1950.

Johnson, V. Webster, and Barlowe, Raleigh, *Land Problems and Policies,* McGraw-Hill Book Company, Inc., New York, 1954, Chap. XIV.

Kraenzel, C. F., and Parsons, O. A., *Agricultural Planning: Its Economic and Social Aspects,* Montana Agricultural Experiment Stations Bulletin 391, Bozeman, Mont., June, 1941.

Lorwin, Lewis L., *Time for Planning,* Harper & Brothers, New York, 1945, Chaps. I–VII and XVII.

Mackenzie, Findlay (ed.), *Planned Society, Yesterday, Today, and Tomorrow,* Prentice-Hall, Inc., Englewood Cliffs, N.J., 1937, Foreword, Introduction, and Chaps. XIX, XXII, and XXV.

[33] Galloway, *op. cit.,* p. 667. See also M. L. Wilson, "Beyond Economics," and W. E. Hocking, "A Philosophy of Life for the American Farmer and Others," in U.S. Department of Agriculture, *Yearbook,* 1940, pp. 922–937 and pp. 1056–1071.

National Planning Board, *Final Report, 1933–34,* Government Printing Office, Washington, D.C., 1934, pp. 12–14, 35–38, and 74–84.

Parkins, A. E., and Whitaker, J. R. (eds.) *Our National Resources and Their Conservation,* John Wiley & Sons, Inc., New York, 1936, Chaps. XXII and XXIII.

Perloff, Harvey S., *Education for Planning: City, State, and Regional,* The Johns Hopkins Press, Baltimore, 1957.

Shepard, Ward, *Food or Famine: The Challenge of Erosion,* The Macmillan Company, 1945, Chaps. III, IV, V, and VI.

Soule, George, *A Planned Society,* The Macmillan Company, New York, 1932.

U.S. Department of Agriculture, "Farmers in a Changing World," U.S. Department of Agriculture *Yearbook,* 1940, Government Printing Office, Washington, D.C., pp. 922–937, 1125–1156.

Von Mises, Ludwig, *Planned Chaos,* The Foundation for Economic Education, Inc., Irvington-on-Hudson, New York, 1947, 90 pp.

LAND REFORM

LAND REFORM AND ECONOMIC PROGRESS

The Meaning of Land Reform—Agrarian Revolt and Agrarian Movements—Land Reform and Agricultural Development—Land Reform and Economic Development

DEFECTS IN THE AGRARIAN STRUCTURE

Farm Size and Layout—Tenancy—Estates and Plantations —Land Titles—Communal Tenure—Credit and Agricultural Indebtedness—Taxation Policies

LAND REFORM MEASURES

Land Redistribution—Land Settlement—Conditions of Tenancy—Conditions of Rural Employment—Economic Holdings—Land Registration—Agricultural Credit—Fiscal And Other Measures

EFFECTS OF LAND REFORM PROGRAMS

Immediate or Short-Run Effects—Long-Run Effects

THE FUTURE OF LAND REFORM

Obstacles to Progress—Recommendations for Future Action

ABOUT TWO-THIRDS of the people of the world live in what have commonly come to be called *underdeveloped* countries. These areas are underdeveloped in the sense that only a segment or two of their economies are developed and but to a very limited degree. Underdeveloped economies are predominantly agricultural. In some countries such as Thailand, nearly nine-tenths of the labor force is engaged directly in tilling the soil, and in all Asia and Africa about three-fourths of the population is agricultural.[1] This is in sharp contrast to a highly developed and diversified economy such as that of the United States, where only a tenth of the population is engaged in agriculture.

The underveloped areas are characterized by *low productivity, instability,* and economies operationg at *near-subsistence levels.* Productivity or output per person in agriculture is very much lower than in the highly developed industrial countries, because the density of farm population per acre is much greater while the acreage yield per acre is less. Since the underdeveloped areas are predominantly rural in character and the inhabitants depend so completely on agriculture for a living, they are especially vulnerable to the vicissitudes of the weather and crop production conditions. Such countries do not yet enjoy the benefits of modern technology, and poverty, illiteracy, ill-health, and disease are widespread.

LAND REFORM AND ECONOMIC PROGRESS

The heavy dependence of underveloped areas on agriculture means that hopes for a better life are tied directly to the system of land tenure, or the relationships established among men in the control and use of land. In most instances these relationships must be reformed or changed by removal of faults or abuses if ignorance, illness, and poverty are to be eliminated or largely overcome.

THE MEANING OF LAND REFORM

Fundamentally, land reform comprises improvement in all the economic and social institutions surrounding farm life. Under this definition, land *reform* is broader in coverage than land *tenure.* Land reform covers all the aspects of land tenure, such as redistribution, consolidation of land holdings into tracts of sufficient size, reduction of exorbitant rental charges, security of tenure for the tenant, improvement of working conditions for farm laborers, settlement of land titles, reform of the tax system, measures to assure reasonable cost of agricultural credit; and in addition, the establishment of rural industries, coöperative societies for group purchases and accompanying savings, marketing, credit, and related institutions.[2]

Land reform is not new. In fact, it is a very ancient idea which has changed its form gradually as economies have grown toward market specialization with stronger financial institutions, and as the people have been given more authority through the right to vote or participate in

[1] Food and Agriculture Organization of the United Nations, *Yearbook of Food and Agriculture,* Rome, 1950, p. 15.

[2] Roland R. Renne, "Land Tenure Reform as an Aspect of Economic Development in Asia," Chap. XX in *Economics and the Public Interest,* Robert A. Solo, (ed.), Rutgers University Press, New Brunswick, N.J., 1955, p. 299.

government. In ancient China, for example, every few centuries land was redivided and the people started out afresh on a new footing of equality. In early times in the eastern Mediterranean area and elsewhere, land was redivided among the families every seven years or so. Apparently the main idea was to see that land was distributed in such a way that each pair of hands would have an approximately equal opportunity to feed one mouth.[3]

The early concepts of land reform have been modified greatly in recent years. Land reform has come to mean a change in the *form* of rural or agrarian society and emonomy in regard to the right of land use and possession. The variety and intensity of land reform measures proposed in various parts of the world and analyzed later in this chapter reveal the wide range of problems of rural societies being attached under the general classification of land-reform activities.

AGRARIAN REVOLT AND AGRARIAN MOVEMENTS

It is probably correct to say that there have never before been so many dissatisfied people in the world. This is not caused by an increase in disease, starvation, and misery, but by the increase in knowledge and improvements in communication and transportation. These have caused peoples who formerly lived in isolated communities with only local standards of comparison to become aware of ways of living vastly different from their own. News of events elsewhere reach local inhabitants, and information and propaganda spread with increasing facility. Poverty, ignorance, and disease are no longer considered inevitable, and desires for better living levels become more widespread. Resentment against their unsatisfactory, undesirable, and unjustifiable situations develops among peoples of the underdeveloped areas. The resulting discontent is the basis for much of the current political instability and economic unrest.

History is full of accounts of peasant uprisings and agrarian movements to improve the unsatisfactory land-tenure conditions of feudalism. It is only during the past two or three centuries that major progress has been made in actually achieving reforms that brought about freer land-tenure conditions or a wider distribution of ownership rights. The French Revolution of 1789, the agrarian uprisings of 1848, and the end of World War I, all were followed by land-reform programs in various parts of Europe. Likewise, after World War II, land-reform programs were inaugurated in widely separated parts of the globe, the most ex-

---

[3] See Kenneth H. Parsons, "Land Reform and Agricultural Development," Part I in *Land Tenure: Proceedings of the 1951 International Conference on Land Tenure and Related Problems in World Agriculture,* Kenneth H. Parsons, Raymond J. Penn, and Philip M. Raup (eds.), University of Wisconsin Press, Madison, 1956, p. 17.

tensive being undertaken in Asia, and to a lesser extent in Europe, Africa, and Latin America.

In general, agrarian reform movements in the present century have taken the form of a demand for the breakup of large estates and the distribution of land in small parcels to the peasants or operators. In simple terms this is a distributing of "land to the landless" program. The programs in Communist-dominated countries have been characterized by ruthless disregard of the right of landowners and by the forced imposition on the peasants of some form of collective operation. In the free nations, sincere efforts are made to carry out land reform with democratic procedures. For example, confiscation is avoided and expropriated landowners are compensated for their property. In many instances they are permitted to retain for themselves a portion of the expropriated land provided they carry out recommended land-use improvements. Private initiative is further rewarded by exempting from expropriation farms classified as "model farms." [4]

Land reform has become a major political issue throughout many of the underveloped countries of the world today. The most burning issue and the most widespread cause of social unrest in these areas is the insecurity and lack of status of the operator associated with tenancy or the inability to own the land. The question of tenure status is not simply a matter of income or degree of poverty; it is also a matter of human dignity and the right to exercise one's own will. Net income measures the degree of freedom from want, but the kind and amount of tenure rights in land determine the degree of freedom from arbitrary and willful acts of other persons.[5] There is nothing quite like having a limited space on the earth that one can call his own to provide security and dignity for the farmer and his family, and the incentives and inducements for him to improve his production and his land-use practices.

LAND REFORM AND AGRICULTURAL DEVELOPMENT

In underdeveloped areas where land reform programs have been emphasized most, agriculture is usually the main, if not the sole, source of wealth and income. For any significant economic improvement in these areas, therefore, it is obvious that their agriculture must be developed further or improved. Agricultural development includes those processes by which an agriculture becomes more efficient, or by which the total agricultural output is increased.

An increase in food production is absolutely essential in most under-

[4] Lowry Nelson, *Land Reform in Italy*, National Planning Association, Washington, D.C., Planning Pamphlet No. 97, August, 1956, p. 4.

[5] Parsons, *op. cit.*, p. 16.

developed countries for improved living conditions. Many of the underdeveloped countries import food to supplement domestic output, at the cost of limited foreign exchange. The margin for saving to secure capital for development can be created in many countries only by increasing food production in total and per capita.

Underveloped areas may be classified into two general groups: (1) those in which land suitable for agricultural use is scarce relative to the existing farm population; and (2) those in which it is not. In the first group population pressure on the land is severe. The farms are small and inefficient. With more farmers wanting land than there is land to be had, landowners may be able to extract exorbitant rents relative to the returns from the land. Social discontent and political unrest develop rapidly and generally under such conditions. Although much can be done to improve the conditions of land users under these circumstances, the permanent and satisfactory solution rests upon the development of nonagricultural resources and the orderly movement of people from agricultural to nonagricultural occupations.[6]

In those areas where land suitable for agricultural use is in adequate supply, even though undeveloped, agricultural development and improvement of living levels is much simpler. The operating farm units can be developed into sizes adequate for economic production, and other phases of the economy can be strengthened to make possible a more efficient and adequate agriculture. These would include essential public services such as transportation, education, and health facilities.

The United States has been fortunate in having both a relative abundance of good agricultural land in relation to population, and rapid economic development in nonagricultural enterprises. As a result, the proportion of the population engaged in agriculture has been declining while agricultural output has continued to increase. The general economic growth of the country has permitted a rapid rise in the capital investment in agriculture and in output per farm worker. Between 1940 and 1955, productivity per hour of labor in agriculture nearly doubled.

When attempts are made to stimulate agricultural development in underdeveloped areas, many problems not encountered in the United States arise. One of the most important of these is the widespread need for elementary general education. General health and physical vigor for effective agricultural development are very important where malaria and intestinal parasites are common. Standard weights and measures do not exist in many areas of the world. Efficiency in public administration, including civil service tenure and systematic promotions of scientists, adequate salaries, appropriate budget procedures, and efficient admin-

---

[6] Cf. Dennis A. Fitzgerald, "Land Reform and Economic Development," in Parsons, Penn, and Raup, *op. cit.*, p. 45.

istrative procedures, is very important because of the influence these have on public programs in agriculture, education, and health.[7]

In addition to these problems, general characteristics of the various cultures exert great influence on the rate of agricultural development. Economic productivity is a function of the whole way of life of a people.[8] To assume that all the underdeveloped countries need to do to increase agricultural production is to master the techniques and adopt the implements, fertilizers, seeds, insecticides, and other items of the more advanced countries is to invite failure and disappointment. Important noneconomic phases of each regional culture must change along with the changes in techniques and implements if rapid agricultural development is to be achieved.

LAND REFORM AND ECONOMIC DEVELOPMENT

In the last analysis, economic development depends upon the accumulation of capital and its investment in productive uses. In the underdeveloped areas, capital accumulation is hindered by the inability of the average individual to save much or anything from his inadequate income. Too often when savings are made they are hoarded rather than invested.

The source of much of the investment capital needed for undeveloped areas has come in the past from the more advanced areas where saving and investment are more highly developed. Since World War II, the investment climate in many areas has not been conducive to attracting outside venture capital in amounts desired for economic development. This is attributable in large measure to the unsettled political, social and economic conditions in the undeveloped areas. The problems associated with use and control of agricultural lands and land-reform efforts have been major factors in the unfavorable investment climate.

Land reform is but the first step in an effective program of economic development; and the solution to agrarian problems, even if an ideal or satisfactory land-tenure pattern is achieved, ultimately must be sought outside the field of agricultural land economics. An adequate program of economic expansion can be undertaken only through the development of a different resource-utilization pattern, in which activities other than agriculture are established in order to absorb population growth, and to produce necessary capital and consumer goods.[9]

In the end, of course, capital borrowed from more advanced areas must be paid back by increased production and savings in the borrowing

---

[7] A. T. Mosher, "A Review and Criticism of United States Participation in Agricultural Programs of Technical Coöperation," *Journal of Farm Economics,* Vol. XXXVIII, No. 5, December, 1956, p. 1198.

[8] *Ibid.,* p. 1199.

[9] Edmundo Flores, "Agrarian Reform and Economic Development," in Parsons, Penn, and Raup (eds.), *op. cit.,* p. 243.

country. Only if alternative sources of employment are made available will increased efficiency in agriculture be possible, to accumulate food and raw materials for the nonagricultural population and for industrial purposes, and to increase levels of living and the purchasing power of the agricultural population.

The program of economic development, to be successful, therefore, must involve increased activity and expansion in both agricultural and nonagricultural fields simultaneously. Land reform may, and very likely will, be the area in which activity is centered in the beginning, but it must soon be followed with a broad economic development program for the economy as a whole. Thus, land reform may be the catalyst that sets this process of economic development in motion.

The experience of Mexico illustrates the case.[10] Beginning with agrarian reform, an all-around policy of economic development followed. The initial aim of agrarian reform was limited to granting a parcel of land to every adult Mexican through the breaking up of large estates, opening of new lands, and resettlement of the population. This policy of land reform was followed by expropriation of oil lands, nationalization of railroads, and development of the electrical industry, all of which meant a new economic policy seeking development of the country's economy in a more integrated way.

When land reform was initiated, there was a flight of capital from agriculture to the cities. At first much of this capital was invested in speculative urban real estate ventures, but soon became attracted to the construction industry, and gradually spread from there to other industrial branches. The expansion of cities and the development of irrigation and communications (transportation and electricity) stimulated the construction industries and made alternative sources of employment available, which helped to absorb the population displaced from agriculture and at the same time led to the production of essential capital and consumption goods. Thus, as agricultural productivity increases, the need for industrial requisites such as transports, farm machinery, chemical products, and similar items grows; and the strategic factor of expansion shifts from spatial limitations and lack of incentives caused by institutional obstacles, to scarcity of capital and lack of technical know-how and enterprise.

DEFECTS IN THE AGRARIAN STRUCTURE

The most important factor that affects living standards in underdeveloped countries is the *agrarian structure*, or the institutional framework

[10] This brief statement of Mexico's experience is based on Edmundo Flores' article previously noted, pp. 243–246.

of agricultural production. The agrarian structure includes: [11] (1) land tenure, the legal or customary system under which land is owned, (2) the distribution of ownership of farm property between large estates and peasant farms or among peasant farms of various sizes, (3) land tenancy, the system under which land is operated and its output divided between operator and owner; (4) the organization of credit, production, and marketing; (5) the mechanism through which agriculture is financed; (6) the burdens imposed on rural populations by governments through taxation; and (7) the services supplied by governments to rural populations, such as technical advice, educational facilities, health services, communications, and water supply.

The agrarian structure varies from country to country, but certain conditions are common to most if not all undeveloped areas. These include: (1) uneconomically small farm units; (2) antiquated farming methods; (3) inadequate credit facilities; (4) extensive unemployment and underemployment; (5) high farm tenancy; (6) decreasing soil fertility; (7) malnutrition; (8) lack of local self-government; and (9) the failure to provide essential community services.[12] Not all these conditions can be discussed in detail, but the more important features of those selected will illustrate their effects on the well-being of the peoples involved.[13]

FARM SIZE AND LAYOUT

The average farm holding is extremely small in many underdeveloped countries. The minimum size of farm for economic operation varies with the type of cultivation and land utilization in different countries. The acreage that will permit full utilization of the farmer's labor and equipment is less important than that which will provide a subsistence minimum. Moreover, acreage alone is not a satisfactory criterion of minimum size in either case, since there are great differences in the intensity and type of cultivation. Obviously, the minimum size for economic operation will be smaller if the plow is drawn by bullocks or carabao than if it is drawn by a tractor.

Regardless of the method used to determine minimum desirable size of farms, there are many countries in which large numbers of farms are too small to provide a subsistence minimum for the cultivator and his family, or to provide them with full employment; and too small also to permit of any improvement in methods of cultivation.[14] This situation

[11] See *Land Reform: Defects in Agrarian Structure as Obstacles to Economic Development,* United Nations, Department of Economic Affairs, New York, 1951, p. 5.

[12] Renne, *op. cit.,* p. 299.

[13] The discussion of agrarian structure conditions is based on *Land Reform: Defects in Agrarian Structure as Obstacles to Economic Development,* pp. 6–49.

[14] For example, in India there are hardly 2 acres of well-watered land available per average holding. This is less than the subsistence minimum, so a large proportion of holdings is considerably below the average. (See *ibid.,* p. 9.)

may be the result either of extreme subdivision of farms caused by pressure of population on the land, or of inequality in the distribution of land ownership; or it may be the result of a combination of the two. Extreme subdivision of farms tends to promote concentration of ownership because small owners are ordinarily unable to earn a subsistence from their farms, and consequently become indebted to moneylenders who ultimately acquire possession of the land.

The density of agricultural population is very high in some areas, exceeding 1500 persons per square mile or only half an acre of land for each person on farms.[15] In these overcrowded conditions the average farm holding would be small, even if all the land were equally distributed. However, problems of inadequate-sized farm operating units are not limited to areas of high population density. Countries with low population density combined with low technology may have relatively low incomes. Parts of western Europe and Japan may be classed as high-population, high-technology, low-income countries; Asia, excluding Japan, as high-population, low-technology, low-income countries; and Africa, Latin America, and the Middle East as low-population, low-technology, low-income countries.[16] Even in countries of very extensive cultivation with large reserves of land, overcultivated small holdings exist.

In countries at all levels of economic development, a feature of the field layout is the splitting of farm holdings into numerous different plots scattered over a wide area. This *fragmentation of holdings* is not associated with any particular form of land tenure. It can be found in highly developed countries, such as Switzerland, in eastern Europe, in Asia, and in the Middle Eastern countries.

Fragmentation has numerous causes. It originated in early times from the traditional field layout in which holdings were divided into several strips located in different parts of a village. These original strips have been divided and subdivided with the increase of farm population and with inheritance laws that encourage subdivision of land among numerous heirs. In western Europe, where pressure of rural population is not acute, the principle of succession is a major influence, while in eastern Europe and in Asia the pressure of population is the major cause, reinforced by laws of succession.

The evils of fragmentation are obvious. They include waste of time and effort, and the impossiblity of rational cultivation. Consolidation of holdings is a difficult reform to accomplish. The high cost per acre of surveying and exchanging many small plots is a major obstacle, as is also the conservatism of the peasants. But even in advanced nations such as Switzerland, consolidation has been slow and difficult.

[15] J. Lossing Buck, "Fact and Theory About China's Land," *Foreign Affairs*, October, 1949, quoted in *ibid.*, p. 7.

[16] Cf. A. T. Mosher, *et al.*, *op. cit.*, pp. 1197–1234.

TENANCY

The proportion of tenants to the number of farmers varies widely from one country to another. In Asia the proportion is generally high. Until recently, about half the land was worked by tenants utilizing small holdings leased to them by landowners, and the majority of the cultivators were either tenants or part-owners and part-tenants. In some regions, such as the Middle East, statistical data are lacking, but aside from Cyprus, Egypt, Lebanon, and Turkey, where most of the farmers own land, tenancy is widely prevalent. Tenancy is also a prevalent form of tenure in several South American countries, especially in Argentina where some 60 percent of the land is leased to tenants; but in Brazil, tenancy is not common.[17]

Tenancy, in itself, is not a bad form of tenure, provided rents are not excessive and security of tenure is safeguarded by legislation. But, generally speaking, these conditions are definitely lacking in underdeveloped countries, where tenancy systems are characterized by excessive rent charges and lack of security of tenure.[18]

Share renting is the most common form of tenancy, and although the percentage of the crop given the landlord as a rent payment varies greatly among nations and within areas of a nation, equal sharing between landlord and tenant is common practice. Payment of rent in the form of fixed amounts of produce or cash payments are less common, and labor rents are not usual except in some countries of Latin America, in parts of India, and in Asia.

Great insecurity and poverty characterize conditions of tenancy in many underdeveloped areas. Cultivators who hold land under various forms of tenancy, ordinarily hold it on a customary basis, with no legal agreement to define their rights and obligations. In some countries of the Middle East, for example, the peasant does not even cultivate the same plot of land from year to year, since the landlord or his agent give the most fertile plots to favored tenants. The peasant therefore, ordinarily has one aim: to get the most out of the soil during his short tenancy, regardless of the effects on fertility.

ESTATES AND PLANTATIONS

Throughout South America, on the Caribbean, in Southeast Asia, in Ceylon, and in parts of East Africa, the agrarian structure is dominated by large estates, centrally managed and operated, and employing paid labor. This type of farm organization is known as the *latifundia*. The

[17] *Land Reform*, p. 15.
[18] See Generoso F. Rivera and Robert T. McMillan, *The Rural Philippines*, U.S. Mutual Security Agency, Manila, October, 1952, processed, and *Philippine Land Tenure Reform*, U.S. Mutual Security Agency, Manila, 1952, processed, for examples of unsatisfactory conditions associated with Philippine tenancy.

total of such holdings in Latin America, for example, constitutes about 50 percent of all agricultural land.[19] Much of the land is not suitable for crop production, but substantial amounts comprise idle lands that have been held for generations. At the other extreme are the small landowners who do subsistence farming on a few overcultivated or unproductive acres. The bulk of the remaining rural population consists of small tenants and landless laborers.

This land utilization pattern is the reverse of that which market conditions and natural resources require. The hillside land, which is best suited for pasture and woodland, is intensively cultivated by hoe culture, which destroys the top soil, while the valley floors, more suited for arable cultivation, are used for grazing. If medium-sized farms played a larger part in the economy, it is believed agricultural production would increase and so would urban and rural levels of living. The major factor limiting expansion of small and medium-sized holdings is everywhere the shortage of capital, which prevents the small tenant or subsistence cultivator from enlarging the size of his holding.

LAND TITLES

In some countries, occupying owners of land have no legal title to the land they occupy, because no system of registration of titles exists, or registration offices are two or three years behind in their work and endless delays confuse and delay the small owners. This is a very serious defect in the agrarian structure, because lack of title means no security of tenure and causes continual disputes over ownership. This condition occurs in several Latin American countries. In the Middle Eastern countries a complicated situation exists, for registration of title is not yet completed and the legal position as to water rights is highly confused. Both in Syria and Iraq, large areas of land remain as government domain, in which title has not been settled. Unless the costs of survey and court fees are kept low, however, settlement of title may work against the small occupier and in favor of the large landowner.

COMMUNAL TENURE

Under communal tenure, control over land is exercised through a social group. Systems of this kind are to be found surviving in parts of Southeast Asia, India, and the Middle East, Africa, in some of the Caribbean countries, and in the northern and western republics of South America. The question of settlement of title arises when such a system disintegrates.

Various forces are contributing to break up the communal system.

[19] See *Land Reform*, p. 19.

Among those which are changing the communal system into more individual forms of land tenure, the most general is the introduction of cash cropping. In some areas shortage of land has been a determing factor, while in others new crops and new methods of cultivation have played a part. Expansion of industrial employment has also been a disruptive influence.

The rapid extension of cash cropping and the growing influence of a money economy have led to a more intensive use of land, and thus given rise to the need for improved techniques in agriculture. These developments are exerting a profound influence on indigenous agricultural society and on land usage. The development of individual tenures with registered titles has deepened upon the growth of cash cropping by which land acquires a commercial value. In French West Africa, for example, registrations have been frequent in and around urban centers and in the coastal regions where cash cropping has been most fully developed.

CREDIT AND AGRICULTURAL INDEBTEDNESS

High interest rates and a high burden of farm debt are characteristic features of the agrarian structure in many underdeveloped countries. These features may reflect a chronic insufficiency of farm income and a permanent tendency for consumption to outrun production. The creation of special agencies to furnish agricultural credit in appropriate forms may correct structural deficiencies, such as the banking system, which is not being adapted to the needs of the small farmer. But the provision of a better form of credit dispensing organization will not solve a shortage of credit that reflects a retrogressive condition in agricultural production.

In many underdeveloped countries, the unsuitability of existing credit agencies is a major obstacle to expansion of output on small farms. As a result, the financing of small-scale agricultural production requires the provision of credit through special agencies. In Asia and the Middle East, the peasant cultivator must obtain credit from one of three sources: (1) The village shopkeeper who gives credit on day-to-day purchases at rates of 100 percent to 250 percent per year; (2) the landlord who lends to tenant cultivators against the security of the crop, and (3) the middleman or moneylender.[20]

An example of the exaction of usurious interest rates, in spite of legal provisions setting 12 percent as the maximum rate in the Philippines, is the common arrangement for advances of rice to the tenant.[21] The landlord or moneylender may require that an extra cavan of palay be returned at harvest for every one, two, or three cavans borrowed. Or the

[20] Ibid., p. 38.
[21] Rivera and McMillan, op. cit., p. 129.

lender may charge the borrower as much as 12 to 16 pesos for a cavan of palay, but allow him only six to eight pesos per cavan at harvest time, five or six months later. Or the farmer may borrow in cash, agreeing to repay in cavans of palay at harvest time. Or moneylenders may transact a preharvest purchase of palay through advancing cash or palay to the borrower at prices considerably under prevailing market prices.[22]

The farmers' incapacity to borrow cheaply in underdeveloped countries is not to be resolved solely through reform of lending institutions. This is evidenced by the fact that the average farmer does not produce enough to feed his family from one harvest to the next. Small farms, low productivity, and conditions associated with farm tenancy make the average farmer in the underdeveloped areas a perennially poor credit risk. Thus, credit shortage is the effect of poverty as well as its cause in Asia, the Middle East, and other areas. The vicious circle of poverty, debt, and high interest rates can only be broken by measures that increase productivity of the holding and lessen the rent and tax burden.

In some countries a major problem is the lack of well-organized capital markets in which land or debentures can be sold to get loan funds to provide credit for farmers at lower interest rates. In underdeveloped countries the task of mobilizing savings is especially difficult even where there is economic and political stability. Low levels of production and income, dense and rapidly increasing populations, and inflexibilities in the social structure significantly limit savings and investment. Since the basic economy in these countries is agricultural, a major source of capital accumulation must be agriculture itself. Therefore, a larger share of the wealth produced on farms should be reserved for agricultural development and credit, rather than drained off by excessive exploitation. Some type of forced savings at the farm level, such as reserving a part of the interest charge for capital accumulation, should have a place in the formulation of capital in underveloped countries, and should be an important consideration in mobilizing capital for an agricultural credit system.[23]

Another important aspect of rural credit results from the breaking up of large estates. In carrying out a land-redistribution program, a difficult and frequently strategic problem is the transference of funds in land to other types of investment. In underdeveloped countries wealth is generally held or controlled by a relatively few people, and land is the principal source of capital investment. Returns from investments in land are generally high, but capital accumulation is low. Landlords tend to spend heavily on consumption goods. Consequently, the forces operating

[22] Renne, *op. cit.*, p. 303.
[23] V. Webster Johnson and Raleigh Barlowe, *Land Problems and Policies,* McGraw-Hill, 1954, p. 393.

for general economic development and overall economic progress in underdeveloped countries are weak.[24]

TAXATION POLICIES

Both land taxes and taxes on agricultural products are levied in many underdeveloped countries. These taxes have been and can be used to achieve changes in land use and ownership as well as to raise revenue. Both of these forms of taxes are regressive in that they are levied at flat rates per acre or per quantity marketed, and consequently fall heaviest on poor farmers and tenants where output per acre or per man-hour of input are lowest.[25]

A wide variation exists in the method of assessment, administration, and collection of both land taxes and taxes on agricultural produce. Farm lands are taxed according to tax rolls, which are prepared on the basis of assessed income or value of the land. This method of assessment is presumptive in all underdeveloped countries where the absence of land registration and the difficulties of determining farm output and local prices make assessment of real income administratively impossible.[26] Usually an assessment is made for a particular year and the resulting tax liability is used as the basis for taxation for a period of time, without revision for as long as 30 or 40 years. This fixity in the amount of taxes makes the tax burden disproportionate to income when prices change.

Taxation of agricultural produce is generally assessed on the basis of the products marketed, and not on the total farm output. Inaccessibility of farming areas and the high cost of taxation at the point of production help explain this procedure in underdeveloped countries. Sometimes the same product is taxed repeatedly on its way to market as it moves through different towns and ports. This pyramiding of the charges widens the cost margin between producer and consumer, and discourages regional specialization in production.[27]

Regressive taxes tend to comprise a relatively high proportion of the total taxes in underdeveloped areas, and introduction of progressive taxes, such as personal income taxation with progressive rates, creates problems because of the difficulties of assessing agricultural income. Flat-rate taxation, such as product taxes, gives no consideration to personal status and number of dependents, resulting in heaviest burdens on small farmers. A high percentage of illiteracy prevails among small farmers in underdeveloped areas, no records are kept, and consequently administration or enforcement of any taxation based on income is diffi-

[24] *Ibid.*, p. 395.
[25] Renne, *op. cit.*, p. 304.
[26] *Land Reform*, p. 44.
[27] *Ibid.*

cult. Nevertheless, some of the Asian countries, such as the Philippines, now have progressive taxes, including personal income and corporation taxes with progressive rates.

Land taxes have been tried at times to break up large estates or to discourage concentration of land holdings by using graduated and progressive tax rates in accordance with the size or value of holdings. However, administrative difficulties and the political power of large landowners in keeping land taxes low have prevented their successful use as a counterconcentration force.[28] In the United States, legal doctrines such as "uniformity clauses" have discouraged the use of graduated and progressive land-tax rates. Nevertheless, if desired, such taxes can be used to break up large holdings and to force underdeveloped lands into more intensive use. Inheritance taxes can also be used to break up large holdings. The "death duties" of England are an example of such use.[29]

LAND REFORM MEASURES

In general, the nations in temperate zones are not involved in major land-reform programs, with the exception of southern Europe. And, although the contrast between different countries in the need for reform is evident, some common objectives occur. The most pronounced of these is family-farm ownership.

LAND REDISTRIBUTION

Some 16 countries reported measures since 1945 to provide wider opportunities of ownership through redistribution of land, in a survey made by the United Nations.[30] These are Bolivia, China (Taiwan), Czechoslovakia, Egypt, Finland, Germany, India, Italy, Japan, Mexico, Pakistan, Poland, Puerto Rico, Spain, Turkey, and Yugoslavia. In most of these countries rural overpopulation exists, either general or regional.

In Asian countries the principal consequences reported are improvement in the status of tenant cultivators, and greater security of tenure enjoyed by them as owners. How much agricultural output will increase depends on how far ownership of small holdings encourages more investment in the farm. The problems of underdevelopment can be solved only with a broader program of diversification of the economy.

In European countries and those in the Middle East, the chief social consequences have been gains in income and status for peasant farmers with insufficient land, and for the landless farm laborers. In Latin American countries, reforms benefit principally hired laborers and share

[28] Johnson and Barlowe, *op. cit.*, p. 397.
[29] *Ibid.*
[30] See *Progress in Land Reform,* United Nations, Department of Economic Affairs, New York, 1954, p. 92.

tenants. Where measures for land redistribution have been accompanied by land reclamation and development, as in Egypt, Finland, Italy, Japan, Mexico, Spain, and Turkey, it is expected that agricultural production will increase as a result of more intensive cultivation.

Financial aspects of land-redistribution measures appear to present more serious problems in Asia than elsewhere. The poverty of the cultivators, lack of funds, and the shortage of credit have implied the transfer of ownership to cultivators, because the purchase price of the holding has been fixed at levels that do not permit tenants to acquire ownership in a short period. Only in India is a large-scale movement of voluntary gift distribution of land under way.

It is generally recognized in the countries undertaking land-redistribution programs that additional measures to increase farm productivity, including credit and a better organized farm credit system, promotion of coöperative organizations, consolidation of fragmented holdings and combination of too small holdings, and better agricultural education should accompany the redistribution program. Governments carrying out land redistribution usually include these and other land reform measures.[31]

LAND SETTLEMENT

The types of tenure granted new farmers on lands available for settlement through reclamation or development vary. In the economically advanced nations where land and capital are plentiful, either freehold or long-term leasehold is granted. In the United States new farmers receive fee simple title. In Australia settlers are usually given perpetual lease on Crown lands, which is the predominant form of tenure. In New Zealand, settlers are offered either freehold tenure, or long-term renewable leasehold.[32] In all three of these countries, new farmers are provided with loans through government-sponsored credit programs, and technical advice.

The resettlement policy of Canada is of wider scope than the development programs of most other nations. It is designed to encourage farmers to move off land unsuitable for grain production and relocate on better land or developed land. The vacated submarginal land is then converted into a community pasture under national or state ownership for use of local farmers.

In Africa two forms of tenure are used. In the Belgian Congo the right of usufruct under conditions approximating ownership is granted

[31] *Ibid.*, p. 96. See also *Report on the Center on Land Problems in Asia and the Far East*, Food and Agriculture Organization of the United Nations, FAO Report No. 393, Rome, June, 1955, processed, pp. 19–21.

[32] *Ibid.*, p. 113.

individual cultivators. In the Gezira scheme initiated in 1925 in the Sudan, the government rents lands from landowners and relets to them and others as cultivating tenants on a profit-sharing basis. The Sudan Gezira Board constitutes the agricultural managers, supplies housing, stores, and ginneries, and is responsible for marketing. Part of the profits is spent by the board on social development.[33]

In the Middle East, shortage of water generally limits extension of the cultivated area and prevents more intensive cultivation of land already being cropped. In Iraq the settlement law gives land to cultivators without rent or other charges, conditional on proper use for 10 years, after which freehold title is granted on condition that the land will not be alienated for an additional 10-year period. In Israel, family-farm holdings are granted in long-term hereditary leasehold. Settlements are organized in coöperatives, which handle purchase of supplies and marketing. Twenty-year low interest loans are made available by the Colonization Department for initial equipment needed by the settlers.

In India coöperative forms of tenure are favored, while in Pakistan individual ownership is granted after the full value of the land is paid up. In the Philippines considerable areas in the southern island of Mindanao have been made available after World War II for settlement of dissidents and others from the heavily populated areas of Luzon. Typical acreages are 8 hectares or approximately 20 acres, with full title granted promptly by the government. Clearing and development of the tract is undertaken by the settler.

CONDITIONS OF TENANCY

Progress to improve conditions of tenancy by greater security of tenure is far from universal. Problems of tenant security are very different in the advanced countries from those in the underdeveloped nations. In some of the more advanced countries, the problem now is to reconcile a high degree of security for tenants with efficient farming. In the underdeveloped areas, the problem is to introduce protection for the tenant and to make it effective.

Much the same contrast holds for rent control. In advanced countries rent control, which reduces rents significantly, may cause landlords to cease maintaining fixed capital in the farm and favor inefficient farming. In underdeveloped areas the problem is to reduce rents to levels that will enable the cultivator to make a living.

In the five Asian countries of China (Taiwan), India, Japan, Pakistan, and the Philippines, new legislation providing security of tenure, including right to compensation for improvements and control of rents, has been introduced as part of the general program of land reform. Among

[33] *Ibid.*, pp. 107–108.

other things, the legislation prohibits labor or personal service and other onerous conditions, such as compulsory sales of produce to the landlord. Since very large numbers of cultivators are affected, these measures, if they are successfully enforced, constitute major advances in the improvement of security of tenure, a larger share of the produce of the land going to the cultivator, and improvement in the social status of the operator. They are the most important of all land-reform measures being undertaken throughout the world, except measures to transfer ownership from landlords to tenants, concurrently undertaken in the same countries.

Enforcement in these Asian nations has been entrusted to special administrative machinery, separate from the courts. Apparently these countries regard the creation of a special administrative agency as a condition of successful enforcement.[34]

CONDITIONS OF RURAL EMPLOYMENT

The hired labor force usually occupies the lowest status economically and socially of the agricultural population (owners, tenants, sharecroppers, and laborers). An effective land-reform program, aiming at improvement of the lot of all those engaged in agriculture, must consider the needs of hired workers and include measures for improvement in their living and working conditions.

The proportion of hired workers to the total engaged in agriculture varies greatly in different countries. In subsistence farming the family ordinarily supplies all the labor. Heavily mechanized family farms in advanced countries like the United States employ relatively few permanent hired workers, usually only a few or one or two per farm. In areas of intensive commercial production, hired workers may constitute the majority.

In underdeveloped countries, the problem of regulating employment conditions is very different from that in the more advanced countries where administrative services are well organized; there is often a strong trade union movement; industrial working conditions are regulated; and there is a definite shift of workers from the land. These conditions, which favor the regulation of working conditions in agriculture, are lacking in underdeveloped countries. Where there is a surplus of agricultural labor, resulting in unemployment and underemployment, the individual worker is likely to be more concerned with getting work than with good wages and working conditions. In addition, the lack of trade union organization and inadequate government administrative services make enforcement of regulations difficult.

In underdeveloped areas there is a danger of transposing to these countries measures suited to more advanced economies without proper

[34] *Ibid.*, p. 148.

consideration of the differences in the level of economic and social development. There appears to be considerable leeway for governments in setting standards of wages and other conditions of employment that could be considered absolute minima. Obviously, such action would need to be accompanied by other measures on a broad front, to raise agricultural productivity in general and make possible higher farm income and wages.

Housing for agricultural workers, even in the more advanced countries, leaves much to be desired. More action by governments generally in setting standards and facilitating new construction is needed. In health, education, and social services, rural areas in most countries are less well served than are urban areas. Where social security schemes have been introduced, some progress has been made in extending the benefits to the rural population, but much yet remains to be done.

In many countries measures to provide wider opportunities of ownership have benefited agricultural workers directly by providing them with holdings or facilitating their getting land. Where land redistribution measures do not create new farm units, agricultural laborers do not generally benefit directly. But to the extent that the transfer of ownership improves the economic position of the farmer and leads to more investment in the land, it should increase employment and improve conditions of employment.

Where the agrarian structure is characterized by great inequality in land ownership and extensive cultivation of land as in some Latin American and Middle Eastern countries, there is not much opportunity for workers to improve their conditions of employment or their status. Land-reform measures designed to provide wider opportunities of ownership, or more secure conditions of tenancy, along with more intensive agriculture, increase the demand for labor and contribute to an increase in wages and better working conditions.

Development of nonagricultural occupations through such projects as village improvement and road building, rural industries and, in some cases, large-scale industries, helps to provide supplementary employment and earnings for farm workers and their families while they remain on the farm, and to take some workers out of agriculture permanently. Community development projects now in progress in rural areas in various parts of the world, together with extensive land-reform measures in underdeveloped countries, must be considered as essential for genuine and maximum improvement in the conditions of hired laborers.

ECONOMIC HOLDINGS

Consideration is being given in several countries to measures to increase the number of holdings of economic size, in the two meanings of the term, but generally it is the question of the minimum holding that gets attention. Conversion to optimum sizes that would increase agricultural efficiency is a phase of land-reform policy not generally considered. Nevertheless, the problem is a critical one in many countries where it is necessary to find means of reconciling the presentation of a social structure deemed desirable, such as individual family-farm ownership, with the need for agricultural and economic progress.

In some countries this problem has been attacked by combining the economies of large-scale operation and marketing with the satisfactions of independent farming, as, for example, in the Gezira scheme. But, in general, progress under special measures to deal with uneconomically small holdings has been slight. In rich countries where there is little or no general pressure on land resources, the program may be one of aid to low-income farmers, providing them with credit and advisory services, as in the United States, or resettling farmers from submarginal land as in Canada, or combining small or dividing large farms in accordance with the needs of economic development, as in Australia.

In countries where pressure of population on the land is acute, providing alternative employment to decrease the number of farmers is the only effective means of reducing the number of uneconomic farms. Diversification of the economy through long-term economic development is the only real solution.

Consolidation of small holdings is one of the most important single measures needed to raise farm output and improve levels of living. In India, Pakistan, and Japan, consolidation is being undertaken by the governments through active participation of the population. Legislation, education, and active coöperation of the farm population are essential ingredients of a successful program to reduce fragmentation to a minimum.

LAND REGISTRATION

Maps on which each parcel of land can be identified and an accurate record of the rights held in such parcels are of great assistance in carrying out land-reform measures involving changes in distribution of land or of rights in land. Such maps and records are also useful in land administration including tax assessment and collection. In addition, they give security to landowners who are registered and to all who participate in land transactions, and facilitate all transactions in which land is involved as security.[35]

Maps and records of this sort are completely lacking in many countries, while in others existing records are inaccurate, incomplete, and unsatis-

[35] Cf. *ibid.*, p. 207.

factory. Practically all nations agree that an accurate cadastre and record of rights is highly desirable, but progress in land registration in many areas is very slow.

If registration of land rights is to be effective, it must be compulsory. A system of registration of deeds is not an adequate substitute for registration of title, since it does not establish title. The register of deeds is frequently the only public record of existing rights in land even in the more advanced countries. In the United States, for example, introduction of the Torrens Title System, and public abstracting services in some countries help expedite and reduce the costs involved in the transfer of rights in land, especially land titles, but progress has been quite slow. In many countries cadastral surveys are being undertaken, and title registration procedures set up, but many areas are not yet surveyed, and registration is even less complete.

AGRICULTURAL CREDIT

Most countries now have some form of public institution for provision of credit to farmers, but the part played by such institutions varies with the extent of development of the country's economy. In the more advanced countries, public institutions are principally designed to meet special cases which, for various reasons, are not adequately served by existing private sources. Since the mid-thirties, these public institutions have played an increasingly important part in complementing and regulating private credit. Thus, in the United States, where commercial banks are the largest single source of agricultural credit, government credit assistance is available through two programs: (1) the Farm Credit Administration, established in 1916 and greatly expanded in 1933 to (a) furnish long-time mortgage credit at reasonable interest rates for attainment of farm ownership, (b) furnish production credit tailor-made to fit the farmer's needs, and (c) make funds available for the development of farmers' coöperatives; and (2) the Farmers Home Administration, which increasingly has been making loans to low-income farmers for development and operation purposes.

In the less developed countries of Europe, as well as those in Asia, Africa, and Latin America, governments have found it necessary to play a more active part in providing agricultural credit either directly to farmers or through coöperatives sponsored by the government, or greatly encouraged and aided by it. Usually one or more public agricultural banks or credit corporations is established to supply credit. For example, the Philippine government created the Agricultural Credit and Coöperative Financing Administration (ACCFA) in 1952 and authorized in separate legislation establishment and operation of rural credit banks. The goal of the ACCFA, which has an authorized capital of 100 million pesos, is "to bring every small farmer within its fold and spare him from the clutches of usurers and unscrupulous middlemen." [36]

In several countries the capital of public banks or credit corporations is supplied wholly by the government by appropriations or special funds. Additional measures have been taken in some countries to tap other sources of money, including acceptance of private deposits, issuance of bonds guaranteed by the state, and association with private banks or institutions, such as insurance companies.

Many governments of underdeveloped countries have tried to supply all three types of credit requirements of agriculture: (1) *short-term* for seasonal expenses, (2) *medium-term* (up to five or seven years) for livestock and equipment, and (3) *long-term* for purchase of land and structural improvements. Shortage of funds or legal or institutional difficulties have often forced them to confine their efforts to one or two of these three types of credit. As a rule, long-term credit has tended to be least well provided for.[37]

In some countries legislation has been passed to cancel or scale down farm debt, fix maximum interest rates and installment periods, and enforce provisions that total interest on a loan may not exceed the principal amount lent. These have provided substantial relief to agriculturists in some countries.

FISCAL AND OTHER MEASURES

Little use has been made of taxation as an integral part of land-reform policy in so far as measures to transfer ownership of land are concerned. In Egypt, however, a supplementary tax of five times the original tax is imposed on landholdings in excess of 200 acres.[38] Several countries have adopted tax measures to impede accumulation of land and break up large estates. In some countries absentee landowners are taxed more heavily than resident owners, unearned increments of land value are subject to special taxation, or to a tax on capital gains; death taxes may force owners to dispose of part of an estate to raise the amount required in taxes; and land taxes are highly progressive as well as taxes on agricultural incomes.

In several countries tax measures have been adopted to promote certain forms of ownership or types of organization. In India and Belgium, for example, exemptions from registration fees and stamp duties in cases of exchanges of land are made to promote consolidation of scattered holdings. Some countries grant tax remissions or exemptions to coöperative

[36] Amando M. Dalisay and Isidro S. Macaspac, "Guiding Principles of the Philippine Agricultural Program," *Economic Research Journal,* University of the East, Manila, Vol. II, No. 2, September, 1955, p. 57.
[37] *Progress in Land Reform,* p. 220.
[38] *Ibid.,* p. 261.

farms. In the United States several states' have enacted laws exempting homesteads from taxation.

Fiscal measures designed to stimulate agricultural development include taxing untilled or undercultivated land at higher rates, partial or total tax exemption of newly cultivated land or land being improved, higher depreciation allowances on capital investment, and use of fiscal measures to encourage certain lines of production.[39] Although the scope of these measures is generally small and their impact on the economy slight, it appears that there is need for fiscal reform in underdeveloped countries, because taxes weigh heavily on the rural population through emphasis on consumption taxes, such as customs and excise duties, and lack of steeply progressive income taxes.

Other measures to improve living standards and social status of the farm population are numerous and extensive. These include depression and drouth relief, agricultural price supports, bulk purchase agreements, guaranteed loans to primary producers in marketing agricultural products, assured markets, subsidized agricultural improvements such as drainage and farm water supply, subsidized soil improvements such as lime and agricultural research, education, and extension programs.

In the United Kingdom the Minister of Agriculture has powers of dispossession against an owner or occupier who after 12 months of supervision fails to show satisfactory improvement in his standard of management or husbandry. Dispossession of an occupier is by means of termination of his tenancy, and letting the land to a tenant approved by the County Agricultural Executive Committee.

EFFECTS OF LAND REFORM PROGRAMS

Proponents of land reform generally assume its introduction in a country will result in higher income and better living levels for small cultivators, and improved total income for both the agricultural and nonagricultural segments of the economy. These assumptions deserve careful analysis. Obviously the effects of a simple land redistribution program will be considerably different from those of a complex program of land redistribution combined with land settlement, tenure improvement, credit, marketing, taxation, and other complementary policies and programs.

IMMEDIATE OR SHORT-RUN EFFECTS

The income from agriculture may decline immediately after introduction of land redistribution, tenure improvement, and other supplementary measures of land reform for any of several causes acting singly

[39] *Ibid.*, p. 265.

or in combination: [40] (1) decline in the rate of agricultural investment resulting from reduction in rental rates and land taxes as required by land reform; (2) decline in agricultural output where there are no incentives for improving traditional or low-consumption habits and for stimulating greater production, (3) too large a gap in family consumption levels before and after immediate introduction of land reform and/or pressure of scarcity prices of essential consumer goods which serve to nullify any increase in farm production caused by land reform; and (4) lack of adequate organization among the new owners and/or tenants which will make the land-reform policies more effective and widespread, and the adequacy of public instrumentalities to deal with the problem or assist farmers in various ways.

Capital investment in agriculture will decline sharply in the beginning stages of land reform because (1) the new owners or tenants will not have for some time the means to compensate for the loss of investment formerly made by the landlords, resulting from low compensation; or (2) reduced rents may also cause lower investment rates in nonagricultural fields. Unless special credit measures are inaugurated, the low rate of agricultural investment will persist for a considerable time. And, if the new farm operators continue without excess income above their consumption needs, the rate of capital investment will continue to be very low. All this means low income for the agricultural population.

Farm production will increase only when farmers can command the essential consumption goods that their increased production will enable them to buy for the satisfaction of themselves and their families. Otherwise, there is no incentive to produce more than their needs for home use. This is particularly true in areas far removed from commercialized production, which make up much of the underdeveloped areas.

If land reforms are to be beneficial, both for increasing farm production of the people affected and for improving their real income position, credit assistance must be made available to the tenants and new owner-operators as a means of capital accumulation, but more especially as an incentive for increased production for the market. If the excess income above consumption requirements is to go into capital formation, the government must supplement the rate of agricultural investment by grants, land improvement projects or production, and equipment loans to farmers.

The undesirable effects of land reform programs in the short run may be mitigated somewhat by: [41] (1) choice of the means and manner of

[40] See Amando M. Dalisay, "The Effects of Land Reform on Income Distribution," *Economic Research Journal,* University of the East, Manila, Philippines, Vol. II, No. 2, September, 1955, pp. 61–62.

[41] *Ibid.,* p. 63.

compensation and repayment in land redistribution; (2) types of rent or tax in land-tenure improvement; (3) proper implementation of such supplementary measures as advice and education in improved production techniques, credit, and other assistance for land improvements and new capital formation; and (4) proper combination with the overall economic development program, along with public policies encouraging a rapid rate of capital formation both within and outside agriculture.

LONG-RUN EFFECTS

In the long run, when various land reform measures have had time to work out their effects and supplementary measures have been developed, increased production and income for agriculture will result. This comes about by three main factors: [42] (1) increased economic efficiency of individual farm units; (2) improved social organization in rural communities, resulting from better organization among farmers, which in turn has favorable effects on credit, marketing, and other services for agriculture; and (3) improved public administration of agricultural programs, including more effective techniques in agricultural education and extension, research, and working relations with farm groups.

It is assumed, of course, that people in underdeveloped areas where population pressure is acute will be able and willing to carry out more than strictly institutional reforms to achieve a better allocation of resources and, in spite of limited savings, pursue an effective general economic development program. Increases in agricultural income may come from measures for improving agricultural techniques to raise farm output and encourage further diversification and/or intensification of agricultural production. The main difficulty, however, is that in countries that have no more uncultivated land for distribution, farms of economic size and with opportunities for full employment of the farm population cannot be provided. Efforts to correct defects in the agrarian structure (high rents, high interest rates, uneconomic holdings, insecure tenure, fragmentation, etc.) are usually nullified by the lack of capital and land relative to the labor supply which continually puts economic pressure against enforcement of legislation to correct these defects.[43]

This points up the fact that increases in farm income in agriculturally overpopulated countries, in the long run, must inevitably lie in the direction of measures outside agriculture that bring about a better allocation of resources between agriculture and other segments of the economy. Only by such means can agriculture achieve a higher absolute increase in income or higher productivity per worker. Industrialization may be the major alternative available in some areas, but all possible alternatives

[42] *Ibid.*, p. 64.
[43] See *Progress in Land Reform*, pp. 288–291.

for providing employment opportunities for the surplus farm population should be considered.

It is frequently assumed that in countries where land resources relative to population are abundant, but where capital is scarce, comprehensive land-reform programs are not necessary. However, in such areas, extension of the cultivated area and control of land use are not sufficient for increasing agricultural production and promoting general economic development. In countries such as Indonesia, the Philippines, and Thailand, for example, where land is not in short supply, the antiquated land-tenure system and weaknesses of the agrarian structure, with its economic maladjustments and social inequalities, prevent expansion in agricultural output and hinder general economic growth.[44]

One further point. Continual increase in agricultural production with higher economic efficiency per worker, soon reaches a point where further production means lower farm prices and incomes. Further investment of individual savings in agriculture merely aggravates the problem. The excess farm production and excess labor on farms must find outlets outside agriculture if farm income is not to be depressed permanently. Thus, just as in the agriculturally overpopulated and underdeveloped areas, the solutions to problems in underdeveloped countries with abundant land resources cannot be found inside agriculture alone. Basic land reforms in both these types of countries must be accompanied by integrated economic development programs including other institutional reforms and improvements outside agriculture, if increased income for agriculture, better income distribution, and balanced economic growth are to be achieved.

THE FUTURE OF LAND REFORM

The problems of land reform have assumed increased international significance in recent years, attributable largely to three factors: [45] (1) improvements in communications and transportation facilities, (2) the rapid growth and influence of international communism, and (3) the division of the world principally into two armed camps, each struggling for political and military supremacy. In this setting land reform programs or agrarian movements in any nation, large or small, may transcend their local or national boundaries and have international repercussions.

Under these conditions it is imperative that every possible effort be made through joint action of governments, as well as by action of individual governments, to develop and promote conditions of sound economic and social progress in all underdeveloped areas. A comprehensive

[44] Dalisay, *op. cit.*, p. 65.
[45] Nathan L. Whetten, "Land Reform in a Modern World," *Rural Sociology*, Vol. XIX, No. 4, December, 1954, p. 329.

attack on major economic and social problems by a combination of measures appears most likely to achieve desired results, rather than single measures applied in isolation without other measures to reinforce and sustain them.

Comprehensive economic development programs require coördinated and integrated economic planning. National economic councils and planning commissions are essential for preparation of integrated economic development plans, determination of priorities in development, and allocation of scarce resources among development projects. These planning agencies can be instrumental in proposing necessary institutional adjustments to make land reform measures more comprehensive and effective for general economic development. Working with international organizations and their regional agencies, these planning bodies can utilize all available resources more fully and plan for economic progress based on world-wide information and appreciation of common needs and problems. In most underdeveloped countries, these planning agencies need to be strengthened greatly and given adequate support for effective staff operations.

OBSTACLES TO PROGRESS

The principal obstacles to effective land reforms may be classified in three main groups: (1) the *administrative and technical,* (2) the *political and social,* and (3) the *economic and financial.*[46]

An administrative obstacle that is very apparent in underdeveloped areas is shortage of trained staff. Lack of data concerning agricultural conditions, including agricultural labor, is another administrative obstacle. Lack of sufficient technical knowledge concerning sound agricultural development and settlement is a serious technical obstacle in many countries.

Opposition of landowners to land reform in underdeveloped areas is a strong political obstacle. It is logical that vested interests would oppose attempts to adjust maldistribution of lands. In many areas landholders exert powerful political and economic influence. Social conservatism in rural communities is an obstacle, especially to reforms such as consolidation of holdings. Almost universally farmers are traditionally individualistic and desire maximum freedom from government interference. Nevertheless, increasing numbers of people, especially farm folk, recognize the necessity of reform measures and are anxious for social and economic progress. Obviously, no reform can be permanent or successful unless it is recognized as necessary by the peoples concerned.

The financial and economic obstacles are the most serious of all, however. In fact, in some areas they are, for the time being at least, in-

[46] *Progress in Land Reform,* p. 292.

separable. Lack of financial resources seems to be the most common. Financial burdens imposed on governments because of payment of compensation and setting up of new agencies connected with reforms aimed at transferring land ownership, combined with heavy development expenditures for other parts of the economy at the same time, impede introduction and completion of reforms. The inability of tenants, because of lack of personal resources and shortage of credit facilities, to pay for acquisition of ownership rights and other reforms, is a closely related financial obstacle. Costs of land survey and settlement schemes involving land reclamation and development are invariably high.

Measures to promote wider opportunities for ownership need not involve prohibitively heavy burdens to the State, provided the terms on which farmers acquire holdings are fixed in accordance with their means or ability to pay. But, since many governments, especially in the most distressed areas, view land reform as a comprehensive policy, and properly so if an adequate job is to be done within a reasonable period of time under existing world tensions and conflicts, the financial requirements are tremendous. Such comprehensive policies include land development, consolidation of holdings, provision of credit, expansion of coöperatives, provision of machinery and other means of technical improvement, and expansion of agricultural research and advisory services. Obviously, in many areas lack of financial resources is the limiting factor in the attainment of such programs.

RECOMMENDATIONS FOR FUTURE ACTION

Several governments have recommended the creation of a special land reform fund to be established under the United Nations to provide necessary financial assistance to member States, either directly or indirectly, to effect land reform, or creation of an international fund to finance measures of land reform and to increase agricultural output in underdeveloped countries.[47] Some governments recommend comprehensive international action including creation of storage facilities and markets, provision of credit, standardization of working hours, fixing of minimum wages for workers, preparation and adoption of a *Declaration on Land Reform* similar to the *Universal Declaration of Human Rights,* and technical and political assistance to member States engaging in land reform programs.

Other specific suggestions for future action in land reform covering both improved systems of land tenure and better farming methods, include: (1) *technical fields*—cadastral surveys and land title registration, security of tenure including compensation for improvements and adjustment of rents, consolidation of fragmental holdings, and administrative

[47] *Ibid.,* p. 297.

implementation of legislation; (2) *social fields*—housing, gradual extension of social security legislation to the whole agricultural population, and more adequate health, educational, and welfare services; and (3) *economic fields*—strengthening of agricultural credit institutions, promotion of credit and marketing coöperatives, improvement of fiscal systems, provision for increased investment in agriculture, and integration of land reform in a wider framework of general economic development.[48]

Much yet remains to be done to achieve satisfactory living conditions and adequate standards of living for peoples in underdeveloped areas, especially rural populations. In fact, hardly more than a good beginning has been made. Vigorous and intelligent action by individual nations and joint action by free nations in land reform measures and general economic development programs are essential if the hopes of the masses in underdeveloped countries who are struggling for land and freedom from poverty, disease, and ignorance are to be realized, and if world peace and progress are to be achieved. This is indeed a worthy and adequate field for application of the talents of the well-prepared land economist.

REFERENCES FOR FURTHER READING

Dalisay, Amando M., "The Effects of Land Reform on Income Distribution," *Economic Research Journal,* University of the East, Manila, Philippines, Vol. II, No. 2, September, 1955, pp. 61–67.

Food and Agriculture Organization of the United Nations, *Report on the Center on Land Problems in Asia and the Far East,* FAO Report No. 393, Rome, June, 1955, processed.

Getty, Ronald, "Consolidation of Farming Lands in France," *Journal of Farm Economics,* Vol. XXXVIII, No. 4, November, 1956, pp. 911–922.

Hill, George W., Beltran, Gregorio, and Marino, Cristino, "Social Welfare and Land Tenure in the Agrarian Reform Program of Venezuela," *Land Economics,* Vol. XXVIII, No. 1, February, 1952, pp. 17–29.

Johnson, V. Webster, and Barlowe, Raleigh, *Land Problems and Policies,* McGraw-Hill Book Company, New York, 1954, Chap. XV.

"Land Settlement: The Making of New Farms," *International Journal of Agrarian Affairs,* Oxford University Press, London, Vol. I, No. 5, September, 1953.

Mosher, A. T., *et al.,* "A Review and Criticism of United States Participation in Agricultural Programs of Technical Coöperation," *Journal of Farm Economics,* Vol. XXXVIII, No. 5, December, 1956, pp. 1197–1234.

Nelson, Lowry, *Land Reform in Italy,* National Planning Association, Washington, D.C., Planning Pamphlet No. 97, August, 1956.

Pak, Ki Hyuk, "Outcome of Land Reform in the Republic of Korea," *Journal of Farm Economics,* Vol. XXXVIII, No. 4, November, 1956, pp. 1015–1023.

[48] For a more detailed analysis of these recommended further actions, based on replies to questionnaires sent member governments, see *ibid.,* pp. 298–302.

Parsons, Kenneth H., Penn, Raymond J., and Raup, Philip M. (eds.), *Land Tenure: Proceedings of the 1951 International Conference on Land Tenure and Related Problems in World Agriculture,* University of Wisconsin Press, Madison, 1956, Parts I–X, XV, and XVII–XX.

Pronin, Dimitri T., "Land Reform in Poland: 1920–1945," *Land Economics,* Vol. XXV, No. 2, May, 1949, pp. 133–145.

Renne, Roland R., "Land Tenure Reform as an Aspect of Economic Development in Asia," Chap. XX in *Economics and the Public Interest,* Robert A. Solo (ed.), Rutgers University Press, New Brunswick, N.J., 1955.

Rivera, Generoso F., McMillan, Robert T., *The Rural Philippines,* U.S. Mutual Security Agency, Office of Information, Manila, October, 1952, processed.

United Nations, *Land Reform: Defects in Agrarian Structure as Obstacles to Economic Development,* Department of Economic Affairs, New York, July, 1951.

United Nations, *Measures for the Economic Development of Under-Developed Countries,* Department of Economic Affairs, New York, May, 1951, Chaps. II, III, IV, and VIII.

United Nations, *Progress in Land Reform,* Department of Economic Affairs, New York, January, 1954.

Whetten, Nathan L., "Land Reform in a Modern World," *Rural Sociology,* Vol. XIX, No. 4, December, 1954, pp. 329–336.

INDEX

Ableiter, J. K., 51
Abrams, Charles, 252, 290, 335, 339
Ackerman, Edward A., 530
Ackerman, Joseph, 392
Adams, Thomas, 556
Ad valorem taxes, 303
Agrarian movements, 560, 561
Agrarian revolt, 558, 560, 561
Agrarian structure, defects in, 564; reform of, 572–580
Agricultural Adjustment Administration, 21, 23, 152, 441
Agricultural Conservation Program Service, 527
Agricultural Extension Service, 527
Agricultural land, amount of land suitable for, 62; amount required, 110; arid agriculture, 443–450; importance of agriculture, 438, 439; peculiarities of, 456–458; physical factors determining suitability, 57; supply of, 57; the prospect, 113; trend in utilization of, 110
Agricultural land economics, 7
Agricultural land taxation, 294–300
Agricultural land tenure and tenancy, see Farm tenancy
Agriculture, credit requirements of, 257; distinguishing characteristics as an industry, 450–456; physical frontiers of, 31
Allen, R. H., 369, 387
Allgeyer vs. *Louisiana,* 322
Allodial land, 367
Alsberg, Carl L., 90
American Forestry Association, 180
Antaeus Clubs, 337
Antleuropa, 37
Appraisal of land, methods, 249–252; purposes of, 249
Appropriation doctrine of water rights, 422
Appropriation of land, see Land appropriation
Area diversification, 449
Arid agriculture, 443–450
Assessment of land, improvement of, 296
Atwood, W. W., 180

Babcock, F. M., 249, 252
Bagley, William C., 362
Bailey, Rex R., 267
Baker, O. E., 31, 40, 58, 64, 108, 383
Ball, Carleton R., 552, 553, 554

Banfield, Edward C., 556
Barlowe, Raleigh, 14, 20, 21, 24, 55, 87, 108, 134, 206, 267, 310, 311, 362, 556, 570, 571, 572, 586
Barnes, C. P., 43, 47
Basin Interagency Committee, 529
Bassett, Edward M., 355, 362
Bauer, Catherine, 432
Baumol, William J., 153, 227
Bean, L. H., 232, 247
Behre, C. E., 117
Beltran, Gregorio, 586
Bennett, H. H., 206
Bequests, 334
Berle, A. A., Jr., 282, 339, 556
Best land use, 12
Bird, Frederick L., 295
Birth and death rates, 98, 102
Black, A. G., 16, 20, 139, 153
Black Death, 330
Black, J. D., 16, 103, 139, 153, 267, 369, 387
Blackstone's Commentaries on The Laws of England, 322
Bonbright, J. C., 252
Boulder Canyon Project Act, 516, 518
Boulding, K. E., 148, 153
Bowman, Isaiah, 33, 34, 38, 54, 106, 108
Brandt, Karl, 546
Brauer, Karl, 269
Brewster, John M., 111, 113
Brinegar, George K., 267
Brinkman, Carl, 329
Britton, Roy F., 306
Brown, Harry G., 290
Brownlee, Oswald, xii
Bruce, A. A., 544
Bryson, Lyman, 92
Buck, J. Lossing, 566
Bunce, A. C., xii, 179, 184, 185, 186, 187, 189, 190, 193, 206
Burgess, E. W., 322
Bye, C. R., 220, 221, 227

Call, L. E., 554
Carbut, Arthur H., 530
Carey Act, 498
Carr-Saunders, A. M., 94, 98
Carver, T. N., 206
Case-Wheeler Act, 501
Cassels, John M., 139, 140
Cavin, J. P., 112
Chamberlin, E. H., 147, 148, 227